A Decade of the Commonwealth, 1955-1964

Edited by

W. B. Hamilton, Kenneth Robinson,

and C. D. W. Goodwin

Published for the
Duke University Commonwealth-Studies Center
Duke University Press, Durham, N. C.
1966

23183

Library of Congress Catalogue Card number 65-28466

Printed in the United States of America
by the Seeman Printery, Inc., Durham, N. C.

Preface: Ten Years of Rapid Change

The decade under discussion in this book was yet young when the Commonwealth was shaken by the Suez crisis; as it ended, an acute problem had to be faced in Southern Rhodesia, where a determined white-settler minority held out against Africanization. In between, all the rest of the Empire in Africa became independent states, along with Malaya and the Mediterranean islands, almost tripling the number of members; South Africa was led to withdraw its application for continued membership as a republic; and Britain shook the association with two measures: application to join the Common Market and restriction on free immigration. Paradoxically, though the centrifugal forces seemed to increase during the ten years, at their end proposals were implemented, backed chiefly by the African members, for a Commonwealth secretariat and a formalization of the exchange of professional people. (Both were instituted in 1965.)

To confront the great winds of change and either analyze their effects for a moment in time or even describe the objects they sweep with or before them is an exhilirating experience, if a somewhat hazardous one. The authors of this book, however, watched from many vantage points, and they sought to maintain the detachment proper to good scholars even when they are involved in the events under study. They write largely about members of the Commonwealth, not about the Commonwealth, and in knowledge, attitudes, and function there is little apparent difference between those who are Commonwealth citizens and those who are not. "The non-exclusiveness of which the Commonwealth has boasted since the idea of a bloc was finally

rejected two decades ago has run so far that the question might
be implied as to whether there is anything left to write of.
Rejected is the old concept of the Commonwealth as the overseas projection of England and Englishry, its vigor judged by the
prevalence of wigs, cricket, and the left-hand drive—rejected
most forcefully not by Canadians or Indians but by the English
(or are they Welsh)."

It is clear that diversity has become a motif of the Commonwealth. The decade was marked by continued development of
the course taken in 1947 when the Commonwealth became multiracial. It was transformed from a cozy club into another international association, which might be considered a holding company for groups of regional associations, might be sublimated
by the United Nations—perhaps. Its multifarious members began to set patterns of government different to some extent from
the Westminster model, raising the question "whether the genius
of the Westminster legacy might not be proved more by its
adaptability than by its perpetuation of inapplicable forms."
Diplomatically, the Commonwealth has not spoken as one voice
at least since World War I. Of late it has developed more voices,
but they sometimes are heard in intra-Commonwealth duets
or larger groups (as with "the Delhi-Ottawa axis"), demonstrating that if the organization is still in the pattern of a rimless
wheel, with London at the hub, there is the possibility nonetheless of bilateral or multilateral concert that cuts across regional
themes, or across the old versus the new. The exchange of high
commissioners, however, except with London, has not kept pace
with the growth of members, and consultation among members'
delegates to the United Nations may well be less effective.
Common citizenship as British subjects has long since disappeared, and autochthony is the rage in constitutional law.

The catalogue of disparateness in institutions, of forces that
seem to divide and weaken, could be extended. It is remarked in
this book that the Commonwealth has no machinery for settling
disputes between two of its members (e.g., India and Pakistan)
and that some people believe, and others fear, that Britain has

tired of her own brood or might be driven by fiscal stress to throw off the burden of holding the Commonwealth together— for the center of it she still remains. To so extend the catalogue, however, would warp the truth. The Commonwealth, in the views of its members, serves useful functions. Its role as teacher and exemplar to the world and as the medium of diffusion of "an Anglo-American way of looking at things" makes it valuable to the United States, which has to foot a lot of the bill for the protection and development of its members.

The authors of these papers, moreover, were able to make just as long a list of the ties that bind. Besides the Prime Ministers' Meetings there are all sorts of gatherings of officialdom, from clerks of parliaments to chief finance officers and vice-chancellors of universities. The non-governmental associations, formal and informal, are legion. Common ideas have been widely diffused by the expansion of Britain. (The devotion to some common models such as that of the British university is said in this volume to be only too slavish.) The common training, in the past, of the armies of members has made them able to co-operate easily in international peace-keeping expeditions. British law furnishes concepts, attitudes, and ruling cases in much of the old Empire, whether there was settlement or not. The English language is a common cement, at least for the rulers, in most of the Commonwealth, and it offers members the best vehicle for science, development, and government.

A heritage left by the British to the successor states was the higher civil service, an ascriptive body, generalist in training and outlook, with a pronounced "ethos" of its own. One view is that this ethos is declining rapidly in the East, a prey to rapid nativization and the necessities of economic planning, and probably should be supplanted by American-type training for the civil service. Mr. A. L. Adu, on the other hand, himself an experienced civil servant in Africa, thinks that the British tradition is more valuable. The postwar patterns of the colonial service effected a welding of the old CAS and new technical, professional, and scientific disciplines into a new elite cadre:

In those African states where there has been time for the creation of an indigenous service, the spirit of the former Colonial Administrative Service—its integrity, *esprit de corps*, its power of quick decision and sense of responsibility, its independence and impartiality and its flexibility and deep loyalty—has infused the new cadres that have emerged and has absorbed these into a new elite bureaucracy that is operating in consonance with the new economic development dynamism.

In economic matters, too, change in the Commonwealth during the decade under consideration contained elements which contributed both to stress and to unity within the association. Demographically the Commonwealth was altered substantially as an area for the free movement of people. Problems of rapid and uncontrolled increase of population in most of the newer Commonwealth states, together with undiminished differentials in living standards among the nations, led to a strengthening of some old barriers to intra-Commonwealth migration and to the creation of new techniques of restraint. Limitation by the United Kingdom of immigration from the Commonwealth after 1962 was the most noteworthy single development. Certain long standing intra-Commonwealth flows of persons, particularly between countries of the old Commonwealth, such as from Britain to Australia, did remain unencumbered and significant in size.

The Commonwealth had its economic roots in a colonial system designed to provide Britain with uses for surplus wealth and labor, sources of raw materials, and markets for goods; it survived economically with the help of such artificial stimuli as Commonwealth preferences and from the force of old habits. The economic ties of the Commonwealth lasted chiefly because they continued to provide a framework of relationships which answered the complementary needs of members. Intra-Commonwealth flows of capital, skills, and trade were facilitated by the rapid postwar recovery of Great Britain and the advancement toward maturity of several newer members. As a result of the successful Marshall Plan and rapid re-establishment of a broad three-cornered trade among the United States, western Europe, and the former colonial possessions, Britain was able to retain her dominant role as major trading partner and supplier of capital and trained personnel for most Commonwealth members. As one aspect of the economic relationship the sterling area—born of the international supremacy of British currency and formalized when London went off gold in 1931—survived as a vital institution of the new Commonwealth, even though it was threatened seriously after World War II both by the new international status of the dollar and by a rising tide of nationalism among members. The mechanism of sterling, based on London as a financial metropolis, was retained as a means for facilitating flows of products and resources and withstood successfully the critical scrutiny of most new nations of the Commonwealth.

At least two major problems have appeared in economic relations within the Commonwealth, both of which are rooted not in uniquely Commonwealth conditions but in worldwide tensions between the more and the less developed nations. First, free mobility of private resources among states has not always brought location where the need is greatest. Rather, there has been a paradoxical and "perverse" movement outward from some developing countries both of capital and trained personnel. This movement is understandable in terms of differing levels of private marginal returns among nations; but it can barely be tolerated by countries seeking rapid development, and it may portend greater controls on factor mobility in the near future. A second problem which has appeared in intra-Commonwealth economic relationships is the continuing heavy dependence by newer members on the vagaries of raw material production. In particular, steadily worsening terms of trade for certain staple producers have led to mounting international frictions. Despite the existence of these problems, the dominant feature of Commonwealth economic relationships by the early 1960's was their mere survival after the turmoil of war, the trauma of new nation building, and the dislocations of rapid economic change. This survival may reflect in part the failure of other groupings to materialize; it also indicates, however, the tendency of these estab-

lished economic relationships to persist so long as they continue to have demonstrable value.

External assistance played an important role in this decade
of the Commonwealth as a counterbalance to some of the reverse flows of private resources noted above. Britain as the main
intra-Commonwealth contributor of aid assumed the position of
beneficent partner, assisting in friendship territories which only
a short time before had been dependent. The impact of the aid
process on the Commonwealth structure was mixed. A major
proportion of foreign assistance to Commonwealth countries
came from outside the Commonwealth, mainly the United States,
although toward the end of the decade such countries as the
Soviet Union and China were getting into the act, and inevitably
conflicting ties and allegiances were established. Moreover,
throughout the decade grave questions were raised about the
future of all aid programs. As the period ended, external aid in
massive form from the more developed to the less developed
countries had come to be recognized as no panacea for the world's
ills. Responsible observers were forced to admit that the aid
process was still only a hopeful experiment in international relations; two decades of experience had shown an early trial in
postwar Europe to be conspicuously successful, while later efforts in Africa, Asia, and Latin America were more questionable.
Donor countries came increasingly to raise the question of attaching controls to aid, while recipients insisted on full freedom of
action. Mr. F. J. Pedler points out that for many new African
nations not the quantity, but the administration, the terms, and
the distribution of aid within countries need improvement. Programs of multilateral external assistance among Commonwealth
nations, such as the Colombo Plan, gave promise of providing
a model for overcoming many objections to foreign aid. Both
givers and receivers of aid have come to give weight to special
factors present in the Commonwealth relationship, such as
mutual confidence, understanding, and respect.

The single most uncomfortable and oppressive characteristic
of this decade of the Commonwealth was the immense economic

distance between the have and the have-not members. The gap
not only failed to narrow but continued to grow. Many reasons
can be suggested for this fact: the unsolved problem of population increase, inadequate social infra-structure in most of the
underdeveloped areas, the chaos generated by rapid nation
building, the smallness of most local markets, excessive military
expenditures, and failure to take advantage of unique opportunities to retain and attract foreign private investment and to
integrate within their societies expatriates with special skills.
But the position reached by most policy makers was one of
skepticism about the existence of simple solutions for problems
of rapid modernization and growth. Survival of the Commonwealth itself as a friendly association of nations and of the economic systems which make it up may depend upon whether answers can be found to these problems of narrowing the gap in
the decade ahead.

Mr. Adu believes it is precisely in the attack upon the problems of economic growth that the Commonwealth can find its
most effective mission. If it cannot satisfy the financial needs
for development, it can go a long way toward alleviating the
shortage in skills plaguing development programs:

If then, the Commonwealth can organise an economic and technical cooperation programme, perhaps by building on the Special
African Assistance Plan and the Commonwealth Education and Training Plan, and if this were conceived as a bold and imaginative venture,
it would receive the enthusiastic support of all the newer members of
the Commonwealth. They would see in this venture a meaning and
purpose for the Commonwealth and they would support an effective
machinery to ensure its success.

Once this machinery for Commonwealth economic cooperation is
established and member states have accepted it, it should not be too
difficult to make it discharge wider areas of responsibilities which are
bound to become apparent as the whole venture evolves.

This statement breathes a pragmatism, a resilient acceptance
of change, characteristic of British government in the past when
it has been working most successfully. It also strikes a note of

optimism, in the face of reasonable cause for pessimism, which reflects to a degree the tone of this volume and of the conference-seminar out of which it originated.

June 29, 1965

W. B. HAMILTON
KENNETH ROBINSON
C. D. W. GOODWIN

The Conference at the Villa Serbelloni

This volume is a product of a conference held at the Villa Serbelloni, Bellagio, Italy, June 29 through July 4, 1964, jointly arranged by the Institute of Commonwealth Studies of the University of London and the Duke University Commonwealth-Studies Center. Professor Kenneth Robinson, then director of the Institute, in opening the conference, graciously adverted to the celebration by the Center of its tenth birthday, as one of the rationales of the conference and its theme.

The following attended:

Amishadai L. Adu, *United Nations Technical Assistance Board Representative in East Africa and Deputy Secretary-General, Commonwealth Secretariat*

Dennis G. Austin, *Senior Research Fellow, Institute of Commonwealth Studies, University of London, and Royal Institute of International Affairs*

Ralph Braibanti, *Professor of Political Science, Duke University*

The Hon. Alastair Buchan, *Director, Institute for Strategic Studies*

Sir Miles Clifford, *Director, Leverhulme Trust Fund*

Taylor Cole, *James B. Duke Professor of Political Science and Provost, Duke University*

Zelman Cowen, *Dean of the Faculty of Law, University of Melbourne*

Stanley A. de Smith, *Professor of Public Law, London School of Economics and Political Science, University of London*

Craufurd D. Goodwin, *Associate Professor of Economics and Secretary, Duke University*

William B. Hamilton, *Professor of History, Duke University*

H. Field Haviland, Jr., *Director of Foreign Policy Studies, The Brookings Institution*

John W. Holmes, *Director General, Canadian Institute of International Affairs*

Calvin B. Hoover, *James B. Duke Professor of Economics, Duke University*

Nurul Islam, *Professor and Head, Department of Economics, University of Dacca; Director, Pakistan Institute of Development Economics*

Douglas M. Knight, *President, Duke University*

Alan K. Manchester, *Professor of History and Dean of Trinity College, Duke University*

Nicholas Mansergh, *Smuts Professor of the History of the British Commonwealth and Fellow of St. John's College, Cambridge University*

W. H. Morris-Jones, *Professor of Political Theory and Institutions, University of Durham (now Director, Institute of Commonwealth Studies, London)*

F. J. Pedler, *Director, Unilever Ltd.*

Alan Pifer, *Vice-President, Carnegie Corporation of New York*

Don C. Piper, *Executive Secretary, 1962-64, Commonwealth-Studies Center, Duke University*

M. S. Rajan, *Professor and Head, Department of Commonwealth History and Institutions, and Director Indian School of International Studies*

Kenneth Robinson, *Professor of Commonwealth Affairs and Director Institute of Commonwealth Studies, University of London (now Vice-Chancellor, University of Hong Kong)*

Andrew Shonfield, *Director of Studies, Royal Institute of International Affairs*

T. E. Smith, *Secretary, Institute of Commonwealth Studies, University of London*

Joseph J. Spengler, *James B. Duke Professor of Economics, Duke University*

Brinley Thomas, *Professor of Economics, University College of South Wales and Monmouthshire*

J. S. G. Wilson, *Professor of Economics, University of Hull*

Robert R. Wilson, *James B. Duke Professor of Political Science and Chairman of the Committee on Commonwealth Studies, Duke University*

Four persons were prevented from attending, but sent papers, which appear in this volume:

G. W. St. J. Chadwick, *Assistant Under-Secretary of State, Commonwealth Relations Office*

Frank T. de Vyver, *Professor and Chairman, Department of Economics and Business Administration and Vice Provost, Duke University*

Sir John Lockwood, *Master of Birkbeck College, University of London*

P. N. C. Okigbo, *Economic Adviser to the Government of the Federal Republic of Nigeria and Nigerian Ambassador to the European Economic Community*

The participants represented seven Commonwealth countries and the United States, which, Mr. Holmes permitted himself to say, "whether or not it is a card-carrier, pays more than dues, and is heavily involved in the ex-imperial club from which it prematurely resigned." All those present who are represented by papers in this book doubled as leaders of discussions, and Mr. Adu (twice), Sir Miles Clifford, Messrs. Cowen, Knight, Manchester, Pedler (twice), and Pifer wrote formal discussion papers of such merit that only the already unwieldy size of this book prevented the editors from requesting them for publication. Mr. Piper presented a background paper on "Enforcement of Foreign Judgments in the Commonwealth" which will appear elsewhere. The conferees remain indebted to Messrs. Cowen, Holmes, and Islam for summations and criticisms of the material of the conference, delivered at its last session. The editors have leaned heavily on their comments in writing the Preface, sometimes borrowing their words without even the grace of quotation marks.

Financial support for the conference was generously provided by the Rockefeller Foundation and the Leverhulme Trust. The Rockefeller Foundation also made available for the conference its international conference facilities at the Villa Serbelloni, where Mr. and Mrs. John Marshall made most agreeable and knowledgeable hosts. The two benefactors, of course, bear no responsibility for any statements in this volume.

Those charged with the long task of arranging the conference wish to thank especially Dr. Piper of the Center and Misses Margaret Beard and Patricia Devonald of the staff of the Institute for a tireless year's work.

K. E. R.

W. B. H.

Contents

Part I

The Commonwealth: A Retrospective Survey, 1955-64

Nicholas Mansergh[*]

On February 8, 1955, Sir Winston Churchill presided for the last time at a meeting of the prime ministers of the Commonwealth. All the member-nations—Canada, Australia, New Zealand, South Africa, India, Pakistan, Ceylon—were represented by their prime ministers, and, by customary special invitation, the prime minister of the Federation of Rhodesia and Nyasaland was there as well. Mr. St. Laurent, as befitted the representative of the most senior of overseas members, spoke a farewell tribute, and Sir Winston was said to have replied with "a few moving words" on what "the fraternal association" of the Commonwealth had meant to him.[1] This little exchange, of no moment even if pleasing to recall, may be taken to mark the close of a brief, but momentous, period in Commonwealth history—a period which opened with Winston Churchill's accession to office on May 10, 1940, embraced that memorable year when the Commonwealth stood alone, saw the working out first in war and then in peace of that continuing conference of cabinets, in which Mackenzie King believed[2] the inner spirit of Common-

[*] Smuts Professor of the History of the British Commonwealth, fellow of St. John's College, Cambridge University.

1. *The Annual Register of World Events* (hereafter cited as *The Annual Register*), *1955* (London, 1956), p. 74.
2. See his speeches of January 31, 1944, to the Canadian House of Commons, Canada, *Parl. Debs.* (Commons), I, 39-42 and to members of both Houses of Parliament of the United Kingdom on May 11, 1944, both reprinted in Nicholas Mansergh, *Documents and Speeches on British Commonwealth Affairs, 1931-52* (2 vols.; London, 1953), I, 579-85 and 587-89 respectively.

wealth co-operation found its true practical expression, and
witnessed what may well prove to have been the greatest triumph
of the Commonwealth idea, in the addition to its membership by
the free and deliberate choice of their own governments of
ancient, populous, and in the case of India and Pakistan, great
Asian states. Much certainly had changed, but more seemingly
still remained. While Britain's power was evidently in decline
the moral stature hardly won by endurance in the war from
its onset to its victorious close continued to obscure the measure
of that decline. In 1943 Field Marshal Smuts had correctly
foretold that the position of Britain after the war would be
"one of enormous prestige and respect . . . but she will be poor."[3]
Yet so long as something of that prestige remained as, so to
speak, a politically marketable asset, the bleak consequence of
comparative poverty in men, money, and resources might be
mitigated, and its existence discreetly veiled. By 1955 foreigners
for the most part may have made their harsh reassessments;[4]
but the Commonwealth, at whose prime ministerial gathering
Sir Winston presided, to most outward appearances at least, continued against the changing pattern of power to think in terms
of a scale of British responsibilities, to which the resources of
Britain were no longer equal. With revealing irony, it was Britain
herself, under other leadership, that within little more than a
year compelled the Commonwealth overseas and, even more,
many of her own people, to come to terms with painful contemporary realities.

"My Government will maintain and strengthen consultation
within the Commonwealth for the fulfilment of common aims
and purposes."[5] So it was stated in the Queen's speech from the
throne at the opening of Parliament in June, 1955, and so it
had been said with variations in phrasing on similar occasions

3. Mansergh, *Documents* . . . , 1931-52, I, 570.

4. Cf. Hans J. Morgenthau, *Politics among Nations* (New York, 1948), p. 274:
"In the metaphorical language of the balance of power one might say, rather
crudely but not without truth, that while in the Russian scale there is a weight
of seventy, the weight of the American scale amounts to a hundred of which
seventy is the United States' own strength, ten that of Great Britain, and the
remainder that of other actual or prospective allies."

5. G. B., 5 *Parl. Debs.* (Commons), DXLII, 42, June 19, 1955.

in preceding years. But since 1956 it has not been repeated. The Suez crisis, among other and no doubt more important things, saw to that. Yet for a Commonwealth becoming accustomed to thinking of consultation, or, when time did not allow for that, of the prompt communication of information about immediate intentions, as the foundation of its informal system of interstate co-operation, the deliberate failure to consult by the senior partner marked a departure from principle and a breach in practice, which signalized lack of confidence on the part of the British government in its power to persuade its Commonwealth partners even to acquiesce in the enterprise on which it was resolved, and added to the sense of outrage with which many of them first received news of it. Of course consultation or no consultation, there would have been open and undisguised conflict of opinion within the Commonwealth, but with consultation something of the dangerous edge of acrimony might well have been blunted. In the Canadian press, more critical generally than that of any other in the old dominions, it is true that even as things were, the tone of most of the correspondents, disposed to disapprove of the Anglo-French action at Suez, was said to be one of pain and sorrow rather than anger, "almost tearful," as the correspondent of the *Economist* observed, "like finding a beloved uncle arrested for rape."[6] But in initial Asian reactions surprise and regret little softened the sharpness of judgment. The prime minister of India "after fairly considerable experience in foreign affairs" could not think "of a grosser case of naked aggression" and felt that in the middle of the twentieth century "we are going back to the predatory method of the 18th and 19th centuries."[7] The Government of India dispatched a formal protest to London; Rajagopalachari, that most respected of elder statesmen, recommended that India should leave the Commonwealth;[8] and to Mr. Lester Pearson, as to many others less well

6. Quoted in James Eayrs, *Canada in World Affairs, October 1955 to June 1957* (Toronto, 1959), pp. 187-88, from the *Economist,* Nov. 10, 1956.
7. Quoted in James Eayrs, *The Commonwealth and Suez: A Documentary Survey* (London, 1964), p. 194.
8. In a statement issued in Madras on November 4, 1956, and reprinted in Mansergh, *Documents and Speeches on British and Commonwealth Affairs,*

informed, it seemed in the first days of the fighting as if the Commonwealth had been brought to "the verge of dissolution."[9] Nor did feelings all run one way. It is difficult for governments, as for individuals, to accept rebuke without resentment, even when its expression is deemed sincere and the scales of judgment evenly balanced. In one respect the Indian condemnation seemed, even to those predisposed to concur in it, somewhat partial, and Sir Anthony Eden retrospectively laid emphasis upon this apparent defect. "The Indian reaction," he wrote,[10] "was remarkable." Mr. Nehru declared in a speech that whereas in Egypt "every single thing that had happened was as clear as daylight," he could not follow "the very confusing situation" in Hungary. The Indian prime minister's studied restraint in judgment upon the Soviet action in Hungary, which might be regarded as a part of the price of the Suez diversion, in fact supplied retaliatory ammunition for its protagonists. A campaign of recrimination without parallel in Commonwealth history was opened; how and when would it close?

If the British advance to Suez was precipitous, the retreat was masterly. It was eased by the re-emergence of a near-consensus of Commonwealth views. "Britain's action, I personally say—and I will say it if I am the only one left to say it—was brave and correct."[11] So Mr. R. G. Menzies expressed himself as early as November 12, 1956—and his choice of words betrayed his isolation. Apart from Sir Anthony Eden, soon to withdraw from public life, Menzies was left alone among leading Commonwealth statesmen to say it. For the rest, whether initially supporters or critics, two broad considerations prompted restraint and calmer reappraisal. On the one hand, the prospect of possible dissolution enhanced appreciation of the value of the Commonwealth and, on the other, there was recognition

1952-62 (London, 1962), p. 521, and in Eayrs, *The Commonwealth and Suez*, p. 256.

9. Canada, *Parl. Debs.* (Commons), 4th (spec.) Sess., Nov. 27, 1965, pp. 52-55; reprinted in Mansergh, *Documents . . .* , 1952-62, p. 515.

10. *Full Circle: The Memoirs of the Rt. Hon. Sir Anthony Eden* (Cambridge, Mass., 1960), p. 610.

11. Quoted in Eayrs, *The Commonwealth and Suez*, p. 168.

that the Suez adventure was not only out of character with the pattern of recent British policy overseas, but out of line with the realities of her power position. In conjunction the two encouraged Commonwealth policies outwardly restoring the *status quo ante* but inwardly marking a readjustment in intra-Commonwealth relations. For the Commonwealth overseas, Britain remained the principal and predominant partner but with a leadership less likely than hitherto to secure backing, or at the least acquiescence, in doubtful or disputed issues; while in Britain itself, and especially within the ranks of the ruling Conservative party, the traditional assumption that the Commonwealth was an asset for the first time came in for questioning that was often distressing but nonetheless persistent. Even though the changing pattern of trading interest in itself sufficed to explain the British application for membership in the Common Market six years later, the traumatic experience of 1956 contributed to the psychology and even the manner of the approaches.

Sir Winston Churchill had spoken in 1955 in terms of "a fraternal association." This was a description that came readily to the lips of those who had worked together closely over the years as representatives of a comparatively small group of sovereign states, all governed in accord with the principles of the British parliamentary system. It was perhaps peculiarly appropriate in the brief years of exclusively Eurasian membership when mother-daughter analogies were outdated;[12] there existed a fresh and lively sense of an experiment in equal relations between peoples and governments of different races. There was also a total membership of only eight, which Englishmen at least, with youthful memories of King Henry V before Agincourt —"We few, we happy few, we band of brothers"—reinforced no doubt by some more substantial considerations, were apt to

12. "The Report of the Committee on Representational Services Overseas, appointed by the Prime Minister under the Chairmanship of Lord Plowden 1962-3," Cmnd. 2276, Dec. 2, 1963, G. B., *Parl. Paps.* (hereafter referred to as the Plowden Report) observed that "before the war, the relation of Britain to other Commonwealth Countries was still largely a maternal one in the sense that Britain's Ambassadors in foreign countries normally looked after the interests of the Dominions as well" (pp. 3-7).

think at once reassuring and fitting, almost as though a numerous band and happiness were self-contradictory. Between 1955 and 1964 the number of the self-governing states of the Commonwealth rose, however, from eight to twenty, and it is not to be doubted that this expansion in numbers complicated the relationship[13] and coincided with a dilution of its character, though not necessarily of its value. By 1964 the use of "fraternal association" would have seemed forced and an Australian writer, Professor J. D. B. Miller, came nearer to reflecting the spirit of these later years when he wrote of the Commonwealth as a "concert of convenience."[14] "I am sure that most of our countries are like Ceylon plain sober and realistic," the High Commissioner for Ceylon told the Royal Commonwealth Society in 1960, "and do not experience a spiritual ecstasy and elation as such at being in the Commonwealth. We are quite down to earth in being there and in wanting to be there. Our sentiments towards the Commonwealth are rational not emotional."[15] That indeed was the strength of the expanded Commonwealth—a strength often overlooked or discounted. The newer partner states in particular were in the Commonwealth because they saw advantage in becoming and remaining members of it. In the old dominions, and most significantly of all in Britain herself, as the pull of sentiment diminished the calculations of national advantage increasingly and publicly prevailed. In brief the Commonwealth, continuing to exist for the individual and mutual advantage of its member states, was "designed for use, rather than for ostentation."[16]

Newer attitudes to the Commonwealth found expression in many ways—in increased emphasis upon the organization of intra-Commonwealth aid for welfare and development, in a wholly new departure in the fields of technical and university

13. The Plowden Committee was much impressed with this new element of complication. See Plowden Report, p. 7.

14. J. D. B. Miller, *The Commonwealth in the World* (London, 1958), p. 275.

15. H. E. Gunasena de Soyza, "A Very Effective Instrument for World's Greater Good," *Commonwealth Journal*, New Series, IV, No. 5 (Sept.-Oct., 1960), 191.

16. Cf. Edward Gibbon, *The History of the Decline and Fall of the Roman Empire* (8 vols.; London, 1825), I, 212.

education following the *Report of the Oxford Conference of 1959*,[17] in the work of professional organizations and interchanges of many kinds, in sustained co-operative endeavors to raise living standards in South and Southeast Asia under the aegis of the Colombo Plan, the first decade of whose working was completed in 1960,[18] and in 1964 dramatically, if unexpectedly, in the contribution of military assistance to help to maintain communal peace in Cyprus and to sustain political authority in Tanganyika, Uganda, and Kenya against the threat of domestic, military seizures of power. These were all things that represented in greater or lesser degree a break with tradition and the most recent of them suggested to one writer,[19] at least, that if there were not a Commonwealth, it would be necessary to invent one.

The political transformation of the continent of Africa dominated Commonwealth, and indeed world, affairs in the decade 1955-64. That an African revolution should succeed to the greater Asian revolution was not in itself surprising. This is not to say that independence in Africa came as a by-product of the ending of colonialism in Asia, though unquestionably the Indian struggle for independence eased the way for independence in Africa without protracted struggle in many cases and without struggle at all in some. Even in the age of late Victorian imperialism, British expansion in Africa was largely determined by British preoccupation with the stability and security of the Indian empire[20] and the premise, therefore, that policy in Africa should be conditional upon developments in South Asia was well grounded in British thinking. What requires explanation is not, therefore, the fact of change, so much as the pace of it. Ghana became the first African member of the Commonwealth, on achieving independence in 1957. Nigeria followed

17. Reprinted in Mansergh, *Documents* . . . , *1952-62*, pp. 702-14.
18. "Colombo Plan for Co-operative Economic Development in South and South-East Asia. 10th Annual Report of the Consultative Committee." Kuala Lumpur, Cmnd. 1600, Oct.-Nov., 1961, G. B. *Parl Paps.*, 1961-62, X. See Mansergh, *Documents* . . . , *1952-62*, pp. 672-700. For a brief account of plans for mutual aid, see Duncan Sandys, *The Modern Commonwealth* (London, 1962).
19. *The Round Table*, March, 1964, p. 118.
20. This is the principal theme of R. E. Robinson and J. Gallagher's *Africa and the Victorians* (London, 1961).

after a three-year interlude in 1960 and then in quickening succession came Sierra Leone and Tanganyika in 1961, Uganda in 1962, Kenya and Zanzibar in 1963, with Nyasaland, Northern Rhodesia, and Basutoland to follow in 1964-1965. Why was the process not more protracted? Two reasons may be offered. One, the more obvious, was the clamant nationalism of many of these African states and the pressures of anticolonial powers at the United Nations and anticolonial opinion in the world at large. What was less evident, but no less real in the later phase, was the resolve of a British Conservative government to end its colonial responsibilities.

On February 3, 1960, Mr. Harold Macmillan told a joint session of the South African Houses of Parliament that the most striking of all the impressions he had formed on his African travels was "of the strength of this African consciousness. In different places it may take different forms. But it is happening everywhere. The wind of change is blowing through this Continent."[21] It was true. But it was also true that there was a change of wind in Downing Street. Of this, however, Mr. Macmillan understandably preferred to say nothing. British settlers in Kenya and Central Africa, however, were soon to feel the breath of what one of them later termed *So Rough a Wind*,[22] and to which another retrospectively attributed responsibility for the wanton destruction of the Federation of Rhodesia and Nyasaland.[23]

Conservatives are well placed under the British party system to carry through radical measures, as Parnell well understood, when he sought first a Conservative alliance to carry Home Rule for Ireland in 1885. It was accordingly without domestic opposition that a Conservative government was able to wind up British colonial responsibilities in Africa, Southeast Asia, the West Indies, and elsewhere at a pace which surprised the majority and shocked a minority of its own supporters, and inci-

21. Mansergh, *Documents . . . , 1952-62*, p. 347.
22. The title Sir Michael Blundell chose for his autobiography (London, 1964).
23. Sir Roy Welensky, *Welensky's 4000 Days: The Life and Death of the Federation of Rhodesia and Nyasaland* (London, 1964), p. 463.

dentally outdistanced many of its critics—Professor Easton of the City College of New York, for example, who in a work published in 1960 admonished the British for "a failure in historical insight and a certain moral blindness at the human level" in their colonial policies, while he evidently remained wholly oblivious of the fact that the British government's concern by that time was how to grant independence in an orderly and responsible way to its remaining colonial possessions, whether in Africa or elsewhere, in the shortest possible time.[24] At the Malta Independence Conference held in London in July, 1963, the secretary of state for the colonies, Mr. Duncan Sandys, found it necessary to reassure Maltese delegates by saying, "We have no desire to hustle Malta into independence . . . ," while at the British Guiana Conference later in the year he spoke with every sign of mounting irritation about the need to settle domestic differences so as not to delay the plans of Her Majesty's Government for an early transfer of power.[25] For the Tacitean "divide and rule" of empire, there was substituted an injunction more appropriate to commonwealth—"unite and abdicate."

The virtual completion of the policy of transforming an empire into a commonwealth accounted for a new assurance, even asperity, in British reactions at the United Nations to anti-colonial critics. In a debate on colonialism in the United Nations General Assembly, on October 1, 1963, the British foreign secretary, the Earl of Home, after alluding to "the vicious attack on us" by Indonesia following the establishment of the Federation of Malaysia and the rupture in diplomatic relations between Somalia and the United Kingdom because of the disputed Kenya frontier, went on to say that these events "seem to us to be strange by-products of the grant of independence which is urged upon us as a policy by every Asian and African country." For Britain the only issue was not *whether* any country should become independent, but only *when*. "The only check on the transfer of

24. S. C. Easton, *The Twilight of European Colonialism* (New York, 1960), p. 519 and generally.
25. Held in London in July and November, 1963, respectively. See Cmnd. 2121, Annex A, G. B., *Parl. Paps. 1962-63*, and Cmnd. 2203, Annex A, G. B., *Parl. Paps. 1963-64*.

power from the United Kingdom to the government of the country concerned is that we want to be sure that, when independence is granted, the country will be able to make both ends meet economically and that it was accepting a constitution, from the day of independence, which will work for the well-being of every section of society. . . ." He hoped Britain could "go along with the majority of the United Nations in these colonial matters" since it accepted the principles of "unqualified self-determination, majority rule and safeguards for minorities."[26]

Lord Home's contribution to the United Nations deserves attention for three reasons. There is always a time lag in reputation and the conviction that a Western imperial power was deliberately divesting itself of the remnants of empire was too unexpected to strike quick roots. The anticolonialists continued to campaign, slow to understand that the campaign in respect of Britain was concluded. The second reason why Lord Home's speech merits attention flows from the first. In the years following Indian independence it was widely maintained, not least in the United States, that a Commonwealth divided between colonialists and anticolonialists could not endure. This view, which *inter alia* discounted the strength of anticolonial, pro-Commonwealth sentiment within Britain and especially within the then dominant Labour party, is now evidently without substance. We are all anticolonialists nowadays as we were all socialists in Harcourt's time. True, this means there are some very odd figures in the ranks, looking for their chance to break away, but the solid mass of opinion keeps them more or less in formation. And no doubt, in bringing about this new measure of agreement on a potentially divisive issue, the influence of Asian membership in the Commonwealth has been pronounced. In that sense, as Professor Rajan maintains,[27] it is a Commonwealth new in character that came into existence in 1947.

Finally, Lord Home's assertion that the issue for Britain was not *whether*, but *when*, any country should become inde-

26. *Commonwealth Survey*, IX (Oct. 22, 1963), 885-88.
27. M. S. Rajan, *The Post-War Transformation of the Commonwealth* (Delhi, 1963).

pendent may serve as a touchstone for reviewing British policy over the whole decade. Certainly it was not universally true at the outset of the period. On July 28, 1954, the minister of state for colonial affairs, Mr. Hopkinson, told the House of Commons that Her Majesty's Government had decided that the time had come to take "a fresh initiative" in the development of self-governing institutions for Cyprus, but it emerged under questioning that this development was not intended to lead to self-government. On the contrary, in the words of the minister, "there are certain territories in the Commonwealth which, owing to their particular circumstances, can never expect to be fully independent."[28] As Louis Napoleon once observed: *"en politique on ne doit jamais dire 'jamais,'"* and neglect of such elementary political prudence on this occasion exacted its harsh price. Elsewhere there was no parallel to such a policy of negation; and elsewhere, with the questionable exception of Kenya, there was no organized national revolt against British imperial rule. Once again, therefore, as in Ireland in 1919-21, it happened, not perhaps altogether fortuitously, that the most bitter conflict was between peoples not of different but of the same race.

In the earlier years of the decade there was a disposition to transfer power by stages—internal self-government with certain powers reserved, full domestic self-government, the chief minister becoming prime minister with a cabinet responsible to an elected assembly, consideration of administrative needs and internal security, inquiry into the position of minorities (the Willink Commission report on Nigeria being the classic document of the period in this field),[29] the holding of a constitutional conference preparatory to agreement on a constitution and the inclusion in it of any necessary entrenchment, as in the Nigerian Constitution of 1960,[30] of minority rights, then independence embodied in an independence act of the British Parliament with all the

28. G. B., 5 *Parl. Debs.* (Commons), DXXXI, 504-5, reprinted in Mansergh, *Documents . . . , 1952-62*, pp. 213-18.

29. Nigeria, "Report of the Commission Appointed to Inquire into the Fears of Minorities and the Means of Allaying Them," Cmnd. 505, G. B., *Parl. Paps. 1957-58*, IX. See Mansergh, *Documents . . . , 1952-62*, pp. 57-66.

30. *Nigeria (Constitution) Order in Council*, S. 1, No. 1652, 1960.

governments of the Commonwealth being invited to concur in Commonwealth membership. Time was allowed for each advance to be tested and for misgivings, notably on the part of minorities, to be expressed, and this was coupled with mistrust of a timetable, defining and committing the British government in advance. In more recent years this phased transfer of power, with either implied or stated conditions for each further advance, has given way to transfer with time as the first priority. If this reflected chiefly a change, if not in outlook at least in temper, on the part of the metropolitan power, it was assisted by growing experience. In the past twenty years the Commonwealth collectively has probably produced the largest number of written constitutions ever composed in so short a period. All the devices of federalism, all the varying balances between executive and legislature, all the machinery of judicial control were there to be copied or exploited as occasion demanded. One thing was lacking—and it was evidently in some demand—and that was a blueprint to serve as the prototype for the creation of a one-party state.

Given the will, the liquidation of colonialism, that is to say of imperial rule over other peoples, presented problems that were largely technical in character. But the liquidation of imperial rule in territories where there were colonists in the Graeco-Roman sense was quite another matter. In South, Central, and East Africa, British colonists had settled, with the encouragement of their fellow countrymen in most instances, and had become in varying degrees a privileged, influential, or ruling minority, differing in cultural background and above all in race from the indigenous majority. Usually, but not invariably, well-intentioned spokesmen encouraged thoughts of partnership, but while this commended itself warmly to liberal opinion, the principal protagonists were more preoccupied with power. That, at root, and *pace* Sir Roy Welensky, accounted for the collapse of the long-considered, but at the last somewhat hastily improvised, federal experiment in Central Africa. Two quotations, the first from the "Report of the Nyasaland [Devlin] Commission of Enquiry, 1959," and the other from the Monckton Commission, 1960, suffice to explain the ever-hardening resolve of the African majority that the Federation should be liquidated. "Federation means the domination of Southern Rhodesia: the domination of Southern Rhodesia means the domination of the settler; the domination of the settler means the perpetuation of racial inferiority. . . ."[31]

It is inevitable and natural that the prospect of independence, seven years ago unthinkably remote, should now appear to many Africans to be a right from which they should be no longer debarred: and racial feeling, far from having merged into a sense of multi-racial nationhood, has grown sharper and stronger. It now appears to many Africans that only the presence of the European community politically entrenched behind the Federal Constitution stands between them and the form of freedom already granted to their fellow Africans in most other parts of the continent.[32]

The entrenchment was removed, the Federation dissolved on December 31, 1963, and in Nyasaland and Northern Rhodesia, as already in Kenya, the privileges and the power of the colonists were ended. But in Southern Rhodesia, the colonists, whose privileged, minority position the British government deemed politically expendable and the African majority desired to see politically expended, were more numerous and prepared to be recalcitrant. For a multiracial Commonwealth their resistance to the winds of change remained in 1964 to present some delicate, possibly dangerous, issues, touching on sensitive, racial chords.

The most important Commonwealth development of the decade was the elevation of race equality, or multiracialism, as a basic principle, perhaps indeed the one basic principle shared by this community of states. In an earlier period allegiance to the Crown, and then, after 1949, the practice of responsible parliamentary government had been accepted or generally considered

31. "Report of the Nyasaland [Devlin] Commission of Enquiry 1959" Cmnd. 814, G. B., *Parl. Paps.* 1959-60, XI. See Mansergh, *Documents* . . . , 1952-62, pp. 133-40.

32. "The Advisory [Monckton] Commission on the Review of the Constitution of Rhodesia and Nyasaland," Cmnd. 1148, G. B., *Parl. Paps.* 1959-60, XI.

conditions of membership. But following the Indian precedent, Asian and African states adopted republican forms of government until by 1964 the number of republican and monarchical member states was roughly equal. If numbers again were counted, about one-third of the members by that date no longer practiced parliamentary government on the Westminster model, and it was accepted, though not in some instances without misgiving, that this was a matter of domestic concern. But in respect of the ordering of race relations, such a plea was conclusively rejected. South Africa provided, as had been long foreshadowed, the test case, for as the Commonwealth moved towards equality and multiracialism, the government of the Union enforced within South Africa a theory of racial separation, little distinguishable in practice from racial discrimination. The test, as it happened, came in such a way as to associate older constitutional with newer and now dominant racial issues.

When the prime ministers of the Commonwealth met in London on March 8-17, 1961, they had before them an application from the government of the Union for South Africa's continued membership of the Commonwealth after she became a republic on May 31. The decision to become a republic had been approved in a referendum (in which voting was restricted to Europeans) in 1960, and the republican constitution, substituting a state president for the governor general, was given a first reading in January and later duly approved by the South African Parliament. Commonwealth precedent in respect of India, Pakistan, Ceylon, and Ghana suggested that a request couched in conventional form for continued republican membership would be acceded to, if constitutional considerations alone were at issue. But while the desirability of distinguishing the constitutional from broader political considerations was recognized by most of the Commonwealth prime ministers—Mr. Diefenbaker of Canada being, however, a notable exception—South Africa's application was made the occasion, as public opinion in many Commonwealth countries demanded, of a general debate upon South Africa's racial policies. This debate, as a brief communiqué issued on March 15 recorded,[33] took place with the consent of the South African prime minister, Dr. Verwoerd. Subsequent accounts given by prime ministers to their individual parliaments reveal something of its fluctuating course and dramatic conclusion.[34] At the heart of it lay the simple fact that Dr. Verwoerd was prepared to make neither apology nor concession. Apartheid, in his view, was not a matter of convenience or expediency: it was an expression of the right view of race relations and as such had to be defended with the uncompromising zeal of a religious conviction. There would be no change in practice or direction and his Commonwealth colleagues, thus faced with the prospect of acquiescence at the threatened price of division among them or of pressing home their criticisms, adopted the latter course. Dr. Verwoerd foreshortened debate by announcing the withdrawal of South Africa's application and thereby fixed May 31, the fifty-first anniversary of the Act of Union, as the date when South Africa's membership in the Commonwealth would lapse.

Dr. Verwoerd subsequently stated that he took this step with "great regret." South Africa's request had been made in the expectation that it would have been willingly granted, "as was done on behalf of South Africa in the previous cases of India, Pakistan, Ceylon, Ghana . . . in spite of our great differences with them," but he had been amazed at, and shocked by, the spirit of hostility and even vindictiveness shown towards his country. This had made it clear that South Africa's continued membership would no longer be welcomed. He believed it marked "the beginning of the disintegration of the Commonwealth." The comments of his fellow prime ministers, other than Mr. Menzies, who confessed himself "deeply troubled," were regretful but also in varying degrees expressed relief at South Africa's departure. The President of Pakistan thought that, as a result, the Commonwealth would emerge as a stronger organization; Mr. Diefenbaker said South Africa's withdrawal was unavoidable, because discrimination in respect of race or color could

33. Reprinted in Mansergh, *Documents* . . . , *1952-62*, p. 365.
34. See *ibid.*, pp. 365-400.

not continue if the Commonwealth was to be "a force for good"; Mrs. Bandanaraike of Ceylon saw in it "a dramatic vindication of the equality and human dignity for which the Commonwealth stands"; Mr. Nehru, though he wondered, and it would seem not without cause, whether the decision would in any way benefit non-Europeans in the Union, had little doubt that the effect "will be to strengthen the Commonwealth," and Mr. Macmillan, for whose policy the outcome represented the frustration of initial aims, spoke more simply of regret that circumstances had made the breach inevitable. Implicit in all that was said was the conviction that a turning point in Commonwealth history had been passed, and hope predominated over anxiety as to what it might portend. It was widely noted that this was the first occasion on which the views of a United Kingdom government had not prevailed in a matter of major importance in Commonwealth internal policy.[35] Unnoted was the fact that the issue was decided by the prime ministers themselves in fluctuating debate and in a tense atmosphere in London seemingly without continuing conference of cabinets.

The decade 1955-64, while recording no change in the foreign relations of Commonwealth members comparable to the developments in their domestic composition and outlook, nevertheless saw significant reinforcement for policies of non-alignment and neutralism. The member states who were aligned in treaty relations with the United States, with other nations, and with one another in 1954 remained without exception so associated in 1964, but the non-aligned, or neutralist, states within the Commonwealth were much increased by a general African adherence to their number. Both Ceylon among older Asian members and Nigeria among newer African states abrogated their defense agreements with the United Kingdom in 1956 and 1962 respectively.[36] The Chinese attack on India in 1962 had, however, a profound impact and, while not modifying Indian attachment to the principles of *Panch Shila*, caused some sharp reassessment

35. Cf. *The Annual Register, 1961*, pp. 63-64, for an account written by the author on which this record is based.
36. See Mansergh, *Documents . . . , 1952-62*, pp. 573-75 and 581-83.

of political and strategic needs.[37] While therefore the pattern of Commonwealth foreign policies remained unchanged, the impact of what did not happen, namely Britain's joining the European Common Market, had repercussions more profound than anything that did.

It was on June 13, 1961 that the British prime minister, Mr. Macmillan, announced that three senior ministers were to visit Commonwealth capitals to consult with Commonwealth governments about Britain's relations with the European Economic Community. The three emissaries—Mr. Sandys in New Zealand, Australia, and Canada; Mr. Thorneycroft in Singapore, Malaya, Ceylon, Pakistan, and India; Mr. John Hare in Ghana, Nigeria, Sierra Leone, and the Federation of Rhodesia and Nyasaland, however, proved more successful in eliciting misgivings about the effects, political as well as economic, for the Commonwealth overseas of Britain's membership in EEC, than in persuading overseas Commonwealth governments of its desirability. While the economic and political strengthening of western Europe was recognized to be a general Commonwealth interest and while it was explicitly conceded in communiqués[38] issued after the talks that Britain's membership in EEC was a matter for decision by the British government, Australian ministers, to take a not unrepresentative example and to quote the communiqué issued on July 11, expressed their concern at "the weakening effect they believed this development would have on the Commonwealth relationship," and while they "did not feel entitled to object to the opening of negotiations by the British Government," they made it clear that "the absence of objection should in the circumstances not be taken as implying approval." When the question was considered collectively by Commonwealth ministers attending the meeting of the Commonwealth Economic Consultative Council at Accra, September 12-14, such strong language was used by the Canadian delegates

37. Indian thinking about China in 1954 was reflected at the Fifth Unofficial Commonwealth Relations Conference held at Lahore, March 17-27. See a report by N. Mansergh entitled *The Multi-Racial Commonwealth* (London, 1955), pp. 83-85.

38. Cmnd. 1449, reprinted in Mansergh, *Documents . . .* , 1952-62, pp. 634-45.

as to suggest that the Canadian government considered that Britain had to make a choice between the Commonwealth and EEC. The official communiqué[39] itself spoke "of the grave apprehension and concern" of all overseas Commonwealth representatives regarding "the possible results of the initiative taken by the United Kingdom."

The Accra communiqué represented a position more extreme than was in evidence in the subsequent negotiations or at the Commonwealth Prime Ministers' Meeting in September, 1962.[40] Though the reasons for it might be debatable,[41] the fact that Britain's trade with the rest of the Commonwealth had declined was something that could not be gainsaid. Yet there remained many in the Commonwealth overseas, especially in the old dominions, who accepted the truth of much that was said by General de Gaulle on January 14, 1963,[42] when he used his country's power of veto to terminate negotiations. They were disposed to agree that Britain was in fact insular, maritime, bound by its history, its political, financial, and trading systems to many and distant countries. While they had become generally reconciled to the thought of Britain's membership in the Common Market with hardly negotiated safeguards and with reservations of their special interests, her complete absorption in the European community, which the General professed to consider a necessary condition of membership, was something which other member states of the Commonwealth would have viewed with dismay. Resentment, therefore, at the brusqueness and lateness—after months of thought and bargaining in which all Commonwealth governments had been in some measure involved—of General de Gaulle's pronouncement was not wholly dissociated from a sense of relief. Yet there remained cause for continuing reflection. In the middle of the nineteenth century

39. *Ibid.*, pp. 650-51.
40. For an official record of the negotiations, see *Commonwealth Relations Office List 1964* (London: H.M.S.O., 1964).
41. To some extent this was a party issue in Great Britain. See, e.g., speech by Mr. Harold Wilson, G. B., 5 *Parl. Debs.* (Commons), DCLXXXVIII, 1367-91, Feb. 6, 1964.
42. Mansergh, *Documents* . . . , 1952-62, p. 667.

Great Britain, carrying through her own commercial revolution, "had in effect broken away from her own Empire";[43] was she in the later twentieth century likewise to break away from a Commonwealth which, while no longer her own, she had nonetheless brought into being?

43. D. G. Creighton, *Dominion of the North: A History of Canada* (Cambridge, Mass., 1944), p. 256.

Part II

The Birth of States

2

The Transfer of Power in Historical Perspective

W. B. Hamilton*

What then is the true test of the historical importance of events? I say, it is their *pregnancy* or in other words the greatness of the consequences likely to follow from them. [SIR JOHN SEELEY, in *The Expansion of England*, 1883.]

To propose that Great Britain should voluntarily give up all authority over her colonies, and leave them to elect their own magistrates, to enact their own laws, and to make peace and war as they might think proper, would be to propose such a measure as never was, and never will be adopted, by any nation in the world. [ADAM SMITH in *The Wealth of Nations.*]

If wisdom alone were listened to, the ordinary object of contention would be reversed—the mother-country would desire to see her children powerful, that they might become free, and the colonies would fear the loss of that tutelary authority which gave them internal tranquility and security against external foes. [JEREMY BENTHAM in *Manual of Political Economy.*] (The last two quotations from Klaus E. Knorr, *British Colonial Theories, 1570-1850* [Toronto, 1944], pp. 188, 266.)

The transfer of power in the British Empire, if adequately treated, would demand the eloquence of a Macaulay, the canvas

* Professor of history, Duke University. I acknowledge indebtedness to Professor Kenneth Robinson for criticism of this essay and for contributions to it, but do not imply that he shares any responsibility for the views expressed in it.

of a Gibbon, and the creative imagination of a Maitland. The
theme is a grand one: out of territory controlled or seed planted
by the inhabitants of a little island cluster off the coast of
Europe there has grown an impressive array of states: the
United Kingdom and dependencies, the United States, Ireland,
Canada, Jamaica, Trinidad and Tobago, Sierra Leone, Ghana,
Nigeria, South Africa, Southern Rhodesia, Zambia, Malawi,
Tanzania, Kenya, Uganda, Sudan, Somalia (in part), Egypt—
shall we count[1] Israel, Jordan, Iraq—Pakistan, India, Ceylon,
Burma, Malaysia, Australia, New Zealand, Cyprus, Malta, and
the Gambia. Approaching thirty, several of these are themselves
great federations or amalgamations! Bermuda and the Bahamas
are internally self-governing, and British Guiana is in-again-
out-again. We doubtless have several more to go in this remarkable act of creation, although it may be hoped we shall stop
short of Tristan da Cunha or Sark.

If an effort to tell the tale of this creation in an essay were
not ridiculous on the face of it, we are sternly warned off pedes-
trian detail by the author of our first epigraph, who calls such
history "the newspaper treatment of affairs," which would consider the loss of America "important because it brings down
the North Cabinet."[2] Fortunately, it is a familiar tale for the
most part, with a very ample bibliography, although its telling
in a single work that can be *read* awaits the reincarnation of the
men named in our first sentence.

Blinded by mercantilism, the British in the eighteenth
century did not ponder Turgot's metaphor about ripe colonies
either to examine its truth or to consider what to do about it.
It remained for Britons overseas to suggest a remedy. "Like so
many other practical gadgets for making life on this planet more
efficient and more comfortable," writes a Canadian, "the British
Commonwealth was invented in America."[3] He is referring to

1. In view of the brevity of the experience recounted by Elizabeth Monroe,
Britain's Moment in the Middle East, 1914-1956 (London, 1963).
2. Seeley, *The Expansion of England* (2nd. ed., [18th printing]; London,
1911), pp. 167, 170.
3. Frank H. Underhill, *The British Commonwealth: An Experiment in Co-
operation Among Nations* (Durham, N. C., 1956), p. 3.

the schemes of American leaders for some form of union[4] between England and new Englands long practiced in the arts of self-government, and proficient to a sophisticated degree in the skills by which my colleague J. W. Cell slyly identifies a ripe colony: one in which the inhabitants are capable of violent and sustained agitation. Obtusely, the British met the situation in the manner of a charging bull and fifteen of the American colonies were lost.[5]

If the British at home lost for the moment their genius for combining ideals of freedom with good pragmatic political action,[6] not so their seventeenth-century cousins in the rebellious colonies. One is lost in admiration—and not, one hopes, out of chauvinism—for the Founding Fathers of what Sir Winston used to call the Great Republic. Even before they had struck off their federal constitution, they had faced the question of colonies and what to do with them when they were ripe. Their recipe was to govern them at the outset as crown colonies, permit a rapid progress toward self-government while not giving the colonists so much power over the imperial governors and judges as the British had given *them*, and as they became ripe admit them into the Union as equal partners,[7] without, as it

4. R. G. Adams, *Political Ideas of the American Revolution* (Durham, N. C., 1922).

5. The following offer keys to the bibliography and recent interpretations: Jack P. Greene, "The Flight from Determinism: A Review of Recent Literature on the Coming of the American Revolution," *South Atlantic Quarterly*, LXI (Spring, 1962), 235-59; Edmund S. Morgan, "The American Revolution: Revisions in need of Revising," *William and Mary Quarterly*, 3rd Ser., XIV (Jan., 1957), 3-15; Morgan, *The American Revolution: A Review of Changing Interpretations* (Washington, 1958), a new edition of which is at pp. 38-55 of *Interpreting and Teaching American History*, ed. W. H. Cartwright and R. L. Watson, Jr. (Washington, 1961).

6. Simultaneously with the loss of the American colonies, agitation forced Westminster to take some steps in Ireland (1782) toward legislative freedom while trying to maintain executive control, and then to the experiment of union. I am not sure that the English reasoned from their Irish expedients toward an analogy with more distant colonies, or vice versa.

7. The Northwest Ordinance, July 13, 1787, confirmed by Act of Congress, August 7, 1789, 1 Stat. 50-53. A somewhat purer text is in *The Territorial Papers of the United States*, ed. Clarence Edward Carter (in progress, Washington, 1934-), II, *The Territory Northwest of the River Ohio, 1787-1803* (Washington, 1934), pp. 203-4. *Vide* Clarence E. Carter, "Colonialism in Continental United States," *South Atlantic Quarterly*, XLVII (Jan., 1948), 17-28, where at p. 28 he lays claim to "the most successful experiment in the administration of colonies that the modern world has witnessed."

turned out, the right of secession.[8] On this scheme the new republic proceeded to build one of the great nineteenth-century empires, and to hold it.[9]

What did the British, or more precisely British governments, learn from the loss of the American colonies? Nothing immediately, or rather a little of the wrong lesson. Chief Justice William Smith of Quebec could write that

> The truth is that the Country [the U.S.] had outgrown its Government, and wanted the true remedy for more than half a century before the Rupture commenced. . . . it belonged to the administrations of the days of Our Fathers to have found the Cure, in the Erection of a Power upon the Continent itself, to control all its own little Republics, and create a Partner in the Legislation of the Empire. . . .[10]

He could advocate such a union, such a treatment, of all North America that was left after the American secession.[11] But all government at home could think of was a titled, hereditary upper house for a new Canada, on the theory that America was lost because the aristocratic principle was absent; a tighter control over the colonies remaining; and the pursuit of more territory—in India and at all the crossroads to it, in the West Indies, and in Spanish America, which by 1806 the British greedily thought to swallow whole at a gulp,[12] or at least to detach from Spain.

8. Seeley held out this feature to the British as an example. (*Expansion of England*, pp. 18-19, 346 ff.) J. W. Cell points out that in the middle of the nineteenth century Molesworth, Russell, Gladstone, and Grey were mindful of the United States' experience, and were influenced by it, especially as interpreted by de Tocqueville, and that J. A. Roebuck's *The Colonies of England, a Plan* (1849) drew upon the N. W. Ordinance. ("British Policy toward Developing Nations: Introduction," an unpublished paper, Duke University, 1964. I am indebted to Dr. Cell for permission to use this paper, which he plans to develop.) See also Wakefield on American land policy.

9. True it is that the Philippines were freed in 1946—or were they evicted from the sugar free-trade area? And for Puerto Rico, the U.S. has adapted the dominion idea of Great Britain. Julius W. Pratt, *America's Colonial Experiment* (New York, 1951); Whitney T. Perkins, *Denial of Empire: The United States and Its Dependencies* (Leyden, 1962).

10. To Dorchester, Quebec, Feb. 5, 1790, *Statutes, Treaties and Documents of the Canadian Constitution, 1713-1929*, ed. W. P. M. Kennedy (2nd. ed.; Toronto, 1930), pp. 190-91.

11. *Ibid.*, pp. 192-93; Chester Martin, *Foundations of Canadian Nationhood* (Toronto, 1955), p. 214.

12. Klaus E. Knorr, *British Colonial Theories, 1750-1850* (Toronto, 1944),

Henceforth for almost a hundred years, the British could accept without blinking the situation that their theorists, the intellectuals, the chief politicians, the under-secretaries in the Colonial Office—a whole host of the prominent, were either actively opposed (they said) to the retention of the colonies or pessimistic about their remaining in the Empire, but that no colony was ejected, none seceded. The free-traders, the economizers (as well as economists), the antimilitarists, the Radicals, the Manchester School, all embraced and advocated separatism or pessimism.[13] Or so they said. The nineteenth-century story is one big paradox. Not only was no colony lost, but during the earlier part of the century, the age of supposed indifference or hostility to the acquisition of territory, there was inexorable expansion (e.g., India, Ceylon, Australia, the Cape, the West Indies, Singapore, Lower Burma, Aden, Hong Kong, New Zealand, the Gold Coast, Natal, Orange Free State, Vancouver and British Columbia, Lagos). The Victorians were reluctant expansionists, yes, but expansionists. For further contrast between theory and fact, between preachment and action, there is the comedy of the anti-imperialist Gladstone sending two armies into Egypt. If an addition were made, the odds are that the Liberals after mid-century would outstrip in annexation the "imperialistic" Conservatives.[14]

We are not done with contradictions. After 1815 a victorious country without a naval rival held to expensive strategic posts. Liberal evangelical humanitarians, in defense of natives and colored people, fought self-government by their emigrant

pp. 209-13 *et seq.*; Helen Taft Manning, *British Colonial Government after the American Revolution, 1782-1820* (New Haven, 1933); Vincent Harlow, *The Founding of the Second British Empire*, I (Oxford, 1952), second, posthumous volume expected; R. Coupland, *The American Revolution and the British Empire* (London, 1930); on the South American venture, tangential to our theme, the author has read manuscripts in the P.R.O. (W. O. 1/161, for example), in the Grenville papers at Boconnoc, and others.

13. Views made familiar by Knorr, pp. 155-349; and C. A. Bodelsen, *Studies in Mid-Victorian Imperialism* (1924, here used in reissue, London, 1960), pp. 11-75.

14. For example, first steps in Malaya and Fiji, forward policy in Afghanistan, chartering of the North Borneo and Royal Niger companies, southern Nigeria at Berlin Congress, New Guinea, Bechuanaland, the decision to remain in East Africa and Uganda, northern Malaya and Johore, German Africa.

brothers, or fought emigration and expansion one day and in changed circumstances pushed British expansion to protect their charges. Promoters of the welfare of the poor by emigration demanded expansion and contested with the defenders of the welfare of the native. Adherents of the religion of laissez faire could in turn inveigh against any colonization, try to refuse the right of colonists to do as *they* would in economic matters, and advocate grabbing territory to keep protectionists out. Some reformers thought colonies economic nonsense at best, but rather liked having such big outdoor laboratories. They thought independence inevitable, but did not see how they could abandon peoples to their own folly and the rapaciousness of outsiders.

No matter how much all the liberal groups and most of the public officials spoke of the necessity for extending self-government or responsible government to the European settlers, no one in power made any strong effort to do so on any comprehensive plan. On the contrary, most advances in self-government were wrung out of Whitehall by contumacious pressure from the colonists, or were slipped over by governors on the spot. Nova Scotia is the exception that merely proves the rule.

To none of these colonial 'crises' [of the 1850's, writes Dr. Cell] did the [Colonial] Office bring a systematically conceived plan. In each case the resulting solution was a compromise worked out, though with the Canadian precedent always in mind, largely on an *ad hoc* basis, among the legislature, the governor, and the authorities in London.[15]

There was not even much logic. Blatchford (Sir F. Rogers) complained of Grey that he could not see that it was impracticable to give representative institutions without going on to responsible government.[16] In the end, of course, it was to prove impracticable to "grant" responsible government without creating an independent nation. No matter how loud the prattle of inevitable independence (by which most persons meant seces-

15. J. W. Cell, "British Policy toward Developing Nations," Introduction, p. 4.
16. Quoted in Kenneth N. Bell and W. P. Morrell, *Select Documents on British Colonial Policy, 1830-1860* (Oxford, 1928), p. xxxix.

sion) no one really contemplated it. (And, indeed, of the colonies populated by persons of British origins—the ones they had in mind in the last century—none has yet seceded.)[17] The process of instituting thorough independence was gradual, drawn out over nearly a hundred years.

We do not have to refresh our minds with many details to illustrate the gradualness. After demands by Papineau and Baldwin, and after the Durham Report, Lord John Russell asserted in the House of Commons in June of 1839 that it was impossible to grant to the Canadas the responsible government exercised in Great Britain,[18] and so advised the governor, Poulett Thomson, on October 14. Two days later he unwittingly opened the road to the practice, if not the grant, by instructing Thomson that tenure of colonial offices during good behavior must cease.[19] Lord John's speech evoked some cogent responses from Joseph Howe, leader of the majority in the Nova Scotian Assembly. The upshot of his contentions was the installation of limited responsible government, on the instruction of Grey.[20] It remained for Elgin to install it in Canada, and the procedure was sealed and dramatized by his assent to the bill indemnifying losses in the rebellions.[21] He was backed by Grey.

Elgin desired not only to install government by the leaders of a majority in the assembly, but to translate to North America the British system as it had evolved recently in England, rather than the American type of government, which represented to him an arrested development, the product of a colony's having quit the Empire under an outworn colonial system, before the growth of parliamentarism.[22] Thus we might underscore Pro-

17. Ireland's unhappy history must always be accounted an exception. South African membership is a casualty more of the multiracial Commonwealth than even of the dogged separatism of the Boers, and the English were not a majority of its European population anyway. Professor Nicholas Mansergh has commented upon the compliment paid by the Afrikaners in applying for membership when they formed a republic.

18. Kennedy, *Documents*, p. 382.

19. Russell to Thomson, Oct. 14, Oct. 16, 1839, *ibid.*, pp. 421-24.

20. To Lt. Gov. Sir John Harvey, Nov. 3, 1846, *ibid.*, pp. 494-96.

21. Elgin to Grey, April 30, 1849, *ibid.*, pp. 501-5.

22. Elgin to Grey, Toronto, March 23, Nov. 1, Dec. 17, 1850, Kennedy, *Documents*, pp. 509-12; Chester Martin agreed: *Foundations of Canadian Nationhood*, pp. v, 97 ff., 203.

fessor Underhill's point that "the real empire builders were the Victorian liberals, most of whom did not believe in empire,"[23] by whom he means the best of the grand Whiggery, the Radicals, the free-traders, the Utilitarians, and the Liberals. It can be added that the colonists' demands (as well as the rulers' yieldings) were reflections of late eighteenth- and early nineteenth-century ideas in England—a transmission of a climate of opinion —just as the earlier rebels overseas had fed on the political ideas of the seventeenth century.

Is it likewise true that there were not any feasible alternatives for Whitehall? To the already larrikinalian Australians, and the slightly less pushing New Zealanders, the North American example only added fire. By 1855, rejecting Grey's halfway measure of 13 and 14 Vic. c. 59, amidst considerable democratic political change, the antipodean colonies had attained a version of responsible government, taking control of the crown lands with it.[24]

Britain had transferred considerable power, but by no means all. Again the word "gradual" is the key to the devolution. It is not necessary to try to summarize the late A. B. Keith's massive *Responsible Government in the Dominions*.[25] The reader will remind himself that while the control of trade insofar as it related to customs was given over to responsibly governed colonies by 1857, shipping was controlled by imperial regulation into the twentieth century; that as for control over lawmaking the Colonial Laws Validity Act of 1865[26] removed certain prohibitions but legislative power remained at Westminster, and the

23. *The British Commonwealth*, p. 15.
24. J. D. McNaughtan, "Colonial Liberalism; 1851-92," in *Australia: A Social and Political History*, ed. Gordon Greenwood (Sydney, 1955), pp. 98-130; Keith, *Responsible Government in the Dominions*, I, 22-27; II, 773.
25. The second edition, revised and rewritten to 1927 (Oxford, 1928) runs to 1939 pages. Herbert Vere Evatt in *The King and His Dominion Governors: A Study of the Reserve Powers of the Crown in Great Britain and the Dominions* (London, 1936) offers supplementary matter and takes issue with Keith on several points. Alpheus Todd, the librarian of the Canadian parliament, was the author in 1880 of an older work, *Parliamentary Government in the British Colonies*, which pronounced a rather broad view of the imperial power and its governors, and itself became an influential historical document.
26. 28 and 29 Vic. c. 63. Conveniently printed in *Imperial Constitutional Documents, 1765-1952, A Supplement*, ed. Frederick Madden (Oxford, 1953), pp. 67-70.

governors could still disallow and reserve; and that the prerogatives of the Crown (which Evatt thought as late as 1936 wanted definition) remained and were the subject of piecemeal altercation and adjustment between assemblies and governors.

In 1879 Canada sought to send to London a quasi-diplomatic agent to have a voice in concerting actions where the imperial and the dominion jurisdiction met. This privilege was granted, but in a report on the office of high commissioner the Canadian privy council acknowledged that "Her Majesty's [U.K.] Government is unquestionably the supreme governing power of the Empire. . . ," and that it held "general authority as rulers of the entire Empire."[27] As for diplomatic representation in other countries, Ripon (colonial secretary) remarked in 1895: "To give the Colonies the power of negotiating treaties for themselves without reference to her Majesty's Government would be to give them an international status as separate and sovereign States, and would be equivalent to breaking up the Empire into a number of independent States. . . ."[28] When in 1920 Sir R. Borden announced that the British had agreed to Canada's dispatching a minister plenipotentiary to Washington, the other old dominions shook their heads. Canada did not send a minister until 1926, and the Irish had preceded her by two years.[29] The national spirit engendered by World War I and the revelation at its end of discrete interests in foreign policy had taken their toll. But British power shaded still that of the dominions.

Of the results of the Imperial Conference of 1926, Keith, at a time when there had been little opportunity for perspective, was rather scornful: no repeal of the Colonial Laws Validity Act, 1865; no freedom from the shackles of the Merchant Shipping Act, 1894; no change in the governor general's duty as

27. "Report of a Committee of the Honourable the Privy Council for Canada, approved by his Excellency the Governor-General, on the 22nd December, 1879," printed in Kennedy, *Documents,* pp. 678-679, and *Selected Speeches and Documents on British Colonial Policy, 1763-1917,* ed. A. B. Keith (Reissue, 2 vols. in one; London, 1948), II, 151-55.

28. Circular letter to governors, June 28, 1895, printed by Keith, *Selected Speeches,* II, 156-66 (at 159), and Kennedy, *Documents,* pp. 680-83 (at 681-82).

29. Keith, *Responsible Government in the Dominions,* II, 893 ff., 1233. Documents in Kennedy, *Documents,* pp. 699-713.

to the reservation of bills; no independence in international affairs. "In view of these facts even autonomy is perhaps an exaggerated expression; independence is absurd."[30] The Statute of Westminster cured such of these ills as were onerous; the evolution of independence was accelerated by it and by the war. The prohibition in 1949 of appeals from Canada to the Judicial Committee of the Privy Council[31] and Mr. Pearson's scheme in 1964 to remove to Canada from Westminster the power to amend the Canadian constitution might serve as a climax to a long process of the transfer of power.

Had England contributed to the building of nations in the old Commonwealth? Certainly. Not directly, consciously, as a logical projection of views such as those of Durham and of Palmerston's fondness for nationalism. The English resist logical projections; if they did not, there would be no Commonwealth. But they contributed the ideas and the institutions. And for reasons of their own, they consistently encouraged amalgamation and federation, so that the European colonies emerged into independence as more or less viable states. True, they failed at first in some efforts at federation: Grey in Australia in 1850, Carnarvon in South Africa in the 1870's. But the English role in Canadian federation was not minor; Buckingham and Chandos and other Englishmen were determined to make it go.

It was [wrote Martin] the undisputed parliamentary supremacy of Great Britain at that time that enabled a group of far-seeing Canadian and British statesmen to carry the *B.N.A. Act, 1867* "per saltum," as Macdonald advocated, thus cutting at one stroke the Gordian knot of state sovereignty which had dragged the United States through the horrors of civil war.[32]

In South Africa, despite a "national" convention and ratification by provincial assemblies (plebiscite in Natal), the Union was

30. Keith, *Responsible Government* (revised to 1927), II, 1233.
31. The documents are in *Documents and Speeches on British Commonwealth Affairs, 1931-1952*, ed. Nicholas Mansergh (2 vols.; London, 1953), I, 39-62, flanked by ones of similar effect for India, South Africa, and Pakistan.
32. *Foundations of Canadian Nationhood*, p. 82.

still thought of as an imposition from without.[33] In the last years of the raj, Britain tried to introduce federalism into India by the Act of 1935, which later served as the structure for the republic.[34] Thus her federalizing efforts carried on into the new Commonwealth, failing in East Africa and the West Indies, but succeeding in Malaya and (if Fate is kind), after some fancy and fast footwork, in the large state of Nigeria, and now making a poor try in Malaysia.

It is easy, in these anticolonial days when every evening sees the announcement of a new state, to write of the long developments in the old British Commonwealth as a devolution *from* something, a dissolution. Maybe so. On the other hand, it is possible to view it as a unique evolution, a growth, *toward* an association unique in world history, much stronger, more inspiring on the eve of World War II than it had been a hundred years before, at the time of Durham's report. We are too close to the new Commonwealth of Nations to say where it will lead. It can just as well be the beginning of something as the end.

The incorporation of the Asian and African empire into the structure, the tradition, constitutes a miracle. As with Dr. Johnson's female preacher, the quality of the performance is not the question; the remarkable thing is that it has been done at all. The salvaging of any kind of order from a revolution is an attainment, an attainment made possible by the British genius for illogical pragmatism, and by the lip service, on which we have remarked, that was for so long paid to anticolonialism and to self-government—some day. When *mañana* forcibly became today, the British did not have to retreat from principles; they had only to change practices.

They had to change practices at a rate of speed and in areas they had not seriously contemplated. As guardians over lesser breeds, they had the responsibility of not letting their wards go.

33. L. M. Thompson, *The Unification of South Africa* (Oxford, 1960) is standard. See Kenneth Robinson, "Autochthony and the Transfer of Power," in *Essays in Imperial Government Presented to Margery Perham* (Oxford, 1963), pp. 279-80.

34. K. M. Panillar, *The Foundations of New India* (London, 1963), p. 153.

The slave trade, barbarous customs, communalism, man's inhumanity to man, all had to be rectified. It was illiberal to talk of freeing them, and Professor Thornton thinks the nineteenth-century builders did not seriously contemplate doing so.[35]

Of Africa, Lord Lugard could in the early 1920's report the verdict of scholars and administrators alike "that the era of complete independence is not as yet visible on the horizon of time."[36] Even Labour, before 1945, thought its mission, too, lay in better conduct of trusteeship; it had not "faced the full implications of, or formally suggested, the liquidation of the Empire."[37] Interestingly enough, the author of that assertion, a Fabian Socialist, could not in 1948 and 1949 give up the tutelary idea. Agreeing with Bentham's and Mill's fears of what would happen if colonies were given up, she suggested that the British stay in, by agreement, "until the people had achieved a national unity which could find expression in their own political institutions. . . ."[38] "I can regret," the great Africanist and student of empire, Miss Margery Perham, said in 1960, "that the white man has not been allowed another fifty years at least in which to build his civilization in Africa."[39]

The independence of the Indian subcontinent was less unthinkable but still remote. Earlier pronouncements of intent to let go were stilled by the Mutiny, but as Eastern empires went, it was an enlightened date when the Round Table leaders could contemplate independence in the second decade of the twentieth century. "If we manage to create in India a self-governing, responsible dominion," said Philip Kerr in 1912, "and if India, when it is responsible and self-governing, elects

35. A. P. Thornton, "Decolonization," *International Journal*, XIX (Winter, 1963-64), 7-29.
36. Sir F. D. Lugard, *The Dual Mandate in British Tropical Africa* (the preface to the first edition was signed December, 1921; the statement still there in the fourth edition, Edinburgh and London, 1929), pp. 197-198. A former colonial officer, writing in 1960, recalls how unthinkable independence seemed not too long ago: Sir Charles Jeffries, *Transfer of Power: Problems of the Passage to Self-Government* (New York, 1961), pp. 23-24.
37. Rita Hinden, *Empire and After: A Study of British Imperial Attitude* (London, 1949), pp. 114 ff.
38. *Ibid.*, p. 181.
39. Quoted, Robert Heussler, *Yesterday's Rulers: The Making of the British Colonial Service* (Syracuse, 1963), p. 208.

to remain within the British Empire, we shall have solved the greatest difficulty which presents itself to the world today."[40] Lionel Curtis, among others, worked at just that during the decade, which was crowned by the statement of the secretary of state, E. S. Montagu, in the House of Commons, August 20, 1917:

The policy of His Majesty's Government, with which the Government of India are in complete accord, is that of increasing association of Indians in every branch of the administration and the gradual development of self-governing institutions, with a view to the progressive realisation of responsible government in India as an integral part of the British Empire.[41]

Thence England proceeded to the Dyarchy and the Act of 1935 by agonizing stages, yielding ground unwillingly as respected British interests, fearfully as respected Indian ones.

In Ceylon in the interwar years there was likewise concession, again to agitation. The constitution instituted in 1931 as a result of the report of the Donoughmore Commission provided for a very wide suffrage indeed, and set up a clumsy machinery introducing Ceylonese into administration. It did not work, but it led to the Ceylonization of the civil service, and thus prepared the Ceylonese for independence.[42]

In the extent of their governmental experience, the Ceylonese were far in advance of any of the African and any other Asian colonies of any country. The British were remiss in training their subjects for self-government. The Englishmen in the older colonies got their own training in their assemblies. The use of Indians in the I.C.S. or most other government service was slowly adopted, widening somewhat between the wars.[43] Unofficial members were only recently admitted to the executive council in the African colonies, e.g., the Gold Coast in 1942. There was

40. Quoted by S. R. Mehrota, "Imperial Federation and India, 1868-1917," *Journal of Commonwealth Political Studies*, I (Nov., 1961), 40 n.65.
41. G. B., 5 *Parl. Debs.*, XCVII, 1695.
42. Sir Charles Jeffries, *Ceylon: The Path to Independence* (New York, 1963), especially pp. 48-74.
43. See Ralph Braibanti's figures on the elite cadres, below: on eve of independence, Ceylonese only 19 per cent British, Indian 48 per cent, Malayan 66 per cent.

as a matter of fact retrogression in using "natives" in the Colonial Service. Non-Europeans were for awhile barred from the service in the Eastern colonies (not India) by fiat of the secretary of state in 1904, and Professor Robinson writes that during Chamberlain's time there was an "emphatic Europeanisation of the civil service" in Africa.[44] All through the colonial empire, Britain was committing the folly of permitting, or even encouraging, education which brought men into contact with Western ideas, with English liberalism, but giving them little outlet in positions and experience. The people of the African territories, the Labour party proclaimed as late as 1933, "are in a condition which could make it impossible for them to take over the government of their country on modern lines. In such cases, what is required is education and preparation with the definite object of training the population in self-government."[45] Nobody was listening.

Indirect rule, an economic and military necessity, saved a staff, but was not instituted to train in self-government. In practice, of course, it insisted on propping up traditional rulers—the princes of India, the emirs and chiefs in Africa. This practice was elevated in Africa after the Northern Nigerian experience into a cult, the English flattering themselves it was sound, humane sociology and politics not to disturb the indigenous culture. They even made chiefs where none existed so that they could rule through them. The trouble was they were educating to demand power quite different persons, the new group who saw in princes as large an obstacle to their rise to power as the raj or the governor were. The procedure does not seem very intelligent at this distance, but in Africa the British were at least honestly mistaken. The charge that they upheld the tribal chiefs in order to divide and rule is false.

The British administrators were not interested in transferring their own democratic and parliamentary institutions. They were

44. Drawing upon figures in Richard Symonds, "Reflections on Localisation," *Journal of Commonwealth Political Studies*, II (Nov., 1964), 223.
45. *The Colonial Empire* (report adopted at the annual conference, October, 1933) (Transport House, Nov., 1933), p. 6.

there to assert order and then to maintain the status quo. They were prefects bent on keeping order in school. If anyone wished to observe that in doing so they exhibited integrity, dispassionate concern for their charges, and "good" government, and, having observed, to emulate, that was all right. But the natives were not to be proselytized for the English ways of life in culture, industry, or government. The administrators were aloof, confident gentlemen, not missionaries, and, alas, not technicians either, or teachers.[46] Admittedly devoted, in their way, to the peoples they served, nonetheless they were interested in their own security, resisted independence, and feared nativization of the service; and it became a race, at independence, to see whether they would leave first, with pensions, or be thrown out by the Africans or Asians hungry for their jobs. They wanted the security of being British office-holders if they stayed to tide the new government over, but a Commonwealth civil service was not established.[47]

We therefore had no long, gradual devolution in Africa and only a short and piece-meal one in Asia. World War I in India, the Second in the rest of the empire, produced circumstances making for such inexorable pressure that the British, lacking the will, the stomach, or the money to stay in, left precipitately. It may be reasoned that no amount of those commodities would have sufficed anyway. The colonies were bent on freedom, and there was no way to keep them. It is useless to try to find reasons why the English let them go, such as supposing a fit of anticolonialism or liberalism, or preoccupation with creating their own welfare state, etc. It does not help to point out, as Professor Thornton does, that the British had lost their faith; that the intelligentsia had lost touch with tradition, the Public School with confidence, the classes with each other in the old relationships.[48] All this presupposes complete free will in London, whereas it was what had been going on in Asia and Africa that mattered more. It would be dangerous to assert that British

46. Heussler's book, *Yesterday's Rulers,* on the Colonial Service between the wars, is the most suggestive work of recent years on the British ruler.
47. Jeffries, *Transfer of Power,* pp. 106-12.
48. A. P. Thornton, *The Impartial Idea and Its Enemies: A Study in Imperial Power* (London and New York, 1959), chap. vi.

colonial policy was always made by the men on the spot and then accommodated to in Whitehall, but, modified a little, the assertion will explain much colonial history. Thornton's more general thesis, that war, nationalism, and democracy have done in the Empire of the late Victorian imperialists, is more on the mark.

At any rate, from not intending to give up anything, wrote Strachey, Britain changed her mind and gave in gracefully, thereby saving herself economically and psychologically.[49] Her purpose then, "if there was one, was not so much to create new states as to find some way of keeping in the family the new states which insisted on being created."[50]

If the British could not create states at leisure, they did play for as much time as they could get to tidy up before they left, as in Nigeria. Burma gave no time and cut off the association. The peaceable departure of the British is the last peaceful scene the Burmese have witnessed. The do-it-yourself tidying up of the Muslims and the Hindus was dreadful to watch. The Sinhalese have yet to agree with the Tamils. Minorities are scarcely safe in the African states, all of which have grave economic problems. There was no hundred years available in which to create viable states in the new Commonwealth.

A noticeable difference between pre- and postwar creations in the Commonwealth is that in the latter there is no wish for a constitution made in Lancaster House, or even for one made in Nairobi and passed by the Parliament at Westminster. The government must be homemade, a "national form" and seen to be so. Thus it has been in Ireland, India, Pakistan, Ghana, Nigeria, South Africa, Tanganyika, and so on. The forms and expression of power, as well as the power, must be "national." K. C. Wheare entitles this phenomenon "autochthony."[51] All this reflects the fact,

49. John Strachey, End of Empire (New York, 1960), pp. 204 ff.
50. Jeffries, p. 16.
51. The Constitutional Structure of the Commonwealth (Oxford, 1960). Professor Kenneth Robinson has explored this theme in two essays: "Constitutional Autochthony in Ghana," Journal of Commonwealth Political Studies, I (1961), 41-55; and the one referred to in note 33, in which he sketches recent developments in Ceylon, South Africa, and Tanganyika.

as Professor Robinson points out, that by the sensible legerdermain at which the British are so skilled, India was made a member of the Commonwealth in 1949 as a sovereign republic.[52]

Abrupt and complete transfer of power, with no strings whatsoever, has not destroyed the Commonwealth. It is evolving with such speed now that we shall not have to live as long as Queen Victoria to see substantial changes in it. Hasty interpretation of what we see will not enhance our reputation.

52. Documents in Mansergh, *Documents* . . . , *1931-1952*, II, 838-78.

3

Political Institutions in New Commonwealth States

*W. H. Morris-Jones**

I

It is as well at the outset to raise a radical doubt about the scope of this survey: how useful for the study of political institutions is the category "new Commonwealth states"? That there are marked differences in political developments in new member states as compared with the old is clear. What is not at first sight so evident is how far Commonwealth membership contributes features to the new states of Asia and Africa which distinguish them from their non-Commonwealth neighbors. In terms of political institutions, is there not more in common between two new states, one of which is a Commonwealth state and the other not, than between two Commonwealth states, one of which is a new state and the other not?

The question is easier to put than to answer. To some, no doubt, the matter presents little difficulty. This would be the case, for instance, with those for whom the Commonwealth has become "the God that failed." This mood of disenchantment was well expressed in the widely noticed articles by "A Conservative" in *The Times*[1]: "the Commonwealth has really become a gigantic farce," "a transparent fiction." Such a sentiment may not be confined to a few and it would be a mistake to think that it could not be shared by non-Conservatives. It derives much of

* Professor of Political Theory and Institutions, University of Durham.
1. April 1-3, 1964.

its strength from the observation that in many new Commonwealth states there has been a marked failure to maintain (or even properly to establish) free and parliamentary forms of rule, coupled with the conviction that likemindedness in the matter of political forms is essential to a genuine association. Only ten years ago this conviction was the established view. But, quite logically, those who believe that the Commonwealth is still a genuine association have had to relegate this aspect into the background.[2]

From another viewpoint there would also come ready answers of the same kind. It seems that there has been of late some swing of opinion as regards the developing areas—or at least some pessimistic voices are making themselves more loudly heard than before. Whereas we had often been invited to regard the new nations as fundamentally like older ones but merely less advanced, we are now urged by many to realize how enormous and appalling is the gap between backward and modern.[3] The leaders of new states may be men in a hurry, but history cannot be thus hustled. The result of the attempt to do so entails only deception and self-deception on the part of the elites concerned. Modernization is a superficial façade and the reality is preindustrial despotism modified by inefficiency and rendered bearable only by the continuing shelter of traditional ways. Only the

2. At the Unofficial Commonwealth Conference at Lahore in 1954, it was ironically enough the then prime minister of Pakistan who expressed the then orthodox view that "the common practice of responsible self-government is the strongest bond of Commonwealth unity." Professor Mansergh as conference rapporteur endorsed this, pointing out that the mechanism of relations between member states was bound up with the practice of parliamentary cabinets and adding that "it is doubtful whether states adopting other forms of government would continue to find membership congenial." The change in the decade is recorded in Professor Mansergh's paper in the present volume, in which he states that departure from parliamentary government has been "accepted, though not in some instances without misgiving, [as] a matter of domestic concern." He suggests that by now "perhaps the one basic principle shared by this community of states" is multiracialism. He does not, of course, say that the Commonwealth would accept *any* departure from parliamentary government as compatible with membership, only that it has so accepted such departures as have so far taken place.

3. I have in mind in particular three rather striking recent publications: I. R. Sinai, *The Challenge of Modernisation* (London, 1964); F. H. Hinsley, "Living with the Insoluble," *The Listener* (May 7, 1964); H. Tinker, "Broken-backed States," *New Society* (Jan. 30, 1964).

liveliest Western imagination can reach across to this other side, for it is a world we left too long ago. Moreover, the distance between us does not diminish but grows: they move backwards as order collapses and disintegration replaces rule, we move faster onwards as science and organization usher us into undreamed of realms. The picture presented is one of historical fate playing the parable of the talents with a vengeance. This view reinforces that which sees the Commonwealth as hopelessly incoherent: even where the appearance of constitutional decency is preserved in any new state, the reality is bound to be so different as to destroy all sense in talk of common objects or common attitudes; where new constitutions have killed constitutionalism by enshrining autocracy, they have at least the merit of honestly registering the abyss.

However, we may reject such gloomy views—on the ground, for instance, that the "façade" verdict implies too simple a view of the impact of modernization and that the historical parallels with European history take too little account of the changes in the rate of change. In that case, the initial question remains, open and difficult. It is a question alike for practicing politicians and for students of politics, a question as how best to act and a question as to how best to understand what is being enacted: how far is the Commonwealth present in the politics of its new states? It seems a question about the importance of history, a teasing battlefield, like that on which heredity and environment fought, supported by armies of scholars surging now this way now that. Like that other war, this one too will be deadlocked so long as we seek one general answer; it is altogether too serious a business to be left to the generalities.

To say that it is a matter of the importance of history is to say that if there are features which distinguish Commonwealth new states from other new states, these will be discovered by looking for a deposit from the past. That is, continuing Commonwealth membership of itself contributes no fresh features to the political lives of the member states.[4] Even so, the

4. I am, of course, not saying that continuing membership has no effect on the survival power of the legacies from the past. Even this, however, may

search for the impact of the past is not simple. It must obviously include in its purview all elements directly bequeathed by the colonial power. But, further, it cannot neglect those features of present political life which can be traced to the character of the nationalist movements, for these, too, were shaped by the particular nature of British rule. Moreover, any thorough search must not confine itself to things overtly political: educational systems, the English language, legal terms and procedures— even committee practice[5]—can exert great influence over working politics.

On the other hand, not all history is, even indirectly, colonial; Commonwealth new states may enjoy legacies from a pre-British period and these will be particular rather than common. Just how important as a continuing influence such earlier indigenous civilizations may be depends on their own level of development and richness and on the duration of the intervening imperial period. On the whole, it has so happened[6] that these factors have canceled each other out: the great civilizations of Asia are separated from the present by very long periods of British rule, while the lesser civilizations of parts of Africa are separated from independence by less than two generations.[7] In almost all Commonwealth new states, however, some pre-British heritage comes through. The forms vary greatly. In Uganda, Northern Nigeria, and Malaya, traditional rulers have so well survived as to be significant elements in the new political systems. In the renaming of many states and in similar symbolic gestures and

be difficult to assess; it is at least not inconceivable that an ex-member might feel less obliged than a member to display independence by throwing away all traces of the former connection. On balance, though—and with some support from Ireland and Burma—it is probable that the maintenance of links helps rather than hinders the maintenance of legacies.

5. Professor Robinson tells me that ex-French and ex-British Africa have very different notions as to how a meeting is to be conducted.

6. Perhaps this makes it sound more a matter of chance than it was?

7. This is one reason which might justify the suggestion that the distinction should be between not simply "old" and "new" but rather "old," "middle-aged," and "new," with "middle-aged" referring mainly to Asia and "new" to Africa. The other reason for such a nomenclature would be the varying lengths of preparation periods (on which a little is said below); the "middle-aged" experienced not only longer periods of colonial rule but also longer periods of transfer of power.

signs, an attempt is made to simulate continuity from an age of earlier independent glory. In the search for a polity in consonance with the "genius" of the people, appeal will be made to earlier systems—as in the use of the "village republics" notion in connection with Indian democratization of local government.

Assessing the Commonwealth "presence" in its new states' polities becomes, then, a matter of weighing the significance of the preserved elements of British- and colonial-period manufacture against that of the other elements which come from other sources, whether these latter be the real or imagined legacies of a pre-British past or the pressures (also both imagined as well as real) of the present circumstances.

II

The next difficulty is that of defining the nature of those "preserved elements" whose significance is to be weighed. An obvious but important preliminary point here is that we should not imagine that all these states set off from the same base line or that the starting point for any of them was some perfectly reproduced liberal democracy. As the pace towards independence has quickened, one of the consequences has naturally been the dramatic narrowing of the interval between paternalistic bureaucracy and the final constitutional conference. During the decade here under review, some of the new states have moved through almost all the intermediate stages, with a year or so to spare. Of most of these new states it can hardly be said that they have moved away from the Westminster style: they scarcely got there in the first place. The new Commonwealth in Africa neither claimed nor was granted independence on the ground that it could run parliamentary democracy. The contrast here with the "middle-aged" Asian members is marked. For Africa, independence constitutions have not been recognized stopping-places; the train of state has had too much momentum to do more than snatch the freedom bag as it thunders through.

It is in any case no easy matter to say what constituted the Westminster model of parliamentary government which was reckoned a common possession of all member states. As Professor de Smith has pointed out,[8] if we mean by this phrase the main features of the British constitution, then "some are not reproduced in the constitution of any other Commonwealth country." Further, most modern Commonwealth constitutions contain features which, though they may be designed "to capture the spirit and practice of British institutions"—judicial review, listed fundamental rights, independent public service and election commissions—are in themselves alien to British experience. Professor de Smith suggests that we take the phrase to mean a

system in which the head of state is not the effective head of government; in which the effective head of government is a Prime Minister presiding over a Cabinet composed of Ministers over whose appointment and removal he has at least a substantial measure of control; in which the effective executive branch of government is parliamentary inasmuch as Ministers must be members of the legislature; and in which Ministers are collectively and individually responsible to a freely elected and representative legislature.

He adds that some or all of these characteristics are absent from the constitutions of Ghana, Cyprus, Pakistan, and Tanganyika;[9] and he proceeds to discuss the three "presidential regimes" (Cyprus is treated as *sui generis*) in a separate chapter.

The "presidential regimes," presented thus as exceptions to an otherwise general pattern, suggest one way of answering our question—and indeed de Smith's impressive book stands forth as an answer of this kind: apart from a few exceptions, it is indeed possible to present the constitutional systems of the new Commonwealth states as composing a group with sufficient common features to be distinct from those of other new states. This is satisfactory as far as it goes, and from the standpoint of constitutional law it goes far enough. However, even the least narrow of

8. *The New Commonwealth and Its Constitutions* (London, 1964), p. 77.
9. The list now (August, 1964) requires the substitution of Tanzania for Tanganyika. Mr. Kenyatta's announcement promised that Kenya would join the list in December, 1964. Dr. Banda's Malawi is likely to follow suit.

constitutional lawyers agrees that the standpoint of the student of political institutions is rather different. Without the space to argue the case fully, we may propose some reasons which the political scientist might have for wishing to press the matter further and along different lines.

First, it appears likely that even in terms of constitutional forms, the number of clear exceptions will increase. While the campaign for the restoration (or, rather, the genuine establishment) of parliamentary democracy in Pakistan has not died, it shows no signs in the near future of succeeding—although after Ayub it may be another story. Other presidential regimes seem even less likely to change, at least in a parliamentary direction. On the other hand, the group may well receive new recruits from African states. Second, however hard we may try to resist "façade" theories of politics (and rightly), we have to admit that constitutional forms may, in new states more than in established ones, tell too little of the truth about the political system to be relied upon as the main tool of examination. For while it can seldom be safe to dismiss the procedures of parliament and of the courts as mere forms—they color and shape the forces that work through them—they may certainly be reduced in relative importance as indicators of the nature of politics. Their place tends to be taken by the institutions of the political party and the bureaucracy about which constitutions say little. Third, and by way of continuation of this point, the student of the politics of new states is bound to take account of the two-way connections of social relations and social change with political behavior. These connections, everywhere significant, have peculiar importance in new states where, almost by definition, polity and society are in relations of tension.

These, then, are reasons prompting us to approach the political institutions of new Commonwealth states with the aid of categories which in themselves ignore the Commonwealth as a common factor.[10] All that can here be attempted is a sketch with illustrations.

10. It would of course be odd if an examination of the whole range of new states failed to disclose some respects in which Commonwealth members con-

III

The political experience of new Commonwealth states during the past decade can be usefully examined in terms of the relation between the problems with which they have been confronted and the resources (and in politics this means chiefly the skills) which they have been able to call upon. To put matters thus is not to present things in deterministic language.[11] For even if the problems are substantially given, skills are not simply so; they can be used well or squandered, cultivated or neglected. It may be useful to try to identify these skills.

This is still the study of political institutions. (The novelty of behavioral studies of politics has been exaggerated.) Behavior is the exercise of skills, but institutions and skills are inseparable. Institutions are changed by the changing skills that men bring to their operation; at the same time an institution will stimulate some skills and kill others.

Political skills must be related to political problems. Economic and social problems are not political problems, though they condition them. It is therefore a dangerous telescoping that is entailed in talk about the extent to which a political institution is well fitted to cope with some economic or social challenge. Political institutions and the skills they embody are to be measured against political challenges and none other. An economic problem remains an economic problem unless and until something is added to it through human hopes and fears; it may then perhaps become a factor in a political problem, not otherwise.

Moreover, political challenges and tasks are not value-free. A standard of living may conceivably be one standard to all men (though this does seem at least questionable), but a standard of governance is nothing if it is not debatable. The undisputed

---

stituted a fairly coherent subgroup. The most comprehensive survey of this field is G. A. Almond and J. S. Coleman, eds., *The Politics of the Developing Areas* (Princeton, 1960), where the examination is by regions and the Commonwealth as such is ignored.

11. We are still, it is to be hoped, keeping away from the two "absurd" extremes (as J. S. Mill described them) of supposing that forms of government are entirely to be taken as given or that they are a matter for free choice.

"core" of political standards is in one sense not worth argument and what matters is the area over which men may choose whether or not to recognize and accept political challenges.

New states are distinguished from others in the nature of their political situations, not by their having different problems, but rather by their having to start to face the problems for the first time, at the same time, and with their own relatively untried and hastily assembled resources. It is not easy to find advanced states which have had no experience of these problems. The problems are two. Both can be presented in fashionable language as problems of integration, the one perhaps horizontal, or concerned with the creation of the national group, the other vertical, or having to do with the bringing into effective existence of "the people," and they are sometimes distinguished by the terms "integration" and "mobilization" respectively.

This formulation, however, does not fully describe the problems. By striving for objectivity it slides over the inseparability of means and ends; it fails to grasp a further dimension of the problems. For the problem is not simply to achieve integration and mobilization in *any* manner. The how of it matters; to be value-free is to be error-bound. This is not to argue that there is really a third problem—viz., how to achieve free politics. It is instead to argue that this is part of the two problems themselves. Integration is a combining of parts; it simply is not integration if one part is wiped out in the process. Neither gas chambers nor liquidation will integrate; so far from solving the problem, they abolish it. Similarly, by mobilization is meant not drafting into slavery but incorporation into citizenship. It may be said that gas chambers and slavery are extremes beyond the pale. Just so; these are means which destroy the end, means which point to a different end. But this is a matter of degree, and thus the invasion of facts by values cannot be prevented.

This being so, it is better to choose terms that show this. The first problem may be called composing the legitimate state and the second, composing the citizen body. This takes that despairing relativism—"Ah well, they do as they do"—out of political analysis and prompts a genuinely critical examination of our data.

IV

It is a familiar and indeed obvious point that new states are often faced with grave problems of nation-building. Useful as it is to remember that no state is without factors of diversity as well as of unity, it has to be acknowledged that the elements of diversity in new states are frequently of awful dimensions, so much so that there can be real ambiguity and uncertainty as to what the nation is that is to be built. Commonwealth new states have their full share of such problems: Malaya (and, equally, Malaysia), Pakistan, Ceylon, Nigeria, Kenya, Uganda, and Sierra Leone all have (in perhaps that diminishing order) acute difficulties. Tanganyika (before the union with Zanzibar) and Jamaica have been more fortunate. All states are no doubt shaped by accidents of history and, in some, defiance of geography, but some are more accidental than others. But the order of difficulty does not remain constant. Against an unpromising deposit of racial plurality, communications, internal migration, and economic relations can operate to bind a territory together. The role of colonial government may—if only by consolidating opposition—have worked in the same direction. But most factors are in themselves ambivalent: economics and colonial rule could also accentuate differences. Each problem of diversity has its own dimensions and its own special features, and each is a political problem.

The size and nature of the problem of shaping the state can also be influenced by the moods which prevail among all concerned at the period of the transfer of power. Sometimes representatives of the ruling power have wanted to see to it that the imperial donation of territorial integrity could be maintained intact. Wavell, though he failed, made such an attempt. Sometimes the emphasis has been on careful protection of minorities.

The pattern of the initial constitution negotiated with White-hall can do a certain amount to set the course and—so fluid may be the conditions in new states—it is not necessarily a pattern that will be swept away after independence. But it is possible that leaders of different sections within the area will be committed in very different degrees to the constitution, and also that they will have quite contrary expectations as to how it will operate. The first of these exercises, entailing assessments of the immediately feasible and the permanently durable, was the scheme of the Cabinet Mission in 1946 for India, which broke down before it was used. In the past decade constitution-making has been a thriving occupation and some difficult and delicate constructions such as those of Nigeria and Malaya have lasted better than some more straightforward models such as those of Ghana and Tanganyika. At the present time uncertainty hangs over the working out of the constitutions of Kenya and Southern Rhodesia.

The political institutions of the new state (whether or not determined and given by the constitution) play a role in relation to the problem of integration but analysis of the connections is far from easy. If we take a federal structure for instance, there can be no simple general rule as to how it bears on the integration situation; it may either check or assist disintegrative processes. It may even be difficult on occasion to decide which it is doing, for it will never be the only factor at work and its influence will seldom be readily separable. Have the federal systems of Nigeria and India stimulated or have they tamed regional loyalties? If in Nigeria there has been a stepping-up of regionalism, this is not to say that a unitary constitution could have been a starter; and it is less the federal constitution than the form taken by parties, especially the failure to develop cross-region appeal, which offers the explanation. In India even the wholesale boundary changes to create linguistically more homogeneous states have been safely contained—not by the rather desperate sloganizing about "national integration" but by the co-operative federalism of the planning process coupled with the preservation of the all-India character of the main parties and top bureaucracy. Pakistan in this connection has an enticingly laboratory appearance, with its experience inside a short period of two kinds of federal structure and one unitary one, but too few factors remained constant to permit safe generalizations. Even more hazardous is the attempt to judge whether there were any attainable conditions under which a West Indian federation could have been made to last.

Federal devices have obvious relevance to integration problems but clearly their exact bearing can vary according to other circumstances. The same is true of other political institutions. A central, nationally recruited bureaucracy can, and normally will, have a strong unifying effect. But even national recruitment can be sectionally uneven and in that case the effect may be opposite. The civil (and military) services in Pakistan tend in the eastern wing to be so identified with the distrusted other half that the mere existence of "national" services only aggravates the sentiment of diversity. The point has been important in a milder fashion in Nigeria; it is said[12] that in both the Northern regional and federal services Nigerianization was slowed down because Northernization was the real objective.

Again, a national parliament has been acclaimed—in India as in Tudor England—as a great unifier of all parts of the country. It can indeed, by its combination of representational and educational roles, translate an input of diversity into an output of unity. In India this happens, but this need not always be so. Parliament may be reduced to a position of such insignificance in the political system that it can contribute nothing. Worse, its members can become so frustrated—perhaps in face of a remote and unresponsive executive—that they devote themselves solely to the exposure of regional differences which thus achieve wider publicity.

Most important of all is the party system, and here too there are no simple rules. One-party systems are often defended in

12. J. Donald Kingsley, "Bureaucracy and Political Development with particular reference to Nigeria," in J. La Palombara, ed., *Bureaucracy and Political Development* (Princeton, 1963), p. 305.

terms of their contribution to integration. But this is only one of the many points at which the category one-party system covers too much. Integration will not be helped if the roots and supports of the single party are markedly weaker (or different in character) in one region as compared with another; this was the case with the Muslim League in Pakistan and this situation will be avoided with difficulty in relation to Kenya's KANU. Moreover, if the single party goes about its integrating work by means of suppression, it surely defeats its declared end; the integration is either hollow or it is productive of fresh hostility. This may be the case in Ghana. On the other hand, two- or multiparty systems need not always offer encouragement to fissiparous tendencies; the Nigerian parties solidified into regional blocs, whereas the main parties in India maintain a nationwide role even though their internal structures are often of a loose federal kind.

It does not follow from the above that political institutions have no independent influence, that they are no more than vehicles for the transmission of social or economic pressures. All that follows is that we have to look at particular cases, precise characteristics, and detailed contexts if we are to see aright their interacting influence.

V

The other major political problem of new states is that of constituting the population into a citizen body, that of vertical integration. Here the elements which are to be related are not geographical but social. In part the problem presents itself in the new states of today as a bringing together of styles or modes of social and political behavior, most frequently those of a Western-influenced elite and those of a populace who live by the rules of religion and custom and move along the traditional ways of social conduct. In a way it is a matter of closing gaps, among them the gap between rulers and ruled, and of doing so by the discovery and creation of intermediaries as much as by direct changes in the character of the extremes. The temptation to indulge in historical analogies is strong; the education of our masters and the escape from the tale of two cities have indeed something to do with the case. But the differences in the situations are notable. The societies of the new states are not mainly encountering rapid change generated from within. Rather, the pace and extent of social change is often less than the leaders imagine and prepare to cope with, while the political revolution which is prior owes much to inspiration from outside. Moreover, the divisions that demand to be conquered are not simply those of class. The political incorporation of the workers and peasants of Europe was surely (unless sociological history has surprises in store for us) a less complex task than that which faces new states. For in the latter the segments often seem to be comprehensive societies, communities within the great community.

Although the problem is common to all new states, its dimensions vary. As with horizontal integration, economic history has a good deal to say on such important matters as the size and nature of the middle classes and the character of the links between urban and rural areas. But the type of indigenous social structure has also to be reckoned with—the difference, for instance (and very crudely) between the localism and independence of tribal and village units as contrasted with the at least regional affiliations and interdependence of an institution like caste. (Tribalism, like some forms of communalism, thus differs from caste in that the latter does not so easily work in such a way as to cause the problems of national and social integration to coincide and reinforce each other.)

Here again, however, when economic history and sociology have had their say, there remains much for politics to explain. The factor of special significance is the relation in time between the advent of popular politics and independence. In some new states independence came either after a short period of struggle or (as in Ceylon) no struggle at all. In others, notably India, the political movement has had to push down deep roots long before the transfer of power. In these latter instances, the incorporation

of the populace as citizens, although very incomplete, had made
a start. The national movement had itself become a shadow polity
before independence. The most important consequence of this
is that middle-level intermediaries and political persons have
emerged; the chain that joins the rulers to the ruled is firmly
carried by a number of well spaced and securely established
posts. The shocks of, for example, adult franchise can then be
taken comfortably; those to whom power was transferred can
manage to hold it. There can even be a mature system for widening gradually the basis of recruitment to the political elite. Where,
on the other hand, the preparation period has been short—and,
after all, it is only in the decade 1945-54 that political organization of practically any kind began in the African states[13]—the
choice is often between a markedly elitist party which runs the
risk of being pushed away from below, and a mass party created
at breakneck speed. The latter type—of which Ghana's is still the
leading example in the Commonwealth—is highly organized,
ambitiously active, and all-absorbing both of the energies and
loyalties of its members and of all other organizations, such as
trade unions and youth clubs.

The timing of mass politicization and independence is not
the only political conditioning factor governing the size of this
second problem. Like the first, it is affected by the political institutions which exist. Whether or not there can be an effective
incorporation of a public, so that no section feels permanently
excluded from influence and permanently barred from participation, depends on several factors: how far the bureaucracy is
fairly recruited (though it has to be allowed that the populace's
notions of fairness may not be those of a public service commission), how far it has the authority that commands respect
without the powers that produce fear, how far there is a representation system not only or even mainly at the capital but also
in the form of local self-government bodies.

Above all, perhaps, it depends on how "open" is the party
system. By this last phrase is meant not necessarily a genuinely

13. See for example Thomas L. Hodgkin, *African Political Parties* (Harmondsworth, 1961), especially chap. iii.

competitive multiparty situation with chances even, but something less exacting and more attainable: a system in which even if there is one dominant party, it is still open to others to enter into business; in which the texture of the main party is loose and openly so; and in which there is an interaction between the small parties and sections within the main party. With such an open party system there can be some competition, if not for voters directly, at least for intermediaries who in turn may compete. No more than in economics is the model of perfect competition necessarily the target, but, as in economics, there is something in the argument about the consumers' choice: an open party system is likely to make the citizen discover ways towards what he wants; a closed system makes him want the sole article on offer. Through the publicity of criticism faults can be remedied before heads have to fall; the same publicity is some guarantee that rulers will consult more than their own interests. A totalitarian one-party system, on the other hand, does not serve the purpose here referred to; the populace becomes incorporated, but in the party rather than the body politic; people are made less into citizens than into party members.

That there is a close relation between the two problems or facets of integration has been clear all along. Not even in all parts of Europe has it been possible to tackle them one at a time and with a breathing space in between; certainly in today's new states both come together. Moreover, routes towards a solution of one often lead away from a solution of the other. The politicization problem can often receive such attention that the national integration problem is aggravated—as in Ceylon. The integration problem may be met by means which imply abandonment of the citizenship—as in Pakistan and Ghana.

VI

In setting out the two major political problems, some indication has been given as to how they can be conditioned by attendant political circumstances. In doing so, it has not been possible to avoid entering at some points the question of the resources available for meeting the problems—meaning by "resources" the attitudes and skills of the personnel of politics.

What is comprised in this category? Prior place must be given to the commitments of ideology entered into by the ruling elite(s). Of course, these may be difficult to assess and may indeed not amount to a great deal. Most new nations' leaders in any case are highly eclectic in their ideological stand. The majority begin with no pronounced general outlook on politics. Even here, however, it may be worth trying to distinguish between two kinds of "openness": (a) an undiscriminating absence of attitude, an unprincipled vacuum into which ideologies of the closed society may enter and take root, and (b) an attitude of "openmindedness in principle" which has as corollary the exclusion of closed-society outlooks. But some leaders come to power with clear intellectual dispositions. Nehru is perhaps the outstanding example, and in his case part of the make-up of his mind was a disposition to find solutions consistent with some sense of free politics. Where such a disposition is present it can—in a situation where so much depends on the standards set by very few—have decisive effect. So can its absence. This factor can be the one which determines the difference between the Nkrumah type of answer and the Nehru type. The difference between an open one-dominant-party system and a closed one-party situation is a political world of difference, but in new states the situation can be so fluid and balanced that the determining factor is not to be found in economic or social situations but at the back of the minds of a small number of men.[14]

Relevant, too, is the extent to which traditional authority can be made available to play its part in the new non-traditional settings. Abdul Rahman is Tunku and even Nehru was Pandit. Confidence is a great part of the work of ruling, and being accustomed to the respect of others is a safeguard against the

14. One of best essays on this subject is F. G. Carnell, "Political Ideas and Ideologies in South and South East Asia," in Saul Rose, ed., *Politics in Southern Asia* (London, 1963). See also Paul Sigmund, ed., *The Ideologies of the Developing Nations* (New York, 1963), Introduction.

uncertainty which is often a prelude either to failure or the abandonment of free politics. What is true of the top holds for the lower levels of political leadership too. Much of the intolerance (at best) and violence (at worst) which characterize the politics of some new states show nothing more than the uncertainty and insecurity of men with little experience or tradition of rule. If elements from traditional elites are able to adapt themselves to modern politics, they not only ease the path of social change for the class from whom they come but also bring to political life the confidence that it requires if its operations are not to be brutal.

Mainly, however, the resources are matters of know-how or skills. Here these can only be summarily listed. Most widely recognized are the administrative skills. What is not so widely recognized is that it is not only the administration that needs to have them. The mechanical side of a legislature's business needs them. Above all, parties need them. It may be true that it is inefficiency which saves the totalitarian parties of Africa from being in reality the sinister machines which such designation implies, but it is also true that open party systems require for their effectiveness a modicum of administrative skill.

The availability and distribution of these political skills in new states depend on many of the factors mentioned in the outline already given of the nature of the problems. The nature of the nationalist movement has an influence: a movement of long duration and considerable complexity is likely to have endowed its leadership with skills of negotiation and representation as well as the more useful skills of mobilization. The training given through colonial institutions can also vary with significantly different results: administrative skills and skills of representation will be widely present if the local elites have been offered experience of a bureaucratic or parliamentary kind. The indigenous cultural background and type of social structure will, even more obviously, condition the nature and amount of skill available as well as its distribution. The distribution is particularly relevant to the matter of intermediaries or middle leadership.

If we look at the political situation of new states in terms of avaliable skills to meet given problems, we may perhaps be offering an explanation of the political outcomes we find. Men cannot do more than they are equipped to do. By their routes to power we should be able—as Machiavelli pointed out—to understand what they do with power. If the leader who has had little opportunity to master any of the skills of politics except those required for mobilizing mobs proceeds after independence to move towards the solution of his problems by mobilizing mobs, we should not be surprised. Could we not construct a scale of new states in terms of the degree to which their political systems are constituted and open? And could we not explain the position of each according to the relation between the demands of its problems and the supply of its skills?

VII

But while this kind of explanation may appeal to some by virtue of its being a political explanation for a political phenomenon, is it really any less deterministic than the sad explanations offered in terms of economic and social equipment? If it is by their routes that we shall know them, what can by now be done about it? It has to be admitted that political resources cannot be easily lend-leased or grant-aided from outside. Public administrators can be sent away for training or experts can be brought in to do the training on site. But who ever tried to communicate the skills of parliamentary or party political life? How can there be a political "operation bootstrap"?

Some time ago, at a period of greater optimism about the Commonwealth, a bold affirmative answer to this last question might have been offered: the Commonwealth is itself a school of politics. Such an answer would now seem presumptuous. And yet membership in this association may still count for something so far as each member state's internal politics is concerned. If it is not a school, it may be an old-boys' association. Each goes his own way, but not without a recollection of certain standards and an uneasiness at departing too markedly from them. Each makes new friends in other circles, but so long as these very special links are maintained at all, a great deal can be communicated through them—no longer as from master to pupils but rather among all as equals. The problems they meet in their new careers have much in common and the skills associated with the school are not irrelevant to their successful confrontation.

4

Commonwealth Federations Old and New: Canada and Nigeria

*Taylor Cole**

Recent re-examination of federalism has resulted in varying definitions, different authors emphasizing special aspects. It has been seen as "a doctrine, a system or a principle."[1] However viewed, the stress may be on the nature of the constitutional division of powers, or the autonomy of federating units, or structural features carried over from confederations, or a community of interests of interdependent political communities, or on a combination of these. But such emphases may contain static implications, and stress form at the expense of process.

Without minimizing the importance of the examination of forms, federalism, for our purposes, will be broadly conceived as the process of realizing a continuing adjustment or dynamic equilibrium between the centrifugal and centripetal forces in a society. Put in political context, federalism may be viewed as the process by which, under the impact of centrifugal and centripetal forces, a continuing adjustment is made in the relationships between the central government and the regional governments of the constituent units of a political system. "Federalism is thus not an absolute but a relative term," William S. Living-

* James B. Duke Professor of Political Science and provost, Duke University. This paper, in its original form, was prepared for discussion at the International Political Science Association (IPSA) Round Table Conference on Federalism and Decentralization at Oxford University, September 19-24, 1963. The author wishes to express his indebtedness to Dr. Don Piper, sometime executive secretary of the Duke University Commonwealth-Studies Center, for his assistance.

1. K. C. Wheare, "Some Theoretical Questions about Federalism," paper prepared for IPSA Conference, p. 3.

ston has appropriately commented; "there is no identifiable point at which a society ceases to be unified and becomes disunified. . . . All communities fall somewhere in a spectrum which runs from what we may call a theoretically wholly integrated society at one extreme to a theoretically wholly diversified society at the other."[2] For inclusion within this continuum, there must be involved an element of constitutionalism, some common values, interests, and beliefs, and some common organizational features. National and supranational federalism are consequently not viewed as alternatives but as part of the federal process.

So considered, the Commonwealth of Nations offers three inviting opportunities for the study of federalism as a process. The first of these is an examination of the ever-shifting relationships between the United Kingdom and the other independent member states which constitute the Commonwealth. The second is a study of federalism within selected members of the Commonwealth. Within the confines of the Commonwealth, Australia, India, Malaysia, Cyprus, Pakistan, the defunct Federation of the

2. *Federalism and Constitutional Change* (London, 1956), p. 4. Cf. the observations of C. J. Friedrich: "From an empirical standpoint, an effectively centralized government, a decentralized government, a federal government, a federation, a confederation or league of governments (states), an alliance, an alignment, a 'system' of independent governments (states), and finally completely unrelated governments,—all these should be represented as differences of degree in the relation of governments to the persons subject to their rule and to the territories they occupy. The two extremes are unitary control by the rulership, and complete separateness of control by distinctive rulers, both being marginal cases. Federalism as a process needs to be seen as linking a number of the systems of interrelationships in the middle section of this series." "Federalism, National and International, in Theory and Practice," paper prepared for IPSA Conference, pp. 19-20. A comparable position has been taken in Robert O. Tilman and Taylor Cole, *The Nigerian Political Scene* (Durham, N. C., 1962), p. 62.

There is a general recognition of the nebulous distinctions frequently drawn between federalism, viewed as a process, and of decentralization, defined as a process. One of the major difficulties in the consideration of decentralization has been mentioned by James W. Fesler in a paper on "Some Approaches to the Study of Decentralization," prepared for the IPSA Conference. "All discussion of the problem," he rightly observes, "is handicapped by the circumstance that our language dichotomizes so that we have 'centralization' and 'decentralization,' which easily convert into a polarization and antithesis which poorly serves political science. We appear to have no term that embraces the full continuum between the two poles nor a term for the important middle range where centralizing and decentralizing tendencies are substantially in balance. For this and other reasons, much of the discussion of decentralization should be considered as a part of the federal process" (p. 21).

West Indies, and the developments in East Africa[3] all illustrate unique features of the federal process. However, Canada, the oldest and one of the more developed federations, and Nigeria, one of the newest and least developed members, have been selected. The third is a consideration of the effects of Commonwealth membership upon the internal developments of these two members. Since all of the papers published in this volume deal in one way or another with the first of these topics, it will be omitted from the following discussion; detailed consideration will be devoted to the second; and passing attention will be given to the third. It is obvious that only the most cursory analyses can be attempted, but it is hoped that these may provide illustrations of federalism as a process in the Commonwealth.

Canada

The history of Canadian federalism has been covered so frequently that it offers a wide selection of approaches for consideration.[4] At the same time, there is lacking any substantial amount of Canadian theorizing on federalism. Canadian concepts of federalism have been developed by extrapolation out of the empirical data, such as court decisions, which Canadian political evolution has cast up. Today, in consequence, the Canadian union can be characterized in various ways, and several distinctive concepts of Canadian federalism have found some effective application. Two of these concepts can represent a starting point for this brief excursion into Canadian history.

Advocates of the compact theory, widely accepted in Quebec, have held that the Canadian union rests on a compact between provinces. Though there is no evidence of Calhoun's influence, the compact theory has a similarity to the views on the nature of the union held by the leaders of the Confederacy before the

3. Particular mention might be made of the new Republic of Tanzania and the E. A. Common Services Organization.
4. See Alexander Brady's comprehensive, critical bibliography on "Federalism in Canada," in William S. Livingston, *Federalism in the Commonwealth* (London, 1963), pp. 11-28.

Civil War in the United States. It is true that the debates on the Quebec Resolutions of 1864 included occasional references to treaty relationships, and these references have been used to support the tenuous basis for considering the B.N.A. Act as an embodiment and a legalization of this "treaty." But whatever be the historical basis, the compact theorists place great stress upon the original rights of the provinces, look with concern upon protecting the sphere of powers delegated to them, such as education and civil rights, and insist upon unanimity among them for amendments. These positions provide us with a stage from which to view briefly Canadian federalism since 1867, as it has evolved under the pressures of the centripetal and centrifugal forces existent in that century.

It is clear that the participants in the Quebec and London Conferences in 1864-66 believed that their resolutions would result in the creation of a highly centralized system, and the provisions of the resulting enactment, the B.N.A. Act, bore out these anticipations. The Act granted the provinces in Section 92 only those powers which were of "local" concern, and left to the central government all powers not otherwise assigned. The power of the central government to disallow provincial legislative enactments, the position of the lieutenant governor in the provinces, and the provisions regarding the selection of federal judges all supported this interpretation. Section 91, which gave to the central government the power "to make laws for the Peace, Order and Good Government of Canada" in respect to all those matters not specifically delegated to the provinces, gave added evidence of the intentions of the constitutional framers. Needless to state, this interpretation cannot be reconciled with the conclusions drawn by the compact theorist in Quebec, who, as Alexander Brady has observed, has "remained consistently attached to a strict federalism as a protector of his own culture and the cultural dualism of Canada."[5]

As late as 1882, the privy council was interpreting the B.N.A.

5. "Quebec and Canadian Federalism," *Canadian Journal of Economics and Political Science*, XXV (Aug., 1959), 260.

Act in the light of the intentions of its framers, but proceeded thereafter in a series of tortuous decisions to whittle down the federal powers with respect to trade and commerce, fisheries, agriculture, international treaties, and the residuary clause. At the same time, it developed the provincial power over "property and civil rights" to include labor legislation, social insurance, exploitation of natural resources, and other matters. In short, as Frank R. Scott has so frequently asserted in bitterly reviewing this chapter in the history of the privy council, the concept of common interest, clearly in evidence in the Quebec and London Resolutions, had been lost.[6] Where a "looser federalism in the United States was unified by the judgments of a Marshall," he comments in reference to the period after 1884 in Canada, "a stronger union was decentralized by a Watson and a Haldane."[7] Or, as characterized by A. R. M. Lower, "the just-short-of-unitary state that Macdonald thought he had achieved was cut down to something just short of a confederacy."[8]

But this period of strict construction of the Constitution in favor of the provinces and of judicial direction of the federal process was destined to end. The reasons for the change cannot be attributed to a major change of heart on the part of the courts, but to a change in the circumstances which produced a new empire for the federal system. Some of these factors have been analyzed by J. A. Corry: (1) There were the improvements in transportation and communications which were to provide unifying bonds for Canada with frontiers extended to the Pacific. Canadian economic historians of the "Innis School" have stressed the importance of the growth of transport facilities, from canals, to railways, to pipe lines, as a special unifying force in Canada. (2) There was the shift from the impact of the individualistic, legalistic, and laissez-faire ideas which were in vogue when the Canadian federation came officially into being to the more collectivist views which were to precede the later government in-

6. "French-Canada and Canadian Federalism," in A. R. M. Lower *et al.*, *Evolving Canadian Federalism* (Durham, N. C., 1958), p. 71.
7. "Centralization and Decentralization in Canadian Federalism," *Canadian Bar Review*, XXIX (Dec., 1951), 1104.
8. Lower, p. 40.

tervention in the form of social welfare legislation, taxation, and "overall guidance of the economy." During the period of the Great Depression, their impacts can be seen not only in the Rowell-Sirois Report of 1940, but in an extreme form in the Green Book proposals which were prepared in Ottawa for the Dominion-Provincial Conference on Reconstruction in 1945[9] and in such writings as Maurice Lamontagne, *Le Federalisme canadien*.[10] (3) The wartime mobilization during both World War I and World War II, coupled with the subsequent fiscal and economic measures necessary to provide for Canadian defense, has played its significant part. (4) Finally, there has been the nationalizing of sentiment among the elites, and especially among the business elites which want "stability in prices, in labor relations, in monetary, fiscal, and other governmental policies, so that they can engage in long-range planning for their industry." Even a resistant province could not help being "caught up in the logic of the interdependent economy and of large-scale industrial enterprise" and could hope in the long run only to play "variant melodies within the general theme" of national design.[11] The federal umpire of this new game or process is no longer the courts, cogently argues Professor Corry, but this role is now played by the politicians who are basing their decisions on policy grounds.

The heyday of classical federalism had passed, and the epoch of centralist and co-operative federalism was at hand. The centralist can point to the developments in such diversified fields as that of finance, where the full implications of the unlimited power of taxation of the federal government to pre-empt in fact tax fields open to the provinces have been recognized, and to the almost limitless possibilities of the grant-in-aid, which has grown progressively in use since 1912. Assistance, with the consequent indirect controls of varying types, has been provided for programs in agriculture, highways, technical education, old age pensions, public health, employment services, hospitals, and

9. Ottawa, 1946.
10. Quebec, 1954.
11. J. A. Corry, "Constitutional Trends in Federalism" in Lower, pp. 108-12.

other areas.[12] Even in the cultural sphere, the report of the Massey Commission in 1951 anticipated a much greater involvement of the federal government, despite the constitutional provisions reserving most educational affairs to the provinces.

Consistent in general with these centralizing trends and developing concurrently in point of time has been the emergence of a number of collaborative relationships involving the provinces and the federal government. This collaboration has been referred to with growing frequency as co-operative federalism.[13] On the horizontal plane, there have been an increasing number of interprovincial contacts to secure more agreement on joint standards and to encourage the enactment of reciprocal legislation. These contacts have been deepened by the annual Interprovincial Premiers' Conferences, which have been meeting since 1960.

There are those who consider the development of co-operative federalism as providing simply another cloak for the growing centralization and who view co-ordinate federalism as added terminology and rationalization for the centralization trends. But the better position is that co-operative federalism is designed to strengthen both levels of government and, in consequence, will at some point be restrictive of continuing centralizing trends. In any case, co-operative federalism was here to stay, asserted J. A. Corry in 1958, even if the provinces were to become "dignified and haughty pensioners rather than partners of the national governments."[14]

However, recent events have thrown doubt on whether all of the provinces are willing to remain "dignified and haughty pensioners." An appraisal must consequently be made of the centrifugal forces which are at work in Canada and which are outlining the contours and conditioning the direction of the federal process. First of all, the recent reactions and strong views held

12. In 1959, almost 25 per cent of the total fund transfers from the central to the provincial treasuries was represented by grant-aided programs. Edwin R. Black, "Canadian Concepts of Federalism" (unpublished dissertation, Duke University, 1962), p. 93.

13. *Ibid.*, pp. 84 ff. Black prefers "correlative federalism" to the more widely used "co-operative federalism."

14. Lower, p. 124.

in one of the two most populous provinces, Quebec, must be given particular attention. "Some of the noise in today's Quebec is the sound of exploding myths, some the noise of a society working furiously to modernize itself, and some an old noise rejuvenated:nationalism," writes Ramsay Cook.[15] These noises have produced what the Royal Commission on Bilingualism and Biculturalism in Canada has called "the greatest crisis in its history."[16]

The setting for this crisis is provided by the social and economic changes which have occurred during the postwar period and particularly during the past decade. Demographic considerations in Quebec, with a birthrate now below the national average; the growth in industrialization; the development of mass communications; the rural exodus in the 1950's and the rapid urbanization; and the effects of an improved educational system coupled with the growing secular influences in Canadian society have all had an impact on French-Canadians who wish to preserve a culture rooted in a common religion, law, and language.[17] The fears of cultural subversion through alien pressures and the unrequited desires for rapid social and economic improvements have helped to strengthen the belief that French Canadians have been subjected to serious discriminations by English Canadians under the existing constitutional system.[18] Whatever be the explanations therefor, it is clear that an emergent

15. "The French-Canadian Question," *Political Quarterly*, XXXVI (Jan.-March, 1965), 8.
16. *Preliminary Report of the Royal Commission on Bilingualism and Biculturalism* (Ottawa, 1965), p. 13.
17. Michael Oliver, "Introduction," in Frank Scott and Michael Oliver, eds., *Quebec States Her Case* (Toronto, 1964), pp. 1-11; Nathan Keyfits, "Canadians and Canadiens," *Queen's Quarterly*, LXX (Summer, 1963), 163-182; Hubert Guindon, "Social Unrest, Social Class and Quebec's Bureaucratic Revolution," *ibid.*, LXXI (Summer, 1964), 150-162.
18. For varying interpretations, which are pertinent, see D. V. Smiley, "The Two Themes of Canadian Federalism," *Canadian Journal of Economics and Political Science*, XXXI (Feb., 1965), 80-97; Kenneth D. McRae, "The Structure of Canadian History," in Louis Hartz, ed., *The Founding of New Societies* (New York, 1964), pp. 219-274. McRae minimizes somewhat the role of industrial and economic factors, which receive more stress in the writings of Smiley. He finds the roots of French-Canadian unity to lie in the peculiar historical evolution of a "fragment" extracted from the absolutist society of Louis XIV and transferred to the New World where its "ethos," and basic institutions of the family and the church, were preserved without fundamental changes in the new environment.

group of middle class intellectuals and professional people, with new conceptions of the positive role of the state, are providing the political leadership to bring about the rapid transformation of the province.

The disaffections and desires among these leaders and the vocal elements in the province as a whole (little being known about the attitudes of the rural farmer and urban semiskilled worker) find reflection in various attitudes toward the Canadian constitutional system and Canadian federalism. The conflicting viewpoints range from those who favor separation from the Confederation (some 12-13 per cent of the population of Quebec and two out of eight French Canadians in Quebec, according to polls) to those who insist upon an "associate state" status for Quebec in a very loose confederation;[19] those who accept the theory of a "dual state" and demand the decentralization of federal powers and the transfer to the provinces of greatly augmented fiscal resources with corresponding adjustments in the present co-operative arrangements; and those who, like L. S. St. Laurent, the retired federal prime minister, in practice at least have supported a theory of concurrent majorities not entirely different from that once expounded by John C. Calhoun. The most widely accepted theory in French-Canadian intellectual and political circles today is probably the "dual state" or "dual alliance" theory. With an earlier historical origin, it came into its own during the Duplessis period, and it represented a fundamental premise of the Tremblay Report in 1956.[20] It finds today strong expression in the Liberal Government in Quebec headed by Premier Lesage. In contrast to the compact theory, which emphasizes the original compact between all of the *provinces*, the dual state theory places the stress upon a compact between two *cultures* or *nations*. In accordance with this theory, which per-

19. The "associate state" relationship has been advocated by the Société Saint-Jean Baptiste, the Créditistes, and the Parti Socialiste du Quebec. See Ramsay Cook, "Quebec and Confederation Past and Present," *Queen's Quarterly*, LXXI (Winter, 1965), 468-484.

20. *Report of the Royal Commission of Inquiry on Constitutional Problems* (4 vols.; Quebec, 1956). Professor Black, in his "Canadian Concepts of Federalism," has found differentiating criteria for the dual alliance, compact, co-ordinate, correlative, and centralist concepts. On the dual alliance concept, see chap. vi.

mits of some latitude in interpretation, the Confederation document of 1867 was agreed to by two cultural groups, and Quebec as an equal partner in a dual state has become the political base and center of one of these groups.

Consonant with his views on co-operative federalism in a dual state framework, Premier Lesage has stated the *minimum* demands of Quebec on several occasions. They are that, first, French must be a "teaching language" for French-Canadian minorities outside Quebec[21] and a "working language" in the federal public service; second, there must be a genuine "decentralization of powers, resources and decision-making in our federal system."[22] These minimum demands, he maintains, will result in greater equality of professional and economic opportunity and preservation of the French-Canadian language and culture.

Two comments may be ventured. On the one hand, the successful pressures being exerted by Quebec are, as is to be expected, beginning to produce countering repercussions in a number of English-Canadian provinces, especially in the western part of Canada. These pressures could under certain circumstances deepen the internal fissures in Canada. On the other hand, there is growing evidence from a number of quarters that a Quebec counterrevolution may have had its beginnings during the past year or two, at least among more moderate elements, which are motivated by the concessions to Quebec made in Ottawa in the light of the probable economic and political costs of a very loose confederation, and, especially, of separation. But, at the least, the "quiet revolution" has already made a basic centrifugal impact on the federal process in Canada.

In addition to the impact of the developments in Quebec,

21. The percentage of French Canadians in the total Canadian population of over 18.2 million in 1961 was 28.1 according to language and 30.4 according to ethnic origin. Over 17 per cent of the French-Canadian population lived outside the Province of Quebec. See Appendix V of the *Parliamentary Report of the Committee on Bilingualism and Biculturalism* for data on French-Canadian minorities outside Quebec.

22. Ramsay Cook, "The Canadian Dilemma," *International Journal*, XX (1965), 20; Jean Lesage, "A Modern Approach to Civil Service Administration," *Civil Service Review*, XXXVII (March, 1964), 28; New York *Times*, March 19, 1965, p. 10.

there are other centrifugal forces which provide support for provincial autonomy in Canada. Other provinces besides Quebec share the concern about central controls over the taxing power. "Provincial autonomy," carefully defined, also finds vigorous defenders in academic circles.[23] Again, there are specific pressure groups in Canada, including those which are engaged in the exploitation of certain natural resources now subject solely to provincial regulation, which would prefer the status quo to change. The more rapid growth of provincial and municipal, as compared to national, expenditures has been evident. The thoughtful interpretations of Frank Underhill deserve mention, though he went too far when he asserted that the provincial governments provided the only real centers of political opposition to the government in power in Ottawa.[24] His contention was that the Canadian electorate voted one way in provincial and another way in federal elections in order to create a balance. Others have cited the "federalization," i.e., the accepted provincial "representation" in the federal cabinet, as serving a similar purpose.

Canada is still in some respects a collection of provinces each of which has its own political characteristics. "The most important thing about Canadian politics," says J. R. Mallory, "is that they are parochial rather than national. This is at once the greatest weakness and the greatest source of strength of our national political system. It is a weakness [which] threatens from time to time to destroy the very idea of a Canadian nation."[25] This parochialism is even evidenced at times by idle threats of an occasional public official in Saskatchewan or British Columbia that these provinces should leave Canada and become states in the United States. In any case, there are operative outside

23. D. V. Smiley, "The Rowell-Sirois Report, Provincial Autonomy, and Post-War Canadian Federalism," *Canadian Journal of Economics and Political Science*, XXVIII (Feb., 1962), 69.
24. See Denis Smith, "Prairie Revolt, Federalism, and the Party System," in Hugh G. Thorburn, ed., *Party Politics in Canada* (Toronto, 1963), p. 133. For recent observations on the "federal structure of Canadian parties," see Leon P. Epstein, "A Comparative Study of Canadian Parties," *American Political Science Review*, LVIII (March, 1964), 50.
25. "The Structure of Canadian Parties," in Thorburn, p. 29.

Quebec many factors and forces which are serving collectively to bridle early trends toward centralization and to modify the co-operative aspects of Canadian federalism.

Nigeria

There are understandable reasons why neither Nigerians nor outside observers have yet produced any distinctive theories of Nigerian federalism. The fact that the Federation of Nigeria became an independent state on October 1, 1960, would be at least one of them. Nonetheless, there has been a great deal of speculation as to the nature of Nigerian nationhood and the future of Nigerian federalism.[26] Sir Alan Burns, a former colonial administrator in Nigeria and the author of a well-known history of the country, expressed a then widely held view when in 1954 he asserted that "there is no Nigerian nation, no Nigerian language . . . and no Nigerian tradition. The very name of Nigeria was invented by the British to describe a country inhabited by a medley of formerly warring tribes with no common culture, and united only insofar as they are governed by a single Power."[27]

For this point of view, which essentially denies the basis of any real unity and coherence in the Nigerian federal state and any lasting foundation for the powers being exercised at the center, various types of evidence are offered. The first of these is that Nigeria is a recent creation and owes her official origin to the fiat of a colonial power on January 1, 1900. The uniting of the Protectorate of Northern Nigeria and the Colony and Protectorate of Southern Nigeria in 1914, again by fiat at the behest of Frederick Lugard, provided the basis for the unitary system which existed thereafter for several decades.

26. The following discussion has borrowed heavily from chaps. iii-v by the author in Tilman and Cole, *The Nigerian Political Scene*. On the background, see, in particular, James S. Coleman, *Nigeria: Background to Nationalism* (Berkeley, 1958), and Kalu Ezera, *Constitutional Developments in Nigeria* (Cambridge, 1960). A bibliography on "Federalism in Nigeria" by Grady H. Nunn is included in Livingston, *Federalism in the Commonwealth*, pp. 173-92.

27. "The Movement toward Self-Government in British Colonial Territories," *Optima*, IV (June, 1954), 9.

A second claim is that, legally speaking, the constitutional developments since World War II have explicitly recognized the growing divisiveness which has been inherent in the Nigerian system from the beginning. The three groupings of provinces had been formally recognized in the Richards Constitution of 1946, and the regional divisions were clearly accepted in the following constitutions of 1951 and 1954. Under this latter constitution internal "self-government" was granted the three Regions between 1957 and 1959. The Independence Constitution of 1960, so it is argued, slightly altered in favor of the Federation, but did not fundamentally change, the distribution of powers between the center and the Regions made in 1954. Accordingly, legal diversity was substituted for the legally unified political structure which existed prior to World War II.

A third charge is that the political organization at the center cannot claim to be the respected and accepted central government of a federal political system. Uncertainties and skepticism were compounded by the revision of some of the provisions of the Independence Constitution of 1960 in the new constitution which went into effect on October 1, 1963, when Nigeria became a republic. A new and fourth Region, the Mid-Western Region, came into being during 1963 and its integration in 1964 into the constitutional structure is contributing to current uncertainties in Lagos.[28] The disparity in size and population of the Regions will be in evidence as the Northern Region will continue to occupy about 75 per cent of the territory and to contain about 55 per cent of the approximately 55,500,000 population, if we accept the controversial official census figures of 1963.[29] Certainly, the Northern People's Congress, the dominant political party in the Northern Region, has at the present moment an absolute majority of the members of the national House of Representatives. The reactions in the South against the North because

28. New York *Times*, July 16, 1963. Some of the possible political implications for the federal process in Nigeria are discussed in Donald S. Rothchild, "Safeguarding Nigeria's Minorities," *Duquesne Review*, VIII (Spring, 1963), 46-47.

29. The processing of the national census, which was nearing completion in 1962, was suddenly discontinued after sharp political controversy. The new census was completed toward the end of 1963.

of the exclusion of southerners from the Northern Region public services have been in evidence, and the sectional bitterness was exacerbated by the first election since independence, in December, 1964. Chief Awolowo, the former premier of the Western Region and the former leader of the opposition in the Assembly, and a large number of his followers were sentenced for treason in September, 1963, and there has been no officially recognized leader of the opposition in the federal House of Representatives since their arrest. Instead, Chief Awolowo from prison is widely regarded by a large percentage of the Yorubas as their continuing political leader. The Supreme Court, with original jurisdiction over disputes between the Federation and Regions and between Regions, and with original and appellate jurisdiction in constitutional questions involving regional and federal legislation, has been charged by partisan critics with a lack of objectivity.[30] Various accusations of corruption of ministers and officials have been made,[31] and there have been recognized shortcomings of the civil service.[32] The planning machinery, in terms of organization, composition, and outlook, has been inadequate. And, in terms of prestige, the Minorities Commission in 1958 concluded that the federal government, in comparison with the regional governments, occupied a "secondary place in the estimation of most Nigerians."[33]

A fourth contention is that certain features of its society provide obstacles to any real unification of Nigeria. Its heavy dependence upon agriculture, fishing, animal husbandry, and

30. See Olowole Idowu Odomoso, *The Nigerian Constitution: History and Development* (London, 1963), pp. 257-75; David La Vine Grove, "The Sentinels of Liberty? The Nigerian Judiciary and Fundamental Rights," *Journal of African Law,* VII (Autumn, 1963), 152-71. For a discussion of the background and political implications of the decisions in *F. R. A. Williams* v. *M. A. Majekodunmi,* July 7, 1962, and *Adegbenro* v. *Attorney General and Others,* July 7, 1962, see John P. Mackintosh, "Politics in Nigeria: The Action Group Crisis of 1962," *Political Studies,* XI (1963), 151-54.

31. See Tilman and Cole, pp. 112-13. The Coker Commission's revelations in 1962 of the types of financial practices in the Western Region have caused widespread speculation regarding the other governments of the republic.

32. *Ibid.,* chap. v.

33. "Nigeria, Report of the Commission Appointed to Enquire into the Fears of Minorities and the Means of Allaying Them," Cmnd. 505. G. B., *Parl. Paps.* 1957-58, IX, 519 ff.

forestry, to which over three-fourths of the employment could be attributed in 1950-57, underlines the importance of the rural areas where local and ethnic ties are dominant. The uneven distribution of the low per capita income, with the Western Region in the favored position, and the statistical gap between the North and the South in such matters as school attendance tend to accentuate regional jealousies and suspicions, and accordingly find reflection in the national political picture at the center.

Finally, some of the factors which make for a lack of social cohesiveness thereby provide a flimsy basis for the effective exercise of the powers of a central government. As seen through the eyes of one observer,[34] the factors making for a lack of stability, and hence for disunity, would include "the absence of universally acceptable and understood rationale for the existence and functioning of the state of Nigeria"; the lack of a "substantial Nigerian tradition of nationalist pressure toward existence as a nationally and ethnically independent state"; the inconsistency with a nationalist ideology of "tribalism, religious juxtapositions, regional diversities, and cultural classes"; the lack of legitimacy or of "valid sources of authority" of the political system; the inadequacies of the Nigerian elite, "too small in number, too isolated from their following, too atypical, too transient, too loosely organized, and too inexperienced"; and the absence of an "orientation of political ideas, leadership, interest groups, and procedures and functions toward a framework of values relating to post-independence possibilities rather than the colonial *status quo*."

In short, it is contended that the trend of the past decade and a half has been toward separation rather than unity; that there has been no real emergence of symbols that would attract the loyalties, or even the attention, of the illiterate and impoverished masses; that increasing urbanization, economic development, and social mobility have not as yet resulted in a new social setting on which a national consciousness can be grounded; that polit-

34. Henry L. Bretton, *Power and Stability in Nigeria: The Politics of Decolonization* (New York, 1962).

ical parties and other groups fail to accept the common interests on which ties of national unity can rest; that there are serious shortcomings and inadequacies in the government at the center; and that without the existence of such ties of unity a central government in a Nigerian federal system must either remain as a weak party or disappear entirely.[35]

Recent events culminating in the constitutional crisis following the federal election in December, 1964, have tended to undergird this skeptical point of view, which at its extreme sees Nigeria prepared to divide into separatist political systems. However, I do not believe that this view takes into account certain forces and developments which are resulting in greater social and political integration and which are thereby providing support for the growing strength and role of the central government. And without this unity at the center, to repeat, no federal system could in fact exist.

To begin with, disruptive developments have not diminished the use of the English language; on the contrary, recent developments in education have tended to confirm its importance as the lingua franca for the growing number of literate Nigerians. The outward forms of parliamentary government have been retained, though these may not always reflect the inner realities; and the portentous developments in the Western Region, which lived during a large part of 1962 under the pall of emergency government and federal intervention, cannot be lightly ignored. Though the impact of English law has produced its stresses and strains, it has been a unifying force and has partially superseded customary law in such areas as the law of evidence and procedure. The dissatisfaction with the degree of acceptance in spirit of the recent penal law reforms in the Northern Region cannot conceal the fact that substantial steps have been taken in that Region which will provide greater legal uniformity in criminal law in all Nigeria.[36] The common quest for the Nigeriani-

35. Tilman and Cole, p. 49.
36. J. N. D. Anderson, "Return Visit to Nigeria: Judicial and Legal Developments in the Northern Region," *International and Comparative Law Quarterly,* XII (Jan., 1963), 282 ff. This point of view was strongly presented by Attorney General I. M. Lewis in an interview in Kaduna in June, 1964.

zation of these public services in independent Nigeria has, despite more limited enthusiasm in the Northern Region than in the others, provided one common bond. And the history of most other federations, including that of Canada, points to the effects over a sufficient period of time of the growth of centripetal pressures.

There are other factors and forces which are serving to integrate Nigerian society and to point to the growing role of the central government in the federal system. The most important of these is the impact of certain economic developments which have necessarily underscored the key position of the government at the center. First of all, the central government provides the channel through which the bulk of the revenue for the operation of the regional governments is made available.[37] In keeping with the constitutionally prescribed bases for distribution of these funds, in 1960-61 about 44 per cent and in 1963-64 about 40 per cent of the total revenue of the federal government passed through federal hands to the Regions. Over three-fifths of all regional government revenue is derived from this source. Again the Federal Government Development Program for 1962-68, or the new National Economic Plan, has been hammered out through the joint action of federal and regional agencies, in which the Federal Ministry of Economic Development, the National Economic Council, and the Central Bank of Nigeria have all played leading parts. Federal expenditures under the Program would constitute two-thirds of the total outlays. If the expectations for the ambitious Plan are falling short of realization at this writing, nevertheless, the central government's role in procuring foreign funds by grant or loan and in making certain percentages available to regional governments cannot be ignored. In the eyes of one student of the Nigerian political scene, this National Plan anticipates thereby a growth of federal powers "not by constitutional revision but by the logic of events and the implications of economic development."[38] Another has gone so far as to say

37. Particular mention might be made of W. R. Cotter, "Taxation and Federalism in Nigeria," *British Tax Review*, March-April, 1964, pp. 97-116.
38. K. W. I. Post, "Nigeria Two Years after Independence," *World Today*,

that "an examination of financial and economic policies suggests that in these matters Nigeria is beginning to operate in much the same way as a unitary state."[39]

Support of a special sort for added federal guarantees and controls of such agencies as the police has come in the past from minority groups because of the feared excesses of the dominant political group, particularly political parties, in each of the Regions. Each Region has had a government which has rested primarily upon the political support of certain tribal groups, the Hausa-Fulani in the North through the Northern Peoples' Congress, until recently the Yoruba in the West through the Action Group, and the Ibo in the East through the National Convention of Nigerian Citizens.[40] These fears, and the solutions suggested by the various ethnic and religious minorities, constituting about one-third of the national population, were ventilated in 1958 to a commission "to enquire into the fears of minorities and the means of allaying them." Though this minority agitation is not as vigorous as at an earlier period, it has shown recent signs of revival and some of these minorities (especially the Tiv) would, if opportunity offered itself, prefer federal protection to regional benevolence.

The growing importance of the federal government in the economic realm and the psychological attraction of the federal arena as the place where foreign and defense policies are being decided have induced some political leaders to move from the regional to the national scene. This was true of Chief Awolowo

XVIII (Nov., 1962), 469. Cf. Wolfgang F. Stolper, "Economic Development in Nigeria," *Journal of Economic History*, XXIII (Dec., 1963), 391-413; Victor P. Diegomaoh, *Economic Development in Nigeria* (Princeton, 1965), esp. chaps. iv, vii, viii.

39. John P. Mackintosh, "Federalism in Nigeria," *Political Studies*, X (Oct., 1962), 245.

40. Two national alliances, the United Progressive Grand Alliance with its chief support from the National Convention of Nigerian Citizens, and the Nigerian National Alliance with its chief support from the Northern Peoples' Congress, were bitter rivals in the federal election of 1964. The complicated sequence of events involving the political parties during the pre- and post-election period has been summarized in the issue of the *Morning Post* (Lagos), for January 13, 1965, esp. pp. 8-9, *et seq*. The coalition cabinet which was formed in the spring of 1965 by Prime Minister Balewa was larger and more broadly based, but in its composition it evidenced many similarities to the cabinet before the election (*West Africa*, April 10, 1965, pp. 390, 395, 401; *ibid.*, May 29, 1965, p. 591).

and of Dr. Azikiwe when they were heads of their respective parties. It has not been true of the most influential of these regional leaders, the Sardauna of Sokoto, premier of the Northern Region. But the pull of political gravity toward the center has increased, at least by comparison with the attitudes prevalent among the political leaders as late as a decade ago. However, the "power structures" in Nigeria are still heavily regionally oriented, and there has not as yet been the development at the national level, as there has been at the regional level, of a dominant leadership group which is bound together by common access to the sources of power and privilege.[41] But these groupings are coming into existence and the attractions of the center are increasing.

The constitutional changes embodied in the new autochthonous constitution of October 1, 1963, for the Federal Republic of Nigeria have not visibly affected the federal evolution in Nigeria. The major changes were the substitution of a president, elected by the two houses of Parliament, for the governor general, the abolition of appeals to the privy council, and the elimination of the Judicial Service Commission. The significance from our point of view may lie perhaps more in the failure to incorporate proposals to strengthen the powers of the president, desired by many NCNC adherents, or the strongly advocated provisions to strengthen the detention powers of the central government. But its existing emergency powers are broad, and, with the abolition of appeals to the privy council, the power of the federal government to dismiss regional governments after a declaration of a state of emergency would appear

41. The unpublished seminar paper presented at the University of Texas in 1963 by Richard L. Sklar on this point might be mentioned. In a chapter on "The Nigerian Constitutional System," to appear in a volume on representative government in Africa, edited by Gwendolyn M. Carter, Dr. Sklar adds: "At present the Northern Peoples' Congress joined by former members of the Opposition commands an absolute majority in the Federal House of Representatives. Therefore, what may seem to be a shift of power from the regional capitals to Lagos during the first years of independence, may actually mask the growing influence of regional leaders at Kaduna in Federal affairs." See also his *Nigerian Political Parties* (Princeton, 1963), esp. chaps. ix-xi. cf., Richard L. Sklar and C. S. Whitaker, "Nigeria," in James S. Coleman and Carl G. Rosberg, Jr. (eds.), *Political Parties and National Integration in Tropical Africa* (Berkeley, 1964), pp. 598-665.

to be almost unlimited. Certainly the exercise of the emergency powers, in the light of the precedent in 1962, has great significance as a centralizing force. To this development may be added the growing amount of national legislation in the broad field of concurrent powers, which has reduced progressively the legislative competences of the Regions.[42] The Regions may eventually have to fall back on their reserved powers, which lie primarily in the fields of local government, land tenure, elementary and secondary education, customary courts and chieftaincy, and agriculture.

Other factors deserve mention. The most important of these are the impacts of educational changes in the political socialization of Nigeria. It is probably true that most Nigerian leaders do not as yet look to the schools as instruments for fostering a national consciousness of solidarity, but the indirect influences of the schools are nevertheless substantial. The remarkable and surprising amount of unity, exhibited by the well-organized strikers during the general strike of 1964, represented action which cut sharply across ethnic and regional lines. Though less in evidence in the North, nevertheless the trade-union unity was marked throughout most of Nigeria and suggests the importance of the role of the trade unions in the future. The growth of the mass media, including newspapers, radio, and television, has added an important element; but the link between the mass and informal systems of communications, while in evidence, is still a somewhat tenuous one.[43]

The various "pulls" toward the center, some economic ones, some based upon the fears of minorities, some psychological ones reflecting a common pride in Nigerian control of her defense and foreign policies, and some reflecting impacts of educational and

42. Note, however, the decision of the Supreme Court of Nigeria in *T. U. Akwule and Ten Others* v. *The Queen*, May 23, 1963, Appeal No. F.S.C. 325.

43. For an informed discussion of education and political socialization, consult Ayo Ogunsheye, "Nigeria," in James S. Coleman (ed.), *Education and Political Development* (Princeton, 1965), pp. 123-143. On the role of the mass media in the election of 1959, see K. W. J. Post, *The Nigerian Federal Election of 1959* (Oxford, 1963), p. 320. The results of a national public opinion survey in the fall of 1962 are analyzed in Lloyd A. Free, *The Attitudes, Hopes and Fears of Nigerians* (Princeton, 1964).

other political socializing forces, are tending to counterbalance the regional and separatist attractions. They are producing not only a modest centralizing trend, but also, as in Canada, they are accompanied by the faint beginnings of co-operative federalism. Various arrangements have been made for increasing the collaboration between the federal and regional governments. In most cases, the initiative has been taken by a federal ministry or agency in Lagos. Such areas as fisheries, agriculture, civil aviation, and others have offered the occasion for federal-regional conferences and for other types of continuing consultation at the ministerial levels. In education, a whole series of agencies and commissions has come into existence within recent years. These have included the Federal Scholarship Advisory Board, the Joint Consultative Committee on Education, and the West African Examination Council, all in existence prior to 1960, and such bodies as the National Manpower Board and the National Universities Commission, which have been more recently established following the report of the Ashby Commission. The potentialities of grants-in-aid are still to be as fully explored in Nigeria as they have been in Canada. Nevertheless, foreign experience is not unknown in Nigeria, and a White Paper of the federal government has anticipated a comprehensive system of grants-in-aid for certain purposes, including the establishment of an expanded system of secondary education.

Regional, rather than federal, pressures will explain the regional "representation" provided by statute on various public corporations, such as the Electricity Corporation and the Nigerian Railway Corporation. Various advisory councils such as the Postal and Telegraph Advisory Council and the Federal Labor Advisory Council, though set up under the authority of federal ministers, do in fact provide for membership to reflect regional points of view. This regional "representation" on the boards of statutory corporations and on other joint consultative bodies provides forums where an exchange of regional and specialized points of view can take place under the aegis of a national body in search of agreement on issues of national concern. In short, this development represents a modest counterpart to the Canadian one toward co-operative federalism.

It is well to recognize that power can be concentrated at the center at the same time that the whole political system in Nigeria may be facing a period of crisis, possibly involving major adjustments, if all of the possible implications of the expected constitutional revision are realized. Even complete separation of the constituent parts or complete legal unification coupled with some revivals of past autocratic systems[44] cannot be ruled out as theoretical extremes on a continuum. For the moment, the pressing economic problems, the uncertainties involved in constitutional revision during the transition to a republic on October 1, 1963, the unsettled political situation in the Western Region following the termination of the emergency government at the end of 1962, the census fiasco in the same year and the bitterness generated by the census of 1963-64, the corruption and treason trials or investigations in 1962-63, the political implications of the general strike of June, 1964, and, particularly, the uncertainties during and following the federal election in December, 1964[45] have necessarily dulled the optimism we reflected in a book published two years after Nigerian independence. Nevertheless, in our view, the unifying forces are still increasingly in evidence, and the interplay of centripetal and centrifugal factors has dulled but not eliminated the prospects for the maintenance of one viable federal system south of the Sahara.

This point of view finds confirmation in the recent observations of Kalu Ezera, one of Nigeria's leading constitutional authorities. In appraising the federal developments in Nigeria, and with a particular reference to the significance of the use of emergency powers, he has commented:

44. Note the prediction of M. G. Smith in his outstanding book, *Government in Zazzau* (London, 1960), pp. 292-93, regarding the Fulani empire.

45. Richard L. Sklar observes: "The federal election saw an almost naked North-South confrontation. The North sees no future except in managing to stay in power; the East feels threatened; the West is bitter; and the Mid-West is uncertain. Though the immediate crisis after the election has been resolved, we should be wrong to think that longer term problems have been dealt with." *Nigerian Opinion*, I (Jan., 1965), 2.

First, a federal structure for Nigeria, however unbalanced the units may be, has been evolved from the original unitary set-up. Secondly, the equal and coordinate relationship between the centre and the regions, once weighted in favour of the latter, has been gradually modified, by centripetal forces, in the direction of national centralisation; and the regions, though still regarded as autonomous component units of a federal state, are, in increasing measure, becoming the subsidized administrative organs of the federal government. Thirdly, under the pressure of domestic emergency, Nigerians have not only become unduly familiar with the inducements of 'constitutional government' which tended to weaken their respect for constitutional limitations and to undermine their belief in popular government, but also made them realize that, in their federal structure, ultimate power lies not in the regions but in the centre. This awareness has, in turn, greatly strengthened centripetal forces making for the unity of the country. All these features tend to suggest that federalism, at least, in Nigeria, has entered a new phase in which cooperation and central leadership and not necessarily equality and independence between the units are the guiding principles.[46]

Conclusion

Membership in the Commonwealth has had little influence in the recent evolution of *internal federal* relationships in either Canada or Nigeria. The reserve constituent powers of the Parliament of the United Kingdom will be recognized so long as some final agreement cannot be reached within Canada as to the exercise of the amending power.[47] The amending power provides at least a focal point for discussions of the distribution of federal-provincial powers. The provinces continue to maintain agents-general in London to look after particular provincial interests, such as trade and investment matters. It might be added that the activities in London of these agents-general, who for obvious

46. "Federalism and the Quest for National Unity in Africa, with Particular Reference to Nigeria," paper prepared for the IPSA Conference, pp. 18-19.

47. See F. R. Scott, "Our Changing Constitution," *Proceedings of the Royal Society of Canada*, Third Series, LV (1961), 94-95. In 1965, a petition was forwarded to the Queen by the federal cabinet at the request of the Lesage Government in Quebec, requesting an amendment of the provisions of the provincial Constitution dealing with the Legislative Council (The Montreal *Gazette*, May 8, 1965, p. 4; *Daily Telegraph* (London), June 18, 1965, p. 22).

reasons are not appointed to any other Commonwealth countries, have increased in recent years. The provinces, through the External Aid Office in Ottawa and other channels, have been providing some assistance, particularly in the educational field, to the developing countries of the Commonwealth. The province of Quebec has continued to insist upon her right to enter into treaty relationships with foreign powers in areas within her legislative competence and has actually concluded with one non-Commonwealth country a cultural "agreement" which has led to sharp controversy. But these illustrations have limited application for our purpose.

In Nigeria, as well, the *internal federal* developments since 1960 have apparently been little affected by Nigerian membership in the Commonwealth. It is true that Nigeria's membership in the Commonwealth has had a number of legal consequences and has raised certain questions. For example, Sections 14, 15, and 16 of the Constitution of 1963 make provision for Commonwealth citizens as distinguished from aliens. Companies which are registered in the Commonwealth have the same power as Nigerian companies for holding land. Special provisions for the reciprocal return of fugitive offenders, including persons charged with political offenses, have long been in effect and have recently received controversial application. The new Merchant Shipping Act, 1962, distinguishes between Commonwealth ships and those of foreign registry. The Immigration Act, 1963, discriminates in favor of Commonwealth citizens. Perhaps as important as these legal provisions has been the utilization in Lagos of Commonwealth ties, as in the period leading to the withdrawal of South Africa, to contribute to national awareness and unity.

But these constitutional provisions and acts have had little, if any *direct* bearing on the internal federal developments since independence. Only two or three cases in point can be cited. One of these was the settlement of the issue of the monarchical vs. republican form of government. The agreement by NPC leaders and Prime Minister Sir Abubaker that Nigeria should become a republic on October 1, 1963, provided at least an official solution to this problem which had been a source of North-South tension. The Northern Region's abandonment of an earlier preference for the status quo might thereby evidence some change in its attitude toward central-regional power relationships. A second item was the decision in 1963 by the privy council in sustaining the contentions of Chief Adegbenro in his appeal from the decision of the Nigerian Supreme Court holding that Chief Akintola had been legally reinstated as premier of the Western Region. This decision led to sharp criticism in Nigeria on both legal and political grounds and added to the pressures which resulted in the abolition in the new constitution of appeals to the privy council.[48] These illustrations suggest that the Commonwealth tie may eventually be ignored in analyses of the federal process *within* Nigeria, as in Canada.

48. Ezera, IPSA paper, p. 17; see also *The Times*, July 27, 1963, p. 7. It might be noted that the name of the "Ministry of Foreign Affairs and Commonwealth Relations" was late in 1963 changed to "Ministry of External Affairs."

Part III

Intra-Commonwealth Relations

5

The Intergovernmental Machinery of Commonwealth Consultation and Co-operation

*Kenneth Robinson**

The Residue of Empire

The Commonwealth is the product not merely—or mainly—of choice but of history. "If it did not exist," Dr. Wheare wrote in 1952, "you could not invent it."[1] From this flow not only its realities but also its weaknesses. Three consequences of its historical origins have been central to our subject: an initial assumption about the nature of the association, a distrust of central machinery, and an increasingly diverse membership.

The governmental machinery of Commonwealth relations was originally shaped at a time when all members were united (most of Ireland and much of South Africa albeit reluctantly) "by a common allegiance to the Crown." How then could their mutual relations be those of foreign states? On this basis a doctrine was propounded, mainly by Britain, which asserted that Commonwealth relations were neither international relations nor governed by international law. This *inter se* doctrine was firmly opposed by the Irish Free State and never accepted in international law. Its importance in determining some of the forms in which Commonwealth relations have been conducted

* Vice-chancellor of the University of Hong Kong, formerly professor of Commonwealth affairs and director of the Institute of Commonwealth Studies, University of London.
1. K. C. Wheare, "The Nature and Structure of the Commonwealth," *American Political Science Review*, XLVII (Dec., 1953), 1016.

should not therefore be exaggerated;[2] nonetheless for most people in most of the original member states, those relations rested on a sentiment, more immediate than any legal theory, that Commonwealth countries were not foreign to each other, even if they did not all agree about the formal consequences this might entail. This sentiment rested on the existence of a relatively dense network of interrelationships between people in Britain and those in the other members, especially among the ruling, professional, and trading groups. A recognizably similar nexus was slowly developing between Britain and people in other parts of the Empire, notably India, though the classes involved were a much smaller fraction of the population. Such relations accordingly might well not survive the transfer of power and would certainly be transformed by it.[3] The *inter se* doctrine was already obsolete when the acceptance of a republican India as a member removed the most obvious basis on which it could be argued. But vestiges of the notion on which it rested remained. A significant stage in their disappearance was marked by the abolition (in 1962) of the unrestricted right of immigration into Britain (and absolute freedom from deportation therefrom) which citizens of all Commonwealth countries had hitherto enjoyed.[4] Other stages have been exemplified, as we shall see, in

2. For the *inter se* doctrine, see James E. S. Fawcett, *The British Commonwealth in International Law* (London, 1963), chap. iv. The doctrine was in some respects a substitute for the assertion of the "diplomatic unity of the Empire" when dominion assertion of autonomy made that untenable.

3. An important factor in the disintegration of an existing political entity (especially a multinational state or empire) has often been "a substantial increase in political participation on the part of populations, regions, or social strata which previously had been politically passive" (Karl W. Deutsch, *et al.*, *Political Community and the North Atlantic Area* [Princeton, 1957], p. 161). This process has its counterpart even within so loose an association as the Commonwealth, in member states in which power was transferred to an existing nationalist leadership which often had close ties with Britain but thereafter sooner or later found itself under pressure from sections of the population hitherto politically inert. Ceylon since 1956 affords a striking example.

4. Commonwealth Immigrants Act, 1962 (10 and 11 Eliz. II, 21). The rights previously enjoyed by Commonwealth citizens as regards immigration to, and deportation from, Britain were a relic of the earlier common code of British nationality, long abandoned in these and other respects by other members. For a brief account of the evolution from a common code to a common status of Commonwealth citizen and the legal effects of the latter, see R. R. Wilson and R. E. Clute, "Commonwealth Citizenship and Common Status," *American Journal of International Law*, LVII (July, 1963), 566-87.

the development of the governmental machinery of Commonwealth relations in this decade.

All members of the Commonwealth were once part of the British Empire. The character of the subordination to London that implied (for all except Britain), as well as the manner in which freedom from it was achieved, naturally look different in different countries, especially as seen in a retrospect of varying length in each. But the prescriptions for mutual consultation in regard to foreign affairs, which were spelled out at the Imperial Conferences of 1923 and 1926, derived more from the determination of some dominions not to be bound by British commitments than from a desire to share in shaping them.[5] More recently, the disinclination of the newer members to accept any Commonwealth machinery which might be interpreted as a continuation of the imperial relationship by other means has been reinforced by greater determination to demonstrate positive independence in foreign policy, especially freedom from any commitment to either of the power blocs which have dominated international relations since the war. It was thus a consequence of its historical origins, as well as more immediate pressures, that throughout the history of the Commonwealth some members were "inflexibly opposed to the establishment of any . . . centralized machinery for consideration of political questions, especially foreign policy and defence."[6] The proposal of the Prime Ministers' Meeting in 1964 for the establishment of a Commonwealth secretariat, recruited from member countries and financed by their contributions, was seen by some as a decisive break with this habitual distrust of centralized machinery, signifying a "mutual determination" among the non-white states "to take over part of the operating responsibilities of a revised Commonwealth as-

5. Australia's successive proposals for some kind of more formal Commonwealth machinery, such as those for a consultative council put forward by Sir Robert Menzies at the Prime Ministers' Meeting in 1957, may be regarded as continuing her earlier preoccupation with securing a share in formulating a common policy. (Cf. Gordon Greenwood and Norman Harper, eds., *Australia in World Affairs, 1956-60* [Melbourne, 1963], p. 45-46.)

6. This phrase has appeared in each edition of *The Commonwealth Relations Office List* since 1956. E.g., *1964*, p. 126.

sociation."[7] Others emphasized the limited tasks prospectively assigned to it:

to disseminate factual information to all member countries on all matters of common concern; to assist existing agencies, both official and unofficial, in the promotion of Commonwealth links in all fields; and to help to coordinate, in cooperation with the host country, the preparation for future meetings of Commonwealth Heads of Government and, where appropriate, for meetings of other Commonwealth Ministers.[8]

The secretariat was established in June, 1965. The decision registers the ending of another of the idiosyncrasies of the old Commonwealth club—the anomaly whereby the inescapable functions of management continued paradoxically to be discharged by Britain. It marks a further stage in the transformation of the club into an international association which, like others, will have an international secretariat. Its functions, like theirs, will depend on what the members can agree that the association should do.

A third consequence of the historical origins of the Commonwealth is the diversity of its membership. The naval and maritime basis of the Empire resulted in its successor states being scattered round the world and including numerous peoples with widely different social and cultural institutions. Such geographical discontinuity and social diversity are naturally reflected in the diversity of economic, political, and strategic interests and preoccupations of members, a diversity which can only be expected to grow as their experience of independence lengthens.[9] Of this aspect of diversity there was already fair recognition by the early fifties.

But of others there was much less. Although there was room for doubt about the extent to which the political institutions

7. P. Keatley, "The Commonwealth Prime Ministers Conference," *The World Today*, XX (Aug., 1964), 321.

8. Commonwealth Prime Ministers' Meeting, July, 1964, Final Communiqué (Cmnd. 2441), p. 9.

9. This is well illustrated in the discussion of the evolution of an independent New Zealand foreign policy in T. C. Larkin, ed., *New Zealand's External Relations* (Wellington, 1962).

adopted at independence by India, Pakistan, and Ceylon would prove sufficiently strongly rooted in, or adapted to, the social environment in all three countries, a cautious optimism at first prevailed. That optimism, called in question by the long delay in adopting a constitution in Pakistan and by the Ceylon elections in 1956 (though these were not at once understood as delayed nationalist reactions against the dominance of the "English-educated" elite), was severely shaken by the military seizure of power in Pakistan in 1958. Ghana's repudiation of the Westminster model in 1960, after only three years of independence, was the more significant because, of all the former British territories in tropical Africa, she was the best endowed with modern cadres and the basis of a modern economy, and also because it could not be claimed to be the result of any failure of the parliamentary system to provide a stable majority.[10] Tanganyika's still more rapid repudiation of her independence constitution in 1962 served notice that the new Ghana model, which she largely adopted, could not be dismissed as an aberration resulting from the political style of Dr. Nkrumah. For a system of consultation which had been epitomized as "a continuing conference of cabinets" and had been thought to depend on some degree of predictable similarity of political behavior on the part of statesmen and officials of the various members, the significance of such developments seemed likely to be far-reaching.

A third aspect of diversity became more evident towards the end of the decade. A maritime-based empire naturally included many small islands as well as some mainland bases originally acquired for naval and strategic purposes. Until quite late in the fifties, it was widely assumed in Britain that, whatever future the accelerating process of decolonization might hold for such countries, it could hardly be sovereign independence,

10. In Ghana power was transferred to a nationalist party led neither by the traditional nor the English-educated elite but by those who had always been strongly critical of both on what might be described as populist grounds. In my opinion, this is crucial for an understanding of developments in the years immediately after independence.

and, even less, full membership of the Commonwealth.[11] Some might become, by integration, federation, or some looser form of association, part of a larger unit with other territories, British or foreign. But for others geography or politics precluded any such solution. Such of them as had attained "maximum internal self-government," the British government suggested in 1959, might be found "to have a distinct identity and a special place in the Commonwealth."[12] Next year, the Commonwealth prime ministers "reviewed the constitutional development of the Commonwealth with particular reference to the future of the smaller dependent territories" and "agreed that a detailed study of the subject should be made for consideration by Commonwealth governments."[13] Whether in this they were moved by the possibility[14] that after independence Cyprus (pop. 577,000) might decide to seek membership has not been divulged. The general problem was studied at the official level[15] but no further reference has been made to that review, and at their next meeting in March, 1961, the prime ministers welcomed Cyprus to membership. With the admission of Zanzibar[16] (pop. 300,000) in 1963 and Malta (pop. 330,000) in 1964, any attempt to find "a special place" for such small territories seemed to have been abandoned. At their 1964 meeting the prime ministers heard a

11. *Labour's Colonial Policy, 3, Smaller Territories* (London, 1957), p. 19, declared that territories "so small and scattered" were "unlikely" to be "accepted by the prime ministers as full members of the Commonwealth." Cf. Sir Hilary Blood, *The Smaller Territories* (London: Conservative Commonwealth Council, 1958), p. 19, where "a new 'class'" of dependency—"The Internally Self-Governing State" which "might be grouped . . . in some form of loose organisation which would bring their chief Ministers into touch with the Sovereign and with Ministers in this country" was recommended. The State of Singapore (1959) and the State of Malta (1961) exemplified moves towards such a conception. Both were, however, short-lived, Singapore becoming part of the new Federation of Malaysia in 1963 and Malta an independent member of the Commonwealth in 1964.

12. G. B., 5 *Parl. Debs.*, DCIII (1959), 1369, reproduced in Nicholas Mansergh, *Documents and Speeches on Commonwealth Affairs, 1952-1962* (London, 1963), p. 290.

13. Final communiqué (text in *ibid.*, p. 555.)

14. This had been made clear in an official statement of January 20, 1960. *Ibid.*, p. 276-277.

15. Government of India, Ministry of External Affairs, *Report 1960-61*, p. 41.

16. This was only one item in the catalogue of disasters in the decolonization of Zanzibar. See Humphrey Berkeley, "How Not to Decolonise," *The Spectator* (London), May 1, 1964.

British statement enumerating a number of territories on the way to independence (two of which had populations of 300,000 or less), four others which "enjoyed a wide measure of self-government" (two of which had populations of 100,000 or less), and went on to refer to a further nineteen territories (only two of which had populations exceeding 100,000). Although "no uniform pattern would fit" the territories in the second and third groups, "some might feel strong enough to proceed to independence on their own."[17] Membership, it seemed reasonable to conclude, would be available for some of them.

This development, with all its implications for the increasing diversity of stature and stability, as well as the increasing number, of members, could be seen as a further example of the assimilation of Commonwealth relations to those of international politics: it paralleled a similar process in the United Nations, the outcome of the same forces at work in international society.[18]

The International Context

To describe some features of international relations since 1945 as amounting to the "Commonwealthizing" of international politics would be misleading as well as paradoxical. But to do so might suggest why some of them have had so considerable an impact on thinking about the Commonwealth nexus.[19] Especially in the area of aid, technical assistance, and scientific, educational, and cultural co-operation, the scope of international relations has been greatly widened. The machinery for their conduct, bilaterally as well as multilaterally, on a regional as well as on a worldwide basis, has become more pervasive. If, in some areas, the cold war set strict limits to the process, in others it extended and accelerated it. Commonwealth countries that became parties

17. Cmnd. 2441, p. 4. See n.4, above.
18. Some aspects of this line of thought are pursued in J. E. S. Fawcett, "The Commonwealth in the United Nations," *Journal of Commonwealth Political Studies*, I (1962), 123-35.
19. John Holmes in this volume touches on the same point when he suggests that the UN has "internationalized the Commonwealth mission."

to NATO, ANZUS, or even SEATO seemed, for example, to be engaged in more far-reaching and mutually pervasive forms of common action than any demanded by Commonwealth membership. Even those of them that embraced non-alignment as an alternative reaction to the tensions of the cold war seemed to be developing a forum in which their leaders reached conclusions on matters of general interest and, in promulgating them to the world, achieved an impact that eluded the Commonwealth prime ministers.[20] Yet it was possible to suspend judgment on the long-term significance of some of these developments, the product as they were of particular objectives which might come to be assigned different priorities in a rapidly changing international scene.[21]

Apart from such specific military or economic pressures (as in NATO or OEEC) a new realization of the size of the economic base required if modern technologies were to be fully exploited, and of the limits imposed on the political power of small states, combined in some parts of the world with the fluidity resulting from the disintegration of the western European empires, led to an awareness of new links of affinity or aspiration in such regions as western Europe, the Arab world, Africa, and Latin America. Countries seriously concerned with regionalism[22] face a choice between the development of organizations in which ultimate control of the nature and extent of regional co-operation remains with each member state, and integration on a supranational basis, whether by merger, federation, or more novel devices like those pioneered by the various European communities. The first type of regionalism merely added, in principle, one more to the number and variety of international organizations to which a member might belong but the second,

20. A point made by the Australian prime minister after the 1957 meeting in relation to Bandoeng. See Greenwood and Harper, p. 47.

21. Cf. "The O.E.E.C. did indeed achieve a degree of cooperation that was never attained within the Commonwealth. But in 1959 the O.E.E.C. was brought to an end, when its limited purposes had been achieved." Patrick C. Gordon Walker, *The Commonwealth* (London, 1962), p. 370. Whatever their ultimate significance may be, recent developments have manifested a striking change in the cohesiveness of NATO from those assumed a few years ago.

22. How seriously they were concerned to promote regional integration is considered *infra* by Dennis Austin in "Regionalism and the Commonwealth."

to the extent that supranational integration was actually achieved, seemed inconsistent with the very notion of the Commonwealth, based as it has been on the unfettered sovereignty of each member. Such objectives (and the uncertainties they evoked) brought into sharper focus the extent to which the older Commonwealth conception had rested on the assumption of a stable international order of states satisfied, indeed determined, to maintain their separate identities, between some of whom, linked, mainly but not exclusively through Britain, by ties of affinity and ties of advantage, it had seemed a notable, some claimed a unique, achievement even to maintain "a style of conversation."[23]

No discussion of Commonwealth affairs in the later years of the decade fails, sooner or later, to mention the dramatic decline of the relative power of Britain in the world. For at least a decade after World War II its full consequences were obscured by the survival and enlarged membership of the Commonwealth, by the apparently greater decline in the power and influence of the major states of western Europe, by the continued existence of a sizable colonial empire in which British power and responsibilities in a period preoccupied with decolonization paradoxically engaged greater international and domestic attention, and by British self-confidence (or complacency), which showed little inclination to ponder unduly the realities of power.[24] The Suez debacle by no means ended this phase but its effect was traumatic. The greater part of the decade we are considering has therefore been marked by a belated awakening to this central reality and by growing uncertainty about its implications for Britain's future international position, sharpened by the emergence of the European Economic Community as a major economic force in the world and the failure of successive British attempts to secure an accommodation between her interests (and

23. The phrase of a speaker at the Seventh Unofficial Commonwealth Conference at Lagos in 1962, this was intended to contrast the "static" objects with which Commonwealth consultation had usually to be content, with the dynamic purposes of regionalism, especially that of the Six. (Charles E. Carrington, *The Commonwealth in Africa* [London, 1962], p. 39).

24. Cf. Nicholas Mansergh, *Survey of British Commonwealth Affairs: Problems of War-time Cooperation and Post-War Change, 1939-1952* (London, 1958), p. 419.

those of her Commonwealth partners) and those of the Six, even when she had at last braced herself to what seemed to some the desperate remedy of joining them.

The increasing scope and density of international relations, the pressure of regional aspirations, the decline in British military and economic power have, for the Commonwealth, been three significant aspects of the world in which it has lived in the last decade. Increasingly it has been confronted with the problem of finding a role in a world in which all members claim at least as close (often a closer) association with states outside as with other members. For a varying body of opinion in all member countries, it has been easy to conclude that there is no continuing role which it can fulfil. The outcome of the Prime Ministers' Meeting in 1964 suggested that the newer members in initiating, and the older members in accepting, the proposal for a Commonwealth secretariat remained of the opinion that the association had, at any rate for some time to come, a role to play. The hard negotiation embodied in the communiqué suggested that the "style of conversation" would in future have rather different aims while the other Commonwealth activities recommended suggested a new willingness to attempt a more distinctly Commonwealth character in the furtherance of developmental objectives. "They want a limited Commonwealth and that is what they have," Professor Miller wrote in 1958.[25] If the 1964 communiqué implied a more realistic admission of the limits of the association, it also implied more positive action within those limits and a fuller acceptance of responsibility by the members for a more evidently multinational association. Whether these new initiatives would survive the tensions which threatened in Africa and Asia only the future would show.

The Machinery of Day-to-Day Relations

"Day to day questions are dealt with either by direct correspondence between governments or through the representatives

25. J. D. B. Miller, The Commonwealth in the World (London, 1958), p. 304.

(High Commissioners) whom Commonwealth governments maintain in other Commonwealth capitals." In its suggestion that the machinery of day-to-day communication between Commonwealth governments still differs from that between foreign governments, this sentence, which has appeared in all editions of *The Commonwealth Relations Office List* since 1957,[26] reflects, if only vestigially, the conception that underlay the *inter se* doctrine and also British preoccupation with that conception. Whether any similar statement would be made officially by another Commonwealth government may well be doubted.

In the early fifties, Professor Mansergh has recorded, direct government-to-government communication "continued to be extensively used," but the United Kingdom, Canada, and India increasingly adopted the practice of cabling, not direct to the government with which it wished to communicate, but to their high commissioner in the member state concerned. Some Commonwealth governments used their high commissioners as intermediaries less than others but it was "important not to overlook this channel of communication."[27] By 1963 an official British account of *Consultation and Cooperation in the Commonwealth* said roundly, "Nowadays most written communications are routed to the recipient government through High Commissioners."[28] In fact, the high commissioner channel is now virtually universal although one or two Commonwealth governments still communicate direct on certain specific (and technical) matters. Professor Mansergh thought that the use of high commissioners "helped to make consultation less formal than when reliance was placed on intergovernmental communication alone." But it undoubtedly represented an assimilation of the method of communication to that generally in use between foreign governments.

All this reinforces the importance of the way in which high commissioners are regarded and do their work. Formally, while

26. E.g., *1964*, p. 126.
27. Mansergh, *Survey* . . . , *1939-52*, p. 409.
28. Great Britain, Central Office of Information Reference Pamphlet 25 (London, 1963), p. 3.

ambassadors are accredited by the head of state to a head of state, high commissioners were originally appointed by one government in the territory of another. After India became a republic, however, her high commissioners presented letters of commission from the President to the Queen. A similar procedure was adopted when Malaya (a separate monarchy) became a member in 1957. It has since been adopted by other members which have become republics. British high commissioners and those of other countries which are "realms" of the Queen likewise present letters of commission from Her Majesty to the heads of state of the republics and of Malaysia. Although the form of letters of commission is somewhat different from that of letters of credence, the tendency to assimilate the formal position of high commissioners to that of ambassadors is clear. The same tendency is also to be seen in the decision, after discussion at the Prime Ministers' Meeting in 1948, that they should be accorded a status and precedence similar to that of ambassadors, and in legislation in a number of Commonwealth countries conferring on Commonwealth representatives the diplomatic immunities and privileges accorded under international law to a foreign envoy and giving power to modify or withdraw them where the sending country does not give corresponding treatment.[29]

Turning to the practical, as opposed to the formal, position of high commissioners, the Commonwealth Relations Office informed the Select Committee on Estimates of the British House of Commons in 1959 that

the principal difference . . . between a High Commissioner and a foreign Ambassador in a Commonwealth capital is that whereas the Ambassador must do all his business through the Department of External Affairs, the High Commissioner is entitled to deal direct with other departments of Government. The result is that the High Commissioner and his staff at appropriate levels have contacts of an informal sort throughout the machinery of Government.[30]

29. See on this Fawcett, *The British Commonwealth in International Law*, pp. 199-201.

30. Great Britain, House of Commons, "Third Report from the Select Committee on Estimates" (H. of C. 252, *Parl. Paps.*, 1958-59, V, p. 56. Reproduced

The extent to which this is so no doubt varies in different parts of the Commonwealth and as regards different member countries' representatives. In its memorandum to the Estimates Committee, the Commonwealth Relations Office asserted that "the U.K. High Commissioner has closer and more frequent contact with the Prime Minister of the Commonwealth country in which he is serving than is the case with foreign heads of mission." Practice on this point, it admitted, naturally varied, and instanced Australia as a member state in which "on all important matters and whenever a formal approach is called for, the High Commissioner deals direct with the Prime Minister." While it would be wrong to suppose that such a special position was never accorded to British high commissioners in newly independent member states, there were difficulties in such a situation in some countries, not only because of natural concern lest it might represent a continuation of a colonial relationship in a disguised form but also because of the conflicting pull of anxiety to demonstrate non-alignment and of aspirations for closer regional association with other countries. These were illustrated, for example, in Nigeria in 1961 and 1962 in considerable public criticism of the special position which the Nigerian government was alleged to accord to the British high commissioner.

How far in practice such less formal access to officials of other departments than that of External Affairs is extended to, or made use of by, the high commissions of other Commonwealth countries in member countries besides Britain is hardly documented. An Australian parliamentary committee is reported to have found in the later fifties that in ten departments of the Australian government "officials had regular contact with people from other parts of the Commonwealth in doing their work" while the official witnesses to that committee "agreed that,

in Mansergh, *Documents and Speeches, 1952-1962*, p. 751). On the basis of experience as British High Commissioner in Canada, 1961-63, Lord Amory, a former chancellor of the exchequer, made a similar point in a debate in the House of Lords in 1964: "the kind of work done by a High Commissioner and his staff is different in a subtle way from that normally performed in an Embassy overseas. It is less formal, it is more widely pervasive, and often goes deeper down. Few people realise how much day to day consultation on a wide variety of affairs goes on . . ." (G. B., 5 *Parl. Debs.* [Lords], CCLVII [1964], 55).

with the exception of the United States, Australia's relations with the newer Commonwealth countries were in many respects more intimate than with non-Commonwealth countries."[31] The exception for the United States suggests that more intimate and informal access even at the official level may rest more on the realities of foreign relations than on any special status assigned to high commissioners.

While high commissioners have become the normal channel for communications between Commonwealth governments, some limits must be set to this process by the fact that Britain is the only member represented by high commissioners in all other member states. It is therefore important to consider the development of intra-Commonwealth representation in this period. At the beginning of the decade, Britain, Canada, and Australia were represented in all member states, India and Pakistan in all except South Africa, although—a significant development—their high commissioners in New Zealand resided in Australia, Ceylon was represented in four member states (not in Canada, South Africa, or New Zealand), while South Africa and New Zealand were each represented in only three. (The limited South African representation in Commonwealth countries did not, like that of its New Zealand counterpart, reflect modest external representation in general but unwillingness to exchange representatives with certain Commonwealth countries.) By 1963, when the number of members had risen to 17,[32] Britain alone was represented in all of them, Canada in 13 (11 resident), India in 12 (11 resident), Australia 10, Pakistan 10 (7 resident), Ghana 9, Ceylon 8 (7 resident), Nigeria 7 (6 resident), New Zealand 6 (5 resident), Malaysia 6 (4 resident). None of the other members was represented in more than 3 while 3 of them (Tanganyika, Cyprus, and Uganda) were represented only in Britain. Even when allowance is made for the future growth of representation on the part of the newest members, it is evident that if Commonwealth consultation and co-operation depend on the

31. Carrington, pp. 42-43.
32. Excluding Zanzibar, which became independent in December, 1963, and joined Tanganyika to form the United Republic of Tanzania in 1964.

mechanism of mutual representation, it must, for some members, be mediated through a very small number of others, notably Britain.

The diplomatic representation of the Commonwealth in foreign countries showed a similar trend and a similar pattern. Leaving the 17 members of the Commonwealth out of account, in 1963 Britain was represented in 103 of the remaining 112 independent countries in the world and maintained resident representation in 91 of them, India in 68 (47 resident), Canada in 63 (36 resident), Pakistan 51 (27 resident), Ghana 38 (34 resident). At the other end of the scale were Commonwealth countries like Sierra Leone 5, Tanganyika 1, Jamaica 1, Trinidad 2.[33] In that context the potential significance, at least for the smaller countries, of the permanent representation of all states at the United Nations was evident.

Any account of the governmental machinery of Commonwealth relations in the earlier years of the decade would have mentioned the regular meetings of the Commonwealth high commissioners in London with the Commonwealth relations secretary in London which were also attended by a Foreign Office minister. These had been held since the later thirties, their frequency depending on the needs of the moment.[34] Similar meetings of the Commonwealth ambassadors in Washington were held "every fortnight except in the summer" at the British Embassy in Washington, and, Lord Franks wrote in 1955, "discussed everything. . . . Even difficulties between individual members, like Kashmir, . . . with conviction but without heat."[35] Both kinds of meetings had been preceded by meetings of dominion

33. All Commonwealth figures calculated from information in the *Commonwealth Relations Office List 1955* and *1964* respectively except those for Britain, which are from "Report of the Committee on Representational Services Overseas, appointed by the Prime Minister under the Chairmanship of Lord Plowden 1962-63," Cmnd. 2276, Dec. 2, 1963, G. B., *Parl. Paps.*, 1963-64. (Hereafter cited as the Plowden Report.)

34. For the origins of these meetings, see Nicholas Mansergh, *Survey of British Commonwealth Affairs: Problems of External Policy, 1931-39* (London, 1952), p. 433, and for later developments, Mansergh, *Survey, 1939-52*, p. 402.

35. Sir Oliver Franks, *Britain and the Tide of World Affairs* (London, 1955), p. 17.

delegations at Geneva with the United Kingdom delegation during the sessions of the Assembly of the League.

By 1964, the meetings in London and Washington were no longer held.[36] Commonwealth delegations to the United Nations continued to hold regular meetings (roughly monthly) in New York. After 1963 the chairmanship rotated each month, alphabetically, though a member of the British delegation still acted as secretary. In UN terms, of course, the Commonwealth is not a group[37] and there is no question of a Commonwealth line. Even in 1960, a not unfriendly British critic had pointed out that the Commonwealth meetings in New York were "concerned more with the tactics of presentation than the substance of individual policies." Such a distinction should not, he said, be pressed too far but suggested "how limited a purpose the meetings served"; the Asian and African members probably attached, he thought, "no very great intrinsic importance to them" but viewed them "benevolently as a public affirmation of a relationship which they still" wished "to preserve."[38] Intra-Commonwealth disputes were "almost never" raised and there was "generally little if any" discussion of other issues on which members were known to be deeply divided. Colonial issues, on the other hand, have been discussed, and early in 1964 Southern Rhodesia was the subject of a meeting. Although the increased claims of regional groups as well as the large number of new members might be expected to have imposed further limits on the breadth and effectiveness of the meetings, a report early in 1964 claimed "almost universal appreciation" of their value among Commonwealth ambassadors.[39]

In the interwar Commonwealth, British subjects of one Commonwealth country resident in another were not considered

36. Meetings were held in London during the negotiations for British entry into EEC. Although no longer held, they might be revived if an issue of similarly general importance arose.
37. Cf. the Assembly decision in December, 1963, to omit reference to the Commonwealth as an area in relation to the composition of its steering committee or in its proposals for an enlarged Security Council.
38. G. L. Goodwin, "The Expanding United Nations, I," *International Affairs*, XXXVI (1963), 178-79.
39. "The Commonwealth at the U.N.," *Spectator* (London), May 15, 1964.

to require consular services since they could rely on the normal facilities of the Commonwealth country where they lived. As a result of the development of separate citizenships in each Commonwealth country and even more of the increasing diversity of membership, such a conception "is no longer realistic."[40] In India, Pakistan, Nigeria, and Malaysia there are British deputy high commissioners in several cities besides the capital and where such additional facilities do not exist U.K. citizens resident elsewhere than in the capital have had recourse to information and trade commissioner offices, though they do not enjoy consular recognition or facilities. Similarly, both Ceylon (in 1959) and Malaya (in 1960) opened assistant high commissioner offices in Madras to deal with passport and other matters relating to Indian migrants, who mostly come from that part of India and return to it for periods of varying lengths.[41] In 1964, the Plowden Report recommended that British commercial, representational, and day-to-day consular services in such outstations should be unified and "where local susceptibilities permit" consular styles and procedures adopted, though elsewhere it might be preferable to keep the title deputy high commissioner for the head of the post.[42]

A further, though not yet final, step towards assimilating the forms of Commonwealth relations to those of international politics was the decision of the British government, announced in February, 1964, to establish, as recommended by the Plowden Committee, a single diplomatic service which would provide the staff for both the Foreign and Commonwealth Relations Offices as well as their respective overseas posts. The Committee went further. It stated:

40. Plowden Report, p. 73. Cf. the remarks of the permanent under-secretary of the C.R.O. to the Estimates Committee ("Third Report from Select Committee on Estimates," p. 14): "Take Calcutta, which has with the adjoining provinces 13,000 United Kingdom citizens. That is in quite a different position from Alberta in Canada, or in an Australian state, where United Kingdom citizens will be indistinguishable from an ordinary Canadian or Australian and there would not be the same need to look after particular minor business interests . . ." Similar issues arise in regard to Pakistani and Jamaican residents in Britain.

41. Indian Ministry of External Affairs, *Report 1959-60*, p. 65 and *Report 1960-61*, p. 59.

42. Plowden Report, p. 74.

The logic of events points towards the amalgamation of the Commonwealth Relations Office and the Foreign Office. . . . This must, in our view, be the ultimate aim. However, to take such a fundamental step now could be misinterpreted as implying a loss of interest in the Commonwealth partnership. We therefore hesitate to recommend the establishment of a single Ministry of External Affairs as an opportune step to take at the present time, although this is the practice in all other Commonwealth countries.[43]

This could be represented as a purely domestic issue about the machinery of British government. The Lord Chancellor, in defending the decision to establish a single diplomatic service but not a single ministry of external affairs, told the House of Lords that "No other Commonwealth capital" had "anything like the turnover of Commonwealth business there is in London."[44] One might nevertheless ask whether, if the Dominions Office had not existed, the Commonwealth Relations Office would have been invented. The decision to retain it could be defended on the purely practical ground that the burden of a single ministry of external affairs would in any event be too great for one minister, just as the case for a single ministry could be based on the equally practical ground that a coherent British foreign policy could not be arrived at "unless we are able to take fully into account the non-Commonwealth interests of Commonwealth countries and deal with them in their regional or world context," which the dual system "did not make easy."[45] But the Lord Chancellor defended the British government's decision explicitly on a familiar version of the *inter se* doctrine. The Commonwealth, he said, was a family in which Britain occupied a central position. Her links with individual members varied in strength. With some they were very strong, with others "we hope that the years will strengthen them." The family did not always agree but problems were discussed in a family atmosphere; it had a tradition of a constant informal exchange of views on all topics and not just of meeting to negotiate a point of disagreement. While that re-

43. Plowden Report, pp. 12-13.
44. G. B., 5 *Parl. Debs* (Lords), CCLVII (1964), 117.
45. Plowden Report, p. 12.

lationship existed, it would be "quite wrong to treat those countries as if they were not in a special position, to treat them in the same way as foreign countries" which was what those who supported a single ministry of external affairs were asking.[46]

Throughout the decade the system of day-to-day communication was thus becoming more "diplomatic" in form; in content, it was being stretched to include not only many more countries (seven in 1954, twenty-one in 1964) but much more diverse ones. How did it work?

In 1956 it could be claimed that all members shared

a general understanding, affirmed at past Imperial Conferences, and given formal expression in the External Affairs Agreement with Ceylon,[47] that Membership of the Commonwealth carries with it an obligation to inform or consult, as may be appropriate, all the other Members on any projected action which might affect their interests, especially in relation to foreign affairs, and thus to give them the opportunity of expressing their own individual views.[48]

In pursuit of this general understanding, the Commonwealth Relations Office accepts that it is one of the duties of British high commissioners "to keep the Commonwealth Government informed of all current developments especially in the sphere of international affairs, particularly those in foreign countries where that Government maintains no diplomatic representation."[49] In 1961 Britain was, for example, "in frequent communication" with other Commonwealth governments on such subjects as "the negotiations over Laos, the control of nuclear tests, and the problems of the Congo and Berlin."[50]

46. G. B., 5 *Parl. Debs.* (Lords), CCLVII (1964), 116-17. Defending the establishment of an African affairs secretariat in Ghana, the foreign minister (Mr. Kofi Baako) said, "Why is it that in Britain they have got the Commonwealth Relations Office. It is because they think of the Commonwealth nations as a family. They regard Commonwealth countries as distinct from other foreign countries. . . . we think of the unity of Africa as the unity of a family. . . . African affairs are nearer to domestic policy than to foreign policy." Ghana, *Parl. Debs.* XXIII (1961), 984.

47. Nicholas Mansergh, *Documents and Speeches on British Commonwealth Affairs, 1931-1952* (2 vols.; London, 1953), II, 750-51.

48. *The Commonwealth Relations Office List, 1956*, p. 11.

49. "Third Report from Select Committee on Estimates," p. 57, reproduced in Mansergh, *Documents and Speeches, 1952-62*, pp. 751-52.

50. Duncan Sandys, *The Modern Commonwealth* (London, 1962), p. 9.

How far is there a reciprocal flow of information to Britain from other Commonwealth countries and how much exchange takes place between other Commonwealth capitals? Assessing the position in the early fifties, Professor Mansergh recorded that other Commonwealth governments had been slow to provide London with information on a considerable scale but that in 1951 there had been "a greater volume of communication from Canberra to Delhi than from Canberra to any other Commonwealth capital except London and not excepting Wellington."[51] Little information is available on either point. Mr. Sandys claimed in 1962 that "other Commonwealth governments keep us constantly posted about these and other matters which are of special concern to them."[52] In his well-informed study of the machinery of Canadian foreign policy, Professor Eayrs wrote in 1961 that "as a senior Member of the Commonwealth of Nations," Canada occupied "a central position in the far flung communications network linking thirteen countries in one of the most remarkable, if unpublicised, intelligence systems in the world."[53] Speculation is idle but it is relevant to recall in this context the great disproportion between the foreign representation of the older members and that of most of the newer ones and also the difficulties which confront many of the latter in building up administrative machines capable of dealing with their major responsibilities in both domestic and foreign affairs.

How full and frank can such an interchange be when, to put it mildly, some members belong to military alliances with the United States and other foreign countries while others are non-aligned? Professor Eayrs observes that "not much of interest flows indiscriminately throughout the entire Commonwealth communications network, each member instead deciding for itself which, if any, of the others are to be favored recipients of political secrets."[54] As the Permanent Under-Secretary for Commonwealth Relations put it to the Estimates Committee in 1959, the British

51. Mansergh, *Survey, 1939-52*, p. 409.
52. Sandys, *loc. cit.*
53. James Eayrs, *The Art of the Possible* (Toronto, 1961), p. 150.
54. Eayrs, p. 145.

were "broadly speaking . . . most anxious to pass out all the information we can. If we have information which we have only been given on certain understandings, we are naturally bound by those understandings" but it was "an implicit understanding that is well known, that we are anxious to keep our Commonwealth colleagues as fully informed as possible."[55] Nor is it only foreign governments that sometimes specify that information is not intended to be passed on to other Commonwealth governments. Mr. Heath, for example, told the British House of Commons in 1961 that "information given to Her Majesty's Government by an individual Commonwealth Government is sometimes confidential between the two Governments and cannot be made known to others."[56]

Nothing like the agreement on external affairs with Ceylon has been concluded with any member admitted subsequently. In the aftermath of Suez (when Ghana and Malaya joined) such a document could only have seemed cynical or have called for an elaboration in drafting which was no doubt best avoided. For the Suez invasion involved a deliberate decision by Britain not to consult any other member. This breach of the "general understanding" was defended at the time on the ground that "our friends inside the Commonwealth, and outside, could not, in the very nature of things, be consulted in time. You just cannot have immediate action and extensive consultation as well."[57] But, in his memoirs, Lord Avon has made it clear that this was not the only consideration:

Whatever the outcome of such consultation, it would have smoothed our path. On the other hand, however sharply pressed, such consultation was not possible within a matter of hours. It must take days at least. Nor was there any chance that all concerned would take precisely the same view of what action must follow consultation. As a result there would be attempts to modify our proposals to reach some compromise between divergent points of view and before we knew where we were, we would be back at an

55. "Third Report from Select Committee on Estimates," p. 16.
56. G. B., 5 *Parl. Debs.*, DCL (1961), 40.
57. Sir Anthony Eden, Nov. 3, 1956, reproduced in James Eayrs, *The Commonwealth and Suez* (London, 1964), p. 213.

eighteen power conference once more. This was the last thing in the world we wanted, because we knew quite well that once palavers began, no effective action would be possible.[58]

This was not, of course, the only occasion on which the British government had not consulted Commonwealth governments on a major development in British policy, the most notable earlier example being the not insignificant one of the decision in 1939 to offer unilateral guarantees to Poland, Greece, and Romania. The suggestion that the obligation to consult was absolute was another example of the overselling of the Commonwealth by some of its apologists, but Professor Miller's conclusion that "the whole notion of informing or consulting fellow-members rested, and rests still, on a prior assumption that the interests of the member in question must not be subordinated to any supposed obligation to consult" is less to the point than his rider that members might "consider that their own long term national interest in the preservation of the Commonwealth" outweighed "some short term national interest."[59] The significance of developments in this decade was the extent to which they suggested changes among the members in the priority among national interests they assigned to the factor of consultation in the preservation of the Commonwealth.

When in 1958 Ghana and Guinea agreed to constitute their two states as the "nucleus of a Union of West African States" other members were informed only on November 22 that negotiations were in progress and a joint statement would probably be issued next day. The Ghanaian foreign minister (then Mr. Botsio) was later reported as stating that the plan had been announced without prior consultation because of the need to demonstrate West African solidarity in the light of Guinea's "very serious internal difficulties" since independence.[60] The Ghanaian insistence that the action they were taking, though "inspired by the example of the thirteen American colonies" in constituting

58. *Full Circle: The Memoirs of Sir Anthony Eden* (London, 1960), p. 526.
59. Miller, p. 69.
60. Great Britain, Central Office of Information, *Commonwealth Survey*, IV (1958), 1098-99. *Daily Telegraph* (London), Nov. 26, 1958.

themselves "into a confederacy which ultimately developed into the United States," was in no way designed to prejudice Ghana's "present or future relations" with the Commonwealth suggests that they may have entertained some doubts about the reaction of other members; even if they were persuaded, as the British government claimed to have been during its negotiations with EEC, that the two associations could, at any rate during a transitional period and perhaps even ultimately, be reconciled, they were not prepared to risk jeopardizing what was regarded as a major national interest by observing the "general understanding."

That the Commonwealth relationship called for an exchange of information and consultation between members to a greater extent than would be called for in the normal course of friendly diplomatic relations or in pursuit of particular objects of policy was, no doubt, widely admitted. But with the steady increase in the size and diversity of membership (ten members in 1959, twenty-one in 1964) the problems involved in both seemed certain to increase. If more small territories were admitted, greater "specialisation" in the exchange of information seemed likely to result, together with a mounting pressure against the maintenance of consultation on anything like a full scale.[61] The scope of both exchange and consultation varied not only from one member to another but also, for any one member, vis-à-vis different members and within limits determined by the relative priorities assigned to other objects of international politics and the relationships with non-Commonwealth states that ensued from them. In a period of rapid change in membership it was not surprising that the priority assigned to the Commonwealth relationship should be questioned in many member countries. The outcome appeared to be a continuing tendency towards the assimilation of Commonwealth

61. G. B., 5 *Parl. Debs.* (Commons), DCXC (1964), 659. It would be naïve to suppose that the much criticized delay in recognizing the revolutionary regime in Zanzibar, which involved an unprecedented expulsion from a Commonwealth country of the British high commissioner there, was greatly increased by British insistence on consultation, but as Sir Alec Douglas-Home told the House of Commons "it takes a little time" and even so Cyprus and Sierra Leone had not recognized it when at length Britain and most other members did so. (The three East African members recognized the regime almost immediately.)

relations to those of international politics even though it would be an exaggeration to claim that the assimilation was complete.

Ministerial Meetings

At the apex of the intergovernmental arrangements are the Prime Ministers' Meetings, first held in 1944 and still so called in 1964 although in four of the nineteen countries represented no such office existed. The 1964 communiqué indeed implied that they might in future be denominated "Meetings of the Commonwealth Heads of Governments."[62] "By tradition convened by the British Prime Minister,"[63] these meetings have, in spite of many suggestions that they might sometimes take place in other Commonwealth capitals, so far always been held in London, presumably because this has been found generally convenient.[64] In 1958 the British government offered to provide a center for Commonwealth meetings in London and in 1962 the prime ministers met for the first time in Marlborough House, which the Queen had placed at their disposal for that purpose.[65] In the last decade meetings were held in 1955, 1956, 1957, 1960, 1961, 1962, and 1964. That held in 1964 extended over eight days, that in 1955 over nine, that in 1960 over eleven, and all the others over ten.[66]

"It has long been recognized that the only persons who at-

62. Commonwealth Prime Ministers' Meeting, August, 1964, Final Communiqué, p. 9.

63. G. B., 5 Parl Debs. (Commons), DCXCIV, 583-586, 1964 (Sir A. Douglas-Home).

64. Prime Minister Menzies (The Changing Commonwealth [Cambridge, 1960], p. 16) says it is not "just because" of this, but one may doubt whether many would agree that it is "more significantly" because "London is where the Queen is."

65. Marlborough House also provides offices for the Commonwealth Liaison Committee and the Commonwealth Educational Liaison Unit. See The Commonwealth Relations Office List, 1963, pp. 121-22.

66. In the previous decade there were six (1944, 1946, 1948, 1949, 1951, and 1953), but all the prime ministers except those of India and South Africa also attended the Commonwealth Economic Conference in 1952, at which several other Commonwealth countries not yet independent were also represented. This is apparently not regarded as a Prime Ministers' Meeting, but if one takes it into account, prime ministers in fact met on seven occasions in each decade.

tend these meetings as of right are the Prime Ministers of the fully independent countries of the Commonwealth."[67] The prime minister of Southern Rhodesia (Sir Godfrey Huggins, later Lord Malvern), who had attended the Imperial Conference of 1937 as an "observer,"[68] some sessions of the 1944 meeting, and those in 1948, 1951, and 1953, was, after consultation with other Commonwealth prime ministers,[69] invited to attend that of 1955 when he had become prime minister of the Federation of Rhodesia and Nyasaland, which, like Southern Rhodesia, was not an independent state. Taking this "into account" the prime ministers at their 1956 meeting agreed to "the continued participation of the Prime Minister of the Federation,"[70] and Lord Malvern's successor, Sir Roy Welensky, was thus enabled to attend the meeting in 1957 and subsequent ones until the dissolution of the Federation in 1963.

The claim advanced by Mr. Smith, then prime minister, that Southern Rhodesia had a right to be invited to the 1964 meeting because "it had assumed the rights and privileges of Commonwealth membership which it had before these were surrendered to the Federation"[71] was accordingly not well founded. The British view was that if Mr. Smith informed them of his wish to be invited, they would consult the other prime ministers since "before issuing invitations to the Prime Minister of any other country which is not independent" they had "always thought it right to satisfy themselves that this would be generally acceptable."[72] Even before the British prime minister's statement both India and Ghana had, however, made it clear publicly that they would not favor such an invitation.[73]

67. Statement cited in footnote 63. As some have no prime minister this should presumably be interpreted as "only the fully independent countries of the Commonwealth have a right to be represented."
68. As did the chief minister of Burma. See "Imperial Conference 1937, Summary of Proceedings," Cmnd. 55482, G. B., *Parl. Paps. 1936-37*, XII.
69. *The Times*, December 14, 1954.
70. Prime Ministers' Meeting 1956, Final Communiqué (Mansergh, *Documents . . . , 1952-62*, p. 132).
71. Statement issued in Salisbury, April 20, 1964.
72. G. B., 5 *Parl. Debs.* (Commons), DCXCIV, 583.
73. Mr. Nehru in Lok Sabha, April 27, and Ghana Government statement, April 25.

The attendance of Lord Malvern and Sir Roy Welensky at Prime Ministers' Meetings as prime ministers of a country not yet independent must be recognized as an anomaly. In 1962 the precedent set by the Commonwealth Economic Conference in 1952, when the British colonial secretary had as advisers representatives of twelve colonial territories,[74] was followed and he was accompanied by advisers from eight of them including senior ministers from seven, who were present at "certain sessions."[75] A rather different device was adopted in 1960 when the prime ministers had an "informal meeting" with the prime minister of Nigeria, which was about to become independent.

Although it has often been asserted that the meetings have "no set agenda"[76] this seems to turn on a rather fine verbal distinction which has now lost whatever force it may once have had. The 1961 communiqué recorded that it "had been agreed" that "on this occasion" discussion should be concentrated on "a limited number of specific problems . . . , namely disarmament, the structure of the United Nations, and certain constitutional problems affecting the Commonwealth itself"[77]—an item which included the continued membership of South Africa after it became a republic. There was, however, to be "at the outset a general review of the international situation as a whole, in order to set those particular problems in the perspective of current world events." In 1964 an attempt by the United Kingdom to place the Southern Rhodesian issue late in the agenda (in the hope that discussion of other topics would by then have generated a feeling of mutual confidence) met with strong objection from African members and some observers claimed that their antipathy to British "manipulation" of such procedural issues was a factor in the initiation of the proposal for a secretariat.

74. Great Britain, *Commonwealth Survey*, Dec. 5, 1952. J. D. B. Miller, "Commonwealth Conferences 1945-1955" in *The Year Book of World Affairs 1956* (London, 1956), p. 162, refers only to some of the territories so represented, and makes the representation appear more arbitrary than it was.

75. *The Commonwealth Relations Office List 1963*, p. 116.

76. E.g., Menzies, *Changing Commonwealth*, p. 18. Sir Alec Douglas-Home said "it is not our practice to reveal details of the agenda. . . ." G. B., 5 *Parl. Debs.* (Commons), DCXCIV, 589.

77. Final Communiqué, 1961 (Mansergh, *Documents . . . , 1952-62*, p. 555).

In 1960 "the traditional practice that Commonwealth conferences do not discuss the internal affairs of member countries"[78] was reaffirmed after a meeting in the course of which much time had in fact been taken up with "informal meetings" between the South African foreign minister and some of the prime ministers and then by a private meeting (without advisers) of all except the prime minister of Malaya, who was incensed by the intransigence of Dr. Louw in a public speech made while these exchanges were in progress. The principle was again confirmed in the 1961 communiqué, which expressly stated that the racial policy of South Africa had been discussed with its prime minister's consent.[79] Similarly, it seems to be established that disputes between one Commonwealth country and another will not be discussed except with the consent of the parties to the dispute. Experience in 1951 of taking part, even in a separate and informal session, in talks with India and Pakistan on Kashmir, at the insistence of the Pakistani prime minister, only confirmed the prime ministers in their reluctance to attempt to reconcile differences between any two of them, and subsequent discussion of such issues appears to have been at separate sessions "outside" the meeting and confined to the parties concerned.[80] The doctrine seems likely to have been reinforced by the storm of criticism in India aroused by the implied reference to Kashmir in the 1964 communiqué which, after noting "friendly public statements" by the president of Pakistan and the prime minister of India, expressed the hope that "the problems between the two countries will be solved in the same friendly spirit." Separate meetings of various degrees of formality outside the official sessions have also been used to discuss matters in which only some members were concerned or

78. Final Communiqué, 1960 (*ibid.*, p. 362).
79. Final Communiqué, 1961 (*ibid.*, p. 365). Cf. Lord Normanbrook, "Meetings of the Commonwealth Prime Ministers," *Journal of the Parliaments of the Commonwealth*, XLV (July, 1964), 251: "What was really at issue then was the effect of that policy on South Africa's relations with other members of the Commonwealth and whether that effect was such as to preclude South Africa's continuing membership."
80. E.g., in 1956 India and Pakistan had "a cordial and friendly exchange of views" on Kashmir, the Canal waters, and the property of evacuees; and in 1957 South Africa and Britain discussed the High Commission Territories.

not all were willing to discuss.[81] In its inclusion of countries not yet independent whose economic importance or problems made their representation necessary, the 1962 meeting resembled the special Economic Conferences of 1952 and 1958 rather than a typical Prime Ministers' Meeting, and it might be unwise to infer too much from the fact that at this meeting the special interests of particular groups of members were more formally recognized within the meeting itself, in arrangements for four "Group studies" concerned respectively with temperate foodstuffs, Asian problems, Associated States and tropical products, and sugar. Nonetheless, considering the increasing number of members and their increasing diversity of stature as well as interests, future meetings might have fewer full sessions and more meetings of various groups with interests in common.[82]

What do the prime ministers talk about? Their communiqués, which provide the only official indication, have been variously described as "traditionally laconic,"[83] "peculiarly tedious,"[84] and "anaemic." They may be supplemented by the speeches some prime ministers make when they return home and, more uncertainly, by what journalists are able to piece together at the time.[85] The 1962 and 1964 communiqués, however they may be assessed, could not be characterized as "laconic." They suggest, indeed, that the earlier ideal of bland, if platitudinous, agreement has been discarded in the face of determined insistence on the recording of the peculiar preoccupations of various mem-

81. In 1955, for example, India and Britain considered the Formosa crisis, and, with Canada, Indochina; in 1956 Britain and Australia, the revision of the Ottawa agreements. In 1957 there was a series of meetings on regional defense, each attended by those whose forces might be operating in the region (none, accordingly by India or Ceylon) in respect of which a separate communiqué was issued. Britain and Pakistan also discussed Kashmir and the Canal waters at an informal meeting "outside" the official sessions.

82. Normanbrook, "Meetings of the Commonwealth Prime Ministers," p. 253 (published after the Bellagio meeting for which this paper was prepared), expresses the same opinion and explains that such a development was inhibited when the membership was much smaller "because we did not wish to appear to be excluding one or two members from a particular meeting." (Lord Normanbrook was secretary of the British Cabinet, 1947-62.)

83. Eayrs, Commonwealth and Suez, p. 3.

84. De Smith, New Commonwealth and Its Constitutions, p. 31.

85. In 1962 they were supplemented by regular press handouts of major speeches, but it may be a mistake to regard this as indicating a new trend.

bers, or groups of members, with an eye on opinion elsewhere. In this decade, however, something like a pattern of discussion emerges: international affairs, economic issues, and intra-Commonwealth constitutional problems. Of the international topics, disarmament has featured in every communiqué since 1953, and in 1961 something like a consensus could be registered in the relatively detailed declaration on that subject annexed to the communiqué. The reduction of international tensions and the major issues of the East-West conflict (e.g., Formosa, Indochina, and more recently Laos); the United Nations' role and structure; the international problems of areas of special Commonwealth concern (western Europe, the Middle East, Southeast Asia, and more recently Africa, especially the Congo)—most of these get a mention in every communiqué. In the economic sphere there has been a gradual shift of emphasis from "stability and sterling" to economic development, its capital and manpower needs, trade and especially commodity problems, and the place of Commonwealth countries in a wider international system. (Nothing was said of economic problems in 1961, no doubt because of the bilateral talks with the United Kingdom ministers which had just taken place on the subject of British negotiations with EEC.)

In the third group of "constitutional questions relating to the membership of the Commonwealth" the issues formally before the prime ministers were the continued membership of those which had become republics or the admission of new members as a result of continuing British decolonization. Although not mentioned in the communiqués, it seems that in 1957 and 1960 at any rate they heard from the British colonial secretary a review of constitutional developments in the colonial territories[86] and, as has been mentioned above, agreed in 1960 that officials should make a detailed study of the future of the smaller territories in relation to the Commonwealth. The admission, the next year, of Cyprus and, in 1963, of Zanzibar suggested that the officials had found no alternative to full membership compatible with the demand for independence. In 1964 a British statement

86. In so doing, he was continuing, or resuming, the practice of a general survey of colonial problems at the Imperial Conferences.

on the progress of the remaining territories towards that goal showed that at least 18 had populations of less than 100,000 and contemplated that for some of them a solution other than separate independence might be acceptable.[87] That issues within this third group of constitutional questions resulting from British decolonization might still, as it neared its end, pose problems of the greatest difficulty for the future of the association was indeed amply demonstrated at this meeting at which the future of Southern Rhodesia was the major issue.

Prime Ministers' Meetings do not pass resolutions, they have "never cast votes,"[88] and they do not issue reports. In them, indeed, more even than in its other arrangements, the Commonwealth has manifested itself as an association which seeks to maintain "a style of conversation" between an increasing number of increasingly diverse states.

It is not their function, nor is it the object of this communiqué [the prime ministers recorded in 1957[89]] to record agreed decisions or formal resolutions. Their value lies in the opportunity which they afford for a full and candid exchange of views in the light of which each Commonwealth Government can formulate and pursue its separate policies with deeper knowledge and understanding of the views and interests of its fellow members.

In 1961 Mr. Sandys still saw the "climax" of the system of consultation in the meetings of the prime ministers, "who sit and talk together privately and informally."[90] But the Prime Ministers' Meetings of course pose the same problem as those of "consultation" at the day-to-day level: how "full and candid" can they be? On the one hand are the reiterated assertions of their intimate and outspoken style of conversation, on the other the inevitability that what is disclosed should be limited by considerations of

87. It mentioned *inter alia* an alternative of "independence with a treaty of friendship" as exemplified in the arrangements made between Western Samoa and New Zealand. See New Zealand Treaty Series 1962, No. 5. Also J. S. Davidson, "The Transition to Independence: The Examples of Samoa," *Australian Journal of Politics and History*, VII (1961), 15-40.

88. Menzies, *Changing Commonwealth*, p. 18.

89. Final communiqué, 1957. (Mansergh, *Documents* . . . , 1952-62, p. 534.)

90. Commonwealth Parliamentary Association Conference 1961, *Report of Proceedings* (London, 1961), p. 10. (Mansergh, *Documents* . . . , 1952-62, p. 767.)

national interest, including those imposed by special relationships with non-Commonwealth countries. To these we must add the likely consequences of the mere increase in numbers and diversity, and we should not overlook the short time available for what are very wide-ranging discussions or the fact that it has not increased at all in this decade though the numbers have risen from seven to eighteen. Severe limitations on "full and candid" discussion may be imposed by mere lack of time or inclination to raise issues not mentioned.[91]

One possible development which might mitigate this problem, the further use of special sessions of interest to some, but not all, members has already been discussed. Another device has also been used which might serve the same end, whether or not that has been its purpose in the past, namely meetings, not of heads of governments, but of ministers concerned with a particular field. In the first decade after the war, there were, for example, meetings of foreign, defense, supply, and finance ministers. Of these only meetings of finance and trade (or economic) ministers have continued since 1954, but these have taken place in every year since then except 1962. In 1955, 1956, and 1957 they were held about the same time as the annual meetings of the International Monetary Fund and the World Bank. In 1958 they took the form of a full scale Commonwealth Trade and Economic Conference in Montreal. In terms which recalled those in which the prime ministers had in 1946 rejected suggestions for more formal organization the Conference communiqué noted "with satisfaction the absence of rigidity and formality" in existing arrangements for economic consultation and affirmed their wish "not to change in any way their consultative character."[92] They agreed, however, to co-ordinate the existing machinery under the name Commonwealth Economic Consultative Council. At the highest level this would consist of the finance and economic ministers meeting as required, and official level meetings would be held to prepare for them.

91. See the comments of Dr. Eayrs (*Commonwealth and Suez*, p. 13-18) on the prime ministers' discussion of the Middle East at the 1956 meeting.
92. Final Communiqué, 1958 (Cmnd. 539) (Mansergh, *Documents* . . . , 1952-62, pp. 537-53).

All Commonwealth governments later agreed[93] that the Council should be regarded as incorporating the Commonwealth Liaison Committee and the Commonwealth Economic Committee. The former, set up in 1948, consisted of U.K. officials and members of the high commissioners' offices in London, meeting to discuss economic and financial problems. The latter, originally established in 1925 and financed by all Commonwealth governments, provides economic and statistical services on Commonwealth production and trade. As a result of a review of its activities initiated by the Prime Ministers' Meeting in 1957 proposals for expanding its activities were approved by the Montreal Conference in 1958, including the provision of information on the progress of development and its financing.[94]

Ministerial meetings of the Commonwealth Economic Consultative Council were held in 1959 and 1960 in London,[95] in 1961 in Accra, in May and September, 1963, and in March, 1964 in London. At the meeting in 1960 it was decided to initiate a Special Commonwealth African Assistance Plan, which is reviewed annually by the Council. At the 1961 meeting all Commonwealth countries except Britain "expressed grave apprehension and concern" regarding the possible results of the British decision to negotiate with EEC. British membership would, they feared, "weaken the cohesion of the Commonwealth as a whole."[96] The meeting in May, 1963, was attended by trade ministers and was largely concerned with preliminary discussion of the subjects on the agenda for the ministerial meeting of G.A.T.T. which it immediately preceded.[97] Similarly, the meetings in September, 1963,[98] and March, 1964,[99] were concerned with discussions preliminary to the meetings of the I.M.F. and the I.B.R.D., the "Kennedy round" of trade negotiations, and the

93. *Commonwealth Survey,* V (1959), 391.
94. Commonwealth Economic Committee, *Annual Report 1958-59* (London, 1959), pars. 4-9.
95. No communiqué was issued in 1959, *Commonwealth Survey,* V, 850-51. For that for 1960, see *ibid.,* VI (1960), 924.
96. Mansergh, *Documents* . . . , *1952-62,* pp. 650-51.
97. *Commonwealth Survey,* IX (1963), 468.
98. *Ibid.,* IX (1963), 855.
99. *Ibid.,* X (1964), 372.

UN Conference on Trade and Development. Particularly at the 1964 meeting, it seemed that a fair consensus emerged on the issues to be discussed at the U.N. conference.

Intergovernmental Arrangements for Specific Purposes

No account of the intergovernmental machinery of Commonwealth relations would be complete which ignored the existence of a considerable group of organizations with quite specific though limited areas of activity. To attempt to examine their working in detail, or even to list their activities during this decade would be impossible within the scope of this paper.[1] They range from bodies concerned with the systematic supply of specialist information, such as the Commonwealth Economic Committee and the Executive Council of the Commonwealth Agricultural Bureaux (responsible for the administration and finance of three research institutes, besides the eight specialized bureaus which are clearing houses for the dissemination of information about research in their particular fields), through advisory bodies representative of the relevant national authorities in Commonwealth countries, such as the Commonwealth Telecommunications Board and the British Commonwealth Scientific Committee, to regular conferences of such Commonwealth officials as survey officers, auditors-general, chief veterinary officers, or the Commonwealth Advisory Committee on Defence Science.[2]

Perhaps the most notable developments of this kind during the decade were the completion of the first two stages of the Commonwealth Round the World Telephone Cable and the initiation

1. There is a list of Commonwealth conferences, 1946-62, in *The Commonwealth Relations Office List 1963*, pp. 143-49; and a further list for 1962-63 in *ibid. 1964*. These lists include, however, many unofficial meetings.
2. All of these have met regularly during the decade; the British Commonwealth Scientific Committee replaced the Standing Committee of the British Commonwealth Scientific Conference (which was abolished in 1958). Under its aegis are the British Commonwealth Scientific Offices in London and Washington and a number of specialist committees.

of construction of the third (agreed upon at a conference in Kuala Lumpur in 1961), the costs being met by the Commonwealth governments concerned,[3] and the establishment of the Commonwealth Education and Training Plan as a result of the Commonwealth Education Conference held in Oxford in 1959.[4] Although the plan rests on bilateral arrangements between member countries, a Commonwealth Education Liaison Committee and a Liaison Unit were established in London with carefully circumscribed functions. A second Commonwealth Education Conference was held in Delhi in 1962 and a third in Montreal in 1964. The Prime Ministers' Meeting in 1964 agreed in principle that a similar initiative should be taken in the field of medicine.

Conclusion

The most evident feature of the decade was that relations between Commonwealth countries continued to become less "exclusive." The factors making for a "special relationship" between members, and notably between Britain and other individual members, remained substantial but their relative importance continued to decline as other relationships with foreign countries developed. This was so in trade and finance, aid, technical assistance, and education, and that it should be so is part of the meaning of independence. What remains is not necessarily unimportant to any member country, and may even be a major factor in its external relations, but any sharp distinction between Commonwealth relations and foreign relations has become increasingly unreal. The growing diversity of membership as its numbers increased has made it more difficult—especially perhaps at the highest level—for the existing machinery to func-

3. A good account is in *The Commonwealth Relations Office List 1964*, pp. 161-65.
4. "Report of the Commonwealth Education Conference" (London, 1959), Cmnd. 841, G. B. *Parl. Paps.*, 1958-59, XI; "Report of the Second Commonwealth Education Conference" (London, 1962), Cmnd. 1655, *ibid.* 1961-62, XI; *Report of the Third Commonwealth Education Conference* (London, 1964), Cmnd. 2545.

tion well, even for the limited—but not therefore necessarily insignificant—purposes it is supposed to serve.

Where Commonwealth countries want to co-operate, there was at the end of the decade still much that facilitated their doing so in the network of interrelationships inherited from the past and in varying degrees maintained today. If they do not wish to do so, it is idle to suppose that such similarities will substantially affect the issue, still more that different machinery would somehow make them change course. Until the dramatic proposal for a Commonwealth secretariat recorded in the 1964 communiqué the traditional hostility to any central machinery had shown little sign of weakening. Interpretation of this development is hazardous, but the long-standing fear that it must strengthen British influence seems to have been replaced by the conviction, on the part of the newer members, that only so could they ensure for themselves a full share in the management of the association and the maximum opportunity of shaping the policies of all members especially, perhaps (if so Anglocentric a note may be permitted), of Britain itself. But if this development thus implied no major change in what Professor Miller called a "limited Commonwealth" and was indeed to be seen as a further step in its decolonization and transformation into an international organization, there were signs that, within those limits, members were willing to seek new purposes to which they hoped to give a distinctively Commonwealth character and thereby strengthen the links between themselves. If the Commonwealth proved able to meet the challenge of interdependence on a basis that all members could come to accept as one of genuinely mutual co-operation, its role, limited though it must be by the limited resources available, might yet provide an experience of major importance to its members and to the world.

6

Intra-Commonwealth Relations
Non-governmental Associations

John Chadwick, C.M.G.*

... The Commonwealth is not just an association of governments. It is an association of peoples, between whom there
are countless connections which need to be continuously re-
freshed and strengthened. There is a vast network of personal and business contacts. . . . There are close links between
professional men. . . . Valuable connections have grown up
between us through art, sport and other activities. . . . In
addition there are the strong links forged by the churches.
There exist also numerous bodies which bring together from
different Commonwealth countries people with similar interests and experience.[1]

Finally, the Conference noted that the Commonwealth
was an association of peoples rather than an organisation of
Governments. While there is much that Governments can and
should do, the real strength of the partnership lies in the ties
of friendship that bind its peoples together. In the modern
world of easy travel, the degree of personal contact between
individuals in every walk of life, throughout all Commonwealth countries, is increasing rapidly. . . .[2]

Today no thesis is easier to sustain than that the Commonwealth is expanding itself to extinction. Nostalgics will point

* Assistant under-secretary of state, Commonwealth Relations Office.
1. Rt. Hon. Duncan Sandys (then secretary of state for Commonwealth relations), *The Modern Commonwealth* (London, 1962), pp. 10-11.
2. *The Future of the Commonwealth: A British View.* Report of a conference
held at Ditchley Park, Oxfordshire, under the auspices of the Commonwealth
Relations Office, April, 1963 (London, 1963), p. 7.

to its racial and political diversity and to the collapse of the tightly knit, like-minded, white club; purists to a lowering of administrative, ethical, and "Western" standards; jurists to breaches of the rule of law. The economist, pondering over changes in the traditional pattern of trade, may argue that Britain can no longer be of both the Commonwealth and Europe. It will suit her, therefore, to sacrifice the Commonwealth relationship. Sections of the press and of public and parliamentary opinion also tend to the short-term (and short-sighted) view that the Commonwealth has now outlived its use and meaning. What, they ask, is the significance of a group of nations which, as its number increases, brings in its train more disputes, more unfriendly votes at the United Nations, further burdens for the British taxpayer, and no countervailing political advantages? One apparently influential politician has gone so far as to comment that "The Commonwealth has really become a gigantic farce."[3]

Yet, as one speaker has said, "Those who pick the Commonwealth to pieces never examine the probable outcome if they prove themselves right. The position is not static. What will happen is not to be assessed by analysis but to be achieved by action." Among the acts which Britain herself should take to ensure a fuller understanding of the Commonwealth, the same commentator listed as "in the long run perhaps the most important of all, the resolute development and extension of the network of educational links, exchanges and assistance programmes, which are part of the very fibre of the partnership."[4] It is with these non-governmental links that this paper is concerned.

Until quite recently apologists for the Commonwealth tended to explain its significance solely in terms of a special relationship between governments, based on a common language, shared administrative and judicial practices, and a political like-mindedness. From these flowed naturally a habit of close and informal consultation which took place either bilaterally or in a wide

3. *The Times*, April 2, 1964, p. 13: "A Party in Search of a Pattern: No. 2— Patriotism Based on Reality Not on Dreams," by "A Conservative."
4. C. S. Leslie, "Has the Commonwealth a Future?" *The Listener*, Feb. 6, 1964.

range of committees and *ad hoc* meetings from those of the prime ministers downwards. The habit of consultation remains of the highest importance: without it and its supporting machinery, the special relationship could not survive. The official means of consultation have been often and exhaustively analyzed. But we still lack a parallel survey in depth of the Commonwealth's unofficial links. If "the Commonwealth is not just an association of Governments, [but] of peoples,"[5] it is time that the omission was repaired.

The Commonwealth Relations Office in a recent annual handbook[6] devotes nearly sixty pages of close type to "organisations and societies in Britain concerned with various aspects of Commonwealth relations." Even this list, which underlines the difficulty of differentiating official from unofficial bodies, is far from exhaustive. All that can be attempted, in a paper of this compass, is to select, somewhat arbitrarily, certain broad fields of human activity in order to bring home the extent to which the Commonwealth prospers through its unofficial relationships. If, in the upshot, the pattern that emerges seems a highly Anglocentric one, this is only in part due to the fact that most Commonwealth-wide organizations had their genesis in Britain. There are indeed a growing number of national organizations in other Commonwealth countries linked in various ways with their counterparts in Britain and elsewhere, as well as a constant and healthy increase in exchanges between Commonwealth members other than Britain.

That these unique links, or indeed the Commonwealth itself, have weathered the storms of growth is at root due to two factors, language and a commonly shared administrative tradition—what may be loosely described as "the British Legacy." For the Commonwealth is above all else a vigorous social organism, drawing its real strength and meaning from the extent to

5. Sandys, pp. 10-11.
6. *The Commonwealth Relations Office List, 1963*, pp. 61-118. Since this paper was written the United Kingdom Committee of the Federation of Commonwealth Chambers of Commerce has promoted the publication of the first comprehensive *Handbook of Commonwealth Organisations* (London, 1965) based in Britain.

which its peoples have "become pretty well mixed up together." As the association expands, more and more dangers will lurk in its path. Nationalism and regionalism may weaken like-mindedness. The sharing of a common tongue is an asset which will survive in some of the newer member countries only if the desire that it should do so persists. As new generations grow to power in Asia and Africa standards and practices which in previous days seemed the acceptable goal may be adapted beyond recognition to suit domestic needs. Nonetheless the personal, cultural, business, and professional links are strong and widespread. It would take much to demolish them.

The Field of Education

Despite nationalist aspirations and the growth in the number of independent countries, the demand throughout the Commonwealth for education and training in Britain, far from slackening, increases year by year. The British may count it as their singular good fortune that their own educational system is divorced from politics and that the legacy of learning which they have offered to the Commonwealth is not, therefore, identified with imperialism. The record speaks for itself. In 1944 the Commonwealth student population of Britain amounted to 2,500; today it is close on 50,000. No longer are these students predominantly the sons and daughters of rich parents from the old Dominions. Of them 90 per cent now come from the tropical Commonwealth. They are studying, not only at British universities, but at teacher-training and technical colleges, in business and industry, or for the liberal professions. Much of the aid to students comes from government sources, both in Britain and the other Commonwealth countries. But this is far from the whole story. In the non-governmental field teachers are increasingly exchanged between local education authorities in Britain and other parts of the Commonwealth. The League of the Commonwealth arranges for upwards of 100 Commonwealth teachers to exchange their respective jobs for a period every year. At university level it is common for appointments to be made from other Commonwealth countries. Oxbridge itself is a prominent example. There are at present over a thousand British university teachers serving in the universities of the developing Commonwealth. Influential contacts are maintained between universities, university colleges, and technical colleges. The Association of Commonwealth Universities, which represents no fewer than 133 institutions throughout the member countries and the dependencies, and the Inter-University Council for Higher Education Overseas,[7] both of them independent associations, provide contacts between their members, help to recruit teaching staff, facilitate interchanges of teachers and students, and promote the exchange of ideas and methods of teaching. The Association of Commonwealth Universities[8] publishes an invaluable *Commonwealth Universities Yearbook*, and organizes quinquennial congresses of universities throughout the Commonwealth, while in the intervening years its Executive Council has since 1949 met on nine occasions in Commonwealth countries other than Britain for discussions on matters of common interest. It also provides the secretariat for the Commonwealth Scholarships Plan in Britain and for the Committee of Vice-Chancellors and Principals of British Universities.

Some British universities, particularly London, have taken a special part in assisting the development of new university institutions in Africa and the Caribbean by making arrangements whereby such institutions prepared their students for degrees of the British university concerned. Teachers of the overseas colleges took a full part, with their British colleagues, in the examination of their own students and syllabuses were modified to meet local needs. Such "special relationships" developed by the universities of Durham, London, and Birmingham now exist with only one or two colleges, the others having become fully independent degree-granting universities. But the informal links

7. The membership of the IUC includes all British universities and some of those in developing countries of the Commonwealth. It recruits over two hundred teachers a year, mainly for universities in Commonwealth Africa. For its history, see Sir Alexander Carr-Saunders, *New Universities Overseas* (London, 1961).

8. Sir Eric Ashby's *Community of Universities* (Cambridge, 1963) is a lively short account of the history and activities of this Association.

between the academic staffs of the British universities concerned and the new universities overseas remain particularly close.

Other expressions—often overlooked—of similar links can be seen in the work of examining boards, themselves based on British universities, which conduct examinations in the overseas Commonwealth at levels which are strictly those adhered to in Britain. Numbers of candidates for the examinations of any one board vary markedly, but it is noteworthy that close on 90,000 candidates take the Cambridge local examinations each year. There are also a number of reputable British correspondence colleges which, through their work in preparing candidates for these and other examinations, form a further Commonwealth link. As time passes, some of these direct links may be formally severed and bodies like the West African School Examinations Council may be set up in the Commonwealth countries themselves. But standards and practices so established will undoubtedly remain influential.

British church and missionary societies also contribute men and money to educational programs in the developing Commonwealth. A recent survey by the Overseas Development Institute[9] of eighty-five missionary societies shows that in 1962 almost 900 British nationals were engaged in educational work under Protestant auspices. A further 158 combined some educational work with pastoral duties.

For some years past "school-leavers" have been sent overseas for a year's service in developing Commonwealth countries. The main private organization concerned has been Voluntary Service Overseas. More recently a scheme to send overseas graduates and people of similar qualifications has been operated by voluntary societies. Some 72 per cent of these graduates have gone abroad to teach. The Overseas Appointments Bureau and the Catholic Overseas Appointments Bureau are further examples of non-profit-making, voluntary agencies inspired by ideals of service to the developing Commonwealth. In 1961-62 the former recruited 106, and in 1962-63 the latter some 60 teachers.

9. Overseas Development Institute, *Educational Assistance* (London, 1963).

British foundations and trusts have also provided financial help for education in developing Commonwealth countries. About half the annual income of the Dulverton Trusts (£180,000) is thus spent. The Leverhulme Trust contributed over £110,000 in the three years 1959-61, and the Nuffield Foundation £254,000 in 1961-62. The Wolfson Foundation has given considerable help to colleges and universities in Britain to which developing countries turn for help and for professional advice. There are many others, including private bequest funds, devoted to strengthening Commonwealth educational links.

British private firms with overseas interests have also spent large sums on education and training on behalf of developing Commonwealth countries. According to the Overseas Development Institute[10] the number of industrial trainees in Britain from the developing countries may be in the region of 5,000 a year. The Federation of British Industries' Overseas Scholarship Scheme, which has so far provided industrial training for about 200 Commonwealth citizens out of a total of 600 scholars, is financed by some 500 British firms. Two British oil companies gave Nigeria £500,000 at independence for technical education. The Indian Institute of Technology has received £250,000 worth of equipment from British industry with the promise of more to come. The Centre for Educational Television Overseas and the Overseas Visual Aids Centre are further non-governmental organizations devoted to training, advice, and research in their subjects for the benefit of educational development in the Commonwealth.

There is also a considerable interchange in the arts field. Many Commonwealth students come to Britain to study music and the other arts. Conversely, there is an outward movement of teachers from Britain, not least of examiners from the Royal Schools of Music, the Trinity College of Music, and the Royal Academy of Dancing. Throughout the Commonwealth appetites are stimulated by visits, often under commercial sponsorship, of artists and musicians and of dramatic companies such as the Old Vic and

10. *Ibid.*

the Royal Ballet and through the establishment of such organizations as the Stratford, Ontario, Shakespeare Company and the Elizabethan Trust of Australia.

Even so brief a survey should also mention the Institutes of Commonwealth Studies of the universities of London and Oxford. These play a prominent role in encouraging collaboration at the postgraduate level between research workers from Commonwealth countries engaged in Commonwealth studies, with particular reference to the social sciences, administration, and economics. Queen Elizabeth House, Oxford, provides accommodation and facilities for academic work over a wide range of Commonwealth problems. The Indian School of International Studies has established a Department of Commonwealth History and Institutions engaged in postgraduate training and research. Also active in this field are the Council for Education in the Commonwealth, with headquarters at the British House of Commons, and the Africa Educational Trust. The Council aims to create an informed public opinion on the problems of education in the Commonwealth and organizes discussions between Commonwealth ministers of education and experts. The Trust promotes special forms of training for Africans, supports similar organizations in Africa, and, in particular, arranges postgraduate nursing courses in Britain for African women from Southern Rhodesia.

The Legal Field[11]

The continuance of English common law as the basic system of law in the great majority of Commonwealth countries leads to strong and widespread links in the legal field. Though many of the newer Commonwealth countries are rightly intent on building up their own law schools and examination systems, British universities and the Inns of Court continue to attract thousands of Commonwealth law students annually. In many

11. This subject, including the interchange of substantive law among courts within the Commonwealth, is discussed at length in Professor S. A. de Smith's chapter, *infra*.

Commonwealth countries there are special arrangements for admitting English barristers and solicitors to practice. Conversely, barristers and solicitors from other Commonwealth countries may be exempted from the examinations and some of the other requirements in England in order to be admitted to practice there.

One example of Commonwealth-wide initiatives in the legal field was the launching in 1962 with assistance from the Wolfson Foundation of a Commonwealth Legal Assistance Scheme for Law Revision. This is operated by the British Institute of International and Comparative Law. It disseminates information on new developments of special interest in law, and particularly in law revision, throughout the Commonwealth; and arranges for assistance between Commonwealth countries in the preparation of legislation or the study of legal problems. Several of the newer Commonwealth countries have already sought and received help from the Institute, and a series of special surveys of interest to the Commonwealth and in particular to the developing countries is being prepared under the scheme, the first being a survey of hire-purchase law and credit-financing.[12] It is significant that the majority of requests so far put to the new body have been for information on legal developments in other parts of the Commonwealth connected with projects of law reform or legal reorganization.

Legal links are also strengthened by the continuous interchange of visits by distinguished judicial personages. The Commonwealth and Empire Law Conference, which will be holding the third of its quinquennial meetings in Australia in 1965, is a significant example of members of the same profession coming together from the length and breadth of the Commonwealth to discuss subjects of mutual interest. Mention should also be made of the Council of Legal Education, which, as the body holding examinations for the English bar, frequently advises on problems of legal education in the developing Commonwealth.

12. *Report* by the director on the activities of the British Institute of International and Comparative Law, 1963-64 (London, 1964), pp. 12-14.

Medicine and Allied Disciplines

Medicine is perhaps the best developed of the Commonwealth freemasonries. The British General Medical Council recognizes upwards of fifty medical qualifications granted by other Commonwealth countries. No less than 17,273 doctors appear on the Commonwealth List of the British Medical Register. While no differentiation is made in the Council's parallel Home List, it clearly contains a considerable number of names of doctors from other Commonwealth countries who have qualified in Britain itself. This is about 17 per cent of the grand total, to which foreign doctors contribute less than 2 per cent. Nearly all other Commonwealth countries, with the exception of certain Canadian provinces, grant reciprocal treatment to British doctors. The General Medical Council is also ready to advise other Commonwealth countries which are establishing their own medical schools on questions relating to the recognition of their degrees by the Council. From this move towards mutual self-help sprang the Commonwealth Medical Association, which was established in 1948 and has since held meetings annually. For its part, the British Medical Association has a widespread oversea organization. It is affiliated with similar bodies in Canada, India, Pakistan, Ceylon, and Malaysia and has branches in many other Commonwealth territories. The College of General Practitioners has faculties in Canada, Africa, and Australasia, and the Royal College of Obstetricians and Gynaecologists regional councils in the older Commonwealth countries. The Royal College of Surgeons conducts examinations and has reciprocity of examination regulations in certain member states, while the Royal Society of Tropical Medicine and Hygiene maintains touch through local secretaries with problems of mutual concern in at least nine of the independent Commonwealth countries. The Royal College of Veterinary Surgeons has members throughout the Commonwealth,[13] while the British Veterinary Association,

13. On December 31, 1963, the *British Veterinary Register* had on it 180 Commonwealth names.

a voluntary body which looks generally to the interests of individual members of the college, is in affiliation with similar organizations in a large number of other member countries.

The dental and nursing professions follow the same cooperative path. While the *Register*[14] of the former shows names for the most part European, the British General Nursing Council recognizes any Commonwealth qualifications imposing standards similar to its own. It would require much detailed research to assemble statistics covering the movement of qualified nurses and trainees between the Commonwealth countries, but all evidence points to the fact that this is a constantly growing and mobile guild. To give only two random examples: in 1962-63 580 nurses trained in Australia and 40 trained in Nigeria were entered on the British Register. Australia and Canada in turn open their gates to trainees from Malaysia and the Caribbean.

Voluntary bodies in the medical field are the British Chest and Heart Association, which is in touch with affiliated societies in most other Commonwealth countries and awards scholarships to doctors, nurses, and medical workers from within the the Commonwealth; the British Leprosy Relief Association, which works within the Commonwealth through grants and loaned staff; the Royal Commonwealth Society for the Blind, whose mobile teams are active in Commonwealth Africa and which operates a Commonwealth scholarship fund and trains teachers and welfare workers from many Commonwealth countries; and the Commonwealth Society for the Deaf, whose aims are to promote the welfare, education, and employment of deaf people throughout the Commonwealth. In the lay field the Institute of Hospital Administrators arranges long courses of practical training for Commonwealth officers, while the St. John's Ambulance Association and Brigade operate first-aid and nursing courses throughout the Commonwealth and can boast outside Britain of a Commonwealth membership of 120,000

14. On January 1, 1963, the *Dentists Register* under its Commonwealth List showed 684 persons from universities in the Commonwealth as registered under the Dentists Act, 1921.

uniformed and disciplined voluntary workers in the Brigade's many branches.

Learned Societies and the Interchange of Scientists

Today governments are increasingly obliged to shoulder the financial burden of scientific research. Yet the learned societies still retain their traditional function of spreading the communication of scientific knowledge. They continue to have a profound influence on the development of scientific research throughout the Commonwealth. Fellows of the Royal Society of London and of other learned British societies are drawn from the whole Commonwealth.

The Journals of these Societies are open for publication of scientific work of Commonwealth scientists who also freely participate in their meetings. Many have local sections in other Commonwealth countries and local correspondents who encourage links with United Kingdom scientists. An outstanding example of Commonwealth scientific collaboration is provided by the Royal Society Empire Scientific Conference of 1946 which was attended by representatives from all Commonwealth countries.[15]

Thus the Royal Societies of Canada and New Zealand, the Australian Academy of Science, the National Institute of Sciences of India, and the Science Association of Nigeria—to name only a few—are bodies which maintain close and continuous links with each other and with their counterpart societies in Britain. The Rutherford Memorial Lecture established by the Royal Society of London is delivered biennially in other Commonwealth countries, while meetings of the British Association for the Advancement of Science are held not only in London but in other Commonwealth countries. The Royal Society of Arts for its part holds examinations in commercial and industrial subjects which are taken widely throughout the Commonwealth.

15. Central Office of Information, *The Promotion of Science in the Commonwealth* (London, 1962), p. 2.

The interchange of scientists is also largely aided through non-governmental channels. Thus, the Nuffield Foundation provides grants for fellowships and scholarships for scientists from other Commonwealth countries as well as giving direct support for research in the Commonwealth. In addition, the Foundation, in collaboration with the Royal Society, operates a further bursaries scheme designed to enable "investigators of proven worth" to pursue research and learn new techniques in any Commonwealth country.

The Royal Institute of International Affairs also deserves mention under this general heading. While not restricting itself to Commonwealth affairs, its library and research facilities are available to Commonwealth scholars; it holds frequent meetings and study groups on Commonwealth problems, commissions studies on the Commonwealth, encourages similar activities within the Commonwealth, and has, with its sister institutes in other member countries, organized eight unofficial Commonwealth Relations Conferences since 1933. The last such conference, at which Commonwealth representatives from twelve member countries were present, took place in Delhi in 1965.

Other Professions

No paper of this length could do full justice to the extent of Commonwealth co-operation in the professional fields. Nor is it possible within so short a compass to define precisely the varying relationships which exist between differing sets of professional bodies in this country and their counterparts or associates in other Commonwealth countries. Some are exclusive and recognize only their own national qualifications; others enjoy a thoroughgoing freemasonry. But each linking set of bodies or associations owes its origin to a common appreciation of British professional standards. This in turn stems from widespread experience of the British educational system and training methods. Such shared experience has had two main consequences. First, many thousands of Commonwealth students continue to travel to Britain to obtain their professional qualifications, to become members of British institutes, and perhaps to start their careers there. Second, professional bodies in one Commonwealth country will in many cases recognize the qualifications granted by another, will include holders of these non-national qualifications on their own registers, and permit them to practice without their having to undergo prescribed national examinations. Thus the overseas Commonwealth membership of the Institute of Civil Engineers amounts today to over 4,500. Those of the Institute of Chartered Accountants, the Institute of Cost and Works Accountants, and the Royal Institute of British Architects are of the same order. The last institute inspired the creation in 1963 of a new intra-Commonwealth body—the Commonwealth Association of Architects—whose declared aim is to maintain professional standards and to assist the architectural profession throughout the Commonwealth. For its part, the Chartered Institute of Secretaries offers an outstanding example of a body vigorous in its activity throughout the Commonwealth. In a recent brochure[16] it refers to the four major overseas divisions of the Institute, each with its own secretariat and local organization, in Australia, Canada, New Zealand, and Southern Africa. The examinations syllabuses in these countries take full account of the local law and practice, and a student who emigrates may complete his studies under the law of the country of his adoption. Of the Institute's total membership of 28,500, over 13,000 members are in these four divisions. In addition there are smaller and less formal organizations known as associations with a growing membership in a number of other Commonwealth territories. Twice annually over 5,000 students are examined throughout the Commonwealth. The Institute, through these and other activities, fully lives up to its claim to be "a Commonwealth body."

Further examples[17] may be taken at random. For instance,

16. Chartered Institute of Secretaries, *The Career of a Chartered Secretary* (London, 1963).

17. Much useful information on organizations in Britain providing facilities for development activities will be found in Overseas Development Institute, *Development Guide* (London, 1962). However, with rare exceptions this publication does not make clear which of the five hundred organizations referred to work exclusively in the Commonwealth field.

trainees throughout the Commonwealth follow the syllabuses of the British Institute of Radio Engineers, which also helps applicants from Commonwealth countries over apprenticeship and trainee courses. The Chartered Insurance Institute offers correspondence courses to students in the developing Commonwealth and conducts examinations in most Commonwealth countries for its diplomas. The Institution of Chemical Engineers has advisory committees in Australia and India, and its examinations are also held widely within the Commonwealth. The Institution of Mining and Metallurgy has local sections in several Commonwealth countries in Africa and Malaysia. That of Municipal Engineers allows candidates from the Commonwealth to study for its examinations. As a final example, the Institution of Structural Engineers holds examinations twice yearly in a number of the developing Commonwealth countries and in many of them has official representatives ready to advise on local problems.

Parliamentary Activities

The Commonwealth Parliamentary Association, founded in 1911 to promote the exchange of visits and information between Commonwealth parliamentarians, is one of the best known and most powerful of the unofficial organizations of the Commonwealth. It now has over eighty branches in the legislatures of the Commonwealth, and its offices at Westminster have become a regular meeting place for Commonwealth legislators. Similar privileges are extended by the branches overseas. The Association convenes annual meetings in various capitals of the Commonwealth, while its yearly course on parliamentary practice and procedure at Westminster is attended by some thirty members invited from various Commonwealth legislatures. The General Council of the Association, which was formed in 1948 and now meets annually, provides an effective link between all branches of the Association and performs the co-ordinating functions previously undertaken by the British branch. To date nine plenary conferences of the Association have been held. At each there are wide ranging discussions on such matters of common interest as economic relations, migration, international affairs, and defense. In 1964 the branch of the Association in Jamaica was host to the annual meeting of the General Council. It is of interest that the American-British Group of the Congress of the United States now constitutes an Associated Group of the CPA.

Banking, Commerce, and Industry

While the commercial importance of Britain to the rest of the Commonwealth has declined since the nineteenth century, London remains the banker for the sterling area and Britain the best customer for the majority of member countries. Sheer self-interest therefore dictates that bankers, businessmen, and industrialists throughout the Commonwealth should take a direct and personal interest in all matters likely to influence market opportunities in each other's countries.

The outlook of bankers is understandably international, but the central banks of the Commonwealth are in constant touch with each other. The Institute of Bankers in Britain conducts professional examinations which are still widely taken within the Commonwealth. It has centers in East Africa and Malaysia and members in many Commonwealth countries. The Commonwealth Development Finance Company has as its particular aims financial assistance to Commonwealth countries for development projects, the provision of ready access to British industrial, financial, and commercial experience, and the investment of funds, raised principally through private sources in Britain, in Commonwealth projects which are unable to attract sufficient capital from governmental sources. The company is also a channel through which Commonwealth countries are able to seek advice and assistance on development problems.

In the business field, the Federation of Commonwealth and British Chambers of Commerce acts as a link between the cham-

bers of every Commonwealth country. It is concerned in promoting trade and investment within the Commonwealth and
helps in the organization of trade missions, exhibitions, and
fairs. It is also working in co-operation with other member chambers towards the introduction of a unified system of examination
throughout the Commonwealth with the long-term objective
of establishing a recognized standard of commercial education.
The Federation convenes Commonwealth congresses biennially.
Its latest and twenty-second meeting took place in Trinidad in
April, 1964. It is also active with the Royal Commonwealth
Society in promoting the commercial education of the business
communities throughout the Commonwealth as well as in encouraging the development of training facilities.

In the regional field the Western Hemisphere Exports Council promotes British exports to Canada and the Caribbean Commonwealth countries as well as to the United States. The India,
Pakistan, and Burma Association maintains and expands British
manufacturing and business connections in those countries, while
the Ceylon and the Malayan Commercial Associations have
similar aims. Comparable committees of business interests are
active in the West, East, and Central African fields and in the
West Indies. Nor in this short recital should one forget the links
forged between Commonwealth businessmen in the shipping
and civil aviation worlds and the personal two-way influence
resulting from the presence in one Commonwealth country of a
powerful business community representing another, e.g., Canadians in London and Liverpool, British in Calcutta and Bombay,
Australians in Singapore.

Voluntary Societies

Grouped (with others) under the Joint Commonwealth Societies' Council, the work of such bodies as the Royal Commonwealth Society, Royal Overseas League, Victoria League for
Commonwealth Friendship, and the English-Speaking Union of

the Commonwealth need little introduction. Their value lies as much in the fact that they have branches and committees in many parts of the Commonwealth as in the work they perform in London in promoting knowledge of the Commonwealth and in their reception of visitors from overseas. There is also in Britain a wide range of regional and bilateral voluntary organizations,[18] such as the British-Nigeria Association, the British Association of Malaysia, the East India Association, the Pakistan Society, the Royal African and Royal Central Asian Societies, and the Women's Council. It is the general aim of all these bodies to encourage intra-Commonwealth activity and understanding in their various fields of interest and to offer facilities and hospitality to Commonwealth visitors to Britain.

The Press, Broadcasting, and Television

The press is a powerful if sometimes rough strand in the relationships between Commonwealth countries. Reuters, which is owned jointly by the British press and two Commonwealth news agencies, serves virtually the whole Commonwealth. There are sizable British interests in newspaper publishing in a number of other Commonwealth countries. Over six hundred of the most important newspapers, periodicals, and news agencies in the Commonwealth are grouped together in the Commonwealth Press Union, which holds annual conferences in London and quinquennial conferences rotating between other Commonwealth cities. The Union has autonomous sections in many of the member countries. Each section nominates representatives to a central council which governs the Union. The CPU has established committees on various aspects of press activities such as the defense of press freedom, telecommunication services, and the training and exchange of journalists throughout the Commonwealth. It has also established a traveling fellowship scheme to enable young Commonwealth journalists to study methods of

18. Fuller details of these and other bodies will be found in the *Commonwealth Relations Office List, 1964,* pp. 61-118.

journalism in other Commonwealth countries. A further organization, the Journalists Training Centre recently founded by Mr. (now Lord) Thomson, though not exclusive to the Commonwealth, has on its courses a strong and wide Commonwealth representation.

To a similar degree broadcasting has its unofficial links spreading widely through the Commonwealth. By means of its External Services, the British Broadcasting Corporation beams programs in both English and local languages to a wide range of Commonwealth countries. It maintains close relations with its overseas counterparts. Many of the broadcasting corporations in the new Commonwealth countries were established with help from the BBC, which continues to second personnel and to train Commonwealth officers at its own Staff Training School. The Corporation, through its transcription service, makes available to other Commonwealth organizations a wide range of its sound output. It is also common for the various organizations to extend to each other facilities in the use of studios, recording channels, and the like. As a collective venture, the corporations in the independent Commonwealth hold regular Broadcasting Conferences. The fifth of them took place in Montreal in 1963. The next is likely to convene in Africa. At the 1963 conference the decision was taken to establish a conference secretariat in London for an experimental period.[19] This body is designed to ensure continuity in the interchange of technical information, programming, administration, and engineering. There has also been established in London a Centre for Educational Television Overseas, which advises on educational programs, particularly on behalf of the newly created television services in the developing Commonwealth. Finally, as a joint venture between the BBC, its Canadian and Australian counterparts and the Rank Organization, a Commonwealth International News Film Agency has been set up to provide a service of international news on film for Commonwealth subscribers.

19. The conference communiqué is in *Commonwealth Survey*, IX (1963), 603-4.

Personal Links

No survey of this kind would be complete without some reference, however brief, to the less tangible bonds which link individual Commonwealth citizens to one another. Some, such as a military career perhaps involving shared experience in the Commonwealth Brigades in Korea and Malaya, training and exchange courses or service with other Commonwealth forces,[20] may in the strict sense result from government action. Others such as participation in the Scouting, Girl Guide, or Boys' Brigade movements, in the special Commonwealth schools or training courses of the Outward Bound Trust, or in a wide range of sporting activities whose highest manifestations are the Commonwealth Games, or those peculiarly Commonwealth sports, cricket and (*pace* the French) Rugby, stem from wholly voluntary effort. Nor should the effect of migration be neglected. It is a truism that the strength of the old dominions was built on the outward movement of people from the British Isles. Today migration within the Commonwealth is to a great degree controlled and financed by governments. But there is still much voluntary effort, notably by bodies such as the Women's Migration and Overseas Appointment Society, the Australian Big Brother Movement, and various church societies. Many migrants moreover travel within the Commonwealth without any help from governments.[21] The sum total of their individual experiences, the links which they maintain with their homeland and the further flow of visits which their own remove encourages within their family circle all serve to spread knowledge (although admittedly not always appreciation) of the Common-

20. Citizens of other Commonwealth countries often hold commissions in the British defense services, many such officers reaching high rank. Thus the present British Chief of Air Staff and the British Air Officer Commander-in-Chief, Far East, are both New Zealanders.

21. "A steady flow of people has been going from Britain to the Commonwealth since the War, numbering at the end of 1963 1,470,000." Mr. R. P. Hornby, under-secretary for Commonwealth relations, speaking in the House of Commons on March 26, 1964. G. B., 5 *Parl. Debs.* (Commons), DCXCII, 752.

wealth *inter se*. Even out of the heated controversy to which permanent Commonwealth immigration to Britain has given rise on social and economic grounds, there emerges the hard fact that the British health and transport services could hardly keep going adequately without the injection of labor which they have had from the West Indies, West Africa, and Asia. Apart from these settlers, it is estimated that in the last few years over 300,000 Commonwealth citizens have come annually as students or temporary visitors to the United Kingdom.

Conclusions

In this survey it has been possible only to glance at the activities of some of the numerous non-governmental organizations working in the Commonwealth field. There is clearly room for a far fuller study. Meanwhile, perhaps enough has been said to refute Lord Casey's view that in the "growing-up" process "The Commonwealth countries have lost a series of important professional links with Britain and with each other."[22] On the contrary, the Commonwealth should be in a strong position to to meet the challenge of a General Assembly Resolution[23] (sponsored by Britain herself) which appealed "to all non-governmental organisations to put their increased enthusiasm, energy and other resources into a world campaign in the basic human fields of food, health and education (including training) to start in 1965 and to continue for the remainder of the U.N. Development Decade." Meanwhile, as the former Minister for Public Works and Building said recently in accepting the presidency of the newly formed Council of Commonwealth Municipalities, "We must seek throughout the Commonwealth exchanges of people and views on a massive scale through such activity as unofficial conferences and commissions and the 'twinning' of towns, schools, universities and youth organisations."[24]

22. Lord Casey, *The Future of the Commonwealth* (London, 1963), p. 115.
23. UN General Assembly Resolution No. 1943 (xviii), Dec., 1963.
24. Rt. Hon. Geoffrey Rippon, M.P., reported in *The Times*, Feb. 20, 1964.

Of necessity, government-sponsored action and government aid will always take the lion's share of Commonwealth joint or bilateral endeavor. But Britain and the older Commonwealth countries between them enjoy a long and solid tradition of voluntary effort. They are rich in private institutions and organizations of all kinds. Governments themselves must often rely on the individual citizen for the specialized knowledge and experience they need to further their own programs. In almost every human activity the Commonwealth can offer some example of collective endeavor in the non-governmental sector. Such effort may not be in the international sense exclusive. Nor can the survival of the Commonwealth rest solely on it. But, to quote the President of the Canadian Institute of International Affairs,

. . . if the Commonwealth survives the difficult times ahead, it may well be because thousands of teachers, scholars and administrators working or studying in each other's countries—Australians and New Zealanders in Malaysia, or the Canadian military training mission in Ghana—strengthen the fabric of an association in which people get along better than government.[25]

By way of preparation for the 1964 Prime Ministers' Meeting, the Commonwealth Relations Office in April of that year invited representatives from some thirty British professional organizations and other non-governmental bodies to discuss the whole complex of intra-Commonwealth relations in the unofficial field. On the eve of the Prime Ministers' Meeting, a second discussion was held under the aegis of the Royal Commonwealth Society and a third planned. In their communiqué, the prime ministers recorded that

. . . it might be desirable to establish a Commonwealth Foundation to administer a fund for increasing interchanges between Commonwealth organisations in professional fields. This Foundation could be administered by an independent Board; and, while it could be financed by contributions from Commonwealth Governments, it would also welcome support from all quarters, whether public or private.

25. John W. Holmes, *The Times*, Jan. 7, 1964.

In January, 1965, senior officials of Commonwealth governments met in London to draw up a precise scheme for such a Foundation. Their proposals were examined by Commonwealth Heads of Government at their conference in London in June, 1965, and were then formally adopted. The communiqué issued at the end of this meeting recorded that "The Prime Ministers approved a report by officials and an agreed memorandum on the establishment and functions of the Foundation."[26]

Subsequently the British government published a White Paper summarizing the aims and terms of reference for the Foundation. This made clear that with general Commonwealth agreement the Foundation should be directed by a chairman—a distinguished private citizen of a Commonwealth country appointed with the approval of all member governments—and that there should be a board of trustees on which all subscribing governments would be represented. There will also be a full-time salaried director, appointed by Commonwealth governments collectively. Member governments would subscribe to the cost of the Foundation on an agreed scale. Of the initial annual fund of £250,000, the British government undertook to subscribe half.

It was accepted that the Commonwealth Foundation should be an autonomous body whose general task it would be to administer a fund for increasing interchanges between Commonwealth organizations in professional fields throughout the Commonwealth. Within this broad purpose, the Foundation would encourage fuller representation at conferences of professional bodies within the Commonwealth, facilitate the exchange of visits among professional people, stimulate and increase the flow of professional information, assist when requested with the setting up of national institutions or associations in countries where these did not already exist, and promote the growth of Commonwealth-wide associations or regional Commonwealth associations in order to reduce the present tendency towards the centraliza-

26. Commonwealth Prime Ministers Meeting, 1965, *Final Communiqué*. Cmnd. 2712 (London, 1965).

tion of such bodies in Britain. To avoid the risk of duplication, the Foundation would not, however, at the outset assume any functions in relation to cultural activities or to the press.[27]

It is now expected that appointments to the Commonwealth Foundation will be made in the near future and that the new body will be established in its headquarters at Marlborough House, London, early in 1966.

27. *Agreed memorandum on the Commonwealth Foundation.* Cmnd. 2714 (London, 1965).

7

Relations between the Old and the New Members

M. S. Rajan*

The development of multilateral relations among members of the Commonwealth (as opposed to bilateral relations between each member and the United Kingdom) is largely a phenomenon of postwar Commonwealth relations. Before the war, Commonwealth-Empire relations were essentially conceived as bilateral relations between each of the dominions on the one hand and the United Kingdom on the other. Only in the United Kingdom, for instance, were all the dominions represented for many years by their respective high commissioners. Intra-Commonwealth relations then, to use a stock simile, were like the spokes from the hub of a wheel—the hub being London—but without a rim.

With the addition of the first batch of three new members from Asia during 1947-48 a new phase opened in the history of the development of the Commonwealth. An important aspect of this new phase is the growth of multilateral intra-Commonwealth relations among members other than the United Kingdom.

International Relations

Broadly speaking, relations between the old and the new (postwar) members, both in nature and volume, are basically

* Professor and head, Department of Commonwealth History and Institutions, and Director Indian School of International Studies.

determined by the general outlook and role in world affairs of the two groups of nations. In the case of some sets of old and new members, however, (e.g., Malaysia and Australia, India, and Canada) and of relations between each of the new members and the United Kingdom, there is a significant correlation between intra-Commonwealth relations and international relations. In the case of relations between South Africa (until it left the Commonwealth on May 31, 1961) and all the new members, on the other hand, there was practically no difference between intra-Commonwealth relations and international relations, both being very cold in nature and very small in volume.

All the present four old members are aligned with the Western bloc through bilateral or multilateral military alliances. South Africa used to operate, and was treated by other nations, as a member of the same bloc. During the period 1955-64, thirteen of the fourteen new members have remained, or have claimed to be, non-aligned with either bloc. The one exception (since 1954), Pakistan, has been a member of SEATO and CENTO (the former Baghdad pact), apart from having a bilateral military aid agreement with the United States. Especially at the height of the cold war, this basic divergence naturally inhibited the two groups from working together more closely in world affairs, particularly on questions and situations involving the cold war or the leading states in the two camps. It has also been responsible for continual stresses and strains between individual old and new members, e.g., as between India and the United Kingdom, Ghana and the United Kingdom.

The nature and extent of relations between the two groups are also determined by the status enjoyed and the influence exercised in the society of nations by individual nations of the Commonwealth, their geographical proximity to other nations, and the degree of their active role in world affairs. The fact that the United Kingdom is the only great power and permanent member of the UN Security Council in the Commonwealth (*ipso facto* with world-wide interests) and hence plays the most active role in world affairs (apart from being the most important mem-

ber of the Commonwealth, both historically and functionally)
naturally explains the close and most substantial relations
that every one of the new members has with that country. Likewise, the cordiality and strength of Indo-Canadian relations are
largely explained by their being two of the leading medium-
sized powers and by their very active and somewhat parallel
roles in world affairs both within the United Nations and without.
Common participation in international organizations or in such
international machinery as the International Commission for
Supervision and Control in Indo-China and the UN Emergency
Force in the U.A.R. has reinforced their mutual relations and
friendships. Geographical proximity to the Caribbean area
(among other reasons) has meant close and substantial relations between Canada and the two new members in the Caribbean—Jamaica and Trinidad-Tobago. Likewise, relations between Australia and New Zealand and the new Asian members
are much closer and more substantial than relations between the
former and the new African and Caribbean members.

Two more factors determining the nature of relations between the new and the old are their respective attitudes toward
colonialism and racialism. All four of the remaining old members are largely of European origin. On the other hand, most of
the fourteen new member nations are colored and have experienced many decades of political subjection under a white
nation, and have unpleasant memories of their colonial past as
well as of racial discrimination suffered under that rule. Hence,
two basic principles of their foreign policies are the promotion of
self-determination for all colonial peoples and the removal of
racial discrimination all over the world. Although all the old
members (with the possible exception of South Africa), especially the United Kingdom (their former imperial ruler), are in
agreement with the principle of self-determination for all colonial
peoples, there have in practice been wide differences between
the two groups as to when, and in what circumstances, colonies
should be granted self-determination. For many years, these
differences have been persistently brought out at the United

Nations. The division has been especially deep between the United Kingdom, Australia, New Zealand, and (so long as it was a member) South Africa on the one hand, and most of the new members on the other. During 1961, for example, relations between the United Kingdom and some new members, particularly India and Ghana, suffered severe strains owing to acute differences over the nature of action to be taken by the United Nations to integrate Katanga province with the rest of the Congo. Towards the end of the same year, when India forcibly annexed Goa, all the old Commonwealth nations (even Canada) severely criticized the Indian action, while all the new (except Pakistan) supported India.[1] Most of the new members were critical at various times of Australian and New Zealand policies towards their UN Trust Territories. More recently most of the new and all the old members were acutely divided over the Southern Rhodesian question in the United Nations, and some of the new members, notably India and Ghana, strongly criticized the British government's stand thereon. The division of opinion in the Commonwealth over the British military action in Suez (1956) (which, in the opinion of the new members, was a colonial-type action) cut across the division between old and new members. Australia and New Zealand fully supported the British action while India and Ceylon were strongly critical of it. While Canada supported the two Asian members, Pakistan's official stand was at best equivocal. Such divergences on colonial issues are a constant source of stresses and strains in the relations between the two groups in international affairs.

Likewise, on all racial questions and in particular the racial policies of a fellow member of the Commonwealth, South Africa, the new and old members have been acutely divided. The United Kingdom, Australia, and New Zealand in particular were opposed for many years even to the discussion of the subject in the

1. Indian official and unofficial opinion was persistently critical of the British stand over Portuguese colonial territories in India for many years before as being pro-Portuguese and anti-Indian. Hence (*inter alia*) from time to time, and especially during the years 1954-56 there were demands by the opposition parties for the withdrawal of India from the Commonwealth.

United Nations, on the ground that the matter was essentially
within South Africa's domestic jurisdiction under Article 2 (7)
of the Charter. This acute division of Commonwealth opinion was
somewhat mitigated when both old and new members joined
hands at the March, 1961, Commonwealth Prime Ministers' Conference in bringing pressure on South Africa to alter its racial
policy—as a result of which South Africa left the Commonwealth.
The old and the new members are, however, still divided on the
nature of international action to be taken to make South Africa
alter its policy. As long as this division on a matter of the
greatest importance to the new members remains, relations between the two groups are likely to be subjected to great and
and recurring stresses and strains.

Two other issues which somewhat divided most old and most
new members were the importance to be given to the Asian-
African nations in the councils of world affairs and the extent of
economic and technical assistance to be extended, especially
through international action, to the development of the new
members, all of whom are either developing or underdeveloped
countries.

It is very difficult to assess how far these differing approaches
to general world problems have determined the nature and
volume of intra-Commonwealth relations between the old and
the new members. In general, they have had the least adverse
effect in respect of the United Kingdom, because of its status
both in the society of nations and within the Commonwealth and
the invaluableness of British friendship for all the Commonwealth nations. Nor have these differences adversely affected
relations with Canada, partly because that country has shown
great understanding and accommodation on questions affecting
the new nations. Perhaps one of the several reasons for the inability of Australia (since the Liberal-Country party came to
power at the end of 1949) and New Zealand to promote very
close or substantial relations with the new members (with the
exception of Malaysia) is the persistent differences between

the two groups of Commonwealth nations on these two basic issues.[2]

Besides these common issues which divided in different degrees all the old from all the new members, certain others have affected the bilateral relations between some new and some old members. Perhaps the most notable example is the Kashmir question, which has persistently bedeviled India's relations with the United Kingdom for many years. This dispute has periodically imposed severe strains on Indo-British relations and even led to demands that India should leave the Commonwealth. Relations between India and three other old members (Canada, Australia, and New Zealand) were also somewhat adversely affected from time to time because of critical press and public opinion in those countries against India's stand on Kashmir, as well as the intervention of the Australian prime minister at one time (1951) in the dispute within the Commonwealth framework and Australian sponsorship or support of certain resolutions of the UN Security Council to which India was opposed. Another instance of this kind is the persistently critical attitude of sections of the British press and public opinion to internal developments in Ghana.

Intra-Commonwealth Relations

When the new members joined the Commonwealth, they were practically strangers to the old members other than the United Kingdom—one notable exception being that of India and South Africa, which for many years before India's independence had had direct dealings with each other regarding the treatment of South African citizens of Indian descent. For a few years after

2. In this context, the significance of Australian economic aid and cultural co-operation to the promotion of better understanding with Commonwealth Asian countries is more limited than Australian statesmen (but not Australian scholars) are wont to claim. On the other hand, substantial Australian military aid to Malaysia for many years and the very modest aid (and sympathy) to India since the Chinese attack in October, 1962, has had greater success in promoting good will and understanding for Australia in these two new Commonwealth nations. On this point, see also Gordon Greenwood and Norman Harper, eds., *Australia in World Affairs, 1956-1960* (Melbourne, 1963), pp. 92 ff.

their accession to independence and Commonwealth membership, therefore, intra-Commonwealth relations between the two groups of members consisted essentially of relations between each of the new members and the United Kingdom alone among the old. Partly for financial reasons, it was some time before the new members and the other old members established mutual representation and discovered and pursued matters of common interest in the Commonwealth as well as outside. In fact both for financial reasons and because of very limited common interests, most of the newer members have yet to establish representation in all the old member nations.[3]

In the relations between the new members and the United Kingdom the position was quite different. Immediately upon independence, as before, the new members had numerous matters of common interest with the United Kingdom. Moreover, the new members depended heavily on the U.K. government for many things: for introduction to, and political support in, international forums; for information and consultation on foreign policy questions; for temporary diplomatic representation in other Commonwealth and foreign states until the new members could find the men and financial resources to set up their own diplomatic establishments; for British economic and technical assistance for internal economic development; for defense stores and the training of their defense personnel; and so on. Apart from Cyprus, all the new members continued to be monarchies

3. An index to the cordiality or strength of relations between the old and the new members can be found in the extent of their reciprocal diplomatic representation in each other's territories. According to the data provided in the *C.R.O. List 1963* the position was thus: All the new members were represented in the U.K.; reciprocally, the U.K. was represented in all the new members. Leaving this apart, among the new members only India, Pakistan, and Ceylon (incidentally, the first batch of new members) were represented in all the three other old Commonwealth countries. Ghana was represented in only one, Malaya in two, Jamaica in one, and Trinidad and Tobago in one, of the other old member nations. Nigeria, Cyprus, Sierra Leone, Tanganyika, and Uganda had no representation among the old members other than the U.K. Conversely, Canada was represented in 11, Australia in 7, and New Zealand in 3 of the 12 new members (i.e., excluding Kenya and Malawi, for which data is not given in the source cited above). It is hardly necessary to add that South Africa (as long as it was a member of the Commonwealth) was not represented in any of the new member nations; nor was any new member except India represented in South Africa, for some years after India's independence. But it was a special case.

for varying periods after independence and, except for Malaya, the British monarch continued to be their Head of State and in some of them, of course, Queen Elizabeth remains Queen.[4] This bond reinforced their other material and sentimental bonds with the United Kingdom. The new members gradually established relations with the other old members (except South Africa, with which they found it impossible to establish even formal diplomatic representation) but this did not adversely affect relations with the U.K. On the contrary, these seemed to broaden and deepen along with the establishment and promotion of closer relations with Canada, Australia, and New Zealand.

Attitude to new membership

Relationships between new members and old in the context of the Commonwealth were partly determined by what little contact they had with the old and also by their image of the old (e.g., South Africa) when they became independent. But more importantly, they were determined by the reception the old members accorded them in a Commonwealth which until 1947 was an association of white nations centered in the United Kingdom. The most cordial and unreserved welcome came from the most important and influential of the old members—the United Kingdom—but for whose lead, the other old members might have had serious misgivings about the accession of the new, and perhaps even objected to their admission. Apart from warmly welcoming the new members initially, British official spokesmen have from time to time since then reiterated the value of their membership to the Commonwealth, especially by praising the crucial value of India's membership.

All the other old members publicly welcomed the new members, even though some of their leaders at least seem to have had privately some reservations about the admission of the Asian-African members, on the ground that it would change the character of the old Commonwealth as a family of nations bound

4. Ceylon (which, however, announced its intention of becoming a republic as long ago as 1956), Sierra Leone, Jamaica, Trinidad-Tobago, and Malawi.

by racial and cultural ties. More disturbing, however, was the fact that in later years some Commonwealth leaders, official and unofficial, as well as some writers on the Commonwealth, publicly criticized the membership and role of some of the Asian-African members, and alleged that the Commonwealth had been weakened by the addition of the newer Asian-African members and had become less fruitful or purposeful in function. Two of the official critics were indeed prime ministers of the old members—Mr. (as he then was) Robert Menzies of Australia and Dr. Daniel Malan of South Africa. Undoubtedly the attitude of the Australian Prime Minister was one reason why the newer members (except Malaysia) were unwilling or unable to establish any close and cordial ties with Australia. Malaysia apart, such views had a fairly self-defeating effect on the avowed post-war Australian policy to promote closer relations with the Asian members of the Commonwealth. Contrarily, it was the great appreciation and exuberantly friendly attitude of Canadian leaders towards the membership and role of the new members that enabled Canada and some of the new members to establish and promote close and cordial relations and numerous ties. At least in the case of India and Canada, it is this Canadian attitude that led basically to what was once known as the Indo-Canadian entente.[5]

Structure and function of the Commonwealth

Another factor that determined the nature and volume of relations between the old and the new members was the positions they adopted on the structure and function of the Commonwealth. The U.K. government has seldom sought to make any distinction between the old and the new members, in spite of its obvious sentimental, racial, and cultural ties with the

5. See M. S. Rajan, "The Indo-Canadian Entente," *International Journal*, XVII (1962), 364-65. It is worth noting, however, that although the then Canadian prime minister, Mackenzie King, publicly welcomed India's independence and Commonwealth membership in August, 1947, according to one of his biographers King "was horrified at the thought of an Asiatic majority dominating the Commonwealth." Bruce Hutchison, *The Incredible Canadian* (Toronto, 1952), p. 424.

other old members. But as recently as 1956 the Australian prime minister, Mr. Menzies, conceived of the post-1949 Commonwealth as a two-tier structure—an inner circle of old members ("the Crown Commonwealth") within a "total Commonwealth" of the old and the new.[6] Notwithstanding such a distinction, and contrary to the fears of some statesmen and writers, the Commonwealth has not operated in practice in two racial blocs. Nor has the prophecy that the relations between the two groups of members would not be quite so intimate as the relations of the older members with each other come true. Likewise, the fears of some writers that the relationship of a republican member (and all the republican members are new members) would inevitably possess a character different from that of the older monarchical members have not materialized.[7]

On the question of the basic function of the Commonwealth, there has been a flood of proposals, mostly from unofficial sources. Among those made by official sources, perhaps the most significant and responsible have come from the Australian Prime Minister. In 1957, at the Commonwealth Prime Ministers' Conference Menzies reportedly proposed a Commonwealth consultative committee similar to that his predecessor, Curtin, had suggested in 1944. He has also been fertile in suggestions for improving Commonwealth machinery and for causing the Commonwealth Prime Ministers' Conference to influence international developments by publicly declaring (like the Bandung conference) their conclusions on current international questions.[8] Once he went so far as to say that it would be a "disaster" if the Commonwealth became a mere series of unrelated nations with no joint opinions to give to the world.[9]

6. See Menzies' two articles under the title "The Ever Changing Commonwealth" in *The Times* (London), June 11 and 12, 1956.

7. For a discussion of these points, see M. S. Rajan, *The Post-War Transformation of the Commonwealth* (Bombay, 1963), pp. 32-38.

8. See *Australia in World Affairs 1956-1960*, pp. 44-45 ff. See also a cogently argued old article of his (which now seems to have been forgotten by scholars), "The Commonwealth Problem: Union or Alliance?," *Foreign Affairs*, XXVII (1948-49), 263-73.

9. In a speech at the Australia Club, London. *Daily Telegraph* (London), July 10, 1956.

Such views, so very out of tune with informed and prevailing opinions among even the other old members, were not merely not shared by the new members (with perhaps one curious exception) but were completely opposed to their whole outlook towards the Commonwealth as an association of nations.[10] The exception (at least at one time, if not today) was the somewhat similar view of the Malayan prime minister, Tunku Abdul Rahman, who opposed the practice of unanimity at the Commonwealth Prime Ministers' Conferences. He expressed himself in favor of tighter links among members, a "united front" on major issues of world concern, and of majority decisions. Unless the principle of agreement by majority was accepted by the Conference, the Malayan prime minister felt, there was a danger of the loosely knit association's becoming "a farce, degenerating into a coffee-house discussion because of indecision."[11] It is very doubtful if the Malaysian prime minister still holds this view of the structure and function of the Commonwealth, especially since it is not shared by any of the other leaders of the new Commonwealth or of the old except perhaps Sir Robert Menzies.[12] Both the old and the new, however, equally share the belief in the value of more extensive and intimate consultation on problems and matters of mutual interest, but (a cynic would say) that is not saying a great deal, because the nature and extent of consultation is something largely left to each individual member to decide for itself.[13]

10. During a visit to Canada in December, 1956, Prime Minister Nehru said he was opposed to uniform Commonwealth policies and that an "artificial unity of policy" among Commonwealth countries was less important than mutual understanding. Commonwealth Survey (London), III Jan. 8, 1957, p. 7.

11. Straits Times (Singapore) Oct. 26, 1960. See also another speech of his in which he said that unanimity was an impediment and out of date in today's Commonwealth Prime Ministers' Conferences and should therefore be discarded. Sunday Times (Singapore) May 15, 1960, and The Guardian (London), May 14, 1960.

12. For an authoritative Canadian dissent from the Malayan Prime Minister's view, see Vincent Massey, Canadians and their Commonwealth (Oxford, 1961), pp. 16-17. For a concurring Australian view, see Lord Casey, The Future of the Commonwealth (London, 1963), p. 48.

13. J. D. B. Miller has remarked: "They need consult nothing but their convenience." The Commonwealth in the World (2nd ed.; London, 1960), p. 276.

Settlement of intra-Commonwealth disputes

An issue that, at one time, cut across the division between old and new members is the role of the Commonwealth in the settlement of intra-Commonwealth disputes. Until about 1960, Pakistan for many years urged the case for a positive collective role of the Commonwealth in the settlement of such disputes, in particular the Kashmir question. There have also been some Pakistani official and unofficial proposals to create Commonwealth machinery for the settlement of intra-Commonwealth disputes and stop the general Commonwealth practice of excluding from the jurisdiction of the International Court of Justice intra-Commonwealth disputes.[14] Perhaps Menzies alone of the other Commonwealth leaders shared (at one time at least) the view that it should play a collective role in the settlement of disputes like that over Kashmir; in 1951 he took some part in attempting a settlement and even proposed the sending of a Commonwealth force to Kashmir to supervise the plebiscite. But no other Commonwealth government then shared the view that the Commonwealth has any collective role to play in the settlement of such disputes or that any standing Commonwealth machinery should be created for the purpose,[15] and Pakistan too has now abandoned it.

Attitude toward racial discrimination

Until the 1961 Commonwealth Prime Ministers' Conference, there was some doubt among the new members whether the old members (Canada and New Zealand until about 1958) had the same strong objections to the *apartheid* racial policy of the South African government or whether they shared the view of the new members that it was blatantly at variance with South

14. For details, see the present writer's article "India and Pakistan as Factors in Each Other's Foreign Policy and Relations," *International Studies*, III (1961-62), 373-75.

15. On this point, see the report of the Plenary Session of the Sixth Unofficial Commonwealth Relations Conference, Palmerston North (New Zealand) in C. E. Carrington, *The Commonwealth Relations Conference, 1959* (mimeo) (London: R.I.I.A., 1959), pp. 31 ff.

Africa's obligations as a member of a multiracial Commonwealth, and her practices formed one of the persistent objections to Commonwealth membership in many of the new member states. Only when South Africa was forced to withdraw from the Commonwealth were the new members finally convinced that all the old members (with perhaps the exception of Australia) believed (as the new do) that promotion of racial equality (both within and without their territories) is a new and additional Commonwealth obligation.[16] Australia's position is in doubt not because her prime minister, Sir Robert Menzies (or the Australian government) has any sympathy with South African racial policy (the contrary is true), but is rather due to the bad Australian image created by the long-standing Australian objection (based on the issue of domestic jurisdiction) to UN discussion of, or action on, South African racial policy and is further reinforced by the fact that Menzies alone of the Commonwealth prime ministers expressed the view that the Commonwealth had "been injured and not strengthened by the departure of South Africa."[17] The Australian stand is presumably based on the possibility of international cognizance of her restrictive and discriminatory immigration policy, and on the fear that Australian support of international discussion of South African policy might create a precedent for similar international action on Australian immigration policy.

Undoubtedly South Africa's departure strengthened the Commonwealth by removing a major divisive issue between the new and the old members, enabling the existing new members to retain their membership, and leaving the trend towards additional membership of other colored Commonwealth countries unaffected. Henceforth, it is inconceivable either that any of the

16. On this issue, see Rajan, *The Post-War Transformation of the Commonwealth*, pp. 17-20. For the contrary view see Miller, *The Commonwealth in the World*, pp. 286-88; and his "South Africa's Departure," *Journal of Commonwealth Political Studies*, I (Nov., 1961), 69.

17. *Current Notes on International Affairs* (Canberra), April, 1961, p. 23. Also his speeches in London indirectly criticizing the stand of the new members on South Africa's membership in the Commonwealth tended to give the impression (in the words of the adjournment motion moved in the Australian House of Representatives by the Leader of the Opposition on March 22, 1961) of "lining up Australia as a junior partner of *apartheid*."

existing members would enforce any discriminatory racial policies and yet continue to remain within the Commonwealth, or that any newly independent Commonwealth country which does so would be admitted as a member. In this sense, the Commonwealth now provides a better example as a multiracial association than the United Nations.

Immigration policy

On the related question of immigration policy towards citizens of other Commonwealth states, the new members have generally objected to any restrictions based even implicitly on racial considerations though practically all Commonwealth governments have restrictive policies of one kind or another against citizens of other (including Commonwealth) states. Although none of the governments of new member states has formally objected to Australian and New Zealand immigration policies, there has been occasional unofficial criticism on the ground that they discriminate against non-white Commonwealth citizens. The new nations are not readily convinced that Australian and New Zealand policies are wholly inspired (as Australians and New Zealanders are apt to stress) by economic and social considerations and the desire to avoid future international complications like those in South Africa. The one significant exception to this chorus of criticism from the new members is Malaysia.[18] Quite obviously in order to reciprocate Australian goodwill, defense support, and economic and technical aid, Malaysian leaders have refrained from objecting to the Australian immigration policy; on the contrary, they have expressed great understanding of the Australian stand, if not actually supporting it. Replying to criticism some years ago of the Australian immigration policy by an opposition leader in the Malayan House of Representatives, Tunku Abdul Rahman said it was "entirely a domestic matter

18. According to Gordon Greenwood, some other Asian nations too did not raise any objections to Australian policy. See his *Australian Attitudes towards the Commonwealth* (mimeo) (Melbourne: Australian Institute of International Affairs, 1959), pp. 22-23.

[for Australia]."[19] In March, 1961, the Tungku reiterated this position even while expressing the strongest objection to South African racial policy and satisfaction at the withdrawal of South Africa from the Commonwealth.

Another old member, Canada, has been moving away from racial discrimination in its immigration policies and practices. For some years past, it has set small quotas for the admission of Indians, Pakistanis, and Ceylonese, as well as West Indians. Under the new regulations introduced in January, 1962, Canadian immigration policy was greatly liberalized so as to remove altogether any racial discrimination (but, though they are no longer necessary, the previous quotas for certain Commonwealth countries have not yet been abolished). Naturally, therefore, what little criticism there was of the Canadian policy in years past in India (and there are in Canada some four thousand citizens of Indian descent) has now completely died away.

Almost all the new members have strongly criticized the restrictions imposed by the U.K. government since the middle of 1962 under the Commonwealth Immigrants Act, 1961, which in effect discriminates against the immigration into the United Kingdom of the colored citizens of other Commonwealth nations. Many of them also felt that this restriction of a traditional right of Commonwealth citizens of free entry into the "heart of the Commonwealth" was (in the words of the official Labour party amendment to the Commonwealth Immigrants Bill) "calculated to undermine the unity and strength of the Commonwealth."[20] Indeed, they were inclined to agree with the opposition leader, the late Hugh Gaitskell, that it was "a plain anti-Commonwealth measure in theory and a plain anti-colour measure in practice." Fortunately, in the implementation of the measure since July, 1962, the U.K. government has kept its promise that it would not be operated in practice on the basis of color, thereby miti-

19. *Straits Times*, Dec. 1, 1959. See however Peter Boyce, "Twenty-one Years of Australian Diplomacy in Malaya," *The Journal of Southeast Asian History*, IV (1963), 75-78.

20. E.g., Prime Minister of Jamaica in a statement on November 14, 1961, strongly criticized the proposed restrictions and remarked that "the Commonwealth will never be the same again."

gating a divisive issue between the new members and the United Kingdom.

Links of affinity

The nature and strength of intra-Commonwealth relations between the old and the new is partly determined by the continuing efficacy or otherwise of the "links of affinity" and "links of advantage" (to use Mr. Gordon Walker's neat phrases) between the two groups of members. Many of these links are still real and substantial. To say as "A Conservative" recently said in the London *Times* that both the old and the new members "have no present real ties with Britain [and, he might well have added, with each other] other than such as history might have left between any two foreign nations,"[21] is to take a very cynical and superficial view. It is these links among the Commonwealth members that mark them off from the non-Commonwealth states, and together constitute an "invisible frontier" (Gordon Walker's phrase) between the Commonwealth and non-Commonwealth states.

These links include sentimental attachment towards the United Kingdom, the former imperial ruler; allegiance to the British monarch or recognition of that monarch as "the symbol of the free association of independent member nations and, as such, the Head of the Commonwealth"; the common heritage of British culture—the English language, British ideas, ideals, and institutions (including especially the common system of parliamentary government); a network of communication links; various economic links such as Commonwealth preference, membership in the sterling area, intra-Commonwealth trade, British private investment; and extensive personal contacts, official and unofficial.

Many of these links between the old and the new members have, in some of the latter at any rate, been somewhat weakened as, for example, by the replacement of English by Sinhalese as the official language in Ceylon and the abandonment of the

21. "A Party in Search of a Pattern," April 2, 1964.

parliamentary system of government in Pakistan, Ghana, Tanzania, and Cyprus. But I think the links of affinity have not been weakened to an extent which would affect the stability and efficacy of the Commonwealth. Pessimism about the future of the Commonwealth on this score, therefore, is not quite justified.

Links of advantage

The fact that all members, old and new, unanimously desire to remain in the Commonwealth would imply that they derive a variety of benefits from this association, though the volume and nature of those benefits vary from member to member. All of them greatly value the benefits of exchange of information and consultation and co-operation on matters of mutual interest. Although, in terms of volume, such exchanges are largely bilateral between individual members and the U.K., in recent years a certain amount of intra-Commonwealth exchange and consultation has also developed among members other than the U.K. Membership in the Commonwealth no doubt gives an added stature (and consequently the ability to influence other nations) to most members, new and old, as well as a sense of belonging to a cozier, more intimate, association of nations without formal treaty commitments of any kind. For the new members, it is an additional source of economic and technical assistance. While the new members, like the old, are all opposed to a Commonwealth defense policy, all continue to co-operate with the old in matters of defense. The dependence of the new members on the U.K. is especially heavy for defense stores and the training of their defense personnel. Ceylon and Nigeria at one time had, and Ceylon and Malaysia still have, defense agreements with the U.K., and Pakistan is associated with the U.K. in SEATO and CENTO. The nature and extent of co-operation in defense between the old and the new members were significantly, and somewhat spectacularly, demonstrated in three recent instances: the prompt British, Canadian, and Australian military assistance to India at the time of Chinese aggression in October-November, 1962; the British commitment in

July, 1963, to defend Malaysia and the Australian and New Zealand promise to go to her aid if and when necessary; the request for British troops in January, 1964, by the governments of Tanganyika, Uganda, and Kenya to quell actual or potential revolts among their own forces and the British government's compliance with this request. The fact that this last request was made at all to the former imperial ruler and the latter's prompt compliance with it suggest that military co-operation still has an important place in Commonwealth relations.

Prospects of Relations between the Old and the New Members

The fact that prewar Commonwealth relations were on the pattern of a rimless wheel did not indicate any weakness of the then Empire and Commonwealth. With the great postwar expansion of the Commonwealth, and that by nations of immense diversity, the situation was altogether transformed, and the prewar pattern of Commonwealth relations became a source of weakness in the postwar Commonwealth. As a former New Zealand prime minister, Walter Nash, put it: "The Commonwealth bond is in danger of being a rather brittle one," if much the strongest intra-Commonwealth relationship of individual members is with the United Kingdom.[22] British official spokesmen have gone a little further: Mr. Duncan Sandys when he was Commonwealth secretary in Britain, for example, wrote that "if the Commonwealth is to attain its full stature, it is essential that the other members [besides the U.K.] should develop closer and more direct links with each other."[23] Countering a remark of the South African Prime Minister (to the effect that for South Africa Commonwealth membership primarily meant close links with the U.K.), he said on an earlier occasion that for the U.K. government the Commonwealth meant something more than a number of separate bilateral links. It meant "a collective multi-

22. See Carrington, *The Commonwealth Relations Conference, 1959*, p. 66.
23. *Commonwealth Relations Office List, 1963*, p. 156.

racial relationship in which we all consult together, think together and, as far as possible, work together, for the advancement of broad, common objectives."[24]

If intra-Commonwealth relations (other than the bilateral
relations of individual members with the U.K.) are of such importance for the strength, stability, and survival of the Commonwealth, the relationship between the old and the new groups of
members is, I suggest, of more crucial importance than cross-ties
among the old or among the new members alone. The development of such relations among the old members is easy, natural,
and not at all surprising, considering their common racial and
cultural ties, their advanced economies and common domestic
political patterns, their low density of population (except in the
U.K.), and finally the coincidence (usually) of their views on
foreign policy. Similarly, the development of such relations
among the new members is equally easy (in most cases at least)
and natural and not at all surprising, because of their erstwhile
common colonial subjection to a single European imperial
power and, in the more important of them, nationalist struggle
for independence from that power, their being colored peoples
of different shades, their largely non-Christian religions and non-
European cultures, the backwardness of their economic and
social development and, in most cases, high densities of population, and finally their non-alignment in the cold war and opposition to colonialism and racialism. But precisely because the
promotion of relations within the two respective groups is easier
and more natural, such a development is of limited significance
to the strength and stability of the Commonwealth as an association of nations. Of greater consequence to the Commonwealth is the development of intra-Commonwealth relations between the old and the new groups of members.

The uniqueness of the postwar Commonwealth lies in that
it is a multiracial, multicultural, and multilingual association of
governments as well as of peoples—one in which, in general,
intimacy and mutual understanding prevail to a degree that hardly

24. 5 *Parl. Debs.* (Commons), DCXXXVII, 526-27, March 22, 1961.

exists in any comparable forum. The Commonwealth also serves as an ideological and economic bridge between two groups of nations. Equally, it operates as a bridge and channel of communication between two groups of nations with broadly different foreign policy orientations in a (still largely) bipolarized society of nations. The development of relations between these two groups within the framework of the Commonwealth is therefore of the greatest importance to the strength and even the survival of the Commonwealth. The prewar Commonwealth could survive and function in spite of the prevalence of merely bilateral relations between each of the members and the United Kingdom because of its smaller membership, common racial and cultural ties, and broadly similar internal patterns and external interests. The postwar Commonwealth, with its large membership and tremendous diversities, cannot survive long without the development of cross-ties, especially between the old and the new members.

What factors inhibit or promote relations between the two groups at present and in the future? Are there any things that members of either group could do to sustain existing relationships where they are already well-established and create fresh ties?

For many years and until recently, relations between most of the new and most of the old members were somewhat inhibited because of the divergence of their basic outlooks on foreign policy due largely to the cold war and all that it meant in practical international relations. With the present *détente* between the United States and the Soviet Union as well as acute division within the respective ideological camps headed by them, it ought to be possible for the two groups of members to be better able to understand, if not sympathize with, each other's objectives in foreign policy.

Likewise, with colonialism on its last legs, and no disagreement between the two groups of members over the principle of self-determination for colonial peoples and increasingly less disagreement in practice (excepting Southern Rhodesia at present), another hurdle in the way of better relations between the old and the new is now in the final stages of disappearance.

For many years after their hard-won (in many cases) independence, the new Commonwealth nations were unduly cautious in promoting relations with the old members because of the association (directly and indirectly) of colonialism and racialism with the old "European" members. Today, this sensitivity has largely gone among practically all the new members and there is an increasing desire to promote relations with the old members, as with other nations outside the Commonwealth. It is now quite clear that the demand for external economic assistance for the development of the new nations is so pressing and large that the rest of the Commonwealth nations would never be able to meet their needs. Therefore the edge of their grievance against the more advanced old Commonwealth nations for not helping them adequately could be said to be blunted to a large extent.

In the context of the Commonwealth, the views and ideas persistently expressed in the past in the old member nations, such as that the Commonwealth would necessarily be grouped on a racial basis or that the relations of the new non-European members with the older European members will of necessity not be quite so intimate as the relations of the older members with each other, or that the republican members are less devoted or faithful to the Commonwealth than the monarchical members (all of which reflect unconscious race prejudice and are also not based on the actual practice of intra-Commonwealth relations), have not been heard recently. Now that it is accepted by all Commonwealth governments, both within the Commonwealth framework and in general international relations, that the factor of race has little relevance to the promotion of interstate relations and that racial equality is a worthy ideal to be promoted by all nations of the world (with the sole exception of South Africa), it should be easier to promote intra-Commonwealth relations without any inhibition by race prejudices on either side.

For many years, and until recently, there was a feeling both among the old and the new members that the Commonwealth was primarily a proprietary interest of the old members even after the new members became more numerous and vastly more populous. This feeling perhaps inhibited, more unconsciously than consciously, the development of greater intra-Commonwealth relations between the old and the new, because the old members gave the impression of running the Commonwealth and the new members did not have a sense of equal and full participation or influence in Commonwealth affairs. Perhaps the decision of the March, 1961, Commonwealth Prime Ministers' Conference to let South Africa leave the Commonwealth, rather than agree to its remaining a member as a republic without any change in its racial policy, put an end to these old feelings on both sides and thus destroyed the psychological and subconscious barrier between the peoples of the two groups of members. Henceforth, relations between the old and the new members ought to be completely uninhibited and free.

There is now, however, the opposite danger that precisely because the postwar Commonwealth has ceased to be a cozy racial and cultural community the older members may lose interest in it and in safeguarding and promoting its interests as a factor in their respective foreign policies and relations. Because the present Commonwealth owes "more to Gandhi than to Balfour and Durham" as a Canadian has pithily put it,[25] there seem to be some influential circles in the old Commonwealth (especially in the U.K. and Australia) who not only no longer claim any proprietary interest in the Commonwealth but are quite willing to abandon it as an unwanted baby.[26] It is a strange irony that today it is some influential sec-

25. See Carrington, *The Commonwealth Relations Conference, 1959*, p. 45; and John Holmes, "The Impact on the Commonwealth of the Emergence of Africa," *International Organization*, XVI (1962), 297.
26. See Rajan, *The Post-War Transformation of the Commonwealth*, pp. 49-51. According to Lord Casey there is very little interest in the U.K. in the Commonwealth. See *The Future of the Commonwealth*, pp. 10 and 85 ff. According to the celebrated article by 'A Conservative' in *The Times*, April 2, 1964, p. 13, "the Commonwealth has really become a gigantic farce." However, and on the contrary, at a conference held in April, 1963 in the U.K. the consensus of the official and unofficial participants was that "the Commonwealth still had within it the potentialities of having an immense force for good in the distracted world of today and that Britain as the founder member should respond to the chal-

tions among the old members that need to be persuaded by the new that the Commonwealth is still worth preserving and promoting for the good of both its members and the society of nations as a whole. That the interest of some of the founder members has become lukewarm will not encourage the new members to promote intra-Commonwealth relations with them. It seems it is a new task for those who, both among the old and the new members, still cherish the Commonwealth and all it stands for to inject some faith in it into the faint hearts of some people in the old.

"In the ideal Commonwealth, there will be a complete nexus, providing equally firm ties of each with each. It will not be completely realized; some threads will always be absent from the pattern or fragile. But it is reasonable to expect that, as more of the new states feel their feet in world affairs, the new threads spun or strengthened will be more numerous than the old ones cut."[27] That ideal situation cannot be realized because of several inhibiting factors. Briefly, intra-Commonwealth disputes, like those of India (and Pakistan) with South Africa over the treatment of people of Indian descent, and those between India and Pakistan, are bound to render it difficult for the other Commonwealth countries to promote equally close and cordial ties with the disputant members—as the U.K. has found with respect to India and Pakistan. Even when there is mere disharmony between two of the members (as in the case of Ghana and Nigeria) it is not easy for other members to deal with them, especially when (for reasons altogether unrelated to that disharmony) the sympathies of the other members lie mostly with one of the two members.

Absence of free institutions in member states (as in Pakistan and Ghana) is a second factor inhibiting relations between them

---

lenge by herself showing imagination and courage and by encouraging others to do so too." *The Future of the Commonwealth: A British View* (London: H.M.S.O., 1963), p. 1. However, that conference could well be less significant than might appear at first sight. In Australia, according to Gordon Greenwood, the Commonwealth looms less large than before in official thinking (*Australia in World Affairs, 1956-1960*, pp. 55-56).

27. *The Round Table*, L (1959-60), 338.

and the old members. If "free institutions are its [the Common-wealth's] life blood," as the 1926 Balfour Report stated, it is not easy for one set of states who still ardently believe this to deal with those members who have little or no faith in it.

Thirdly, any cynical disregard of the vital Commonwealth obligations to exchange information with and consult other member states on matters of common interest (such as that of the U.K. in respect of the use of force in Suez and Ghana in respect of the Ghana-Guinea Union in 1958) is bound to inhibit the extent as well as the intimacy of intra-Commonwealth relations between the old and the new. Fourthly, if any member behaves contrary to the unstated belief that the Commonwealth is an instrument of international peace and security (as the U.K. did in respect of Suez and India did in respect of Goa) there will be little enthusiasm to promote greater intra-Commonwealth relations between the old and the new members.

Beyond all these factors, the volume and cordiality of relations between the old and the new members will be basically determined by geographical remoteness (e.g., Australia and the Caribbean members), limited financial resources for more extensive diplomatic representation (for, without such representation, it is difficult to develop any substantial relations), and finally lack of specific common interests (for without them, and merely because of their common membership of the Commonwealth, they cannot have much to do with each other). But these rockbottom considerations have not yet been reached in most cases, and there is still a great deal that is both desirable and possible to do in the promotion of intra-Commonwealth relations, as much in the mutual interests of the members as in the interests of the Commonwealth as a whole.[28]

28. For a recent listing of many proposals for the development or fresh establishment of relations between the old and the new members, see, e.g., Derek Ingram, *The Commonwealth Challenge* (London, 1962); Lord Casey, *The Future of the Commonwealth*; and *The Future of the Commonwealth: A British View.*

8

Some Questions of International Law in Commonwealth Relations

Robert R. Wilson*

The Commonwealth has developed against a background of public law, some elements of which have wider than national application. Included are rules of international law, which a well-known British jurist has described as comprising "the sum of the rights that a state may claim for itself and its nationals from other states, and of the duties which in consequence it must observe toward them."[1] For the states that have become independent members of the Commonwealth such rights and duties include some that were inherited, some that flow from the fact of independence, and some that rest upon commitments made subsequently to independence. The claiming of rights and the acknowledgment of duties have of course been a matter not of turning to law for its own sake, but of utilizing the rules to serve economic, social, and political ends. The fact that for newer Commonwealth states the period of transition to viable statehood may be a long one need not preclude an examination of legal questions that have already arisen in connection with their foreign relations.

To attempt a summary statement touching *all* of the public law acknowledged by Commonwealth states in their relations *inter se* or with outside states would be to go far beyond the present purpose. It is proposed to deal selectively with four

* James B. Duke Professor of Political Science, chairman Committee on Commonwealth Studies, Duke University.
1. J. L. Brierly, *The Outlook for International Law* (London, 1944), p. 5.

subjects: (1) state succession, (2) citizenship, (3) judicial assistance, and (4) application of international law as municipal law. Each of these matters would of course merit much fuller examination than the limitations of a brief inquiry permit. Pronouncements by chiefs of state and foreign offices, positions taken in diplomatic correspondence, and decisions by courts will receive relatively greater attention than will opinions of publicists.

State Succession

A state succession—such as occurs when a community that has been a part of a larger community becomes independent —commonly gives rise to many legal questions. When there is a complete break-up (which, as some claim, was the situation as to Austria-Hungary after World War I) the situation is different from that which exists when there is simply a withdrawal of one or more parts of a continuing monarchy. In the latter case disposition of public property, liquidated or unliquidated tort claims against the new government, pension claims by civil servants who previously served the undivided state, bonded indebtedness of the former colony, and other types of claims may present questions for municipal courts, international tribunals, or diplomatic agencies. The status with respect to nationality of residents of the new state will normally require clarification. The arrangement of such matters may be affected (if not in the formal legal sense, in a psychological one) by the spirit of revolt against so-called "imperialism" or "colonialism." The emergence of a new entity may be attended by something less than an outpouring of gratitude for past benefits.[2]

The kind of succession in the Commonwealth which is here to be considered is state succession, not merely governmental

2. This is illustrated in such a statement as that of a delegate from Ghana to the United Nations. "On looking back upon the history of Africa, I remain convinced that it was unnecessary for the Europeans to colonize Africa in order, as the argument goes, to introduce the benefits of Western civilization" (Alex Quaison-Sackey, *Africa Unbound* [New York, 1963], p. 9).

succession. The recent transitions in the Commonwealth have not been abrupt ones, but there have been some incidents that have apparently occasioned sharp feeling between former officials and new authorities, such as one in Uganda which resulted in the deportation of six British persons and a formal expression of regret by Britain to Uganda.[3] For the new order in some cases there have been legal problems that would appear to be quite simple. Thus the Supreme Constitutional Court of Cyprus was asked to decide upon the legality of a criminal action against a defendant whose alleged offense had been committed during British rule, the fact of it not being discovered until after Cyprus had become independent.[4] Another case, arising in India after the partition of that country, involved a person who had been tried and convicted in a part of India that remained Indian territory after partition, but who had been sent to prison in a part of India that later was territory of Pakistan.[5]

Some expression of opinion by spokesmen for new African states in the Commonwealth has seemed to *anticipate* state succession and put in question rights under (international) claims by other states. President Nyerere, for example, has questioned the basis for Portuguese title to territory in Africa which Portugal has occupied for more than a century. Portugal's domination of Mozambique for more than a hundred years, he asserted, did not make Mozambique any less an "occupied" territory than if the Portuguese had held it for only five years. A "statement" from Lisbon that Mozambique was an integral part of Portugal, Nyerere submitted, did not move the territory from Africa to the Iberian

3. *The Times* (London), Dec. 24, 1963, p. 52.
4. Counsel for the accused argued that the act, if committed against the "Crown," was *not* committed against any authority which was any longer existent in Cyprus, but this argument did not persuade the judges. *Republic* v. *Charlambos Zacharia of Ypsonas,* Supreme Constitutional Court of Cyprus, 2 *Report of Cases,* (1961), 1-7.
5. There was in this instance an unsuccessful invocation of international law by counsel who sought an order for the prisoner's release. Under the circumstances it could not be argued that the "Crown" as a legal authority had disappeared, nor could the matter be brought under any rule of international law concerning "foreign" judgments. It was held that the accused, having been regularly charged and convicted before partition, was properly serving his sentence in what had come to be a foreign country. *Mohammad and Others* v. *The Crown Int. Law Rep.,* 1948 (published 1953), p. 72.

Some Questions of International Law 175

peninsula.[6] The position is comparable to that which India's representative at the United Nations took concerning Goa—to the effect that there had been an occupation by the Portuguese and that, notwithstanding the four and a half centuries of Portuguese rule, no valid title resulted from such occupation.[7] Traditionally, the doctrine of prescription in international law has recognized that legal title may result from long and uncontested occupation.[8]

There has been one instance in the new Commonwealth of a member state's being partitioned, with resulting effect on pre-existing treaties and on membership in a world organization. When Pakistan became a state separate from India, an equitable arrangement assigned to Pakistan obligations under treaties which called for performance in what came to be Pakistan territory, and left to India those which looked to performance in the territory that remained Indian. Pakistan did not succeed to membership in the principal world organization, but had to seek admission as a new member of the United Nations. Pakistan's position had been that the privileges of the old government of British India were inherited (automatically) by both Pakistan and India.[9]

Newly emerging states may inherit treaty rights and obligations as under the type of agreement which the United Kingdom and Ghana made in an exchange of letters on November 25, 1957. By this agreement,

(i) all obligations and responsibilities of the Government of the United Kingdom which arise from any valid international instruments shall henceforth, in so far as such instruments may be held to have an application to Ghana, be assumed by the Government of Ghana;
(ii) the rights and benefits heretofore enjoyed by the Government

6. Publication of the Tanganyika Information Service (undated), with text of the Tanganyika President's address to Norweigan students in Oslo. The President distinguished territory in South Africa from that in Mozambique, saying that an enactment by the British Parliament had made South Africa a sovereign state; but this, he said, did not affect the validity of the movements underlying the freedom movements of Africa.
7. SCOR, Plenary Meeting (987th Meeting, Dec. 18, 1961), pp. 7-10.
8. In the Venezuelan boundary dispute at the end of the nineteenth century, to which the United States was not a party but in which it assumed great interest, fifty years of uncontested possession was considered a reasonable time. C.8439, Treaty Series No. 5, 1897, G. B., Parl. Paps., 1897, CII.
9. J. M. Jones, "State Succession in the Matter of Treaties," British Year Book of International Law, XXIV (1947), 360-75.

of the United Kingdom in virtue of the application of any such international instruments to the Gold Coast shall henceforth be enjoyed by the Government of Ghana.[10]

It is obvious that such phrasing will not necessarily set at rest all questions of rights and duties under British-made treaties that were in force before the emergence of a new Commonwealth state. In some areas, for example those which have been mandates or trust territories, the limited legal capacity of the former administering authority may be a factor. Thus in Tanganyika there arose a question of the continuance in force of agreements between the United Kingdom and Belgium, made in 1921 and 1951, relating to port facilities in Kigoma and Dar es Salaam.[11] Under the Ghana-type inheritance agreement it might seem that legal duties would devolve upon an independent Tanganyika. The 1921 agreement between the United Kingdom and Belgium related to transit across Tanganyika for persons and goods coming from or going to the Congo and Ruandi Urundi; the 1951 undertaking had to do with the exchange of the site at Dar es Salaam and the provision of a new site. Concerning the obligations involved, the Prime Minister of Tanganyika said in the Tanganyika National Assembly in 1961:

We would not object to the enjoyment by foreign states of special facilities in our territory if such facilities had been granted in a manner fully compatible with our sovereign rights and our new status of complete independence. . . . No one can give away something that is not his own. When Great Britain made the 1921 Agreement it should have known that Tanganyika was not a territory under its full sovereignty and that its status was about to be regulated by

10. 287 UNTS 234. The United Kingdom made similar arrangements with Ceylon ("Ceylon: Proposals for Conferring on Ceylon fully responsible status within the British Commonwealth of Nations," Cmd. 7257, G.B., Parl. Paps. 1947-48, XXI), Cyprus ("Cyprus," Cmnd. 1093, ibid. 1959-60, XXVII), Jamaica ("Jamaica: International Obligations . . . ," Cmnd., 1918, ibid. 1962-63), and Nigeria ("Federation of Nigeria: International Rights and Obligations. . . ," Cmnd. 1214, ibid. 1960-61, XXXIV), respectively. See A. P. Lester, "State Succession to Treaties in the Commonwealth," International and Comparative Law Quarterly, 4th Ser., XII (1963), 475-507 at 503-6. Contrast statement by D. P. O'Connell, The Law of State Succession (Cambridge, 1956), p. 48.
11. "Convention between Great Britain and Belgium. . . ," Cmd. 1327, Treaty Series No. 11, G.B., Parl. Paps. 1921, XLII; "Agreement . . . ," Cmd. 8240, Treaty Series No. 38, ibid., 1950-51, XXXII.

the mandate agreement with the League of Nations. One of the principal purposes of the mandate system was to assist territories which were not yet able to stand by themselves. The words "not yet" appear in the Covenant of the League of Nations and I emphasize them. They make it clear that the mandate system was not intended to place territories under the permanent rule of the authority. . . . Under the Charter of the United Nations it is even plainer that the right of an administering authority in a trust territory will exist only for a limited period. It is clear, therefore, that in appearing to bind the territory of Tanganyika for all time, the United Kingdom was trying to do something which it did not have the power to do.[12]

The Prime Minister continued by saying that the government of Tanganyika would notify the Belgian government that the rights to leases granted by the United Kingdom were not valid, that the Belgians would have to give up the port sites, and the East African Services Organization would thereafter operate buildings and wharfs and facilities on Tanganyika's behalf. It was proposed to compensate the Belgians for their investment, after subtracting the amount which they had already recovered by way of amortization of this investment. The Prime Minister observed, concerning this last point, that all or part of the compensation might be payable to Burundi and Rwandi (as successors to Belgium); distribution of the compensation, he suggested, might be a matter for arbitration between the authorities concerned.

The international commitments affected by the "inheritance" agreements are perhaps distinguishable in a technical sense from treaties made in the past by the British in behalf of members of the old Commonwealth on the ground that, for the latter, some treaties were made before independence was fully achieved.[13] All questions as to what treaties shall bind whom will perhaps not be immediately and fully answered. Uganda, a former pro-

12. Tanganyika, National Assembly, *Debates*, 37th Sess. (6th Meeting), Nov. 30-Dec. 2, 1961, p. 10.

13. On the point that the king or queen as a contracting party to the United Kingdom treaties is a different legal person from the sovereign as contracting on behalf of other Commonwealth states that are monarchies, see A. B. Keith, *The Constitutional Law of the British Dominions* (London, 1939), p. 528, and D. P. O'Connell, "The Crown in the British Commonwealth," *Int. and Comp. Law Quar.*, VI (1957), 103-25.

tectorate, provides an example of a new Commonwealth member that has sought to arrive at a list of its treaties in force. That the rules of international law are acknowledged in this connection is indicated in the wording of a communication sent to the Secretary-General of the United Nations on February 12, 1963:

Prior to Uganda attaining independence . . . treaty relationships were entered into, on its behalf, by the Government of the United Kingdom. The Government of Uganda now wishes to make clear its position in regard to obligations arising from those treaties entered into prior to 9th October, 1962, by the protecting Government. . . .

2. In respect of all treaties validly concluded by the United Kingdom on behalf of the Uganda Protectorate, or validly applied or extended by the former to the latter, before the 9th October, 1962, the Government of Uganda will continue on a basis of reciprocity to apply the terms of such treaties from the time of its independence, that is to say, 9th October, 1962, until the 31st December, 1963, unless such treaties are abrogated, or modified by agreement with the other high contracting parties before the 31st December, 1963. At the expiry of this period, or of any subsequent extension of the period which may be notified in like manner, the Government of Uganda will regard such treaties, *unless they must by the application of the rules of customary international law be regarded as otherwise, surviving*, as having terminated.

3. The declaration in the previous paragraph extends equally to multilateral treaties; and during this period of review any party to a multilateral treaty which was validly applied or extended to Uganda before the 9th October, 1962, may on a basis of reciprocity as indicated above, rely on the terms of such treaty as against the Government of Uganda.

4. It is the earnest hope of the Government of Uganda that during the aforementioned period, the normal processes of diplomatic negotiations will enable it to reach satisfactory accord with the States concerned upon the possibility of the continuance or modification of such treaties. In the case of multilateral treaties, the Government of Uganda intends, before the 31st December, 1963, or such later date as may be subsequently notified in like manner, to indicate . . . the steps it wishes to take, whether by way of confirmation of termination, or confirmation of succession or accession, in regard to each such instrument.[14]

14. Sess. Paper No. 2 of 1963, *Treaty Obligations.* (Emphasis added.) Certain changes were made in the Constitution of Uganda by the "Constitution of

There has been occasion for a judicial finding that a party to a treaty has become extinct. This involved an extradition treaty which the British government made with the Tonk state in 1869. When the case was before the Supreme Court of India that tribunal had to decide whether application of the Extradition Act of 1903 (as to an appellant who lived in what had been Tonk) could proceed, notwithstanding a provision in the Act whereby nothing should derogate from the provisions of any treaty for the extradition of offenders. There was a question of whether the treaty had lapsed as from August 16, 1947, when Tonk became a member of the Dominion of India. The Court held that Tonk had ceased to exist and the term "subject" of Tonk no longer had any meaning.[15]

The continuance of rights and of obligations under treaties that were originally made by the government of Great Britain and that have subsequently come to be applied in the wider territory have naturally involved understandings with "third" states. The handling of commitments involved is illustrated in diplomatic correspondence of the United States with respect to the Anglo-American Extradition Treaty of 1931 as applied by a note of 1939 to named Malay states. By agreement between the United States and the Federation of Malaya in 1958 the treaty provisions were to apply to all the states of the Malayan Federation. Furthermore, when Malaysia came into existence five years later (with the addition to the federation of three new states), all external relations were held by the government in Kuala Lumpur to be continued by Malaysia; no new recognitions were necessary by outside states, since diplomatic relations which had existed with Malaya were held to apply automatically to Malaysia.[16]

Uganda (First Amendment) Act," which is No. 1 of 1963, but Sec. 46 of this Act made it clear that any treaty, agreement, or convention with any country or international organization made or affirmed by Uganda on or after the 9th Oct., 1963 (the day prior to the date of the amending Act), or to which Uganda was otherwise a party on Oct. 8, 1963, was not to be affected by the constitutional changes made in the amending Act.

15. *Babu Ram Saksena* v. *The State, Int. Law Rep., 1950* (1956), p. 11.

16. M. M. Whiteman, *Digest of International Law* (In progress; Washington: Department of State, 1963-), II (1963), 999-1000.

It is obvious that state succession may give rise to still other questions, such as those involving citizenship, elements of municipal law and, generally, responsibility of succeeding states to foreign governments for treatment (by the succeeded state) of aliens and alien-owned property. The first two of the topics here suggestively mentioned invite more detailed consideration.

Citizenship

The breakup of the British Empire in the twentieth century would have been less complete (in a practical sense) had some vestige of a common nationality been retained. There was a considerable effort in this direction. From the period of a common code, the transition had been to a common status within the Empire, i.e., the status of British subject. In certain situations a British subject who sojourned in a Commonwealth state other than his own (i.e., other than that in which he principally exercised the privilege of citizenship and acknowledged obligations attaching thereto) might be permitted in the other Commonwealth state to exercise such privileges as that of the suffrage. He might also be held, by the other state, to compulsory military service, if municipal law provided for this.

The Canadian Citizenship Act of 1946 marked the beginning of a new, although somewhat looser, arrangement than that which had existed in the Empire under the common code. The British Nationality Act of 1948 mentioned not only British subjects and Commonwealth citizens, but also another category of persons (although a transitional one), i.e., those who were British subjects without citizenship.[17] The British Nationality Act of 1964 makes provision for resumption of United Kingdom citizenship by individuals who have previously renounced it, and also

17. Robert R. Wilson and Robert E. Clute, "Commonwealth Citizenship and Common Status," *Amer. Jour. Int. Law*, LVII (1963), 566-587. On the non-recognition of a common nationality status in Ceylon, although British subjects are not defined as "aliens," see statement by Sir Kenneth Roberts-Wray in J.N.D. Anderson, ed., *Changing Law in Developing Countries* (London, 1963), p. 56.

sets out conditions under which such citizenship may be renounced.[18]

The adoption by various states in the Commonwealth of a republican form of government (instead of a monarchical one) presumably had some psychological effect upon the concept of "subject." While Eire upon becoming a republic was constrained to leave the Commonwealth fold (although its nationals continue to have many of the benefits which citizens of Commonwealth states enjoy), republican models in India and Pakistan seem to have been achieved with no great stir in other Commonwealth countries. Ghana, Cyprus, Nigeria and others have followed a similar course. While in the new republics of the Commonwealth the classification of persons as "subjects" was perhaps less natural than in the states retaining the monarchical form, there was considerable latitude within which legislative policy could accord to "citizens" of other Commonwealth states (or to "subjects" in the broader sense) treatment more favorable than that accorded to ordinary aliens. In this matter, however, there is complete self-determination by the respective Commonwealth states. The very optionality which exists makes it possible for a state such as India to set conditions upon the enjoyment by persons of another Commonwealth state of better-than-ordinary-alien treatment. It was perhaps inevitable that reciprocity should be a basic condition set by states that had in the past protested against restrictive (and particularly white) immigration policies. Practice such as that of Australia, which in the past had occasioned sharp discussion at Imperial Conferences, did not terminate with the attainment of statehood by Commonwealth communities that had in the past resented such policies.[19]

Toward the end of the decade under review even the United Kingdom broke a long tradition of allowing free entry to British subjects from other parts of the Commonwealth when Parliament enacted the Commonwealth Immigration Act, 1962.[20] This provides a quota basis for admission of citizens from other Com-

18. 12 & 13 Eliz. II. c.24.
19. Wilson and Clute, pp. 576-81.
20. 10 & 11 Eliz. II.

monwealth countries who have in view no employment in
Britain, have no special skills, and are unable to support themselves without working. Whatever regret there might be on policy
or sentimental grounds for such legislation, there is no conflict
with international law, which still leaves to each state the determination of what aliens shall enter its territory. Nor does that law
preclude discrimination. Commonwealth states may therefore
continue to accord in this matter more favorable treatment to
persons from other Commonwealth countries (and even to Eire,
which is not a Commonwealth country but for some purposes
is treated as if it were one) than that accorded to ordinary aliens.
In the utilization of the most-favored-nation clause Commonwealth states for several decades have followed the practice
of inserting the limiting word "foreign" before "nation" in order
to protect imperial preferences. So far as international law is
concerned, most-favored-nation treatment (or any variant of it)
still flows from agreement and not from customary rules.

As to discrimination directly affecting persons rather than
goods, the development of a distinctive nationality for each
Commonwealth state has not in itself precluded the distinction
made in legislative policy between citizens of other Commonwealth states and "other" foreigners. The three-tier classification
—citizens of the local state, persons identified with other Commonwealth states, and other persons—is a reminder of the dream
of one common status within the Commonwealth, which was
never completely realized. For the purpose of establishment
matters, such as the practice of professions, distinctions may still
assume considerable practical importance.

In the period since World War II Great Britain has, in its
handling of reclamations with states such as Yugoslavia and
Hungary, included clauses which permitted the British government to espouse the claims of broad categories of British subjects
and Commonwealth citizens. This has not meant, however, that
the now-independent states of the Commonwealth could not
themselves bring reclamations in behalf of their respective citizens; in some instances they have done so.[21]

21. Wilson and Clute, pp. 581-85.

The legal status of particular persons or categories of persons in Commonwealth states has sometimes been a subject of judicial determination. For example, in the case of the Japanese Canadians, involving war measures which Canada had taken, the Judicial Committee of the Privy Council held that Canada could deprive the persons concerned of their status as Canadian citizens, but that legislation under view would deprive them of their status as British subjects only *in so far as the law of Canada was concerned.*[22] In a case before the Supreme Court of Trinidad and Tobago (decided before the country became an independent member of the Commonwealth) persons who were citizens of the United Kingdom and colonies were found not to be citizens of Trinidad and Tobago in the sense of being entitled to enjoy any special rights or privileges reserved therein for those who belonged to the Colony by virtue of the qualifications specified in the Colony's Immigration (Restriction) Ordinance. Answering applicants' argument, the Court said that "the power residing in Colonial legislatures to over-ride the common law is derived from the Colonial Laws Validity Act, 1865, which remains unaffected by the 1948 Act. . . ."[23]

A development in the Commonwealth during the latter part of the period under review involved status of persons in an area that has recently emerged from trusteeship (although its people have not assumed complete control of their own affairs). As of January 1, 1962, the constitution of the independent state of Western Samoa came into force. By a treaty of friendship with the government of Western Samoa effective August 1, 1962, the government of New Zealand undertook the diplomatic protection of Western Samoans and the performance of consular functions on their behalf.[24] The Citizenship Ordinance enacted by Western Samoa's Legislative Assembly on September 8,

22. *Co-operative Committee on Japanese Canadians* v. *Attorney-General for Canada* [1947] A.C. 87.
23. *Musson and Musson* v. *Rodriguea, Int. Law Rep.*, 1955 (1960), p. 60. Cf. decision in *Sudali Andy Asary* v. *Van den Dreesen* (Ceylon Supreme Court, Feb. 22, 1952), *Int. Law Rep.*, 1952 (1957), p. 61.
24. New Zealand Treaty Series, 1962, No. 5. See also "Samoa Comes of Age: The Development of Independence," *The Round Table*, Sept., 1961, pp. 347-64.

1959, having made no mention of British subjects or citizens of other Commonwealth communities, the Western Samoan citizens will presumably be assimilated to citizens of New Zealand (for the purpose of their status in other Commonwealth states) during the continuance in force of the 1962 treaty.

Judicial Assistance

Between states that are members of a federal union or a confederation, as well as between completely independent entities, there is need for co-operation looking to effective administration of justice in municipal courts. At least some of the processes involved come within private (rather than public) international law. Others proceed on the basis of treaties, so far as legal obligations are involved. Between newly independent states there may be, without treaty commitments, hold-over arrangements dating from the time when all were under a common sovereignty. Such arrangements may serve in lieu of formal treaties and customary international rules. This has been and is the case in the Commonwealth.

One of the yields to people of the Commonwealth from their unique association has been the working out of a statutory basis for the two types of judicial assistance to be mentioned here—the enforcement in one jurisdiction of a judgment that has been obtained in another, and the return of accused persons to the country where they have been charged with crime. On the enforcement of foreign judgments there is no universally applicable rule of customary international law. A rule that has been widely applied, as, for example, by the Supreme Court of the United States,[25] is that of reciprocity. This, however, is open to the valid objection that it fails to take into account the intrinsic merit of the judgment or the competence of the court from which it emanates. Without reciprocity, the judgment may be considered as prima facie evidence of an enforceable decision. Practice in the Commonwealth has developed what would appear

25. *Hilton* v. *Guyot*, 159 U.S. 113 (1895).

to be a rational system for the recognition of a judgment obtained elsewhere within the Commonwealth and invoked for the purpose of securing enforcement by the court before which it is invoked or for the purpose of evidence.[26] United Kingdom legislation of 1920 and 1933[27] provides a set of criteria which may be adopted by any Commonwealth state or any province within such a state. This system of registration and enforcement has been widely, but not universally, adopted.[28]

As is well known, extradition between Commonwealth members still proceeds upon the basis of a British statute, the Fugitive Offenders Act, 1881.[29] There is under this system clear divergence from general international treaty practice. The most striking divergence lies in the absence (from the statute) of provisions making exceptions for fugitives whose offenses are political in character. That the omission of such a clause was intentional is shown from the legislative history of the Act. To a question raised on the point in the House of Commons on August 20, 1881, the attorney general replied:

Of course, the reason why, as between Nations, the one did not recognize political offences committed against the Government of the other, was because the one Government did not inquire into the laws of the other. But, as regarded the Mother Country and her Colonies, the authority of the Crown extended over the whole.[30]

In the decade under review this part of the 1881 Act received much attention in connection with the return from Great Britain

26. H. E. Read, *Recognition and Enforcement of Foreign Judgments in the Common Law Units of the British Commonwealth* "Harvard Studies in the Conflict of Laws," II (Cambridge, Mass., 1938).

27. 10 and 11 Geo. V, c. 81; 23 & 24 Geo. V, c. 13.

28. A study by Don C. Piper, to be published in a volume of the Duke University Commonwealth-Studies Center, indicates the extent to which the statutory plan is in use. See J. E. S. Fawcett, *The British Commonwealth in International Law* (London, 1963), pp. 63-65, on the contrast between the existing system in the Commonwealth and an arrangement by which orders and judgments of a European court might be treated as orders or judgments of a court of co-ordinate jurisdiction with the High Court in England.

29. 44 & 45 Vict. c. 69. By legislation of 1916 (5 & 6 Geo. V, c. 39) there was extension to protected states. For application of the legislation, see Robert E. Clute, "Law and Practice in Commonwealth Extradition," *Amer. Jour. of Comp. Law*, VIII, No. 1 (1959), 15-28.

30. 3 *Parl. Debs.*, CCLXV, 599.

to Nigeria of Chief Anthony Enahoro, an ex-minister of the Western Region of Nigeria. Treason and felony come within the offenses for which persons can be returned to the requesting country under the Act, and the home secretary has discretion as to the surrender of an individual requested. Enahoro's application for habeas corpus having been dismissed and likewise a petition for leave to appeal, the question was raised in Parliament of whether the Fugitive Offenders Act should not be changed so that Commonwealth citizens would be as favorably treated as aliens in extradition cases. There was a rumor that Nigeria threatened to break off relations with Great Britain if Enahoro were not returned. The Attorney General of Great Brtiain reportedly said that, since there could be an appeal from Nigeria to the Judicial Committee of the Privy Council, there was (at that time) the possibility of a review of judicial action against Enahoro after his trial in Nigeria. The fugitive was returned. The Home Secretary said he proposed, in consultation with the secretary of state for the colonies, to examine the 1881 Act afresh from the point of view of its relationship to the future pattern of the Commonwealth.[31]

The Enahoro incident seemed to suggest need for a change in the Act or for a shift to the ordinary international law standard through the conclusion of appropriate treaties. The reason for exceptions in the case of political offenders would seem to be as strong as it was when John Stuart Mill assigned such great importance to it.[32] The conclusion is reinforced if account is taken of the trend (as developed since the inclusion of wording on the matter in the Universal Declaration of Human Rights) toward some realistic definition and establishment of a right of asylum.[33]

31. *The Times*, Jan. 15, 1963 (12d), Jan. 16, 1963 (12d), Feb. 7, 1963 (17a), March 13, 1963 (15c), March 25, 1963 (11c), March 29, 1963 (12c), April 10, 1963 (13c).

32. *Autobiography* (3rd ed.; London, 1874), pp. 299-300. It might be argued in opposition to this view (that political offenders should not be extraditable) that this would permit one who, for example, had been a spy in Australia to find refuge in the United Kingdom. Under present conditions, however, the act of spying in Australia might be much less dangerous to Western security than would such an act in the United States. There is, under international law, no obligation to surrender fugitives, apart from treaties.

33. See Alona E. Evans, "Reflections upon the Political Offense in International Practice," *Amer. Jour. Int. Law*, LVII (1963), 1-24.

Enforcement as Municipal Law

The decade under review, while marked by widespread supersession of British governing authority by local legislative and executive authority, has not been a period of complete replacement of municipal law previously enforced in the respective new states. The very fact of statehood has implications for public law, international as well as constitutional. The effect of transition to statehood has been described, in the case of Israel, as follows:

The declaration of independence gave the new State access to the international laws and customs which all states enjoy by virtue of their sovereignty, and enriched its legal system by the accepted principles of the law of nations. We no longer need to obtain those principles second-hand, through specially provided secondary channels, for today we are able, by virtue of Israel's membership in the family of nations, to go to the fountain-head by virtue of the closing passage of the . . . Law and Administration Ordinance (which prescribes the law that is to be in force in Israel after the declaration of independence "with such modifications as may result from the establishment of the State and its authorities") or even without that section and without any reference to it.[34]

In 1774 the Continental Congress in America declared "that the respective colonies are entitled to the common law of England. . . ."[35] In the case of new states that were previously British colonies and are now Commonwealth members, it is instructive to note (1) the manner and extent to which the common law of England was made applicable in the respective colonial areas, and (2) the law of nations as a possible element of the common law as thus extended. On the first point the record is fairly clear, as illustrative enactments will indicate. On the second point legalists appear to be not completely agreed.

34. *Stampfer* v. *Atty.-General*, decided Jan. 4, 1956, by the Supreme Court of Israel sitting as a Court of Criminal Appeals, *Int. Law Rep.*, *1956*, p. 284. On the general subject, see O'Connell, *The Law of State Succession*, pp. 213-16, and Shabtai Rosenne, "The Effect of Change of Sovereignty upon Municipal Law," *British Year Book of Int. Law*, XXVII (1950), 267.

35. *Journals of the American Congress from 1774 to 1788* (4 vols.; Washington: Way and Gideon, 1823), I, 21.

In the case of Jamaica, after considerable uncertainty in the last half of the seventeenth century the situation appears to have been regularized by the British Parliament's confirming that the laws of England applied in the island.[36] The common law of England was apparently extended to the Gold Coast by Parliament as the law existed on July 24, 1874, but the Criminal Code of 1892 excluded the common law.[37] In Northern and Southern Nigeria were made applicable the common law, the doctrines of equity, and the statutes of general application in England on January 1, 1900; native custom was to be regarded in proceedings between natives.[38] The common law of England was extended to Tobago; also in force in that island were local ordinances; some of the latter introduced English statute law. Trinidad and Tobago were united by an Order in Council of November 17, 1888, which was made in pursuance of the Trinidad and Tobago Act, 1887.[39] In Trinidad Spanish law that had been in force prior to cession of the island to Great Britain appears to have been gradually displaced by local enactments; the latter are reported to have been shaped along the lines of English law; however, as late as the early part of the twentieth century elements of the old (Spanish) law still governed certain relationships in private law.[40]

The British acquired Sierra Leone not by conquest or cession but by occupancy. It had at first the status of a "plantation," with the common law of England prevailing, along with the statute law comprising ordinances, certain imperial acts, and all acts of general application in force in England on January 1,

36. See Bryan Edwards, The History, Civil and Commercial, of the British Colonies in the West Indies (3rd ed., 3 vols.; London, 1801), I, 215-220.
37. William Burge, Commentaries on Colonial and Foreign Laws, as reprinted in Colonial Laws and Courts, with a Sketch of the Legal Systems of the World and Tables of Conditions of Appeal to the Privy Council, ed. A. W. Renton and G. G. Phillimore (London, 1907), p. 264.
38. Ibid., p. 268. On the goal of attaining a fully integrated "common law" for all the citizens of a given colony, see T. Oliwale Elias, British Colonial Law (London, 1962), p. 299.
39. 50 & 51 Vict., c. 44 (which repealed, insofar as it related to Tobago, 39 & 40 Vict., c. 47).
40. Burge, as in n.37, pp. 247, 248.

1880.[41] In the maritime provinces of Ceylon, where Holland governed before ceding the area to Great Britain in the early nineteenth century, the Roman-Dutch law applied. This was modified by local enactments. Under English rule it was also modified by judicial decisions that followed in certain cases rules of English law. The resulting body of law apparently applied to all inhabitants except in cases where personal law was applicable.[42]

Extensions of the common law to colonial areas could acquire significance for international law through Blackstone's doctrine that the law of nations is a part of the common law of England.[43] With the exception of those areas (such as Southern Rhodesia, the Transvaal, the Orange Free State, Natal and Quebec) where the civil law had prevailed prior to British rule, courts in British colonies from an early date applied some law which, according to a widely held view, embodied as one of its elements the law of nations. There resulted for courts (1) a rule of construction and (2) a rule of evidence. If there were more than one possible interpretation of a statute, that interpretation would presumably prevail which was consistent with the law of nations. When invoked, a rule of international law would not have to be proved in the same manner that "foreign" law must be proved when invoked in a municipal court.[44]

Another method of arranging the relationship between international law and municipal law is by the inclusion of wording in constitutions. There is considerable variance in the language of such provisions.[45] Instead of a clause of definite incorporation

41. *Ibid.*, p.273, citing Ordinance No. 14 of 1904. See also *Jour. of Comp. Legis.*, I, 181.

42. *Ibid.*, pp. 186-87.

43. Blackstone, *Commentaries on the Law of England* (1876 ed.; Philadelphia), Bk. IV, chap. v, pp. 6-7.

44. Hersch Lauterpacht, "Is International Law a Part of the Law of England?" *Transactions of the Grotius Society*, XXV (1940), 51-88. Cf. D. C. Vanek, "Is International Law Part of the Law of Canada?" *Univ. of Toronto Law Jour.*, VIII (1949-50), 241-297. Contrast W. S. Holdsworth, "The Relation of English to International Law," *Minnesota Law Rev.*, XXVI (1942), 141-52, and statement by J. E. S. Fawcett, *British Commonwealth in International Law*, p. 18, to the effect that there is no general addition or incorporation of international law into English law.

45. Examples, some of them from Commonwealth states, are mentioned in

there may be a general directive. India's Constitution, for example, sets forth in its article 51(c) that the state shall "foster
respect for international law and treaty obligations. . . ." As
to the effect of this, one publicist, after noting that according to
Articles 12 and 36 of the constitution the word "state" in 51(c)
includes the Government and Parliament of India and the
government and legislature of each of the states in that country,
suggests that the wording of 51(c) is of little significance to
Indian judges in their application of the Blackstone doctrine.
He adds, however, that "as the doctrine is part of common law
which became . . . part of Indian law under British rule, the judges
tend to accept the same inter-relationship between municipal
law and international law as prevails in English law." He goes
on to say that it would be difficult to imagine that the judges
could ignore the doctrine. Taking a specific subject for the
purpose of illustration, he notes that while there is no general
statute on diplomatic immunities in India, foreign envoys do in
fact enjoy privileges which international law requires.[46] In the
case of any given subject matter the appeal to common law alone
would not be effective unless it could be shown that there was
existing international law that had, through the process of incorporation in the common law, become the law of the state.

   Aside from customary law that may be invoked in Commonwealth courts in the manner that has been suggested, there is
also the matter of treaties given the force of law under constitutional arrangements. The latter may make treaties a part of
the law of the land (as in Cyprus, where the condition of reciprocity on the part of the other party state must be met), or
may (as in Canada) assign to treaties no effect as parts of
municipal law unless there has been implementation of the
treaties through municipal legislation. A Canadian judge in

Robert R. Wilson, "International Law in New Constitutions," *Amer. Jour. Int.
Law,* LVIII (1964), 432-36.
   46. C. H. Alexandrowicz, *Constitutional Developments in India* (Melbourne
and London, 1957), p. 215. See also, on the relationship of English common
and statute law to Indian law, M. C. Setalvad, *The Common Law in India* (London, 1960), p. 117, and M. K. Nawaz, "International Law in the Contemporary
Practice of India," *Proc. of the Amer. Soc. of Int. Law, 1963* (Washington, 1963),
pp. 275-290.

1932 did make a statement to the effect that for the purpose
of municipal courts a treaty has the "effect of law, quite independently of legislation," but a court in a subsequent case declared this to be unacceptable without important qualifications.[47]
The fact that a state (whose constitution does not specify that a
treaty is a part of the law of the land) has not implemented the
treaty through legislation would not change the fact that the
treaty would continue to be binding in the international law
sense. There may be constitutional questions as to the meaning
of statutory provisions referring to treaties, as will appear from a
decision of the Supreme Court of New South Wales in 1956, concerning the meaning of the words "arising under any treaty"
in Australia's Trading-with-the-Enemy Act.[48]

Conclusion

It might be argued that there has been little that is distinctive
about the positions that Commonwealth states have taken with
respect to the law of nations. To the extent, however, that this
law depends upon some sense of community (however short
the present international reality falls of being such a community)
the background of recent Commonwealth history suggests a situation conducive to co-operation through legal arrangements that
are wider than national in their application. Little may be gained
through praising the unique association which is the Commonwealth as the "first united nations organization," as an enthusiastic member of the Canadian Parliament once did.[49] Yet
the experience of the past decade would seem to indicate some
special proclivity on the part of these states for handling their
relations with one another and with outside states on the rational
basis which legalism presupposes.

47. *Bitter* v. *Sec. of State of Canada*, Exchequer Ct., Canada, 1944, *Int.
Law Rep.*, 1943-45 (1946).
48. *Bluett* v. *Fadden*, *Int. Law Rep.*, 1956 (1960), p. 477. The decision is
the subject of comment by Fawcett, *British Commonwealth in International Law*,
pp. 25-26.
49. Canada, *Parl. Debs.* (Commons), 2nd Sess. (20th Parl.), I, 797, April 11,
1946.

In the past Commonwealth states have in their relations *inter se* operated under various British-provided arrangements, at least some of which would now seem to be outmoded in light of modern international practice; the experience with extradition provides illustration. In contrast, the course followed with respect to citizenship (despite continuing resentments in parts of the Commonwealth concerning racist policies and restrictive immigration) may point the way to constructive international practice. The retention of a kind of common status as to citizenship, while capable of being made the basis for discrimination against "foreign" persons in such matters as professional work and shipping, suggests the possibility of a stage of development in the wider international community when alienage will be less of a bar to rights and to opportunity than it presently is.

It was to be expected that the new Commonwealth states in Asia and Africa would reflect the general feeling against colonialism and imperialism that has found such sharp expression at the mid-twentieth century. As it affects international law, this feeling has been directed against such a concept as that of prescriptive right. The new states have naturally been more receptive to the idea, which appears to be widely held by writers on international law in England, that in general a new state enters the family of nations without being unduly bound by pre-existing treaties that have applied to its territory.

Distinctive citizenship has been achieved in the respective Commonwealth states, but there is room for more effective arrangements (and perhaps dramatic innovations) in certain forms of judicial assistance, such as recognition and enforcement of foreign judgments. The rules of international law are not static, and adherence to them does not commit states to indefinite subscription to norms that, through force of custom, have become outmoded.

In the decade under review Commonwealth states have at times been ranged on different sides of issues touching international law, such as those in the Suez crisis.[50] Some of them

50. That this did not preclude their co-operation with each other is illustrated in Canada's extension of good offices to Australia; with the concurrence

have at other times been vocal in behalf of modernizing the law on such matters as territorial waters and fisheries rights. Their spokesmen have on occasion had part in efforts to influence the development of international law on responsibility of states, diplomatic immunities, and rights in polar regions.[51] The English common law heritage with its claimed ingredient of rules that touch international legal rights could conceivably be a continuing and significant factor in the further extension and strengthening of the existing body of international law.

---

of the Egyptian government, the government of Canada agreed to the attachment of an Australian official to the Canadian Embassy in Cairo, the arrangement being designed to assist the return to Australian owners of property that had been sequestrated by order of the Egyptian government. *Current Notes* (Australia, Department of External Affairs), XXIX, No. 7 (July, 1958), 432.

51. Three Commonwealth states are parties to the 1959 treaty concerning Antarctica (402 UNTS 71) and to the multilateral agreement on measures (effective in 1963) in furtherance of principles and objectives of that treaty (T.I.A.S. [U.S.A.] 5274).

· 9 ·

Commonwealth Military Relations

*Alastair Buchan**

I

"Time as he grows old teaches many lessons," wrote Aeschylus. And one that is relevant to our purpose is that it is a mistake to make judgments about the future of so plastic an association as the Commonwealth on the basis of a particular conjunction of policies and events. For twenty years it has been accepted that the reality and value of the Commonwealth is not to be measured by its effectiveness as an organization for mutual defense. Ten years ago it seemed probable that the development of regional alliances to which some members of the Commonwealth adhered but which were rejected by others might undermine the central foundation of political co-operation and consultation on which the validity of the idea of Commonwealth rested. Writing in 1959, Mr. Brian Tunstall admirably summarized the sense of doubt about where the development of NATO, SEATO, and the other regional alliances might lead the Commonwealth.

The whole idea of defence by regions has about it a disruptive quality in so far as arrangements entered into by certain members of the Commonwealth are seen as unnecessary and dangerous by others. To this the best answer may be that the survival of the whole depends on the survival of the parts, and that the strains involved by creating these organisations are part of the necessary price for the Commonwealth's continued existence.[1]

* Director, The Institute for Strategic Studies, London.
1. W. C. B. Tunstall, *The Commonwealth and Regional Defence* ("Common-

Yet, as matters have turned out, these forebodings have not been entirely justified. Developments within the two great power blocs have somewhat blurred the distinctions between the militarily aligned and the non-aligned members of the Commonwealth. National irredentism has in some cases, notably East Africa and southern Asia, become as much a threat to the peace as Communism. The development of a complex strategic stalemate between the United States and the Soviet Union has limited the freedom of military action of the great powers and has tended to place a premium on the services of those who can act in an emergency, several of whom, notably Canada and India, are members of the Commonwealth. And the rise of many new nation states, both within and outside the Commonwealth, has laid emphasis on a new aspect of defense co-operation, helping to assure the internal stability of young political regimes as well as to defend them against external enemies, to which the common practices and techniques evolved within the Commonwealth have an especial relevance. Ten or even five years ago, one might have been justified in assuming that if the Commonwealth survived the doubling of its membership and did succeed in creating a viable system of collaboration among multiracial societies in five continents, the factor of military co-operation would be of marginal significance. I am not certain that this view is any longer correct, and I will attempt in this paper to justify a different opinion.

II

Ten years ago, the reorientation of Commonwealth defense arrangements on the basis of regional alliances which had been foreshadowed in the British White Paper of 1946,[2] when the ghost of the Committee of Imperial Defence was laid to rest, had been completed. Britain and Canada had for six years been

wealth Papers," No. VI [London: Institute of Commonwealth Studies, The Athlone Press, 1959]).

2. "Statement Relating to Defence," Cmnd. 6743, G. B., *Parl. Paps.,* 1945-46, XX.

members of NATO. Australia and New Zealand had since 1951 been allied to the United States in the ANZUS Security Pact. In the previous year, 1954, Britain and Pakistan had become linked by treaty, as well as the unspecified obligations of the Commonwealth, to Australia and New Zealand (and to the United States, France, Thailand, and the Philippines) by the Manila Treaty which created the South East Asia Treaty Organization. In 1955 itself Britain and Pakistan had acquired mutual defense obligations to Persia, Turkey, and Iraq under what was then called the Baghdad Pact (rechristened CENTO in 1959 after the withdrawal of Iraq). Thus by 1955 Britain had become linked to Canada by treaty in a defense system that embraced North America, western Europe, and the Mediterranean countries in a highly organized alliance with an automatic provision for collective action and a permanent central military command system. She had become linked to Australia, New Zealand (who had earlier acquired a formal military guarantee of military assistance from the United States), and to Pakistan in a much less highly formalized security system covering southern Asia, and again to Pakistan in a similar arrangement covering Russia's southern flank. The other two members of the original multiracial Commonwealth, India and Ceylon, were in none of these alliances and disapproved of them.

This system of regional alliances has remained unaltered, as far as membership is concerned, ever since. Though the number of sovereign countries in the Commonwealth has almost tripled since then, none of the new members has adhered to the multilateral treaty systems that came into being in the first ten years of the cold war. One further potential regional arrangement, for Africa and the southern Middle East, foreshadowed in the Anglo-South African agreement of 1955, gradually fell to bits as it became clear that South African racial policies would permit of no co-operation with central African nations, as the Central African Federation collapsed, and when South Africa left the Commonwealth in 1961. A second attempt to develop a more explicit defense arrangement with an African member of the Commonwealth, though in a more local context, proved abortive when the British-Nigerian defense agreement was abrogated in January, 1962, fifteen months after Nigeria became independent.

Although the British concept of Commonwealth defense had since 1946 been based on an explicit encouragement of regional defense associations, the actual system that had emerged by 1955 had only an incidental relationship to the Commonwealth. The prime mover in its creation had been the United States (except for the abortive African arrangement and for ANZUS, which in effect had been an Australian condition for acceptance of the Japanese Peace Treaty), and the military and political center of the system was clearly Washington rather than London. Moreover the United States had no great patience at that time with emphasis on the value of the Commonwealth association. It looked as if Britain's strategic or military relationship to another Commonwealth country might be significant only insofar as both of them had a close relationship with the United States, and as if the latter had entirely inherited Britain's mantle as the prime guarantor of the security of the other Commonwealth countries with the Strategic Air Command as the successor force to the Royal Navy.

Most events in the later 1950's reinforced the view that any unified conception of Commonwealth defense with Britain as its center was at an end. For one thing it became doubtful whether she had the means to come to the assistance of a Commonwealth country in an emergency, even though up to 1960 she still had a large number of overseas garrisons. Not the least deplorable aspect of the Suez fiasco was the revelation that Britain's capacity for swift sea and air reinforcement, even in the Mediterranean, as well as her amphibious capability, had become sadly run down in the postwar years. One result of Suez was the imposition of the Arab air barrier and Egypt's control of the canal, which complicated the reinforcement of the Indian Ocean area, and this in turn reinforced the latent doubts of Australia and New Zealand as to whether Britain could play an effective part in SEATO or in their own defense in the event of a crisis in southern Asia. The attempt to develop a secure route by means of a defense agreement with Libya, staging rights in the Sudan, and the construction of an air base at Gan in the Maldive Islands seemed a poor substitute for the old imperial highroads.

Moreover, until 1962 British defense policy seemed to imply that the security of Britain's Commonwealth partners, especially those not linked to her by mutual security treaties, was sinking in her list of priorities. The Five Year Plan launched in 1957 was based on the twin assumptions that conscription was to be ended as soon as possible and that Britain must regain her influence in the world by increased emphasis on her nuclear striking force. The 1957 White Paper scarcely mentioned Commonwealth defense and subsequent ones made only a cursory reference to it, until in 1960 no mention at all was included in the government's annual statement of its defense policy. The focus of British debate became increasingly centered upon the problems of constructing a credible nuclear force, of the strategic relationship with the United States, and the defense of Europe and its implications. To the other Commonwealth governments, expenditure of £600 million on the Bluestreak missile hardly seemed to reinforce their own security, while the reduction of the British Army from 375,000 to 175,000 affected it directly. In 1958 the idea of an overall British plan for the defense of the Middle East was officially abandoned in favor of bases in Cyprus and Aden, and the imperial garrisons began their retreat from Africa, the Caribbean, and the Far East. Fifteen years after the war it was commonly assumed by defense experts in London that by the end of the 1960's there would be no overseas garrisons except in Hong Kong, and possibly in Aden; that Britain would become primarily a European military power, with some shadowy system of floating bases in the Indian Ocean; and that the vacuum left by her withdrawals would be filled by the United States. This sense, throughout the Commonwealth, that British defense was becoming increasingly NATO-centered was reinforced by the British government's growing preoccupation with its relationship to Europe which led to the decision to seek entry to the European Economic Community in July, 1961.

The only exception to this general trend in British and Commonwealth policy concerned the defense of Malaya. Since 1953 an informal system of co-operation entitled ANZAM has existed between Britain and Australia, New Zealand, and Malaya. In 1955, two years before Malaya became independent, a Commonwealth strategic reserve consisting of a British-Australian-New Zealand infantry brigade was created and stationed in Malaya and was later supplemented by an Australian air wing. This was negotiated between the three Prime Ministers at the Commonwealth Conference of 1955. In 1957 Britain negotiated with Malaya an agreement on External Defence and Mutual Assistance under which she assumed specific responsibility for assisting in the external defense of Malaya and the training of the Malayan forces. In return Malaya granted Britain the right to station forces on her territory with special safeguards that they would not be used from Malayan bases for SEATO purposes without her consent. Australia and New Zealand associated themselves with this agreement. The doubtful element at the time of its signature was how long it would be possible for Britain to continue to remain in Singapore, and how useful a force she could then maintain in Malaya without it.

III

The note of doubt about the reconcilability of a series of local defense systems with the broader ideal of Commonwealth which I have quoted from Mr. Brian Tunstall is qualified by the following passage:

On the other hand it would be erroneous to suppose that the members of the Commonwealth possess no capacity for joint strategic planning even though the means to pursue such plans may lie in a different sphere. Consultation and inter-communication at the political level, together with an elaborate system of joint services representation in each other's countries, staff conferences, interchange of officers for training and interchanges of technical information, serve to help those members of the Commonwealth who wish it, to keep in close strategic touch with each other.[3]

It is precisely because the fabric of joint training and military co-operation has remained largely unaffected by the break up of the Commonwealth into regional defense systems, into aligned and non-aligned countries, that, as its external environment has begun to alter again, it has proved possible to reknit the threads of common policy.

It is worth examining this system in some detail in order to appreciate the continuing utility of the Commonwealth system in the new age of strategic deadlock. Its center is still primarily in the United Kingdom and its most important aspect is the training of senior Commonwealth officers. Some twenty-one officers who are on their way to the top of their profession come to the Imperial Defence College in London each year for a year's course; an average of fifteen go to the Joint Services Staff College at Latimer. The essential point about these two colleges is that they embrace officers from both the old and the new Commonwealth, and there must be nearly five hundred senior officers at or near the top of the Commonwealth armed forces who have thus lived and worked together. In addition each year six more junior officers go to the Royal Naval Staff College, six to the RAF Staff College and twenty-one to the Army Staff College, to which double that number would be sent (mostly from new Commonwealth countries) if it could handle them. Including technical courses there are generally some seven hundred Commonwealth officers in British schools at any one time and nearly as many non-commissioned officers. (The U.K. contributes to their costs.) They are mainly soldiers, though the maritime members of the new Commonwealth such as Malaysia send an appreciable number of sailors and air force officers. Finally, some twenty British officers a year do their staff training in Commonwealth staff colleges in Canada, Australia, India, Pakistan,

3. Tunstall, *The Commonwealth and Regional Defence*, p. 65.

and sometimes New Zealand; some Canadian officers go to Australian staff colleges and vice versa.

On top of this basic structure of joint training, there is a regular system of consultation among those who make military policy. There is a biennial conference in Britain of all Commonwealth chiefs of staff, and in the intervening years each of the British chiefs of staff holds a conference with his opposite numbers from the other countries. The Commonwealth Advisory Group on Defence Science has been operating since 1947 and from it the Anglo-Australian agreements on the Woomera Missile Base emanated. For some years this seemed likely to run into the sands as Britain and Canada, and to a lesser extent Australia, became increasingly inhibited from discussing any aspect of nuclear science or strategy with scientists from other Commonwealth countries. However, as the non-nuclear aspects of warfare and therefore science have regained importance, the symposia on defense science held in rotation throughout the leading Commonwealth countries have become significant.

There were in 1963 over eight hundred British officers and non-commissioned officers serving in the countries of the new Commonwealth, some on secondment and within the national command system, some acting as training teams outside the national system of command. The U.K. contributed nearly a million pounds to the cost of such officers in 1963 and over two and a half millions in 1964. But these arrangements are no longer purely bilateral with the United Kingdom. Canada has a thirty-man training mission in Ghana and is responsible for the Ghanaian Military Academy. The Ghana Air Force was founded with the help of Indian (and Israeli) officers. The Malaysian Navy is partly trained by Australia and is commanded by an Australian.

Finally, no Commonwealth country has abandoned the basic British system of staff duties and organization. Canadian organization has, of course, been closely geared to that of the United States but has never been modeled on it. Australia adopted the American pentomic structure for her army, but has had to rebuild her own system again since the United States abandoned it.

And the Pakistan forces are now so dependent on American equipment that a change in their military organization may be inevitable. But the remarkable fact remains that there are at present more than twenty countries whose soldiers and sailors at every level speak a common argot and instinctively obey identical commands and signals. Perhaps the most striking fact of all is that the Commonwealth countries that bound the Indian Ocean, whether aligned or non-aligned, Ceylon or Australia, Pakistan or Malaysia, exercise annually with the British Far Eastern fleet.

It is important not to overestimate the continuing strength of the military fabric of the Commonwealth. For one thing, unity no longer applies to equipment, and, certainly as far as aircraft and other major armaments are concerned, Britain is merely a middle-sized, fairly high-cost producer in a buyer's market. Canada long ago ceased to be dependent on British equipment (I can remember the dismay in 1939 of the Canadian General Staff, of which I was then a very junior member, on discovering that if anything should happen to Woolwich Arsenal they could get no ammunition for the coast defense guns at Halifax nearer than Singapore, nine thousand miles away) and is herself a major producer. No other Commonwealth country is in that position, but as Australia's recent rejection of the TSR2 in favor of the American TFX and her decision to buy two American destroyers shows, it is no longer felt that the Commonwealth association involves any obligation to buy British. Nor does Britain tie her training assistance to the local purchase of British equipment, as France does for the Community countries. British military aid is given where the new country has clearly inherited an external security problem as a result of Britain's own past policies, as in Malaysia, in Kenya, and in a sense, in India. If, through remarkable incompetence, Britain ceases to be able to meet the bulk of the defense equipment needs of the Commonwealth countries, especially of the newer ones, then the system of joint training and staff duties must become gradually eroded. But so far the system is only frayed at the edges, not impaired.

IV

The demonstration of the utility of the Commonwealth as a military system in recent years has taken two forms, co-operation for the actual defense of territory and co-operation to maintain the peace, either bilaterally or under the United Nations.

Neither Britain nor any other member of the old Commonwealth has ever formally renounced its obligation to come to the assistance of other Commonwealth countries, whether linked to them by security treaties or not. But a right becomes open to doubt if it is never exercised, and in the first fifteen years or so of the cold war it was never put to the test. The Chinese attack on India in October, 1962, was therefore of crucial importance as a test case, and the speed with which Britain reacted with an offer of assistance to India proved that this obligation is still regarded as valid. It is true that Britain acted in concert with the United States and the extent of the British offer of military assistance was, and still is, concerted with Washington. But several aspects of the Indian emergency suggest that the Commonwealth obligation was felt to be of great importance. For one thing though the original amount of military assistance, $60 million, was *pari passu* with that offered by the United States, it represented a much greater sacrifice in British than in American terms, particularly since Britain has no contingency funds allocated for military aid. Second, the Indian emergency brought an offer of technical and military assistance from Canada and Australia, though the security of neither was directly affected. Third, and most important, though Britain took rapid action to assist India, this occurred despite the fact that her planners did not share either the American or the Indian view about the seriousness of the Chinese threat to Indian security. I think there is no doubt that if it had proved to be a full-scale invasion Britain would have mustered as much force as possible to assist India, particularly in the form of air support. Though India now shops throughout the world for military equipment, military co-operation is easier with her Commonwealth partners than with other countries.

The second instance in recent years of a Commonwealth defense effort has been in Malaysia. This has involved not merely a change in the external threat but an alteration in the British perspective about her ability to play a continuing military role in South Asia. As mentioned earlier the reason why it was thought that the 1957 Defence Agreement might be of short duration was that if Britain left Singapore she would be unable to fulfil her share of the bargain. But when the Singapore government decided in 1961 to adhere to a greater Malaysia, Britain was presented not only with the need to help construct this larger state but also provide it with the means to do so, as the tenant of one base in a big country rather than as the dominant element in an island colony. The clash with Indonesia, which the incorporation of the Borneo and Sarawak territories into Malaysia has involved, implies a protracted British defense effort in support of Malaysia (which is heir to the 1957 Malayan Defence Agreement). And the natural desire of Australia to contain Indonesian ambitions in general is leading to a gradually increased Australian association with this effort. Few people now envisage Britain's withdrawing from her Far Eastern commitments during this decade, that is until Malaysia has trained stronger indigenous forces, and until Australia, which has hitherto had a very modest defense effort in relation to her wealth, is in a position to play a stronger part in the security of the area.

Two factors in particular have affected this change in British policy and attitude. One has been the modernization of her air and sea mobile forces, and her enhanced ability to move rapidly across the world. Even if the routes through the Middle East and Africa should become precarious, the fact that she is no longer pursuing a colonial defense policy but helping to maintain order in a sensitive area gives her a common interest with the United States which makes it possible to consider moving British forces west-about with American co-operation. The second was the decision of the Kennedy-Johnson administration to limit

American commitments in Asia, and to encourage Britain to continue playing an active military role in the Far East, even if it meant limiting her contribution to the security of Europe. Britain now spends one-third of her defense budget east of Suez and little is to be heard for the moment of a purely European-centered strategic policy.

Since the Nigerian experience Britain has been chary of entering into specific defense agreements with new members of the Commonwealth. Mr. Sandys was careful to describe the results of his conversations with East African leaders after the meetings as "arrangements." The sole documents were published summaries of the talks. A defense agreement has been negotiated with Malta because of her central strategic importance.

With the development of a strategic stalemate within a continuing ideological conflict, which renders overt war less likely but which makes situations of civil unrest and subversion abnormally dangerous, the distinction between defense and the maintenance of internal order in new countries becomes less sharp. Hence, when the British government was asked in January, 1964, to intervene in Kenya, Uganda, and Tanganyika to disarm mutinous elements in the forces of those countries, it was widely accepted that all concerned were using the techniques of Commonwealth co-operation to nip a potentially dangerous situation in the bud. Moreover, the role of the military in the political evolution of the new countries gives especial significance to a sophisticated international system of training for senior officers.

But the sphere in which Commonwealth military co-operation has been most strikingly illustrated has been in the peace-keeping activities of the United Nations. The first instance occurred at the lowest moment of Commonwealth solidarity—in 1956—and it is an ironic fact that the speed with which the United Nations could deploy a force in Gaza to expel and replace the British forces was almost entirely due to the fact that Canadian and Indian staff officers used common, that is British, procedures. Similarly, in the Congo the most efficient collaboration of national contingents was among those of Ghana, Nigeria, Malaya, the Canadian signalers, and the forces of a former member of the Commonwealth, the Irish Free State. For the past few years the Secretary-General has had an Indian officer as his military adviser with a Canadian deputy for air problems. It is not wholly accidental that in another situation where military forces had to be deployed rapidly in a delicate role, namely in West Irian in 1962, a Commonwealth country, Pakistan, was asked to supply the necessary officers and men.

On the other hand, the operation in Cyprus has revealed the limitations of Commonwealth co-operation under the UN, for Archbishop Makarios's preference for a force composed entirely of Commonwealth units could not be met, since Commonwealth forces acceptable to him were not forthcoming in sufficient numbers. But the relative ease with which an Indian UN force commander could assume command of five thousand British troops and one thousand Canadians, and the fact that the force was to be organized on British lines even when the full Scandinavian and Irish contingents were deployed, again indicates the value of the Commonwealth military system as a practical instrument of UN policy.

V

It is important not to overstate the importance of Commonwealth military relationships, and to avoid any complacent suggestion that a new form of Pax Britannica is emerging. Any such idea is nonsense. Britain's capacity to come to the aid of any of her Commonwealth partners in a situation of serious aggression remains strictly limited, and cannot be effectively exercised without the co-operation of the United States. Though Canada has a unique role to play in peace-keeping operations around which, judging from her latest White Paper, she intends to organize much of her strength, she cannot replace British or American power; and it will be some years before Australia can do more than contribute to the defense of Malaysia. The Himalayan crisis revealed the weakness of India as a military power, and obscurantism has removed from the service of the Commonwealth and world peace the only indigenous country capable of exercising a decisive military influence in Africa.

It may, as I have suggested, be difficult to maintain this Commonwealth defense co-operation in the face of national ambitions and requirements. But far down the road one can envisage a system which is no longer purely British centered, but in which Australia accepts the principal responsibility for underpinning the security of the Malayan area, Britain with Nigeria for Central Africa, in the same way that New Zealand explicitly assumes responsibility for the security of Fiji and the South Pacific islands. Canada may accept some responsibility for the West Indies, or may concentrate on UN security forces. Such a prospect, of course, assumes that the interests of the United States and the Commonwealth march in common.

The world of the mid-1960's is very different from that of a decade earlier. It is, as Walter Lippmann has said, one of less danger but of greater trouble. If one is right in thinking that the effect of the nuclear stalemate has been to depolarize international relations and to give greater freedom of action to the middle and smaller powers, then the need for a variety of means of averting and controlling local conflicts in a world of nearly 120 sovereign states needs no emphasis. In this situation the system of Commonwealth co-operation (provided that it is not attenuated by problems of national secrecy or equipment) has a real value, not to serve primarily British interests, or even solely Commonwealth ones, but as one instrument among several at the disposal of the UN and of responsible groups of countries to prevent internal friction, subversion, and the communal tensions which are the legacy of Empire from threatening a peace that is still precarious.

Part IV

Samplings of the Interchange of Institutions and Culture

10

The International Diffusion of Economic Ideas within the Commonwealth

J. J. Spengler*

> Society can only be understood through a study of the messages and the communication facilities which belong to it. [NORBERT WIENER, *The Human Use of Human Beings*, chap. i]

This essay, essentially a *mise en scène*, treats of the diffusion of economic ideas within the British Empire and its successors, the old and the new Commonwealth. These ideas played a major role in shaping the Commonwealth and setting the stage for its future as well as for its past decade.

Sources of Ideas within the Commonwealth

The main source of the ideas and practices transmitted to members of the British Empire prior to World War I was the United Kingdom; and even in more recent years the main source has been the English-speaking world. The bearers of these ideas and practices, therefore, were influential, because of their provenance if not also for personal reasons. Yet, for close to a half century after the Napoleonic Wars British spokesmen did not, as a rule, attempt vigorously to transplant domestically developed economic ideas and practices, except in India. To it,

* James B. Duke Professor of Economics, Duke University. He wishes to thank Ralph Braibanti for a number of helpful suggestions.

at first under the auspices of the East India Company (most of whose agents had some training in economics) and later under successor auspices, was transmitted a revenue system largely Physiocratic, Smithian, and Ricardian, together with an essentially English set of laws and a limited educational program intended to supply the Company and later the British raj with indigenous administrative personnel as well as to prepare India for self-government.[1]

A number of factors made for the absence of pressure upon potential transmitters to diffuse British economic ideas and practices. Because of the prestige of their political economy and industry, Britons apparently supposed that British economic ideas would be welcomed even in the absence of British pressure. Furthermore, under the influence of Smithian and other classical economists, both the climate of British opinion and governmental inclination were unfavorable to aggressive mercantilist colonial and related undertakings. It was deemed preferable that commerce be free and that costly governmental efforts to extend political sway and protected markets be avoided. While it was

1. Eric Stokes, *The English Utilitarians and India* (Oxford, 1959), esp. chap. ii on land revenue. Adam Smith's views supposedly were reflected in the Permanent Settlement authored by Sir Philip Francis, who also corresponded with Sir James Stuart on Indian mometary policy. See B. Natarajan, "Economic Ideas Behind the Permanent Settlement," *Indian Journal of Economics*, XXII (Jan., 1942), 708-23; also S. R. Sen, *The Economics of Sir James Stuart* (Cambridge, 1957), chap. x. Ranajit Guha finds, however, that British governors adopted mainly Physiocratic principles with the intention of "transforming a vast Asian countryside." See his *A Rule of Property for Bengal* (The Hague, 1963). Ram Mohun Roy (1772-1833), first Hindu to break the East-West barrier, create a vernacular press, establish a college giving instruction along Western lines, and seek modernization of India through Westernization, found both the Zamindari and the Ryotwari settlements to be very burdensome, but, believing a prosperous intermediate or middle class of Indians conducive to India's progress, favored the Zamindari type. See Bimanbehari Majumdar, *History of Political Thought from Rammohun to Dayananda (1821-84)*, I (apparently no more published. Calcutta, 1934), 67-68; [*The Life and Works of Raja Rammohun Roy*], ed. R. Chanda and J. K. Majumdar (3 vols.; various titles; Calcutta: Calcutta Oriental Book Agency, 1938-41), III, *Raja Rammohun Roy and Progressing Movements in India, 1774-1845*, pp. xcvii-cii, 479-504. Regarding late eighteenth-century theory, see J. C. Sinha, "Economic Theorists among the Servants of John Company (1766-1806)," *Economic Journal*, XXXV (March, 1925), 47-59; also, H. R. C. Wright, "Some Aspects of the Permanent Settlement in Bengal," *Economic History Review*, VII (Dec., 1957), 204-15. On arguments regarding European colonization in India, see A. K. Sen's study based on Company and governmental archives, "Settlement of Europeans in India: The First Phase (1766-1833)," *Calcutta Review*, CLXIX (Oct., 1963), 17-29.

possible to build a case for colonies on Ricardian principles as well as on Wakefieldian ones, it was believed that dominion status must be conferred upon colonies as soon as practicable. Then they would find continuing membership within the Empire politically tolerable and Britain would find the cost of the colonies economically tolerable; for such status entailed dominion responsibility for internal and non-military external affairs and for resulting governmental costs, together with partial responsibility for the planning and support of defense. E. G. Wakefield's scheme for making emigration self-financing was in keeping with this colonial philosophy in that it minimized Britain's economic responsibility while providing an outlet for her surplus capital and population and enlarged her external sources of produce and raw materials not easily producible in land-short Britain.[2] British inclination to let trade and settlement develop "naturally" and almost without the stimulus of governmentally supported inducements was manifest in British disinclination to expand Cape Colony and move into other parts of Africa until after frontier problems had made it advisable and gold discoveries had made it more feasible economically.[3]

Only in India was it expected that Britain could make benefits and costs balance in the aggregate. That this expectation was fulfilled is to be doubted.[4] Concern respecting Indian matters

2. E.g., see Goodwin's studies cited below; K. E. Knorr, *British Colonial Theories 1570-1850* (Toronto, 1944), chap. ix, also chaps. viii, x-xi; Brinley Thomas, *Migration and Economic Growth* (Cambridge, 1954), chaps. i, xiii; R. N. Ghosh, "The Colonization Controversy: R. J. Wilmot Horton and the Classical Economists," *Economica*, XXXI (Nov., 1964), 385-400. D. N. Winch, "Classical Economics and the Case for Colonization," *Economica*, XXX (Nov., 1963), 387-99; Bernard Semmel, "The Philosophical Radicals and Colonialism," *Journal of Economic History*, XXI (Dec., 1961), 513-25; my "John Stuart Mill on Economic Development," in B. F. Hoselitz, ed., *Theories of Economic Growth* (Glencoe, 1960), pp. 130-47; Asa Briggs, *The Age of Improvement* (London, 1959), pp. 381, 385-93. According to W. D. Grampp, only one group within the "Manchester School" was "opposed to colonies and empire." See his *The Manchester School of Economics* (Stanford, 1960), pp. 7-8.

3. J. S. Galbraith, *Reluctant Empire* (Berkeley, 1963), chap. iv; S. H. Frankel, *Capital Investment in Africa* (London, 1938), chaps. ii-iii; Ronald Robinson et al., *Africa and the Victorians* (New York, 1961), chaps. i, iii, xiv-xv; H. M. Robertson, "150 Years of Economic Contact Between Black and White," Part 2, *South African Journal of Economics*, III (March, 1935), 3-25, esp. 9 ff., 13-15. The classical economists, it should be noted, usually qualified their support of free trade. E.g., see Grampp, *passim*.

4. India in the early nineteenth century "was a military empire in an unim-

continually influenced British foreign policy and prompted un-economic undertakings. Investment of capital, manpower (though small in numbers), administrative skill, and diplomacy in India diverted these from the fuller development of the temperate-zone dominions and southern Africa. The resulting heavier in-flux of manpower and capital into these areas might have made them much more powerful and certainly far more reliable and far less expensive than are the successor states to Britain's African and Asian colonies.[5]

In the late nineteenth and early twentieth centuries, British climate of opinion and external-policy orientation began to change, under the threat of German and other rising industrial competition, the fear that England's economic progress might slow down, and the belief that England's military situation might become less secure. In association with this change in opinion there emerged the view that England must seek military and economic security within the framework of a British confedera-tion of nations rather than within that of an empire of loosely affiliated members situated in a world in which trade was only partly free. It was also recognized that Britain's continued progress was dependent upon her increasing investment in in-dustrial research, upon her extending education to the entire British population, and upon modernization of her university curricula. Moreover, the economic role of the state in both domestic and international affairs must be greatly enlarged. The resulting trend toward greater economic intervention by

perial age, a vast commitment dubiously balanced by its actual commercial value to English industry." Stokes, p. xi.

5. In "Imperialism and Socialism," *The Nineteenth Century*, VII (April, 1880), 726-36, Frederic Seebohm stressed the absurdity of pursuing "some Imperial phantom in Asia" instead of developing "the new Englands beyond the oceans in the West and South, the temperate zones of the world, where her [i.e., En-gland's] people can live" and in time multiply to and beyond a billion, to the great advantage of the British Isles. On the impact of India on British policy in Africa, see Robinson *et al.* Had Seebohm's policy been applied in southern Africa, demographic balance with, if not ascendancy over, the Bantu peoples would have resulted; we are thus afforded a measure of the cost of British short-sightedness. As it was, the importance of Cape Colony long derived from its being viewed as the key to the mastery of India. See Frankel, p. 41. South Africa's present-day strategic importance derives in part from threats to British Middle-East bases.

the state, under way in the decades just before 1914, was accentuated during and after World War I and still more during and after World War II, in part because of changes in ideology and in the body of economic knowledge. In recent decades, therefore, English economic thought has become much more collectivistic than it was even in the 1920's; it has also been diffused more vigorously and effectively to students within the Commonwealth, whether studying in the United Kingdom or enrolled in colleges affiliated with British universities. Other modes of communication have also been intensified. Today, therefore, diffusion is at a much higher rate than it was in the thirty to forty years preceding World War I or even in the 1920's.[6]

Media of Transmission

The linguistic media employed in the old Commonwealth have not greatly interfered with the reception of economic ideas, since English has been the dominant tongue. Only among the French Canadians and the Afrikaner has the rate of diffusion of economic ideas been lower than in the English-speaking population, and then mainly because educational levels have been lower in these two groups. In most other parts of the Commonwealth (with the exception of English-speaking West Indies) the tongues used by the majority of the population (e.g., in India, Pakistan, Ceylon, and West and East Africa) are lexically unequal to the task of communicating economic thought. From at least the middle third of the nineteenth century, for example, British administrators and educators in India were deciding whether, even if attention were given to the vernaculars, they ought not to proceed (as they did) upon the assumption that, as one author put it, "English alone possessed a sufficiently supple

6. On the changes in attitude, ways of thinking, etc., noted in this paragraph, see Robinson, *et al.*, esp. chaps. i, xi, xiii-xv; G. M. Young, *Victorian England* (London, 1961), pp. 93-99, 114, 119-20, 141, 176-84; Bernard Semmel, *Imperialism and Social Reform* (Cambridge, 1960); D. S. Landes, "Some Thoughts on the Nature of Economic Imperialism," *Journal of Economic History*, XXI (Dec., 1961), 496-512; Alfred Marshall, *Industry and Trade* (1919) (London, 1927), pp. 104-6, 159-62.

and extended vocabulary for conveying the elements of the Western sciences."[7] This assumption was generally taken for granted in underdeveloped parts of the Empire, though not in a way to assure linguistic and politico-cultural homogeneity and loyalty to the state.[8] In the Commonwealth up to now, therefore, English has been the medium of most educated persons with an interest in economic affairs, but the disposition and the capacity of some populations to use this medium has been quite limited and may decline. Should this happen, the various local languages will not prove adequate for the transmission of economic ideas, being short of item count. Moreover, they will hardly become adequate so long as there are so few people with the skill to introduce enough items to meet the needs of economic analysis; even were there enough such people, there would still remain the prohibitive task of producing the infrastructure of scientific communication in the vernacular, namely, journals, teaching materials, translations, etc. It is advisable,

7. See on this language controversy, C. E. Trevelyan, *On the Education of the People of India* (London, 1938); B. D. Basu, *Education in India under E. I. Company* (2d ed.; Calcutta, 1934), pp. 54-146; H. H. Dodwell, ed., *Cambridge History of the British Empire*, V (New York, 1932), esp. pp. 118-19, also 109-17, 355-56. See also Crane's papers, cited below in note 25, and K. Ballhatchet, *Social Policy and Social Change in Western India 1817-1830* (London, 1957), chap. x. Some Indians, among them Ram Mohun Roy, shared the British view that English was essential to the modernization of Indian society, in part because Sanskrit was both difficult and a repository of matter unfavorable to modernization. See P. C. Mittra, *A Biographical Sketch of David Hare* (Calcutta, 1877), pp. 10-14; Arthur Mayhew, *The Education of India* (London, 1926), pp. 91-92; E. Thompson and G. Garrett, *Rise and Fulfillment of British Rule in India* (London, 1939), pp. 314-15. In the 1950's the replacement of English by Sinhalese in universities was opposed on the ground that the latter is not suitable for instruction in natural and social science. See Henry Oliver, *Economic Opinion and Policy in Ceylon* (Durham, N. C., 1957), pp. 33-34, also 10-11; also Ivor Jennings, *Problems of the New Commonwealth* (Durham, N. C., 1958), pp. 16-18, 88-90.

8. In India, for example, as A. K. Dutta feared, the English-speaking intelligentsia became separated from the masses to whom they sought to transmit (or transmitted) neither English nor the modern knowledge English conveyed. The British hope of gradually Anglicizing the Hindu population thus went unrealized. See B. Majumdar, pp. 145-46, 275-76; also Mayhew, pp. 91-92; and R. V. Parulekar, ed., *Selections from the Records of the Government of Bombay: Education (1819-1852)* (2 parts, titles vary, as do years covered; Bombay, 1953-1955), I, 183-87. Some Indian scholars believed that vernacular languages might be fitted for modern communication by including words built upon Sanskrit roots. See J. Ghosh, *Higher Education in Bengal under British Rule* (Calcutta, 1926), pp. 90-91, 217-18.

therefore, either that English be made the main language of science and administration (an object easier of realization in African states without a written literature than in Asian states with a native literature), or that English be made co-ordinate with the native tongue and serve as the language of the schools and the educated. It is not likely, however, given the demands of nationalism, that the latter course will be followed, and it is probable that the effective use of English will decline in some parts of the Commonwealth.[9] If so, the communication of economic ideas may be retarded, at least temporarily.

Content of That Which Is Transmitted

The international transmittability of sets of ideas is conditioned by their content, especially by the complexity of this content, and probably above all by the extent to which this content is ethically or religiously oriented and permeated by essentially ultimate or non-instrumental values. While objects are divisible into means and ends, it is possible for a means to be wanted for itself as well as because it is a means. We may, therefore, assign every object an index value representing the ratio of its "meansness" to its "endsness"; this ratio, or (simply) means-ends ratio, will range in value from infinity in the case of pure means to zero in the case of pure or ultimate ends. Objects may then be ordered in terms of the ratio of their "meansness" to their "endsness." Similarly, we may order diverse sets of ideas along a means-ends continuum, with sets ranging from those denoting referents with a high means-ends ratio to those at the opposite pole. Given such orderings, the significance of objects will be derivative—that is, dependent upon their capacity to function as means or instruments—in proportion as their means-ends ratio is high. Similarly, the significance of sets of ideas may be said to be derivative in proportion as the means-ends ratio of

9. See T. H. Silcock, *Southeast Asian University* (Durham, 1964), chap. v; also N. Thirtha, *Babel; Language Dilemma in Indian Schools* (Masulipatam, 1962); J. Ornstein, "Africa Seeks a Common Language," *Review of Politics*, XXVI (April, 1964), 205-14.

their referents is high. It is highly probable, moreover, that the ease of transmittability of a set of ideas from one culture to another under relatively similar conditions will be associated positively with the magnitude of the means-ends ratio of this set and its referent. For, if the means-ends ratio of a given set of ideas were high, its introduction into another culture would tend to be relatively welcome, or at least not unwelcome, as long as it could serve purposes already approved in that culture; and it would probably do this since the number of diverse purposes that a given means can serve tends to be positively associated with the magnitude of its means-ends ratio. If, on the contrary, the means-ends ratio were low, the set of ideas designating a more or less "ultimate" value, its assimilation into a new culture might be expected to entail a significant change in the system of values regnant there, and hence would probably be resisted.

Western economic ideas proved relatively introducible into non-Western cultures, inasmuch as they had to do, not with higher values and ends, but with means to generally approved material ends. Comprehension of their content, even when largely empty of empirical illustration, must often have been handicapped, however, by the traditional character of economies outside the European sphere of culture. The acceptance of Western economics may have been retarded also by the great significance it attached to material purposes, rewards, and motivation oriented thereunto, and by its favoring modern forms of organization at variance with those found in traditional societies.

While the content of economic opinion in the dominions as in India was somewhat influenced by indigenous conditions, it also tended to reflect changes in English economic opinion, especially in more recent decades, and above all after the 1930's. Of this parallelism there is evidence in Indian and dominion journals and even in Ceylon.[10] While it is to be expected that in

10. "Ceylonese intellectuals have adopted or altered economic philosophies expounded at Oxford [etc.]; Ceylonese trends of thought have paralleled, although they have not exactly reproduced, trends in Britain. In general, economic opinion has become more interventionist and more egalitarian with the passing of the decades." Oliver, pp. 35-36; also 61-65 on Asian etatism.

the immediate future economic opinion may be even more interventionist and etatistic than now in Asia and Africa, this tendency will undergo some leavening through the impact of local cultural elements. This impact will be greater in Asia, with its traditional value systems (Moslem, Hindu, Buddhist) and supporting literature and priestcraft, than in African states into whose cultures these value systems have not become imbedded. Everywhere, however, the secular administrative state will exercise a powerful countervailing influence, and this will strengthen the demand for economically trained personnel to manage the apparatus of economic control and plan its evolution.

The Milieu of Potential Receivers

The potential receiver as well as his milieu has much to do, as has already been suggested, with the degree to which sets of ideas are introduced from abroad and diffused within a country. The effectiveness of the receiver as a secondary transmitter, though conditioned by his expositive skill, depends also upon the prestige which he derives from his socioeconomic status and from the source of the ideas which he is introducing. The energy with which he diffuses these ideas will be conditioned by advantages he hopes to realize from his diffuser role, and their reception will be conditioned by the advantages which domestic receivers expect from their acceptance.

Tightly knit, well-integrated systems of social thought are less pervious to sets of ideas external to the system than are more loosely knit systems. The Scholastic and the Physiocratic systems of economic thought were much less congenial to new economic ideas than was the relatively diffuse mercantilist system; nominalistic philosophy was much more congenial to the thought system associated with capitalism than was philosophical realism;[11] and Confucianism and at times Marxism have been particularly impervious to the infiltration of foreign ideas. While

11. E.g., see Werner Stark, *Sociology of Knowledge* (Glencoe, 1958), pp. 38-41; also his *The Fundamental Forms of Social Thought* (London, 1962).

Indian systems of thought were not so well integrated, they sometimes were hostile, even as was Confucianism, to incorporating new ideas. A system of thought, even though well integrated, can, of course, absorb change much as did economic analysis when it converted statics into a special case of general dynamic analysis.[12] Indeed, the post-1900 systematization of economic and social thought has been accompanied by the belief that deliberate change-producing activities can be institutionalized, with the result that both socioeconomic systems and the bodies of theory designed to explain their behavior have become dynamic.[13] The capacity of Indian systems of thought to absorb foreign ideas—much greater, for example, than the Confucian system—appears to be associated more with its relatively amorphous and nonsystematic character than with its other properties. Whatever the formal cause, India's thought systems prove fairly congenial to Western ideas.

In Canada, Australia, and New Zealand demographic factors were more favorable to the importation and reception of British economic ideas and practices than in South Africa and decidedly more favorable than in Asia or elsewhere in Africa. The aboriginal population was small in Canada and the antipodes, and migrants from Britain came in a small but continuing stream, though long offset in Canada by heavy emigration to the United States. Moreover, the English-speaking population was sufficiently large and concentrated to support internal diffusion of newly acquired ideas and to attract considerable British investment.[14] Into South Africa, on the contrary, until the discovery of gold in the Transvaal in the 1880's, there was little migration of people or capital, the country being viewed in Britain as an expensive and unprofitable land, valuable primarily because

12. P. A. Samuelson, *Foundations of Economic Analysis* (Cambridge, 1947), chap. ix.

13. E.g., see J. S. Berliner, "The Feet of the Natives Are Large: An Essay on Anthropology by an Economist," *Current Anthropology*, III (Feb., 1962), 47-61.

14. About 1860, 1880, 1900, and 1920 the white population approximated (in millions): in Canada, 3.2, 4.3, 5.4, and 8.8 (of whom in the neighborhood of three-tenths were French); in Australia, 1.2, 2.3, 3.8, and 5.4; and in New Zealand, 0.1, 0.5, 0.8, and 1.2. On investment, which also carries with it economic practices, see Thomas, *op. cit.*

it guarded the route to India. The population remained small and little urbanized, although three-fifths literate as early as 1860. Indeed, as late as 1891 less than one-seventh of the European population were European born; the rest were descended from the nearly 14,000 Dutch enumerated in Cape Colony in 1793, progenitors of roughly three-fifths of present-day South Africa's 3.2 million whites. As late as 1904 natural increase and British immigration, though nearly ten times as high in 1881-1913 as in 1843-80, had elevated South Africa's white population, about 322,000 in 1873, to only 1,117 thousands in a total population of 5,174 thousands.[15] In India, and to a greater extent elsewhere in Asia and Africa, demographic factors were unfavorable in that the English population was very small and the number of natives who were functionally literate and knew English well was also very small. In 1931, for example, there were but thirty-four Englishmen for every hundred thousand Indians and the number had not been much higher in 1911, perhaps a peak year.[16] Until after 1931 less than one-tenth of the population were literate; the proportion literate in English was below 1 per cent until in the 1920's, while literacy in other tongues was distributed among many languages and scripts.[17] Elsewhere, outside the dominions, literacy and education were even less advanced, as a rule.

Countries differed in relative amounts of incentives that make for economic education. Incentives productive of demand for such education were of two sorts. Education might be viewed as essentially a consumer service. In this category may be placed education which conferred social status, which familiarized the student with secular elements in his culture, or which gave him access to the symbolism and ideology, and perhaps the philosophy

15. See *Cambridge History of the British Empire*, VIII (London, 1936), 759, 769-73; Thomas, p. 57; H. M. Robertson, "South Africa," in Brinley Thomas ed., *The Economics of International Migration* (London, 1958), chap. xii; Robinson *et al.*, pp. 6 n., 57 n. On the impact of the discovery of diamonds and gold in South Africa, see Frankel, chap. iii.

16. Kingsley Davis, *The Population of India and Pakistan* (Princeton, 1951), p. 96. Over half these were military personnel. British made up 90-96 per cent of the Europeans in India.

17. *Ibid.*, pp. 151, 157-59.

and rationale, of his religion; it did not include economics. Education might also be viewed as an instrumental or producer service, as it would be if it were sought because it fitted the student for governmental employment, or for professional employment, or for supposedly productive employment in the private sector; indeed it was so viewed by the "competition wallahs." The potential suppliers of education were either Britain and her agencies in the Empire or the Commonwealth or indigenously supported institutions. Britain and her educational agencies seem to have been most interested in fitting students for posts in government and in introducing Western culture and tastes making for demand for British goods and services and associations. Indigenous institutions were initially concerned to supply consumer-oriented education, together with fitness for some types of public and private employment. Provision for economic education was long most likely to be stimulated by the belief that it made for effective public and private administration and hence gave access to employment and wealth—a belief that was not very powerful in the nineteenth century, even in advanced countries. That trained economists could contribute importantly to the solution of problems in the private sector and to the formulation of effective national economic policy as well as assess proposed legislation relating to trade, length of the working day, etc., apparently was not widely taken for granted until later in the nineteenth century.[18]

Differential Progress in Diffusion

Because of variation in internal milieu from one component to another of the British Empire as well as for other reasons, the knowledge and application of economic science spread and developed at quite different rates. This progress was greatest in the dominions, though much more pronounced in Canada and

18. Even so, before 1850 English classical economists did contribute to policy formation. See Lionel Robbins, *The Theory of Economic Policy* (London, 1952) and George J. Stigler, *Five Lectures in Economic Problems* (New York, 1950), chap. iii.

Australia than in the others; it was much slower in Asia and negligible in sub-Saharan Africa until very recently, when English higher education began to be introduced. After all, regnant value systems were much less favorable to economic science outside than inside the English-speaking dominions. Moreover, it had not come to be widely recognized that knowledge of economics might confer on its possessor professional and material advantages comparable with those conferred by knowledge of engineering, medicine, or forestry; indeed, economics probably was viewed as essentially a consumer-good component of a liberal arts education.

In India, prior to 1850, little effort was given to the diffusion of economic science, though village schools, especially those in Hindu regions, had long trained pupils to "read and write and cast accounts and carry on business correspondence."[19] The vast majority were indifferent; values prevailing in the Hindu and the Moslem aristocracy seem not to have prompted much of an interest in economic science, the relevance of which to their own material concerns was not even widely perceived by the middle class until the nationalist independence movement got under way.[20] Hence political economy did not serve as a major vehicle of Western educational penetration, though it was taught in Roy's Hindu College in the 1830's and in several colleges perhaps as early as in the 1840's, and practical economic questions (e.g., transport) were commanding attention.[21] Those interested

19. Basu, pp. 160-74, 186-94; H. R. Mehta, *A History of the Growth and Development of Western Education in the Punjab 1846-1884* (Lahore, 1929), pp. 6-8; J. Ghosh, *Higher Education in Bengal*, pp. 10-12, also pp. 105-6 n., where it is indicated that the Pandits were not opposed to using Sanskrit translations of works relating to commerce. Capacity to count and compute had long been considered even more important than writing as it facilitated commerce, calculation of interest, etc. See D. G. Apte, *Our Educational Heritage* (Baroda, 1961), pp. 71-72.

20. Vikas Mishra concludes that although institutions and attitudes of Hinduism had at one time helped rather than hindered economic growth, they became brakes upon it with the advent of Western industrialization. *Hinduism and Economic Growth* (Bombay, 1962), pp. 205-6.

21. B. Majumdar, pp. 79-80, 161 n.; P. J. Thomas, "The Late Professor V. G. Kale," *Indian Journal of Economics*, XXVII (1946-47), 333; J. Ghosh, pp. 113, 126 n., also pp. 59-60, 124-26, 131 on cultural resistance to Western ideas. On transport estimates and policy, agriculture, and income in India, see Daniel and Alice Thorner, *Land and Labour in India* (Bombay, 1962); Daniel Thorner, *In-*

in Western learning preferred a literary to a professional education, in part because lack of training in economics was not a barrier to employment in administrative and clerical posts, perhaps because there were few qualified persons available in the 1830's and for some time thereafter.[22] Fifty years later, despite the increasing Indianization of administration, long demanded by Indian authors, there were said to be more college graduates than public and professional employment could absorb, albeit too few appropriately trained for commerce and industry,[23] whose growth was retarded then as later by a dearth of businessmen.[24] The number of students enrolled in India's technical or arts colleges was too few, had their program included economics, as it seems rarely to have done, to have contributed notably to the diffusion of economic knowledge.[25] This is not surprising,

vestment in Empire (Philadelphia, 1950); Simon Kuznets, et al., Economic Growth: Brazil, India, Japan (Durham, N. C., 1955), chaps. iv, ix, xv-xvi.

22. B. Majumdar, p. 160; B. T. McCully, English Education and the Origins of Indian Nationalism (New York, 1940), chaps. ii-iv; Cambridge History of the British Empire, V (1932), 116-18, 342, 349-50; J. Ghosh, pp. 96, 119-21, 146-49, 152, 155, 171; Mittra, p. 45; Bijoy Bhattacharya, Bengal Renaissance [1800-58] (Calcutta, 1963). I am drawing also upon two papers by my colleague, Robert I. Crane, "The Transfer of Western Education to India," in W. B. Hamilton, ed., The Transfer of Institutions (Durham, N. C., 1964); "Technical Education and Economic Development in India before World War I," to be published in C. A. Anderson and M. J. Bowman, eds., Education and Economic Development (Chicago, 1965), Part II, chap. v.

23. J. Ghosh, pp. 166-67, 171, 178-84. Indianization of the Indian Civil services was advocated by Ram Mohun Roy and others, in part on the ground it would reduce the costs of government inasmuch as the salaries of Indian civil servants were much below those of comparable Europeans serving in India. Majumdar, pp. 70, 200-201, 214, 217, 230, 299, 380-81. By 1931, all but 12,000 of the posts in the administration of India were filled by Indians. See John and Ruth Hill Useem, The Western-Educated Man in India (New York, 1955), p. 129. Some Indians, among them A. K. Dutta (1820-1886), believed technological education essential to India's industrialization. B. Majumdar, pp. 145, 154-56. The comparative costliness of a scientific education remained a deterrent, however, to its acquisition even as in present-day underdeveloped countries. See J. Ghosh, p. 182.

24. Ghosh, pp. 238 n., 240-41 n.; also p. 239 n., on Indian preference for "soft-handed labour."

25. In 1916-17 when India's population numbered some 306 millions, only about 14,000 students were enrolled in technical or industrial institutions, and only some 45,000 in arts colleges. See Crane, "Technical Education . . . ," cited in note 22. Early in the present century the National Council of Education included among the college-level programs it endorsed one providing specialization in economics in the form of an elementary and an advanced course. See Haridas and Uma Mukherjee, The Origins of the National Education Movement (1905-1914) (Jadavpur, 1957), pp. 53, 56.

for the study of economic problems had received but negligible attention in either Hindu or Moslem education, and what there was in pre-British times seems to have been oriented to administration rather than to analysis or policy formulation.[26] Such discipline as English-style universities came to exercise over the colleges seems not to have had a notable influence upon economic education.[27] Dissatisfaction respecting the teaching and the content of economics in the colleges seems to have been widespread in India in the present century if not also earlier,[28] and there was complaint that too little use was made of Indian economists on commissions of economic inquiry.[29] To these complaints may be added the widespread complaint that economics were not included in curricula, that Indian universities had too few economists and too little equipment, and that economic research received little support.[30] B. K. Sarkar added that Indian

26. See Bal-Krishna, "Economics in Ancient India," *Indian Journal of Economics*, II (1918-19), 629-49. N. N. Law included "economics" in the list of "sciences" studied in Mughal times. See his *Promotion of Learning in India* (Bombay, 1916), pp. 161-62. Under Muslim rule revenue administration was mainly carried out by Hindus, some of whom wrote books of rules for the guidance of administrators. See Syed Sulaiman Nadvi, *The Education of Hindus—Under Muslim Rule* (Karachi, 1963), pp. 114-15. The Laws of Manu were directed against the Zamindari system and the *śastras*, rationally interpreted, were described as useful. B. Majumdar, pp. 127-28, 132, 211.

27. Three English-style universities were established in 1857, another in 1882, and yet another in 1887, at which time college students in India numbered about 12,000, or approximately one in 26,000. In the early 1880's, there were at least 61 arts colleges, 14 law colleges, 4 engineering colleges, and 3 medical schools, and 133 schools offering some technical training. See Crane, "The Transfer . . . ," cited in note 22 above; *Cambridge History of the British Empire*, V, 118-19, 336-56. The number of Indian students studying in Europe rose from below 100 before 1880 to 1,761 in Britain alone by 1929. *Ibid.*, p. 354.

28. E.g., see H. S. Jevons, "The Teaching of Economics," *Indian Journal of Economics*, I (1916), 96, 98, sect. III; *idem* and Gilbert Slater, "Higher Economics Courses," *ibid.*, II (1918-19), 92-100; unsigned, "A New Economics Course," *ibid.*, III (1920-22), 63-83; also Ras. Sahib K. S. Pucholy, "Whitherward Ho?," on the content and teaching of economics in Indian universities, *ibid.*, XI (1930-31), 513-34.

29. V. G. Kale, "Economics in India," *ibid.*, IX (1928-29), 608-11, 624. On Kale's role as a follower of Ranade, see *Indian Journal of Economics*, XXVII (1946-47), 323-33.

30. See C. N. Vakil, "The Formation of Economic Opinion in India," *Indian Journal of Economics*, XV (1934-35), 758-84; the *Report* of the Calcutta University Commission, 1917-1919 (13 vols.; Superintendent, Government Printing, Calcutta, 1919), XI. See in *ibid.* especially the replies to questions on subjects omitted from curricula, pp. 3, 4, 7, 9, 13, 14, 17, 22, 28-30, 32-34, 36, 38-39, 44, 45, 47, 49, and replies to questions on research, pp. 201, 203-7, 219, 227, 234. There is an occasional complaint too that use of English as a medium of instruction greatly limits the diffusion of knowledge. E.g., see *ibid.*, p. 42.

economists were often badly trained and too inclined to be anti-British.[31]

Interest in economics and economic problems began to develop notably in India in the third quarter of the nineteenth century, and by the first quarter of the present century books as well as many articles (some in English in dailies, weeklies, and monthlies, and some in vernaculars) were being published.[32] Initially this interest assumed classical form, perhaps because Indian students (e.g., at the Hindu College) found in Smith and Bentham a basis for attacking English and other restrictions on Indian trade and industry, removal of which, some believed, would make possible India's industrialization, and in J. S. Mill grounds for advocating temporary tariff protection for Indian industry. The classical ideology also lent support to a fairly widely held view that the introduction into India of skilled English colonists, especially cultivators and industrial personnel, would accelerate India's progress.[33]

With the growth of interest in India's economic progress, Indian economists apparently qualified their support of laissez faire even more than had Ram Mohun Roy. Dadabhai Naoroji

31. See Shib Chandra Dutt, *Conflicting Tendencies in Indian Economic Thought* (Calcutta, 1934), pp. 190-92. Sarkar participated in the Swadeshi movement, however. See Haridas Mukherjee, *Benoy Kumar Sarkar* (Calcutta, 1953), pp. 3-7.

32. The English-language journal *Dawn* published 114 articles on economic subjects in 1898-1912. See Mukherjee, *The Origins*, pp. 332-39. S. C. Dutt includes a bibliography of Indian writings in 1898-1932 in *Conflicting Tendencies*, chap. ii. Dutt contrasts the economic opinions of Benoy Kumar Sarkar with those of Mahatma Gandhi, who emphasized the spiritual aspects of economic life. Gandhi's opinions have been assembled by J. S. and A. S. Mathur, in *Economic Thought of Mahatma Gandhi* (Allahabad, 1962). Gandhism, described as "the philosophy of the isolated individual or of a small group, peasant or artisan, not of the industrial masses," did not give rise to a school. See P. K. Gopolakrishnan, *Development of Economic Ideas in India (1880-1950)* (New Delhi, 1959), chap. vii, esp. pp. 203-4. This work amounts to a second edition of the work of the same title, exclusive of chap. vii, published in 1954. Ashakant Nimbark finds in Gandhian economics a keystone concept of trusteeship "strangely allied with the classical Hindu concept of Dharma." See "Gandhism Re-examined," *Social Research*, XXXI (1964), pp. 109-13.

33. B. Majumdar, pp. 70-80, 111, 127, 161 n., 261, 309, 312; also 74, 95-96, 196-97, 231, 338 on "colonization." Roy favored partially replacing land taxes by luxury taxes and the standing army by a militia. *Ibid.*, p. 70. See also on "colonization" J. K. Majumdar, pp. lxxvii-lxxxvii, 407-66. A. K. Dutta, a follower of Ram Mohun Roy, advocated deferment of marriage as a means of checking undue population growth. See B. Majumdar, p. 154.

(1825-1917), though a social philosopher under the influence of British economists (notably, J. S. Mill), adopted the famous "drain theory" according to which Britain drew more economic resources out of India than she invested there, a theory supported already by Ram Mohun Roy and perhaps first enunciated in 1825 by Serampore missionaries; he apparently was led to this conclusion by his studies of Indian finance, taxation, and income formation.[34]

Mahadev Govind Ranade (1842-1901), so-called father of Indian economics, advocate of vernacular instruction in the universities, and founder of the Prartha Samaj (which resembled Ram Mohun Roy's Brahmo Samaj) and (along with Naoroji) of the Indian National Congress, made the economic development of India his main theme. An early graduate of Bombay University with a residual interest in economic issues, he played a major role in shifting economic thought and policy in India from one based on the ideas of Smith and the classical economists to one based upon the etatistic and economic-development-oriented views of American and German economical writers, from 1878, when he began to publish economical papers in the *Journal* of the Sarvajanik Sabha.[35] Believing the solvent of Indian

34. Naoroji came to England for a time and won a seat in Parliament as a Radical member. On his economics, see Gopalakrishnan, chap. ii. Naoroji estimated Indian per capita income in the 1860's at 40 shillings or Rs. 20. *Ibid.*, p. 44. It was put at Rs. 23-24 by others and at Rs. 30 in 1901. *Ibid.*, p. 51. His and other estimates are discussed in V. K. R. Rao, *The National Income of British India, 1931-32* (London, 1940). The "drain theory" was popularized by William Digby in *Prosperous British India* (London, 1901). While Romesh C. Dutt said the "drain theory" was foreshadowed in the mid-nineteenth century, B. Majumdar (p. 71) traces it to 1825. See Dutt, *Economic History of India* (6th ed.; London [1911?]), p. 127, first published in 1904 as *India in the Victorian Age*. On Indian income estimates and trends, see Daniel and Alice Thorner, chaps. v-vii; also Colin Clark, *The Conditions of Economic Progress*, (3rd. ed.; London, 1957), pp. 204-7. Clark endorses the view that real income per head, very low in the early nineteenth century, fell to even lower levels by the 1890's, thereafter to rise until 1931, though never to attain seventeenth-century levels. *Ibid.*, pp. 205-7.

35. R. C. Dutt, chap. iii; G. D. Karwal, "Mahadev Govind Ranade—His Economic Views," *Indian Journal of Economics*, XIII (1932-33), 643-68, XIV (1933-34), 53-78; Kale, pp. 605-28, esp. 624-26; K. Anantaran, "Ranade, The Economist," *Indian Journal of Economics*, XXII (1941-42), 387-93; K. N. Sen, "Economic Thinking in the Indian National Congress," *ibid.*, pp. 689-707, esp. 693; B. Datta, "The Background of Ranade's Economics," *ibid.*, pp. 261-75; James Kellock, "Ranade and After: A Study of the Development of Economic Thought in India," *ibid.*, pp. 245-60. J. C. Coyajee, in "Ranade's Work as an

poverty lay in industrialization, he indicated that it was to be accomplished through capable entrepreneurship variously assisted by the state, and perhaps facilitated by emigration and by social and institutional reform.[36] He favored, as did S. Ghosh (1840-1911), temporary protection of native manufactures based upon India's undeveloped resources; in this opinion he had the support of some but not all contemporary and later economists.[37] His stress upon "Indian economic problems," reflected in the frequently used book title, "Indian Economics," persisted in Indian economic-journal literature,[38] though in a form usually unfavorable to the development of empirical, theoretical, and methodological aspects of economic inquiry in India.[39]

Ranade's emphasis upon economic development, if not his protectionism, was continued by G. K. Gokhale (1866-1915), critic of unproductive expenditure (e.g., on the Indian Army) and advocate of use of governmental expenditure and monetization of the Indian economy as means to its modernization.[40] R. C. Dutt (1848-1909), in his economic history of India, lent support to Naoroji's attack on the "annual economic drain from India" and to a development program based on land-tax and

Economist," *ibid.*, pp. 307-30, acclaims Ranade "as the ablest writer on Indian economics since the days of Kautilya." Ranade's collected *Essays in Indian Economics* (Madras) appeared in 1898.

36. Gopalakrishnan, pp. 104-22; D. G. Karve, "Ranade and Economic Planning," *Indian Journal of Economics*, XXII (1941-42), 235-44; Kellock, pp. 250-55; Coyajee, pp. 309, 316-21, 328-30; Karwal.

37. Ranade's protectionism was anticipated in 1869 by Chandranath Bose, proponent of manufacturing development in Bengal, and in 1873-74 by Bholanath Chandra (1822-1910), advocate of protectionism and father of the "Swadeshi movement, in its purely economic" form. See B. Majumdar, pp. 276-82, 375-79, on Bose, Chandra, and S. Ghosh. See also M. C. Munshi, "Protectionism and Indian Economic Thought," *Indian Journal of Economics*, XXII (1941-42), 331-56, esp. pp. 335-38 on the views of G. V. Joshi and R. C. Dutt; P. S. Lokanathan, "The Economics of Gokhale," *ibid.*, XXII, pp. 225-34.

38. Kellock, pp. 258-60.

39. T. M. Joshi, "A Critique of 'Indian Economics,'" *Indian Journal of Economics*, XXII (1941-42), 276-79; D. H. Butani, "The Quality and Perspective of Indian Economic Thought," *ibid.*, XXII, 280-89. Nearly all the economic articles published in *Dawn* in 1898-1912 dealt with Indian subjects. See Mukherjee, *The Origins*, pp. 315-58, esp. 332-339.

40. Gopalakrishnan, chap. iv. Ram Mohun Roy, S. Ghosh, and others wanted to cut military expenditures. B. Majumdar, pp. 69-70, 380-81. Gokhale, president of the Indian National Congress in 1905, believed, as did others, that protection was to the disadvantage of the Indian people. See Lokanathan, also, McCully, chap. v, on the ideas of Indian economic nationalists.

agrarian reform, together with complementary industrialization.[41]
B. K. Sarkar later presented a much more balanced view of
problems of Indian development and the role played therein by
foreign capital and personnel.[42]

In South Africa, economic science, such as it was, long received its expression outside a virtually non-existent university
world.[43] South African College, forerunner of the University of
Cape Town, so designated in 1918 after eighteen years as University College, became a college of sorts eight years after its
founding in 1829, but it did not function effectively until some
years later. While Stellenbosch was established in 1870 and
Rhodes about three decades later, it was not until the present
century that higher education began to flourish.[44] Some attention
apparently was given to political economy in these institutions
and, as early as 1882, in the gymnasium-like predecessor of
Pretoria University, on the ground that public servants required
economic knowledge.[45] In the nineteenth century and for some
time thereafter, however, it was mainly in official reports on transportation, agriculture, industry, tariff, as well as on labor, native
and related questions, together with public comments on these,
that economic analysis was manifest.[46] Here as in other dominions
and apparently elsewhere (above all prior to the establishment
of British-connected university colleges) economic science and
analysis long received expression principally in policy-oriented
discussions of current issues.

41. Gopalakrishnan, chap. iv. Dutt, a member of the Indian Civil Service,
1869-97, was president of the Indian National Congress in 1899.
42. Shib C. Dutt, chaps. v-vii. Sarkar stressed the importance of vocational,
technical, and other relevant education, the example of Japan, and the fallacies
underlying the "drain theory."
43. H. M. Robertson deals with the development of economic science in
South Africa in a forthcoming monograph.
44. F. C. Metrowich, *The Development of Higher Education in South Africa—
1873-1927* (Cape Town, 1929), chap. i and pp. 26, 76-80; *Cambridge History
of the British Empire*, VIII, 364-65, 380, 650-51, 855-57; Lord Hailey, *An
African Survey* (revised 1956; London, 1957), pp. 1135-42. See also E. G.
Malherbe, *History of Education in South Africa, 1652-1922* (Cape Town, 1925).
45. Metrowich, p. 28.
46. Some of these are listed in Volume VIII of the *Cambridge History of the
British Empire*, in conjunction with chaps. xxix-xxx on economic development
and tribal-life change. The second edition of this work, edited by E. A. Walker
(Cambridge, 1963), does not contain much new information.

It was in Canada and, above all, in Australia among the dominions, both initially collections of provinces, that economics made most progress. The relatively rapid urbanization and industrialization of Australia, together with its distance from England and its freedom from powerful influences emanating from a nearby power, stimulated discussion there and fostered an eclecticism capable of mixing received orthodox economics with Marxism, Pope Leoism, and other economic "isms."[47] In both countries similar problems gave rise to similar analyses and discussions, with policy questions dominating inquiry and with universities beginning to play an important role no earlier than late in the nineteenth century (if then), much as in South Africa. Many authors in each country professed to be familiar with English classical economics, drawing on these writings when they could be drawn on for support of opinions put forward, but otherwise turning to German or American authors when these better served. In Canada as well as in Australia, with land the most abundant factor, the disposal, settlement, and taxation of land long commanded attention. In Canada how to price and tax land and thereby avoid undue population dispersal was treated by R. Gourlay and his partial disciple, E. G. Wakefield (who came to Canada with Lord Durham), and later by followers of Henry George. Although Wakefield never went to Australia, his proposals regarding the pricing and settlement of land there were much defended and attacked, usually from motives of self-interest, with the attackers (among them young W. S. Jevons) sometimes effectively employing monetary, price, and other theories, often in part of classical derivation. Later the advantages and disadvantages of land nationalization and Henry George's proposals for land taxation commanded attention.

International commercial policy was continually the subject of attention in both countries. In Canada, freedom of trade was defended by merchants, carriers, and doctrinaire laissez-faireists, usually with arguments drawn from the English classical school;

47. My discussion of Canada and Australia is based upon two outstanding works by my colleague Craufurd Goodwin, *Canadian Economic Thought* (Durham, N. C., 1961), and *Economic Enquiry in Australia* (Durham, N. C., 1966).

it was attacked by advocates of protection—industrialists, home-market agriculturalists, antidumpers, growth-stimulators, etc.—who advanced both *ad hoc* arguments and arguments based mainly upon Carey, List, and Scottish John Rae, Canada's outstanding nineteenth-century economist. In Australia, though it was protected by a longer sea voyage than was Canada, commercial policy was the most common subject of economic discussion. Expositions of free-trade theory were usually inspired by protectionist arguments (which began at least as early as 1819) in need of refutation and by the fear of rising etatism after the gold discoveries. For many decades a considerable volume of literature was devoted to the promotion of protection, arguments in support of which ranged from advocacy of a balanced, home-market economy to emphasis upon the need to develop infant industry and an industrial demand for labor. Much (and often illicit) use was made of J. S. Mill's views as well as of the views of American and German protectionists, especially Carey, List, and the historical school. The most skilful of Australian treatments of the merits of protectionism, the famous report of 1929, was prompted largely by the attacks made by university economists in the 1920's upon the less tenable props of the tariff structure that had by then been erected in Australia.

With the sometime exception of international trade, no economic subject tended to command as much attention in the dominions as did monetary problems and the seemingly related problems manifest in price and activity fluctuation, usually more severe and less cushioned in relatively export-oriented economies. In Canada, monetary discussions, dominated by bankers, rested largely upon the English "Banking" or "Currency" schools, though Rae, in discussions not appreciated until university economists became ascendant, stressed the connection between banking and economic development. In Australia, far more than in Canada, a variety of circumstances, among them falling export and domestic prices in the later nineteenth century, prompted much perceptive discussion of means whereby the money supply might be increased (e.g., bimetallism, greater currency or credit issue, more lending on long-term collateral) and of the causes of economic fluctuation. Indeed, one found in Australia not only a climate of opinion favorable to the emergence of a Keynesian approach but several macroeconomists, the work of one of whom (influenced in part, as was Keynes, by the phenomenon of export leakage) developed a kind of matrix-type multiplier a half century before Keynes's simpler model won him world-wide fame. Because of concern with economic growth and stability, there developed an extensive literature relating to population policy, the significance of evolutionary theory for social inquiry and policy, transportation problems, the role and treatment of labor, the contribution of the state to economic growth, and the amassing and use of statistical information. The volume was much greater in Australia than in Canada, in considerable part because Canadians relied more than did Australians upon American and British writings and perhaps also because the United States, which drew so many immigrants from Canada, may have attracted many persons who might otherwise have entered the learned professions in Canada.

In both Canada and Australia the universities were mainly responsible for the transformation of problem-oriented economic discussion and "doctrine" into a disciplined economic science. This transformation proceeded quite slowly, however. In Canada the universities early included economics in their curricula but even as late as 1880 they exercised little influence, in part because the teaching of the subject was not departmentalized until after World War I, long after the burgeoning of the Canadian economy in and after the 1880's had enlivened interest in the subject and taken its presentation out of the hands of dull clerics and college administrators. Yet only after World War I did the universities begin to provide environments calculated to attract and hold able foreign-trained scholars and to promote the development of economics. In Australia too the development of economics was retarded by that allergy to hard economic thought, present in most men, not only among practitioners of traditional disciplines but also among those who live by the public hustings and have need of economic science if they would promote economic growth, as Australian legislators wished to do. Though occasionally taught as early as the 1860's and 1870's and in some measure thereafter, for a long time mainly by non-professional economists, economics did not flourish in the Australian universities until after World War I.

The tardiness with which economics won an important place in the dominion universities is not so striking when compared with the failure of economics to begin really to flourish in university settings in the United Kingdom or the United States until the last quarter of the nineteenth century. Nor is it surprising that so little was accomplished in the colonies through the establishment of university colleges, given the very small number of persons educationally eligible in Africa, Asia, and elsewhere (outside Canada, Australia, South Africa, New Zealand, and India).

Comments

Our discussion prompts a number of concluding comments. (1) It is striking how much familiarity with English and even other economic literature, albeit often inaccurate, residents in the dominions early manifested, very frequently though by no means always because they had come from abroad. At the same time, it seems establishable that a really disciplined approach to economic analysis awaited the development of a university system, in the absence of which looser though often perceptive treatments by publicists predominate and the distinction between economic science and mere discussion of economic policy remains obscure. (2) Interest in economic science initially arises in societies with the emergence of problems whose solution involves implicit or explicit knowledge of typical economic relationships or sequences. In India as well as in the dominions economic discussion originally related mainly if not entirely to local problems; in these parts even as in England, America, and western Europe men thought most economically about that which was troubling them economically, responding thereto somewhat homeostatically, though how they thought about this depended upon the economic theories, categories, tools, data, etc., at their disposal. We may say of economic ideas, much as Von Neumann said of mathematical ideas, that it is approximately true that they "originate in empirics." In time, however, certain socioeconomic conditions come into being; secondary students increase in number; there is pressure for higher education, and an economic surplus for its support; and there may be doubt, a doubt fed by the recurring exudation of destabilizing intellectual proletariats, that universities may entirely neglect serviceable subjects, to concentrate on those which, though innocuous, are of little practical application. Then sciences, among them economic science (even though it was long wedded to moral philosophy), may come to be taught in higher educational institutions. Indeed, if conditions remain propitious, economics may emulate mathematics and "live a peculiar life of its own," though perhaps never as completely divorced from the empiric.[48] This sequel had to await the advent of the middle third of the present century. (3) Every member of the British Empire and the successor Commonwealth early manifested a strong propensity to economic as well as political autonomy and to seek in economic science for supposedly supportive argument. (4) It is to be expected that economics will flourish much more in the future even than in the recent past of the Commonwealth, both because it can now serve the needs of many decision-making private units as well as those of a more or less collectivistic state faced by macro- as well as micro-economic problems. (5) Until now economics has flourished only in those members of the Commonwealth in which English has been widely enough understood in educational circles to serve as a vehicle, and even here lack of an adequate economic-educational infrastructure retarded the development and spread of economic science

48. See John von Neumann's remarks on mathematics in "The Mathematician," in James R. Newman, ed., The World of Mathematics, (4 vols.; New York, 1956), IV, 2063.

until the present century. (6) The Commonwealth would be strengthened and the prospects of its African members would be greatly improved were they to adopt the English language, and thus have access to the economic and other scientific infrastructure of the English-speaking world and hence to means for overcoming long-time non-viability. A somewhat similar argument may be advanced in respect of India, Pakistan, and Ceylon.

11

The Interchange of Institutions: Law

S. A. de Smith*

If one were drawing up a list of factors explaining the survival of the Commonwealth association, one would surely not fail to mention the pervasive influence exerted by the spirit and substance of the common law. Yet the part played in Commonwealth relations by the institutional machinery of the law is of small importance; the formal legal links between the members of the Commonwealth are little more than a miscellany of random connections; and one may search in vain for a corpus of fundamental Commonwealth law. The Statute of Westminster was the lawyers' swan song; the "singularly lawless association"[1] of the 1930's is even less lawyer-like in the 1960's. One is told that not so very long ago a house in Lincoln's Inn Fields in London bore a plate directing "tradesmen and attorneys" to use the side entrance.[2] In the modern Commonwealth, tradesmen regularly use the front entrance; attorneys (and barristers) are saved from indignity, but their welcome is likely to be unenthusiastic and their appearances on the scene tend to be discreet, inconspicuous, and infrequent.

I

Many years have elapsed since the Commonwealth shed its international personality, and it is difficult to imagine any cir-

* Professor of public law, London School of Economics and Political Science, University of London.
1. R. T. E. Latham, The Law and the Commonwealth (London, 1949), p. 513.
2. R. M. Jackson, The Machinery of Justice in England (4th ed.; Cambridge, 1964), p. 243.

cumstances in which it would re-emerge as an integrated political entity. That the Commonwealth as such might develop its own legislative and executive organs of government in the foreseeable future seems to be an idea too preposterous to merit discussion notwithstanding the recent decision to establish a Commonwealth Secretariat. Nevertheless, there are those for whom the problem of devising a new supreme court for the Commonwealth remains an issue worthy of solemn deliberation. Ten years ago the notion of a perambulating Judicial Committee of the Privy Council, forever on circuit, was still being fitfully canvassed; and even today its echoes reverberate in unexpected places. If Canada had abolished the appeal because it had felt the Judicial Committee to be the House of Lords in disguise, could not the image be transformed by swamping the Anglo-Scottish element with an influx of judges from other Commonwealth countries? Or could one perhaps hope to change the image by changing the name of the Judicial Committee as well as its composition?[3] Or should one aim at superseding, or complementing, the Judicial Committee by a Commonwealth Court of Human Rights?

Glibly to dismiss each of these visions as a chimera might be injudicious, but one would be surprised to see any of them translated into reality. Everybody agrees that the Judicial Committee has done valuable work as a detached appellate tribunal[4] setting and enforcing high minimum standards of judicial administration and promoting the uniformity of laws insofar as uniformity was an objective to be aimed at; yet the valedictory compliments paid to it have seldom concealed dissatisfaction with its modern role. And the valedictions (which have not invariably been complimentary) have been numerous. By 1955 it had been deprived of jurisdiction to entertain appeals from Canada, South Africa, India, and Pakistan. In 1959 it was pos-

3. Cf. Edmund J. Cooray, "A Commonwealth Court," *Journal of the Parliaments of the Commonwealth*, XLIII (Oct., 1962), 347. The writer, representing the government of Ceylon, had put forward a proposal for a new Commonwealth Court at the meeting of Commonwealth Prime Ministers in 1960.

4. Though Winston Churchill's description of the Judicial Committee (in the debates on the Government of India Bill, 1935) as "the most august court that has ever been in existence in modern times" (G. B., 5 *Parl. Debs.* [Commons], CCC, 150, April 1, 1935) may be regarded as over-colorful.

sible to envisage an expansion of its jurisdiction in constitutional matters; for Ghana and the Federation of Malaya had retained the appeal after independence, and a comprehensive list of justiciable fundamental rights had been incorporated in the Nigerian Constitution. Indeed, since 1960, most of the constitutions with which Commonwealth countries have been equipped on the attainment of independence have embodied not only an entrenched bill of rights, but also an entrenched right of appeal to the Judicial Committee on questions of constitutional interpretation. Nevertheless, by the end of 1963 appeals from the republics of Ghana, Cyprus, Tanganyika, and Nigeria had been abolished[5] and it was to be expected that other new African states (and possibly Ceylon) would soon follow the same path.

If the objections to the retention of the appeal had been based on the fact that the process of appeal was often dilatory and expensive, or even on the patent unfamiliarity of so many members of the Judicial Committee with the problems involved in interpreting written constitutions and with the content of exotic systems of private law, they might have been overcome by displacing the Judicial Committee from its permanent seat in London and adding several Commonwealth judges to its regular membership.[6] But in many of the new states the objections ran deeper. It is doubtless correct to say (as the Judicial Committee recently had occasion to affirm) that "true independence is not in any way compromised by the continuance" of the appeal;[7] yet the very existence of an appeal from the highest domestic court to an external authority could affront nationalist sentiment. When, moreover, that external authority was Her Majesty in Council, it would appear reasonable to terminate the right of appeal at the same time as a republican constitu-

5. Appeals still lie from Malaysia, although it is not part of Her Majesty's dominions. The advice of the Judicial Committee is tendered direct to the Yang di-Pertuan Agong, the Supreme Head of the Federation.

6. The appointment of new members from Australia, New Zealand, and Nigeria was announced in 1963, but none of them has sat regularly as a member of the board. Cf. *Commonwealth Survey*, VIII, No. 20, Sept. 25, 1962, p. 781.

7. *Ibralebee* v. *R.* [1964] 2 W.L.R. 76, at p. 90 (*held* that the power of the Judicial Committee to entertain appeals in criminal matters from Ceylon had not been impliedly abrogated by the granting of independence).

tion was adopted. If the appellate body had been a different kind of tribunal, free from the taint of "terminal colonialism," it is unlikely that enthusiasm for the retention of its jurisdiction would have been appreciably warmer. The political embarrassment suffered by the federal government in Nigeria as a result of the Judicial Committee's decision in the *Akintola* case[8] would have been no smaller if the judgment had been handed down by a new Commonwealth court. And one cannot imagine that the government of Ghana would be willing to accept the determinations of any Commonwealth tribunal on the validity of its acts.

In short, nationalism does not stop short at the frontiers of adjudication. If a new Commonwealth court were to be established, it would be accorded jurisdiction over part of the Commonwealth only. To Sir Alec Douglas-Home the idea of a Commonwealth court is "immensely valuable,"[9] but there are good reasons for doubting whether the replacement of the Judicial Committee by such a court would be worth while. *A fortiori,* a Commonwealth Court of Human Rights would be an inappropriate institution for the Commonwealth of 1964. Optimists may still persuade themselves that by 1974 all members of the Commonwealth will have agreed to submit to the jurisdiction of a supranational court, analogous to the European Court of Human Rights, delivering contentious judgments on politically sensitive issues.

II

In 1955, as in 1964, the basic rules of the Commonwealth association were concerned mainly with the acquisition and discontinuance of membership. They were rules of convention, not rules of strict law; and, like other conventions, they could be

8. *Adegbenro* v. *Akintola* [1963] A.C. 614. The effect of the decision was immediately nullified by a retroactive constitutional amendment.
9. G. B., 5 *Parl. Debs.* (Commons), DCLXXXVIII, 1366, Feb. 6, 1964. The principle was to be discussed at the Third Commonwealth Law Conference in 1965.

(and have been) reshaped by political practice.[10] Legal dogmas which, twenty years earlier, had appeared to be inseparable from the definition of the Commonwealth, had already been enfeebled to the point of atrophy. The fundamental doctrine of common allegiance to a common Crown had been deprived of its universality by the recognition of India's republican membership of the Commonwealth. Its corollaries—the denial of a right to separate neutrality in war or to unilateral secession, the principle that all citizens of Commonwealth countries were British subjects, and the curious *inter se* doctrine of Commonwealth relations[11]—were dead or dying ducks. Since then the disintegration of the concept has been manifested in two ways. In the first place, the Indian precedent (which in 1959 was not officially recognized as having set a precedent at all) has been followed by a number of other countries. In June, 1964, those non-Britannic members of the Commonwealth owing allegiance to the Crown no longer commanded a majority. They were balanced by the republics of India, Pakistan, Ghana, Cyprus, Tanganyika and Zanzibar, and Nigeria (and more to come), monarchical Malaysia, and innominate Uganda. Secondly, most of the new Commonwealth members do not designate their own citizens as British subjects or even as Commonwealth citizens; several prohibit the holding of dual citizenship; and the status of citizens of other Commonwealth countries is being gradually assimilated to that of aliens.

On the whole, constitutional lawyers did not agree that the Statute of Westminster had effectively terminated the sovereignty of the imperial Parliament in relation to the dominions; for Parliament was inherently incapable of fettering its own freedom of action, and in any event the statute had merely purported to regulate the manner in which future legislative authority was to be exercised. The essential provisions of the

10. See generally K. C. Wheare, *The Constitutional Structure of the Commonwealth* (Oxford, 1960); J. E. S. Fawcett, *The British Commonwealth in International Law* (London, 1963), chap. x; S. A. de Smith, *The New Commonwealth and its Constitutions* (London, 1964), chap. i.

11. Fawcett, *The Inter se Doctrine of Commonwealth Relations* (London, 1958).

statute were reproduced in the Ceylon Independence Act, 1947. But in the same year the Indian Independence Act evinced a clear intention that subsequent Acts of the United Kingdom Parliament were never to have effect *ex proprio vigore* in the laws of India or Pakistan.[12] This would not relieve English judges of their obligation to apply an Act of Parliament clearly designed to alter the law of India or Pakistan; but it could be treated as conclusive authority for Indian and Pakistani judges to adopt a different view, assuming that they needed any authority to recognize the severance of their own legal systems from the imperial root. Now the pattern of independence legislation has become demonstrably incompatible with any suggestion that the paramountcy of the United Kingdom Parliament remains the ultimate legal principle of a Commonwealth legal order. The acts passed in pursuance of the attainment of independence by the Federation of Malaya (later Malaysia) and Zanzibar made no reference to future United Kingdom legislation for those countries; the Independence Acts for Nigeria, Sierra Leone, Tanganyika, Jamaica, Trinidad and Tobago, Uganda, and Kenya stated explicitly that no future United Kingdom act was to extend to those countries as part of their laws.[13] Today no voice would be raised outside Canada, Australia, and New Zealand to assert the continuing hierarchical superiority of the United Kingdom Parliament in the municipal legal order; and even in the older members voices would be muffled and discordant.

Not only have the legal systems of the newly independent Commonwealth countries been released from formal subordination; to an increasing extent their constitutions have become autochthonous,[14] or home-grown. India, Pakistan, Ghana, Tan-

12. Indian Independence Act, 1947 (10 & 11 Geo. 6, c. 30), s. 6(4): "No Act of Parliament of the United Kingdom passed on or after the appointed day shall extend . . . to either of the new Dominions as part of the law of that Dominion unless it is extended thereto by a law of the legislature of the Dominion."
13. E.g., Kenya Independence Act, 1963 (c. 54), s. 1(2).
14. For variant formulations of the principle of constitutional autochthony, see Wheare, *The Constitutional Structure of the Commonwealth*, chap. iv; Kenneth Robinson, "Autochthony and the Transfer of Power," Robinson and Frederick Madden, eds., *Essays in Imperial Government* (Oxford, 1963), p. 249.

ganyika, and Nigeria have followed in the footsteps of the Irish Free State and have adopted constitutions which are purely local in origin. Zanzibar's singularly short-lived constitution of December, 1963, was also a domestic product. The Cyprus Constitution of 1960 was of mixed parentage, but Britain was not among its progenitors. It is to be expected that by the end of the present decade most of the constitutions of the Commonwealth will have local roots. Nevertheless, several of them will doubtless be recognizable by a close resemblance in content to Westminster's export models.

III

Britain's endeavors to transplant the Westminster model of parliamentary democracy in inhospitable soils are inevitably being criticized today. But too often one has the impression that the critic's aim is misdirected, for he usually lacks any clear conception of what a typical Westminster-style constitution contains. In fact, it will contain many devices which have no place in the textbooks of British constitutional law. It will codify conventions of responsible cabinet government in the form of potentially justiciable rules of strict law, but the rules may differ materially from those of the model on which they have been based.[15] Moreover, it will embody entrenched sections, alterable only by a special procedure; it will normally provide for the limitation of legislative sovereignty, judicial review of the constitutionality of legislation, guarantees of fundamental human rights; it will incorporate institutional safeguards, unknown at Westminster, for protecting the independence of the judiciary, the police, and the public service and for insulating the process of prosecution and the conduct of elections from political inter-

15. See generally de Smith, *The New Commonwealth* . . . , chap. iii., Appendix. In *Adegbenro* v. *Akintola* (note 3, *supra*) the Nigerian Federal Supreme Court had held by a majority that the scope of a Regional governor's power to dismiss a premier was to be construed by reference to the corresponding conventions of the British Constitution; but the privy council, reversing the decision, declined to invoke British conventional rules and preferred to confine itself to interpretation of the express wording of the constitutional text.

ference. To a lawyer the constitutional provisions relating to the judiciary, prosecutions, and human rights—provisions which became common form only in the late 1950's and early 1960's— must be of special interest.

The judiciary

In England superior judges are appointed by the executive and are removable upon an address presented by each House of Parliament in pursuance of a simple majority vote. The fact that "political" appointments are now almost unknown is not attributable to any rule of law. The fact that the judges enjoy an extraordinary degree of freedom from outside pressure in the discharge of their functions, and virtually complete security of tenure, is attributable mainly to the interplay of constitutional conventions, political practice, professional tradition, and public opinion.

As a matter of strict law, both the appointment and the removal of colonial judges fell within the area of executive discretion.[16] But to introduce the British legal framework upon the granting of self-government might not afford an adequate safeguard for judicial independence in a climate charged with political tension. In the spring of 1957 it became apparent from the Report of the Singapore Constitutional Conference[17] that fresh and imaginative ideas had been conceived within the Legal Division of the Colonial Office.[18] The conference agreed that under the new constitution superior judges (other than the chief justice) would be appointed on the advice not of the executive but of a predominantly judicial body, and that they were to be removable only for infirmity or misbehavior in pursuance of a report of a judicial tribunal of inquiry and a subsequent reference of the case to the Judicial Committee of the Privy Council. The new procedure for making judicial appointments was trace-

16. See *Terrell* v. *Secretary of State for the Colonies* [1953] 2 Q.B. 482.
17. Cmnd. 147, G. B., *Parl. Paps.*, 1956-57, XX, p. 107, par. 46.
18. See generally Sir Kenneth Roberts-Wray, "The Independence of the Judiciary in Commonwealth Countries," *Changing Law in Developing Countries*, ed. J. N. D. Anderson (London, 1963), p. 63.

able to precedents set in Ceylon and Ghana; the proposal to give judges the exclusive power to decide whether judges should be removed from office was a novelty, though reference of these issues to the Judicial Committee had taken place in the past. After 1957 every constitution drafted in Great Smith Street for an independent or internally self-governing Commonwealth country provided for a judicial service commission, under the chairmanship of the chief justice, with authority to determine senior judicial appointments, and with full power to appoint, promote, transfer, discipline, and remove other judicial officers; and the new method of safeguarding the tenure of superior judges was gradually incorporated into the constitutions of all territories in the Commonwealth.

It is perhaps too early to predict the durability of these arrangements, but where the principles of constitutionalism are rejected they will be thrown out with the bath water. In 1957 Ghana embarked on independence with a Judicial Service Commission; superior judges were to be removable for infirmity or misbehavior in pursuance of a two-thirds' majority vote in the National Assembly. In 1959 the Judicial Service Commission was abolished and judicial appointments thereafter were made in the discretion of the executive. Under the republican Constitution of 1960 judicial appointments were to be made by the president, and the chief justice (who was head of the Judicial Service) was removable as such in the president's discretion. In December, 1963, after a special court composed of three judges had acquitted three out of five men who had been accused of treasonable offenses, President Nkrumah dismissed Sir Arku Korsah, the chief justice.[19] As a result of a constitutional amendment in February, 1964, he acquired power to dismiss all superior judges in his discretion without any parliamentary address, and in March he dismissed three judges of the Supreme

19. By Act of Parliament he was also granted power to nullify the verdict of a special court, and he proceeded to quash the verdicts of the court in question. Cf. Rousseau, *The Social Contract*, Book IV, chap. vi: "If . . . the peril of such a kind that the paraphernalia of the laws are an obstacle to their preservation, the method is to nominate a supreme ruler, who shall silence all the laws. . . . In, such a case, there is no doubt about the general will."

Court. Tanganyika, on the other hand, retained a Judicial Service Commission under its republican Constitution, though its functions no longer extended to appointments and promotions; and it retained the safeguard whereby superior judges were removable only upon an adverse report of a judicial tribunal of inquiry. In October, 1963, however, Nigeria abolished all judicial service commissions, and also substituted removal upon parliamentary addresses for the judicial tribunal of inquiry procedure. These changes (which, apart from the replacement of the governor-general by a president, were the most striking departures from the constitutional scheme of 1960) do not necessarily foreshadow political dominance of the judicial branch of government; they may be regarded simply as an indication that Nigerians prefer the Westminster model to Westminster's export model; nonetheless, they afford another reason for doubting whether the policy of rigorously delimiting politically neutral zones can be effectively implemented in Africa today.

Prosecutions[20]

Under the British system the attorney general is a politician, lacking security of tenure, and the director of public prosecutions is a civil servant acting under the attorney general's directions. In deciding whether to institute criminal proceedings, or to give leave for proceedings to be instituted, or to enter a *nolle prosequi* in order to stop a trial on indictment, the attorney general need not blind himself to political considerations or deafen himself to the voices of his political colleagues, but the discretion is his alone and he must not accept dictation from any quarter.

In general these principles have worked satisfactorily. But if they are to be transported to a newly self-governing Commonwealth country they must be given constitutional status in an appropriately adapted form. Since 1957 two main types of constitutional provisions have been employed, the choice depending on whether the attorney general is to be a public officer or a politician. If he is to be a public officer, the constitution will lay

20. de Smith, *The New Commonwealth*, pp. 143-45, 252, 298, 300.

down that in instituting, conducting, taking over, continuing and discontinuing prosecutions he is not to be subject to the direction of any other person, and that in the exercise of all of these functions other than commencing prosecutions his responsibilities are to be exclusive. He will be removable only for inability or misbehavior on the recommendation of a predominantly judicial tribunal. If, as is usual, the attorney general is to be a minister, the independent constitutional functions that would otherwise be vested in him will normally be vested in the director of public prosecutions, who will also be afforded special security of tenure.[21]

Political conflict in new states will often find expression in prosecutions of opponents of the government for political offenses, and to expect that constitutional devices designed to screen the process of prosecution from political influence will survive indefinitely is to display a naïve optimism. The attorney general in Ghana and the D.P.P. in Tanganyika are now fully subject to presidential directions. In Nigeria the functions formerly vested in the D.P.P. have been transferred to the attorney general (who is a minister) on the same basis of personal independence; the D.P.P. no longer enjoys a constitutional status differentiating him from other public officers.[22] Here again Nigeria has preferred to revert to the original Westminster model; the distrust of the political executive manifested in the structure of the discarded export model was not shared by the framers of the republican constitution.

Bills of rights[23]

Guarantees of fundamental rights were written into the Indian Constitution of 1950. But the Colonial Office was not inspired by the Constituent Assembly's example. It had been unmoved by the adoption of the Universal Declaration of Human

21. For an early example of these devices, see sections 228-33 of Nigeria's pre-independence constitution, as inserted by section 106 of the *Nigeria (Constitution) (Amendment) Order in Council 1958*, S. I., 1958, No. 429, 1958.
22. Constitution of the Federation (1963, No. 20), ss. 88, 104.
23. de Smith, *The New Commonwealth*, chap. v.

Rights; it remained unmoved by Britain's accession to the European Convention on Human Rights and by the extension of its terms to the dependent territories in the early 1950's. Not until 1959 was a comprehensive bill of rights written into a colonial constitution; but the Nigerian precedent (which had its origins in the peculiar difficulty of devising any generally acceptable constitutional safeguard for the interests of minorities and individuals) has broadened downwards with startling rapidity. Among the Commonwealth countries which have achieved independence since 1959, only Tanganyika has spurned the suggestion of a constitutional bill of rights. In a recent period of two months, Northern Rhodesia, the Bahama Islands, Swaziland, and Mauritius joined the legion of territories whose constitutions paraded a bill of rights, and it was certain that there would be further recruitment.

From the point of view of a majority party, a bill of rights may well seem the most innocuous, the least inhibiting of constitutional guarantees. One is reminded that at the Nyasaland Constitutional Conference of 1962, Dr. Banda rejected proposals for a second chamber, a council of chiefs, a council of state and an ombudsman, but accepted a constitutional bill of rights.[24] One has also observed that in Nigeria the opponents of the federal government have drawn cold comfort from the list of fundamental rights.[25] Parliamentary democracy and the rule of law would have survived in India during the Nehru epoch without constitutional guarantees of fundamental rights. Constitutionalism can exist without a bill of rights, and a bill of rights cannot ensure the maintenance of constitutionalism; but a bill of rights tends to buttress the practice of constitutionalism by prescribing high minimum standards, educating public opinion, and interposing an obstacle in the way of legislatures and governments which are disposed to make piecemeal encroachments upon the enjoy-

24. "Report of the Nyasaland Constitutional Conference . . . ," Cmnd. 1887, pp. 7-9, G. B., *Parl. Paps.* 1961-62.
25. D. C. Holland, "Human Rights in Nigeria," *Current Legal Problems*, XV (1962), 145; David La Van Grove, "The 'Sentinels' of Liberty? The Nigerian Judiciary and Fundamental Rights," *Journal of African Law*, VII (Autumn, 1963), 152.

ment of basic rights and freedoms. In a revolutionary situation, or in a society where the legitimacy of organized dissent is denied, a constitutional bill of rights will be valueless as a safeguard for the political nonconformist.[26] In a relatively tranquil climate where political pluralism is accepted as a fact of life, it is potentially a valuable shield against oppressive or manifestly unreasonable action by the state and its officials.

Constitutional bills of rights in the Commonwealth today fall into four classes. First there is the Indian prototype, which has yet to be copied elsewhere but which will doubtless facilitate the interpretation of other bills of rights; for instance, the Maltese Court of Appeal used a judgment of the Indian Supreme Court as a persuasive authority in constructing the meaning of "freedom of expression."[27] Secondly, there are the Nigerian-style bills of rights. The Nigerian model, which, with minor adaptations—for example, tighter guarantees against expropriation without proper compensation, better safeguards for persons placed in preventive detention during an emergency, and qualified guarantees of freedom to leave the country and freedom from expulsion—has been reproduced in a number of other constitutions, was itself based on the European Convention on Human Rights, and also bears some resemblance to the Indian guarantees. The characteristic pattern is one in which the enunciation of a general right (freedom of association and peaceable assembly) is followed by a list of the circumstances in which derogation from the right is permissible. To be valid, derogation must also conform to a standard of reasonableness determined in the last resort by the courts. These unexciting recitals have been labeled "bills of exceptions"; their practical efficacy will vary from one country to another. Thirdly, the Southern Rhodesian declaration of rights stands alone because of the peculiar form and far-reaching scope of the exceptions to the guarantees.

26. Though it may have some value in politically non-contentious situations, e.g., by prescribing the minimum requirements of a fair trial.

27. *Buttigieg* v. *Minister of Health*, *The Times* (London), Jan. 14, 1964, p. 17 (*held* a government ban on health department employees taking to work newspapers which had been condemned by the church authorities contravened the constitutional guarantee of freedom of expression).

Its terms will not be reproduced in other constitutions, but one feature of the new framework—an independent constitutional council charged with the duty of drawing public attention to contraventions of the guarantees—did reappear ephemerally with a change of costume in Northern Rhodesia.[28] Lastly, there is the Canadian bill of rights, different in form, proclaiming broad generalities in sonorous phrases but lacking the quality of constitutional entrenchment. It has provided the model for Trinidad's constitutionally entrenched bill of rights, and it may soon be reproduced in New Zealand. American lawyers will find much that is familiar in its terminology, but its teeth are blunted.

IV

Eighty-five years ago the Judicial Committee of the Privy Council asserted that it was "of the utmost importance that in all parts of the empire where English law prevails, the interpretation of that law by the Courts should be as nearly as possible the same."[29] In 1963 the Lord Chief Justice of England thought it "of importance, to say the least, that the common law should develop homogeneously throughout the Commonwealth."[30] That "lawyers' law" should be essentially uniform throughout the common-law jurisdictions of the Commonwealth has indeed been a persistently recurrent theme over the years. Why it ought to be uniform has seldom been made clear. Divergence is assumed to pollute a pure spring of jurisprudence, to weaken the Commonwealth connection, to make life inconvenient and untidy. But the possible advantages of creative experimentation, and the need for adaptation to local conditions, are too often overlooked by the conservative idealist. Uniformity does not always make for harmony, and harmonization permits a wide tolerance of diversity. Now that the migrant common law speaks

28. *Northern Rhodesia (Constitution) Order in Council, 1963*, S. I., 1963, No. 2088, chap. ii. The constitution of independent Zambia does not reproduce this provision.
29. *Trimble* v. *Hall* (1879) 5 App. Cas. 342, at p. 345.
30. *Attorney General* v. *Clough* [1963] 1 Q.B.773, at p. 792.

in a variety of local accents, one may glance back briefly to survey its passage and settlement overseas.

The extent to which English law was applicable in colonies was partly dependent on the method by which a territory had been acquired by the Crown: in general, settled colonies received English law as it stood at the date of acquisition, and conquered and ceded colonies retained their own systems of law subject to certain modifications and exceptions. However, in a number of territories the reception of English law was determined by reference to a specified date. In the Gold Coast, for example, the courts were directed to apply the common law, the doctrines of equity, and the statutes of general application in force in England on July 24, 1874;[31] these rules of law could be changed by local enactment, save insofar as they were contained in United Kingdom legislation which already applied directly of its own force in the colony. The volume of United Kingdom legislation extending directly to dependent territories has never been substantial,[32] but a great many rules of English law have been transported by the vehicle of local referential enactment.[33]

Once the substance of English law had been incorporated into a colonial legal system, deviations from the metropolitan pattern might well occur, for there was no formal machinery expressly designed to secure the maintenance of uniformity. Nevertheless, a high degree of harmony was preserved. In the first place, subsequent United Kingdom law reform Acts would usually be adopted (sometimes tardily) by the local legislatures; where an Act was considered suitable for local adoption its terms would be circulated in a Colonial Office despatch to all governors.

31. For the difficulties arising in the interpretation of this provision, see Antony Allott, *Essays in African Law* (London, 1960), pp. 7-10, 31; F. A. R. Bennion, *The Constitutional Law of Ghana* (London, 1962), pp. 391-98. See also A. E. W. Park, *The Sources of Nigerian Law* (London, 1963), pp. 20-29; W. C. Ekow Daniels, *The Common Law in West Africa* (London, 1964), chaps. v, vi, xii.

32. For illustrations, see 5 *Halsbury's Laws of England* (3rd ed.; London, 1953), 703-8.

33. For the method of introducing English commercial law into Malaya and Singapore, see *Malaya and Singapore: The Development of Their Laws and Constitutions*, ed. L. A. Sheridan (London, 1961), p. 28. See also Daniels, *The Common Law*, pp. 130-34.

Secondly, on complex issues model ordinances, based on but not identical with the English rules, would be prepared in London from time to time for local enactment. Thirdly, at the apex of the judicial system the decisions of the Judicial Committee of the Privy Council, which bound all colonial courts, ensured uniformity on particular topics. Fourthly, decisions of the superior courts in England on common-law doctrines and the interpretation of statutes enjoyed the highest persuasive authority in colonial courts. The formulation of the doctrine of judicial precedent in relation to the colonies has given rise to inconclusive controversy,[34] but it was hardly conceivable that a colonial court would refuse to follow a decision of the House of Lords or even the Court of Appeal. And as late as 1914 the High Court of Australia, one of the most eminent judicial tribunals in the world, ruled that, in the interests of imperial legal harmony, it would follow a decision of the House of Lords if it conflicted with one of its own.[35] Fifthly, English law was used as a residual source of law. Where there were gaps in a developing legal system they were generally filled by rules of English law. Similarly, where the local courts were directed to apply native customary law only insofar as it was not repugnant to "natural justice, equity and good conscience," the yardstick most frequently employed was the existing English common law.[36] Sixthly, judges, magistrates, and law officers were to an overwhelming extent English lawyers reared at the Inns of Court, sharing assumptions absorbed during their legal education, and turning instinctively to English law as a source of innovation and a secure anchorage; and the

34. Helpful analyses have been published by Allott, *Essays*, chap. ii; T. O. Elias, "Colonial Courts and the Doctrine of Judicial Precedent," *Modern Law Review*, XVIII (July, 1955), 356; and Daniels, *The Common Law*, pp. 186-95.

35. *Piro v. Foster (W) & Co., Ltd. (1943)* 68 C.L.R.313. See further Zelman Cowen, "The Binding Effect of English Decisions upon Australian Courts," *Law Quarterly Review*, LX (Oct., 1944), 378; G. W. Paton in *The Commonwealth of Australia: The Development of Its Laws and Constitution*, ed. Paton (London, 1952), pp. 11-14.

36. See, e.g., J. Duncan M. Derrett, "Justice, Equity and Good Conscience," in *Changing Law in Developing Countries*, ed. Anderson, p. 114; Bennion, *The Constitutional Law*, pp. 408-11; Allott, *Essays*, p. 11; M. C. Setalvad, *The Common Law in India* (London, 1960), pp. 23-24, 53-57, 61, 62; Park, *The Sources of Nigerian Law*, pp. 69-75; Daniels, *The Common Law*, chap. x.

cases cited before them by practitioners (who would also be products of the Inns of Court) would be predominantly English cases.[37] And the mobility of members of the Colonial Legal Service was a factor of incalculable importance in the harmonious development of legal systems in the Commonwealth. A crown counsel in Fiji might become solicitor general of the Gambia, attorney general of Hong Kong and then a judge in British Guiana. On his travels the common law would be his ever-present companion, and insofar as he had responsibilities for molding the shape of the law his intellectual world would be Anglo-centric.

The effects of the reception of English law have not invariably been felicitous. It was hardly appropriate to extend to Malaya the English rules governing testamentary gifts in partial restraint of marriage.[38] Nor do Nigerians rejoice in the fact that their law of real property is largely based on a United Kingdom statute which is out of print and unobtainable.[39] But the common law has provided a firm basis for a host of emergent legal systems. England's legacy may prove to be as enduring as was Rome's. And the common law is not merely a body of substantive rules; it is also, indeed primarily, a method of administering justice,[40] with the judge presiding as a detached and impartial arbiter.

V

Sooner or later, however, political independence becomes incompatible with a continuing juridical dependence. To end Privy Council appeals is the most obvious form of self-assertion, but there are other, less spectacular, methods of proclaiming the autonomy and unique identity of a legal system.

37. For criticisms of excessive reliance on English decisions, see Sheridan, *Malaya and Singapore*, p. 20; Park, *Sources of Nigerian Law*, p. 44; G. V. V. Nicholls (Canada), *Law Quarterly Review*, LXXVI (Jan., 1960), 75.

38. *Leong* v. *Chye* [1955] A.C.648.

39. B. O. Nwabueze, *The Machinery of Justice in Nigeria* (London, 1963), p. 18.

40. A. L. Goodhart, *Law Quarterly Review*, LXXVI (Jan., 1960), 46.

Legislation

There is little evidence that law-reform legislation in Commonwealth countries has made a significant impact in Britain. The reports of the Law Reform Committee and the Criminal Law Revision Committee indicate that scant attention has been paid to Commonwealth precedents as a source of inspiration. On the other hand, there is ample evidence that United Kingdom law-reform Acts have influenced law reform in other Commonwealth countries. And in recent years Britain has often taken the lead in reform—for instance, in modifying the law of occupiers' liability, in mitigating the rigor of the law of homicide, and in removing the taint of criminality from suicide. Yet when Commonwealth experience has been available to draw on, it has tended to be ignored. The example set by New Zealand in restricting freedom of testation in the interests of family dependents was disregarded in Britain for nearly forty years. The first Commonwealth country in which the idea of an ombudsman was seriously canvassed was Britain, but it was left to New Zealand to import the institution while the British Conservative government dismissed the whole notion as constitutionally objectionable and administratively undesirable. However, in 1964 a change of government in Britain brought with it a more sympathetic approach to this problem. New Zealand has also preceded Britain in introducing a scheme of compensation for the victims of crimes of violence, though here the mother-country did not lag far behind.

In many of the new Commonwealth countries a dearth of legal advisers and draftsmen and the pressing urgency of other tasks are likely to retard the conception and implementation of thoroughgoing law reforms. Ghana, however, has already made a striking impression with the scope and originality of its law reform program; in particular its new company law, based on the Gower Report,[41] will assuredly attract emulators elsewhere. One may safely predict that the general pattern of reform in

41. *The Commission of Enquiry into the Working and Administration of the Present Company Law of Ghana, Report* (Accra: Govt. Printer, 1961).

new states will be characterized by simplification and the elimination of technicalities. To an increasing extent one may expect legislation in the older Commonwealth countries also to digress from familiar paths; the Australian Uniform Companies Act is by no means a carbon copy of its British parent.[42] To hope for uniformity, or even perhaps close harmony, in the laws of the Commonwealth in the 1970's would be unrealistic. What is important is that Commonwealth countries should be in a position to make use of the experience of others for their own purposes; and this necessarily implies that they should have access to relevant information about legislative developments throughout the Commonwealth.

Case law

For Canada the Judicial Committee of the Privy Council lies dead and buried, but its constitutional precedents have continued to rule the Supreme Court from the grave. Elsewhere it can be taken for granted that Privy Council and House of Lords decisions will long exercise strong persuasive, if not binding, authority after juridical independence has been achieved. Their binding force can, of course, be abrogated by explicit legislative or judicial pronouncements. Ghana has made it clear that decisions of the House of Lords and the Privy Council no longer have binding force, and has named the common law, but not merely English common law, as a source of the law of Ghana;[43] but English and Privy Council precedents are still cited in Ghanaian courts. Recent developments in Australia have taken a different turn but are of even greater general interest. The High Court, flinching from its self-imposed obligation to apply the much-criticized doctrine of "murder by negligence" laid down by the

42. Geoffrey Sawer, "Federal-State Cooperation in Law Reform: Lessons of the Australian Uniform Companies Act," *Melbourne University Law Review*, IV (Nov., 1963), 238; and see generally Richard H. Leach, "The Uniform Law Movement in Australia," *American Journal of Comparative Law*, XII (Spring, 1963), 206.
43. Constitution of 1960, arts. 40, 42(4); Interpretation Act, 1960 (C.A.4), s.17.

House of Lords in *Smith's* case[44] has deliberately changed direction and has departed from its policy of applying House of Lords decisions in preference to its own.[45] Australian and New Zealand courts,[46] like the Supreme Court of Canada,[47] have also declined to follow the views of the House of Lords[48] on the virtually unqualified power of government departments to withhold relevant documents from disclosure in legal proceedings. It appears that these recent Antipodean decisions, which were discussed approvingly in the best-known English law journal,[49] have had an indirect effect on the attitude of the English courts themselves to claims to Crown privilege; and the critical comments of the English Court of Appeal on the existing state of English law[50] have at last moved the British government to consider the need for amending legislation. This is surely an entirely healthy state of affairs.

Until the last two or three years Commonwealth precedents were seldom cited or relied on in English courts. Lately, however, partly because of the increasing tendency of English legal writers to draw attention to Commonwealth experience on doubtful and controversial points of law, there has been a perceptible change of emphasis. On issues as diverse as tortious liability to child trespassers,[51] technical matters in patent law,[52] the privilege claimed by journalists to be immune from the duty to divulge their sources of information in judicial proceedings,[53] and unre-

44. [1961] A.C.290.
45. *Parker* v. *R.* [1963] Argus L.R.524, at p. 537 (*per* Dixon C.J.).
46. *Bruce* v. *Waldron* [1963] V.R.3; *Corbett* v. *Social Security Commission* [1962] N.Z.L.R. 878; though cf. *Nash* v. *Commissioner for Railways* (1963), S.R. (N.S.W.) 357.
47. *R.* v. *Snider* [1954] S.C.R.479.
48. *Duncan* v. *Cammell, Laird & Co.* [1942] A.C.624.
49. *Law Quarterly Review*, LXXIX (1963), 37, 153, 313. See also *Cambridge Law Journal*, Nov., 1962, p. 174.
50. *Merricks* v. *Nott-Bower* [1964] 2 W.L.R. 702. In the subsequent case of *In re Grosvenor Hotel, London* (*No.* 2) [1964] 3 W.L.R. 992 a majority of the members of the Court of Appeal were of the opinion that the *ratio decidendi* of *Duncan's* case had been too widely stated and that the relevant rules of English law were those expressed in the Commonwealth decisions referred to at notes 46 and 47, *ante*.
51. *Videan* v. *British Transport Commission* [1963] 2 Q.B.650; though see now *Commissioner for Railways* v. *Quinlan* [1964] 2 W.L.R. 817 (J.C.P.C.).
52. *R.* v. *Patents Appeal Tribunal, ex p. Swift* [1962] 2 Q.B.647.
53. *Attorney-General* v. *Clough* [1963] 1 Q.B.773.

solved problems in the field of criminal law,[54] one has found that Australasian precedents in particular have been given a great deal of weight. Belatedly, a pattern of interchange extending to England itself is being created. That it will spread to other areas of the law is beyond doubt.

The personnel of the law

When independence came to the Commonwealth countries of West Africa, most of the judicial offices were occupied by English lawyers. In East Africa there was not a single indigenous African judge at the time of independence; indeed, in 1960 there were only thirty qualified African lawyers in Kenya, Uganda, and Tanganyika.[55] Since independence the general trend has been to fill judicial vacancies by the appointment of local lawyers if suitable persons are available, to recruit expatriate lawyers from Commonwealth countries other than Britain if they are not, to take immediate action to set up local university law faculties and professional law schools, and to provide some legal training for unqualified African magistrates.

The drive towards Africanization is likely to lead to the growth of integrated hierarchical judicial systems, with regular promotions from the lower ranks to the higher (especially in East and Central Africa), so that direct recruitment from the bar to the superior judiciary will be unusual. Of the new judges, an increasing proportion will not have been trained in England; their outlook will not necessarily be orientated towards England; in some countries they will feel the weight of political pressure. It remains to be seen what ethos the new law schools will generate. At present most of them are headed and staffed by men steeped in the English legal tradition, which will inevitably be disseminated among the students during the early years; and the example of India suggests that it is a tradition with unusual

54. E.g., *Bratty* v. *Attorney-General for Northern Ireland* [1963] A.C.386 (defense of automatism); *Connelly* v. *D.P.P.* [1964] 2 W.L.R. 1145 (plea in bar of "issue estoppel").

55. *Report of the Committee on Legal Education for Students from Africa,* Cmnd. 1255, G. B. *Parl. Paps. 1960-61,* xviii, 719.

qualities of persistence. A sprinkling of graduates of the local law faculties will proceed to further legal studies in England. And there will always be a number of local men and women who will wish, for one reason or another, to obtain a first law degree or professional qualifications in England. But as other countries follow Ghana and Nigeria in insisting on locally obtained qualifications as the condition for entry into professional practice, the surge of African students into the four Inns of Court will gradually recede. There are signs that the tide is already on the ebb.[56]

VI

Nobody is likely to deny that it is in the general interest for close co-operation to be maintained between Commonwealth countries in legal matters and for each country to be helped to draw on the experience of others. Nobody with a sense of political realism is likely to assert that these objects can be achieved today by means of supranational institutions endowed with supranational authority. Would it be unrealistic to explore the suggestion, put forward by Mr. Diefenbaker in 1960,[57] for the establishment of a Comonwealth Law Institute, modeled on the American Law Institute? Such an institute, supported by governments and equipped with a permanent staff and panels of expert volunteers, would presumably aim at promoting the harmonization, even the unification, of aspects of private law in the Commonwealth by drawing up restatements and perhaps model codes. In the present climate of Commonwealth relations the pursuit of this goal would probably be overambitious. But there are other

56. The intake of Commonwealth students to the four Inns of Court in 1963 has been compared with the corresponding figures for 1959 by inspecting the entry forms. From the information there disclosed, it appears that the number of Ghanaians has declined from 90 to 27 and of Nigerians from 271 to 158. The intake from the East African countries has declined (surprisingly, although the establishment of a law faculty at Dar es Salaam and a professional law school at Nairobi possibly explains the fall) from 59 to 44. The figures for the Central African territories show an increase from 11 to 31. There has also been a substantial increase in the number of students from Malaysia and Pakistan.

57. *Record of the Second Commonwealth and Empire Law Conference, Ottawa, 1690* (London, 1962), pp. 85-88.

means of enlarging legal contacts and diffusing legal experience within the Commonwealth. Already educational interchange is being stimulated by the excellent schemes for the award of Commonwealth Fellowships and Scholarships and by the recruitment of law teachers from Britain and the older Commonwealth countries to staff the new law schools. The secondment of draftsmen and legal advisers is being arranged at the official level. At the unofficial or semi-official level there are the successful Commonwealth Law Conferences, and the visits paid by members of the judiciary from one Commonwealth country to another. Perhaps the most promising of recent developments has been the establishment of a Commonwealth legal advisory service in London, under the auspices of the British Institute of International and Comparative Law. This is essentially an information bureau, which receives requests from Commonwealth governments contemplating measures of law reform and wishing to obtain access to relevant legislation adopted by other countries on the matter in question. The answers are compiled on the basis of material supplied by governmental sources. The British Institute, acting in conjunction with the Oxford Law Faculty, is also to sponsor an Annual Survey of Commonwealth Law. There are many other gaps to be filled, many other forms of contact to be developed, but the wider dissemination of legal information may be an essential preliminary to bolder projects.

12

The Transplantation of the University:
The Case of Africa

Sir John Lockwood*

A backward look to the year 1954 is discouraging for believers in the reliability of prediction in the field of education. The educational picture of the Commonwealth today is very different from that of ten years ago. Wherever you turn your eyes, things have happened which were barely credible, if they were even thought of. Who, for example, would have believed that a series of Commonwealth education conferences would be set in train by governments to provide for such things as the invaluable scheme of interchange of graduate scholars? Who, too, would have been prepared to contemplate the idea of the radical change in the financing of universities of Australia,[1] or the existence of five universities in Nigeria, or of three university institutions in East Africa, Ghana, Central Africa, within so short a time? Who would have put any faith in a prophecy that there would be Chinese universities in Hong Kong and Singapore? To come nearer home, who in his wildest dreams would have expected the academic upheaval in the United Kingdom which the seismic force of Robbins has created?

For the purposes of the present discussion, Africa will be the main center of interest, with minor excursions into Southeast Asia, since selection is inevitable from so wide a range of prob-

* Sir John Lockwood, master of Birkbeck College, University of London, died in July, 1965. He was knighted for his services to higher education in the Commonwealth, especially in Africa.
1. See *Report of the Committee on Australian Universities* (Canberra, 1957) and *Reports of the Australian Universities Commission*, 1960 and 1963.

lems. Even for Africa, it will be necessary to single out a few of the chief issues which the countries have had to meet and will continue to face for a long time to come. Africa has its peculiar attraction in the present context since politics and education have become so closely intermingled during the approach to national independence and its realization, and international interest has been excited in both alike.

Three passages in an inaugural lecture by Lionel Elvin in December, 1956, will serve as a starting-point because they pinpoint an important aspect of the African situation: (i) "The distinctive and overriding factor in colonial educational development at this moment is surely the political one. No view of it at present could make much sense if it ignored the rapid changes in the political scene." (ii) "Imitation English education is unlikely to be good education in Africa." (The use of the word "English" is possibly intentional and is certainly significant.) (iii) "It would therefore be foolish as well as wrong to fight some last-ditch battle of cultural imperialism when political imperialism has gone."[2]

What Elvin said in (i) is almost truer now than when he propounded his statement. Apart from the internal nationalist ambitions in all the British or former British countries in Africa, the various movements for the grouping of African states and Pan-African ventures are exercising influences in varying degrees. The arrival of UNESCO through the Addis Ababa (1961) and Tananarive (1962) conferences[3] and educational missions to, e.g., Lagos (1961)[4] and Lusaka (1963)[5] has added a new politico-educational dimension.

In a situation as sensitive as the present, the questions confronting the educational planner south of the Sahara are urgently different from those of the more leisurely days of the colonial

2. *Education and the End of Empire* ("Studies in Education," No. 8 [University of London Institute of Education, 1956]).

3. The Conference of African States on the Development of Education in Africa (Addis Ababa, May, 1961) and the Conference on the Development of Higher Education in Africa (Tananarive, Sept., 1962); see its report *The Development of Higher Education in Africa* (Paris: UNESCO, 1963).

4. Chairman, Jean Capelle. See *Report of the UNESCO Advisory Commission for the Establishment of the University of Lagos* (UNESCO, 1962).

5. See *Education in Northern Rhodesia: A Report and Recommendations prepared by the UNESCO Planning Mission* (Lusaka, 1964).

past. A nation on the move, aiming hopefully at far more rapid development than its economic position can possibly warrant and assuming that external aid will come to the rescue of its exchequer, cannot rest content with systems which have no built-in respect for urgency and for the acceleration of progress. With the advantage of hindsight we have no difficulty in being critical of what was done and in being proud of our recognition of what was not done. The past is, however, by no means indefensible, as the wilder, extremist views sometimes claim. In sober fact, the defense that can be put up is strong, if looked at in the light of contemporary conditions of the past. Over the last generation the fault which lay at the heart of the concepts which are now subjected to attack was the serious misjudgment of the time-scale of the national independence process by successive governments. There seemed little reason to challenge the traditional habits and forms of education which had been transplanted from their native soil, and education has not always been as popular and desirable in the eyes of the African as now.

Thomas Hodgkin described the transplantation of academic institutions as exemplifying the "policy of identity," that is, the "policy of exporting European, or Western, institutions to Africa"—"models with the least possible modification." He goes on to say of this policy that "African opinion was, on this issue at least, wholeheartedly in support. . . . The leaders of African opinion in the 1940's unhesitatingly rejected substitutes."[6] They got what they wanted, even to the extent of having begowned students, high tables, and both the outward appurtenances of the medieval type of university and its inward awkwardnesses. African students appeared to like all the external trappings, which thereby, presumably, gain some justification.

But what of the late 1950's and the 1960's? Could the African choice of the 1940's be any longer wholly valid? From 1948, when the University College of Ghana was established, until the opening of the University of Nigeria in 1960, the university institutions had been steadily moving forwards and upwards

6. "The Idea of an African University," *Universities Quarterly*, XII (1958), 376 ff.

through the general degrees to honors and special honors degrees, reproducing with an admiring faithfulness the British patterns of the last forty years. All had progressed from lowish to high entrance requirements (except the University College of Rhodesia and Nyasaland, which had begun immediately with the high). We gave them our full support in the direction they took. Our reasons were not always identical. Some acted from a deeply ingrained sense of academic purism. Others, anxious to produce Africans in the best European mold, could see no alternative procedure. Yet others were not wholly unactuated by more or less conscious motives of regard for the importance of giving the expatriate staff similar teaching opportunities to those at home so as to facilitate ease of return to universities in the United Kingdom. Doubtless there were other additional reasons, but these will suffice.

By the mid-1950s the first grumblings of doubt became audible. Some of us had already questioned the wisdom of the University College of Rhodesia and Nyasaland's beginning with high entrance requirements. Rumors about the character of the promised University of Nigeria which one day was to be founded were disquieting to the traditionalists, who regarded the project as, at the best, contemptible and, at the worst, ridiculous. The rigid conservatism of the conformist could only be scandalized by the thought of an academic institution which was deliberately setting as its goal the creation of something which was to be specifically Nigerian in outlook and philosophy. But the British traditionalist ought to have been provoked by the doctrine of Dr. Azikiwe into asking himself honestly the obvious question: How far can any sensible, thinking person accept the too-little-questioned principle that a system of education which has grown successfully and flourished in one national society must be expected to succeed equally, by a kind of automatically self-perpetuating genius, in an alien society, particularly when that society has different roots, different traditions, different customs, a different economy, and is in a far different stage of development? The question seems so obvious now in the middle 1960's that it may hardly be worth asking, and the answer may also appear self-evident. But there are still countless people in the academic world for whom the question is repellent and the answer obvious but different from mine. Blinkers are not the monopoly of the patient horse. American campuses are as familiar with the doctrine that the type of the land-grant college, with its earlier special relevance to the developing U.S.A., is bound to succeed in any other developing country, especially if the country is largely agricultural, as we are with the widely held and frequently expressed conviction that sixth forms, A levels, and special honors degrees offer the only valid passport to a modern society of the highest order educationally, nationally, and economically. For the U.S. academic, the emphasis is on the transfer of an assumed special relevance, for the British the transmission of a quasi-mystical concept of high standards, which often possess a narrowness directly proportionate to their so-called height. (It is also an odd paradox that standards are at their highest when a subject is studied in depth.) It would be an interesting and valuable operation to examine for the whole Commonwealth the actions and interactions of imported educational models and alien copyings of educational systems. The balance-sheet of advantages and disadvantages, and the profit and loss account of virtually unmodified imports would be illuminating documents. This is not the moment for indulging in detailed accountancy procedures, and a few salient factors are all that can be suggested.

First of all, it is important not to forget what has been achieved, and what there is on the credit side. Whatever opinion is held about their defects, nobody will deny that academic institutions such as those at Ibadan, Legon Hill, Makerere, Singapore, and Kuala Lumpur have made their mark on the world scene. The import or copying of the British academic order of things was instrumental in establishing their reputations. Anyone who visits universities in the countries of Southeast Asia and studies their present academic habits may be excused for an enhanced affection for some of the qualities of our tradition, as seen in Singapore and Kuala Lumpur, when allied to flexible attitudes. Similarly, in the schools, the gearing to the examinations of Cambridge and London, even after a heavy discount on the ground of the restrictive nature of these tests, provided a stimulus to better teaching and to a sense of quality of work. Without the stimulus and the educational guidance of the examining bodies, schools might have been left floundering with no course charted.

Secondly, what have been the major weaknesses of past practice? They have been several in number. It has imposed the classificatory structure of the British educational system, with its somewhat arbitrary view of what is and what is not regarded as respectable enough to be included within the field of university studies and what should be shut away in another type of institution. In doing so, it did not a little damage to the needs of technical and technological education and of the training of teachers. By the introduction of higher entrance requirements, it effectively barred many potential students from finding a place in the university institution in their own country. It created an impression, through its selectiveness, of discriminating against too many, as indeed it could not avoid doing when sixth forms, the channel to the higher ranges of education, were too few. An almost pedantic rigidity of adherence to certain standards for entrance was one of the causes of some of the troubles which the University of Ghana has suffered during the last few years. Also, and it is especially sad to say this, the story of higher education in Central Africa might conceivably have been more comfortable, if, in pursuit of standards, the formulae of the United Kingdom for university entrance had yielded more to the demands of the social needs of the African community. It is an agonizing reflection that, from the viewpoint of the opportunity for the African in the now defunct Federation, a link-up with the University of South Africa, had it been politically possible, through its external degree system could have opened more doors than the relationship with the University of London in the form in which it was agreed. The original decision on entrance requirements was taken largely on political grounds, but the continuing acceptance of the restrictive entrance requirements in face of the social needs and the political awakening of Africans and their demand for advancement was no longer tolerable, and, in consequence, has forced urgent changes in the structure of higher education in Central Africa. These changes may have been inevitable in any case, but they were made easier by an academic policy in Salisbury which looked temporarily sound but was shown to be shortsighted and which the malicious or unthinking critic could readily and without much patently extravagant invention interpret as allied to, and also as contributory to, the illiberal racial policies of the federal government. This kind of criticism can be overdone and to recall and repeat it is to do some injustice to the men of great liberal spirit whose eagerness to promote the best in education and whose passion for excellence could not escape from the tentacles of the political milieu in which they pursued their ideals.

Outspoken comment on the imported pattern grew with the increasing success of nationalism. Thanks to the largely European character and content of the academic curriculum, it was a sitting target for attack; it gave the appearance of being wedded to a substantially non-African world. As Dr. Biobaku said at the Fourah Bay Conference in 1961: "This is a point that worries the layman and governments. They expect the university to be in the front line of change in the community. They do not expect the university to be the place where one talks about the past or about Western civilisation and so forth."[7] This attitude is inevitable in countries concerned with the acceleration of the developmental process. The urgency of their ambitions demands that education should be providing the machinery for boosting the speed of growth and that higher education should concentrate more on local problems and the mechanics of material progress than has seemed to be the case hitherto. Universities are not remarkable for their rapidity of adjustment to the need for change except when external pressures compel them.

7. M. Dowuona and J. R. Saunders, eds., *The West African Intellectual Community* (Ibadan, 1962), p. 74.

Nowadays, we talk enough of the need for manpower assessments as a precondition of prudent educational planning, and in so doing we are doing little more than recognizing the justice of the attitude mentioned by Dr. Biobaku. Professor Harbison performed a fine service for Sir Eric Ashby when he applied his techniques of analysis and projection to Nigeria at a vital point in its history. Guy Hunter's surveys in East Africa[8] and Southeast Asia,[9] and the investigations of the needs of Central Africa offer similar aids and stimuli to countries concerned about the dynamic equilibrium of their educational systems, as seen in the light of their desired economic programs. Studies of the economics of development, growing in number with the increase of appointments in this field, will lead to better bases on which manpower assessments can be constructed and removed to a greater degree from the sphere of crystal-gazing to that of prediction. When national resources are small, there can be no excuse for planning which is not investment-minded, whether in education or any other sector of public activity. To take a simple case, internal political influences and international pressures call upon governments of all countries to promote universal primary education. A country's most urgent needs happen to be for a substantially stepped-up program of secondary education for its immediate development purposes. The country cannot afford both. Since the issue is not merely one between the numbers of pupils involved but is tied up with the types of teachers to be trained and secured for the several tasks, the only sound basis for decision must be, as it were, profitability. What split of the investment will pay off the better? In a country which still stands low down on the foothills of progress, financial stamina should not be wasted. It was gratifying to find this doctrine reiterated in the recent report, *Education for Development*, on education in Malawi.[10] The first recommendation of the survey team also

8. *Education for a Developing Region* (London, 1963).
9. *High-Level Manpower for Development* (Consultant's Report for the UNESCO-International Association of Universities' Study of the Role of Institutions of Higher Education in the Development of Countries of Southeast Asia [1964]).
10. *Education for Development* (Report of the Survey Team on Education in Malawi [1964]).

needs to be taken along with the third: "Continue the Government policy of steady progress toward the *long-term goal* of universal primary education, with due regard to the requirements of educational balance which give higher immediate priority to the rapid expansion of secondary schools and the introduction of higher education." The third recommendation is particularly interesting, whatever view may be held about the rights or wrongs of the proposal: "Extend the principle of self-help, local initiative, and responsible local planning, by requiring local governments to bear a fixed proportion, however modest, of the rising cost of primary education on a grant-in-aid basis with local matching funds, perhaps with an equalisation principle to take account of genuine differences in District ability to contribute."

This is a pointed reminder of the realities which have to be faced, since they could be ignored only by the optimistic politician who expects external aid to relieve him of all his discomforting burdens. Priorities need to be firmly established. Education cannot be other than a slow process, and spectacular leaps cannot be assured.

Many cultural barriers must be overcome if Western technology is to be the instrument of development. Centuries-old customs and traditional practices do not yield readily to the influx of alien ideas and foreign methods. The tension between the old and the new offers the strongest reason for the encouragement of African studies in the African universities. While it is clearly necessary and indisputable that the education of a people should be generally grounded in its life, beliefs, habits, and historical experience, education in an African society or an Asian society should not, any more than in a European or American society, be an author of a static corpus of attitudes. If a university in a country which is seeking to industrialize itself—and this appears to be the hope of all alike—does not concern itself with the conflicts and tensions which this kind of development shows signs enough of producing, it will be neglecting an important social duty. Institutes of African studies, so rightly supported by the Tananarive Conference, have a special place as the focus of all interrelated investigations covering the whole range of public and private life and conducted in the context of a national community subjected to novel stresses and influences. While they clearly must devote themselves to researches into history, archeology, law, cultural anthropology, and economics, they have another important responsibility. Theirs is a sociological task of some magnitude. They will be not only the guardians of the country's past but also, more important, at the heart of the struggle for the future. It has been said that anthropologists have confined themselves excessively to traditional tribal societies and that in consequence we know far too little of the urban industrialized societies. Research methodologies from outside can assist them to formulate the principles of their studies, but upon themselves rests the responsibility for exploiting the principles with enterprise and vigor. And they should be stimulated by the timeliness of their task. The recent Gardner Report[11] on AID's relationship with the academic community recognized the size of the undertaking which such a task must involve: "The means for making the changes in cultural patterns necessary for development without destroying important human values are only beginning to be understood." It recognized also that a country has to work out its own salvation: "The problems of the developing nation cannot, in any fundamental sense, be solved from outside." But this should not be taken literally to mean that external aid and guidance can only scratch the surface. Educational assistance will be at its best when it is given, not in any narrowly constricted compass of view, but in the total context, or at least the largest possible context of development. To plant a dozen foreign agriculturalists or veterinarians, or hydrologists in an educational program, without any concern for all the side effects of the injection, if it is successful in its immediate objective, could seem irresponsible. A subject which would be worth examining, if it were practicable, is partially germane to what has just been referred to. For many years there has been a steady stream of students to the U.S.A. and Europe. In an article of some years

11. John W. Gardner, *A.I.D. and the Universities: Report to the Administrator of the Agency for International Development* [Washington, 1964].

ago about students who had been to the U.S.A., Mr. Pifer said that "we know very little about these students and especially about what has happened to them since their return." He went on to ask a number of questions:

How many in fact have returned to the colonies from which they originated? What are they doing now? Are they in the civil service? education? business? the professions? politics? Has their American education been useful to them or has it been a liability? Have their American degrees been recognised? Are there special difficulties about medical registration or other professional qualifications? Has indeed the large expenditure of human energy that has gone into the traffic to the "mecca" of American higher education been worth the effort to those concerned and their countries?

It is not proposed to answer any of these questions now. They provoke further questions: Are they contributing in a different way to their country's growth by the particular character of the education they received than if they had not gone abroad? Have they become deracinated to such an extent that they are potential or actual sources of the cultural tensions that have been mentioned? How far have their training and instruction made them more *or* less adaptable in the life of their own country?[12]

The prevalent doctrine in the U.S.A. and the U.K. is that students ought to pursue their undergraduate studies in their own country, wherever possible. Two main grounds justify this doctrine: the necessity not to prevent the development of local university institutions by starving them of students, and the pragmatic prudence of not uprooting students from their own society until they have matured through their undergraduate education. There is a growing view that an element of danger may exist in sending large numbers overseas for postgraduate work, since the institutions will equally suffer from inability to expand their research activities, if their better graduates are siphoned off elsewhere, with the further risk that many will not return home after the completion of their studies. Some compensating factors are to be found in the increasing movement of

12. "Education and Research in British Dependent Territories—The Role of the United States," *Universities Quarterly*, XII (1958), 399 ff.

graduate scholars in the reverse direction, as the opportunities for special research in the universities of the developing countries become better known. The help given by certain foundations and by the Commonwealth Scholarships Plan have encouraged this intercountry movement. All these happenings have assisted the development process, however marginally. Other policy directives and tendencies, on the other hand, may have a braking power. For example, the introduction of a national language, which may have a praiseworthy purpose as a national cohesive force, brings with it educational problems. In Malaysia, if Malay is to replace English as the medium of instruction in higher education, library difficulties present themselves. But the democratization of university entry enforces the use of the national language. The University of Malaya may have to face the same problems as the University in Bangkok, where the lectures are given in Thai, but most of the books are in other languages. Linguistic policies, of course, run down into the schools in Malaysia, with the result that while in primary school a Malay boy has to learn English, an English boy Malay, a Chinese or Indian boy has to learn Malay and English. To those of us who have occasionally questioned enforced bilingualism in Wales and the Republic of Ireland as a confusing impediment for some children, a policy of compulsory trilingualism seems to have peculiar hazards.

To return to the main theme of this paper, that of the contribution of education to the life of a nation: it deserves notice that the three reports on higher education in Africa[13] and Mauritius[14] published in the last six months or so have all paid special attention to the developmental need; to the essential principle of responsiveness to the real, existent needs of the country; and, therefore, to a view of higher education which counts human resource development as, for the present and the early future, the prime duty of the educator and of the educational planner. This does not mean that education is to be just a mere tool.

13. See notes 5 and 10, above.
14. Colin Leys, *The Development of a University College of Mauritius.* Mauritius, Legislative Assembly Sessional Paper No. 4 of 1964.

"Education cannot be reduced to terms of the market-price and it cannot be a mechanical response to man-power statistics." All three reports, in spite of their preponderant emphasis on what some might criticize as the purely material side of a nation's life, are conscious that there are other things in the life of a people than the mere satisfaction of manpower requirements. the problems of Northern Rhodesia, Malawi, and Mauritius are sufficiently similar to provoke a roughly similar approach to their solution. In his report on Mauritius Professor Colin Leys put the case with considerable force:

I should emphasise one general assumption about further education which is reflected in my approach, namely that the 'investment' aspect of education must be paramount. This is far from applying only to countries faced with economic crises. Development at any level can only be sustained in a scientific age if resources are constantly invested in research and training in branches of knowledge and skills. When this is reinforced by an economic crisis, however, as in the case of Mauritius, the argument becomes irresistible: if more resources are to be devoted to education, education should be as directly productive, in terms of making possible increases in future output, as if those resources went into (say) building factories. This is a tough test, and one hard for educationalists (such as myself) to accept, but I would feel quite unjustified in making any recommendation which I did not think could pass it. One consequence of using the test is, however, that any academic institution founded on it enjoys an exciting and justified sense of being important to the community which pays for it.

All three reports put agriculture and education (i.e., the preparation of teachers) as leading priorities, because, apart from the Copper Belt, the three countries have agriculture as their chief productive industry and are deficient in the proper quality or quantity of teachers. They all set a high value on studies in administration, on extramural opportunities, and on in-service training. What is perhaps most important, they all press for a rationally co-ordinated scheme for postschool education, with the Northern Rhodesian report stressing the essentiality of provision for possibilities of transfer from aspect to aspect within the comprehensive plan, with appropriate adjustment or equalizing

courses on transfer. "The main object of the pioneer development [in the Northern Rhodesia case] is that the catchment
area for the University's work is widened to embrace *all* ex-
secondary school pupils of reasonable standard and not merely
those who have reached the 'grammar school' level of attainment." Proposals such as these have taken a good deal of swal-
lowing by British academics, because they seem to be not only
diversifying the traditional form of a university but also in some
way degrading its very concept. But Colin Leys neatly rounds
on this distaste: "Happily the days when academic snobbery
dictated the growth of universities are past. Fashions change.
Once upon a time universities were centered on schools of the-
ology but no one today supposes that the many universities which
did not offer such training do not deserve the name of university." Special pleading in favor of the new approach is surely
no longer necessary, and it is perhaps a moribund horse that is
being flogged.

If a university and an educational system can marry their
general cultural responsibility for preserving the past history,
traditions, and intellectual life of the nation to meeting the immediate needs of the present and aspirations for the future, they
will fully justify their place in their society. If they depress the
element of national need in their planning and their work, they
may cease to merit the full freedom which they have a normal
right to expect. Governments, as Ghana has shown, are likely
to have limited patience if the university shows too little overt
interest in national goals. The analysis of the arguments against
unrestricted academic freedom produced in *The Spark* in March
of 1964 as a reply to a convocation address by the vice-chancellor
of the University of Ghana has more than local significance.
Even democracies in Africa are more authoritarian than in
countries where they have flourished longer, and universities will probably have to rethink their position. That is why
they should refuse to hark back to ideals of absolute freedom
and, in taking a new stand as occupying a central role in national
development, exercise a freedom of decision and an enterprise

which does not attract interference. The new universities can set the pace in such thinking. This is what I hope will be the result of the foundation of the universities in Zambia and Malawi, and what will be the fruit of the earlier establishment of the University of Nigeria. These are lines of growth which deserve external aid and will surely win it in plenty.

13

Elite Cadres in the Bureaucracies of India, Pakistan, Ceylon, and Malaya Since Independence

*Ralph Braibanti**

The elite cadres of the Commonwealth countries in Asia comprise about three thousand of the ten million persons engaged in governing the half billion people of India, Pakistan, Ceylon, and Malaya. These four cadres, now called the Indian Administrative Service (IAS), the Civil Service of Pakistan (CSP), the Ceylon Unified Administrative Service (CUAS), and the Malayan Civil Service (MCS) are derivative in concept and, to a lesser extent, in structure from the old Indian Civil Service. The ICS has a familiar history[1] which, although amenable to much more research and analysis, cannot be sketched in this paper.

Conceptually, the elite cadres are related to Confucian and Platonic canons and to the characterization given by Max Weber

* Professor of political science, Duke University. The author wishes to record his indebtedness to participants in the conference at Bellagio, especially to T. E. Smith for his helpful suggestions on Malaya, and to A. L. Adu. He is also indebted to R. O. Tilman and R. S. Milne for help on Malaya, and to Robert N. Kearney and Sir Charles Collins on Ceylon.

1. The voluminous literature includes: Government of India, "Report of the Public Service Commission, 1886-87" (Aitchison Report) I, esp. chap. ii, C. 5327, G.B., *Parl. Paps. 1887-88*, XLVIII; "Report of the Royal Commission on the Public Services in India," (Islington Report) (20 vols., 1914-1916, var. Cd. nos.) I (1917), esp. chap. i, Cd. 8382, G.B., *Parl. Paps. 1916*, VII; Sir Edward Blunt, *The ICS: The Indian Civil Service* (London, 1937); C. H. Philips, *The East India Company, 1784-1834* (Manchester, 1940); Akshoy Kumar Ghosal, *Civil Service in India under the East India Company* (Calcutta, 1944); Hugh Tinker, "The British Imperial Heritage," and Bernard Cohn, "Recruitment and Training of British Civil Servants in India, 1600-1860," in Ralph Braibanti and associates, *Asian Bureaucratic Systems Emergent from the British Imperial Tradition* (in press); Naresh Chandra Roy, *Indian Civil Service* (Calcutta, 1935).

of both Chinese and Brahminical literati. One of the most appealing issues which awaits further historical definition is the precise relationship between the examination system of China and Western civil service systems based on examination. The relationship was first suggested by Ssü-Yu Têng, who amassed evidence based in part on Earl MacCartney's interest in the Chinese system acquired during his diplomatic mission to Jehol in 1793.[2] Subsequent writings of G. L. Staunton, secretary to MacCartney's embassy, and of his son, G. T. Staunton, reveal extended diffusion of the Chinese concept and advocacy of its extension to India. H. G. Creel, characterizing Têng's paper as "classic," and referring to further research by Donald F. Lach and others, supports the view that the concept of examinations was diffused from China to Europe.[3] The concept of the elite cadre may have less direct diffusional relationship than the institution of examination, however, since the notion of elite cadres is an important part of the scheme of statecraft described in Plato's *Republic*. Indeed, it has not been uncommon for members of the Indian Civil Service to think of their service in terms of Platonic guardianship, as is suggested by Woodruff's panegyric in his "Epilogue" to the second volume of *The Men Who Ruled India*, and, of course, by the volume's title, *The Guardians*.[4] The challenge to subsequent historical research on the diffusion of bureaucratic concepts lies in the possibility that Chinese ideas of the mandarinate may have been fortuitously diffused along with the institution of examination and may have converged with and reinforced the Platonic concept radiated in the West from Greek political philosophy.[5]

Whatever the institutional and ideological antecedents of the elite cadres may be, the nearly two thousand officers who comprised these four systems at the time of independence shared

2. Ssü-Yu Têng, "Chinese Influence on the Western Examination System," *Harvard Journal of Asiatic Studies*, VII (1943), 267-312.

3. H. G. Creel, "The Beginnings of Bureaucracy in China: The Origin of the Hsien," *Journal of Asian Studies*, XXIII (1964), 155-85, especially p.162 and n.46.

4. New York, 1954.

5. See also a provocative effort to relate English public school values to concepts of leadership and to the Confucian system: Rupert Wilkinson, *Gentlemanly Power* (London, 1964).

common attitudinal characteristics, and occupied comparably dominant positions in the bureaucratic power structures of the ex-colonial states. These characteristics may briefly be summarized as follows: The elite cadres were discrete entities, insulated from a variety of other civil services by ethnic differential, superior managerial technology, latency of colonial physical power, higher salary, and related perquisites. Once admitted to the elite cadres by criteria of patronage, achievement, and ascription, the proportions of which varied in time and place, advancement was almost entirely by ascription rather than achievement. It is perhaps not widely enough appreciated that the mere fact of ascriptive status contributed immensely to the power, prestige, and isolation of the elite cadres. It minimized intrabureaucratic rivalries and it permitted courageous action and independence of view to assume postures of inviolability in relation to emerging politicization. As political turmoil increased, ascriptive status prevented the elite cadres from being completely caught up in the maelstrom. Ascriptive status was reinforced by tenure policies which insulated the elite cadre from the vagaries of political recrimination. The Civil Services (Classification, Control, and Appeal) Rules enacted in India in 1930 and a corpus of consequent judicial construction codified the nearly inviolable position of the ICS. This doctrine was premised on assigning removal power exclusively to the appointing power —the governor-general of India. Analogous policies were regnant in Ceylon and Malaya. The upper echelons formed a secretariat with vast powers to make policy and even with the appointment of non-British ministers; British secretaries, theoretically subordinate, actually were superordinate.[6] This control of the foci of power was held by the omnicompetent generalist, a

6. Of the relationship between British secretaries and ministers in India, Subramaniam has said: "But their experience as Ministers in their relation with their departmental secretaries was rather mixed; some Ministers openly condemned the sabotaging activities of the secretaries in approaching the Governor over their heads; many others probably worked out some sort of live and let live arrangements with the civil servants but the general mass of evidence before the Simon Commission in 1929-30 (from Ministers and civil servants alike) about their 'harmonious' relations was mostly polite hypocrisy." V. Subramaniam, "The Evolution of Minister-Civil Servant Relations in India," *Journal of Commonwealth Political Studies,* I (1962), 223-32 at 226-27.

control the more potent and productive of enhanced prestige because it combined judicial and executive powers. The elite were characterized by a style, an attitude, bred by the tremendous and isolated power of the district officer. They were predominantly British, but the gradual addition of indigenous officials had made possible a diffusion of the values and ethos of the British bureaucracy. On the eve of independence 66 per cent of the MCS cadre was British, 53 per cent of the ICS, and, by contrast, only 19 per cent of the Ceylon Civil Service. For all four (Pakistan and India being combined in the ICS figure) the figure was 51.6 per cent British.

Erosion of British Influence

The most immediate and significant change in the elite cadre after independence was, not unexpectedly, a sharp diminution in direct British participation in the services and of British influence in the systems. The break with British service was sharpest in India. Most of the British officers left service, and immediately after independence, of the 451 officers in the ICS, approximately 33 (or 7 per cent) were British. Of these, only 20 were on executive duty, the remaining 13 being judges. Within five years after independence, most of these officers left service and in 1963 only three remained, two as chief justices of state high courts and one on a state board of revenue. Thus, direct influence by British executives in the bureaucracy almost immediately was reduced to negligible magnitude. This was of great significance in analysis of the cadre as an institutional matrix for the diffusion and reinvigoration of British norms.[7] Of equally serious consequence was the decision made not to resume sending new ICS (renamed IAS) recruits to England for training. This practice had already been stopped because of wartime exigencies in 1940, and was not resumed. To be sure,

7. For further analysis, see essays by Braibanti and S. P. Jagota in Ralph Braibanti and J. J. Spengler, eds., *Administration and Economic Development in India* (Durham, N. C., 1963) pp. 1-94.

the 451 officers remaining in the service had been trained in England, and later in India many of these received their apprenticeship under British officers. This group was the sole means of diffusing traditional norms into the new postindependence structure. While, of course, this group continued because of seniority to occupy the crucial senior posts in the bureaucracy, it was numerically overwhelmed by the influx of new recruits. Of equal importance is the fact that nearly 50 per cent of the new recruits entered laterally at an older age, and were not trained intensively at the academy, which was the sole medium for diffusion of the old ICS ethos. By 1948 the total strength of the cadre had doubled and, increasing annually by about ninety officers, it numbered, on January 1, 1964, 1,971.[8] While the number of non-British-trained officers was increasing, the British-trained group was, because of retirement and mortality, shrinking. Figuring retirement at sixty years of age, a loss of 40 per cent of the British-trained officers can be estimated from 1947 to 1970. Thus by 1970 probably only 150 British-trained officers out of a total projected cadre strength of 2,500 will be left in service. From 1970 on, less than 10 per cent of the total cadre will be British-trained officers.

In India this sharp loss in direct British influence is accentuated by the fact that administrative training has been generated under the auspices of the Ford Foundation, which helped establish the Indian Institute of Public Administration. Moreover, the design for administrative reform has been based on the two Ford-financed reports of Paul Appleby. To be sure, instruction at the National Academy of Administration in Mussoorie, where the elite cadre is now trained, is in the hands of British-trained ICS officers, but that training lacks the force, dynamic quality, and élan requisite to successful attitudinal indoctrination. Moreover, it is important to note that there is no mandatory, graded training system which requires all officers to be trained at various ranks beyond the initial Mussoorie course.

8. Authorized strength for the same date was 2,278. (Letter, Ministry of Home Affairs, July, 1964.)

The Indian Institute of Public Administration is probably the best such institute in all of Asia. Its research and publications surpass comparable efforts in other Asian states. Nevertheless, its immediate effect on the IAS is marginal, since it is not articulated into a scheme which requires officers to undergo training at the Institute. No doubt, its long-range influence on administrative techniques and ideology will be great, but its role as a matrix for the continued infusion of Western ideology directly to the heart of the bureaucracy is of lesser significance.

In Pakistan the decline of British influence has been of a different order. Immediately after independence, 34 per cent of the cadre strength was British, as against 7 per cent in India. The cadre grew slowly and British officers left less quickly; hence it was not until 1957 that fewer than 5 per cent of the adjusted cadre strength were British. More important, British officers occupied key positions with respect to molding the attitudes of the Civil Service of Pakistan, as the cadre was called. A British officer was in charge of the Establishment Division almost continuously from 1947 to 1958; and the Civil Service Academy, citadel of the elite corps, was headed by a British officer from 1951 to 1960. Again, unlike India, Pakistan maintained other ties with British values. Virtually all recruits into the CSP entered in the time-honored way between the ages of twenty-one and twenty-four. All were trained for one year at the Civil Service Academy and all recruits from 1947 through 1960 were trained at Oxford or Cambridge for one year, except for one group of thirty officers who were sent to Australia instead. The difference between the situation in India and Pakistan may be seen in this way: in 1963, 70 per cent of the total cadre in Pakistan had received some training in England; in India, 10 per cent were British-trained. These are the bare statistics indicating a significant human phenomenon, i.e., a much firmer attachment to preindependence ICS traditions in Pakistan than in India.

Not only is the British tradition more enduring in Pakistan, but the dynamics of official American influence are far more significant than in India.[9] In India the United States Agency for International Development expended less than half a million dollars on administrative reform. In Pakistan the expenditure has been close to five million dollars. As a result of this activity, which commenced in 1960, three institutes of public administration were established, a department of public administration was established at the University of the Punjab, an advisor to the Civil Service Academy was furnished for two years, and a number of Pakistanis were trained in public administration in the United States. The institutes have so far trained 67 CSP officers, 230 officers of the provincial services, and 240 other officers (a total of 537 officers) in various courses such as management development, conference leadership, and administrative systems ranging from eight days to three months in duration. The present basic plan is for the three institutes to train approximately 180 additional officers each year. The same contract has provided for training in public administration in the United States through the Ph.D. level. Those so trained will staff the institutes upon their return. Thus far, one Ph.D. candidate, one A.M. candidate, and one librarian have returned to the institutes. There were in mid-1964 fourteen Ph.D. aspirants studying in the United States. All but one of these students were expected to have returned to Pakistan by September, 1965.

A significant outcome of this contract has been the formulation of a comprehensive training policy[10] administered by the Establishment Division of the president's secretariat in the central government. This policy acknowledges that training is a continuous requirement in career planning and states further that such administrative training "should be an important factor in deciding cases of promotion." It establishes a clientele based on rank for the Administrative Staff College, the three national

9. For tables showing expenditures of the United Nations, United States Agency for International Development, and Ford Foundation on administrative reform in India and Pakistan, and for evaluation of these reforms, see Ralph Braibanti, "Transnational Inducement of Administrative Reform: A Survey of Scope and Critique of Issues," in John D. Montgomery and William Siffin, eds., *Politics, Administration and Change: Approaches to Development* (in press).

10. Establishment Division, *Memorandum No. 2/17/61-A-IV*, dated at Rawalpindi, Oct. 31, 1961. Subject: Public Administration Training Policy.

institutes of public administration, and the two village development academies. In a newly developing state which inherits the
literary-generalist tradition of the ICS and which implicitly re-
jects the necessity for technical administrative training for
statecraft, this training policy is a significant accomplishment for
the United States Agency for International Development. Another direct result of that agency's activity has been the professionalization of public administration through research and
publication activities. The National Institutes of Public Administration at Dacca and Karachi have reprinted several earlier
reports on administrative reform, and each of the three institutes
publishes a journal.

Since 1962 there has also occurred a strengthening of the
public administration division within the Pakistan mission of
the agency, which now consists of six persons (excluding public
safety and statistical advisors). Significant basic work is being
done by these officials in such fundamental activities as the
preparation of a census of government employment and furnishing advisory services to a vigorous O and M wing which is starting to deal with specific operational problems.

British influence in Pakistan is thus being replaced by American influence, or at least the two influences are jostling in a
highly dynamic matrix of diffusion.

In Ceylon there was no mass exodus of British officers in
the elite cadre immediately after independence, but by 1963
all had left the service, and the cadre was completely Ceylonese.
No systematic training program for new recruits in the service
was started nor is there an active American or British program of
training and administrative reform. In 1957 a training center
was established under the Colombo Plan with a British advisor,
but the Perera Commission, deploring the absence of such training, doubted that so small an undertaking "could make any impact on training in the immediate future."[11] The dimunition of
British influence is, therefore, a normal attritional process, un-
accelerated by unusual factors.

11. Government of Ceylon, *Report of the Salaries and Cadre Commission,*
1961, Part II, p. 12.

In Malaya the British percentage of the elite cadre dropped to 41.2 immediately after independence, and in 1963 only five British officers remained in service. The Japanese occupation during the years 1942 to 1945 broke the continuum of diffusion of British bureaucratic values. This break was more serious than independence in 1957. As in Ceylon, no new influences have emerged in Malaya to regenerate British or other Western norms of administration. This is especially curious since Malaya (in contrast to India, Pakistan, and Ceylon) has a highly developed social organization, a sophisticated commercial structure, and a prosperous economy. These otherwise favorable factors may very well have dulled the awareness of any acute necessity to improve administration drastically. It is probably also of some significance that in both countries American influence through the Agency for International Development is non-existent. Whatever the reasons, the failure to continue British influence and the failure to regenerate British norms through some institutional means may create serious problems, the nature of which will be suggested below.

Size and Distribution of Power

As in the days of British rule, the size of the elite cadre remains small, totaling for the four countries a mere 2,924 officers in a bureaucracy of nearly nine million employees.[12] Yet the strength of the cadre for all four countries has nearly trebled since independence, the largest increase being in India. The cadre retains its hold in crucial positions of power at all levels and has demonstrated its preindependence versatility by extending its competence to such new activities as planning, diplomacy, government corporations, and training functions, although two activities—government corporations and community development —that were designed to circumvent the law-and-order mentality of the cadres have used them very little. The largest group of

12. The size of the cadres in 1964 was: India, 1,974; Pakistan, 432; Ceylon, 203; Malaya, 315.

officers continues to be assigned to district administration in India and Pakistan, where nearly one-third of the strength is thus occupied. In Ceylon and Malaya, however, more than one-half the cadres are in the central government secretariat. That none is assigned to judicial functions in India, Ceylon, or Malaya, reflects the fact that judicial and executive functions have been separated in those countries. In Pakistan this separation has not occurred, and nearly 4 per cent of the cadre is assigned to the judiciary. The pattern in Pakistan also differs in that a greater proportion of officers are undergoing training (16.7 per cent) and are in control of training institutions. Significantly, staff lists for Ceylon and Malaya reported no officers undergoing training in 1959 and 1962 respectively.

In India district administration is firmly in the hands of the elite cadre, yet it is conceded generally that the power of the district officer and of the elite cadre generally has been curtailed substantially by the maturation of the political process at all levels. The same appears to be true in Ceylon and Malaya. In Pakistan the power of the elite cadre has increased rather than diminished in strength largely because of martial law. The abolition of party politics has had the consequence of reducing harassment of division commissioners and district officers by politicians. In the provincial secretariats there were no ministers; hence secretaries to government functioned as ministers as well as executives. In the central government there were ministers, but the turnover was great, the level of competence was minimal, and in many cases one minister held several portfolios. The consequence was concentration of both political and administrative power in the hands of the secretaries, a return, in a sense, to the situation under British rule. Even the end of martial law in 1962 did not change the power status of the CSP substantially; the political process is still too feeble to present an effective countervailing force. The increased politicization of Basic Democracy units, the re-emergence of political parties in 1962, and the role of both in the presidential election of 1965 suggest the beginning of an erosion of autocratic power wielded by the CSP. There is a final difference in the development of the cadre in Pakistan. Each year from 1960 to 1963 five military officers of the rank of captain have entered the service. They have come from distinguished military families and nearly half of them had been on foreign assignments. This effort to permeate the civil structure with the values and outlook of the military has been of considerable importance in imparting a tone of discipline and sophistication to the CSP cadre.

Differentials in Social Status and Remuneration

Each of the four countries here considered dealt with the problem of differential status of the elite cadre in a somewhat different way. In India there was no serious outcry against maintaining the separate status of the IAS. Not until several years after independence was there serious talk about abolishing the cadre by unifying all the services. This suggestion, made both by Asok Chanda and Paul Appleby, was never taken seriously and at no time did it become a burning issue in discussions of Indian administration.[13] The tight exclusiveness of the old ICS was broken by the heterogeneity of postindependence recruitment and by common training of all the central superior services in the same course at the National Academy.

In Pakistan the continued existence of a tightly knit elite cadre continued to be an issue of some importance. When the National Assembly reconvened in 1962 after forty-four months of martial law, politicians attacked the CSP with almost as much vigor as before martial law. Maulvi Akhtar Ali of West Pakistan claimed that CSP officers were not "sympathetic to the rural population" and he likened their caste consciousness to the Freemasons Society. "Even [President] Ayub," he continued, "does not enjoy the powers that these people possess. All the hatred in the hearts of the people against any Government is due mainly

13. Asok Chanda, *Indian Administration* (London, 1958), p. 127; Paul Appleby's comments appeared in the *Sunday Statesman* (Delhi), April 16, 1961, p. 4.

to the self-conceited and haughty behavior of these function-
aries."[14] The CSP, nevertheless, in 1965 has succeeded in maintaining its identity and its superiority to all other services and
successfully fought off the recommendation of the Second Pay
and Services Commissions headed by Chief Justice A. R. Cornelius, which allegedly would have merged it with other services.

Ceylon has taken the most drastic step—that of abolishing
the Ceylon Civil Service and merging all administrative grades
into a common Administrative Service. This had been recommended by the Perera Commission, which noted that "the existence of two sets of officers on different salary levels and with
different promotion prospects [has] . . . created . . . a 'caste'
system which, besides being a constant source of irritation and
discontent, has created a division in an important level of the
Public Service."[15] Thus Ceylon was the first country of the four
to abolish the structural distinction between the covenanted
and uncovenanted services.

In Malaya the MCS continues as the senior service but there
appears to be no sharp antagonism to it. This is probably due to
the fact that it has absorbed MAS officers, just as the Indian Administrative Service absorbed state service recruits. The relative
prosperity and alternative means of professional employment have
engendered a much less antagonistic attitude toward the services than is found in Pakistan, India, and Ceylon.

All four countries have reduced somewhat the sharp dispari-
ties in remuneration. The Rs. 4,000 salary of the preindependence
secretary has been nearly halved and other salaries have been
raised somewhat. The disparity which continues to exist between
the lowest rank and the highest is the inevitable reflection of
caste-structured societies in which modes of life are entirely
different for various groups. Even with such disparity reduced,
the prestige of the elite cadre remains immense. The posts they
occupy were formerly held by their British rulers and mana and
charisma have been transferred along with independence.

14. National Assembly of Pakistan, *Debates*, June 20, 1962, pp. 221-22.
15. *Reports of the Salaries and Cadre Commission 1961* (Colombo, April, 1961),
Sessional Paper III—1961, Part I, p. 161.

Concluding Observations

1. Perhaps the most obvious issue which is suggested by the foregoing remarks is the persistence of the concept and structure of elite cadres in three countries for seventeen years and in Malaya for seven years after independence. Although passing adverse references to the system have been made in India, Ceylon, and Malaya, only in Pakistan has a serious, major effort to reconstruct the total bureaucracy on different conceptual premises emerged. That effort was due to the single-minded persistence of Chief Justice A. R. Cornelius, who was chairman of the second Pay and Services Commission, which submitted its three-hundred-page report to President Ayub in 1962. This controversial report has not been released either to the public or to the National Assembly. Its recommendations have not been concurred in by the Establishment Division, hence have not been implemented; indeed, public discussion of the basic issues involved has been minimal.[16]

The earlier equivalent commission in India, headed by Shri Justice Jagannadha Das, which submitted its report in 1959, refrained from dealing with the Indian Administrative Service upon advice of the Ministry of Finance, which ruled that the Indian Administrative and the Indian Police services were outside the commission's terms of reference. The Perera Commission in Ceylon, although recommending abolition of the CCS, did not expound at length on the concepts implicit in the suggestion. In Malaya the problem has not been systematically dealt with, although it is reported that since Malaysia was formed some thought has been given to abolishing the MCS.

It is not difficult to suggest the reasons for failure to abolish

16. Since the report has not been released, its recommendations are not known except by the few government officers who have read it. Members of the National Assembly periodically inquire when the report will be presented for their consideration. In the course of such inquiries, Qamarul Ahsan stated that it "envisages a basic change in the structure" of the services and Mahbubul Huq stated that it recommended "unification of services." National Assembly of Pakistan, *Debates*, Dec. 5, 1962, p. 413; *ibid.*, April 13, 1963, p. 1807.

the basic structure of which the elite cadres are the keystone. First, the division of the total bureaucracy into discrete entities with a complex pattern of allegiances to various ministries is so deeply enmeshed in so intricate a pattern of relationships that it is difficult to make any evolutionary change. In fact, the tendency in India, Pakistan, and Ceylon has been to multiply entities such as a Taxation Service, Scientific Service, and Administrative Training Service rather than to amalgamate them. Secondly, the separate existence of cadres performs the function which professionalization in non-government fields accomplished in other societies. Since professionalization of such activities as medicine, education, and engineering has occurred in all these countries except Malaya within the public bureaucracy rather than outside of it, the bureaucracy has tended to be structured into components analogous to the professions. Thirdly, the discrete entities reflect more or less the caste-structured societies of which they are a part, and the hierarchy of entities is often correlated with levels of education and social status. Fourthly, none of these countries has known any other possible organization of a bureaucracy. Contact with the American model has been limited even in Pakistan, where American influence is greatest. Fifthly, members of the elite cadres are usually in control of reform in all four countries and hence may be less interested in drastic structural revision than others might be. Sixthly, a natural reluctance to tamper drastically with what appears to be a functioning system is a consequence of the political uncertainty which has characterized all four states. As these six factors assume varying degrees of relevance in social change, the status of elite cadres may be similarly modified.

2. It is commonly said that the elite cadres have impeded development; this sentiment is keenly felt, especially by Americans who have worked with them. This is an oversimplification of a complex problem. In the first place, it is impossible retrospectively to assess the role of order in development and the role of elite cadres in maintaining that order. Secondly, governments

have not depended exclusively upon the cadres for development; hence it cannot be said they have been tested and have failed; much initiative in development has come from the corporate device and from the rural development movement. Thirdly, in some instances, elite cadre officers have done heroic work in development activities. It is not the intent here to defend the concept of elite cadres as agents of economic and political growth. In fact, I have misgivings as to their continued adequacy to meet the demands of development, but suggest that it is futile, in terms of evidential corroboration, to engage in retrospective polemics regarding past accomplishments when the magnitude of the relevant variables is only partially apprehended and still less understood.

The one crucial question to ask regarding elite cadres in developing states is whether they constitute an effective medium of intake for the aggregation of manpower with skills technologically and ideationally relevant to bureaucratic needs in development. An answer is suggested by the following analysis, which may be called (for want of a better designation) the aggregation and intersectoral permeability of skills in asymmetrical development. Analysis of this concept requires keeping in focus the central characteristic of elite cadres, namely, that they constitute a closed system for aggregating managerial and policy-making skills in the public bureaucracy. Determination of such skills is made by achievement criteria between the ages of twenty-one and twenty-four (except for minor variations in India and Pakistan in age to accommodate backward classes) in all four states for at least 75 per cent of the cadre (the typical allowance for lateral entry from state and other services being 25 per cent). In a relatively static society, this fixation of skill has minimally deleterious consequences. However, all four of these states are no longer static in development and are experiencing highly uneven rates of development between institutional sectors. By development in institutions I mean (a) the assimilation of norms of modernity; (b) the capacity of the institution to formulate norms and to relate positively such formulation to its institutional objectives and its structure; (c) the capacity to maintain internal efficiency and viability through time; (d) the efficiency of the institution as a source for diffusing its norms among other institutions; (e) the capacity of the institution to receive, assimilate, and integrate competing norms with its own norms; and (f) a cosmopolitan view of the relation of selfish to group interests. When we view the development of such institutions as public civil bureaucracy, public military bureaucracy, non-public commerce, education, ecclesiastical entities, medicine, judiciary and practice of law, voluntarism, the political process, and interest groups, an extremely uneven attainment of these characteristics is evident.

When the growth of these institutions (or "sectors") is viewed in terms of the indices listed above, it is evident that their development is highly differential or asymmetrical. The asymmetry occurs not only in the relation of one sector to another but in relations of subsectors within a sector. Thus, for example, within the public bureaucracy we find differing rates of development of the higher bureaucracy and the lower bureaucracy. This phenomenon may be called intrasectoral as distinct from intersectoral differential. There is also a characteristic which we may call substantive differential. That is, various characteristics of development advance at differential rates in the subsectors as well as the sectors. As a consequence we find a complex pattern of differential rates, some changing rapidly, others slowly. For example, the officer subsector of the military bureaucracy may be permeated with modern norms at a much faster rate than the enlisted subsector or than other major sectors, yet may be behind other subsectors or sectors in assimilating and integrating competing norms. Such asymmetry appears to have characterized the development of most states although the asymmetry may have been less differential in some. It is clear, for example, in the United States that, for a variety of reasons, private commerce developed faster than did public bureaucracy, and the political process faster than the administrative process. In India, Pakistan, and Ceylon, public bureaucracy developed faster than the political process or private commerce. In Malaya, largely because of the economic consequences of rubber and tin, these differentials appear not to have been as acute.

Asymmetrical development is probably inevitable; even in rigidly planned societies perfect control seems impossible to achieve. Be that as it may, asymmetrical development poses serious problems, not the least of which is the uneven burden assumed by some sectors or subsectors which, by design or by default, compensate for the slower development of companion sectors. But the problem most crucially related to elite cadres is that of intersectoral permeability of technology and norms. The elite cadres should be the medium for absorbing superior technological and normative competences from other sectors. They should manifest sufficient flexibility to extend an intake apparatus to whatever sectors are productive, at any given time, of superior, though not necessarily surplus, competences. It is clear, for example, that managerial technology in India and Pakistan is developing at a much greater pace in private commerce than in public bureaucracy. It is conceivable that technological output of engineering, agricultural, and economic institutions may soon be superior to those of the orthodox university structure. Many of these differentials are caused or accelerated by foreign technical assistance. Whatever the cause, the differentials exist. The problem is to structure the intake media to accommodate to the differential output. I should point out in passing that this is important not only to bring into the public bureaucracy talent from other sectors but also to bring into such sectors as the political process, bureaucratic talent which might articulate better with the needs of politics than with the new dynamism of administrative development. The crucial need in developing states is the opening of means of intake so that newly emerged talent may have mobility. Even so, this must be done with care lest public bureaucracy monopolize such emerging talent. There is also a risk that the *élan* or *esprit* generated by the elite cadre as a closed entity may be overwhelmed completely by Philistine selfishness. Of equal importance with capturing the output in talent from faster developing sectors is the problem of maintaining within the higher bureaucratic structure a highly dynamic medium for the diffusion of new technology. The closed intake system which now exists in all four states depends exclusively on internal training for such diffusion. Such training is virtually non-existent in Ceylon and Malaya and is introverted and disarticulated in India. In all three states we may very well witness an atrophy of administrative viability caused by the autonarcotic effect of living exclusively on fading standards of the past. An administrative system cannot derive its exclusive generative impulse from its own past without atrophy. Of course, the opposite has its dangers; in Pakistan the intake of a new technology is so fast and so dynamic that not atrophy but other disorders may be the consequence. Closely related to diffusion of technology is inculcation of an ideology capable of continuous generation of viability. Intrastructural training, properly conceived and implemented, and supported by institutions, is, in my view, the best medium for diffusion of norms and technology. In the absence of such training or in the presence of imperfect training, intersectoral intake is essential. The possibility of such intersectoral intake may be reduced by the elite cadre structure.

There is another risk in the elite cadre concept carried to the extreme, namely, an ideological one based on a concept of concern for human dignity made manifest in uncertainty regarding human capacity for growth and in progressive enlargement of the scope of opportunity for such growth. All four states have implicitly accepted such ideology in their postindependence constitutional political forms. But so long as they support institutionally a structure which decrees that a majority of the bureaucratic makers of policy shall be chosen between the ages of twenty-one and twenty-four, and no one else may later join their ranks, they perpetuate an extreme in elitism which may militate against implementation of an ideology which presumably should be the fruit of independence. This articulation of apparatus with ideology has occurred most completely in India, ostensibly in Ceylon, to some extent in Malaysia, and almost not at all in Pakistan.

3. The elite cadres continue to serve as makers of policy in all four states, although this function is affected by the rise of politicization. It is likely that too rapid an intake may destroy the corporate sense, or *élan*, which, if properly contained, is one of the chief advantages of the *corps d'élite*. It is possible, also, that erosion of British influence and a rise in American influence in administration, already significant in Pakistan, becoming significant in India, and likely to be important in Malaysia and Ceylon, may convert the elite cadres into a corps of management specialists. Such an eventuality would destroy one of the advantages of the institution, namely, its humanistically oriented generalism. It is important to consider whether policy-making is essentially a mechanistic process or whether it is a phenomenon involving judgment, insight, and discretion. If policy formulation is a mechanistic process, the utility of elite cadres is limited, for this function can be adequately performed by average administrators who have mastered a set of techniques. If, on the other hand, it is a phenomenon closer to art than to science, elite cadres perform a crucial role in statecraft. It is here contended that policy-making is more of an art than a science.[17]

Mechanistic policy formulation places such emphasis on technique, procedure, and consensus that it neglects value, independence, creativity, eccentricity. In its extreme form in the United States, it may be a corruption of the dogma of participative democracy whereby participation as such becomes an end rather than a means. The process has become labeled "science" and has invoked the concepts of "policy science" which have developed over the last three decades in its support. The curiosity is that this is a fundamental misconception of the concept of policy science. It is true that a crucial aspect of policy science empha-

17. Cf. Robert Presthus, "Decline of the Generalist Myth," *Public Administration Review*, XXIV (1964) 211-17; John D. Montgomery, "The Role of Induced Elite Change in Political Development," *Public Policy: A Year Book of the Graduate School of Public Administration, Harvard University, 1964*, XIII, ed., John D. Montgomery and Arthur Smithies (Cambridge, Mass., 1964), 133-52.

sizes techniques for managing empirical data and modes of eliciting from groups and individuals an interpretation of data which results in decision. It is further true that this effort to empiricize decision-making is the chief characteristic distinguishing policy science from armchair judgment. But this is only a part of the process of policy science—a part seized upon by those who support a mechanistic training for public administrators. The views of Lasswell, for example, which for three and a half decades have pushed out the frontiers of scientific policy-making, do not support an exclusively mechanistic view. To be sure, Lasswell has emphasized the need to identify and assemble all possible facts bearing on a decision and has specified in minute detail devices for storage and recall of data and for stimulating imagination.[18] But in devising his developmental constructs, Lasswell pleads for the inclusion of values and, in so doing, in Eulau's words, "deviates from the positivistic bias of much of social science."[19] Lasswell states that his concept of rational decision-making depends on "a clear conception of goals, accurate calculation of probabilities, and adept application of knowledge of ways and means."[20] Such decision-making depends on assessment of details and forecasting possibilities; as estimates they involve insight and creative imagination. Recognizing this, Lasswell states that "even in an automatizing world some top-level choices must be made. In that sense at least discretion is here to stay."[21]

While policy-making executives, then, do not perform mechanistic functions in formulating policy, do they not devote a large measure of their effort to management functions, which are also mechanistic in nature? An illuminating analysis of this problem is that of Banfield,[22] who contends that a science of organization

18. See especially Harold D. Lasswell, "Technique of Decision Seminars," *Midwest Journal of Political Science*, IV (1960), 213-36.

19. Heinz Eulau, "H. D. Lasswell's Developmental Analysis," *Western Political Quarterly*, XI (1958), 237.

20. Harold D. Lasswell, "Legal Education and Public Policy," in *The Analysis of Political Behavior* (New York, 1958), p. 30.

21. Harold D. Lasswell, "Current Studies of the Decision Process: Automation versus Creativity," *Western Political Quarterly*, VIII (1955), 399.

22. Edward C. Banfield, "The Training of the Executive," in *Public Policy: A Year Book of the Graduate School of Public Administration, Harvard University, 1960*, X, ed., Carl J. Friedrich and Seymour E. Harris (Cambridge, Mass., 1960), 16-43.

is of benefit to only a relatively few persons largely engaged in administrative management. He arrives at this conclusion by a perceptive classification of tasks. He divides organizational behavior into (1) substantive or non-administrative, and (2) administrative, i.e., maintaining the relationships necessary to accomplish the substantive tasks. He then divides the administrative tasks into two subcategories: (a) administrative tasks (such as filling out a payroll) and (b) administrative management, which deals with a particular feature of the system of relationships. Employing these distinctions, Banfield concludes that the science of management is the full-time work of only a few persons. Administrative management is mostly part-time work of executives dealing with substantive matters and lesser executives actually performing administrative tasks. Following this analysis, it would appear to be wasteful to train the elitist cadres, who are substantive officials (using Banfield's classification) in administrative management tasks which constitute a minor part of their work. There may very well be a need for British "classical generalism," archaic in its extreme colonial form, to reassert itself in modern form as the dominant ethos of the elite cadres.

4. A fourth issue is the relationship of elite cadres to stability and unity in highly fragmented social orders. A major problem of most emerging states—certainly of India, Pakistan, Malaya, Ceylon, and Malaysia—is the centrifugal force of linguistic, cultural, or religious differences. National unity is difficult to maintain; the emotional force of patriotism is lacking. There is unity in negative attitudes towards former colonial powers or towards historical enemies, but there is little unity of a positive, constructive kind. Not only is political unity difficult to achieve, but cultural fragmentation is usually at the roots of disunity. The homogeneity of, let us say, Japan, is lacking. There is no deeply imbedded concept of *Kokutai*—state polity—with accompanying pride of being *rippana nihonjin*—a splendid Japanese. Elite cadres are often the only entity in fragmented societies which can provide a cohesive force. They usually have a sense

of national destiny and a corporate pride or *élan* which gives form to an expression of that destiny.

Another more tangible unifying force is the insight into various substantive areas and levels of government which their diverse experience is likely to provide. This is bound to result in understanding of other areas and problems which will increase the national perspective and level of generality in policy-making. Officers who move from the districts to posts in co-operative societies, government corporations, provincial establishments, finance, commerce and industry, and education have a perspective on the totality of nation-building which no other group in society has. Related to the issue of national unity is the effect of a centrally oriented, ascriptive bureaucracy on the pattern of federalism. It may well be that constitutional allocations of power between levels of government are functionally affected, perhaps even vitiated, by the power positions of the centrally oriented elite cadre at all levels of government.

5. The perpetuation of the functional characteristics of the traditional elite cadre poses two analytical issues for political science. One is whether or not the continued control of government, especially local government, by that cadre does not prevent the political maturing that direct election of local officials—participation—is said to enhance. At what point in political development should elected officials replace ascriptive bureaucrats? Is there a level of political maturity at which the one system may replace the other? Japan, for example, before the American-induced political reforms in 1945, had a bureaucratic apparatus functionally identical to that now found in the four nations here under review. Although a base for change had been built in the 1920's, the apparatus was politicized in one institutional move rather than gradually and its viability has been amply demonstrated. But this politicization was enhanced by several factors absent from these four nations. The political function was made respectable quickly, moreover, by a transfer of prestige and talent from the higher bureaucracy to the political realm. This has not

occurred in these four nations in which the factiousness of the political process is held in remarkably low esteem, although politicization has effectively challenged local bureaucracy in India. It is ironic that the sovereign states of India, Pakistan, Ceylon, and Malaya have chosen the same policy of gradual maturation of the political process which were resisted in India in the Montagu-Chelmsford Reforms of 1917. Those reforms were based on the assumption of a "friendly partnership" between the district officer and the local governments which theoretically were to so develop in responsibility that the ascriptive bureaucracy would be a sideline advisory group if, indeed, it did not wither away completely. Thirteen years later the Simon Commission reported that this expectation of a new relationship between the ascriptive bureaucracy and local government had been only partially fulfilled. It advocated return, largely because of "a constant watch (which must) . . . be maintained upon extremist movements,"[23] to an ascriptive posture of power. A tutelary, ascriptive relationship exists today between the bureaucracy and the political process. It will be significant to note the process by which one gains ascendancy over the other in each of these four countries.

6. Another major issue is what will be the consequence of massive introduction of American administrative norms on the governmental viability of Pakistan and, to a lesser extent, of India. In Pakistan this influence is more pronounced, because a carefully articulated training apparatus is American-oriented. In India, the training apparatus, as we have seen, is not articulated, and American influence, in any case, is felt in the design of administrative reform rather than in training of officials. The orientation of American inducement of reform to technical and managerial modes may overwhelm the generalist orientation of the earlier British system. Yet the elite cadres will probably have to play a dominant policy role in statecraft for some time to come. In the abstract, there is an optimum synchronization of

23. "Report of the Indian Statutory Commission" (Simon Report) (2 vols.), I, 290, Cmds. 3568, 3569, G. B., *Parl. Paps. 1929-30*, XI.

developments: with rapid politicization, the policy role shifts away from the ascriptive bureaucracy, which assumes more and more technical management responsibilities. But there is no rational projection as to the speed of these progressions. It may be that the policy role may shift away before it can be absorbed in politicization. Another aspect of this problem is that an ascriptive bureaucracy is probably better able to maintain viability in the context of political instability and trauma than is an achievement-oriented bureaucracy. If internal democratization of elite cadres leads to excessive achievement orientation and if this occurs at a rate greater than the stabilization of the political realm, the strains on bureaucracy may be excessive and less viability may be the consequence.

In Ceylon and Malaya, similar consequences may result from different circumstances. Here the question is not the possible erosion of policy skills in the elite cadre because of permeation of American technical norms. Such permeation is virtually non-existent. The problem may be that of progressive deterioration of any bureaucratic norms because of loss of contact with British values and failure to establish training institutions for the diffusion of such values or new values.

7. It is also relevant to examine the relationship of the elite cadre, or orthodox bureaucracy, to the new dynamism of economic development implicit in the new "non-bureaucratic" bureaucracies of rural uplift and government corporations. The emergence of these new bureaucracies is due to the alleged incapacity of the elite cadre, oriented toward law and order, to manifest the creativity and dynamism requisite to development. The proclivity to spawn government corporations is one of the principal characteristics of the four states here considered. There are seventeen in Malaya, twenty-seven in Ceylon, thirty-five in Pakistan, and fifty-three in India. Enlargement of the scope of governmental power has occurred largely within the ambit of the corporate device. Conceivably, this might mean a shift in emphasis of the elite cadre—a retrogression to law and order functions as the

larger development functions become the responsibility of the corporate device. It is possible that a new managerial-entrepreneurial group will emerge, eclipsing the power of the elite cadre. There may occur a syphoning off by natural selection of entrepreneurial talent from the elite cadre to the corporate device. A new bureaucratic elite derivative in part from the old would thus emerge. The challenge and the power of such corporate activity has already been appreciated by the elite cadres, although there has been no spectacular transfer of talent to the new bureaucracy.

The crux of this problem is that of replacing the motivations of British rule with a new bureaucratic ideology capable of continuous generation of improvement in government. The new ideology may be the dynamism of the corporate device or it may be the somewhat less appealing (from the point of view of power) participative humanitarianism of the community development movement, or it may come by reorienting the elite cadre through indoctrination. Finally, the countervailing forces of a vigorous political process, given intersectoral permeability within the society, are likely to modify the disposition and effect of the elite cadre.

8. Finally, the relevance of this essay to the future of the Commonwealth requires some discussion. I assume that wherever there is a serious erosion in British norms or a departure from British organizational forms, or a failure to reinvigorate British organizational forms by continued reference to the wellspring of norms, or the emergence of intellectual ties with nations other than Britain, Commonwealth bonds with the state in which these developments are discerned are to some degree weakened. It would be less than cautious to suggest the extent of such weakening, for there are too many other factors involved. But it is clear that in all four countries, from 1970 on, fewer than 10 per cent of the elite cadres will be officers who have had some direct contact with British administration. In Pakistan, the somewhat higher percentage is vitiated by massive infusion of American

influence. In Ceylon and Malaya there is neither new influence or reinvigoration of old British norms. Moreover, the elite cadres have necessarily (except for Pakistan) become somewhat more egalitarian in their composition. To be sure, British administrative norms are at the base of all four systems, but unless these norms are reinforced by vigorous institutional means, the elite cadre systems will drift farther from the British model. This drift, insofar as it involves crucial policy-makers in government, may be of some significance in a loosening of intellectual and institutional ties between these four ex-colonial states and the ex-imperial power which bequeathed them an impressive administrative legacy.

14

Industrial Relations Systems in the Commonwealth

Frank T. de Vyver[*]

Institutions do not always follow the flag. No clearer example of this assertion is evident than the experience of the Commonwealth countries with systems of industrial relations. All of the countries have trade unions; all have a form of collective bargaining; and all have some governmental regulation. The way these ingredients are put together, however, has led to the development of different systems, even though the same terms may be used.

Professor Dunlop has described an industrial relations system "as comprised of certain actors, certain contexts, an ideology which binds the industrial relations system together, and a body of rules created to govern the actors at the work place and work community."[1] The actors are trade unions, employers and employers' associations, and the state. Sometimes the state becomes an employer and thus reduces the number of actors. The context involves the type of work place, the product market, and the locus and distribution of power. The ideology has to do with the common ideas and aspirations of the groups involved. Finally, that rule making which is so necessary in an industrial society is carried on in various ways by the actors.

In a short paper designed to cover developments in many countries over a ten-year period no adequate analysis can be made of all of these parts of an industrial relations system. I

[*] Professor of economics and vice-provost, Duke University.
1. John Dunlop, *Industrial Relations Systems* (New York, 1958), p. 7.

shall, however, attempt to analyze the different roles of the actors as these roles have developed under different social and historic conditions in Australia, South Africa, India, and Ghana. For each country the roles of the actors will be examined and an attempt made to explain why the industrial relations systems have developed as they have. Finally, I shall try to generalize from the experiences of these four countries to see if there are any patterns which might reveal clues about possible developments in other British areas that have or will become independent.

Australia

The Australian system of industrial relations assigns a major role to government under a unique system of compulsory arbitration.

Starting in 1888 in the sweated industries of Victoria, governmental settlement of wage rates has evolved to become an intricate system of boards, courts, and commissions charged with setting not only wages but also almost every detail of industrial working rules. Over the years since Justice H. B. Higgins' Harvester decision in 1907, which provided a basic wage, government has become increasingly involved. The system has remained viable, and the principle of governmental responsibility for final settlement of labor disputes has remained constant. The other actors may bargain and may even reach a decision, or they may bargain to an impasse. If the agreement is to become generally operative, however, the proper court must approve.[2] If there is an impasse, a court will settle it with an award.

Furthermore, although the Commonwealth Commission may not make a common rule for the entire country, the conditions

2. See Frank T. de Vyver, "The Melbourne Building Industry Agreement," *Journal of Industrial Relations*, I (Spring, 1959), 7. In this case the conciliator refused to approve the agreement between the parties. This refusal meant that the agreement could have only limited application and that builders doing government work could not increase the costs to the government as they could have if the conciliator himself had ordered the wage increase or if he had approved the one agreed upon.

of any award may be extended to all employers in the industry if the unions go through the legal fiction of establishing a dispute with each individual employer. When there are few employers, most of them may have been part of the original dispute. When there are many small employers, as in the clothing industry, the union is faced with the task of developing "roping in disputes" with hundreds of small subcontractors.[3] The net result is the same. When the governmental agency has established wages, skill margins, fringe benefits, and other conditions of employment, all employers in the particular industry are expected to adhere to at least the minimum standards of the award.[4]

Employers as individuals do little bargaining except for the over-award rates which become more important as full employment creates labor shortages. Most of the negotiating is done either through employer associations, of which there are approximately 150, or by chambers of manufacturers or federations of industry. Prior to meeting with the union, representatives of the employers in the particular industry formulate their demands. Broad boundaries are set for the guidance of the employer's industrial officer whose task is to negotiate with the union and to present the employer's case before the proper commissioner or court.

On their side the trade unions are also organized so that they easily fit in with the arbitration system. Government, by establishing broad jurisdictions, minimizes the dual unionism often found in the United States. When a new industry develops, such as plastics, the federal government may have to decide among conflicting claims of unions wanting to represent the workers.

There are approximately 355 unions in Australia.[5] Some have jurisdiction for an entire industry. The textile workers' union

3. See Frank T. de Vyver, "Conciliation and Arbitration in Australia: The Case of the Clothing Trades Award," *South Atlantic Quarterly*, LVIII (Summer, 1959), 457.
4. This brief summary of the place of government has ignored the activities of the several state governments, each of which has similar procedures for settling labor disputes which cannot be brought under the aegis of the federal system. Fundamentally, however, the actors in the state systems have the same roles as those under the federal plan.
5. Commonwealth of Australia, Bureau of Census and Statistics, *Labour Report*, 1961, No. 49, p. 246.

and the clothing workers' union, for example, have the responsibility for representing all or most of the workers in all branches of the two industries. Other unions represent particular craftsmen. There are unions which represent electrical workers, railroad engineers, and various skilled groups in the engineering industries. Finally, there is the Australian Workers' Union, a large conglomeration of workers, many of whom are the unskilled or the rural workers such as cane-cutters and sheep-shearers. Most unions except the Australian Workers' Union are affiliated with the Australian Council of Trade Unions (ACTU), a loose central organization with headquarters in Melbourne. As in the United States the main power control lies with the national union rather than with the federation.

The Australian system of industrial relations is based upon the supremacy of government as the chief actor which takes the lead in establishing the necessary rules. Various factors may account for this line of development. In the first place Australia's principal exports are primary products whose prices are liable to far wider fluctuations than are those of the manufactured products which Australia imports. In such an economy costs must be maintained as low as possible and long interferences with production cannot be tolerated. Although the Australian system developed initially as a way for settling industrial unrest, more recently it has been used also as part of economic policy for development.[6]

A second factor which helps to account for the Australian type of industrial relations system is a characteristic egalitarian ideology. An examination of margins for skills found in various awards provides concrete evidence of this fact. For example, skill margins for fitters in the engineering industry and for cutters in the clothing industry were until recently exactly the same. In the United States these differences in skills receive quite different rewards.[7]

6. With the same type of economic problems, the New Zealand industrial relations system has developed along similar lines.
7. For further discussion of this point, see Frank T. de Vyver, "Concept of Wages in Australia," *South Atlantic Quarterly*, LXI (Summer, 1962), 388.

A third factor in shaping and developing the Australian system of industrial relations is a conviction that over the years it has worked. The Australian industrial relations system has not succeeded in eliminating strikes and lockouts. Some evidence does exist, however, that the system has helped reduce industrial conflict.[8] Certainly, industrial peace has been a declared objective of the system. In his annual report for 1962, the president, the Honorable Sir Richard Kirby, of the Commonwealth Conciliation and Arbitration Commission remarked, "The chief objects of the Act so far as the Commission is concerned remain the promotion of good-will in industry, the encouragement of conciliation and the prevention and settlement of industrial disputes by conciliation and arbitration with a maximum of expedition and the minimum of legal form and technicality."[9]

During the past decade the Australian economy has progressed satisfactorily. Unemployment has been at a minimum; since 1960 prices have remained stable; and the balance of payments has been satisfactory. The extent to which the industrial relations system contributed to these conditions cannot be determined. Nevertheless, being pragmatists, the Australians continue to say of their system, "Keep it viable, and keep it."

Republic of South Africa

Experience in South Africa is another example of the way in which industrial relations systems are shaped by environment. Here the system has many similarities to that of Britain, yet racial problems, recent development of secondary industries, the predominance of the mining industry, and the emergence of a strong central government have all had an impact.

8. Commonwealth of Australia, Department of Labour and National Service, *Industrial Disputes in Australia*, 1958, and Kenneth F. Walker, *Industrial Relations in Australia* (Cambridge, Mass., 1956), chap. xii.

9. *Sixth Annual Report of the President of the Commonwealth Conciliation and Arbitration Commission. For the period 14th August, 1961 to 13th August, 1962* (Melbourne, 1962, mimeographed). See also Kirby's lecture in Percy Clarey Memorial Lectures in Industrial Relations," *Journal of the Australian Productivity Council*, IV (March, 1963), 1.

In South Africa there is a range of form in industrial relations from complete governmental control to plant collective bargaining subject only to general factory acts such as are found in most countries. In general, however, the system is characterized by industry-wide collective bargaining except in situations where weakness among unions or industrial organizations makes the role of government critical.

Employers in the republic are organized into associations with an aggregate membership of approximately seventeen thousand firms.[10] Unlike the Australian system where work agreements are ordinarily negotiated for employer organizations by chambers of manufacturers, the industry trade associations in South Africa do most of their own negotiating with unions through approximately 90 organizations called industrial councils.[11]

About two hundred and fifty unions represent a membership of nearly five hundred thousand workers.[12] In recent years, some of these unions have by law been Balkanized into all white, all Cape coloured, all Asiatic, or all native, but forty-nine unions are still classified by the Labour Department as mixed. The councils negotiate agreements covering wages, hours, and working conditions and provide the first step toward enforcing the detailed regulations the agreements prescribe.

In making such agreements, however, the government plays a more important role than might be expected in the usual industry-wide bargaining found in the United States and the United Kingdom. When an agreement is concluded, the minister of labor, "if he deems it expedient to do so," may publish it in the official *Gazette* and thus give the agreement the effect of law, binding not only upon the members of the organizations making the agreement but also upon all others engaged in the particular industry covered. Furthermore, in most cases the minister extends the terms of the agreement to natives, who, under the Industrial Conciliation Act, are not included "in the

10. *State of the Union Year Book for South Africa 1959-60* (Johannesburg: Da Gama Publications), p. 59.
11. Garfield Clack, "Industrial Peace in South Africa," *British Journal of Industrial Relations*, I (1962), 99.
12. *Ibid.*, p. 96.

definition of the expression employee" and who, therefore, would not be covered by an agreement between employers and employees.[13]

With each industrial agreement subject to governmental approval before its provisions can be published officially and so have universal application, the parties pay particular attention to the minister of labour's representative who sits in on negotiations. A simple "I don't think the minister would approve of that" does more than simply guide the negotiators. In this way a strong central government influences and may bring pressure to bear on the final decisions not only at the micro-level affecting details of plant and industry operation, but also at the macro-level affecting the general wage policy of the nation.

Unlike the Australian situation, there are industries in South Africa in which either the employers or the workers, or both, are poorly organized. For these the government uses a Wage Board modeled on the British pattern and consisting of a chairman and two members—all appointed by the minister of labour. The board recommends to the minister not only wage rates but also other conditions of employment. At the hearings numerous economic factors are considered such as the industry's ability to pay, the cost of living indices, and current practices in the nation with respect to working conditions.

The Wage Board, however, can only recommend. Final authority for publishing recommendations, thus giving them the standing of law, is left to the minister of labour. Again, only "if he deems it expedient to do so," does the minister publish them in the Gazette. If the findings are not published they remain without effect. No statistics are available to determine the extent to which the government has ignored board decisions, but the probability is that most recommendations meet the government's requirements.

Great governmental control is exercised over native workers, who are considered to be wards of the state and are forbidden to form, or to be full members of, trade unions. The Department

13. See Frank T. de Vyver, "South African Labor Relations," Labor Law Journal, XI (Sept., 1960), 837.

of Labour is charged to protect the rights of native workers and has created elaborate machinery for this purpose.

The least governmental control is found among secondary industries such as automobile assembly plants and rubber firms. Here decision making is unilaterally in the hands of employers, and there are few, if any, union members. This area of production is similar to segments of American industry which are unorganized, but in which workers are given protection through factory acts guaranteeing certain basic standards for such matters as hours of work and overtime. Presumably, unilateral decision by employers exists because wages are high enough here to alleviate the necessity for Wage Board action and because no unions have developed to challenge the employers' methods of instituting industrial regulations.

The government's role is also strong in settlement of disputes which arise either in making the basic agreement or in carrying out its provisions. Strikes are generally illegal until all avenues for settlement are exhausted, and every effort is made to help disputants reach a settlement. A conciliation board may be appointed at the discretion of the minister and its decisions may be gazetted and thus given the force of law. Mediation is always available and, all else failing, arbitration may be offered or required, depending upon the circumstances. Arbitration is compulsory for disputes in the government service and utilities. In addition, however, "the Minister of Labour 'may from time to time by notice in the Gazette, notify his intention' of applying the arbitration procedures to those industries supplying or distributing perishable foods or supplying gasoline or other fuels to local authorities."[14] Under this clause the minister brought the whole canning industry under compulsory arbitration and thus made strikes entirely illegal in this industry.

Even in other industries where compulsory arbitration is not in force, strikes are legal only after time-consuming procedures have been followed. Furthermore, unlike the situation in some other parts of the world, the law against strikes is enforced in

14. *Ibid.*, p. 846.

South Africa. An illegal strike is a criminal offense and strikers are often jailed. South African law has developed the cooling-off period to an extreme. This combined with severe penalties for striking during the cooling-off period has meant almost a strike-less system.[15]

In summary, the South African system of industrial relations is dominated by government to a greater extent than that in the United Kingdom and in some important ways to a greater extent than that in Australia. Cause and effect are not always easily distinguished, but certain economic and social factors seem to have shaped the South African situation.

First, because 60 per cent of the population are considered wards of the state, control of the African segment of the labor force has resulted naturally. A large majority of natives in the labor market are unskilled or semiskilled workers, and, lacking trade unions, they have depended on government for protection from exploitation. Unskilled white workers are protected because they are members of the elite. Skilled white workers are in short supply, and they have used their competitive position to obtain at least some of their goals. In this situation a government com-mission concluded with some reason that in South Africa "state policy cannot allow free competition between peoples living on such widely different levels of civilization as the Natives and white population."[16]

Another environmental factor that helps to account for the strong role played by government is the political situation in South Africa. A white minority in a country located in a continent dominated by nationalistic Africans have sought protection of their present status by means of a strong state. They argue that however kindly one may feel toward one's wards, discipline is necessary if the wards are not to become masters. This philosophy has brought the government more and more into the industrial relations system. The split between the minority English and the

15. See Clack, p. 96, for a further analysis of the reasons for industrial peace in South Africa.

16. *Report of the Native Economic Commission*, U. G. 22/1932, par. 845, as cited by Garfield Clack, p. 100.

majority Afrikaners may also have strengthened the Afrikaners' willingness to accept a dominant role for government in the labor relations system.

Finally, it is argued in South Africa that a strikeless society with government playing the dominant role in industrial relations is necessary in a developing economy based to so great an extent upon gold production. Likewise, governmental control, it is reasoned, enables the economy to be diversified more quickly than under a freer system. "Guidance" in industrial relations will provide cost restraints and limited redistribution of income as a palliative to workers.

The South African government, rather than strengthening unions, has chosen to weaken them by seeking one-race unions in a multiracial society. Government in the industrial relations system as elsewhere in the economy is imposing its own prescriptions for development and for all social action.

India

The industrial relations system of India presents to the Western observer the same enigmatic picture presented by other aspects of Indian society. The actors in the drama are all present with their written parts, but often the script appears to have been replaced by improvisation. Officially the system desired is collective bargaining. One observer suggests that "The spirit of collective bargaining took firm roots under the guidance of Mahatma Gandhi, who began his work at Ahmedabad and organized [the] trade union movement in the technical sense." The first collective bargaining agreement in India was arranged as early as 1920.[17] Yet, although the government policy has been "strongly and clearly committed to the method of bargaining," government action has not moved in that direction,[18] or at least not in the direction of collective bargaining, Western style.

17. V. Agnihotri, "Towards Collective Bargaining," *Indian Labour Journal,* IV (March, 1963), 262-63.
18. Van D. Kennedy, "The Conceptual and Legislative Framework of Labor Relations in India," *Industrial and Labor Relations Review,* XI (July, 1958), 487.

Unlike the well-organized movement of Australia and the well-controlled movement of Ghana,[19] the trade-union movement in India is a veritable labyrinth. There are four main federations, each tied closely to one of the principal parties. Although registration of unions is required under a 1926 law, there is no regulation giving the government the right to limit unions to specific jurisdictions. Thus the employer may find himself negotiating with two unions.[20] Not only are the unions separated at the national level, but "a corresponding division and duplication have also taken place at industry, locality, and often plant levels."[21] This situation has led to the formation of about five thousand small unions with an average membership of seven or eight hundred.[22]

Whatever the membership, Indian trade unionism itself seems to be thoroughly dismembered. For this and other reasons, finances are so weak that only a few unions or federations have full-time paid leadership. There are, of course, exceptions. However, one commentator states that "Collective bargaining in India is yet to develop and strengthen its hold on the industry and the labour."[23] Thus, even though a strong trade-union movement is essential for effective collective bargaining, and even though official statements deny the fact, a viable trade-union organization has failed to develop in India.

Management plays its role through associations and by individual enterprises. The character of the actors, however, has modified considerably the actions which might be expected either from association bargainers or those representing individual firms. In the first place, nepotism seems to abound.[24] Another char-

19. Most of the secondary materials for this section are from Charles A. Myers' chapter on India in Walter Galenson, ed., *Labor and Economic Development* (New York, 1959).

20. See, for example, note of a settlement between M/S Burn and Company and their workmen. "Separate settlements were reached between the Management and Magnesite National Labour; Union (I. N. T. U. C.) and Magnesite Workers' Union (A. I. T. U. C.). . . ." *Indian Labour Journal*, IV (February, 1963), 174.

21. Kennedy, p. 490 n.

22. Myers, p. 37.

23. Agnihotri, p. 265.

24. B. B. Lal, "Industrial Management and Economic Growth," *Indian Journal of Economics*, XLI (Oct., 1960), 196. See also Myers, p. 50.

acteristic of Indian management is its paternalistic and authoritative attitude. G. L. Mehta, former president of India's Chambers of Commerce and Industry, has said, ". . . the borderline between authority and autocracy, discipline and docility still seems to elude us."[25] Made in 1947, this statement is still appropriate, although young and dynamic management teams, trained in modern labor relations practices, are changing the character of some management groups.[26] In certain areas and industries, employers collectively negotiate with unions. Since 1920, for example, the Ahmedabad Millowners' Association has been dealing with the Textile Labour Association. This experience, by Western standards, is probably the most successful example of industrial relations in the country. There are other examples, particularly in the textile, engineering, and jute industries. Other producers, however, deal individually with their employees' unions.[27]

As in the other Commonwealth countries examined in this paper, in India the government plays the leading role in the industrial relations system. Under British rule government was a passive regulator of labor aiming to provide minimum protection to workers and to limit disturbances which might threaten the peace and security of the state.[28] In 1947, however, the Indian Industrial Disputes Act was passed, which, with amendments and supplemented by other legislation such as the Industrial Employment Act of 1946 and certain state laws, provides both the framework and the control that the new developing Indian state feels it needs.

At the plant level the 1947 law provides that government may establish works committees, presumably modeled after the Whitley Councils in the United Kingdom. The Act itself is vague about the functions of the committees, with the result that

25. G. L. Mehta, "Industrial Management," in C. N. Vakil, ed., *Papers in Economics* (Bombay, 1947), as cited in Myers, p. 47.
26. Myers, p. 47, and Kennedy, p. 498.
27. Agnihotri, p. 264. In 1955, for example, the Bata Shoe Company, Ltd., signed an agreement with the Bata Mazdoor Union, and in 1956 the Indian Aluminum Company, Ltd., Belur Works reached agreement with its employees' union. See also Oscar A. Ornati, *Jobs and Workers in India* (Ithaca, 1955), p. 146.
28. Myers, p. 58.

"Unionists tend to look upon works committees as rival organizations which lend themselves to employer manipulation for anti-union purposes,"[29] and furthermore, "there is wide-spread opinion in management circles that the committees have been ineffective."[30] Often the committees are used as local grievance machinery and sometimes as consulting groups on production problems. In general, they have not developed as their sponsors apparently had hoped.

Considerable governmental intervention in rule-making is provided by the Industrial Employment Act of 1946. Industrial establishments employing one hundred or more persons must post "a set of certified standing orders defining the conditions of employment in the establishment."[31] The power of government in setting rules for classification of workmen, shift schedules, rules for attendance, tardiness, leave and holidays, discipline for misconduct, and discharge and grievance procedures is implemented by requiring that the orders must conform with the government's model standing orders. Furthermore, the conditions outlined in the law itself may be supplemented by administrative regulation.

Conciliation and arbitration through industrial tribunals are the procedures used ostensibly for the settlement of disputes. However, Indian conciliation has involved considerably more governmental interference than that found in the United States, where a conciliator cannot pass public judgment upon the merits of disputes he is investigating. Before terminating a case Indian conciliators invariably indicate to disputing parties the settlement they personally consider equitable.[32] Because this conciliator may recommend arbitration as the next step, the likelihood is that his suggestion for settlement will be accepted. A considerable number of disputes are referred to arbitration but the exact figure is not available. Of the 487 disputes in 1961, about two-fifths

29. Kennedy, p. 491.
30. Myers, p. 55. See also "Working of the Industrial Employment (standing orders) Act 1946, during 1960," *Indian Labour Journal*, IV (Feb., 1963), 161.
31. Kennedy, p. 491.
32. Kennedy, p. 492.

involved governmental intervention, but only three or four were settled by compulsory arbitration.[33]

The Indian system illustrates well the dilemma involved in labor relations in a developing country. Imbued with a spirit of democracy and steeped in traditions of an independent labor movement, the country has placed few restraints upon union development and collective bargaining. Yet the costs of independent unionism were recognized.[34] Trade unions were not allowed to become militant. Indian workers were allowed only a limited share in the slowly growing national income.

For economic good or ill, the trade-union movement has developed in such a way as to make it difficult for unions to battle militantly for improved conditions. As one Indian writer has said,

the manner in which some [Indian] unions operate gives the impression that, apart from being a lucrative profession, trade unionism is a good grazing ground for all kinds of people such as briefless lawyers, reckless men with political ambitions, and sometimes even semi-educated hoodlums who exploit the poverty and ignorance of the workers. . . . Government must therefore assume some control and exercise some vigilance on the working of the trade unions, especially those dominated by outsiders, so that under the cover of being the champions of the down-trodden proletariat, they do not become a menace to the industrial progress of the country.[35]

Thus far the Indian government, unlike those in some other parts of the Commonwealth, has not followed Palekar's recipe for governing free collective bargaining, but rather has used every effort to encourage worker participation through works councils,

33. "Industrial Disputes in India during 1961," *Indian Labour Journal*, IV (Feb., 1963), 139, 157.
34. Oscar A. Ornati, "Problems of Indian Trade Unionism," *Annals of the American Academy of Political and Social Science*, CCCX (March, 1957), 151. The author described the difficulties of free collective bargaining as urged by V. V. Giri, minister of labour in the first independent government. The government felt forced to overrule the Labour Appelate Tribunal's decision granting higher wages to bank employees on the grounds that implementing the decision would impair banking in the rural areas. Vigorous growth of rural banks, contended the government, was necessary for the development envisaged by the Five Year Plan. Giri resigned from the government, and as Professor Ornati puts it, this "resignation in the bank dispute sounded the death knell of free collective bargaining."
35. Shreekant A. Palekar, *Problems of Wage Policy for Economic Development* (*with Special Reference to India*) (New York, 1962), p. 225.

union-management negotiation, and other methods for mutual settlement of problems. The machinery exists for governmental control of industrial relations, not only industrial tribunals but also standing orders and stated wage policies. The conflict is clear "between lowering consumption standards which are already low and stimulating capital formation,"[36] and thus the maze of free labor mechanisms in India may soon give way to government intervention in the name of development.

Ghana

In 1951 when the Nkrumah Government first came into office it promulgated the following policy towards trade unions, which could have been lifted from the platform of either of the major American political parties:

The Government wishes a strong and healthy trade union movement to be firmly established on constitutional lines in the Gold Coast. . . .

The basis of a sound and effective trade union movement is strong individual unions . . . comprised of the greatest possible number of workers in a trade or industry. . . . Negotiation on wages and conditions of employment is a matter for the individual unions of workers and employers who are primarily concerned. Government is anxious to see the development of sound negotiating machinery in all trades and industries.

The Trade Union Congress . . . should be capable of representing the interests of workers in all matters of national importance affecting them . . . its functions are essentially consultative and advisory.[37]

During the intervening years governmental policy has changed dramatically. One writer has explained, "They [the Convention People's Party] were not prepared to allow the trade unions

36. *Ibid.* Yet V. V. Giri, when governor of Kerale, in an introduction to a book by G. L. Srivastava, speaking of compulsory adjudication, says, "I consider it to be enemy Number One of the working class." *Collective Bargaining and Labour-Management Relations in India* (Allahabad: Bookland Private Limited, 1962), p. 2.

37. J. I. Roper, *Labour Problems in West Africa* (Harmondsworth: Penguin Books, 1958), p. 101.

to become the basis of effective opposition. The primary function of the unions in the new state was to be the same as that of unions in The Soviet Union."[38] This policy change has been paralleled by a change in the system of industrial relations. This shift from a free trade-union movement to a controlled one provides an excellent example of an imported institution being extensively modified by environmental factors, both economic and political.

As a British colony, Ghana came under the policy which encouraged British-type trade unions for possessions. In 1938 a labor department of the colonial government was established, in part to encourage the formation of trade unionism. Legislation passed in 1941 gave legal status to unions and included such basic trade-union principles as recognition of the right to strike and protection of trade-union funds against civil units.[39] The industrial relations system which developed had certain similarities to that in the United Kingdom, and certain distinct differences.

The system consisted of free trade unions negotiating with individual employers except the mining union, which negotiated with a single association—the Chamber of Mines. In some instances, negotiating procedures were supplemented by governmentally appointed wage boards composed of representatives of employers and employees. Like their prototypes in the United Kingdom and South Africa, these boards were empowered to fix wages and other conditions of employment for specified classes of workers. Further, when voluntary effort broke down, the Labour Department provided conciliation when requested, and, with agreement of both parties, the dispute could be submitted to arbitration.

The actors in the system developed their roles in unusual

38. B. C. Roberts, *Labour in Tropical Territories of the Commonwealth* (Durham, N. C., 1964), p. 106.
39. Walter Bowen, *Colonial Trade Unions* (Fabian Research Series No. 167 [London, 1954]), p. 5. Impetus for the new legislation came from passage by the British Parliament of the Colonial Development and Welfare Act, which required that there be reasonable facilities for the establishment of trade unions before money could be spent under the Act.

ways. Although under the 1941 law unions had to be registered, by 1954 of the 113 unions which had registered "18 were inactive, eight had amalgamated to form three unions and 19 had had their certificates of registration cancelled."[40] Two years later 53 registered unions were active with an aggregate paid-up membership of only 53,500. No more than 11 of the 53 unions had a paid-up membership exceeding 1,000.[41] Furthermore, the majority of these were organized as company-wide unions, meaning that all members were employed by the same company or governmental organization.

Unions were established to negotiate with employers or with combinations of employers. However, by 1954 no combination had been registered and presumably all bargaining was with individual employers. Furthermore, "except in the government service, negotiation of terms of employment between employers and union representatives was the exception rather than the rule."[42]

The third actor, government, except for its own operations, rarely appeared on stage. Neither the arbitration machinery nor the wage board provisions were used extensively. Despite an ideological approach of devoted British colonial and trade-union leaders, the industrial relations system of Ghana prior to 1958 was a transferred institution that did not work as expected. Economic and social conditions probably rendered failure inevitable in the absence of long years of trial and error, impossible in a country seeking rapid development.

The Ghanaian industrial relations system was not conducive to tripartite activities. In the first place, conditions were not propitious for development of strong unionism. A tradition of family and tribal ties made membership in a union less essential than in a more modern society.[43] Several additional socioeconomic

40. *Colonial Office Report on the Gold Coast for the Year 1954* (London: H. M. S. O., 1956), p. 26.
41. Douglas Rimmer, "The New Industrial Relations in Ghana," *Industrial and Labor Relations Review*, XIV (Jan., 1961), 211.
42. Rimmer, p. 211.
43. Roper, chap. iii.

factors contributed to lessen interest in unions. The predominantly migratory labor was difficult to organize, agricultural workers made poor union candidates, many of the employed workers were unskilled, and illiteracy was prevalent. Add to these facts the reality that the government employs half of the wage earners of Ghana and it is little wonder that strong unionism did not develop in this particular country.[44]

The organization pattern for carrying out the part unions might be expected to play in rule-making activities has not been satisfactory in Ghana. Many registered unions were too small to be effective. The Trades Union Congress, modeled after the British institution of the same name, was advisory and educational only, with little or no formal authority over affiliated unions. Few union organizations seem to have had money for operations. As one writer summarized the situation in 1954, "without experience, leadership, or funds, the tiny unions face the great colossi of industry and government, sometimes with a feeling of despair, sometimes with violent anger, and often with fear."[45]

On their side, the two largest employer groups, governmental and non-governmental industry, have seemed content to make unilateral decisions on conditions of employment. R. B. Davison has summarized this employer attitude toward bilateral negotiating.

Paternalism dies hard, even if it is not a conspicuously successful policy, and the managerial element has not moved beyond the stage of a somewhat pained bewilderment that the workers are not completely satisfied with what is provided for them. The more out-spoken lay the blame for the 'newfangled' unions at the door of literate malcontents, the British Socialist Government, meddling labor officers, and incompetent intellectuals.[46]

44. Frank T. de Vyver, "The Transplantation of Trade Unionism to British Africa," in W. B. Hamilton, ed., *The Transfer of Institutions* (Durham, N. C., 1964), pp. 216-32. There were, of course, some strong organizations such as the United Africa Company's Employees' Union and the Mines Employees' Union.

45. R. B. Davison, "Labor Relations and Trade Unions in the Gold Coast," *Industrial and Labor Relations Review*, VII (July, 1954), 602.

46. Davison, p. 602.

With weak and ineffectual trade unions and hostile employer attitudes it is little wonder that even before independence, the Ghana government devised a new industrial relations system. Ratified on the last day of 1958, a new law changed the structure and characteristics of the trade-union movement and forced unions and management to negotiate. In this new scene the names of the actors are the same but their positions on the stage are entirely different from the previous arrangement. In fact, the costumes and voices of the actors have been so changed that they cannot be recognized as the same cast. Amendments to the 1958 law have strengthened further the hand of government. The old Trades Union Congress is now the chief spokesman for labor. The number of registered unions has been reduced to sixteen, and, while each has control over its various branches, each is completely subordinated to the Trades Union Congress. Furthermore, union membership is compulsory and the check-off of union dues is generally imposed. No union may exist unless the Ministry of Labour has approved registration. Machinery has been developed for settling disputes with compulsory arbitration as the final step. The amended 1958 law certainly does not meet the International Labor Organization Convention regarding free trade unionism, a fact probably recognized even by the government itself.[47]

Since 1958 employers have extended their organizations, although much of the bargaining is still carried on by individual companies. In addition to the Chamber of Mines there are, among others, a Timber Federation, the Civil Engineers' Federation, and the Port Employers' Association.[48] As an employer the government does not bargain with its workers through unions.[49]

On the surface this new system appears similar to that in South Africa. Strengthened by government, a few unions are

47. Rimmer, p. 212 and Lester N. Trachtman, "Ghanaian Labor Legislation Since Independence," *Labor Law Review*, XII (June, 1961), 549. See also *Comparative Collective Agreements Negotiated to Date by National Unions of the Trades Union Congress in the Cause of Ghana Workers* (Accra: T. U. C. Publication, 1961).
48. *Comparative Collective Agreements*, p. 5.
49. Trachtman, p. 551.

now negotiating wages, hours, and working conditions with individual employers or with employer groups. Rimmer states that "The Act of 1958 could plausibly be regarded as a concordat between organized labor and the government. On the one hand, the trade unions conceded the principle of compulsory arbitration and relieved the government of anxiety about strikes. On the other hand, the government provided legislation designed to increase the organizational and financial strength of the union."[50] Yet, the industrial relations system of Ghana is under the domination of the government, for the "government has the authority to seize the funds of the Trades Union Congress, set the rules for its operation, control its finances and determine its constituent members."[51] Furthermore, the government has used its powers. Confronted by an economic crisis in 1961, the government applied a system of forced savings to workers. A spontaneous strike that followed was declared illegal. Although a number of strikers were jailed, the union took no action to defend the workers in that situation.[52]

The Ghanaian system of industrial relations with its absolutism has developed in part, as Professor Roberts has said, because

the leaders of the triumphant Convention People's Party were concerned to create a trade union movement that would be completely under their control. They were not prepared to allow trade unions to become the basis of an effective opposition. . . . Through a subordinate trade union movement, the government would be able to bring pressure to bear upon employers or to damp down demands from workers for improvements in wages and working conditions to suit the political circumstances.[53]

Certainly Dr. Nkrumah has managed to eliminate most of the opposition, and a trade-union movement allowed to grow strong

50. Rimmer, p. 216.
51. Trachtman, p. 216.
52. William H. Friedland, *Unions and Industrial Relations in Underdeveloped Countries* (New York State School of Industrial and Labor Relations at Cornell, Bulletin 47, 1963), p. 53.
53. Roberts, p. 106.

independently might have been an important source of opposition.

Yet other factors besides a desire for absolute control should be considered. Ghana as a developing nation is beset with the problems of attracting capital, raising productivity, and preventing inflation. These aims can easily be upset by a trade-union movement of the American or British model. Strikes and labor unrest, serious enough in a developed economy, may be disastrous in a developing area. Negotiated wage increases may affect costs adversely and thus hinder exports and the growth of much-needed capital.

Political leaders in Ghana, with considerable acumen, altered substantially the weak trade-union movement which had been developing along British lines to serve the workers better economically, and also to serve as a political arm of the Convention People's party.

Summary and Conclusions

The industrial relations systems of the Commonwealth examined in this paper seem to have common characteristics even though they all have been modified from the British system. Both external and internal forces have helped shape the parts played by the several actors.

Chief among the external factors has been the British background itself. British civil servants and other migrants took to the colonies what they knew at home, which for over a hundred years has been a free trade-union movement with collective bargaining for wages and comparatively little governmental interference in dispute settlement. This factor was not as important in Australia and South Africa, where unionism evolved only a little later than it did in England. In the newer countries of the Commonwealth, however, unions developed after British trade unionism had reached its present status.

To delineate all of the internal factors is too great a task for a short paper. Such a study would be an economic history of each country. Certain factors, however, do stand out. In each situation economic development has been involved. In Australia that factor has been augmented by an egalitarian philosophy. In South Africa differences between the two groups of white settlers and the multiracial society have helped forge that country's industrial relations system. In each country examined government plays the principal role, a part much more important than that played by the government of the United Kingdom. To be sure, there are variations in the playing of the role ranging from close supervision in South Africa to absolute control in Ghana. A very tentative conclusion which might be drawn from this observation is that the importance of the role of government is likely to be in inverse ratio to the country's stage of economic development and its adoption of economic planning. South Africa, a comparatively well-developed and wealthy economy, can afford to allow rule-making to be done by bargaining or by unilateral company action. Australia retains an historic institution, but a considerable amount of free collective bargaining takes place within that framework. Contrasted with these, Ghana and India in their stages of development seem to feel that government must maintain control.

With government the principal actor it is not surprising to find labor unions becoming politically minded. This is a general development in the four countries, and in this instance the development has not been different from that in the United Kingdom. The methods are different. In Australia the Labour party is usually the loyal opposition, although in several states it is the party in power. In Ghana the government has made the Trades Union Congress an arm of the government. In India the four federations represent four shades of political view and are aligned with four political groups. South Africa provides the exception. United in their loyalty to their national origin, the workers of that country have divided along racial rather than political lines.

The three actors in an industrial relations system are constantly on the stage. For better or worse, government plays the lead part in all of these Commonwealth countries. Developing countries apparently fear that they cannot afford the luxury of free trade unions and free collective bargaining. Countries with planned economies plan for work rules as they do for other aspects of economic life. Here, the new look in industrial relations seems to be more the work of Procrustes than of Darwin.

Part V

International Relations

15

Regional Associations and the Commonwealth

Dennis Austin*

It might be thought that if further evidence were needed of the weakening of Commonwealth ties it could be found in the growing interest among several of the member countries in their own regions, some because of trade interests, some because of defense requirements, others again because of an emotional belief in pan-Africanism, or enosis, or pan-Asianism. The phenomenon of "regionalism" is said to be world-wide: "one of the most significant developments of contemporary international relations."[1] Certainly, regional defense groupings have proliferated since 1945—NATO, SEATO, CENTO, the ANZUS Pact, the Warsaw Pact; and hardly a region of the world has not attempted to devise a free trade area or a common market—Latin America, Central America, EEC, COMECOM, East Africa, Equatorial Africa. What is true of the world in general might be thought true also of the Commonwealth, which, over the past decade, by acquiring an impressive number of new frontiers, has raised problems—and opportunities—of regional association. Canada draws ever closer to the United States. The Greeks in Cyprus refuse to abandon the prospect of union with Greece. The African leaders declare their prior commitment to African unity should regional and Commonwealth loyalties conflict. Jamaica

* Senior research fellow, Institute of Commonwealth Studies, University of London, and Royal Institute of International Affairs.
1. R. J. Yalem, "Regionalism and World Order," *International Affairs*, XXXVIII (Oct., 1962), 460, and see Ernst B. Haas, "Regional Integration and Nation Policy," *International Conciliation*, Carnegie Endowment, 1957.

has announced that it may apply for membership in the Organization of American States. Australia and New Zealand are turning more and more to their own part of the globe, hoping to offset in Asian markets what they may lose in Europe. Britain itself has been a suppliant on the threshold of Europe until turned away by France. The picture may be exaggerated in detail, but it can be argued that it is true in substance.

Moreover, if one asks why there should have been a loosening of Commonwealth links in the face of strong regional pulls the answer is clear: the inability of the United Kingdom to bear the weight of global power. The change both in status and stature has come swiftly but (it is argued) unmistakably when one compares the past, even the immediate past, with the present. Twenty years ago, the Commonwealth was a power still; it guarded an immense area of the world and it carried a vast portion of the world's trade. Of the present eighteen independent member countries, fourteen were still subject to Westminster: they were blinkered in their relations with the outside world and scarcely conscious of their neighbors. Moreover, what was true of the dependent territories was hardly less true of the dominions, whose gaze was still fixed on London. After 1945, however, the Commonwealth scene was transformed as Britain began to be displaced by the growth of American and Soviet power. Britain also lost an empire. And the virtual disappearance of empire (it can be argued) produced a familiar situation which the expansion of the Commonwealth has done little to mask. The effect has been as if a powerful magnet had lost the greater part of its power, the consequence being that other fields of attraction have become active whose lines of force must be traced to other poles, many of them with a regional appeal. Thus Canada is obliged to look south, Australia and New Zealand to their own hemisphere, the United Kingdom to Europe. To the newly independent countries, the reduced stature of the United Kingdom perhaps has been a source of comfort, since it has helped to assuage their fears of "neo-colonialist forces." They have, nonetheless, tended to look with suspicion at any sug-

gestion of closer links with Britain, and have participated in new
regional associations which cut across Commonwealth boundaries. Other evidence may be adduced. It can be argued that it
is natural for governments to think in terms of hinterlands and
neighbors, most states having land frontiers and an obsession with
all the troubles that go with them. Regionalism is simply an extension of these interests in a peaceful setting. The concept is
embodied in the Charter of the United Nations, notably in the
sphere of operation of its special agencies. It is also a major element in United States thinking out of a habit born, no doubt, of
its preoccupation with North America and the western hemisphere. If then one looks forward in hope to a future world order
under the United Nations, its substructure may well be thought
to divide logically into geographical areas, as are the regional
provinces of a large federal unit. If, on the other hand, the
realities of global politics are faced, then the future of the world
might well be thought to lie between the two or three major
poles of power—Washington, Moscow, Peking—each primarily
concerned with its own regional hinterland in Latin America,
eastern Europe, Southeast Asia, but engaged also in promoting
its interests in competition with each other in more distant
regions. What place is there in either setting, it may be asked, for
a non-regional Commonwealth whose members are scattered
throughout the world—the product of a now vanished maritime
empire?

Such in outline is the argument for stressing the importance
of regional groupings. How seriously has the Commonwealth
been affected by a general movement in this direction? Its effect
may undoubtedly be detected as one more influence at work,
weakening Commonwealth ties and posing alternative ends, however impractical, for many of its members. The answer suggested
in this chapter, however, is that the trend to regionalism in the
world has been greatly exaggerated. Indeed, if it were not for
one major exception, it might be said that Commonwealth ties,
based on history, have usually been hardly less important than
the geography of the member countries. The exception is of the

greatest importance, however: namely, the United Kingdom's relations with Europe. For here the Commonwealth relationship as a whole is brought into question, thus demonstrating once again that the greatest injury which may be inflicted on the association lies within the capacity not of the newest members but of the oldest, out of what may be thought to be the prior national interest of the United Kingdom.

What have been the main regional associations affecting the Commonwealth in the past decade? Leaving aside regional links between the Commonwealth members themselves, it is possible to list a number of groupings.

One might start with a long-familiar problem: Canada and the United States. Canada resists closer ties with the U.S., it is true, but is it a weakening resistance? No Canadian, certainly no English-speaking Canadian, takes the proof of his national identity for granted, and the search for a clear expression of Canadian nationalism continues. In earlier decades, the pull of the south was counteracted by membership in a Commonwealth in which British power was still strongly expressed, by a cautious adherence to the League, and a calculated aloofness from external affairs. Since the war, however, successive Canadian governments have extended their interests in the outside world, notably through the United Nations: Canada now has more than eighty diplomatic missions abroad where in 1939 it had only ten; it has troops and civilian officers under United Nations authority in troubled areas of the world. Yet despite these efforts to broaden its national outlook, the pace of Americanization has increased, notably in defense and the penetration of Canadian economic life by American trade and capital.

For example, in 1940 the United States government undertook to come to Canada's defense. In 1949 Canada accepted membership in an Atlantic Alliance dominated by the United States. Today the air defenses of the whole of the northern hemisphere are co-ordinated under the North American Air Defense Command. Disagreements may continue over the manning of missile bases and the control of warheads; but Canada has had to face the fact of the armed division of the world between the two great nuclear powers and its own intermediate position in the polar regions. Liberal and conservative governments alike have committed Canada not only to a regional alliance based on the north Atlantic (within which it is one of many, including the United Kingdom) but to a close liaison with the United States on terms that would have been unthinkable before 1945.

Similarly, in terms of trade and investment, Canada continues to submit to the advance of the United States' power. The Diefenbaker Government came to office in 1957, promising to increase Commonwealth trade; but investment and goods still flow in greater quantity, and at a greater rate of increase, across the southern border:

Table 1. *Canada: Imports and Exports* ($ million C)

	Imports from				Exports to			
	1938	1948	1958	1961	1938	1948	1958	1961
Total trade	678	2637	5192	5771	838	3075	4791	5756
United States	425	1810	3583	3866	272	1510	2821	3122
United Kingdom	119	300	527	618	340	687	772	909
Japan	5	3	70	117	21	8	105	232
Germany*	10	2	106	137	18	13	201	213

*After 1948, Federal German Republic
Source: *United Nations Year Book of International Trade*, 1962

The predominance of United States trade becomes clearer when the figures are expressed as percentages of total Canadian trade. In 1938 imports from and exports to the United States were 46 per cent of Canadian trade; ten years later they were 58 per cent; ten years later again, they were 64 per cent. Investment figures show the same pattern. For many years Canada has been faced with a balance of payments deficit which reached its peak of $1,500 million in 1959 and led to devaluation in 1962. The largest contribution to the deficit has been payments of interest and dividends on foreign holdings of Canadian equities and debt securities, largely of American origin. Its worst effects have been counteracted by sales of wheat behind the Iron Curtain and by further investment of foreign capital, largely from America:

Table 2. Control of Selected Canadian Industries 1926-1961

| | 1926 | | | 1961 | | |
Controlled by	Manufac-turing	Mining & smelting	Petroleum & natural gas	Manufac-turing	Mining & smelting	Petroleum & natural gas
United States	30%	32%	n/a	45%	52%	60%
Canadian	65%	62%	n/a	41%	41%	31%
Other countries	5%	6%	n/a	14%	7%	9%

n/a = not available because components were negligible items at that time, and included under other headings

Table 3. Value of Selected Foreign Investments in Canada by Country of Origin, December 31, 1961

I Direct investment 13.7 billion = 100%

United States	−82%
United Kingdom	−12%
Other countries	− 6%

II Portfolio investment 8.2 billion = 100%

United States	−72%
United Kingdom	−19%
Other countries	− 9%

Source: Dominion Bureau of Statistics and National Industrial Conference Board's Chart Survey, "Canada's Balance of Payments," April, 1964

Thus if defense and economic needs alone were the measuring rule of national interest one might be surprised that Canada had not already become part of the American union.

Yet the very strength of the southward pull has evoked its own resistance. Although the Canadian population is increasingly cosmopolitan, it still draws its largest single group of immigrants from Britain; and although French Canadians may dislike the distribution of powers under the British North America Act, they are hardly likely to prefer Washington to Ottawa. The Commonwealth tie may be weaker today than it was in earlier decades— although statements to this effect rarely take into account what the relationship was like in past years—but it is far from clear that this is simply a consequence of *regional* alternatives. On the contrary:

There is still a strong sentiment in favour of the Commonwealth, and little if any positive sentiment against it. The new immigrants, and indeed even the French Canadians, while they may not be enthusiastic supporters, are not actively hostile. To all Canadians it offers an opportunity to be different from the Americans at a time when in all other things Canada is merely a carbon copy of them. To a small population, in close geographic proximity to a huge one, this is no small thing.[2]

Not all Canadians are so mild-spoken. To suggestions that Canada's destiny lay in the Americas, a fate it should recognize and welcome, Mr. John Holmes has replied:

We are now under pressure, not only from other residents of the Hemisphere but also from Europeans, to stop being a world-wide nuisance and settle down in our own region. . . . Here we have the dogmatism of a new European school, which sees in regionalism not only the miracle ingredient of Western Europe's welfare but a doctrine to which all must subscribe. Attachment to an adjacent continent it is now fashionable to describe as internationalism, whereas the retention of links with distant continents is frowned upon as isolationism or nostalgia.[3]

Of suggestions that Canada might once again consider membership in the Organization of American States—if only to interpose between the United States and its restless, southern clients a dispassionate, disinterested "third force"—Holmes was still more scornful. It might be, he argued, that the three Commonwealth members of the hemisphere—Canada, Jamaica, and Trinidad—could offer their good offices "to assist understanding or suggest solutions" of problems facing the Organization of American States; but extravagant talk of a Hemisphere Economic Community, "and even a Hemisphere Parliament," merely exposed the weakness of these vast regional schemes of unity. Pan-Ameri-

2. W. F. Dawson, "Canada and the Commonwealth," unpublished paper given at the Royal Institute of International Affairs, May, 1964.
3. "Our Other Hemisphere," *International Journal*, XVII (Autumn, 1962), 414.

canism might have much to commend it as an exercise in good
neighborliness:

It remains one of the nobler political conceptions of recent history. . . .
A good many noble institutions, however, not least of all the Commonwealth, have been asked to engage in agonizing reappraisals of their
function. The pan-Americans might also be well advised to cut through
the layers of oratory . . . and ask what their function is in a world
vastly changed since the presidency of James Monroe. Canadians too
should probe deeply into the future of pan-Americanism before reaching a decision on their own place in our Hemisphere.

Clearly, regionalism has no appeal in this quarter, in its
North American setting. And, given two major presuppositions,
one may argue that it has very little appeal among any section of
the Canadian population. One is that Quebec's insistence on *le
droit d'être maître chez soi*[4] will not be pushed to the extreme
point where the federation is all but broken and the gravitational
pull of the United States on the English-speaking provinces is
magnified. Until that point is reached, a re-examination of the
British North America Act may have the opposite effect, namely,
a strengthening of the provincial characteristics of the federation against not only Ottawa but the external world (including
the United States) as well. The other supposition (it is discussed later) is that the United Kingdom itself will continue to
see the Commonwealth as a useful field of policy. On this basis,
Canada seems likely for many years to come to see the Commonwealth as a necessary weight in the balance of its own national interests.

What can be said of regional pulls on Australia and New
Zealand? They exist, and both countries are conscious of them
to an extent unimaginable before 1939. But, here too, it is difficult to measure the extent to which regionalism as such is
responsible for the change in Antipodean—United Kingdom
and Commonwealth relations. "For most of its members," said

4. "Il y a un autre point important. C'est le droit d'être maître chez soi. . . .
L'Autonomie, c'est le droit . . . de faire des lois pour nous et par nous, de faire
régler les questions qui regardent Québec par Québec, plutôt que les faire
régler par Ottawa." Maurice Duplessis, as early as 1945, quoted in Herbert Quinn,
The Union Nationale (Toronto, 1963), p. 191.

Menzies, "the association is, in a sense, functional and occasional."[5] This may be so, although Menzies did not say it was true of Australia; but, even if it were, the explanation would surely lie more in the changed nature of the Commonwealth as a whole than in the counterpull on Australia or New Zealand of the United States or Southeast Asia. It is true that the United Kingdom's inability to defend the Australasian area and to maintain its prewar dominance in trade there has seen both New Zealand and Australia look to America for their defense and to Asian markets for their products. To this extent the Commonwealth relationship has had to make room for other interests of an economic and defensive nature. But it would be greatly exaggerating the evidence to argue that a broadening of the base of Australia's and New Zealand's interests implies a particular threat to their very complex ties with the United Kingdom.

What is the evidence? In respect of defense, the decisive date was probably the fall of Singapore. It led to Australian-New Zealand co-operation within an American rather than a Commonwealth framework, a notion of regional areas of strategy further enlarged by SEATO, within which the power of the United States dwarfs that of the United Kingdom or any Commonwealth country. Yet even in defense matters, it can be argued that the very weight of United States power is counterproductive: that is, although Australia and New Zealand must rely on American power and may move in the direction of American equipment, standardization of weapons, and even officer training (though this has not happened yet), the result may nonetheless be that Commonwealth ties will acquire a particular value precisely because they enable wider relations to be maintained with other parts of the world. Mr. Keith Jackson has argued that

New Zealand's relationship with the United States though cordial, [cannot] be semi-institutionalised to the extent that it is in London—there is no New Zealand lobby in Washington. Instead such little effective influence as New Zealand is likely to exert on United States

5. Department of External Affairs, *Current Notes on International Affairs* (Camberra), XXXIII (Oct., 1962).

policies is most likely to be through Commonwealth sources. In this sense, paradoxically, the change in strategic commitment has tended to enhance rather than diminish the importance of the Commonwealth.
. . .[6]

Thus, regional pressures may have weakened some aspects of the former imperial relationship, but they have also added to the value of wider, Commonwealth links.

In matters of trade the simple fact is that the United Kingdom is no longer able to take as large a share of Australian and New Zealand exports as it did before the war, nor have British manufacturers been able to retain their former hold on Australasian markets. The most striking increase, particularly in Australia, has been in the amount of trade with Japan, notably since the Japanese Trade Treaty in 1957. During the past ten years Australian exports to Asia have increased from 13 to 32 per cent of total exports. At the beginning of 1964 Japan had (just) replaced Britain as Australia's best customer, and Communist China was "Australia's fourth largest export market, taking half the wheat surplus and increasing quantities of wool."[7] In addition, the United States now buys more than 80 per cent of Australian beef exports. The long-term pattern may be set down as:

Table 4. *Australia: Imports and Exports* (£A million)

	Imports from					Exports to				
	1938	1948	1958	1961	1962	1938	1948	1958	1961	1962
Total Trade	111	333	792	1088	883	158	410	818	969	1068
United States	18	67	104	217	174	11	35	46	72	108
United Kingdom	46	132	325	341	266	86	156	221	232	206
Japan	5	1	24	65	50	6	3	103	161	187
Germany*	4	0	41	66	52	4	4	33	27	41
New Zealand	2	4	13	17	13	7	15	55	62	59

*After 1948, Federal German Republic
Source: *United Nations Year Book of International Trade*, 1962. *Reserve Bank of Australia Statistical Bulletin*, 1964

6. "New Zealand and the Commonwealth," unpublished paper given at the Royal Institute of International Affairs, April, 1963.
7. *The Times* (London), "Supplement on Commonwealth Trade," April 10, 1964.

Table 5. New Zealand: Imports and Exports (£NZ thousand)

	Imports from				Exports to			
	1938	1948	1958	1961	1938	1948	1958	1961
Total Trade	55,422	128,534	252,800	287,126	58,376	147,821	250,173	283,679
United States	6,864	13,873	17,175	27,023	1,476	7,306	37,169	40,843
United Kingdom	26,533	67,107	132,804	128,455	48,898	107,915	139,105	143,837
Japan	1,209	59	2,832	8,350	593	47	5,514	14,822
France	235	938	1,826	2,838	1,015	8,308	14,680	17,387
Australia	7,159	14,308	43,680	47,015	2,189	3,954	10,266	10,942

Source: United Nations Year Book of International Trade, 1962

This growth of a new direction of trade is obviously of great importance to countries situated on the edge of Asia. Yet it has to be seen in perspective, for on any long-term view the steady market within the United Kingdom for Australian and New Zealand products will continue to be basic to the economies of both countries for many years to come. Moreover, it would be absurd to suppose that a regional interest in new markets or defense arrangements is particularly harmful to Commonwealth ties in general. Indeed, a growing interest by Australia in Southeast Asia may help to increase Commonwealth understanding of its problems after the withdrawal of United Kingdom responsibilities in the area. It is true that, as a consequence, both Australia and New Zealand are likely to have to take a more positive stand in international relations that they did before 1939; and this may lead to political differences with the United Kingdom, as happened in extreme circumstances in 1941.[8] But these, too, have to be seen in their context. Do political differences between governments greatly affect the total framework of relations among Australia, New Zealand, and Britain? Commonwealth ties, at least between these three members, are not simply a political relationship. They are compounded of history, emigration, language, culture—bonds that may be much less disturbed by the search for regional markets, or by an enforced dependence on American military power, than might seem to

8. E.g., over the use of Australian troops in North Africa. Churchill, The Grand Alliance (London, 1950), pp. 328-34.

those preoccupied by the formal relationships between governments.

The Asian members of the Commonwealth have only a shadowy interest in regionalism: pan-Asianism is too cloudy a concept to have any practical effect on national policies, and the primary concern of most Asian leaders is to consolidate the state rather than extend its relations with neighbors of an undefined region. It is hardly conceivable that earlier schemes of an Islamic federation linking Pakistan with its western Muslim neighbors or of a "Maphilindo" union linking Malaya, the Philippines, and Indonesia will clothe themselves in reality. The fact is, India is so large as to be a region in itself; Pakistan is too absorbed in internal divisions and its relations with Delhi to concern itself with wider schemes of union; Ceylon is an island without neighbors other than India. Various regional schemes have been promoted in Southeast Asia—SEATO and, on a wider footing, a measure of economic co-operation among the Colombo Plan and ECAFE countries; but they have been of a functional, fluctuating nature. The one major indigenous effort

at regional association was the Association of Southeast Asian States (ASA). *Asa*, we are told, means 'hope' in the languages of Malaya, the Philippines and Thailand; and this hopeful triune association came into being in July 1961 to promote "close cooperation which would be non-political in character, independent, in every way, of any power bloc, and essentially one of common endeavor for the common good of the region in the economic and cultural fields." Tangible results are not easy to show: an *Asa Express* train runs between Penang and Bangkok, but though this may seem hardly worth mentioning, this is the only regular inter-state communication in SE Asia, other than air links. . . . It appears that any regional organisation for SE Asia is unlikely to emerge at an early date. Attempts at military and political association have met little success. A "Common Market" for the region is improbable. As producers of primary products for the world market, the SE Asian countries are not only competitors amongst themselves, but also face world competition, so that attempts to control price or output would be immediately countered from elsewhere. Almost inevitably, leading countries in the region will continue to have relations with outside powers which are as close as or closer than those with their neighbours.[9]

Fourthly, there is the pan-African movement, an imaginative concept among leaders who are increasingly aware of the difficulties of consolidating their national hold on the territories shaped by colonial rule. The weakness of such schemes, even on a limited regional basis, may be seen in the attempt between 1958 and 1960 at a union in West Africa of Ghana, Guinea, and Mali: it began with a flourish in September, 1958, and faded on the assertion of the national sovereignty of the three constituent states. A preliminary announcement on November 23, 1958, from Accra and Conakry was followed by a formal declaration (May 1, 1959) of a "Union of Independent African States" for which it was proposed to have a common citizenship, flag, anthem, and motto, although each state was "to preserve its own individuality and structure" until it had decided "what portion of sovereignty should be surrendered" to the Union. Eighteen months later, the government of the Mali Republic—having broken its own newly formed link with Senegal—joined with Ghana and Guinea to proclaim a yet wider "Union of African States" as the "nucleus of the United States of Africa." Here, seemingly, was a new departure in Commonwealth membership, involving the merger of two foreign states and a Commonwealth country. Professor Wheare examined the implications and concluded that "on the existing rules of the Commonwealth, the answer was clear. If a Member joined with a foreign country in a union so close that the Member ceased to be a separate independent country, then it could no longer be a Member of the Commonwealth."[10] When questioned in the House of Commons, Mr. Macmillan hedged his words with caution:

Last Saturday, Dr. Nkrumah informed me that negotiations were in progress and that it was likely that a joint statement would be

9. Hugh Tinker, "Regionalism in South-East Asia," unpublished paper given at the Institute of Commonwealth Studies, March, 1964.
10. Kenneth C. Wheare, *The Constitutional Structure of the Commonwealth* (Oxford, 1960), p. 119. Professor Wheare was cautious enough to add: ". . . new situations and new needs would bring new rules. For in the Commonwealth, Members decide what they want to do, and bring the rules up to date."

made on Sunday indicating the intention of himself and the Prime Minister of Guinea to enter into a union. On Sunday, I received the text of the joint declaration issued by the two Prime Ministers in Accra. . . . This is an interesting development which may have political, constitutional, economic and other implications not only for Ghana and Guinea but also for the Commonwealth and other countries. I know that the Government of Ghana value their association with the Commonwealth; and the joint declaration says that the actions which the two Prime Ministers are taking are designed not to prejudice in any way the present or future relations between either Ghana and the Commonwealth or between the Republic of Guinea and the French community. My impression is that almost all the detailed arrangements between Ghana and Guinea which would be necessary to give effect to this statement of intention on the part of the two Prime Ministers have yet to be worked out. . . .[11]

The doubts expressed by Macmillan were sensible, for by 1963 the Union of African States had ceased to exist. At best, it could be argued that it had been merged with the new "Organisation of African Unity" formed at Addis Ababa in May by the thirty-two African heads of states and governments. But the OAU is a very loose association of countries, the Charter of which is designed to protect as much the sovereignty and independence of its members as their joint action. The members' commitment to the Charter is hardly more binding than the practical obligations of Nigeria, Ghana, Sierra Leone, Uganda, Tanzania, and Kenya as Commonwealth members, and much less than the terms of the Yaoundé Agreement linking the eighteen African associated states with EEC.[12] Similarly, disputes between the OAU members (e.g., Ethiopia-Somalia) are hardly less rife than those between Commonwealth countries (e.g., India-Pakistan).

Are the directives embodied in the Addis Ababa Charter likely to raise difficulties for the nine Commonwealth members vis-à-vis their relations with Britain in particular and, thereby, with the Commonwealth in general? Certainly it is possible.

11. G. B., 5 Parl. Debs. (Commons), DXCVI, 556, Nov. 27, 1958.
12. Early in 1964 Nigeria began to negotiate terms on which it might be able to associate itself with the Common Market countries. The Nigerian government declined however to take part in the institutional aspects of the Yaoundé Agreement.

The OAU is not only strongly anticolonial but antiwhite-supremacy rule in southern Africa. A Liberation Committee established by the organization at Dar-es-Salaam agreed at its first meeting (June 25-July 5, 1963) that those countries having "a special relationship" with a particular colonial power should exert diplomatic pressure designed "to hasten the liberation" of colonial Africa (including South Africa); and in September the Ghanaian representative at the United Nations led the attack on Britain in the Security Council over Southern Rhodesia. Similarly, a major clash of policy may develop between some Commonwealth African countries and Britain over Southwest, or South Africa, in respect of the call for sanctions against apartheid. To this extent it must be admitted that the existence of the OAU sharpens the points of dispute between Britain and its fellow Commonwealth African members. Nonetheless, its influence should not be exaggerated. Should any one of these quarrels be pushed to the point of secession from the Commonwealth, the primary cause will lie less in the OAU or the shadowy provisions of its Charter than in the belief held by particular African leaders that such action should be taken "against Britain," or because of pressure exerted domestically by radical groups against a conservative leadership. This may happen. If it does, it will be further evidence of the overriding bilateral aspect of Commonwealth relations. For, in theory at least, there is no essential clash of principle—as might have arisen over the question of a surrender of sovereignty—between the Commonwealth, as an association of states of which some are African, and the OAU, in which some of the states are Commonwealth members.

One should note, too, where the material interests of the African member countries lie: they are overseas, not with their African neighbors; and although the percentage of trade between the African countries and the United Kingdom has declined in relation to their total trade, it is still substantial. Few governments are motivated solely by economic self-interest. Yet even the most radical of the new states cannot wholly disregard, or disrupt, the framework of trade and investment required for the generous schemes of development on which they have embarked. All the Commonwealth African states have important trade ties outside Africa (as may be seen in the selected tables below) as well as a growing network of educational, legal, and social links with Britain and other Commonwealth countries;[13] all of them have a growing list of enterprises for which outside capital, including British capital, is sought.

Fifthly, Cyprus. Enosis is a regional demand of a limited nature which raises issues of sovereignty comparable with those at one

Table 6. *Nigeria: Imports and Exports* (£ thousand)

	Imports from				Exports to			
	1938	1948	1958	1961	1938	1948	1958	1961
Total Trade	8,632	41,215	166,274	222,466	9,286	35,898	132,791	168,536
Germany*	753	2,338	12,258	16,499	1,647	50	11,087	13,231
Ghana	5	5	278	606	172	286	810	1,166
Netherlands	150	813	8,834	10,611	1,001	700	18,224	21,807
United Kingdom	4,713	21,362	72,762	85,188	4,647	29,125	74,943	74,668
United States	694	4,726	9,738	11,889	671	4,402	8,069	19,091
South Africa	5	196	751	98	26	110	171	18

*After 1948, Federal German Republic
Source: *United Nations Year Book of International Trade,* 1962

Table 7. *Ghana: Imports and Exports* (£ thousand)

	Imports from				Exports to			
	1938	1948	1958	1961	1938	1948	1958	1961
Total trade	7,867	31,378	84,593	140,781	6,321	49,550	93,203	102,424
Germany*	454	1,189	4,827	10,772	787	3	16,838	14,184
Ivory Coast	—	—	64	932	—	—	32	6
Morocco	—	—	—	956	—	—	—	—
Netherlands	162	1,751	7,133	10,999	594	2,244	10,192	13,976
Nigeria	179	405	737	708	3	4	178	861
South Africa	6	323	1,541	10	13	635	1,284	228
Togo	—	—	1,108	2,500	—	—	227	48
United Kingdom	4,289	17,647	36,624	51,765	2,554	13,953	26,954	22,069
United States	769	2,165	4,221	9,821	1,346	16,934	20,022	26,991

*After 1948, Federal German Republic
Source: *United Nations Year Book of International Trade,* 1962

13. Including agreements on technical aid, officer training, co-operation in broadcasting and television, Commonwealth scholarships, etc.

Table 8. Kenya: Imports and Exports (£ thousand)

	Imports from				Exports to			
	1938	1948	1958	1961	1938	1948	1958	1961
Total trade	9,667	45,364	77,029	88,672	8,505	25,831	29,300	35,326
Zanzibar	5	119	300	215	48	408	223	284
Sudan	—	8	—	—	32	49	73	194
Egypt	16	—	—	—	32	447	—	—
Congo (L).	423	109	—	—	56	306	358	419
Central African Federation	—	30	209	1,346	—	183	358	172
South Africa	147	1,872	3,216	4,414	146	1,624	1,026	1,214
Germany*	—	34	4,707	4,293	64	11	6,200	5,860
United States	873	2,995	2,641	5,014	397	1,261	3,205	5,018
United Kingdom	4,312	23,600	27,723	30,508	2,790	7,699	8,488	8,505

*After 1948, Federal German Republic
Source: United Nations Year Book of International Trade, 1962

time thought to be implicit in "pan" movements of a wider kind. It can be argued, however, that Cyprus is a very special case. Its position as a Commonwealth member has distant parallels perhaps with Ireland rather than any existing member country, as a state resentful of its treaty relationship with the United Kingdom (and Greece and Turkey) to which it is also tied by an irrevocable defense agreement;[14] but the Cyprus position has no true precedent in the Commonwealth; and few, surely, in the world at large. Two warring communities are extensions of a Greek and Turkish nationalism, either of which it would be extremely difficult to adjust to Commonwealth ways and traditions. Whether Cyprus will in fact achieve union with Greece still remains doubtful; but the doubt arises because of the island's uneasy relationship with Turkey and Greece, not because of Commonwealth ties, which must surely be minimal. The island's trading interests, one might note, are with Britain, Germany, and Italy. Nonetheless, it would probably be a fair assessment of the present situation to say that Cyprus is a member of the Commonwealth only because the rivalry between Greece and Turkey

14. The independence of Cyprus is established by treaty between the Republic of Cyprus, the United Kingdom, Greece, and Turkey; the treaty provides for bases "which . . . shall remain under the sovereignty of the United Kingdom."

prevents any alternative solution. It can hardly be used as evidence of a general trend in the Commonwealth towards regionalism.[15]

Apart from the single instance of Cyprus it might not be too difficult therefore, on the evidence so far adduced, to allay fears that the world is becoming divided into regional groups among which the Commonwealth will find neither appeal nor place. The one major regional problem remaining, however, is the future relationship of Britain with Europe. It is of a different order from those already discussed. For membership in the European Community (as it is constituted at present) carries with it specific obligations of a concrete nature. It implies not only a special relationship among its members but discrimination against non-members: hence the difficult question during the Brussels negotiations of reverse preferences on (*inter alia*) New Zealand dairy products and Asian manufactures. Moreover, in the distance (however uncertain in outline) lies the possibility of political union, a prospect that has dismayed many of the Commonwealth countries. Thus, although the immediate concern of the Commonwealth delegations at Brussels[16] was over the loss of preferences or of the right of free entry, there was also anxiety over the long-term significance of the British application. It was expressed most fully by Menzies:

One of the great intended virtues of the European Community association is that its very existence and its mutual functioning will tend to reduce, and ultimately eliminate, these old hostilities in Western Europe which have twice in this century brought the world to the brink of disaster. Every European statesman will, therefore, naturally wish to see a closer and closer integration of political policies and

15. Is there an "Africanism" comparable with "Hellenism" and, therefore, able to exert a magnetic pull on two or more African states comparable with the attraction of Cyprus to Greece? It is hardly conceivable. The nearest parallel perhaps is the force of Somali nationalism, which ended the association of British Somaliland with Britain. "Africanism" is hardly a comparable force in the continent generally. Despite current interest in the problem, "race" is a poor substitute for history, language, and culture as a unifying force between states.

16. As Professor Miller commented: "The time had long gone by when any experienced Commonwealth country was prepared to trust the negotiation of its trading policy to Britain." "The Commonwealth after de Gaulle," *International Journal*, XIX (1963-64), No. 1.

a closer and closer economic co-operation. Under the new policies now operating, there are large fiscal considerations. A common external tariff needs to be collected and this will mean very great sums of money presumably coming into some central treasury. Variable levies will be imposed on certain imports. These again will have to be collected and handled. Inevitably there will be at the centre of the community a large financial and administrative organisation exercising functions which, as we see them, are functions of government. They are not likely to be left indefinitely to officials, since the control of such great matters by a central bureaucracy would be inconsistent with British democratic ideas.

It seems to me, therefore, probable that unless the association disintegrates, there must be, at the centre, more and more a body of elected persons exercising the powers and performing the administration involved in the further workings of the Treaty of Rome.

The British Government says, and I have no doubt with the utmost good faith, that it is not contemplating a federation in Europe, it looks at its political association in *ad hoc* terms, with periodical discussions between Prime Ministers, Foreign Ministers and the like, but without the creation of federal institutions. I sincerely hope that it works out this way. But I keep remembering the undoubted truth of the proposition that political associations do not tend to stand still, that they go forward until they assume what we would call a federal structure, or even a complete union in certain cases, or they come apart. . . .

. . . .It seemed to me no more feasible to say that Great Britain's position in the Commonwealth would be unaffected by participation as a constituent state in a European federation than it would be to say that Australia could join another great federation and still remain an independent sovereign member of the British Commonwealth. Now, of course, one answer to all this—and it has been clearly made in London —is that Great Britain has no intention of going into a federation. I repeat that this must be accepted, and that if she does not, then much of the comment which I have made disappears. I think that twenty years ago I might have become more impassioned about this matter, but the Commonwealth has changed a lot since then. Its association has become much looser. For most of its members, the association is, in a sense functional and occasional. The old hopes of concerting common policies have gone. Under these circumstances, it may well prove to the fact that even if federation could be achieved in Western Europe, the anomalous position of Great Britain in the Commonwealth which would then emerge would be regarded as no more anomalous than many other things which have been accepted, and with which we have learned to live.[17]

Few who followed the debates in 1961-62 over Britain's application were prepared to assert that Menzies' fears were groundless. The western European countries were merging their economies in a manner unprecedented in history; and no one could be sure what the political limits to such a process might be.

Were the problems raised swept away by the veto on January 14, 1963? At first sight, one might think they were, since it seems unlikely that the Conservative party would risk a second rebuff or that the Labour party would abandon its suspicions. It is also possible to argue that the economic arguments for entry have lost much of their force. A prime motive had been to safeguard a major shift in the growth of British trade. In 1953 exports to western Europe were only 27 per cent of total British exports; but "by 1962 for the first time they began to exceed those to the Sterling area and by 1963 they formed 37 per cent of the total."[18] Here was a new development of great importance, the safeguarding of which (it was argued) required Britain's being within the European Community. Yet the veto on Britain's application (at the beginning of 1963) was followed by an impressive 15 per cent rise (valued at £106 million) in exports to EEC, of which the biggest single increase (£43 million—31 per cent) was to France. Exports also went up to West Germany, the Netherlands, and Belgium by 7, 11, and 9 per cent.[19] Perhaps, then, Britain may still have its Commonwealth cake without forfeit of its share of regional, European prosperity.

So comforting a conclusion might be possible if the situation in Europe or in the Commonwealth were to remain static. But is either likely? If Britain is not drawn to Europe for reasons which appeared convincing to the Conservative party in 1961, it might nonetheless grow increasingly indifferent to the Commonwealth as its membership grows and its ability to act as a whole is reduced to a minimum. Moreover, there is a continuing dynamic

17. *Current Notes on International Affairs*, XXXIII (Oct., 1962), 33-35.
18. Board of Trade figures, given in *Commonwealth Survey*, March 3, 1964.
19. *Ibid.*

in the European situation (or so, perhaps, it might be wise to assume)—a continual groping of the political will after new solutions—that has been absent from the Commonwealth. The difference may be expressed by saying that the uncertainty—most evident in Britain—which clouds the Commonwealth today is one of doubt how best to arrest its decline (and whether it is sensible to try), whereas the uncertainty which now lies over the Community is one of doubt how best to direct its future growth. And he would be a very bold observer who, looking at the Commonwealth and western Europe in 1964, could say unhesitatingly that British interests and policy will never again be thought to lie with Europe rather than the Commonwealth.[20]

Before trying to reach any broad conclusions on the general theme, there is a different aspect of the problem to consider briefly, namely, the extent to which the Commonwealth countries themselves are beginning to explore regional links with each other. Although hopes of new federations on the Malaysian model in the Caribbean or East or Central Africa have faded, one might still hope for the growth of regional associations between a number of member states, thus "strengthening the rim" and not merely the spokes of the wheel. There are, for example, seven contiguous countries in east, central and southern Africa—Kenya, Uganda, Tanzania, Zambia, Malawi, Southern Rhodesia, and Bechuanaland. In East Africa, there are the interterritorial links maintained by the Common Services Organizations; in Central Africa, Zambia and Southern Rhodesia are obliged to cooperate over the joint management of the Kariba Dam complex and the railway. There is perhaps a sense in which all the Com-

20. For a cogently argued account of the advantages and disadvantages of membership of the European Community, by one who "is a child of the Commonwealth and of the Atlantic rather than the European connection," see Alastair Buchan, "Britain Returns to Europe," the third of the Dyson Memorial Lectures, *Australian Outlook*, August, 1962. It is argued there that Britain cannot afford to stand aside from what is happening in Europe however unpalatable the alternative is. Although "the relation between Britain and the original Dominions is . . . a factor of the first importance in international relations," the sad fact is that the "multi-racial Commonwealth. . . is no longer an association of real political significance." Therefore, "Britain must take on more and more of the countenance of a European rather than a world power" and "acknowledge that we are primarily a regional and no longer a world power."

monwealth countries in Africa are in closer touch with each other than with other states, as may be seen in the dispatch of Nigerian troops to Tanganyika, in the help given by Ghanaians to the East African Common Services Organisation and the Nyasaland public service, and in the numbers of Nigerian students in the University of Ghana, or of Ghanaian and Nigerian students in the University of Sierra Leone. Similarly, Australia and New Zealand may be drawn closer together through their involvement in Southeast Asia, as well as by arrangements designed to establish a free trade area between the two countries.[21] There has also been a long-standing interest in Canada in the British West Indies, resulting in financial and technical help and the admission of West Indian students to Canadian universities, on a scale which, though still not very large, would hardly have existed at all but for the formal Commonwealth relationship.

Yet it would be wrong to exaggerate these links, or see in them a new possibility of Commonwealth growth. On balance, the Commonwealth tie may help to preserve contact between members in a particular region, if only because the common base of a similar imperial past enables them to co-operate more easily if the political will to do so exists. It might be argued that the present hostility between India and Pakistan would be worse if it were not modified by Commonwealth membership and an underlying similarity—of the civil service, judiciary, army, and the universities—derived from the past. But animosity between India and Pakistan has so far outweighed their willingness to co-operate; and the most likely direction in which all the new Commonwealth countries of Asia, Africa, and the Caribbean are moving is away from, rather than towards, closer ties with their neighbors. "It was not that we loved others less," Sir Alexander Bustamente said at the Jamaican Independence Conference, "but that we loved Jamaica more." Even where the practical possibility of regional co-operation exists, therefore, it is unlikely to

21. See A. D. Robinson, "An Australian-New Zealand Community," *Australian Outlook*, April, 1964.

offset the honoring of a much older tradition in the Commonwealth—the stress on national sovereignty.

A number of conclusions may now be set down. First, it is very doubtful whether, in fact, the world is "moving towards regionalism," and still more doubtful whether there is any "decline of the territorial state."[22] Outside western Europe, what have appeared to be nascent regional groups have often been no more than local manifestations of United States power operating through defense pacts, or economic groups similarly dependent on American aid. The effect of American power on British policy is profound; it also diminishes the United Kingdom's ability to act as the center of a multiregional Commonwealth: but this has little to do with regionalism as such. Secondly, the truly striking phenomenon of the present age is the appearance of a very large number of new states whose overriding interests are national, not regional. The dissolution of the European empires has seen the proliferation of weak successor states under rulers absorbed in a local struggle for control. (It is the former imperial powers—France, Holland, Belgium, Italy—which, free of the burden of empire, have moved towards a wider regional grouping.) The Commonwealth has its full share of these new states, and is more likely to be emptied of meaning —though this is not to say it will happen—by the assertion of national interests (or brought under attack as an item of controversy between locally competing groups) than challenged by rival regional interests. Thirdly, even where regional pressures are felt they are not wholly negative. Australia and New Zealand are drawing closer together. It is possible that some of the Central or East African Commonwealth members may do likewise. Moreover, even where regional interests do cut across Commonwealth boundaries (as in North America) the Commonwealth relationship may be valued as a counterbalance to them. Fourthly, however, none of the foregoing affects the immediate, though minor and exceptional, problem of Cyprus, nor the long-term,

22. John Herz, *International Politics in the Atomic Age* (New York, 1959), pp. 99-108, in which it is argued that changing technological conditions of an international character are leading to a "decline of the territorial state."

and vital, problem of Britain and Europe. Whereas most regional associations are of the vaguest kind, and pose very little threat to Commonwealth ties, neither characteristic is true of the European Community and its effect on United Kingdom policy. The political will in Europe may continue to bar British entry; political decisions in Britain itself may impede a renewal of the negotiations broken off in 1963. Yet it is equally difficult to believe that Britain and Europe can continue to remain unaffected by the breach between them. Therefore, it is worth restating here the general proposition noted earlier: that those who, looking back over the past decade, puzzle over the future of the Commonwealth—and whether it has a future—are likely to find the answer in respect of regional alignments (as of much else) in Britain—in the estimate placed on Commonwealth ties by the United Kingdom.

16

The Commonwealth and the United Nations

John W. Holmes*

The United Nations and the Commonwealth are two institutions which have profoundly affected the history of the world since 1945. The Commonwealth has played a significant part in the evolution of the United Nations. Individually its members have been from the beginning active and constructive workers. As an institution, the Commonwealth set the pattern for the United Nations' concept of colonial development, and a model, imperfect but tangible, of interracial community. Paradoxically, however, the United Nations has deprived the Commonwealth of certain reasons for its existence. By internationalizing the mission of the Commonwealth, the United Nations provides the framework within which the Commonwealth may eventually be sublimated.

The Early Years of the United Nations

When the Charter was being drafted at Dumbarton Oaks and San Francisco, members of the Commonwealth were among the most influential of the allies who had formed themselves into the "United Nations." Britain participated in the drafting on a footing of equality with the United States, and the British habit of consulting other Commonwealth members was at that time more serious than it became after the Commonwealth had ex-

* Director General, Canadian Institute of International Affairs.

panded into a less cohesive body. Before San Francisco, in April, 1945, a ministerial meeting took place in Downing Street during which Commonwealth representatives discussed all issues arising out of the Charter. The influence exerted by the Commonwealth derived partly from Britain's interest at that time in preserving Commonwealth solidarity as one of its waning assets in the struggle to remain a great power. It was based also on the international prestige and strong will of remarkable men: Field Marshal Smuts, whose rhetoric is embodied in the Charter, and those obstreperous and dynamic Labour party representatives from Australia and New Zealand, H. V. Evatt and Peter Fraser. At San Francisco the influence of Evatt and Fraser was even stronger than at the London session. They were the principal spokesmen of the lesser powers, struggling valiantly, often rudely, but largely in vain, to mitigate the principle of great-power unanimity preordained by the great powers themselves. They were supported ardently but less stridently by the Canadians and Indians in a middle-power bloc that was almost a Commonwealth bloc—a pattern for diplomacy within the United Nations which was to become habitual. Both at the London meeting and at San Francisco the aim was a meeting of minds rather than a united front. There was a remarkable degree of unanimity, nevertheless, among members other than Britain, a feature of the Commonwealth which persisted so long as the independent-minded Labour governments remained in Canberra and Wellington.

The Commonwealth as a group remained an active force during the first decade of the United Nations. One reason was that the focus of crisis was the Far East, on the problems of which there was a rough consensus among Commonwealth countries. There were variations in the positions of Britain, India, Canada, Australia, and others on Korea or relations with China; but the consensus, such as it was, arose from a shared concern not only over China but also over the Asian policy of the United States. The role of India was crucial because it was one of the few channels of communication with Peking. Nehru's influence was strong in Commonwealth capitals, and the concept of partnership with the Asians attracted new support in the old members for the Commonwealth idea. The other Commonwealth countries by no means accepted fully Delhi's estimate of China's policies, and most of them joined the United States in United Nations military operations in Korea. Nevertheless, they grew alarmed over what they considered the rigidity of American attitudes. In such issues as the offshore islands and the attempt to achieve a Korean settlement which dominated United Nations high politics for a number of years, there was, in addition to a harmony of views, collusion among Commonwealth countries at the United Nations on ways of restraining the principal antagonists. India, Britain, and Canada were particularly active in this diplomacy, which extended also to the truce settlements in Indo-China outside the United Nations in which all three were assigned responsibilities to maintain agreements that the United States had declined to sign. The Commonwealth consensus was most notable when the prime ministers met in London in February, 1955, at the time of ratification of the defense treaty between Washington and Taipeh. Their communiqué went unusually far in saying on this issue that they were "united in their conviction that it was necessary that incidents should be avoided while means were sought for a peaceful outcome" and "confident that the intimate and personal discussions which they had held . . . would be a valuable foundation for future consultations with one another and with other countries directly concerned." What amounted to combined representations were made to Washington and, through India, to Peking.

This consensus at a stage when the Commonwealth countries, as new performers in the world of diplomacy, were acquiring a sense of power and influence was fortuitous. It diminished later when the spotlight shifted to the Middle East, where British rather than American policy was under fire. Nevertheless, the Far Eastern crises of the early fifties did establish a habit of common action, a feeling, not altogether unjustified, that there might be a Commonwealth way of looking at world issues; and that the cross-fertilization of Asian and European perspectives was uniquely valuable. To call this an anti-American front would be a distortion; it was non-American rather than anti-American. It is Commonwealth doctrine that its good work must be complementary to that of the United States; and, in fact, the institution could not flourish on any other basis. Nevertheless, its capacity at various stages of its history either by accident or design to set itself apart from the United States has strengthened the agglutinative process. It is a factor which is wisely not mentioned by statesmen and should be restricted for confession to the psychiatrist-historian.

Decline of the Consensus

This consensus was somewhat ephemeral. It left a tradition and a justification of the Commonwealth tie in matters of diplomacy, particularly strong in Ottawa, where the need was felt for associates and supporters in world diplomacy and also for an orientation not anti-American but independent of the United States. It helped to set Canada, and to a lesser extent Australia and New Zealand, in the habits of middle-power diplomacy, although their associates were quite as often the Scandinavians and other independent-minded states as members of the Commonwealth fraternity. India, however, which had played a central role in the earlier consensus, by the mid-fifties was emerging under the forceful if choleric leadership of Krishna Menon as a great power in the United Nations, tacitly if reluctantly recognized as such in the Assembly if not formally in the Security Council. Its role was primarily that of a leader of the Asians and Africans, although it continued to be a force also within the councils of the Commonwealth, largely because of the inclination of Nehru. Curiously enough, Krishna Menon, however much he delighted in scourging the British, Australians, and, of course, the South Africans, remained Commonwealth-minded, perhaps because, his political formation being British, he felt more at home battling with other people of similar background.

Much of Commonwealth diplomacy in the United Nations was among the lesser powers. It is not true, as often stated by the British, that there is little direct association of Commonwealth members and that all contacts run through London. A good deal takes place behind their backs. In the United Nations close personal relations and teamwork, those intangible ties said to distinguish the relationship, have been more notable among Canadians, Indians, New Zealanders, or Nigerians than with the British themselves, embarrassed as they inevitably are by their motherhood. For the British the Commonwealth was often a millstone, whereas for other members it provided opportunities to be taken advantage of or ignored as they wished.

The Suez crisis of 1956 divided the Commonwealth but proved its strength. It did not break up, and in spite of bitterness the tradition of Commonwealth consultation persisted. Regardless of the differences in public positions, Commonwealth representatives in New York worked earnestly together, and the messages exchanged among London, Delhi, Karachi, Ottawa, and elsewhere proved a strong justification of the existence of the Commonwealth. While Washington virtually broke off relations with London, Nehru, Suhrawardy, and St. Laurent worked hard to get the British out of their mess and save the Commonwealth, an endeavor in which they were conscious of the encouragement of powerful forces in Britain and anguished members of the British foreign service who, while loyal to their government, recognized what their Commonwealth associates were trying to do. The disruptive effect of the Suez crisis was mitigated by the fact that differences on the subject among the peoples of the Commonwealth were not strictly along national lines. Even without Britain it was Commonwealth members which formed the core of the United Nations operation, fortunately including old and new members. Although Canada took the initiative in proposing a solution by the establishment of UNEF, it could not have rallied support from the skeptical Arabs and Asians if it had not been for teamwork with India and Pakistan.

Nevertheless, after 1956 the Commonwealth was never quite

the same again at the United Nations. The cause was by no means only the division over Suez. The British lost their confidence and never recovered the leading role they had had in the United Nations up to that time. The Africans began to pour into the United Nations, and the Asian-African bloc was more and more the focus of interest of the new Commonwealth members. Whereas in the earlier stages Britain's enlightened policy of liberation had given the Commonwealth as an institution prestige in the world community, the last stages of decolonization raised hard-core issues: Central Africa, South Africa, Angola, British Guiana, and the bitterest aspects of "colonialism." It became no longer just a question of the colonialists' seeking to propel the willing British towards a goal they had already chosen. Both sides were running into stubborn resistance and disagreed vehemently on the way to dissolve it. The United Nations itself became a cause of division between the British, whose Conservative Government displayed an obvious lack of enthusiasm for the institution, and other members, both white and non-white, whose dedication to the United Nations was intense if not entirely consistent. At the same time what seemed to the British a lack of consideration for their problems in the United Nations on the part of their Commonwealth colleagues encouraged hostility in Britain to the Commonwealth itself as well as to the United Nations, a hostility encouraged by powerful elements anxious to isolate Britain in a European alignment.

The Commonwealth and "Colonialism"

The fact that the Commonwealth has been embroiled over questions of colonialism has obscured the fact that its greatest contribution to the United Nations is its existence. The most important function of the United Nations has been providing a framework within which could take place the transition from an imperial world to one in which over a hundred countries stand on their own feet. The transition has been accompanied by such turmoil and anger that we forget how much more bloody and violent it would otherwise have been. The United Nations Charter, however, went no further than to insist that dependent territories must become independent. What was needed in practical politics was a formula for the peaceful process from dependence to independence. This formula was provided by the Commonwealth.

The idea of a colony's being aided by the colonial power to establish institutions of government and proceed by stages to govern itself in fruitful collaboration with its former master is now widely accepted as the natural progression, but a generation ago it did not seem at all natural or obvious. It was not only Marxists who assumed that independence could come only in a violent break accompanied by hostility. The British Commonwealth had, long before World War II, set a different pattern for white countries, but it was the creation of India and Pakistan in 1947 and their unexpected preference for remaining within the Commonwealth that was decisive. Even if membership within the Commonwealth were regarded as no more than a face-saving formula (a view which would underrate it), it established the revolutionary idea that the path was open for non-European peoples in the Empire to achieve freedom by orderly evolution and agreed stages rather than by precipitate "liberation." This philosophy of the Commonwealth became the philosophy of the United Nations, accepted in the Trusteeship Council and in Assembly debates even by those who at intervals denounced the British for not acting in accordance with the pattern the British themselves had established. The acceptance of the Commonwealth as the norm was neither acknowledged nor conscious, of course. The other imperial powers, France, Belgium, The Netherlands, and even Portugal were expected to follow this pattern even though they had quite different ideas of their own. The application to other powers, and the pressure for speed, did not necessarily have happy results in all cases. It is often argued that the tragedy of the Congo was due to the insistence of the United Nations and the Congolese that Belgium pursue the Commonwealth pattern in too great haste, and it is feared that the enforced application of the principle to Portugal would lead the United Nations into the most dangerous responsibility of its history. Nevertheless, if colonial rule is doomed by history, it was better on the whole that the United Nations fix its confidence on a tried pattern of partnership between the governors and the governed than to have indiscriminately encouraged "liberation." The greatest contribution of the Commonwealth to international society was to prove in practice that this partnership would work, a fact which justifies it for all time, even after it fades from the scene as an institutional entity.

The Commonwealth as a "Caucus"

To what extent is the Commonwealth or has it been a bloc in the United Nations? Mr. Thomas Hovet, in his study of *Bloc Politics in the United Nations*[1] includes it as a "caucusing group," and his analysis of its voting record suggests to him that it is a "loose coalition," with "a very low degree of either identical or solidarity votes." He found it most likely to vote together on matters involving economic, social, and humanitarian co-operation and least likely on questions of self-determination. Not surprisingly, he also noted that it tended to divide into old and new Commonwealth groups, although this has been by no means a fixed division. The pattern of voting since this survey was made has not changed greatly, although it has become more complex with the increase of Commonwealth members, which now include countries aligned neither with the aligned nor the nonaligned. Such statistics present the facts about the "group," but conclusions are misleading which place too much emphasis on unanimity, a concept foreign to the Commonwealth since 1945. Having decisively rejected suggestions that it have a common foreign policy, the postwar Commonwealth made almost a fetish of rejecting the united front. Its object is to promote understand-

1. Thomas Hovet, Jr., *Bloc Politics in the United Nations* (Cambridge, Mass., 1960), pp. 69-73.

ing, to encourage tolerance, and to reduce but not eliminate differences.

On many occasions Commonwealth members have altered their votes in order not to offend another member. Canada would not vote in favor of the resolution which condemned British actions over Suez, although it obviously deplored them. Britain's *volte-face* in its voting on South Africa after the latter withdrew from the Commonwealth proved how much its earlier votes had been conditioned by the obligations of fraternity. The new members have felt less constrained to "loyalty" in their voting, but their positions have been conditioned by a sense of Commonwealth obligation. India, Pakistan, Nigeria, and smaller states as well have often sought to moderate anticolonialist resolutions, partly in order to attract a majority to the middle of the road but also out of regard for feelings in the old Commonwealth. Some countries, or rather some spokesmen, have recognized no inhibition and perhaps been more than usually spleenful to the old master, but this does not invalidate the general conclusions. They have reserved their worst fire for the French, the Belgians, and especially the Portuguese. The old members, except South Africa in its time, have consistently bridled their feelings in public statement about other members. Nevertheless, although the old members charge the new members with failure to recognize a decent obligation to the Commonwealth in the United Nations, the latter have a strong case that the old members, in spite of their soft language, have given a priority to solidarity with their European allies on colonial issues about which the Commonwealth brethren feel strongly. It is hard for the anticolonialists to accept that the cautious attitude of the older members over these issues stems not only from obligations of their alliances but also from a more cautious concept of the function of the United Nations and of the best way of effecting change. In spite of common political and judicial traditions, there is a real difference among Commonwealth members over Article 2(7), which has been as much at the root of their differences as their varying views on colonialism. So strong are the feelings of the African members on this issue now and so intractable the argument over "intervention" that the Commonwealth is seriously threatened by the bitterness of the debate in the Assembly. The position of the old members has stiffened, but not even the "white Commonwealth" is always solid on colonial votes. When Britain remains intransigent, Canada, Australia, and New Zealand sometimes abstain or accept a compromise. This flexibility in the middle alleviates somewhat the sharp division.

The fact that all members of the Commonwealth have regional or other associations to consider and have in most cases given priority to their racial, regional, or defense associations does not necessarily imply the failure of the Commonwealth idea in the United Nations. The Commonwealth is designated as a bridge by which there can be communication and some meeting of minds among the continents and peoples of the world. It is essentially a bloc of a very different sort from the others. It cannot be denied that the single-minded attachment of such countries as Ghana or Ceylon to the Asian-African bloc casts doubt on the theory of a commonwealth of understanding. Ghana and Ceylon are, however, not entirely typical. For most of the members, European and non-European, the Commonwealth association has at least introduced a healthy ambivalence into their orientation, which is all to the good of the United Nations.

It is doubtful whether the Commonwealth should be described as a "caucusing group" at all. During the General Assembly and on other occasions there have been weekly, fortnightly, or *ad hoc* meetings of Commonwealth delegations to discuss the agenda. The purpose has been to exchange information and explore possibilities of agreement rather than negotiate agreed positions. In the early days of the United Nations, when habits of Commonwealth consultation were taken for granted and members were more dependent on the British diplomatic service for information, these meetings were taken seriously. They declined in importance largely because of a tendency to avoid issues on which there were differences and concentrate on procedural questions. For many years they were chaired by the head of the

British delegation, a tactical error which was only in the last few years corrected by a system of alternating chairmen. However, senior members of delegations gave up the habit of attending, and the custom, which with more imagination could be useful, has been hard to salvage. It should not be assumed, however, that the failure of this formal system means a failure of consultation altogether. There is a constant exchange of views on United Nations matters through diplomatic channels and in *ad hoc* meetings which are franker and more fruitful. The representative of the Commonwealth Relations Office normally on the staff of the British mission has acted as a channel and coordinator of information, although any suggestion that he is an aligner of votes has to be scrupulously avoided. Consultation is bilateral or multilateral but rarely in sessions of the whole. Inevitably some members are more addicted to Commonwealth consultation than others, but the prevalence of the habit need not be judged by the practices of the least interested.

The Diplomatic Advantages

One of the reasons new members have chosen to remain within the Commonwealth is that they recognize the value of diplomatic assistance when they are pushed out into the cold world. Naturally they will see a good deal of their regional brethren, and be more inclined to align themselves in that direction, but they find the need of help also from sophisticated relations with well-established communications and a storehouse of information and experience. It is Britain which is, of course, most forthcoming with assistance of all kinds, but the other countries have been increasingly helpful. Before Kenya, Uganda, or Jamaica, for example, joined the United Nations, their officers had been training as members of not only the British but also the Canadian, Australian, and New Zealand delegations, and thus had established among other things personal links and attitudes which reinforce the Commonwealth tie. With rudimentary foreign services, it is impossible for most of these countries to cope with the hundreds of issues in United Nations organs or even to be represented at all meetings. They find themselves more fortunate than unattached new members in having the assistance of countries with established missions which are among the most effective in the United Nations.

Group Representation

The Commonwealth has been officially and unofficially recognized as an entity by the United Nations. According to the unofficial agreement reached among the great powers at San Francisco, one of the six non-permanent seats in the Security Council was to go to a member of the Commonwealth other than Britain. The Commonwealth was accorded a seat because it included five of the then most influential United Nations members: India, Canada, Australia, South Africa, and New Zealand, none of which at that time fitted neatly into any existing regional group. In the first two elections, Commonwealth countries competed against each other, and India was reluctant to be labeled the Commonwealth sitter. However, they came to realize that they had a privileged position, and thereafter Commonwealth members clung loyally to the "gentlemen's agreement" even at the risk of good relations with the United States. The United States had abandoned the agreement on the grounds that it was intended to apply only to the first election, and refused to vote for an eastern European member, but the Commonwealth members more or less consistently respected this agreement because the Soviet bloc abided by the commitment to a Commonwealth representative. In 1957 official recognition was accorded when the General Assembly adopted a resolution on the composition of its General Committee which provided that at least one of the vice-presidents in the Asian-African category or the "western Europe and other states" category would be from a Commonwealth country. It was a somewhat more appropriate way of recognizing the Commonwealth, not as a bloc itself, but as an association significant enough to be represented above and beyond the regional groups.

This was not a situation which could last indefinitely. The original categories do not fit the United Nations of today with its expanded membership of Asians and Africans for whom there was scant opportunity within the San Francisco formula. Both the Commonwealth seat on the Security Council and the provision for a Commonwealth vice-president were challenged at the 1963 Assembly. Older members of the Commonwealth, who did not fall easily into a geographical group, fought hard to preserve these positions, seeing in them not only opportunity of election to office but also a recognition of the Commonwealth as an entity. However, they were not supported by the newer members, who, to a large extent, preferred to take their chances with regional groups. The special proviso for a Commonwealth vice-president was lost. The Assembly also passed a resolution calling for an enlarged Security Council with representatives from four specified areas, with no mention of the Commonwealth. This has not yet come into effect. It must be ratified by the permanent members of the Security Council, and the Soviet Union is opposed in principle to enlargement of any kind at this time. The convention of Commonwealth representation on the Council is, nevertheless, dead. No Commonwealth country was elected in 1964 as a non-permanent member, although Malaysia split the term with Czechoslovakia and took a one-year seat in 1965. The fact is that, with over a hundred members in the United Nations, no member of the Commonwealth, except of course Britain, can expect to be on the Security Council more than once in a generation, and the chances for Canada, Australia, and New Zealand are probably best as compromise candidates.

In other United Nations organs and in the specialized agencies there has been a less explicit acknowledgment of the Commonwealth as a group deserving recognition. One of the older members has normally been elected to the Economic and Social Council and usually one of the newer ones as well. The Commonwealth seat on ECOSOC has alone been maintained after the revisions of the 1963 Assembly. Resolution 1991 (XVIII) called for an expansion of ECOSOC by nine members to be distributed along geographic lines, but this was explicitly "without prejudice to the present distribution of seats." The recognition of Canada, Australia, and New Zealand as a special group is common in most bodies, and in a rough way their representatives are rotated in office. They and the newer members have had more than their share of seats and offices, but they have deserved this recognition because they have been more responsible than most nations in the United Nations. Their record of contribution, both of money for the regular budget and special causes and of men for Korea and the United Nations peacekeeping operations has been unusually good. A "Commonwealth Division" was provided for the United Nations forces in Korea. India and Canada have been involved as major contributors in almost every United Nations peacekeeping body established, and Australia took part in Indonesia and Greece before it lost, after Sir Robert Menzies came to power in late 1949, its reputation for "independence." It is perhaps in the contribution of remarkable men that the Commonwealth has been outstanding. Out of twenty presidents of the General Assembly, five have been from the Commonwealth, a reflection perhaps of the parliamentary tradition and the instinct for compromise which are part of the inheritance.

Intra-Commonwealth Disputes

The most distressing problems for the Commonwealth in the United Nations have been those situations in which members of the Commonwealth were direct antagonists. The most important has been the persistent argument between India and and Pakistan over Kashmir. Other members have consistently tried to maintain an objective position, avoid strong advocacy of one side or the other, and take an active part in prompting reconciliation. In the effort to find an accommodation, Britain has worked closely with the United States, and Australians and Canadians have been likewise involved. In spite of these strenuous efforts to avoid commitment, neither of the parties has appreciated the impartiality of its Commonwealth associates. The Indians, who prefer the status quo, have not liked the efforts of Britain and others to propose new means of settlement and have assumed that Pakistan had the favor of its SEATO allies, Britain, Australia, and New Zealand. Pakistan, on the other hand, has complained bitterly that its brothers and allies have not given the support that was its due. On the other major intra-Commonwealth issue, the treatment of Indians in South Africa, there was likewise an effort on the part of other Commonwealth members to find compromise solutions and avoid denunciation. There is no doubt that the departure of South Africa from the Commonwealth has been a relief to the white Commonwealth countries in the United Nations; since that day they have given up the struggle to be neutral on South African issues, although their actions are still restrained by their reluctance to commit the United Nations to intervention which it could not carry through or which would more likely stiffen resistance in South Africa than induce compliance.

In earlier stages of the United Nations many Commonwealth supporters were offended that an argument between members should come before an international body at all, as they hankered after a Commonwealth court and Commonwealth machinery for settling disputes.[2] The ferocity of the Kashmir dispute did more than anything else to remove that noble idea from the realm of practical politics. The United Nations relieved the Commonwealth of an intolerable problem which could have torn it apart. It would have been a matter of prestige for the Commonwealth to muster the resources of diplomacy and persuasion to promote

2. The judgment of a British expert on this question is as follows: "The experience to be drawn from Commonwealth practice appears to be that Commonwealth countries do not regard intra-Commonwealth disputes as *sui generis*, and outside the purview of the United Nations, and that while certain disputes which might be justiciable by the Court, are excluded from its compulsory jurisdiction, no provision has been made for their regular settlement elsewhere, and further that there are clauses of intra-Commonwealth disputes which are by treaty within the jurisdiction of the Court." J. E. S. Fawcett "The Commonwealth in the United Nations," *Journal of Commonwealth Political Studies*, I (May, 1962), 133.

an equitable settlement. However, the chances of agreement on any terms between India and Pakistan or between India and South Africa were small, and it has been better for the Commonwealth that the blame which the parties attach to all those who have tried to help and to the organs of mediation themselves should have been diffused among many members of the United Nations and heaped upon the Security Council rather than upon any Commonwealth body.

An Appraisal

One's assessment of the record of the Commonwealth within the United Nations depends on one's approach to the institution itself. If the Commonwealth is regarded as a constitutional organization corporate in intent, the judgment is likely to be that it has been ineffectual and its very existence a chimera. It has rarely presented a common front; it has been divided on major and minor issues; and its record of infighting is far from fraternal. The coherence which it had at San Francisco and afterward has dissipated. Insofar as there has been coherence, this has largely been the traditional collaboration among the white members on the one hand and among the Asian and African members on the other, in neither case exclusive. But if one thinks of it as an organism, a heritage, a historical phenomenon rather than a club or bloc, the picture is different. It does not pretend to be a tightly knit group of like-minded countries with obvious common interests which might naturally aspire to unanimity and common action. Although its conventional rhetoric may sound as if that was its aim, no contemporary Commonwealth politician or diplomat has been able to think of it as feasible. The accomplishment is less apparent than in the case of most regional blocs, but the ambition should be recognized as higher. It is an ambition well-nigh impossible to achieve, and success is bound to be limited. Looked upon as a collection of active, devoted, and—according to somewhat varying lights—responsible member states, it has had an impact out of all proportion to its numbers.

It is difficult to estimate how much if any of that success can without strain be attributed to Commonwealth membership, and it is important not to indulge in the kind of illusions that have for too long prevented the Commonwealth from seeing itself sensibly for what it is. Suffice it to say that it has been more than appears to the public eye. The political tradition, the sense of belonging from birth as a nation to a worldwide community, the flow of information, and the continuous dialogue made easier by the sharing, at least partially, of a political language are considerable elements. It is better judged by the personal relations it has stimulated than by the institutions it has spawned, none of which has been very effective. It is a presence within the United Nations working for good. If its accomplishments as a bridge among the races and continents have been limited, these must be set against the difficulties in what is the major task of our time.

One of the difficulties in trying to estimate the function of the Commonwealth in the United Nations is that it is by its nature non-exclusive; it marches in step with other members moving in the same direction. Its mission is shared to such an extent by the United States in particular that it is hard to isolate the significance of the Commonwealth as an entity. Its *raison d'être* is that it has certain historic, familial features which can be exploited in their own way to hold the world closer together. There would be no sense in creating it in this day and age for that purpose, but it was not created; it grew and it exists, and as it exists, advantage can be taken of it to do what the world needs most. The United Nations cannot progress further, either in the creation of more effective institutions or in the solving of disputes, unless the consensus on major issues is widened. The United Nations has not yet divided itself into fixed racial groups warring against each other, and there is reason to hope it never will. If the consensus widens and the United Nations is thereby strengthened, the existence of the Commonwealth will have been a factor of significance in promoting the sense of community.

17

The United States and the Commonwealth

*H. Field Haviland, Jr.**

*Arnold A. Offner***

The significance of the Commonwealth for the American people and their government is difficult to come to grips with, not only because of the peculiarly amorphous nature of this ingenious British invention but because the issues it raises have not usually been regarded as of such burning consequence as to warrant priority attention in Washington and because the leverage which the United States could exercise to influence the future course of the association has seemed marginal at best. Nonetheless, there are solid issues at stake for the interests of the United States; there are political, military, and economic aspects of the Commonwealth relationship which affect American policy; and policies and actions of the United States have profound repercussions on the Commonwealth.

Political and Military Considerations:
The Atlantic Community

The hard center of United States foreign policy is the Western grouping sometimes called the Atlantic Community, with its formal expression in the North Atlantic Treaty Organization and the Organization for Economic Cooperation and Development. It is the effect of the Commonwealth on this vital center,

* Director of Foreign Policy Studies, The Brookings Institution.
** Assistant professor of history, Syracuse University.

especially the roles of the older, more developed members, that weighs most heavily in shaping the attitudes of the United States toward the Commonwealth.

Perhaps the foremost contribution of the Commonwealth to the Atlantic family of nations is that it symbolizes and strengthens the leadership of some of the most successful democracies on earth. These are the states that have been among the world's foremost tutors in the values, institutions, and practices of democratic government. Their continuing collaboration through the Commonwealth furthers the reciprocal reinforcement of their democratic mores and continues to set pioneering standards for other nations, including the more developed states. In this, as in other functions of the Commonwealth, the United Kingdom leads the way, but the other advanced members, Canada, Australia, and New Zealand, contribute significantly. The continuing development of these governments strengthens the voice of constructive and progressive democracy and counterbalances some of the less democratic elements within the Western community.

The U.K. has long been experienced in international relations, and the interrelationships of the Commonwealth, formal and informal, together with the effects of the wars of this century, have schooled the independent members in the conduct of international affairs. Their common military training and traditions, for example, make them peculiarly and interchangeably effective in military operations, as Alastair Buchan points out elsewhere in this volume, particularly peace-keeping missions, such as those in the Gaza strip, Cyprus, Malaysia, and East Africa.

The increasing pull of American power and equipment (e.g., Pakistan, Canada, ANZUS) no less than the decline of British power are, of course, loosening the bonds of this unity, but one should not exaggerate the harmony that exists between the United States and members of the Commonwealth, particularly the U.K. There is as widespread delight in the ancient sport of pulling the tail feathers of the eagle as there has been, say in

Chicago, of twisting the lion's tail. No one pretends that all the members of the Commonwealth think as one, nor, indeed, all people in Great Britain, who find themselves in disagreement over that country's own defense policies.

The fluctuations in temperature over nuclear weapons is an example of that fact as well as of the tides in the U.S.-U.K. relationship. In April, 1957, Britain publicly declared its intention of undertaking "the biggest change in military policy ever made in normal times" by shifting the emphasis in military strategy from conventional to nuclear weapons.[1] The defense secretary, Mr. Duncan Sandys, stated on April 16 that his Government thought it advisable to maintain "an appreciable element of nuclear power" on their side of the Atlantic so that no nation could threaten western Europe with a major attack "without the risk of nuclear retaliation." Eisenhower had already acquiesced in the British decision when he agreed at his March meeting in Bermuda with Macmillan to have the United States supply Britain with intermediate-range missiles that could be equipped with conventional or atomic warheads.[2]

The Kennedy administration infuriated the British in December, 1962, by canceling, partly for reasons of economy, development of the air-to-ground Skybolt missile, which Britain had intended to purchase to use as the basis of its deterrent system. At a meeting at Nassau later in the month, Macmillan could get Kennedy to agree only to sell Britain Polaris missiles without nuclear warheads, which the British would have to arm themselves and install on submarines they had yet to build. Britain further had to promise not to use the missiles as an independent deterrent but as part of a "NATO nuclear force . . . targeted in accordance with NATO plans."[3]

America's reasons for wanting to prevent development of an independent British nuclear deterrent system were bound up

1. Text of British White Paper, April 4, 1957, in New York *Times*, April 5, 1957.
2. New York *Times*, April 17, 1957; text of communiqué in Paul E. Zinner, ed., *Documents on American Foreign Relations, 1957* (New York, 1957), pp. 130-32. Hereafter cited as *DAFR*.
3. Communiqué in *DAFR, 1962*, pp. 242-45.

with the Kennedy administration's effort to create, as a part of NATO, a multilateral nuclear defense force (M.L.F.) consisting of atomic submarines, later changed to surface ships, equipped with Polaris missiles with nuclear warheads, owned and manned by a multinational NATO force.[4] In this way, United States diplomats reasoned, they would halt the spread of independent nuclear systems while giving all NATO nations, including Germany, a share in nuclear weapons and responsibility.

Macmillan's Government, anxious to preserve Britain's nuclear independence, disliked the project. French President Charles de Gaulle was even more hostile. Having determined to exclude both British and American influence from the Continent and to build France's own nuclear force, de Gaulle announced in January, 1963, that France would not join the M.L.F.[5] British Labourites, too, disliked the M.L.F. Six months before his party came to power, Patrick Gordon Walker, who was to become foreign secretary, indicated that a Labour Government would oppose the M.L.F. and German acquisition of nuclear weapons. He proposed instead that Britain share with the United States responsibility for shaping nuclear strategy, but that America remain the sole possessor of nuclear weapons in the West.[6]

At the end of 1964 President Lyndon B. Johnson and Secretary of State Dean Rusk met with the new prime minister, Mr. Harold Wilson, and Gordon Walker for two days of talks. They concluded with a communiqué on December 8 stating that they had agreed to seek arrangements for control of nuclear weapons "which best meet the legitimate interests of all members of the alliance, while maintaining existing safeguards on the use of nuclear weapons and preventing their further proliferation."[7] While there were indications that Britain would agree to contribute some Polaris-equipped submarines to some sort of Atlantic nuclear force, the governments were a long way from working

4. See Kennedy's speech to Canadian Parliament, May 17, 1961, in *DAFR*, *1961*, pp. 272-79.
5. New York *Times*, Jan. 15, 1963.
6. P. C. Gordon Walker, "The Labor Party's Defense and Foreign Policy," *Foreign Affairs*, XLII (April, 1964), 390-98.
7. Text of communiqué in New York *Times*, Dec. 9, 1964.

out the details—as well as solving the problem of de Gaulle's intransigence. The United States quietly abated its zeal for the M.L.F. and awaited the next round.

Political and Military Affairs:
The Developing Countries

The United States must be concerned with the implications of the Commonwealth not only for the comfortably familiar core of present Western power—the Atlantic grouping—but for those turbulent continents that are only approaching the threshold of future power after centuries of somnolent stagnation. One of the most remarkable aspects of the Commonwealth, scarcely dreamed of a few decades ago, is its function as a bridge between the old and the new. The most important contribution of the Commonwealth to Western relations with the less developed countries is to foster a sense of community, to cultivate communication and consensus, between the more and the less developed nations. Through them there can be transmitted to a wider circle of nations the message that there are those in the West who sincerely want to aid the emerging states and who can be trusted as partners. Now that the bulk of the British Empire has achieved independence and, at the same time, has maintained amicable relations with the United Kingdom, this message is more credible than it once was. An important segment of opinion in the new nations, including such leaders as Ayub Khan, Balewa, Mboya, and Nyerere, have recognized that their peoples cannot prosper in isolation from the West, that they need the help of the more advanced states, and that the Commonwealth is an invaluable channel for such collaboration. Similar sentiments are evident in other newly independent territories, but in no other instance have relations between former dependencies and the metropole so successfully weathered the stormy transition from dependence to independence.

This sense of community has very practical consequences in relation to both the long-range development of basic political concepts and institutions and to more immediate political problems. No aspect of the emerging countries' growth is more crucial than the strengthening of their political foundations, and the Commonwealth continues to play a key role in this process. Ideas flow back and forth through countless arteries of communication, both governmental and non-governmental. Key officials, borrowed from the older Commonwealth countries, help to elevate governmental standards as they work side by side with their indigenous colleagues, and local personnel travel to other Commonwealth countries. Joint training programs of all kinds and at all levels improve the quality of governmental performance. In these and other ways, numerous seeds are sown and nurtured as part of the long-term process of political growth. While similar contacts take place with non-Commonwealth nations, the bonds of shared language, education, values, and institutions tend to favor continued collaboration within the Commonwealth.

There are of course counteracting forces to the centripetal tendencies. It is idle to exaggerate the harmony existent between the U.K. and Ghana, ignoring the fact that the forces of nationalism exert a strong pull in the new states, many of whom look to the United Nations rather than to the Commonwealth for a friendly and influential international platform. The United States' involvement in the internal quarrels among the members may be illustrated most forcibly by the Suez crisis, which was the gravest the Commonwealth faced in the decade under review.

The immediate events that led to that crisis are familiar. At the end of 1955 the United States and Britain agreed to lend Egypt $70,000,000 to begin preliminary construction at Aswan on the Nile of a great dam that would provide a tremendous boost to Egypt's agricultural and industrial productivity. The World Bank was to follow with a $200,000,000 loan, which the United States would match to cover foreign-exchange requirements. The Egyptian government then announced in January, 1956, that the Soviet Union offered more attractive financial arrangements. In May President Gamel Abdel Nasser withdrew recognition from the Nationalist Chinese regime and established relations with the mainland Chinese People's Republic. This latter act did not distress the British, who had recognized the Peking regime prior to the Korean War, or such other nations as India, Ceylon, and Canada, who had sought varied arrangements with the People's Republic of China. But Nasser's approaches to Communist nations (e.g., in 1955 he bartered cotton and rice for guns from Czechoslovakia) angered the administration of President Eisenhower, especially John Foster Dulles, whose attitude toward Communist nations, particularly that of Mao Tse-tung, remained unchanged throughout his tenure as secretary of state. "You might say," Dulles declared on April 2, 1957, ". . . that the United States, despite the Korean armistice, exercises certain aspects of belligerency as regards Communist China."[8] Hence, on July 19, 1956, while Nasser was visiting Tito and Nehru, the American government announced that it was "not feasible in present circumstances" to participate in the Aswan project.[9]

The American maneuver, about which the British had not been adequately consulted, intensified tensions long simmering.[10] One week later Nasser announced in an impassioned two-and-a-half-hour speech at Alexandria that he was putting an end to the "State within a State" by nationalizing the Suez Canal Company.[11] The British government next day affirmed to the United States, and the Commonwealth nations through their high commissioners in London, that Britain would oppose Nasser's action. In a telegram to Eisenhower, Eden, doubtful that economic pressure alone would force Nasser to relent, indicated that Britain was ready "in the last resort, to use force to bring Nasser to his senses." The Prime Minister displayed the attitude the British

8. Quoted in Richard P. Stebbins, The United States in World Affairs, 1957 (New York, 1958), p. 223.
9. Text of the statement in Noble Frankland, ed., Documents on International Affairs, 1956 (London, 1959), pp. 69-70.
10. Dulles' semiauthorized biographer, John K. Beal, in John Foster Dulles (New York, 1959), p. 260, says the Secretary acted brutally to expose the "shallow character" of the Soviet Union's foreign economic pretensions. What alternative Dulles left Nasser, and what Dulles expected Nasser to do next, Beal does not state.
11. Speech and nationalization law in Documents . . . , 1956, pp. 77-115.

would maintain throughout the ensuing crisis when he said that the United States and the United Kingdom should not involve themselves in "legal quibbles" about Egypt's right under international law to nationalize the Suez Canal Company and pay compensation to its owners. He urged taking issue on "broader international grounds," that is, the right of nations to navigate the Canal regardless of ownership.[12]

Dulles declined an invitation to confer with the British and French in London, only to make a hasty flight there on July 31 when Deputy Undersecretary Robert Murphy sent alarming reports to Washington. En route the Secretary of State outlined the paper that was to be the basis for the tripartite statement of August 2. This Anglo-French-American declaration summoned to a conference in London beginning August 16 the eight remaining signatory countries of the Constantinople Convention of 1888, which had guaranteed the Suez Canal as an international waterway, and sixteen other nations whose interests or trade patterns involved the Canal. These included Commonwealth members Australia, New Zealand, India, Ceylon, and Pakistan.[13]

At this point American and British policies or, perhaps more properly, tactics, seemed close when Dulles told Foreign Secretary Selwyn Lloyd that Nasser had to be made to "disgorge what he was attempting to swallow," and that world opinion had to be turned against him to make more likely the success of a military operation.[14] Labour leader Hugh Gaitskell, while preferring that an international commission settle the dispute peacefully, on August 2 struck the chord that was to be a subtle but powerful motif in British thinking when he branded Nasser's behavior "exactly the same that we encountered from Mussolini and Hitler in those years before the war." Six days later Eden told a nationwide audience that for Britain "the Canal has always been the main artery to and from the Commonwealth" and, declaring that Britain had no quarrel with the Egyptian people

12. *Full Circle: The Memoirs of Anthony Eden* (Boston, 1960), pp. 476-77.
13. Beal, *Dulles*, p. 266; *Documents . . . , 1956*, pp. 138-39. Egypt declined the invitation but sent an observer; Greece, angry with Britain over the Cyprus dispute, refused to attend.
14. *Full Circle*, p. 487.

or Arab world, labeled Nasser's seizure an unpermissible "act of plunder."[15] As one observer has noted, the Prime Minister thus publicly committed himself to a battle whose logical end was the demise of one of the two protagonists.[16] The stage was set for the first London Conference.

Representatives of twenty-two nations, meeting in London for a week, concluded their work with an eighteen-nation declaration on August 23 that called for establishment of an international Suez Canal Board, on which Egypt would be represented, and an Arbitral Commission to run the Canal and settle disputes.[17] At this point there appeared among Commonwealth nations a conflict in approaches to solution of the problem that would persist in the months to come. Both India and Ceylon, along with the Soviet Union and Indonesia, refused to support the declaration. Nehru's sensitivity to matters of national sovereignty and the slightest traces of "imperialist" techniques was long a matter of record. In Ceylon S. W. R. D. Bandaranaike's coalition Freedom party had taken office only four months before, espousing nationalization of tea and rubber plantations and removal of the British from naval and air bases at Trincomalee and Katunayaka.[18] Hence India and Ceylon favored an international board with advisory powers only.[19]

When Dulles refused his services, Eden called on the Australian prime minister, R. G. Menzies, to lead a five-nation delegation to Cairo to present the eighteen-nation proposal to Nasser. This mission's efforts concluded with a fruitless exchange of letters between Menzies and Nasser on September 7 and 9, with the Egyptian President refusing to agree to have an international board control the Canal.[20]

The divisions between Britain and the United States and be-

15. Gaitskell and Eden speeches in Documents . . . , 1956, pp. 131-37, 151-58.
16. John C. Campbell, Defense of the Middle East: Problems of American Policy (New York, 1958), p. 102.
17. Text of plan in Documents . . . 1956, pp. 175-76.
18. Stebbins, U.S. in World Affairs, 1956, pp. 129-30.
19. The Indian proposals are in Documents . . . , 1956, pp. 174-75.
20. Full Circle, p. 504. The Menzies and Nasser letters are in United States, Department of State, The Suez Canal Problem: July 26-September 22, 1956 (Washington, 1956), pp. 309-22.

tween Britain and influential Commonwealth nations were now becoming more apparent. By September 3 Eisenhower had informed Eden that American public opinion rejected use of force to resolve the problem. Eden on September 6 had likened Nasser's present and future course of action to Hitler's in the 1930's, concluding that if negotiations fail "our duty is plain."[21] Dulles now proposed creation of a Suez Canal Users' Association (SCUA), which would maintain the Canal, hire pilots, and pay Egypt a rental fee from shipping tolls, a plan to which the British reluctantly adhered. But whereas Dulles remarked at a press conference on September 13 that the United States, whatever its rights, would not shoot its way through the Canal, Eden declared in Parliament the same day that no British minister could give such an absolute pledge. This was the crucial rift which Nasser could—and did—exploit, announcing to a correspondent of the Press Trust of India on September 16 that he would not allow the SCUA to function through the Canal.[22]

The second London Conference (September 19-21), in which the eighteen nations subscribing to the proposals of the first conference met to draft a declaration for the SCUA, only deepened the rift between Britain and its Commonwealth associates. Now Pakistan refused to endorse the declaration, insisting that SCUA be used as a basis for negotiations only and that if they failed the Security Council should take up the matter. Japan and Ethiopia concurred in this view.[23] Dulles, who had made impassioned pleas for SCUA, now weakened its chances of Egyptian acceptance when he said on October 2 that "there is talk about the 'teeth' being pulled out of it. There were never 'teeth' in it, if that means use of force."[24] This meant that not only would the United States not shoot its way through the Canal but that American shippers would not be instructed by their government to withhold Canal tolls from Egypt and pay them to SCUA instead.

21. *Full Circle*, pp. 517-21.
22. Transcript of Dulles' news conference in United States, *Department of State Bulletin*, XXXV (Sept. 24, 1956), 476-83; Eden speech in *Documents . . . , 1956*, pp. 219-23; Nasser statement in New York *Times*, Sept. 17, 1956.
23. *Documents . . . , 1956*, pp. 236-40; Herman Finer, *Dulles over Suez: The Theory and Practice of His Diplomacy* (Chicago, 1964), p. 256.
24. Text of news conference comments in *DAFR, 1956*, pp. 337-38.

The British next took the matter to the Security Council, where on October 13 they got unanimous approval of a six-point resolution that called for respecting Egypt's sovereignty, keeping the Canal open to transit without discrimination and "insulated from the politics of any country," letting the users and Egypt determine charges and the proportion of tolls to be used for Canal maintenance, and settling disputes between the Suez Canal Board and Egypt by arbitration.[25] But the Soviet Union and Yugoslavia blocked acceptance of a second part of the resolution calling for establishment of an advisory committee with executive power to settle disputes concerning tolls, discrimination, and other treaty infractions. So far as the British were concerned, as Eden has recounted, the six principles were useless without the independent executive board.[26] Thus, while Dulles left New York confident that the Suez problem would be resolved in the negotiations scheduled to begin in Geneva on October 29, Britain, France, and Israel chose another course of action.

The precise nature of the Anglo-French-Israeli negotiations during October, 1956, is unknown. What is certain is that the nations involved did not consult any other countries about their undertakings at the end of the month, which included the Israeli campaign into the Sinai Peninsula on October 29, the Anglo-French withdrawal ultimatum of the next day to Egypt and Israel (which Egypt refused), and the Anglo-French military operations against Egypt, which began at dusk on October 31 and lasted until the cease-fire on November 6. Eden declared directly in the House of Commons on October 31 that the Canal was "a matter of survival" for Britain, which was not the case for the United States, and he insisted that Britain could not bind itself to seek American support before acting in its own interest. As for consulting Commonwealth nations, Colonial Secretary Alan T. Lennox-Boyd begged the question when he insisted that they had been consulted continuously over the last three months. If that was so, Labourite Philip Noel-Baker remarked later, it was "not consultation as the Commonwealth has known it for thirty

25. *Ibid.*, pp. 342-43.
26. *Full Circle*, pp. 563-64.

years."[27] Eden himself insisted that responsibility for the decision was solely that of Britain and France, and Lloyd argued that under the circumstances prior agreement was impractical.[28]

The new Suez crisis caused the United States and the Commonwealth nations to respond in ways that reflected their national and international interests and obligations. Australia abstained in the Security Council from voting on the American cease-fire resolution and the "Uniting for Peace" resolution, both of which Britain opposed, which put the matter before the General Assembly. In the General Assembly, Australia, with New Zealand and Britain, voted against the cease-fire resolutions of November 2, November 4 (sponsored by India), and November 24. The same three nations abstained from voting on the Canadian resolution of November 4 to send a United Nations Emergency Force to the Suez area, and the Ceylonese-sponsored resolution of November 7 directing Israel to cease fire. India, Pakistan, and Ceylon voted for all the General Assembly resolutions. The Union of South Africa, obviously opposed to resolutions ardently supported by the so-called Afro-Asian bloc but trying to avoid head-on collision with those nations, abstained from voting on the General Assembly resolutions, except the Canadian one, which it supported.[29] Canada throughout sought to display what Foreign Minister Lester Pearson called "an objective attitude . . . a Canadian and independent attitude." Pearson said he knew the nations of Asia and Africa were watching to see if Canada were a "colonial chore boy" or an independent nation.[30] Canada in a sense asserted its allegiance to Britain by abstaining on the November 1 and November 24 cease-fire resolutions. By pressing for the United Nations Emergency Force, Canada did much to raise its prestige as a "middle power" and "honest broker" among nations.[31]

27. *Ibid.*, p. 596; Lennox-Boyd and Noel-Baker comments in G. B., 5 *Parl. Debs.* (Commons), DLX, 289-91, 866, Nov. 8 and Nov. 13, 1956.
28. *Times* (London), Nov. 1, 1956.
29. The resolutions and votes recorded on them are in *Documents* . . . , *1956*, pp. 243-46, 270-71, 274-75, 304-05, 340-41.
30. Pearson quoted in Stebbins, *U.S. in World Affairs, 1956*, p. 247.
31. Lionel Gelber, *America in Britain's Place: The Leadership of the West and Anglo-American Unity* (New York, 1961), p. 220.

The United States had to make difficult and painful decisions. Clearly, American diplomats sought to reassert consideration for the aspirations of the Afro-Asian nations while bolstering United States prestige among them. But, while voting with India, Pakistan, and Ceylon was one thing, voting with the Soviet Union and other Communist nations against Britain, France, and Israel was another. For all his faults, Dulles' remark at the United Nations on November 1 that he spoke with "as heavy a heart" as any other delegate there ever did, knowing that the United States opposed "three nations with whom it has ties, deep friendship, admiration, and respect, and two of whom constitute our oldest, most trusted and reliable allies," should be taken as sincere.[32] True enough, some like Richard Nixon reflected the heat and expedience of the presidential campaign, as well as the old bugaboo about pulling British chestnuts out of the fire, when he remarked on November 2 that for the first time in its history the United States showed "independence of Anglo-French policies toward Asia and Africa which seemed to us to reflect the colonial tradition." But five weeks later even Nixon publicly conceded that it was imperative that history record that "neither we nor our allies were without fault in the handling of the events which led to the crisis."[33] Once an act of aggression had been committed, however, American diplomacy had to follow the path implicit in Eisenhower's declaration that "there can be no peace without law. And there can be no law if we were to invoke one code of international justice for those we oppose, and another for our friends."[34]

The Suez crisis saw its resolution in British and French withdrawal in December, Egypt controlling the Canal and Israel finally withdrawing its troops from the Sinai Peninsula in March, 1957, after being guaranteed the right to navigate the Gulf of Aqaba to the port of Elat. Chief responsibility for bringing on the crisis, as Eden said of the decision to attack Egypt, must rest with Britain and France, with Israel a willing accomplice.

32. *Department of State Bulletin*, XXXV (Nov. 12, 1956), pp. 751-55.
33. New York *Times*, Nov. 3, 1956; *DAFR, 1956*, pp. 55-64.
34. Speech of October 31, 1956, in *DAFR, 1956*, pp. 49-55.

These nations' provocations, particularly Israel's, as American statesmen admitted, were great. But the military undertaking, which particularly in Britain's case probably had some irrational aspects stemming from the decline of the Empire and of British power, ran counter to the history of the twentieth century, as well as to the United Nations Charter and American policy of not linking the Arab-Israeli dispute with the dispute over the Suez Canal.

American diplomats had responded in a manner more moral and legalistic than they would have if the issue had been the Panama Canal instead of the Suez Canal. Then, too, Dulles' diplomacy lacked tact and sensitivity, as his embarrassing Nasser on the Aswan loan demonstrated. All too frequently his grand pronouncements proved to be little more than just that. "Unleashing" Chiang Kai-shek was an empty gesture, and the Republican liberation policy proved to be nothing more than Democratic containment. Similarly, the Users' Association was unworkable if Nasser stood fast, and Dulles did little to move the Egyptian leader toward accepting it. But it would be unfair and unwise to link the shortcomings of American diplomacy in other areas with the fiasco at Suez. The fact was that, unless the United States and other nations agreed to use force in 1956, and later as well, there was nothing they could do to reverse Nasser's *fait accompli* once he decided to exercise his right to nationalize the Suez Canal.

What is remarkable about the episode is that its results were not disastrous. The Commonwealth could have dissolved, yet it did not. British prestige in the Middle East did decline, but the Suez crisis only underscored a decline long in process. Anglo-American relations reached a low point, but even in the course of the crisis their common interests and aims emerged along with their differences. Eisenhower bluntly dismissed Soviet Premier Nikolai Bulganin's proposal of November 5 for joint Soviet-American intervention against Britain, France, and Israel as "unthinkable."[35] On November 29 the United States reaffirmed its support

35. Text of letters in *Documents . . . , 1956*, pp. 292-95.

of the Baghdad Pact, to which Pakistan had asserted its support, along with Iraq, Turkey, and Iran, six days earlier.[36] The American government by then had authorized an emergency plan to supply Britain with oil, and the Export-Import Bank and the International Monetary Fund in Washington provided the British with loans and credits for oil purchases. The United States and Canada waived interest payments on England's postwar loans.[37] Finally, Eisenhower, who had added to British and French anguish when he put off meeting with them in November and December, met with the new prime minister, Macmillan, twice in 1957. They met in March in Bermuda and in October in the United States, where they signed a "Declaration of Common Purpose," affirming that "the concept of national self-sufficiency is now out of date" and pledging their nations to work for progress "in genuine partnership by combining their resources and sharing tasks in many fields."[38]

The declaration notwithstanding, the United States has not seen eye to eye with Britain on many major issues since 1957. Early in that year the American government, fearful of a "vacuum" in the Middle East, put forth the Eisenhower Doctrine, which declared that the United States was prepared to use force to combat aggression in that area. The British did not like the doctrine, and India's Nehru made his position clear when he said that "if there is a power vacuum in West Asia, it has to be filled by countries in that region through their internal strength and unity."[39] Yet when the governments of Lebanon and Jordan in July 1958 requested help to withstand Egyptian and Syrian pressures, the United States and Britain were able to engage in a joint military occupation to stabilize the situation at least temporarily (and as well as could be expected under the circumstances). Significantly, Macmillan could tell the House of Commons that Britain's decision to intervene was taken after "full consultation" with the

36. Communiqués in *ibid.*, pp. 339-42.
37. Gelber, *America in Britain's Place*, pp. 257-58.
38. March 24, 1957, communiqué in *Documents . . . , 1957*, pp. 381-83; declaration in *DAFR, 1957*, pp. 132-36.
39. Quoted in Stebbins, *U.S. in World Affairs, 1957*, p. 176.

United States and with that government's "full support and approval."[40]

The Commonwealth nations divided over this venture largely as they did over the Suez crisis. But India and Ceylon protested much less vehemently than they had two years earlier, for, in addition to the fact that the governments of Lebanon and Jordan had themselves summoned American and British aid, India now had to consider that too great success for Nasser might lead to increased Egyptian belligerency and an outstripping of India's influence among the Afro-Asian nations. Pakistan now supported the Anglo-American maneuver, for the Baghdad Pact stood in jeopardy since Iraq's new leader, by virtue of a bloody *coup d'état*, Brigadier General Abdel Karim Kassim, intended to take his nation out of the alliance, which he did in March, 1959. Hence, amidst the summer crisis, Dulles in London on July 28, 1958, signed a declaration of collective security with Pakistan, Turkey, and Iran. The Secretary of State also committed the United States, which still clings to its policy of not formally joining the alliance, to negotiating in March, 1959, separate bilateral defense and military aid agreements with those three nations in the alliance called the Central Treaty Organization (CENTO) since August, 1959.[41]

Supplying weapons to other nations has got the United States into difficulty with nearly every wing of the Commonwealth. Especially has this been the case where India and Pakistan, themselves locked in a fierce struggle over Kashmir, have been involved. Relations with these nations illustrate how intra-Commonwealth difficulties at times combine with broader international tensions to force decisions on American diplomats bound to anger one country or another. In another way, however, on a more optimistic note, India and Pakistan demonstrate certain flexibilities in foreign policy, characteristic of other nations, too, which might prove assets in the quest for international peace.

The administrations of both Eisenhower and Kennedy sought

40. Macmillan's comments in *Documents* . . . , *1957*, pp. 296-97.
41. Baghdad Pact Declaration and communiqué in *DAFR*, *1958*, pp. 376-78; agreements in *DAFR*, *1959*, pp. 396-99.

to steer a neutral course in the India-Pakistan dispute over Kashmir. Nevertheless, from the time of the formation of the Baghdad Pact in 1955, Nehru accused the United States not only of bringing the cold war to India's borders but of supplying Pakistan with weapons it could use against India. Both the United States and Britain incurred Indian wrath when in June, 1962, they voted for a Security Council resolution, sponsored by Ireland but vetoed by the Soviet Union, urging India to begin new negotiations with Pakistan over Kashmir. Nehru irately declared that the United States had "washed out in one stroke" by a "speech made and a vote cast" all the good will it had managed to build up over the years through steadily increasing economic assistance.[42] In August Defense Minister Krishna Menon, a fierce critic of American foreign policy, announced that his country would accept Soviet aid to bolster India's own strength. Kennedy, more openly tolerant than Dulles of India's neutrality, only remarked cautiously that it was important for India "to attempt to maintain its freedom."[43]

India's quest for military funds stemmed largely from threats Communist China now posed. For three years the Peking regime had been engaging India in border warfare, centering upon the region of Ladakh in Kashmir, through which the Chinese had built a military highway linking Tibet with Sinkiang Province. In September, 1962, China shifted its pressure farther to the northeast, and the following month began a massive assault that inflicted six thousand casualties on Indian forces before the cease-fire of November 21. India sought arms from the United States and Britain. On November 20 Kennedy sent Assistant Secretary of State W. Averell Harriman to India to assess its long-term military requirements. Britain sent Duncan Sandys, secretary of state for Commonwealth relations, on a similar mission. In the summer of 1963 the United States promised to supply India with radar equipment, train Indian technicians in its use, and with Britain agreed to engage in joint training exercises with the In-

42. Resolution in *DAFR, 1962,* pp. 270-71; Nehru quoted in Stebbins, *U.S. in World Affairs, 1962,* p. 180.
43. New York *Times,* Aug. 23, 1962.

dian Air Force as well as consult with India in the event of renewed Chinese aggression.[44] Thus, without formal commitment, America and Britain placed India under protection of an "air umbrella" defense.

The American effort to bolster Indian defenses has had an unsettling effect on United States relations with Pakistan, the only Asian member of both CENTO and the Southeast Asia Treaty Organization (SEATO). In the latter, the United States is defensively allied with Commonwealth nations Britain, Australia, and New Zealand (as well as France, Thailand, and the Philippines), largely against Communist China. India's difficulties with China, and military arrangements with the United States and Britain, opened the way for Pakistan, formerly a stalwart in Commonwealth ranks against Communist China, to seek closer ties with the Peking regime. Pakistan signed its first trade agreement with Peking in January, 1963, reached a temporary frontier settlement in March, and in August disregarded American appeals by becoming the first Western-oriented nation to conclude a civil air transport agreement with Communist China. President Mohammad Ayub Khan has explained his altered course and the reasons for his anger at American diplomacy as stemming from the "serious threat to Pakistan's security" that the United States and Britain have created by arming India. He insists that once it has patched up its difficulties with China, India will revert to its "traditional policy of intimidation of Pakistan," using American weapons.[45] Thus Pakistan, like India, refuses to believe that the weapons America has supplied the other will be used for defensive purposes only, and each nation is displeased with United States policy.

Economic Policy

The international economic policy of the United States in recent years has been to work for a liberalization of trade, a

44. *DAFR, 1963,* pp. 274-75.
45. Mohammad Ayub Khan, "The Pakistan-American Alliance: Stresses and Strains," *Foreign Affairs,* XLII (Jan., 1964), 204, 208.

reduction of national barriers, and an abolition of closed trade areas. She has poured billions of dollars into efforts to improve the basic productive capacity of the underdeveloped nations. In this last aim she is at one with the aims of the Commonwealth, which in its own countries enjoys advantages over the United States: the relative ease of communication and collaboration across national boundaries due to the widespread sharing of common cultural patterns, not the least of which are similar educational systems and the network of unofficial organizations and associations binding the people of the Commonwealth together.[46] It is usually far easier for a British technician than it is for a United States technician to operate in Nigeria or India or Malaysia, and such aid programs can draw talents from any part of the Commonwealth, or beyond it, to meet the special needs of the recipient country. In addition, a well-developed network of private investment injects approximately $420 million a year from Britain alone into the Commonwealth's bloodstream and carries with it a substantial dose of technical training.

The principal complaints leveled against Commonwealth development efforts are that the member states are not sufficiently generous and that there is a tendency to resent and impede investment from outside the family circle. While there is no generally accepted standard to determine what level of aid should be provided, there is significant support for the view that the present level within the United Kingdom of approximately .7 of 1 per cent of the gross national product is too parsimonious and that it should be closer to 1 per cent. There is also concern over the tendency of some segments of Commonwealth opinion to increase discriminatory practices that operate to restrict development contracts to member states. Mr. Harold Wilson has urged in Parliament that

Arrangements should be made for regular meetings to work through the development and capital investment programmes of each Commonwealth country. We should ask for a specific preference in awarding contracts to Britain—exactly as the United States does in its de-

46. See Mr. John Chadwick's chapter for a discussion of these social and professional ties.

fence and Buy America Act programmes—from the Commonwealth.
. . . instead of tariff preferences we should have preferences in the way
of capital contracts. . . .[47]

The subject of aid, however, does not have to be pursued here
because it is considered more fully in the papers of B. Thomas
and C. B. Hoover.

The impact of the American demand for freer trade, for the
abolition of Empire preference, and for Britain's association with
the EEC is also discussed in several other chapters, but some
details might be adduced here because of their importance in
United States-Commonwealth relations.

Britain responded to the formation of the Common Market
by forming the European Free Trade Association, which, unlike
its rival, did not impose external tariffs, hence leaving Britain's
relations with the Commonwealth unimpaired. By 1961, however,
the EEC seemed to have made a resounding success. The Kennedy
administration, in pursuit of its wider trade policies, now had
to choose between Britain and its Commonwealth associates on
the one hand and the Common Market on the other. At a meeting with Macmillan in Washington in April, 1961, Kennedy indicated that America wished Britain to join the EEC.[48] On July 31
the Prime Minister told the House of Commons that his Government would seek to enter the Common Market, provided special
arrangements could be made for Britain's Commonwealth and
EFTA associates, who did not like the decision. Kennedy expressed America's delight with Britain's new course later that
summer. At the conclusion of their talks in Bermuda in December, the President and the Prime Minister limited themselves to
expressing the hope that Britain's negotiations with the EEC
would prove successful.[49]

The Common Market passed a crucial stage in its development in January, 1962, by agreeing on the outlines for a common
agricultural policy. The Kennedy administration stepped up its
pressure on Congress for a new Trade Expansion Act, which

47. G. B., 5 *Parl. Debs* (Commons), DCLXXXVIII, 1380, Feb. 6, 1964.
48. Joint statement in *DAFR, 1961*, pp. 261-62.
49. Communiqué in *ibid.*, pp. 263-64.

would grant the president authority for five years to reduce exist-ing United States tariffs by up to 50 per cent and negotiate across-the-board (as opposed to nation-by-nation) tariff reduc-tions with the Common Market on items for which the United States and the EEC were the free world's chief suppliers. The items to which the across-the-board tariff reductions, or even elimination, would apply were mainly industrial, but there could be few meaningful reductions unless Britain belonged to the EEC.[50] "We must either trade or fade," Kennedy said in a speech on May 4, 1962, and at a press conference that day he talked about "full partnership" with the nations that accounted for "90 per cent of the industrial power of the free world," and had it within their power to create "the greatest market the world has ever known . . . a trillion dollar economy, where goods can flow freely back and forth." Congress passed the Trade Expansion Act a few months later.[51]

The United States had been able to prevail upon Britain to seek entry into the Common Market, and in the summer of 1962 Britain secured promises from the EEC that special considera-tions would be made for tea and manufactured goods from India, Pakistan, and Ceylon, but it could not get similar guarantees for Commonwealth agricultural produce. Unhappy as they were with recent developments, the Commonwealth nations asserted that they would not abandon their association if Britain joined the Common Market.[52] This serious disruption of Commonwealth economic relations was vetoed by de Gaulle.

Concluding Thoughts

For the future of the Commonwealth in relation to United States interests, two fundamental problems are of overriding im-

50. Joseph Kraft, *The Grand Design: From Common Market to Atlantic Partnership* (New York, 1962), p. 41; Stebbins, *U.S. in World Affairs, 1962,* p. 361.
51. New York *Times,* May 5, 1962; official summary of Trade Expansion Act (Public Law 87-794) in *DAFR, 1962,* pp. 496-508.
52. Communiqué in *The Times* (London), Sept. 20, 1962.

portance: the evolving ties between the older and newer members and the relationship between the Commonwealth as a whole and the rest of the world.

The links between the more and less developed Commonwealth nations are significant not only as they directly affect the well-being of the inhabitants of these societies but as they indirectly touch the interests of other people. The Commonwealth makes a vital contribution to the alleviation of the so-called "north-south" problem in its role as a bridge between the richer and poorer members of the association. It is to be hoped that in the future, despite the countervailing pressures reviewed earlier, the Commonwealth can perform this mediatory function even more effectively, and at the same time, by its example and achievement, spread its benefits to an ever-widening circle of communication and collaboration beyond its own boundaries. Sir Alec Douglas-Home, when he was prime minister, emphasized the importance of this task:

Everyone is conscious of the dangers of the horizontal division of the world into the Southern half . . ., which is poor, and the Northern half, which is rich, dangers which will become much more acute should that division harden . . . on racial lines. The modern Commonwealth, if it can make itself into a working co-operative society, is the best guarantee against any such development, which would be a horror worse than anything the world has seen.[53]

Because the United States has a direct stake in this endeavor, it behooves the American people and their government to do what they can to give appropriate support to public and private Commonwealth developmental programs and to assist those individuals and groups that are in the vanguard of such efforts.

The second major problem concerns the relationship between the Commonwealth as a whole and the outside world. Like any group, this association can become introverted, emphasizing its own domestic development, or it can assume a more expansive outlook, stressing the need for external as well as internal co-operation. The then president of the British Board

53. G. B., 5 *Parl. Debs.* (Commons), DCLXXXVIII, 1356, Feb. 6, 1964.

of Trade referred to this ambivalence in a recent parliamentary debate:

There are those . . . who want to see more emphasis on . . . the Commonwealth as a rather more exclusive organization. . . . I do not believe that, today, it is possible, even if it were desirable. Others recognize . . . that the Commonwealth countries . . . are . . . developing their links with the outside world in every possible way, and want to see a conception of the Commonwealth that fits in with their own activities in that direction.[54]

United States policy favors this second alternative, and, if it is to encourage this broader perspective, the American people have a responsibility to do what they can, through policy and action, to help reinforce those tendencies within the Commonwealth that favor a wider outreach, including world-wide co-operation in dealing with international political questions and problems of developmental assistance.

54. *Ibid.*, c. 1465; Feb. 6, 1964.

Part VI
Economic Relations

18

The Population of the Commonwealth: Composition, Growth, and Migration

T. E. Smith*

Introduction

People living in the Commonwealth countries and their dependencies together make up about 24 per cent[1] of world population. The population varies greatly from one major region to another; in Oceania, including Hawaii and other Pacific islands, 93.3 per cent of the population live in the Commonwealth, in Asia 32.6 per cent, and in Africa 30.6 per cent. In Europe and the Americas the proportion is below the world average. The 1961 mid-year estimated figures for the Commonwealth are shown in Table I.

India is by far the most populous country in the Common-

Table 1. *Population (1961) of the Commonwealth by Major Regions*

Africa	79,811,000*
The Americas	22,219,000
Asia	561,478,000
Europe	53,438,000
Oceania	15,670,000
	732,616,000

*The Nigerian figure in the African total is based on pre-1963 census estimates.

* Secretary of the Institute of Commonwealth Studies, University of London.
1. This and other figures in the first two paragraphs are calculated from statistics of population given for each country and territory in the *U.N. Demographic Yearbook, 1962*, Tables 1 and 2. The population of condominium territories has not been counted as peoples of the Commonwealth.

wealth, with just over 60 per cent of the total. Pakistan, with between one-fifth and one-quarter of India's population, stands second on the list, followed by the United Kingdom, Nigeria,[2] Canada, Australia, Ceylon, and Malaysia[3] in that order. No other Commonwealth country, with the possible exception of Tanganyika, contained as many as ten million people in mid-1964. The Commonwealth, excluding India and Pakistan, contains some twenty million people fewer than the U.S.S.R. and some twelve million more than the United States.

From a demographer's point of view, the larger Commonwealth countries (i.e., those with a population of two million or more) can be divided into three main categories. In the first category comes the United Kingdom (with the Channel Islands and the Isle of Man), which has a very largely white population, a low birth rate,[4] a low death rate, and a low annual rate of increase. The second group of larger Commonwealth countries consists of "white Dominions." In these countries, as in the United States, crude birth rates are at medium levels (in the range 22 to 27) and death rates are low. The three "white Dominions" have annual natural rates of increase ranging in the last few years from 1.35 to 1.79 per cent per annum, nearly double the range of western European rates of growth, and this is increased to over 2 per cent by net immigration. The third group of countries consists of the Asian and African countries of the Commonwealth and contains the great majority of the Commonwealth's population; in these countries the white element in the population is very small, the birth rates are high (typical crude birth rates being at the level of about 40), and the rate of natural increase is at a medium or high level (i.e., from 2 per cent to 3 per cent per annum or even higher) according to whether mortality rates are medium or low. The smaller Commonwealth countries and territories (i.e., those

2. There is some uncertainty regarding the relative position of the United Kingdom and Nigeria following publication of the preliminary results of the 1963 census of the latter country.

3. The population of Ceylon probably still exceeds that of Malaysia, but the difference is very small indeed.

4. I.e., crude birth rate below 20.

with less than two million population) will be considered as a separate fourth group, because, unlike the larger countries, emigration is a factor of importance in some of them in determining growth rates.

The United Kingdom (with the Isle of Man and Channel Islands)

Between the 1951 and 1961 censuses the population of the United Kingdom increased by a little under two and a half million people. During the same period the population of Canada increased by nearly four and a quarter million and that of Australia by over two million. The excess of births over deaths accounts for almost all the United Kingdom increase; net migration into the country during the decade was negligible, a net inflow of some half million Commonwealth and Irish citizens and some 150,000 aliens being almost exactly balanced by the net outflow of United Kingdom citizens.

Commonwealth citizens have made up about three-fifths and Irish citizens two-fifths of the non-alien postwar permanent immigrants into the United Kingdom. About three-quarters of the Commonwealth immigrants were colored, the West Indians being the largest group and Jamaicans easily the largest subgroup among the West Indians. Colored immigrants have tended to stay in the United Kingdom for longer periods than white Commonwealth immigrants from Australia, New Zealand, and Canada, who are more likely to come to Britain for a combination of work and travel and to stay for relatively short periods.[5]

In 1961, the last complete calendar year before the Commonwealth Immigrants Act came into force, net immigration rose to 170,000, which was more than twice the 1960 figure and nearly four times the net balance in each of the years 1958 and

5. By definition an immigrant must intend to stay for at least a year. The Economist Intelligence Unit's *Studies on Immigration from the Commonwealth* provide useful information on the characteristics of the immigrant communities. R. B. Davison's *West Indian Migrants* (Oxford, 1962) gives a summary of social and economic data relating to migration from the West Indies.

1959.[6] Before 1958 the net balance of migration was outward. The net inflow of immigrants into the United Kingdom continued in the first six months of 1962 at an even faster pace; many of these immigrants undoubtedly accelerated departure from their homelands in order to enter the United Kingdom before the Act came into force on July 1 of that year. In the first year of the Act's operation the net inflow[7] of Commonwealth citizens was 34,523; immigration from Eire did not come under control as a result of the Act, and the figure given refers to Commonwealth citizens in the strict sense of the term.

Official population projections made by the Registrar General assume a continuation of net inward migration until the mid-1970's. Even if this assumption proves to be correct, the population of the United Kingdom will continue to grow but slowly; projections prepared in the middle of 1961, based on a net inward migration of 50,000 persons a year from 1962 to the mid-1970's and on reasonable assumptions relating to fertility and mortality trends, gave an increase of under ten million between 1961 and 1986 and of about 15 million between 1961 and 2001.

Unofficial estimates give a figure of half a million colored Commonwealth citizens as currently resident in the United Kingdom. No accurate figure can be given because birth and death registration data and census figures (unlike those of the United States) do not differentiate between white and colored. If the figure of half a million is approximately correct, the colored Commonwealth citizen population of the United Kingdom is less than 1 per cent of the total.

Canada, Australia, and New Zealand

Canada, Australia, and New Zealand are alike in containing populations of predominantly European origin, in hav-

6. According to figures given in *Overseas Migration Board Statistics for 1961* (London: H.M.S.O., 1962).

7. "Control of Immigration Statistics, July 1, 1962 to June 30, 1963," Table 1, Cmnd. 2151, G. B., *Parl. Paps., 1963-64.*

ing fairly rapidly growing numbers of people as a result of a combination of natural increase and immigration, and in having low densities of population. They differ in the degree of racial homogeneity and in the proportionate contributions of natural increase and migration towards growth.

For some decades after the Treaty of Paris in 1763 gave Canada to Britain, the former country remained very largely French in population. A wave of migration from the British Isles to Upper Canada between 1820 and 1860 brought the British and French communities into rough numerical balance, the latter community still predominating by four to one in Quebec at the end of this period. Since 1896 the immigrants have come from many European countries. The British Canadians,[8] once in an absolute majority as Table 2 shows, made up 44 per cent of Canada's eighteen and a quarter million people at the time of the 1961 census, whereas the French Canadians have maintained their proportion of the population at about 30 per cent. Other ethnic groups have increased their representation from 11 per cent in 1881 to 22 per cent in 1951 and 26 per cent in 1961; of these other groups, the Germans are much the largest, followed by the communities of Ukrainian, Italian, Netherlands, Scandinavian, and Polish origin. Asians in Canada were considerably

Table 2. *Percentage Distribution of the Canadian Population by Ethnic Groups, 1901-61*

Ethnic group	1901	1911	1921	1931	1941	1951	1961
British and Irish	57.0	55.5	55.4	51.9	49.7	47.9	43.8
French	30.7	28.6	27.9	28.2	30.3	30.8	30.4
German	5.8	5.6	3.4	4.6	4.0	4.4	5.8
Ukrainian	0.1	1.0	1.2	2.2	2.7	2.8	2.6
Italian	0.2	0.6	0.8	0.9	1.0	1.1	2.5
Netherlands	0.6	0.8	1.3	1.4	1.8	1.9	2.4
Scandinavian	0.6	1.6	1.9	2.2	2.1	2.0	2.1
Polish	0.1	0.5	0.6	1.4	1.5	1.6	1.8
Other European	1.1	3.0	4.8	4.8	4.6	4.5	5.6
Asian	0.4	0.6	0.8	0.8	0.6	0.5	0.7
Indian and Eskimo	2.4	1.5	1.3	1.2	1.1	1.2	1.2
Others	0.9	0.7	0.5	0.3	0.6	1.3	1.3

Source: Dominion Bureau of Statistics, *1961 Census of Canada, Bulletin 1*, pp. 2-5.

8. Including those of Irish origin.

less than 1 per cent of the population in 1961, and Indians and Eskimos not much over 1 per cent.

Migrants settling in Australia, like those entering Canada, come largely from Europe (including the United Kingdom); but the contributions made by the various European countries to the populations of Australia and Canada differ in relative importance. The United Kingdom, for instance, has provided between one-third and one-half of the migrants settling in Australia in recent years, but the postwar contribution to Canada has been only one-quarter of total immigration and less than half of immigration from continental Europe. Italy and Greece provide more than half the continental European migration to Australia with further substantial contributions from Yugoslavia, Spain, Germany, and Holland in that order. The movement to Canada relies far more heavily on migrants from northern Europe, though Italy is the leading exporter from the continent to Canada as well as to Australia.

Large-scale immigration of non-British Europeans to Australia is a more recent phenomenon than the similar movement to Canada, and probably some 80 per cent of the present Australian population is of British origin.[9] New Zealand has not so far turned its back on a policy of ethnic and cultural homogeneity. Nearly three-quarters of the long-term immigrants, assisted and unassisted, in New Zealand in the years 1958-63 gave the United Kingdom, Australia, or Canada as their last country of permanent domicile, and it may be assumed (particularly as the U.K. contingent was by far the largest and the Canadian the smallest) that the great majority of those were British.

Australia's outstanding success in attracting immigrants from Europe since the end of World War II can be attributed in part to the large number of assisted immigrants and in part to the

9. The 1954 Australian census gave 86 per cent of the population as Australian-born, 7 per cent born in the United Kingdom and Ireland, and 7 per cent elsewhere. C. A. Price gives a June, 1960, estimate of the ethnic composition of the Australian population as 80.5 per cent British (72.6 per cent Australian-born and 7.9 per cent overseas-born), 18.8 per cent non-British white (10.6 per cent Australian-born and 8.2 per cent overseas-born), and 0.7 per cent non-white in his article "Overseas Migration to and from Australia, 1947-1961," *Australian Outlook*, XVI (Aug., 1962).

pull of Australia, particularly in the case of southern Europeans. Of the one and a quarter million permanent arrivals in Australia in the first twelve postwar years, rather over half were assisted immigrants and nearly half of these were British. The proportion of assisted Italian immigrants was far smaller, and Borrie stated in his Cohen Memorial Lecture[10] given at the University of Sydney in 1958 that "the inflow of southerners [i.e., southern Europeans] would have been considerably greater had landing permits not been restricted pretty closely in recent years to essential workers and immediate relatives of these and of earlier immigrants." Net migration to Australia has not, except for the period from 1949 to 1952, quite managed to achieve the official long-term target of 1 per cent per annum of total population, and in 1961 and 1962, years of growing prosperity in Europe itself, the net migrational inflow was down to 0.59 per cent of total population.

New Zealand, with a relatively low density of population but one which is nevertheless six and a half times that of Australia, has adopted a more cautious immigration policy. Assisted immigration was restricted to unmarried British immigrants until 1950. A new immigration policy announced in that year extended the free and assisted passage scheme to certain categories of married British immigrants with up to two children, later extended to four children. A limited number of non-British single men and women of Dutch, Danish, Swiss, Austrian, and German nationality were also admitted under the scheme, but the recruitment of persons of the last four of these five nationalities was terminated at the end of 1958. Assisted immigration to New Zealand is now once again an almost entirely British affair, 3,474 of the 3,584 immigrants under the scheme in 1962 being of British nationality.

Unlike the migrant streams of earlier years, long-term immigration into Canada, Australia, and New Zealand has not in the postwar years been a predominantly male movement. Indeed females have consistently outnumbered males recently among

10. The lecture appears as the chapter "The Peopling of Australia" in H. W. Arndt and W. M. Corden, eds., *The Australian Economy* (Melbourne, 1963).

long-term immigrants into Canada, and the numbers of the two sexes have been nearly equal, with a small male predominance, among the immigrants into Australia and New Zealand. All three countries still have more males than females in their total populations, however, partly as a result of earlier patterns of migration and partly because of the very low current levels of mortality.

The French community in Canada grew from some 65,000 at the time of the Treaty of Paris to five and a half million in 1961 without any substantial new immigration, and it is the high birth rate of this community which has until recently maintained Canadian fertility rates at a medium rather than a low level. In the last two or three decades provincial—and hence ethnic— differences in birth rates have narrowed, and the inverse relationship between birth rate and income has largely disappeared. As Keyfitz puts it ". . . all statistically recognizable groups seem to be converging on a norm. People exercise their increasing freedom to have the same number of children as their neighbours, in the narrow range of two to four, and to have them at the same ages."[11]

The crude birth rate and the rate of natural increase are rather higher in Canada and New Zealand than in Australia, as Table 3 shows.

Although Canada can show a higher rate of natural increase than either Australia or New Zealand, she is well below Aus-

Table 3. *Crude Birth and Death Rates in Canada, Australia, and New Zealand*

	Crude birth rate			Crude death rate			Rate of natural increase		
	1960	1961	1962	1960	1961	1962	1960	1961	1962
Canada	26.7	26.0	25.5	7.8	7.7	7.6	18.9	18.3	17.9
Australia	22.4	22.9	22.1	8.6	8.5	8.7	13.8	14.4	13.4
New Zealand	26.4	27.0	26.2	8.8	9.0	8.9	17.6	18.0	17.3

Note: Despite the higher crude death rates in Australia and New Zealand, expectation of life at birth is almost identical for the three countries, the expectation figures for both sexes being slightly higher in New Zealand than in Australia and Canada.

11. N. Keyfitz, "New Patterns in the Birth Rate," in V. W. Bladen, ed., *Canadian Population and Northern Colonization* (Toronto, 1962).

tralia (though above New Zealand) in the proportionate contribution which net migration makes to total rates of population growth. Migration as a source of population growth is, of course, much more subject to fluctuation than natural increase, but it is approximately true to say that net migration has produced one-third of total population growth in Australia in the last few years, but rather under one-quarter of Canadian and New Zealand population growth. The high level of migrational gain to Australia (ranging from 60,000 to nearly 100,000 per annum in the decade 1952-62) gives her a total rate of population growth as high as that of Canada and higher than that of New Zealand.

The Larger Commonwealth Countries of Asia and Africa

The countries and territories in this category are listed in Table 4.

The population of all the Asian countries listed in Table 4 is now growing at the rate of more than 2 per cent per year and that of the three smaller countries (Ceylon, Malaysia, and Hong Kong) at a particularly fast pace. It is much more difficult to estimate with reasonable accuracy the growth rates of the African countries, but the indications are that a typical rate is close to 2 per cent per year. Most estimates of the Nigerian rate of growth of population prior to the announcement of the 1963 census figures were put at rather less than the suggested typical rate,[12] while the Ghana and Uganda rates of increase were over 2 per cent per annum in the 1950's. A 2 per cent annual rate of increase, if continued, implies a growth in population of 81 per cent in thirty years and 169 per cent in fifty years.

Most of the larger Commonwealth countries of Asia and Africa contain a plurality of ethnic groups. Although fertility rates are high in all these countries, there are in some of them

12. The recently published Nigerian census figures suggest, however, that the true rate of growth has been higher than any of the estimates made.

Table 4. *Population (1961) of the Commonwealth Countries of Asia and Africa with over 2 Million Inhabitants*

	Country	Population	Average population per square km. *
Asia	India	441,631,000	138
	Pakistan	94,547,000	100
	Ceylon	10,167,000	155
	Malaysia†	10,131,000	30
	Hong Kong	3,178,000	3,082
Africa	Nigeria‡	35,752,000	39
	Tanganyika	9,399,000	10
	Kenya	7,287,000	13
	Ghana	6,957,000	29
	Uganda	6,845,000	29
	S. Rhodesia	3,150,000	9
	Nyasaland	2,890,000	24
	N. Rhodesia	2,480,000	3
	Sierra Leone	2,450,000	34

Source: *U.N. Demographic Yearbook, 1962.* Some of the figures in this table—particularly the African data—are of doubtful reliability.

*For comparison, population per square km. in United Kingdom was 217, Canada 2, Australia 1, and New Zealand 9 in 1961.

†The density in the former Federation of Malaya was 54 in 1961 and that of North Borneo and Sarawak 6.

‡The 1963 Nigerian census gave a total population of 55,653,821. The estimated 1961 figure is obviously far too low.

striking differences between the rates for one such ethnic group and another. The Chinese in Singapore and Hong Kong, for instance, have exhibited recently a definite decline in fertility partly as a result of an increased age at marriage and partly because of the increasing use of modern methods of family planning. In the areas covered by the Family Planning Pilot Project in Ceylon, a drop of one-third in crude birth rates has been achieved.[13]

Some African tribal groups have relatively low fertility rates. As described in more detail elsewhere,[14] the existing evidence suggests that a high proportion of infertile unions, coupled with a good deal of one-child sterility and often with a high incidence of venereal disease, is one of the most important factors associated

13. Information provided at the Asian Population Conference of December, 1963.

14. T. E. Smith and J. G. C. Blacker, *Population Characteristics of the Commonwealth Countries of Tropical Africa* (London, 1963), pp. 30-39.

with such areas of relatively low fertility. Other factors affecting fertility relate to marriage, including age at marriage, marital stability and instability, and the extent to which marital cohabitation is interrupted by labor migration or by the periodic return of wives or husbands singly to their own family homes. Methods of abortion are known in Africa, though there is no measure of their use.

While fertility is not at a uniformly high level in all the countries and among all the communities of Commonwealth Africa and Asia, the present typical birthrate in these countries is probably somewhat higher than the European birthrate before the demographic revolution. A number of Asian governments, including those of India and Pakistan, have given official recognition to the need to restrain the rate of growth of population; thus the government of India, in its statement to the Asian Population Conference of 1963, said that it "is firmly committed to a policy of implementing specific programmes to accelerate acceptance of family planning as a way of life by the people in order to achieve economic strength and social welfare." Over eight thousand centers, including six thousand in rural areas, have been set up in India for contraceptive distribution, and voluntary sterilization has been popularized in some parts of the country. In Pakistan achievements to date in the field of family planning are far from great, despite President Ayub Khan's repeatedly stated views about its importance; in that country red tape and opposition to family planning at lower official levels have contributed to the ineffectiveness of the three demonstration projects in family planning.

Among the Commonwealth governments of Africa, none has as yet developed a policy of attempting to restrict the rate of growth of population. With the present low population density in that continent as a whole, the fairly high rates of population growth are not at present regarded as a source of anxiety. Nevertheless, there are some regions of Commonwealth Africa in which settlement is dense. The Eastern Region of Nigeria is three times as thickly populated as the country as a whole, and the Region's population density is not very far short of that of India. Even in thinly populated East Africa, there are areas of high population density, such as the Kenya highlands, the Kigezi district of Uganda, and parts of the Lake Victoria shore.

Mortality rates have fallen continuously in the Commonwealth countries of Asia during the past decade. In Ceylon, for instance, the crude death rate fell from 12.4 in 1950 to 8.6 in 1960, while the infant mortality rate dropped from 82 to 57 in the same period. The figures for India are less reliable than those of Ceylon, but the indications are that the crude death rate dropped by some 20-25 per cent during the 1950's. The crude death rate for Pakistan, estimated at 16.7 for the year 1962, is at a level similar to that of India, while Malaysian and Hong Kong mortality rates bear comparison with those of Ceylon. It is impossible at present to make any reliable estimates of death rates for the African population of the Commonwealth countries of Africa, but the indications are that crude death rates in African Commonwealth countries are in general higher than in any Commonwealth country of Asia, with the probable range of from just under 20 to rather over 30 deaths annually per thousand population.

Migration does not now make a substantial contribution, positive or negative, to the growth of population of any of the Commonwealth countries of Asia with the exception of Hong Kong, which has been the haven of a very large number of refugees from the Chinese mainland both between 1937 and 1941 and again after World War II. As no population census of Hong Kong was taken between 1931 and 1961 and as most of the refugees have been integrated into the life of the Colony, it is impossible to estimate their number accurately; some indication of the size of the migratory movement can however be gauged from the fact that the 1931 population was a mere 840,000 persons while the 1963 mid-year population has been estimated at 3,592,000,[15] or more than four times the 1931 figure. By contrast for India international migration is negligible compared to the size of the population, while for Ceylon, net migration, which

15. Hong Kong country statement to the Asian Population Conference, December, 1963.

has been consistently outward since the country became independent, has not amounted to more than a small fraction (varying from 2.5 per cent to 7.5 per cent) of natural increase in recent years.

The picture relating to migration is substantially different in Commonwealth Africa, where, unlike Asia, there is a high degree of population mobility. The direction of many of the important long-distance movements of African population has been mapped, though there are no reliable data on the dimensions of these movements. Many of the migrant labor movements are internal rather than international in character, but African migrant laborers working in countries other than their own are nevertheless to be numbered in millions. Examples of international migration affecting Commonwealth countries are the long-continued migration to the Buganda province of Uganda from the area of the former Trust Territory of Ruanda-Urundi and the movement to the Copper Belt of Northern Rhodesia from many areas of Central and East Africa with poorer economic prospects.

The Smaller Countries of the Commonwealth

The countries of the Commonwealth with under two million inhabitants, of which there are a considerable number if both independent and dependent political units are included, tend in general to be either territories with a rather dense population living in a total area of a very few hundred square miles or thinly populated countries with very undeveloped economies.

Many of the compact, densely peopled small territories were the creation of Britain or some other metropolitan power in the first instance and were built up with the help of immigrant labor. The islands of the West Indies, Mauritius, and the Seychelles for instance, were empty or almost empty at the time of initial European colonization, and their developing economies were dependent on the importation of slave labor and later, in some instances, indentured labor. In all these compactly sized territories, public health measures were easier to put into effect than in the larger and more thinly populated countries, and the transition from high death rates to low death rates has for this reason often been very rapid. As an example, the eradication of malaria in Mauritius has been instrumental in a reduction of the crude death rate from 25 to 30 in the period between the world wars to a range of 10.9 to 16.1 in the 1950's and 9.9 in 1961; the rate of natural increase has in consequence climbed from less than 1 per cent per annum to 3 per cent. With already dense populations, high rates of natural increase, and limited possibilities of economic development, the problem facing the governments of many of these small countries is to find homes in other countries for prospective emigrants. As we have seen, many thousands of Jamaicans and other West Indians have come to the United Kingdom in recent years; migrants from the smaller West Indian islands have moved to Trinidad, though this movement has come to a near halt; there are several thousand people of Maltese origin in Australia, the United Kingdom, and Canada. Territories such as Mauritius and the Seychelles are, however, too isolated to be able to export their peoples on any scale, and small Commonwealth countries with non-European populations find the doors of other countries increasingly difficult to negotiate. In many such countries, only a small minority are aware of the significance of the rapid growth of population, and birth control campaigns often run counter both to religious opinion and to entrenched patterns of behavior.

Despite their very small size, these countries often contain a plurality of ethnic groups for reasons arising from the history of their colonization. Mauritius and Trinidad both contain the descendants of African slaves, the descendants of Indian indentured laborers, and other minorities. Further examples of plural societies in small countries are Cyprus and Zanzibar, in both of which independence has failed to diminish ethnic differences and reduce the risk of outbreaks of racial strife.

The Commonwealth countries with small populations thinly scattered on the ground tend to have very different characteristics from those which have been considered in the last two paragraphs. Unlike the compact, densely populated territories, they often contain a high proportion of inhabitants descended from peoples who have inhabited their countries for many generations and can be regarded as indigenous (e.g., Bechuanaland, Swaziland, Basutoland, the Solomon Islands, Gilbert and Ellice Islands, the Gambia). Much of the land in these countries is jungle, mountain, or desert, and development has in some of them been restricted largely to areas contiguous to the main town or towns (e.g., Aden, Bechuanaland, British Honduras, and British Guiana). These lightly peopled small countries of the Commonwealth have suffered neglect in the past as colonies; now their governments can find little comfort in the world tendency for people to concentrate more and more in urban and industrial communities, for they may well need larger populations if they are ever to hope to develop their economies.

Some smaller Commonwealth countries do not fall neatly into either of the groups whose demographic characteristics have been outlined above. The crude birth rates in Malta and Gibraltar, two compact, densely populated territories, are at southern European levels (i.e., just over 20 births per thousand population per annum), and the rate of natural increase is between 1.2 and 1.5 per cent per annum; in the 1950's emigration from Malta and Gibraltar was on a sufficiently large scale to come close to balancing this rather moderate excess of births over deaths. Again, there are some small Commonwealth countries which are neither densely nor thinly populated; some of these, such as Fiji and St. Helena possess certain demographic characteristics (e.g., high rates of natural increase and a lack of adequate outlets for potential emigrants) in common with most of the countries of the compactly sized, densely populated group, while one or two (e.g., Tonga) are more akin to the thinly populated category. Finally, in not every case is the economy of the thinly populated small countries at a low ebb; in Brunei, for instance, the national product is at a high level in relation to the size of the population.

General Considerations

The preceding four sections contain evidence of the difficulties of making generalizations about the demography of the Commonwealth countries as a whole. The range of fertility is virtually as high within the Commonwealth as in the non-Commonwealth countries of the world, though nowhere in the Commonwealth (except in the Isle of Man) is the crude birth rate quite so low as in Sweden, Czechoslovakia, Hungary, and even Japan. The mortality range within the Commonwealth countries is also great, but there is a tendency for Commonwealth countries in Asia, Africa, and the Caribbean to have lower death rates than non-Commonwealth countries in the same region; for example, the crude death rate in Malaysia is probably less than half that of Indonesia and Thailand; that of India much lower than that of Burma; that of Ghana apparently somewhat lower than that of its French-speaking neighbors; and that of Jamaica substantially less than that of Cuba, Haiti, and the Dominican Republic.

The Commonwealth is a meaningful group of countries in the field of international migration. Jamaicans, Indians, and Pakistanis would not now live in the United Kingdom in large numbers if Jamaica, India, and Pakistan had not been members of the Commonwealth. Australia and New Zealand still have an official preference for British-born immigrants, and Canada has at least a sentimental preference for them. International migration within the Commonwealth is in general subject to less restriction than international migration outside the Commonwealth, despite the Commonwealth Immigrants Act and the restrictive policies of a number of Commonwealth countries, though the Communauté would probably not compare unfavorably with the Commonwealth in freedom of movement.

At present one out of every eight persons living in the Commonwealth is white. This proportion seems certain to decrease very slowly for the next few decades unless some of the Asian or African members leave the Commonwealth. From the numerical point of view, the Commonwealth was never British.

19

Intra-Commonwealth Flows of Capital and Skills

*Brinley Thomas**

The last quarter of a century has seen profound changes in the structure of the British Commonwealth and its relations with the rest of the world. New problems of adjustment have had to be faced as a result of the economic impact of World War II, the resurgence of Europe and the shift in the balance of power within the Atlantic economy, and the rapid transformation of the remainder of the colonial empire into a group of independent nations. This paper will examine one aspect of intra-Commonwealth economic relations in this new setting. The main facts about movements of capital and skills between 1946 and 1962 will be set out. The aim is to present broad trends rather than a comprehensive statistical picture. An attempt is made to assess the economic significance of the emerging pattern in recent years and to consider the effects on rates of economic growth in the richer and less developed parts of the Commonwealth.

Reconstruction after the War

In retrospect it is remarkable how quickly the traditional flows of capital and labor from Britain to the overseas Commonwealth countries were restored after World War II. The British economy had suffered severe strains and distortions. As com-

* Professor of economics, University of Wales, Cardiff.

pared with 1938 the volume of exports was reduced by two-thirds; half the prewar tonnage of merchant shipping had been destroyed; the net income from overseas investments in 1945 was only half of what it was in 1938; external liabilities—mainly the sterling balances held abroad—had increased by nearly £3,000 million; Britain's own external assets had been consumed to the extent of £1,118 million; and internal disinvestment between 1940 and 1944 amounted to £885 million. Total losses due to physical destruction on land and sea, together with internal and external disinvestment, were estimated at £7,300 million; this was the equivalent of 25 per cent of the national wealth of the United Kingdom before the war.[1] The grim outlook in 1945 was summed up as follows:

Thus the difficulties to be overcome in restoring financial equilibrium and expanding exports, which are formidable enough in themselves, have to be faced at a time when there are no less pressing demands at home to make good war losses and deprivations alike of industry and of a civilian population whose needs, beyond the barest minimum, have for six years been subordinated to the demands of war.[2]

A summary view of the process of recovery may be seen from the figures of the United Kingdom balance of payments in Table 1.

Table 1. *United Kingdom Balance of Payments, 1946-1950* (£ million)

	1946	1947	1948	1949	1950
Current Account					
Visible trade (net)	−162	−414	−190	−131	−136
Invisibles (net)	−133	− 28	+197	−169	+433
Current Balance	−295	−442	+ 7	+ 38	+297
Special Grants	—	+ 30	+138	+154	+140
Long-term Capital Account					
Balance of long-term capital, monetary movements, and balancing item	+295	+412	−145	−192	−437

Source: *United Kingdom Balance of Payments, 1946-1957* (London, H.M.S.O., 1959), p.16.

1. "Statistical Material Presented during the Washington Negotiations," Cmd. 6707, G. B., *Parl. Paps. 1945-46,* XXI.
2. *Ibid.,* p. 15.

In each of the five years after the war, and particularly in 1947, there was a heavy deficit on visible trade, but the balance on invisible account improved considerably as from 1948. A major factor in the situation was the massive inflow of government loans and grants from the United States and Canada, amounting to a net total of £1,935 million over the years 1946-50, the main constituents of which were the United States line of credit of £930 million, the Canadian credit of £297 million, and the European Recovery Program (net of American share of counterpart) equal to £627 million.

It is against this background that we can explain why the Commonwealth was able to resume so rapidly and smoothly its regime of factor mobility and multilateral trade. The main elements in the United Kingdom balance of payments with the rest of the sterling area in the years 1946-50 are shown in Table 2.

Great Britain was able to resume long-term capital exports to the rest of the sterling area as early as 1947; the total under this heading for the four years 1947-50 was £943 million (in-

Table 2. *United Kingdom Balance of Payments with the Rest of the Sterling Area, 1946-1950* (£ million)

	1946	1947	1948	1949	1950
Current Account					
Current balance	− 26	+128	+256	+299	+283
Special Grants					
Australia and New Zealand gifts	—	+ 30	—	+ 16	—
Long-term Capital Account					
Intergoverment loans by U.K. (net)	+ 10	− 26	—	—	− 3
Intergoverment loans to U.K. (net)	− 5	− 13	−244	− 91	− 10
Other long-term capital (net) and balancing item	+ 55	−282	−260	−206	−195
Monetary Movements					
Overseas sterling holdings	− 30	−117	− 95	+ 3	+391
Balance of long-term capital, monetary movements, and balancing item	+ 30	−438	−111	−294	+183
Interarea Transfers					
Net Rest of sterling area sales of gold in U.K.	− 82	− 77	− 55	− 68	− 98
Other transfers	+ 78	+357	− 90	+ 47	−368
	− 4	+280	−145	− 21	−466

Source: *United Kingdom Balance of Payments, 1946-1957* (London, H.M.S.O., 1959), p. 18.

cluding a small balancing item). Moreover, during the years 1946-48 there was a substantial running down of sterling balances. This achievement would not have been possible without the substantial blood transfusion from North America in the form of government loans and grants. There was also a strong revival in British emigration to the Commonwealth. In the years 1946-50 no less than 577,900 sailed to these destinations, almost exactly equal to the outflow in 1925-29. Of this total Canada took 144,400, Australia 164,300, New Zealand 38,100, South Africa and Southern Rhodesia 94,000, and other parts of the Commonwealth 138,500. It is estimated that in the three years 1947-49 the net efflux of migrants' funds amounted to £60 million; and four out of every five emigrants went to the Commonwealth.

Just after the war there was a high proportion of skill in the migration movements both ways. A sample inquiry based on 1946-49 showed the following occupational distribution of British male emigrants: professions and semiprofessions 22 per cent; proprietors, officials, etc. 18 per cent; skilled workers 28 per cent; semi-skilled workers 4 per cent, and unskilled workers only 7 per cent.[3] The return movement of British nationals to the United Kingdom was about 45 per cent of the outflow to the Commonwealth; three out of every ten immigrants came from the Indian subcontinent, consisting mainly of civil servants and members of the armed forces and their families.

The outstanding fact about the transition period after the war was the emergence of a triangular mechanism linking North America, the United Kingdom, and the outer sterling area.[4] The enormous import of public capital from North America enabled Britain to continue her role as exporter of capital and skills to the overseas Commonwealth, and reasonably free mobility of goods within the sterling area was maintained. This was part of a circular flow connecting the United States, western Europe, and the overseas countries; this provided the basis for the re-

3. Julius Isaac, *British Post-War Migration* (Cambridge, 1954), p. 54.
4. See the present writer's "Migration and International Investment" in Brinley Thomas, ed., *Economics of International Migration* (London, 1958), pp. 3-16, and "Recent Trends in American Investment in Europe," *Three Banks Review*, Sept., 1960, 3-21.

markable progress of the international economy in the 1950's, particularly the economic resurgence of western Europe.

Trends in Commonwealth Investment

The network of Commonwealth investment is so vast and complex that it is impossible to describe it in a brief statement. Since this analysis is confined to movements of capital within the Commonwealth, it will be helpful at the outset to indicate the broad relations between internal and external resources. We shall take advantage of the new statistical material available since 1958 to give a fuller account of trends in the last few years.

The magnitude and sources of the capital absorbed by overseas sterling countries in the decade 1948-59, estimated by Mr. A. R. Conan, are given in Table 3.

Table 3. *Capital Imports into Sterling Countries, 1948-1958*
(£ million)

mporting country	Source of supply				
	U.K.	U.S.A.	World Bank	Other	Total
Australia	400	200	100	100	800
South Africa	500	150	50	100	800
India	175	257	175	75	700
Rhodesia	300	25	50	75	450
Colonies	600	75	25	50	800

Source: A. R. Conan, *Capital Imports into Sterling Countries* (London, 1960), p. 70.

The figures in Table 3 cover capital of all kinds; and the relative significance of different categories, public and private, varies considerably from country to country. In the decade 1948-58 Australia, South Africa, and the colonies absorbed about £800 million of capital each; Britain provided seven-eighths of the colonial intake, five-eighths of the South African, and a half of the Australian. The American contribution to Australia's imports was half of the British; in the case of the colonies, American imports were only about one-tenth of the British. In the case of India the high American contribution consists mainly of government loans.

In August, 1956, the British government decided to introduce a number of measures to improve economic statistics, including those of the balance of payments.[5] With the simplification of exchange control, the trade accounts have now become the basis for the statistics of all imports and exports. Regular inquiries are conducted by the Board of Trade into direct investment by British companies overseas and by overseas companies in the United Kingdom. New estimates of British portfolio investment overseas are provided by the Bank of England's survey, which not only measures capital flows but also gives estimates of the nominal value of a large part of the stock of U.K. portfolio assets. These comprise the holdings of U.K. residents (including companies) in overseas government and municipal loans and in securities of companies incorporated abroad. Thanks to these important developments, it is possible to present a fairly comprehensive and accurate account of capital flows for the years 1958-62.

A summary view of the United Kingdom balance of payments with the overseas sterling area in recent years is shown in Table 4.

The biggest item in the current account balance was the net inflow of interest, profits, and dividends. In 1962 the visible

Table 4. *United Kingdom Balance of Payments with the Overseas Sterling Area, 1958-1962* (£ million)

	1958	1959	1960	1961	1962
Current account balance	+475	+299	+359	+285	+217
Balance of long-term capital	−218	−189	−221	−208	−166
Interarea transfers	− 69	−306	− 44	−176	− 57
Balancing item	− 95	− 9	+126	− 23	− 42
Balance of monetary movements	− 93	+205	−220	+122	+ 48

Source: *United Kingdom Balance of Payments, 1963* (London, H.M.S.O., 1963), p. 2.

5. See Central Statistical Office, *New Contributions to Economic Statistics, Second Series, Studies in Official Statistics,* No. 9 (London, H.M.S.O., 1962), pp. 76-81.

account was adverse to the extent of £45 million, but interest, profits, and dividends brought in a surplus of £284 million. The balance of monetary movements mainly reflects changes in overseas sterling holdings. The net outflow of long-term capital was at an annual average of over £200 million in 1958-60, but there has been a decline since then. We shall now examine the constituents of these items in more detail, i.e., the movements of direct and portfolio investment, overseas sterling balances,

Table 5. *Value of U.K. Companies' Private Investment in the Commonwealth and Elsewhere in 1962 (Excluding Oil, Insurance, and Banking)* (£ million)

	Total net asset value of direct investment	Total net asset value plus depreciation
Canada	607.0	880.8
Australia	401.3	496.7
South Africa	219.3	279.9
New Zealand	75.7	107.0
Total old Commonwealth	1,303.3	1,764.4
India	107.7	221.1
Rhodesia & Nyasaland	83.9	102.9
Pₐkistan	24.6	29.5
S ngapore	5.9	7.9
Malaya	104.2	143.4
Nigeria	66.2	88.1
Sierra Leone	14.5	21.7
Ghana	49.3	66.4
Kenya	15.7	18.7
Hong Kong	16.2	18.6
Jamaica	14.0	19.8
Trinidad	21.1	26.6
Other British West Indian territories	66.4	83.1
Total new Commonwealth	652.7	848.8
Rest of overseas sterling area	143.9	178.5
United States	276.1	344.0
Western Europe	303.9	422.8
Latin America	115.0	145.0
Other non-sterling areas	57.9	77.1
Grand total*	2,853.1	3,780.7
Estimated grand total including allowance for non-response	3,500.0	—

*Owing to rounding, figures may not add through to totals.
Source: *Board of Trade Journal,* Nov. 15, 1963, p. 1080.

and government aid, including technical assistance to the less-developed members of the Commonwealth.

Private investment

New information yielded by the Overseas Direct Investment Inquiry for 1962 is set out in Table 5.

The most comprehensive inquiry yet made reveals that the stock of British companies' direct investment in 1962, not allowing for accumulated depreciation, was £1,303 million in the old Commonwealth and £653 million in the new Commonwealth. The value of direct investment, including depreciation, in Canada alone was greater than the corresponding total for the whole of the less-developed part of the Commonwealth. It must be remembered too that these figures do not include oil, insurance, and banking. It is estimated that two-thirds (£2,250 million) of British direct investment covered by the survey was located in the richer countries of the world; the part located in underdeveloped countries was estimated at £1,250 million, of which £350 million was made available in the years 1958-62.

Space does not permit an analysis of direct investment by overseas Commonwealth companies in the United Kingdom. By far the largest item is the Canadian contribution of £130 million, net of depreciation; the figures for other Commonwealth countries are negligible. Of the total net asset value of all overseas-owned companies' investment in the United Kingdom in 1962, i.e., £1,400 million, no less than £985 million, or 70 per cent, was American.

We shall now look at the course of capital flows and the earnings on capital in the years 1958-62. It is not feasible to present these figures for the countries of the Commonwealth in the form in which Table 5 is set out. The figures of direct investment, which exclude oil, insurance, and banking, need to be supplemented by figures of "other investment," which include portfolio investments and outlays by the oil and insurance industries. Estimates of private investment in this wider sense are conveniently available as between the United Kingdom and the overseas sterling area but not for the individual countries. However, with the exception of the omission of Canada, the overseas sterling area is not very different from the overseas Commonwealth.

The course of private investment by the United Kingdom in the overseas sterling area and vice versa is set out in Table 6.

Table 6. *Private Investment,* 1958-1962 (£ million)

	1958	1959	1960	1961	1962
By United Kingdom					
Overseas sterling area					
Direct†	− 79	−106	−155	−128	−120
Other‡	− 91	− 56	− 36	− 62	− 29
Total	−170	−162	−191	−190	−149
Total all areas	−298	−307	−313	−326	−259
In United Kingdom					
Oversea sterling area					
Direct†	+ 10	+ 8	+ 14	+ 10	+ 8
Other‡	− 24	+ 22	+ 12	+ 47	+ 26
Total	− 14	+ 30	+ 26	+ 57	+ 34
Total all areas	+165	+176	+228	+417	+274
Private investment (net)	−133	−131	− 85	+ 91	+ 15

*Net of disinvestment
†Excludes oil and insurance
‡Includes portfolio investment and investment by oil and insurance industries.
Source: *United Kingdom Balance of Payments, 1963* (London, H.M.S.O., 1963), p.18.

In 1962 about 54 per cent of total overseas direct investment by British companies was in the overseas sterling area, compared with 55 per cent in 1961, 63 per cent in 1960, and 53 per cent in 1959. There was an abnormally large outflow to Australia in 1960. Australia absorbed 27 per cent of the sterling area total in 1959 and 28 per cent in 1961; in 1962, however, the proportion rose to 43 per cent. Unremitted profits as a proportion of total investment in the sterling area went up sharply from 29 per cent in 1961 to 57 per cent in 1962. The volume of other investment, including portfolio and the outlays of oil and insurance companies, has fluctuated between £91 million in 1958 and £29 million in 1962. The net outflow of private capital, direct and other, to all areas fell from £133 million in 1958 to £91 million in 1961, and in 1962 there was a net inflow of £15 million.

The flows of interest, profits, and dividends as between the United Kingdom and the overseas sterling area are shown in Table 7.

Table 7. U.K. Interest, Profits, and Dividends, 1958-1962 (£ million)

	1958	1959	1960	1961	1962
Debits					
Overseas sterling area:					
Direct investment*	2	3	3	4	4
Portfolio investment	38	32	34	35	34
Other†	92	82	107	111	110
Total	132	117	144	150	148
All areas: total	411	416	452	444	455
Credits					
Overseas sterling area:					
Direct investment*	124	149	176	168	186
Portfolio investment	60	62	72	73	79
Other†	205	154	190	187	167
Total	389	365	438	428	432
All areas: total	711	688	688	695	780
Interest, profits, and dividends (net)	+300	+272	+236	+251	+325

*Excludes oil and insurance
†Includes oil and insurance
Source: *United Kingdom Balance Payments, 1963* (London, H.M.S.O., 1963), p. 11.

The income on direct investment covers branch earnings, interest on loans granted, and dividends remitted from subsidiaries, together with the parent companies' share of unremitted profits retained for reinvestment. It must be noted that this last item appears also as "private investment" in Table 6 as a contra item. Estimates of interest and dividends remitted on portfolio investment are based mainly on Board of Inland Revenue records.[6] Table 7 brings out the important part played

6. This explains why these estimates are about 25 per cent higher than those yielded by the Bank of England's survey of portfolio investment. The latter covers, as far as possible, all securities dealt in on the London Stock Exchange,

by the flow of earnings on British investment in the overseas sterling area; the annual total in the years 1960-62 was over £430 million, which was 60 per cent of the aggregate earned in all parts of the world. The outward flow of interest, profits, and dividends to the overseas sterling area in the same period was about £148 million a year, or about 33 per cent of the efflux to all parts.

Overseas sterling balances

At the end of the war the United Kingdom's external liabilities, known as the overseas sterling balances, amounted to £3,567 million, £2,327 million of which was held by members of the sterling area. The rate at which they might be drawn on was a serious problem to Britain in the immediate postwar years, and agreements were arrived at in 1947 and 1948 to set limits to this process. Eighteen years after the war the total of the holdings held by sterling area countries had increased; it was £2,763 million in June, 1963. But the financial significance of these holdings had changed substantially. The wartime accumulations had disappeared, to be replaced by holdings built up from trading surpluses since the war. The use of sterling balances by the underdeveloped members of the Commonwealth has been a potent factor in facilitating development. India, Pakistan, and Ceylon drew down their holdings from £1,352 million in 1945 to under £200 million in 1960, the process being particularly rapid as from 1955. The East, Central, and West African group of countries increased their holdings to a peak of £750 million at the end of 1954 and have used them to finance development plans in recent years. The Middle Eastern and Far Eastern countries have been rapidly adding to their balances from an aggregate of £520 million in 1954 to £1,162 mil-

together with U.S. and Canadian securities quoted abroad, on which information is available through the working of the U.K. exchange control. Other securities quoted abroad are not covered, unless they have a registrar or paying agent in the United Kingdom. See *Bank of England Quarterly Bulletin*, III (June, 1963), 118.

Table 8. Overseas Sterling Countries: Movements in Sterling Holdings (Net) (£ million)

	Total	Australia, N. Zealand, and S. Africa	India, Pakistan, and Ceylon	Caribbean area	East, Central, and West Africa	Middle Eastern countries*	Far Eastern countries†	Other overseas sterling countries
End years								
1945-54	+495	+191	−700	+ 48	+551	+101	+278	+ 26
1954-62	−147	−147	−514	+ 47	−328	+313	+329	+ 39
Holdings at								
end-1962	2,675	452	138	148	427	413	749	348

*Persian Gulf territories, Libya, and Jordan
†Malaysia, Brunei, Hong Kong, and Burma
Source: Bank of England Quarterly Bulletin, III (Dec. 1963), 267.

lion in 1962 and have thus provided a basis for the promotion of economic growth in the near future.

Table 8 summarizes the remarkable changes which have occurred since the war.

In mid-1963 the amount held by non-sterling countries was £1,037 million, of which £376 million was in the hands of central monetary authorities. Although the non-official holdings are apt to be volatile, they are by no means as large as they used to be and are now almost wholly offset by U.K. short-term claims on those countries. The changes over the last decade in the distribution of sterling balances as between different types of holder have added to the strength and stability of the sterling area.

Aid to developing countries

The flow of government aid to the underdeveloped parts of the Commonwealth from the United Kingdom has been much increased in recent years; it doubled in size between 1957-58 and 1961-62. The details are set out in Table 9.

Bilateral aid is given direct to the receiving country, whereas

Table 9. *United Kingdom Aid to Underdeveloped Countries in the Commonwealth* (£ million)

	1957/8	1958/9	1959/60	1960/1	1961/2	1962/3 (provisional)
Bilateral Aid						
Colonial Territories						
Grants	41.4	37.3	40.3	38.9	56.6	40.4
Loans	6.2	11.7	17.3	32.9	38.9	20.2
Total	47.3	49.0	57.6	71.8	95.5	60.5
Independent Commonwealth						
Grants	2.7	5.0	5.0	10.2	12.5	20.6
Loans	2.0	20.8	34.7	35.4	32.0	41.7
Total	4.7	25.8	39.7	45.6	44.5	62.3
Total Bilateral Aid	52.0	74.8	97.3	117.4	140.0	122.9
Multilateral Aid*	18.8	24.0	19.9	21.2	6.3	9.9

*Not all of this went to Commonwealth countries
Source: *Aid to Developing Countries*, Cmnd. 2147 (London, H.M.S.O., Sept, 1963), p. 15.

multilateral aid goes through the medium of international organizations. It is estimated that a quarter of the former is "tied," i.e., loans to independent countries stipulating that the proceeds must be spent on British goods and services. About half the British expenditure on aid takes the form of outright grants, and about 80 per cent of the money provided in the form of loans is made available for twenty years or more at a rate of interest at which the government can borrow on the domestic market. The total of aid to the Commonwealth in 1961-62 was well over £140 million, nearly 70 per cent of which went to colonial territories. Nine territories which were dependent in 1960 (British Somaliland, Nigeria, Sierra Leone, Cyprus, Southern Cameroons, Tanganyika, Jamaica, Trinidad and Tobago, and Uganda) had become independent by 1963; nevertheless bilateral aid to colonial territories rose from £57.6 million in 1959-60 to £95.5 million in 1961-62. One of the important channels of aid is the Colonial Development Corporation, whose outlay on capital investment had grown to £91,838,000 by the end of 1962.[7] (As a result of a decision announced in July, 1962, the name has been changed to Commonwealth Development Corporation.) For reasons of space we must omit reference to aid granted by members of the Commonwealth other than the United Kingdom.

The Circulation of Skills

In addition to the capital flows already described, there are numerous criss-cross movements of what we must call human capital from country to country. Unfortunately, the imperfections of the statistics make it impossible to draw up even a rough balance sheet of the interchange of different categories of skill. The best we can do is to select two Commonwealth countries which have introduced new classifications based on the international standard classification of occupations.

Table 10. *Occupations of Immigrants to Australia and Canada, 1950-54, Group according to the International Standard List of Occupations*

Occupational grade	Australia		Canada		Total	
	No. of immigrants (000)	%	No. of immigrants (000)	%	No. of immigrants (000)	%
Agriculture	46	15	88	20	134	18
Skilled	124	40	120	28	244	33
Laborers	38	12	81	19	119	16
Clerical and administrative	45	14	44	10	89	12
Professional	23	7	31	7	54	7
Domestic service	22	7	43	10	65	8
Miscellaneous or occupation not given	16	5	22	6	38	6
Total	314	100	429	100	743	100

Source: J. W. Nixon, "Occupations of Immigrants into the Principal Countries of Immigration in 1950-54," *International Population Conference,* International Union for the Scientific Study of Population, Vienna, 1959, pp. 652-63.

7. *Colonial Development Corporation, Report and Accounts for 1962* (London, H.M.S.O., May, 1963), p. 4.

From Table 10 we see that the skilled element was 40 per cent of the immigration into Australia and 28 per cent of that into Canada in 1950-54. Laborers were 12 per cent and 19 per cent of the totals respectively. The clerical, administrative, and professional grades comprised about a fifth of the inflow into these two countries. A sample analysis of assisted British migrants to Australia in 1959 revealed that 68.2 per cent of them were skilled, 13.7 per cent semiskilled, 6.1 per cent unskilled, and 12.0 per cent professional and intermediate.[8]

One of the most illuminating surveys of emigration from an underdeveloped country is the *Study of External Migration Affecting Jamaica, 1953-55*, by G. W. Roberts and D. I. Mills.[9] In 1955 the rates of outflow as proportions of gainfully employed workers in various skilled occupations in Jamaica were as follows: carpenters 113 per 1000; masons 211 per 1000; mechanics, etc., 183 per 1000; and tailors 79 per 1000; whereas for unskilled laborers the rate was 13 per 1000.[10] The authors concluded that

... the possibility of unplanned emigration grossly depleting the future supplies of skilled workers has to be reckoned with. And in the present state of the island's development it has to be carefully weighed whether emigration of the type now in progress, even if it does contribute to the reduction of population growth, is an unqualified advantage to a country crying aloud for industrial development.[11]

The report also found that

... the departures of unskilled workers from the island over the three year period strongly suggest that this phase of emigration may be expected to continue its increase into 1956 and that the unskilled, the rural dwellers and the illiterates will appear in mounting proportions in the emigration stream to the United Kingdom after 1955.[12]

The Commonwealth Immigrants Act, which came into effect in the United Kingdom in July, 1962, introduced a system of

8. R. T. Appleyard, *British Emigration to Australia* (London, 1964), p. 126.
9. *Supplement to Social and Economic Studies* (University College of the West Indies), VII, No. 2 (1958).
10. *Ibid.*, p. 70.
11. *Ibid.*, p. 124.
12. *Ibid.*, p. 47.

control which puts a premium on skilled immigrants. The Explanatory Memorandum to the bill stated that admission would be readily granted to "persons who possess training, skill or educational qualifications likely to be useful to this country" and to any person "who can support himself and any dependants without working." The late 1950's had seen a sharp increase in immigration into the United Kingdom; the net balance of migration with the rest of the world changed from −72,000 in 1957 to +170,000 in 1961. In the first half of 1962 the net inflow from the Commonwealth (excluding Canada, Australia, New Zealand, South Africa, and Southern Rhodesia) was as high as 97,000.

Under the new Act employment vouchers are issued at the discretion of the British Ministry of Labour in three categories: A, when the applicant has a job to come to in the United Kingdom; B, when the applicant has a recognized skill required in the United Kingdom; C, others, not included above, with priority for persons who have served in H.M. forces in war. In the first year of the operation of the Act (July 1, 1962–June 28, 1963),

Table 11. *Vouchers Issued for Admission to the United Kingdom under the Commonwealth Immigrants Act, July, 1962-June, 1963*

Country of origin	No. of vouchers issued		Percentage distribution by category		
			A (Job secured) %	B (Skill required) %	C (Quota) %
India	17,419	100	6	18	76
Pakistan	10,734	100	17	18	65
Jamaica	3,084	100	7	2	91
Nigeria	2,982	100	4	27	70
Australia	1,533	100	20	55	25
Canada	1,507	100	10	56	34
Barbados	897	100	67	1	32
Hong Kong	994	100	97	1	1
Malta	887	100	39	6	54
Cyprus	853	100	78	1	21
Whole Commonwealth	44,750	100	16	19	65

Source: Memoradum No. 9, June, 1963, by R. B. Davison, Adviser on Migration, Jamaica High Commission, London, based on statistics supplied by the U. K. Home Office and the Ministry of Labour.

44,720 vouchers were issued and 14,680 of them were used. An analysis of the vouchers issued by category and country of origin is given in Table 11.

Well over half of the vouchers issued were for Indians and Pakistanis; 35 per cent of the total for the whole Commonwealth were in categories A and B. The types of skill included in these two groups are indicated in Table 12.

Table 12. *Occupational Analysis of Employment Vouchers Issued in Categories A and B under the Commonwealth Immigrants Act, July, 1962-June, 1963*

	Percentage distribution of vouchers by occupation	
Occupation	Category A (Job secured) %	Category B (Skill required) %
Teachers	1	20
Nurses	4	5
Doctors	1	5
Other graduates and professionals)	3	38
Draftsmen and higher technicians)		6
Engineering craftsmen)	4	9
Building craftsmen		4
Shorthand typists	1	10
Others	85*	3
	100	100
Total number of vouchers	6,977	8,670

*Including mainly shop assistants, waiters, kitchen workers, domestics, and unskilled factory workers.
Source: As for Table II.

Of the 8,670 vouchers issued under category B, 58 per cent were for the professionals, including teachers, 19 per cent skilled craftsmen, 5 per cent doctors, 5 per cent nurses, and 10 per cent shorthand typists. In category A, for persons who had a job waiting for them, as many as 85 per cent were in semiskilled and unskilled occupations, mainly in the service industries.

With regard to the outward movement of skills from the United Kingdom, we shall deal only with one aspect—the supply of technical personnel to the less developed countries of the

Commonwealth. This was given a strong impetus by the setting up of the Department of Technical Co-operation in 1961. Expenditure on technical assistance, including contributions to multilateral agencies, was estimated at £30.3 million in 1963-64, which is six times more than it was in 1957-58. Half of this total was devoted to the Overseas Service Aid Scheme, which provides satisfactory terms of service for British officials serving in dependent territories to enable their employment to be continued after these territories have achieved independence. Thirty-nine governments participate in the scheme, and 15,400 officials were covered by it in 1963. Then there are the Colombo Plan and the Special Commonwealth African Assistance Plan. There are regular arrangements for the loan or secondment of professional people for skilled posts overseas. Moreover, there are over 60,000 overseas students studying full time at British universities and colleges or as trainees in industry; two-thirds of these come from the less developed countries. These examples of what is being done by the United Kingdom are only a part of the total effort; a great deal of technical assistance on similar lines is also being given by the other developed members of the Commonwealth.

Implications for the Future

We turn now very briefly to some of the implications of the picture which emerges from our statistical survey, bearing in mind that it is unavoidably blurred and incomplete.

From official information recently published[13] it is now clear that the international capital position of the United Kingdom is more favorable than has been generally thought hitherto. At the end of 1962 the U.K. government had a net long-term liability to overseas governments of £1,532 million (a net liability of £1,793 million to non-sterling area countries balanced by a net claim of £260 million against overseas sterling coun-

13. "An inventory of U.K. External Assets and Liabilities: End-1962," *Bank of England Quarterly Review*, IV (March, 1964), 22-33.

tries). The U.K. private sector owned assets abroad in the form of portfolio and direct investments amounting to at least £8,000 million, of which £4,600 million was in countries outside the sterling area and £3,400 million in the overseas sterling area. The corresponding liabilities of the U.K. private sector came to £2,800 million, mainly to non-sterling countries. It is interesting to note that U.K. oil companies owned net assets abroad of approximately £1,100 million, of which £300 million was in sterling area countries, whereas U.S. and European oil companies had net assets in the United Kingdom valued at £700 million.

On short-term account the United Kingdom has liabilities equal to £5,200 million (£2,462 million official and £2,738 million private). To meet these there are gold and convertible currency reserves of £1,002 million, government holdings of marketable securities in non-sterling countries valued at £385 million, and drawing rights on the International Monetary Fund of £876 million (£357 million of which automatically). Thus there is a total of £2,263 million of short-term assets, making about 43 per cent of the short-term liabilities. In commenting on the figures, the Bank of England makes the point that, from the point of view of the balance of payments, the profit and loss account on international investment is more important than the balance sheet of items differing widely in liquidity.

There has been a significant change in the international balance of payments structure of the sterling area. There is no longer a matching, as there was before the war, between the overseas sterling area's surplus and the United Kingdom's deficit with the non-sterling countries. The overseas sterling area now tends to have a deficit with non-sterling countries. The influx of capital from outside the sterling area and the internal output of gold are thus playing an important part in the mechanism of the system.[14] This may contain the seeds of future trouble.[15]

14. See A. R. Conan, *The Rationale of the Sterling Area* (London, 1961), pp. 2-8.
15. This was originally written in April, 1964. Trouble came in October. When the new Labour Government took over in the United Kingdom after the general election, the chancellor revealed that the prospective deficit on external account was running at between £700 and £800 million. About half of this

The main challenge of the future is whether the gap between the average standard of living and the rate of economic growth in the less developed countries and the rich countries of the Commonwealth can be narrowed. Our survey has shown that the great increase in international private investment has been predominantly within the rich sector: in the 1950's only 18 per cent of total private investment in sterling countries went into industries other than oil and bauxite in the least developed parts of the Commonwealth. The growing activity of governments in granting aid is only a partial offset to the strong propensity of private capital to go to the developed countries. Similarly, in the case of skilled personnel, there is an intense demand in North America, Europe, and the developed countries of the Commonwealth. The underdeveloped nations are ill-equipped to compete with the rich countries for the limited supplies of skill. In the Commonwealth, as in the Western world as a whole, there is a two-way traffic of skilled people between the rich and poor sectors. There is, on the one hand, a "perverse" outward movement of trained persons from the underdeveloped to the advanced countries; on the other hand, there is a reverse movement of government-financed technical personnel from the advanced countries to the underdeveloped.[16] In some senses the latter is just an expensive means of plugging the growing leak of indigenous talent from countries which need it most.

We must reject the simple view that the principles of the free society impel us to regard all free international movements of skilled personnel as inherently desirable. The relevant criterion is not marginal private productivity but marginal *social* productivity. Given this criterion, some of these international flows are perverse in the economic sense, and this is probably one of

---

was on long-term capital account. To reduce the trade gap, a surcharge of 15 per cent on the price of all manufactured imports was imposed, and a financial stimulus was given to exports. A severe sterling crisis developed in November, 1964, and strong measures were introduced to cope with it; they included a special Budget, an increase in Bank Rate from 5 per cent to 7 per cent, and the mobilization of $3000 million of special aid for sterling.

16. See the present writer's "International Factor Movements and Unequal Rates of Growth," *The Manchester School of Economic and Social Studies*, XXIX, No. 1 (1961), 1-21.

the reasons why the gap between the low-income and advanced nations is tending to widen. We need much more statistical information on the magnitude and character of these flows.[17]

Finally, there is the central problem on which the attention of the United Nations Conference on Trade and Development was focused. As a group the less developed countries derive between 80 and 90 per cent of their earnings from primary produce; because of unfavorable terms of trade, their export earnings over the period 1954-62 increased by only 30 per cent as compared with a corresponding increase of 70 per cent for the developed areas. As a market for the products of poor countries, Great Britain has a good record. In 1963 about a third of her total imports came from underdeveloped countries; she buys more manufactured goods from these countries than does the whole of the European Economic Community. Any attempt to solve the problem by maintaining artificially high prices for primary produce would be retrograde. If the gain to less developed countries from investment aid is not to be offset by losses on the terms of trade, it is essential that the rich countries should agree on ambitious measures to solve the international liquidity problem.

17. For a brief account of some of the problems involved, see W. Brand, *Requirements and Resources of Scientific and Technical Personnel in Ten Asian Countries* (Paris: UNESCO, 1960).

20

The Creation of Capital and Skills within Commonwealth Countries in Africa

Pius Okigbo*

At the end of World War II the Union of South Africa was the only independent Commonwealth country in Africa. In the twenty years following, Ghana (1957), Nigeria (1960), Sierra Leone (1961), Tanganyika (1961), Uganda (1962), Kenya (1963), Zanzibar (1964), Malawi, Zambia and Gambia (1965) have become independent, adding color and variety to the Commonwealth club. The end of the colonial period in Africa has introduced special problems into Commonwealth relationships and has made all the more urgent the need for assistance for the enlargement of the capital stock and the development of skills. Our purpose in this paper is to assess the magnitude of the problem and evaluate the special contribution that the Commonwealth can make towards its solution.

Any analysis of the current difficulties of the newly independent nations in Africa must recognize two phenomena. First, the absolute level of savings is too low relative to the needs of the territories. The low level of income determines the capacity to save in the economy; however much the countries may be willing to save, the limit on what can be done is imposed by the low level of income. This may be no more than saying that the new countries are poor because they are poor. There is, therefore, little prospect that they can lift themselves up by their own boot

* Economic advisor to the government of the Federal Republic of Nigeria and Nigerian ambassador to the European Economic Community.

straps; they need external assistance to maintain the rate of growth they have so far attained. Second, it may be possible to achieve some economies by a more judicious deployment of current savings. Some reallocation of the existing use of resources may lead to a greater efficiency in resource use and thereby raise the rate of growth of output.

The Colonial Period

The colonial period had similar features and yielded similar results in each of the territories. The tasks of the colonial administrations could be reduced to two broad categories: first, the establishment of an administration for the maintenance of law and order; second, the promotion of trade in exports with a view to making the territories as solvent as possible and with a view to reducing their dependence on the British Treasury for financial support for their day-to-day expenses. Underneath these two objectives was the presumption that following the classical comparative cost doctrine, the territories were singularly suited to produce tropical crops required for the industries of Europe (i.e., Britain) and, in some cases, they were singularly endowed by nature for the production of certain minerals. Consequently, the expansion of production possibilities in respect of crops and minerals was a cardinal plank of colonial economic policy.

In West Africa the colonial governments saw it as their prime duty (consistent with the maintenance of social peace in an area so many times the size of Britain) to protect the land of the natives from alienation to foreigners. Plantation companies seeking new areas for investment were refused land for agricultural development; some of them had to go to the Belgian Congo to realize their ambitions. In East Africa, particularly in the Rhodesias, alienation of land was relatively free. Consequently, there developed in East and Central Africa a settlement of European landed gentry at once removed from the native population except in the relation of landlord and peasant, master and servant. The social tensions that preceded the attainment of independence in Kenya and Nyasaland are therefore in sharp contrast to the relatively pacifist transition in West Africa.

The public authorities accepted responsibility for the provision of those conditions that would enable the private sector to carry out its business with the minimum of government intervention. This role consisted in the establishment of basic (and minimum) infrastructure—roads, railways (sometimes for military reasons), harbors, and communications facilities. Since attention was focused early on agricultural development (by peasants in West Africa and immigrant farmers in East and Central Africa) and on mining development (by expatriate companies), the public sector confined itself to the dissemination of information and provision of facilities for the transport of the output of the fields and the mines from the hinterland to the coast. The railway complex that got fastened on West Africa bears testimony to this principle. Similarly, utilities were developed—water, electricity, telegraph, and telephone—partly to assist the administration but more often in response to keenly felt need rather than in planned development. These installations were therefore often already inadequate at the time they were commissioned.

The colonial era also saw the beginnings of the introduction of education on the British model in the African territories. The needs of the early administrators were relatively simple: there was no question of bringing the natives into direct participation in the higher arts of government. In Nigeria and Ghana the experiment of indirect rule so eloquently argued by Lugard led to the use of existing political institutions for the government of the territories. But in the final analysis, control was firmly exercised by the administrators, all of whom were expatriate. The need for local participation in the functions of the administering authority was for interpreters (for whom literacy in English was the only qualification), clerks, and undifferentiated labor. For the training of such men all that was required was several years of schooling. In East Africa the situation was even worse. The availability of relatively cheap but relatively semiskilled Asian labor (cheap relative to imported British labor), first for the construction of the East African railways and subsequently for the East African technical services, reduced the urgency of training Africans in any skills that went beyond simple literacy.

In spite of these circumstances many Africans triumphed over their handicaps. There were people like Samuel Ajayi Crowther, who rose to be a bishop in the Anglican faith; like Aggrey, who rose to be the vice-principal of Achimota College; or Henry Carr, who rose to be director of education in Nigeria. Such men were exceptional in the sense that they would have triumphed anywhere.

No group recognized the need to have Africans trained in the technical skills more than the technical departments of government. The departments of public works, railways, marine, posts, and telegraphs soon realized that their success as technical arms of government could not be secured simply on a large army of clerks. They opened technical schools that served as pioneers in organized training in the engineering arts and technology. The numbers were few. Some of the graduates rose to the rank of foremen, for the professional engineering cadres were still closed to Africans. It was perhaps only in Ghana that the induction of Africans into the technological arts was more rapid and most farsighted. This is explained by the fact that Ghana had a succession of very forward-looking and progressive governors.

Public Investment Programs

A review of the colonial era cannot end on such a severe note. No one should underestimate the achievement of the period or the difficult circumstances under which the administrators worked. In each territory the colonial administration started from scratch: new towns, roads, infrastructure, and housing had to be established. The rapid growth in some of these African economies today would not have been possible but for the build-up of the social overhead capital in the previous sixty years.

By the end of World War II the colonial governments were under considerable pressure to prepare long-range programs of economic and social development. Under the Colonial Development and Welfare Acts, particularly that of 1945, funds were earmarked by the U.K. government for assistance towards the development of the dependencies. Governments became committed to a policy of conscious promotion of development. Plans were formulated in anticipation of needs and implemented as funds were released. These investment programs were not development plans in the strict sense of the term; there was no apparatus in any of the dependencies in Africa for meshing the sector programs or for relating the individual projects to the overall needs, priorities, and targets of the economy. It should be recalled that national accounting in the colonies was to come several years later, and most of the territories concerned had not yet even established a department of statistics.

The programs presented for finance covered the ten-year span 1946-55. They included both economic development proper, e.g., harbors and railways, as well as social development, e.g., town and country planning, rural water supplies, and health schemes. From Table 1 below we see the magnitude of the programs and the level of achievement in the first five years up

Table 1. *Colonial Development and Welfare Programs 1946-55* (£ million)

	Sierra Leone	Gold Coast	Nigeria	Kenya	Tanganyika	Uganda	EAHC*	Rhodesia	Nyasaland
Total program†	27	143	147	87	81	69	107	84	34
Expenditure by 1950	9	41	64	39	22	25	49	23	7

*EAHC refers to the East African High Commission which had responsibility for the common services like posts and telegraphs, income taxation, customs, railways, and harbors.
†These figures do not include supplementary programs introduced within the period.

to 1950; by that date greater devolution of power to the nationals of the territories had grudgingly but surely become a plank of colonial policy.

By 1950 the governments and public authorities had come to recognize their increasing role as an engine of development. They went into direct action in agriculture. They now adopted a policy of not only encouraging private initiative in industry but also of directly participating in industrial activities. In 1950 only four or five establishments in Nigeria could properly be described as manufacturing on a factory basis. By 1957 there were more than 110 establishments of this sort and government had entered into industrial production, particularly in cement and textiles. Consequently the scope and size of public investment had widened and grown relatively to the private sector.

The contribution of the public sector to the capital investment of the past sixty years was also helped by the willingness of the peasant community to experiment in new ways of doing things. It is so easily forgotten today that in 1900 the exports of West Africa consisted mainly of palm produce and minerals. In 1913 palm oil and kernels constituted 75.2 per cent of all Nigerian exports by value. By 1937 cocoa, cotton, and groundnuts had been introduced on a scale large enough to tilt the proportions. In the introduction of these new crops the colonial governments played an important part by providing seedings and technical information.

If we take only two representative countries, one in the west and the other in the east, we can see the achievement from the following indices:

Nigeria (1960)   roads (41,065 miles), vehicles (57,000), electricity (420.9 million kwt. hrs. generated), railway (1.3 million ton miles per annum), ports (6.5 million tons annually), telephones (38,690).

Kenya (1960)   roads (25,815 miles), vehicles (89,505), ports (4.5 million tons), telephones (39,900), electricity (402.6 million kwt. generated and imported compared with 17.2 million in 1938).

The Private Sector

Historically, foreign private investment in Commonwealth African countries had gone into only three channels: trade, plantations, and mining. Some of the other fields like public utilities and railways had been pre-empted as areas for public investment and were therefore not open for private investment. Consequently, investment has followed the path traced by the contacts between Europe and Africa.

When the slave trade was abolished in the nineteenth century, many of the slave dealers on both sides reverted to the legitimate items of commerce: in West Africa this took the form of trade in palm oil and kernels; in East Africa, in spices. In return for these exports the Africans imported alcoholic drinks, textiles, and glass jewelry. But trade was largely by barter, and the hinterland had not been opened up.

It should be obvious that this form of activity would not require a large investment in fixed capital. Instead, in view of distances and the time lag between order and delivery, accumulation took the form of large inventories of merchandise and heavy working capital requirements. The merchandise trade of the nineteenth and early twentieth centuries did not give rise to significant investment in fixed capital in the African countries. It is of interest that the United African Company, the largest trading firm in Nigeria, had in 1939 only £.75 million in fixed assets and £2.5 million in floating assets. The £.75 million represented nearly half of all the fixed assets standing in the name of the Company in all its business lines in Nigeria and elsewhere. The values for other and smaller companies are negligible. Since World War II, however, the expatriate trading firms have increased their domestic fixed capital investment, partly by modernizing the structures and partly by extending to new lines.[1]

1. The rate of investment in fixed capital has grown significantly since World War II. The U.A.C. and other Unilever Associated Companies spent on capital account £3.7, £3.1 and £4.2 million in 1957, 1958, and 1959 respectively.

The second channel open was agriculture. In West Africa the policy of the territorial governments in not allowing alienation of land to European farmers denied West Africa foreign investment from this source. In East Africa, particularly in Kenya and the Rhodesias where the climate was more suitable for permanent European settlement, the growth of the East African economies depended almost exclusively on foreign investment in agriculture. It is, of course, a matter for debate whether the gain in foreign investment is a price worth paying in return for the complex social problems and tensions that it has generated.[2] The contrast in the routes towards the development of agriculture is striking, but the results have not been too dissimilar. The readiness with which West African peasant farmers have taken over the introduction of new crops that were not native to West Africa has been extraordinary. Between 1900 and 1937 cocoa had taken firm root in Ghana (300,000 tons) and Nigeria (116,000 tons), and groundnuts in Nigeria (285,000 tons). Similarly in East Africa new crops were introduced through European entrepeneurship with the result that crops unknown at the end of the nineteenth century had become staple crops by 1937: sisal (133,000 tons), cotton (200 million lbs.), coffee (87,000 cwt.)

But perhaps the most outstanding example of how European settlement has contributed to the transformation of a hitherto very poor country is the story of Southern Rhodesia. The first European settlement occurred in 1890. By 1919 tobacco had become the main source of income for the territory, mainly as a result of European farming; the net output of European agriculture had risen from £1.98 million in 1925 to £45.1 million in 1957.

In Kenya, which provides another example of private foreign investment in agriculture, *net* investment in agriculture by non-Africans was running in the 1950's, at an average of between £4

The expenditure on industrial undertakings rose from £636,000 in 1957 to £1,885,000 in 1959. Cf. U.A.C., *Statistical and Economic Review*, No. 26, Oct., 1961, p. 53.

2. See my "Factors in West African Economic History," *Journal of World History*, I (No. 4, 1957), 226-30.

million and £5.5 million annually. Non-African farmers accounted in 1960 for £37.9 million, or nearly 80 per cent of a total net output of £47.5 million from all farmers. The picture in Kenya and Southern Rhodesia is in sharp contrast to that in Nigeria and Ghana, where all agricultural output in 1960 was from indigenous peasant production.

The third channel of investment by foreign enterprise is in mining. Apart from coal mining, which was taken on by the colonial government in Nigeria, all other mining activity has been left to private capital. Mining (until oil was found recently in Nigeria and until diamonds became an important source of income in Sierra Leone) has been a more important activity in Central Africa than in West Africa. In the Rhodesias, as Barber has observed,[3] mining has historically been the mainstay of the economy. The range is wide: gold, asbestos, chrome ore, copper, cobalt, lead, and zinc. Investment in Southern Rhodesian mining began with gold, then moved into asbestoes and chrome ore. Northern Rhodesia has consistently specialized in copper production, into which large resources have been committed. Up to 1936, £25 million had been invested in the copper mining industry. Since then expansion has been more from profits than from fresh capital from abroad. Yet the inflow of capital has been substantial compared, for instance, with the capital investment in mining in West Africa. What is indeed remarkable is the ratio of loan to equity capital in the expansion of the mines: the United States has provided £13 million for the expansion of the copper mines, while equity capital from outside has been less than £8 million since the initial development.[4]

In West Africa the most notable source of mineral wealth until the 1960's was tin, produced in Nigeria for more than fifty years. Frankel had estimated the gross foreign investment in Nigeria between 1870 and 1936 at £75.1 million (this makes no allowance for depreciation).[5] Private investment accounted for £40.3 million, representing 53.5 per cent of this total. By

3. W. J. Barber, *The Economy of British Central Africa* (Oxford, 1961), pp. 117-26.
4. *Ibid.*, pp. 124-26.
5. S. H. Frankel, *Capital Investment in Africa* (London, 1938), pp. 158-59.

any measure this is a poor performance. It is clear therefore that the West African countries have had very little investment from overseas for their development and that the progress that had been achieved up to 1936 had to be secured on a shoe string. Since 1946 the search for petroleum, begun in 1937, has been resumed with vigor, and by the end of 1958 a reported £40 million had been spent on exploration.

Investment in manufacturing prior to 1950 was negligible. One major reason is clearly the size of the local markets. Although the past fifty years provide a record of rapid rise in the money income of the territories, each country taken by itself constitutes a relatively small market for manufactures. The minimum economic scale for the production of most commodities that are traded in the territories was often too large for the individual territory. Unquestionably this limitation is imposed by the inward-looking nature of most manufacturing enterprises in Africa—export markets in adjacent or neighboring areas may exist, but they do not enter into the calculation of the investor who reckons on the potential size of the internal market. Consequently the expatriate firms have shied away from manufacturing.

Yet this proposition cannot be wholly true. In 1953 Professor Arthur Lewis reviewed the industrial possibilities of the Gold Coast and found that the Gold Coast market could support a number of manufacturing activities that had hitherto not been taken up seriously.[6] The fact was that the territories themselves did not engage in industrial promotion, in the dissemination of information, and even more important, the firms then operating in Ghana were for the most part trading organizations and could not be expected to spearhead the transition from a purely mercantile to an industrial society.

The attitude of the extraterritorial expatriate firms engaged in trade in West Africa has been described succinctly by Mars.[7] They are in the main branches of firms with headquarters in the

6. See W. Arthur Lewis, *Industrialization and the Gold Coast* (Accra: Govt. Printer, 1953), pp. 3-7.
7. See Margery Perham, ed., *Mining Commerce and Finance in Nigeria* (London, 1947), pp. 67-70.

metropolitan country; they are engaged in trade in imports and exports; they are their own carriers; they have long-standing contracts with manufacturers in Britain and elsewhere and often have an interest in the manufacturing industries in Britain. They understand marketing but not manufacturing. They could not as trading firms therefore encourage investment in local manufactures for it was not in their best interest as merchandise dealers. Nor was it in their interest to tie up their capital in equipment when by investing in inventories they could earn a greater rate of return.

In addition there had developed a myth that African labor was indifferent, irresponsible, and unaccustomed to industrial discipline. It was thought, therefore, that African labor could not be readily taught industrial skills. This belief was current for long enough to dampen the enthusiasm of those who might have wished to invest in industry. Major Orde Browne's study of labor conditions in West Africa[8] went a long way to dispel this notion by establishing that African wage earners responded well to training and adapted satisfactorily to industrial discipline. In Central Africa the existence of a large population of European stock provided a pool from which skilled workers could be drawn. The same situation was true in Kenya and to a limited extent in Uganda and Tanganyika. In addition, the presence of a large Asian population cushioned off the African population from exposure to the higher skills and management.

Because of the common policy in neighboring Northern Rhodesia and Nyasaland, export-oriented industries seemed to have taken root in Southern Rhodesia. Manufacturing accounted for a net output of roughly £37.7 million in 1955. The main activities have been metal manufactures (excluding the processing of minerals), alcoholic and soft drinks, transport equipment, chemicals and chemical products, clothing and footwear, cement, and rubber products. In Nigeria, on the other hand, in 1950 only five establishments could be described as being run on a factory basis, with a net output of less than £3 million. The expansion

8. Major G. St. Orde Browne, *Labour Conditions in West Africa* (London: H.M.S.O., 1941).

in the 1950's has been due to more direct government participation in industry of all types, varying from construction materials such as cement and steel rods to such light consumer
goods as alcoholic beverages and soft drinks.

In assessing the growth of industrial production in the
Commonwealth African countries we must therefore not forget
that this area of activity is relatively new. But it is an area that
is growing rapidly and in which many governments have put
great faith. In view of the importance attached by the public
authorities to the growth of manufacturing industry, we can
ask ourselves whether these African countries can induce a flow
of private investment in the volume required to change the
structure of the economies. In Kenya manufacturing accounts
for 9.7 per cent of the gross domestic product; in Tanganyika for
4.3 per cent. In Nigeria, however, the output of manufacturing accounts for less than 2 per cent of the gross domestic product. To
raise this proportion to 5 per cent would require investment in industry of the order of more than £120 million. It would become
evident that a net inflow of capital of this order of magnitude from
abroad is not likely to be forthcoming in the near future. Unless
resources are released from other areas of activity to enable the
public sector to devote more resources to the growth of manufacturing business, the aspirations of many of the African countries will be frustrated.

Creation of Skills

We have already touched upon the requirements for skills
in the early colonial period. The task of training Africans and
providing the requisite skills was left partly to the government
(whose needs were simple) and partly to the missionaries (whose
needs were even simpler). In the traditional fields into which
European capital had been invested—trade, plantations, and
mining—the need was for a mass of undifferentiated African
labor. Many Africans acquired skills in merchandising, but the
limitations imposed by illiteracy, lack of proper accounting

systems, etc., made it impossible for even the very successful among then to operate on a scale anywhere near the scale of the middle-range European firms.

Perhaps the first attempt at assessing the shortage of skills in any African Commonwealth country was the attempt in Nigeria (1960) to establish the needs for intermediate and higher level manpower.[9] The calculations of Professor Harbison in the resulting report suggest that to maintain a 4 per cent rate of growth of the economy (the rate that has obtained since 1950) Nigeria would need in the decade between 1960 and 1970 various intermediate and higher level personnel of the following magnitude:

Table 2. *Manpower Needs (Nigeria 1960-1970)*

Activity	Senior category	Intermediate category
Agriculture, forestry, and fishing	2,100	4,000
Mining, quarrying, and petroleum	1,200	1,500
Manufacturing	3,000	4,000
Construction	1,800	2,600
Electricity, water services	300	1,100
Commerce	4,000	2,500
Transport and allied services	2,700	4,800
Government	6,000	13,000
Miscellaneous	1,500	1,900
Graduate teachers	8,400	—
Other teachers	—	20,300
Total	31,200	54,700

We have commented on Harbison's method elsewhere;[10] whatever the criticisms we may have, we have to admit that Harbison's data give an idea of the order and magnitude of the needs. The cost of installing the facilities for implementing this program has been estimated at more than £120 million at 1961 prices. In effect, therefore, the training in skills and technology required to sustain the Nigerian economy is clearly beyond the

9. *Investment in Education* (Lagos, 1960), Part II, chap. i. This report is often referred to as the Ashby Report after the chairman of the Commission, Sir Eric Ashby.

10. See my "Criteria for Public Expenditures in Education," paper prepared for the Conference of the International Economic Association, 1963.

resources of Nigeria and will severely tax the resources of the richer nations.

We have taken the Nigerian case only as an illustration of the need. The same problem exists in even greater measure in the countries of East Africa and Central Africa. It is clear that they will have to depend on the assistance from the Commonwealth for a long time to come. There are many ways in which the leading members of the Commonwealth can make their own contribution to the creation of skills in Africa. Outside of government services and the school systems, the private investor can make an important contribution towards the technological change in the newer countries. This, as Fforde has argued, can come through any of four different routes which he has described as the individual route, long-term joint venture, short-term joint ventures, and product-specialized foreign investment.[11] Each of these methods has its special merits and may be more appropriate in one country than in another. The private investor moving along an individual route may not have the opportunity to affect a large number of local people. The scope for the diffusion of technical knowledge and skills through this channel is limited unless there are large numbers of such individual entrepreneurs. Joint ventures, whether short-term or long-term (for a stipulated period), appear to have had a greater impact on skill formation.

The idea of establishing a pool of technicians from which Commonwealth countries, especially the new ones in Africa, can draw to meet their needs has often been canvassed. In our view, for such a pool to be effective it will have to be so large and so varied that its organization and its management will raise problems. The United Kingdom is, in fact, doing what appears similar to this scheme by making available to overseas countries the services of specialists who are difficult to find under normal circumstances. But perhaps the country that can offer more than any other in some of these fields is India. It may well be that technical assistance within the Commonwealth

11. J. S. Fforde, *An International Trade in Managerial Skills* (Oxford, 1957).

should be so organized that funds made available by one country need not be tied to personnel coming from the donor country, for it may be cheaper in the long run for West Africans to use Indian personnel on technical assistance functions and pay for them from funds provided, say, by Canada or the United Kingdom.

However, the needs of the African countries today extend beyond the facilities opened up by the import of specialist personnel. The experience of East Africa and to a lesser extent West Africa is that the most urgent need is to develop elementary and primary skills. The need in agriculture is less for entomologists, agronomists, and plant pathologists than for extension service agents, field staff, and supervisors. In medicine there is need for general practitioners and specialists but the more serious bottleneck is for laboratory technicians, clinical staff, etc. In the construction industry we need masons and carpenters more than architects and engineers. The professional personnel can always be imported (at a high cost admittedly) but the numbers are fewer relative to the supporting staff without whom the professional staff will be unable to devote their time to the more serious branch of their work.

From the foregoing discussion several observations stand out. First, the role of the public sector in the creation of capital and skills in the emergent African states will tend to increase in the future. This conclusion stems from the extension of the scope and sphere of direct government activity. The traditional role of the public sector as providers merely of the infrastructure of development has now given way to a more pervasive role in which the governments of the newer nations have gone directly into agriculture and industry and, in some cases, are even experimenting with retail distribution.

The second observation is that the magnitude of the needs of the new countries suggests a level of assistance beyond the resources of the Commonwealth. The United Kingdom apart, no other Commonwealth country is in a position to offer assistance of the magnitude or form sufficient to make a serious dent in the enormous problem facing the African countries. Even then, the assistance that has been forthcoming from Britain to the independent African countries on a government-to-government basis seems relatively less than what is going to the Commonwealth countries in Asia.[12]

The third observation is that the new countries themselves will have to make far greater efforts to mobilize their own internal resources than they were ever expected or compelled to in the colonial period. One reason for this is that independence has in itself engendered a higher level of expectations. The success of the governments in the newly independent African countries depends in part on the degree to which they cope with the increasing range of economic difficulties that seem now to abound since independence.

If the Commonwealth cannot satisfy the needs for the finance of development, it can go a long way to alleviating the shortage in skills that is plaguing the implementation of development programs. The Commonwealth has a unique opportunity here: the traditions are broadly similar and commercial experience and practices, accounting units and systems, economic institutions, all have the same roots in Britain. It is therefore easier to draw from the experience that is so similar than to stretch across to alien institutions and practices.

Yet the shortages that plague the new nations are also evident in the more mature members of the Commonwealth. No single Commonwealth country is in a position to bear the burden of providing the skills required in African countries. The search for skills must be extended beyond the Commonwealth. But if it were possible to apply the resources of the Commonwealth

12. Between 1951 and 1960 the total United Kingdom government aid to the less developed countries, including non-Commonwealth countries, amounted to £880 million. The annual volume of aid has risen sharply from between £70 million and £80 million in the mid-1950's to £150.6 million in 1960. Private investment has been running at between £140 million and £160 million per annum. The combined government and private assistance investment amounted to £2,800 million (including investment in the oil industry) between the end of World War II and 1960. Of this, government assistance accounted for £1,000 million. Much of this, however, has gone elsewhere than to the Commonwealth African countries, the largest recipients being in Asia—India, Pakistan, and Malaya. See H. J. P. Arnold, *Aid for Developing Countries* (London, 1963), pp. 70-86.

jointly in procuring personnel from all Commonwealth sources, the gap in higher level manpower could be alleviated in many countries.

In fact, however, the bottleneck is at the lower level. This category of skills must be trained locally and on the spot if the cost of skill formation is not to cripple the lean resources of African countries. It is here, more than anywhere else that the new African nations need assistance—in men (teachers), money, and materials. It is here also that the Commonwealth can, as a unit, play a significant role in raising the average level of technology in the newer African countries.

21

The Formation of Capital and Skills in the Commonwealth Countries of South and Southeast Asia

Nurul Islam[*]

Growth of Income and Investment

In the last decade the pace of economic development in India, Pakistan, Ceylon, and Malaysia territories has considerably quickened. The annual rates of growth in the gross national product during 1950-60 were 3.3 per cent in Ceylon, 3.9 per cent in Malaya, 3.3 per cent in India, and 2.5 per cent in Pakistan. During the same period per capita G.N.P. increased at considerably lower rates, i.e., by 0.8 per cent in Ceylon, 1.4 per cent in India, and 0.5 per cent in Pakistan.[1] This is due to a rapidly increasing population, the annual rates of growth of population varying between 2.5 per cent and 4.4 per cent as between different countries.[2]

The increase in investment has been one of the most important determinants of growth. During the same period the average gross investment rates (i.e., investment-G.N.P. ratios) were 12.2 per cent in Ceylon, 16.9 per cent in India, and 7.8

[*] Professor and head of the Department of Economics, University of Dacca; Director, Pakistan Institute of Development Economics.

1. "Population and Economic Growth in the Countries of the ECAFE Region 1960-1980," an unpublished paper prepared by ECAFE, Economic Development Branch, Research and Planning Division (Bangkok, 1963).

2. United Kingdom, Department of Technical Co-operation, *Technical Co-operation under the Colombo Plan, Report for 1962-63* (Colombo, Oct., 1963), p. 9.

per cent in Pakistan.[3] During the period 1955-57 the ratio of gross investment to gross domestic product was 11.0 per cent in the Federation of Malaya.[4] In each of these countries, there has been a rise in the rate of investment starting from relatively modest beginnings in the early 1950's. For example, in Pakistan the ratio of net investment to net domestic product rose from the low level of 2 per cent in 1950 to 8 per cent in 1955 and fell to 6 per cent in 1960. In India the net investment income ratio rose from 6.3 per cent in 1950-51 to 7.5 per cent in 1953-54–1955-56 and to 11.3 per cent in 1956-57–1958-59.[5] Data on domestic capital formation are very scanty for such territories as North Borneo, Sarawak, and Singapore. However, an idea of the rate of investment in these territories can be obtained from the growth of public development expenditures. (See Table 1.)

Table 1. *Annual Average Development Expenditure in the Public Sector* (Three-year averages, £1,000,000)

	1953-54/ 1955-56	1956-57/ 1958-59	1959-60/ 1961-62
North Borneo	2.66	2.33	2.75
Sarawak	3.00	2.96	3.90
Singapore	12.30	16.40	19.50
Burma	38.7	30.3	39.8
Ceylon	25.8	34.8	31.3
India	384.2	748.4	1221.7
Malaya	16.5	59.1	73.8
Pakistan	51.85	122.3	143.5

Source: The Colombo Plan, *Annual Report of the Consultative Committee* (London, H.M.S.O.), 1955 (4th), p. 8; 1957 (5th), p. 8; 1957 (6th), p. 10; 1958 (7th), p. 11; 1960 (8th), p. 11; 1961 (9th), p. 10; 1962 (10th), p. 11.   The figures in national currencies have been converted nto sterling pounds at a constant rate of exchange.   The intertemporal and intercountry comparisons of expenditures on development heads suffer from a number of limitations such as differences in the scope and definitions of development expenditure as well as in the price levels which affect the real value of development expenditures.   The figures for the years 1960-61 and 1961-62 are budget estimates; they usually differ from actual expenditures, figures of which are published only after a time-lag.

3. ECAFE, "Population and Economic Growth."

4. UN/ECAFE, *Economics Survey of Asia and the Far East, 1961* (Bangkok, 1962), p. 23.

5. M. Huq, *A Strategy of Economic Planning* (Karachi, 1963), Table 6, pp. 72-73. Commonwealth Economic Committee, *Commonwealth Development Financing: India* (London, 1963), Table 3, p. 20.

Public development expenditures have recorded a rise in all the territories, more so in Malaya, India, and Pakistan than in North Borneo and Sarawak.

In view of a high import content of investment expenditures in these countries, imports of capital goods may also be treated as a reasonable index of total domestic capital formation in both public and private sectors.[6] It is not only that a large proportion of capital goods is imported from abroad, but also often domestic capital goods industries depend heavily for their requirements of raw materials or intermediate inputs on imports from abroad. As Table 2 indicates, in all the countries there has been relatively

Table 2. *Change in Value of Imports*
(Index for 1958-60, with 1951-53=100)

	Food	Other Con-sumption Goods	Materials Chiefly for Con-sumption Goods	Materials Chiefly for Capi-tal Goods	Capital Goods	Total
Ceylon	100	126	130	109	149	117
Federation of Malaya and Singapore	97	94	118	153	109	107
India	82	76	93	186	213	126
North Borneo	157	220	416	214	242	227
Pakistan	105	69	129	137	133	117
Sarawak	114	120	108	155	149	113

Source: UN/ECAFE, *Economic Survey . . . 1962*, p. 87.

a greater increase in recent years in these two categories of imports, which has accelerated the rate of capital formation. India has recorded a very high rate of increase and so also have countries like North Borneo and Sarawak, which started from very modest beginnings.

6. For example, in Ceylon the imports of capital goods constituted 86 per cent of fixed capital formation in 1952-53 and 74.7 per cent in 1957-59. In India and Pakistan the percentages were 19.2 per cent and 42.2 per cent respectively in 1952-53 and 23.7 per cent and 41.0 per cent respectively in 1957-59. Since data on imports comprise both public and private account imports, they offer an index of capital formation both in public and private sectors. This is relevant especially for those countries which do not have direct estimates of private investment. UN/ECAFE, *Economic Survey . . . 1961*, p. 25.

Pattern of Investment

In most of the countries under review, public investment has played an important and often a critical role in increasing the rate of capital formation. The reasons are various. In some countries, such as Ceylon and India, a general climate of thought tending towards a socialist pattern of economy seemed to prevail with varying degrees of emphasis in the course of the last decade. In other countries, such as Pakistan, the role of public enterprise has been conceived more as a catalyst in the process of economic development. Public enterprise often has initiated new industries which require large capital or a scale of organization which exceeds the limits of ability of a private enterprise. In Pakistan it has supplemented private enterprise, and in some cases public enterprises, after they have become successful, have been transferred to private hands. In the field of social overhead (facilities which need large investments and yield returns only in the long run and in which social returns are usually higher than private returns), public enterprises continue to occupy a dominant position in all the countries. Moreover, the growing importance of foreign aid provided mainly under the aegis of foreign public agencies has contributed in no small measure to the growth of the public sector.

The share of public investment in total government expenditure has generally recorded a rise in the past; the largest increase has taken place in Malaya, Singapore, and Sarawak, increases being two and one-half times, four times, and one-half times respectively during 1951-1962. In 1962-63 public investment constituted about 50 per cent of total government expenditure in North Borneo, Sarawak, and Singapore; 25 per cent in Pakistan; 28 per cent in India and Ceylon; and 37 per cent in Malaya.[7] Moreover, the relative importance of public investment in total domestic capital formation has also increased. In both India and Pakistan, the relative importance of public

7. UN/ECAFE, *Economic Survey . . . 1960*, Part II, chap. v, p. 72; *ibid., 1962*, Appendix, Table 34, pp. 232-33.

investment is increasing through time, while in Malaya there is a certain amount of decline. For example, in India it increased from 24 per cent in 1951-53 to 36 per cent in 1958-60, while in Pakistan it declined between 1950 and 1955 and subsequently rose from 48 per cent in 1954-56 to 60 per cent in 1958-60. The share of public investment in total investment expenditure is the highest in Pakistan (60 per cent), with Ceylon occupying a close second position (48 per cent).[8]

The role of public investment in accelerating the rate of capital formation and its effect on the growth of an economy are more clearly evident from an analysis of the composition of public investment. (See Table 3.)

As Table 3 indicates, an overwhelmingly large proportion of public investment is concentrated on the development of social and economic overhead facilities such as transport, communication, power, irrigation, and water supplies; the proportion of such investment is significantly higher in Malaya, Singapore, Sarawak, and North Borneo than in other countries. Only in Ceylon, India, and Pakistan is there a noticeable public investment in the field of directly productive projects such as the manufacturing industry. The relative importance of public investment in industry, including small- and large-scale industries, has increased in India in the course of the last decade. The largest single element in public investment in all the countries is the investment in transport and communication facilities. The expenditure on health and education has also shown an upward trend in all of the countries.

Investment in economic overheads such as transportation, communication, roads, power facilities, irrigation, etc., has been undertaken both in response to the pressure of existing demand as well as in anticipation of future demand. Such investments generate external economies, for they lower the cost of inputs in, and hence induce the development of, directly productive projects in the fields of industry and agriculture. As a consequence,

8. The figures include changes in inventories except in the case of Pakistan. *Ibid., 1956*, pp. 194-95; *ibid., 1960*, pp. 128-29; *ibid., 1961*, pp. 172-73; and *ibid., 1962*, pp. 190-91. Huq, *A Strategy*, p. 230.

A Decade of the Commonwealth

Table 3. *Pattern of Public Investment* (Per Cent of Total Investment)

	Agri-culture	Power and Energy	Industry, includ-ing Fuels and Miner-als	Trans-port and Communi-cations	Construc-tion	Health and Educa-tion	Others
India							
1950-59	29.0	8.0	13.0	32.0	(a)	16.0	2.0
1956-57/							
1960-61	20.6	9.7	23.4	28.3	(a)	10.3	7.7
Ceylon							
(1950-59)	35.0	8.0	3.0	22.0	13.0	11.0	8.0
Pakistan							
1955-60	14.3	30.0*	13.7	14.3	(a)	5.3	12.4(b)
1960-63	12.3	33.1	10.8	21.6	(a)	8.8	13.4(b)
Federation of Malaya							
1953-55	9.4	(a)	17.4†	22.9	13.2‡	8.1	29.3(b)
1960-62	16.2	(a)	11.4	20.2	28.1§	15.7	8.7(b)
North Borneo							
1955	9.0	(a)	—	35.2		5.5	50.3‖(b)
1960-62	6.1	(a)	—	31.0		12.8	50.0(b)
Sarawak							
1955	8.1	(a)	—	19.30		31.0#	41.70(b)
1962	10.3	(a)	—	30.9		15.5	43.00(b)
Singapore							
1956	0.35	(a)	—	22.29	21.33(d)	14.54	41.48(c)
1962	—	(a)	3.2	9.3	10.3	63.4	13.9

*Including irrigation
†Including power
‡Civil works and miscellaneous
§Civil works
‖Including power and water supplies and civil works
#Including water supplies

Public investment in some cases includes revenue or current expenditure under development heads, while in others it includes only capital expenditures.

(a) The item has been included elsewhere.

(b) The item "Others" includes in the case of Pakistan and the Federation of Malaya construction expenditure on housing as well as expenditures on water supplies, resettlement, and municipal services. In the case of North Borneo, the largest item is "Others" and includes power development, civil works, municipal services such as sewerage and water supplies, etc. In the case of Sarawak, the item "Others" includes development of power, civil works and construction, etc., whereas the item "Health and Education" includes the development of water supplies.

(c) In the case of Singapore, the item "Others" includes municipal development as well as water, power, and public utilities.

(d) Includes only housing and public works.

Source: UN/ECAFE, *Economic Survey . . . 1960,* Part II, p. 75; Commonwealth Economic Committee, *Commonwealth Development and Its Financing,* No. 7: *India* (London, 1963), Table 25, p. 70; Government of Pakistan Planning Commission, *The Second Five Year Plan* (June, 1960), p. 408; Huq, *A Strategy,* Table 50, p. 88; The Colombo Plan, *Annual Report,* 5th-12th reports.

the social return on the investment is higher than the private returns. The projects involved often enjoy economies of scale, have long periods of gestation, and are very durable. They are immobile in the sense that their services cannot be imported and hence they must be produced within the country. Private enterprise seldom foresees these opportunities of profit arising from external interdependence, financial and technical, between different industries on the one hand and social overhead capital on the other. It is only public enterprise which can take into account the external interdependence of investment decisions in various sectors of the economy and undertake investment in social overhead capital on a scale greater than what is warranted by an evaluation of direct and immediate costs and returns. In the countries under review, the investment in social overhead capital has often been pushed in anticipation of future demand. That this policy may have resulted in the short run in losses in some cases and in low profits in other cases is not ruled out. The ultimate test of worthwhileness would be how far a particular project either facilitated investment or removed bottlenecks in the way of investment elsewhere in the economy.

The pattern of allocation of private investment between various sectors differs from that of public investment. Data on the sectoral allocation of either total investment or of private investment are scanty except for one or two countries. Investment in directly productive projects, especially in industry and agriculture, assumes a greater importance in the total complex of capital formation, including both public and private sectors. While in Pakistan the proportion of industrial investment has been high throughout the last decade (about 28-36 per cent), in India the proportion has doubled between the two five-year plan periods (i.e., from 14 to 28 per cent). During the 1950's investment in agriculture increased from 6 per cent to 11 per cent of the total investment in Pakistan, whereas it has remained at about 15 per cent in India.[9] The preponderance of industrial

9. Huq, *A Strategy,* p. 155; Government of Pakistan, Planning Commission, *Guidelines for the Third Five Year Plan (1965-70)* (1963), p. 18; Commonwealth Economic Committee, *India,* Tables 24 and 27, pp. 70-71.

investment is even more evident if only private investment is considered. Investment in industry and that in construction constituted 60 per cent and 32 per cent respectively in Pakistan, whereas in India the corresponding percentages were 34 per cent and 36 per cent respectively during the years 1955-60.[10]

Consequent on the magnitude and pattern of investment which has taken place in the recent past, there has been a change in the economic structure of the various countries under review. The proportion of gross domestic product originating in all the secondary and tertiary sectors, i.e., manufacturing, transportation, and others, increased, with a consequent decline in the proportion of domestic product originating in agriculture. There is no doubt, however, that the change in the course of the last decade has been neither very rapid nor very spectacular. During 1950-60 the proportion of gross product originating in agriculture declined from 58 per cent to 48 per cent in Ceylon, from 46 per cent to 44 per cent in Malaya, from 49 per cent to 46 per cent in India, and from 59 per cent to 56 per cent in Pakistan.[11] In the field of manufacturing industries the rate of growth in the capital goods sector, on the whole, has been higher than that of the rest, partly owing to the small base of capital goods industries with which the countries started out on their industrialization programs. The various branches of capital goods industries enjoyed annual rates of growth in the late 1950's, varying between 8 per cent and 14 per cent in Ceylon, 8 per cent and 21 per cent in Malaya, 8 per cent and 12 per cent in India, and 14 per cent and 19 per cent in Pakistan. As against these the corresponding annual rates of growth of the total manufacturing industries were 8 per cent in Ceylon, 7 per cent in Malaya, 43 per cent in India, and 11.5 per cent in Pakistan.[12] The rate of growth of the intermediate goods sector is also generally higher than that of the consumer goods sector. In

10. Commonwealth Economic Committee, *India*, Table 27, p. 7; Huq, *A Strategy*, Table C-2, p. 260.

11. United Nations, Department of Economic and Social Affairs, *The Growth of World Industry, 1938-1961* (New York, 1963), pp. 122-25, 225-29, 380-94, 587-91.

12. *Ibid.*, pp. 124-25, 228-29, 388-89, and 590-91.

India the industrialization program under the successive five year plans accorded a relatively greater emphasis on heavy and producer goods industries, and there is a similar shift in the later stages of the Second Five Year Plan in Pakistan. The recent emphasis on heavy industries is related to the policy of accelerating the rate of capital formation. So long as the domestic base of capital goods industries is small, the speed of capital formation is a function of the capacity to import. Barring an indefinite continuance of an adequate volume of foreign aid and loans, an increasing capacity to import depends upon a growing value of exports.

Most of the countries under review have been traditionally exporters of primary commodities, the world trade in which has suffered from a relative stagnation in the past. The annual rate of growth of exports in the 1950's has been barely 0.8 per cent in Malaya, 1.3 per cent in Ceylon and India, and 3.8 per cent in Pakistan.[13] The planned expansion of exports in the future in these countries is not much higher. Even in the expansion of manufactured exports they face obstacles both at home and abroad, e.g., relative inefficiencies of infant industries at home and restrictions abroad imposed by advanced countries on their exports. Moreover, the prospects of an efficient industrialization program itself depend upon the availability of capital goods. Foreign aid and loans, while increasing the supply of capital goods in the short run, do saddle them in the long run with the problem of repayment, which has to be made increasingly in terms of exports of manufactures and in the face of sluggish world demand for primary exports. Moreover, it is the exports of heavy manufactures which enjoy a buoyant trend in world trade.

Sources of Financing Capital Formation

A substantial portion of investment expenditures in these countries has been financed by domestic saving, both private and

13. UN/ECAFE, *Economic Bulletin for Asia and the Far East*, XIV (Dec., 1963), 18-19.

public. Gross domestic savings during 1950-59 on an average constituted 13 per cent of G.N.P. in Malaya, 13.4 per cent in Ceylon, and 8.6 per cent in India,[14] with, of course, considerable annual variations. This is especially true of countries heavily dependent on the export sector variations in the income from which have important effects on the distribution of aggregate income between savings and consumption. For example, if there is a greater variation in the income of those who are dependent directly or indirectly on the export sector, the saving-income ratio may record a corresponding variation. The variations in gross savings rates are shown in Table 4.

In Pakistan where gross investment as per cent of gross

Table 4. *Gross Savings as Per Cent of G.N.P.*

	1955	1956	1957	1958	1959	Average
The Federation of Malaya	16.8	16.2	8.2	10.7	—	13.0
India	12.0	11.9	7.0	5.9	6.2	8.6
Ceylon	13.5	13.5	14.8	12.1	—	13.4

Source: UN/ECAFE, *Economic Bulletin*, XIII (Dec., 1962), No. 3, Table 1, p. 1.

Table 5. *Distribution of Increased Revenue in the Government Sector* (Per Cent of Increased Revenue)

	Increase in Total Current Expenditure	Increase in Current De-velopmental Expenditure	Increase in Current non-Developmental Expenditure	Increase in Saving
Ceylon 1950-60	117.1	57.1	60.1	−17.1
Federation of Malaya 1951-59	189.2	89.2	100.0	−89.2
India 1950-60	106.5	73.4	33.1	−6.5
North Borneo 1950-60	54.0	30.1	23.9	46.0
Pakistan 1950-60	77.4	11.4	66.0	22.6
Sarawak 1951-60	83.7	53.3	40.3	16.3
Singapore 1950-60	67.0	55.8	11.2	33.0

Source: UN/ECAFE, *Economic Bulletin*, XIII (Dec., 1962), No. 3, p. 29. These ratios relate to increases in government saving as a proportion of increases in government revenue and not to absolute levels of public savings, which are often substantial. Government saving is defined as the surplus of government revenue over development and non-development current expenditure.

14. UN/ECAFE, *Economic Bulletin for Asia and the Far East*, XIII (Dec., 1962), Table 1, p. 1.

domestic product increased to 9 per cent in 1959-60 and 11.9 per cent in 1961-62 as compared with 8.6 per cent in 1951-55, the gross savings ratio changed from 6.7 per cent during 1951-55 to 6.0 per cent in 1956-60 and 6.9 per cent in 1961-65.[15] Data on overall saving ratios are not available for such state units as Singapore, Sarawak, and North Borneo. However, a rough idea of the saving effort of these territories in recent years can be obtained from the increase in savings mobilized in the public sector. (See Table 5.)

The increase in government saving has been largest in North Borneo, Singapore, and Sarawak. In these countries the increase in non-developmental current expenditure has in general absorbed smaller percentages of the increase in total government revenue than is the case with the rest of the countries. Moreover, of the increase in total government revenue, their current developmental expenditures have constituted a much larger share than non-development expenditures. In Pakistan the increase in government saving has been facilitated by a very small increase in current development expenditure, which has offset a larger increase in current non-developmental expenditure. On the other hand, in Malaya the increase in current non-developmental expenditures has absorbed the whole of the increase in total government revenue; in Ceylon, Malaya, and India the combined increases in developmental and non-developmental current expenditures have left no surplus. In view of a persistent pressure for an increase in social and economic service expenditures, of which there is a considerable backlog, the rate of government saving can be raised only with difficulty and as a result of careful planning. The ratio of government saving to government revenue during the period 1950-60 averaged from 12.6 per cent for India and Pakistan to about 22 per cent for Singapore and Ceylon, with the Federation of Malaya in the intermediate position with an average rate of 16.7 per cent.[16]

Public saving as a source of finance for public development expenditure has increasingly assumed an important role in the

15. Huq, *A Strategy*, Table 5, p. 69.
16. UN/ECAFE, Economic Bulletin, XIII (Dec., 1962), 29.

countries under review. In North Borneo public saving has financed on an average about 44 per cent of development expenditure during 1955-57 and almost 100 per cent during 1960-62. In Sarawak the proportion of development expenditure financed by public saving rose from 28 per cent during 1954-57 to about 66 per cent during 1960-62.[17] In Pakistan public saving financed 12 per cent of the public investment in the first plan and 23.3 per cent of public investment during the first three years of the second plan.[18] During 1956-60 net public saving financed in India 28 per cent and in Ceylon 87 per cent of net public investment.[19]

In spite of the increasing importance of public saving as a source of financing of capital formation, private savings constitute the most predominant component of domestic saving—92 per cent, 85 per cent and 62 per cent in India, Malaya, and Ceylon respectively during the late 1950's.[20] Among the constituents of private saving, household saving appears to be by far the most important source, constituting 86 per cent to 48 per cent of domestic saving. Corporate saving is more important in Ceylon and Malaya than in India. Differences are partly due to variations in the profitability and dividend policies of the corporate sectors and partly due to differences in the relative importance of corporate sectors.

Insofar as the alternative forms of household savings are concerned, there is a great deal of diversity among the individual countries. Financial assets constituted during the late 1950's 66 per cent, 45 per cent, and 39 per cent of gross household savings in Ceylon, India, and Malaya respectively. The rest consisted of tangible assets. Among the financial assets, bank deposits and currency are the least important in Malaya as a medium for household saving as they constitute only 2.2 per cent of total household saving. They are more important in Ceylon and constitute 28 per cent of household saving but are less so in India,

17. The Colombo Plan, *Annual Reports.*
18. Huq, *A Strategy*, p. 137.
19. *Ibid.*, p. 189. UN/ECAFE, *Economic Bulletin*, XII (Dec., 1962), 32-33.
20. *Ibid.*, XIII (Dec., 1962), Table 2, p. 4.

where they constitute 16 per cent. Contractual saving, including life insurance, constitutes about 27-28 per cent of household saving in Ceylon and Malaya, whereas it is only 13 per cent of total saving in India. Corporate and government securities are least important in Ceylon (5 per cent of total savings) and relatively more important in India (12 per cent of total savings). In Pakistan during 1955-62 currency and bank deposits constituted 57 per cent of non-corporate saving (business and household), whereas contractual saving constituted 29 per cent and corporate shares 21 per cent.[21] The relative importance of different financial assets depends partly upon the state of development of capital and financial markets and partly upon the attractiveness of the rates of interest, tax exemptions, etc., offered by the governments to encourage the accumulation of savings. That such a high proportion of household savings is held in the form of tangible assets reflects the primitive stage of development of capital markets in these countries. However, increasingly the financial intermediaries, including commercial banks and specialized financial institutions, are playing an active role in mobilizing as well as in channeling savings into productive uses. While the proportion of household savings directly transmitted to the users via direct sales and purchases of financial instruments is 3.8 per cent of total household saving in Ceylon, 9.5 per cent in the Federation of Malaya, and 12.7 per cent in India, the proportion which is indirectly transmitted to the users via financial intermediaries is 42.5 per cent in Ceylon, 32.0 per cent in the Federation of Malaya, and 32.4 per cent in India.[22]

With the increasing importance of the corporate sector, the share of profit and of savings in national income is expected to go up. The propensity to save of the corporate sector is usually higher than the household propensity to save. In India corporate income after tax comprised less than 1 per cent of national income, and corporate saving accounted for 5.8 per cent of total

21. *Ibid.*, XIII (Dec., 1962), Table 3, p. 6. S. R. Lewis and M. I. Khan, "Estimates of Non-Corporate Private Saving in Pakistan, 1949-62," *Pakistan Development Review*, IV (1964).

22. These are average figures for the period 1955-1959. UN/ECAFE, *Economic Bulletin*, XIII (Dec., 1962), 11.

private saving during the period 1950-59. The share of corporate income in national income is higher in Ceylon than in India owing to a relatively large plantation and export sector; consequently corporate saving contributed over 22.4 per cent of private saving.[23] As between different countries, the range of variation in the saving propensities of households is very wide. One may expect to explain differences in the rates of household saving with reference to the differences in the level, composition, and distribution of disposable income of households—an exercise ruled out in the absence of relevant and adequate data. Whatever scanty evidence is available does not confirm any stable interrelationship among these variables. While in Ceylon the proportion of household income appropriated by entrepreneurial and property income is almost the same as in Japan (about 46-50 per cent), the rate of household saving in Japan is two and one-half times higher than in Ceylon.[24] Even though there are great inequalities of income in India and Ceylon the ratio of household saving to household disposable income was on the average only 5.8 per cent and 4.8 per cent respectively during 1950-59.[25] This tends to confirm that it is not inequalities of income as such but shifts of income in favor of those persons or sectors which have higher propensities to save that will raise the rate of saving. Inequalities of agricultural incomes do not usually contribute to higher rates of saving since high income earners in agriculture have usually higher propensities to consume than others.

From the above it appears that efforts at raising rates of domestic saving in the countries of Southeast Asia have met with only a limited success. The average rates of gross domestic saving are low compared with the rates of saving which the advanced countries experienced during the period of their rapid

23. UN/ECAFE, *Economic Survey . . . 1961*, p. 55.
24. *Ibid.*, p. 56.
25. In Ceylon the top 1 per cent of income receivers received 18 per cent of total income, and the bottom 10 per cent received only 1.4 per cent. In India 1 per cent of non-agricultural income earners receive 20 per cent of non-agricultural income, and 1 per cent of these engaged in cultivation own 16 per cent of agricultural land. "Savings of the Ceylon Economy 1950-59," *Central Bank of Ceylon Bulletin* (Jan., 1961); J. S. Gulati, *Resource Prospects of the Third Five Year Plan* (Bombay, 1960), p. 64; UN/ECAFE, *Economic Survey, . . . 1961*, p. 55.

progress in the past. Most countries are planning to achieve a high rate of economic growth in the future. Ceylon's ten year plan (1959-68) originally projected an annual rate of growth of G.N.P. at 5.9 per cent and scaled it down to 4.8 per cent per annum for the period 1961-62–1963-64. The projected annual rates of growth in the mid 1960's are 4.1 per cent, 5.6 to 6.0 per cent, and 4.4 per cent for Malaya, India, and Pakistan respectively.[26] Over the long run each of them seeks to accelerate considerably its rate of growth. This will no doubt require the realization of higher rates of domestic saving than those achieved in the past. Some countries have succeeded in the very recent past in achieving marginal rates of saving as high as 20 per cent or so. The urgency for increasing the domestic rates of saving is further reinforced by the fact that foreign aid and loans are not expected to continue indefinitely and they have to be repaid in the not too distant future.

Improvement in government saving will depend upon the ability to raise additional tax resources, which until now constituted a small fraction of national income in the majority of the countries under consideration. Restraint on the increase in non-development expenditures is essential. Encouragement of the growth of the corporate sector by means of such incentives as tax rebates, high depreciation, and investment allowances may tend to augment the flow of undistributed profits and consequently the rate of corporate savings. Higher interest rates on saving deposits and securities, greater banking facilities, development of investment trusts and markets for securities, popularization of voluntary or compulsory insurance and pension funds—all will contribute to the mobilization of household savings, especially of the urban classes and middle income groups. An additional means of financing capital formation, especially in the public sector, which has been frequently resorted to is deficit financing. In the late 1950's, budget deficits constituted about 3.3 per cent of G.N.P. in Ceylon, 11.2 per cent in India, and 5.7 per cent in Pakistan.[27] To some extent budget deficits

26. UN/ECAFE, *Economic Survey . . . 1962*, p. 179.
27. UN/ECAFE, *Economic Survey . . . 1962*, p. 59.

have been met by borrowing from non-bank sources, which implies a transfer of sources from the private sector and is not inflationary. During the second plan in Pakistan, non-bank borrowing financed 10 per cent of public investment, whereas in India during the second and third plans its contribution varied between 25 and 30 per cent of public investment.

In Pakistan deficit financing, which met about 8 per cent of the second plan public expenditures, is expected to increase to 10 per cent of the third plan expenditures.[28] During 1950-60 deficit financing in India constituted 6.5 per cent of total public expenditure, which was partly offset by a reduction in the creation of private credit.[29] Though requirements of increased monetization and growth of transactions demand for money have partially offset the effects of forced saving in both countries, there was a rise in prices, partly aggravated by a stagnation in food supply. But nowhere did it develop into an acute competitive bidding for resources, aided by a cumulative creation of new money, on the part of different sectors of the economy. The transfer of income to profit earners consequent on a rise in prices, while it helped the process of capital accumulation, could not avoid entirely the inequitable effects, limited though they may have been, on income distribution. The limited scope for non-inflationary deficit financing can be exploited more effectively provided an adequate supply of food and essential items of mass consumption can be ensured in order to prevent an undue rise in the cost of living and a consequent pressure for increased money incomes. Moreover, a pattern of investment which emphasizes social overhead capital and heavy producer goods industries has the effect of postponing the supply of consumption goods into the future. The consequential increase in output reflects itself largely in investment goods, and income thus created in the investment process may largely be saved in the face of a limited supply of consumption goods. If voluntary saving falls short of investment so undertaken, the gap, of course, has to

28. The Government of Pakistan, Planning Commission, Guidelines (1963), p. 23.
29. Commonwealth Economic Committee, India (1963), pp. 25-28.

be met by public or private creation of money or by increased taxation to restrain expenditure.

Formation of Skill

It is now increasingly recognized that the development of human capital is as important a component of economic development as the accumulation of physical capital. The former enables a productive utilization of material capital and natural resources. In the countries under review there has been a steady but not spectacular development in the spread of education and the growth of technical manpower. For one thing the formation of technical skill and capacities among indigenous people is as difficult and slow a process as changing of their attitudes towards thrift, saving, and investment. Moreover, the gestation period in the spread of education as well as in the training of high level manpower and of technical personnel is usually quite long.

In the process of formation of skill in a wide sense, an improvement of literacy is an important element insofar as the transmission of skill to illiterate persons is more difficult than to literate persons. An increase in the vocational, scientific, and technical content of education even at the primary level not only increases the absorptive capacity of farmers with respect to new techniques or factors of production but also results in a more productive use of existing capital or land. There has been an improvement in literacy in all the countries under review in the past decade. The school enrollment at all levels increased in the decade of the 1950's. It doubled in Sarawak, while it increased by 50 per cent in the Federation of Malaya, by about 30 per cent in Singapore, North Borneo, and India, by 24 per cent in Ceylon, and by only 14 per cent in Pakistan.[30]

An indication of the relative stages of development of human resources in some of the countries can be obtained from Table 6. The Federation of Malaya has the highest percentage of enroll-

30. UN/ECAFE, *Economic Survey . . . 1961*, pp. 32-33.

Table 6. *Human Resource Development*

	Stock of high level manpower			Measures of education development enrollment ratios				Orientation of higher education per cent enrolled		Expenditure on education as per cent of national income
	Teachers 1st & 2nd Levels per 10,000 population	Engineers & scientists per 10,000 population	Physicians & Dentists per 10,000 population	1st Level unadjusted (a)	1st & 2nd Level adjusted	2nd Level adjusted (b)	3rd Level unadjusted (c)	Science & technology	In humanities law & arts	
Pakistan	20	n.a.	0.1	20	29	16.2	1.8	29.9	42.4	1.2
Malaya	29.2	n.a.	1.8	58	62	21.0	0.5	26.0	34.9	n.a.
India	30.2	2.4	1.5	24	35	24.2	2.2	27.3	59.9	1.7

(a) Pupils enrolled in primary education as a percentage of the estimated population aged 5 to 14 inclusive, not adjusted for the length or duration of schooling which vary from country to country.

(b) Pupils enrolled, secondary education as a percentage of estimated population aged 15 to 19 inclusive adjusted for length of schooling.

(c) Enrollment in higher education as a percentage of the age group 20-24.

Source: F. Harbison and C. A. Myers, *Education, Manpower and Economic Growth* (New York, 1964), pp. 45-47.

ment in primary and secondary education, whereas the percentage of enrollment in the higher levels of education is the highest in India, with Pakistan being a close second. The large concentration of students in humanities, arts, and law is evident in all the countries, with India leading. The number of primary school students per million of population is the highest in Singapore (166,862) and is considerably higher in Singapore and Malaya (154,767) than in India (60,737) and Pakistan (52,519).[31] In terms of enrollment in technical schools alone, Malaya ranks the highest, with 1,069 students per million of population at this Singapore has 776 students per million of population at this level. Pakistan has the poorest performance (134) in this re-

31. For India and Pakistan population figures relate to the year 1956 and for Malaya, Singapore, and Ceylon they relate to the year 1961. UN Department of Economic and Social Affairs, *Statistical Year Book, 1961* (New York, 1962), pp. 614-25.

spect. In all the countries except Malaya the enrollment per million of population in the higher stages of education is greater than in the technical schools. In India and Pakistan it is almost ten times the enrollment in the technical schools, and in Singapore it is five times. The largest enrollment per million of population in the higher stages of education is in Singapore (3,351), India following as a close second (2,302), and Pakistan being third in rank (1,481). In Malaya the relative enrollment in the higher stages of education is one-fourth of that in the technical schools. In Ceylon in the 1960's there were 807 students per million of population in the universities as against 443 full time students per million of population in technical schools and 202 in professional courses.[32]

The state of manpower development in the majority of these countries is often unbalanced, with an acute shortage of technical personnel at the intermediate levels such as foremen, supervisors, craftsmen, overseers, and mechanics. This may lead to a wastage of high level manpower insofar as qualified engineers are employed to do the job of draftsmen or supervisors. The relatively meager enrollment in science classes limits the number of entrants in the institutions of higher learning in technical and engineering fields and thus restricts the output of technical personnel. In India, for example, the enrollment in science classes in all colleges was 38 per cent of the total enrollment in 1950-51, declined to 34 per cent in 1955-56, and stayed at 34 per cent even in 1960-61.[33] The number of graduates from engineering colleges increased from 6 per million of population in 1950-51 to only 13 in 1960-61, whereas the output of technical institutes granting diplomas increased from 7 per million of population in 1950-51 to 18 per million by 1960-61.[34] In Pakistan while there has been a 100 per cent increase in enrollment in

32. UNESCO, unpublished materials on educational development in Ceylon, 1964.

33. These enrollments relate to the colleges teaching only arts, science, and commerce. Government of India, Central Statistical Organization, *Country Statement for India, Asian Population Conference* (New Delhi, Dec., 1963), p. 30, Table 64.

34. Government of India, Planning Commission, *Third Five Year Plan* (summary), chap. xvii, pp. 149, 151-64.

the universities and a 114 per cent increase in enrollment in the general arts and science colleges between 1953-54 and 1960-61, the increases in enrollment in technical and professional fields such as medical, engineering, and commerce subjects have been only 58.5 per cent, 31.7 per cent, and 46.4 per cent respectively.[35] The meager increase in enrollment in the engineering and technical colleges and institutions is partly due to the shortage of teachers and equipment. The supply of equipment involves scarce foreign exchange, and in addition it takes time to train teachers for technical subjects.

The programing of the educational expenditure as a whole and in its various components such as primary, secondary, technical, and engineering education, etc., is being increasingly linked up with the whole economy in countries such as India, Pakistan, and Ceylon. Attempts are being made to assess the requirements for various kinds of trained manpower arising from the development programs and to allocate investment funds between various stages of education in order to meet the projected requirements. In both India and Pakistan, the allocation of the public educational expenditures among various forms of education has changed from one plan period to the next in response to changing priorities. For example, there was a decline in the proportion of expenditure on primary education in the second plan as compared with the first; the share of primary education, however, increased in the third plan.[36] This reflects in part the interdependence between higher and lower stages of education; i.e., expansion of secondary and teacher training education was necessary to provide teachers for the expansion of primary education. During the first plan period, India devoted 56 per cent of the total educational expenditure to primary education, and in Pakistan primary education's share was about the same as secondary education's (about 20 per cent), while higher education claimed the largest single share (26 per

35. M. S. Jellani, "Levels of Education Attainment in Pakistan," *Pakistan Development Review*, IV (Spring, 1964), 76-77.
36. *Ibid.*, pp. 150, 160, 212-13. Government of Pakistan, Planning Commission, *Guidelines* (Nov., 1963), Annexure II, p. 119.

cent). This is partly because of a very small base of higher education in Pakistan at the beginning of the first plan and a very acute shortage of higher level manpower in the early years of Pakistan's independent existence. The largest increase took place both in India and Pakistan in the field of technical education. This was necessary because of very modest beginnings. Its share in total expenditure increased from 13 per cent to 25 per cent in India and from 6 per cent to 29 per cent in Pakistan. The relative share of higher education which was any way concentrated on arts and humanities declined in India from 17 per cent during the second plan to 15 per cent during the third plan. It is expected to decline from 25 per cent to 15 per cent in Pakistan in the next, or third plan period.[37]

For a number of countries such detailed statistics as above are not available. Some idea of the extent of skill formation in Malaya in the 1950's can, however, be obtained from the percentage distribution of the labor force between various occupations requiring different levels of skill.

The high level manpower, i.e., those in technical professions and related occupations as well as in administrative, managerial, and executive occupations, constituted only 4.16 per cent of the total economically active population in 1957, whereas the medium level technical personnel constituted about 15 per cent of the labor force. However, as stated earlier, Malaya is expanding her pool of technical manpower at a faster rate per head of population than her bigger neighbors.

One of the endemic problems of the underdeveloped countries in Asia and South Asia has been a pronounced lack of enthusiasm for vocational, professional, and technical education. This is partly due to the inadequate status which these professions enjoy in society and partly due to insufficient financial incentives. The net result has been a critical shortage in the supply of technical manpower, especially of intermediate level of technical and professional personnel. White-collar jobs, especially administrative ones, command greater prestige and also

37. *Ibid.*

are well remunerated. This is reinforced by a certain antipathy towards physical and manual labor on the part of educated persons. The predominance of the non-technical general administrators in the social and administrative set-up is a heritage partly from the colonial days and partly from the past tradition that the maintenance of law and order is the *raison d'être* of public administration. This often has a demoralizing effect on the technical and professional personnel. There is a need for a conscious policy on the part of the public authorities which should guarantee a high social status to technical manpower as well as provide such persons sufficient financial incentives. Since the public sector is an important employer in most of these countries, it can set the pace and the standard for the necessary transformation in status and salary so urgently called for.

In the expansion of the supply of technical personnel, one is faced with a vicious circle: a slow rate of economic development limits the supply of technical personnel while an inadequate supply of the latter retards economic progress. As in the case of social overhead capital, so also in the field of manpower development, because of a long gestation period in the training process it is difficult for an individual to decide on the appropriate amount of investment in the right kind of education. The price mechanism cannot reflect future demand and supply of technical personnel and, therefore, cannot serve as efficiently the allocative purpose to meet the future needs of an economy. It is the responsibility of public authorities to make such appropriate forecasts, to provide training facilities at home and abroad, and then to direct the flow of students into predetermined channels via the provision of financial and other incentives.

While planning the appropriate allocation of limited resources for the formation of technical skill one is often faced with a choice in the short-run between education as an object of consumption and education as a field for productive investment. After all, every choice has a time dimension. Relative emphasis on technical education or on the development of high-level manpower in certain areas of critical shortages in a given plan period does not preclude a shift of emphasis, as resources for educational expenditure expand, towards those levels of education of which the component of consumption is more important than that of investment. Therefore, a choice made in a certain period is not irrevocable and needs to be continuously reviewed in the light of changing circumstance. It may be worth considering whether in view of the very high costs and long gestation periods of some forms of educational investment, on the one hand, and an urgent need for a rapidly expanded supply of their outputs, on the other, it may not be desirable to shorten the periods of and to reduce the costs of training at some sacrifice, no doubt, of the highest standards achieved in advanced countries, at least for some of those engaged in various technical professions. Thus the supply of some grades of technical skills and services can possibly be augmented at a much faster rate to meet the urgent needs of development programs. This is an area of inquiry where the considered judgment of educational specialists is awaited.

Conclusion

The countries in South and Southeast Asia have made modest progress in their attempts to increase the rate of capital formation as well as to enlarge the pool of technical and professional manpower. The public sector plays a crucial role in accelerating the rate of capital formation not only by mobilizing savings but also by undertaking investments financed by public savings as well as by borrowing from private persons and institutions and from foreign sources. Private investment is still shy but is beginning to play an increasing role. Public investment is mainly concentrated on the creation of social overhead capital as a stimulus to growth in the other directly productive sectors of the economy. Private investment is mainly directed towards industry, construction, and to a lesser extent, agriculture, which, in addition, receives a large amount of non-monetized investment undertaken by individual farmers. Private saving constitutes the major source of domestic financing. Household savings, which constitute the most important single component of private saving, are expected to increase with an increasing use of either voluntary or compulsory insurance and pension funds as well as with the development of organized markets for corporate and government securities. The importance of household saving and the relative unimportance of corporate saving imply that there is a greater scope for institutionalized religious characteristics, ceremonial waste, and, in some parts, opposition to usury, to check capital formation. With the growth of large-scale trade and industry the share of profits in national income increases, which in turn is expected to raise the rate of saving. The growth of the corporate sector with its built-in propensity to accumulate surpluses out of undistributed profits is expected to speed up the rate of capital formation. Until that time the state would continue to play a greater role in mobilizing savings.

The major concern in these countries is not that savings are not increasing but that they are not increasing commensurately with the needs of financing an accelerated rate of growth. The alternative is forced saving via deficit financing, a limited scope for which in the countries of South Asia can be exploited with care. The inflationary impact is partly cushioned by the monetization of the subsistence economy as well as by the growth of transactions demand for money in the monetized sector. The poor performance of agriculture in the countries of the region retards development. Because of its predominance in the economies of the region, only a prosperous agriculture can provide a sizable investable surplus. Moreover, the contribution of agriculture to public revenues has been low because of an inadequate tax system. The possibility of accelerating capital formation with the help of underemployed or unemployed labor in the rural areas depends on the availability of additional food or wage goods and equipment. The surplus food aid from the U.S. has helped the introduction in the villages of Pakistan of rural works programs such as roads, irrigation works, buildings, excavation of canals, etc. The major difficulty appears to lie in the organization and administration of such rural works programs which can at the same time generate sufficient enthusiasm on the part of the rural population.

There are two important sources of saving in the economies of the region: the reduction in defense expenditure and the reduction in the rate of growth of population. In at least some of these countries an important source of saving in government expenditure lies in a possible reduction of defense expenditures, which constituted in 1962-63 3.4 per cent of total government expenditure (both current and capital) in Ceylon, 8.1 per cent in the Federation of Malaya, 15.1 per cent in India, and 21.8 per cent in Pakistan. A reduction in defense expenditure to the extent that it is not financed by military aid from abroad will release domestic resources for development. However, capital outlays on defense such as the building up of defense industries which manufacture transportation equipment or other heavy industrial products do give an impetus to the development of subsidiary industries and these products are partly used for development purposes as well. Moreover, expenditures on the training of manpower in the armed forces have contributed to the growth of the largest single corps of trained manpower in the form of engineers, mechanics, and the intermediate level of technicians.

High rates of growth of population have cut into the rate of growth of per capita income and hence of savings; moreover, they greatly increase the need for investment in the provision of such overheads as housing and primary education and thus employs resources which otherwise could have been devoted to productive investment yielding an immediate increase in income. The reduction in the rate of growth of population is a time-consuming process unless drastic measures are adopted. Both this and a reduction in defense expenditures involve political, social, and strategic, as well as economic considerations.

The development of technical skill is a time-consuming process. In all countries its shortage is acute both in terms of intermediate level technicians as well as of high level manpower. Moreover, it cannot be imported on the same scale as physical capital equipment, especially if it is high quality skill which is so urgently needed. There is an increase in the share of total public expenditure on education in general and technical education in particular. Increasingly attempts are being made to forecast requirements of technical manpower arising from development programs and to adjust the educational system as well as investment therein to meet these requirements. No less important is the need to stem and control the reverse movements of skill or trained manpower from the underdeveloped to the developed countries in search of higher wages and greater opportunities of employment. A better integration of educational and economic planning is called for. A combination of mildly coercive and persuasive methods in both the developed and underdeveloped countries to attract trained personnel back to their native lands may alleviate the situation.

There is the need for a conscious policy on the part of public authorities to insure a high social status to technical manpower as well as to provide sufficient financial incentives. It is true that development of technical skill is both a cause and an effect of economic development. If a speedy process of economic development creates excess demand for technical and professional skills and is reflected adequately in the market for technical personnel in terms of rising rewards for them, there is likely to be an increasing flow of entrants to technical professions. This is already happening in many of these countries. However, to wait for the pressure of demand to create its own supply may slow down the rate of progress. As in the case of physical overhead capital, so also in the field of human capital: what is necessary is long-term perspective planning of investment in the creation of skill.

22

Economic Dimensions of the Commonwealth

Craufurd D. W. Goodwin[*]

Change in Economic Dimensions

Measurements of economic growth

A comparison of growth rates of gross national products in the Commonwealth during the 1950's (Table 1)[†] does not reveal

Table A. *Planned and Actual Growth Rates of Gross National Product, 1959-1961*

Country	Plan period	Planned growth rate (per cent)	Actual increase of G.N.P. in constant prices (per cent) 1960	1961
Ceylon	1959-68	5.9	7	4
	1961/62-1963/64	4.8		
Fed. of Malaya	1961-65	4.1	9	5
India	1961/62-1965/66	5.6-6.0	7	–
Pakistan	1960/61-1964/65	4.4	6	4

Source: *Economic survey of Asia and the Far East 1962* (United Nations, 1963), p. 179.

startling disparity among countries. Growth rates of between 3 and 4 per cent were maintained by members at widely different levels of development: Canada, Cyprus, India, Malaya, and Nigeria. Jamaica and Trinidad and Tobago were conspiciously in the lead with growth rates of 8.0 and 9.2 per cent respectively. Pakistan and the United Kingdom achieved rates of less than 3 per cent, similar to the pace maintained by the United States.

[*] Associate professor of economics and secretary, Duke University.
[†] Tables 1-22 are found on pages 480-502.

Growth rates among Asian members have been higher in recent years and suggest that planned growth rates for the immediate future, in all cases above 4 per cent, may not be as unrealistic as indicated by reference to the more distant past (see Table A).

Dampening effects of population growth upon increases in per capita rates were very different among members (Tables 1 and 2). In Canada increase in per capita gross national product was only one per cent; in India 1.6 per cent; in Nigeria .3 per cent. In Pakistan the pressure of population between 1951 and 1959 actually turned a modest increase in absolute levels of production into a slight decline per capita: a negative growth rate of —0.2 per cent. In the United Kingdom, where population increase was relatively slight, per capita G.N.P. increased by 2.1 per cent per year. The broad conclusions of Tables 1 and 2 are worthy of emphasis. The excess of births over deaths, more than any other single factor, prevented the less developed nations of the Commonwealth from gaining on the more developed ones, even relatively.

Table 3 indicates the overwhelming importance of starting points in comparisons of growth rates among nations. Although Canada's output grew relatively slowly during the 1950's, that country began and ended the decade well in the lead in level of per capita G.N.P. (U.S. $1774 in 1961), followed by New Zealand (U.S. $1439), Australia (U.S. $1380), and the United Kingdom (U.S. $1244). In general, older members of the Commonwealth were far ahead of the newer members in levels of productivity. Ceylon, India, Pakistan, Ghana, Kenya, the Rhodesian Federation, Tanganyika, and Uganda each had per capita products in 1961 of less than U.S. $200. Barbados, British Guiana, Jamaica, Cyprus, Malta, Malaya, Mauritius, and South Africa were all below U.S. $500 per capita. Trinidad and Tobago, which more than doubled their total product between 1953 and 1961, almost doubled per capita levels from U.S. $330 to U.S. $643. Viewed in terms of absolute base levels the growth rates set out in Tables 1 and 2 take on new significance. For example, a mere 4 per cent increase in Canada's per capita gross national product today yields an increment equal approximately to the total per capita product on the Indian subcontinent.

Tables 1, 4, 5, 6 and 7 provide information concerning changes in uses and sources of gross national product. In Commonwealth countries for which statistics are available, increases in private consumption kept pace at least proportionately with increases in G.N.P. Members at all stages of development permitted their people to partake of the immediate fruits of progress. Ironically, the old dominions as a group (Canada, Australia, New Zealand, and South Africa) expended annually a larger portion of gross national product on fixed capital formation, between 20 per cent and 30 per cent (Table 5), than did those members which were in desperate need of development. The Asian and African Commonwealth nations provided clear examples of the familiar conflict in countries developing from a low-income base between a desire for long-term growth and immediate and urgent demands for consumption. Fixed capital formation reached a high of only 14 per cent of G.N.P. in Ceylon in 1962 and a high of 12 per cent in Nigeria in 1957. The Caribbean members maintained unusually high rates of fixed capital formation, in two instances exceeding 30 per cent (British Guiana in 1960 and Trinidad and Tobago in 1959 and 1962); in this way they achieved remarkably high growth rates. Expenditures on government consumption increased relatively rapidly in certain newer Commonwealth countries, by as much as 14.9 per cent annually in Cyprus, and by 11 per cent annually in Nigeria.

Agricultural production as a source of gross domestic product fluctuated widely around an upward trend in Australia and Canada, the two most important producers in the Commonwealth of staple agricultural products (Table 6). Fairly steady, although unspectacular, growth was experienced in agricultural sectors of other Commonwealth members. Rates of increase in industrial production are not easily obtainable or reliable; where available, however, they suggest a proportionately greater increase of total production in less developed countries such as Pakistan, which began after World War II with a very low industrial output, than in relatively industrialized nations such as the United Kingdom.

Tables 8 and 9 portray the price movements which accompanied economic growth in the Commonwealth. Most countries experienced a steady upward pressure on prices, greater among consumer goods than wholesale goods. Between 1953 and 1961 consumer prices increased most rapidly in Nigeria, followed by Cyprus, New Zealand, and most of the other Commonwealth countries bunched not far behind.

The labor force

Table 10 suggests that in the Commonwealth no close correlation can be found between level of development and proportion of the population participating in the labor force. For example, a smaller proportion of the population was listed as "economically active" in Pakistan (30.7 per cent in 1951) than in Canada (37.9 per cent in 1951) and much less than in Ghana (73 per cent in 1960). Social, cultural, and other diversities, as well as some statistical error and inconsistency, explain the almost random pattern which appears in this table.

Levels of illiteracy in the Commonwealth, set forth in Table 11, are related inversely to stages of economic development. As many as three-quarters of the population were categorized as illiterate during the 1950's in India, Pakistan, and the African colonies or former colonies. This high proportion was both a cause and a result of low levels of per capita income.

Food shortages as indicated by low caloric intake (Table 12) were a serious problem, in the countries for which statistics are available, only in Ceylon, India, and Pakistan. However, gluttony seems to have characterized other areas where calorie consumption exceeded requirements—in Australia, New Zealand, and the United Kingdom by as much as 25 per cent.

No clear pattern emerges of trends in employment in Commonwealth countries (Tables 13 and 14). In general employment seems to have increased more steadily and evenly in the old Commonwealth than in the new. The general employment index in Canada moved from 92 to 106 between 1954 and 1961, by the same amount in New Zealand, and from 98 to 104 in the United Kingdom. Non-agricultural employment followed a similar pattern, moving in Australia from 94 to 105, in Canada from 93 to 100, in the United Kingdom from 97 to 104, and in South Africa from 89 to 102. Among the newer African states particularly rapid gains in general employment were experienced by Ghana, which moved steadily from 84 in 1954 to 114 in 1960, and in non-agricultural employment by Sierra Leone, which jumped irregularly from 87 to 111. Wide fluctuations and little net gain were characteristic of Northern Rhodesia, Tanganyika, and Uganda. In non-agricultural employment Ghana gained substantially, while Kenya, Nigeria, the Rhodesias, Nyasaland, Tanganyika, and Uganda fluctuated widely. In Singapore a substantial reduction in general employment occurred, from 105 to 88. Moderate gains were made by Cyprus, Fiji, and Malta. Non-agricultural employment in Trinidad and Tobago rose markedly from 85 to 101 in only five years between 1956 and 1960.

Real wages in non-agricultural industries rose proportionately most rapidly in the less developed countries of the Commonwealth (Table 15). Between 1950 and 1961 wages rose by 22 index points in Australia, by 33 points in Canada, by 32 points in the United Kingdom, and by only one point in South Africa. In contrast, over the same period real wages rose by 44 index points in Ceylon and Cyprus, by 39 points over a seven-year period in Singapore, by 36 points over an eight-year period in Trinidad and Tobago, and by 108 points in Tanganyika between 1953 and 1961. More rapid growth rates in wage levels of less developed countries were made possible, in part, by the relatively low base from which these countries began. These rates help to explain the proportionately high levels of consumption and low rates of capital formation noticed in Tables 1 and 5.

International trade

Tables 16 and 17 portray changes in levels of external trade of Commonwealth countries by volume and price between 1948 and 1961. In general it is clear that members took advantage of the gains from international specialization by increasing steadily both imports and exports. Growth of imports was spectacular in several of the newer countries, for example in Ghana and Nigeria, where indices rose between 1948 and 1961 from 41 and 26 to 159 and 129 respectively. The statistics, of course, do not reveal sources of payments for these imports, which included substantial foreign assistance and investment. Exports of most Commonwealth areas followed an erratic upward path, reflecting variations in crop yield and in world demand. For countries where national income statistics are still in a primitive state these statistics are useful as a guide to levels of national productivity.

Commonwealth countries differed from each other significantly as to the effects of changes in the terms of trade $(\frac{\text{export prices}}{\text{import prices}})$. Several areas which exported mainly primary staple products and imported highly manufactured goods experienced noticeably worsening terms of trade. Australia and New Zealand in particular paid steadily rising import prices but received falling export prices. Between 1954 and 1962 prices of export goods from Ghana, East Africa, Nigeria, and the Federation of Rhodesia and Nyasaland all fell erratically, while import prices generally rose. In Jamaica rising export prices failed to keep pace with import prices, which rose even more rapidly. Canada, Ceylon, Cyprus, and South Africa were not affected markedly in either direction by changes in terms of trade over the period. Only Malaya, Mauritius, and the United Kingdom gained steadily in their trade position.

Tables 18, 19, 20, and 21 are matrixes of international trade among Commonwealth countries for the years 1948 and 1959. They indicate changes in the strength of commercial ties among Commonwealth units over an eleven-year period. For most of the Commonwealth these statistics reveal a marked decline in dependence upon intra-Commonwealth trade. The only countries which did not experience a decline in the proportion of exports destined for other Commonwealth areas were those which retained particularly heavy economic dependence on the United Kingdom: Hong Kong, Mauritius, Sarawak, Malaya, Singapore, and Cyprus. Marked declines in intra-Commonwealth exports were recorded by all countries which in 1959 still contributed the bulk of total intra-Commonwealth exports. The proportion of Australia's exports destined for other parts of the Commonwealth fell from 1948 to 1959 from 61.1 per cent to 43.8 per cent; for Canada the decline was from 32.5 per cent to 20.8 per cent, for India from 52.8 per cent to 45.1 per cent, for New Zealand from 79.3 per cent to 64.1 per cent, for the Union of South Africa from 53.2 per cent to 50.1 per cent, and for the United Kingdom from 45 per cent to 40.4 per cent. In both years the United Kingdom was by a wide margin the major contributor to intra-Commonwealth exports; 36.2 per cent of the total in 1948 and 37.3 per cent in 1959. Australia's share fell from 12.2 per cent to 8.4 per cent and Canada's from 12.6 per cent to 10.7 per cent.

Changes in import interrelationships among Commonwealth countries were analogous to the decline in export interdependence. The only Commonwealth units for which proportions of total imports from other Commonwealth countries did not decline between 1948 and 1959 were Malaya, Pakistan, and the United Kingdom. With the exception of the United Kingdom all major contributors to total intra-Commonwealth imports experienced proportional declines in imports from the Commonwealth: Australia from 68.0 per cent to 51.5 per cent, Canada from 18.4 per cent to 14.8 per cent, India from 48.7 per cent to 30.3 per cent, and the Union of South Africa from 46.0 per cent to 45.3 per cent.

The weakening of export and import interdependence in the Commonwealth was the result in part of the failure of intra-Commonwealth trade to keep pace with non-Commonwealth trade. In part this development reflected the relative decline of Great Britain as a dominant world economic power, and in part it arose from the greater maturity of other developing Commonwealth areas. Proportional declines conceal, in some cases, absolute increases in intra-Commonwealth trade. They fail to reveal, moreover, sustained links between significant pairs of countries, and in particular links with Great Britain. Nevertheless, the proportional decline in internal trading relationships in the Commonwealth does point to a potential weakening of ties and emphasizes in a forcible way the continued significance of Britain as the single most important unifying focus in commerce as in other spheres.

Statistics in Table 22 describe balances of trade between parts of Commonwealth countries in 1959 by subtracting exports f.o.b. of each trading partner country to a given Commonwealth country from that country's exports to the partner country. E.g., exports from Australia to Aden in 1959 were $7.1m. and from Aden to Australia were $3.1m. Therefore, by the definition used in Table 22, Australia's balance of trade with Aden was +$4.0m., and Aden's balance of trade with Australia was —$4.0m.

The pattern which emerges from Table 22 is complex. Several of the developing Commonwealth nations maintained a sizable negative trade balance with the Commonwealth, including India and Malaya, each with trade deficits in 1959 of approximately $100m. New Zealand's aggregate unfavorable balance was the largest of all the Commonwealth countries ($—306.9m.), principally because of an excess of exports from the United Kingdom ($190.7m.). Canada was almost in an exact reverse position, having a net surplus of $273.7m., the largest component being a favorable balance of $234.2m. with the United Kingdom. Sarawak, Singapore, and the United Kingdom all received greater export markets from other Commonwealth countries than they provided themselves.

Conclusions

On balance, the statistics examined in this paper do not point to any material tightening of the economic bonds of the Commonwealth. Even though some economic progress was evident in all areas, growth in undeveloped parts was much less in absolute terms than in more prosperous areas and was similar only in terms of growth *rates*. As a result the gulf in living standards between different portions of the Commonwealth failed to diminish, and the only members which began to emerge noticeably from the category of "have-nots" to that of "haves" were islands in the West Indies. International trade among Commonwealth units remained substantial, although a diminishing fraction of total trade for most countries. Substantial imbalances existed, and the continuing importance of Britain as a commercial nucleus remained evident.

The Statistics

The collection of economic statistics in the Commonwealth has been irregular, eccentric, and inconsistent among countries. There is no single central Commonwealth statistical bureau to co-ordinate efforts and to publish results. The statistics presented here were collected by several international organizations as parts of world surveys. Gaps in coverage indicate either incomparability or absence of data, and no attempt has been made by this writer to employ statistical services of individual nations to fill these gaps. Series have been selected which give the most suggestive glimpses of economic conditions in the Commonwealth. In most instances original footnotes which describe minor peculiarities of the statistics have been omitted, but original sources have been identified. For comparison, data have been provided where available for France, the Federal Republic of Germany, the United States, and the U.S.S.R.

The use of these statistics is subject to substantial danger. It is safest usually to regard individual series as indicative of the direction rather than the precise magnitude of change, and to view international comparisons only as a basis for ranking. Despite their limitations, these statistics are the best measures available to describe economic change in the Commonwealth. In some instances they have shown signs of rapid improvement in quality and quantity in recent years.

Table 1. *Average Annual Rates of Growth of Real Gross Domestic Product and Its Components (in Per Cent)*

Country	G.D.P.			Expenditure on G.D.P.			Industrial origin of G.D.P.		
	Period	Total	Per capita	Private consumption	General government consumption	Fixed capital formation	Agriculture	Mining and manufacturing	Other
Canada	1952-60	3.3	0.6	4.4	1.5	3.4			
Ceylon	1952-59	2.9	0.4	3.1	7.7	6.6			
Cyprus	1952-60	3.0	1.2	1.6	14.9	4.8	1.3	2.4	4.5
India	1952-59	3.0	1.3				2.3	2.9	3.9
Jamaica	1954-59	8.0	6.3	6.8	8.8	7.6	5.6	22.4	12.9
Malaya, Federation of	1956-60	3.9	0.7						
Nigeria	1952-56	3.7		4.1	11.0	10.8	2.4	6.1	3.9
Pakistan	1954-60	2.6	0.5				1.9	6.9	2.5
Fed. of Rhodesia and Nyasaland	1955-60	6.0	3.4	4.1	6.9	−1.4			
Trinidad and Tobago	1952-60	9.2	6.0	8.9	3.8	12.7			
United Kingdom	1952-60	2.7	2.2	2.9	2.0	6.5	2.2	3.0	2.6
France	1952-60	4.2	3.4	4.1	2.4	6.0	2.5	4.8	4.2
Fed. Republic of Germany	1952-60	7.2	6.0	7.3	5.2	10.3	1.9	8.9	6.6
United States	1952-60	2.6	0.9	3.4	1.1	2.3			

Notes on Tables

(Derived in part from sources listed after note)

Table 1

The figures shown in this table are computed as average annual geometric rates of growth expressed in percentage form for the periods indicated. They are based on the estimates of real gross domestic product and its components which appear for most countries in the standard tables "Expenditure on Gross National Product" and "Industrial Origin of Gross Domestic Product" of the *United Nations Yearbook of National Accounts Statistics*. Conceptual differences and other details concerning the basic data may be obtained by reference to these tables. It should be noted that the methods used to obtain

Table 2. *Annual Rate of Growth and Index Numbers of Real Per Capita Gross National Product Each Year 1950-1960* (1953 = 100)

Country	Average annual rate of growth 1951-59*	1950	1951	1952	1953	1954	1955	1956	1957	1958	1959	1960
Canada	1.0	91	94	99	100	94	100	106	104	102	103	103
Ceylon	0.5	97	103	104	100	100	104	96	100	101	105	109
Cyprus	2.0	85	85	94	100	99	100	104	115	107	104	98
India	1.6	93	94	96	100	101	101	104	101	106	105	110
Malaya, Federation of						100	95	92	89	97	103
Nigeria	0.3	105	110	100	100	106	108	104	106			
Pakistan	—0.2				100	96	100	98	96	97	101	
Federation of Rhodesia and Nyasaland	0.9				100	110	116	110	105	116	117	
United Kingdom	2.1	95	97	96	100	104	106	109	110	110	113	117
France	3.3	91	96	98	100	104	109	114	119	120	122	128
Fed. Repub. of Germany	6.1	80	87	94	100	106	117	124	129	131	138	148
United States	1.1	90	95	98	100	97	102	103	103	99	104	105

*Average of last three years shown compared with average of first three years shown, compounded annually.

estimates of gross domestic product at constant prices and the years to which these prices relate vary widely between countries.

In order to minimize the influence of single terminal years on the computed growth rates, the estimates of real product were averaged and centered for the first three and last three years of each period for which data were available. For example, the figures shown for the period 1952-1960 represent rates of growth based on estimates of average real product in the periods 1951-1953 and 1959-1961. (*Yearbook of National Accounts Statistics 1962* [United Nations, 1963], pp. 311-312.)

Table 2

The figures in this table relate to index numbers and average annual rates of growth of per capita gross national product at constant market prices. *Gross national product* is the market value of the product, before deduction of provisions for the consumption of fixed capital, attributable to the factors of production supplied by normal residents of the given country. It is identically equal to the sum of consumption expenditure and gross domestic capital formation, private

Table 3. *Estimates of Total and Per Capita Gross Domestic Product Expressed at Factor Cost in United States Dollars 1953, 1958, 1961* (totals in millions of dollars)

Country	1953 Total	P. C.	1958 Total	P. C.	1961 Total	P. C.
Aden			68	64		
Australia	8,848	1,004	11,959	1,215	14,502	1,380
Barbados	41	192	57	251		
British Guiana	104	226	125	235		
Canada	22,581	1,521	30,243	1,767	32,409	1,774
Ceylon	942	114	1,143	122	1,299	128
Cyprus	168	332	225	410	229	404
Fiji			74	200		
Gambia			21	74		
Ghana			986	158	1,285	185
Hong Kong			728	255		
India	23,100	62	27,600	67	31,300	73
Jamaica	299	201	556	357	684	419
Kenya			582	85	629	86
Malaya, Fed. of			1,420	218	1,673	242
Malta and Gozo			106	329	126	383
Mauritius	118	228	133	221	149	226
New Zealand	2,155	1,053	2,923	1,281	3,482	1,439
Nigeria	1,862	60	2,740	81		
Pakistan	6,150	77	4,760	54	5,340	56
Fed. of Rhodesia and Nyasaland			1,275	161	1,572	185
Sierra Leone			154	64		
Singapore			545	360		
South Africa	4,730	316	6,461	385	7,480	414
Trinidad and Tobago	224	330	417	529	552	643
Tanganyika			468	52	523	56
Uganda			411	65	437	64
United Kingdom	41,188	814	55,975	1,084	65,657	1,244
Zanzibar & Pemba			30	101		
France	36,371	853	48,548	1,089	52,825	1,149
Federal Republic of Germany	30,048	611	47,916	920	66,560	1,232
United States	333,249	2,080	406,474	2,324	472,673	2,572

and public, and the net exports of goods and services plus the net factor incomes received from abroad.

It should be noted that the weight base period to which the constant prices relate is not uniform from country to country. For the purposes of this table, however, the index numbers are shown on a common publication base, 1953 = 100.

The figures should be interpreted with caution. The per capita estimates are subject to considerable error and are appropriate for

Table 4. *Annual Rate of Growth and Index Numbers of Real Per Capita Private Consumption Expenditure Each Year, 1950-1960* (1953 = 100)

Country	Average annual rate of growth 1951-59*	1950	1951	1952	1953	1954	1955	1956	1957	1958	1959	1960
Canada	1.8	95	94	97	100	99	104	108	108	108	111	111
Ceylon	6.3	96	104	103	100	96	102	93	102	101	106	112
Cyprus	1.4	75	83	90	100	93	97	113	110	95	96	88
Jamaica	5.6				100	109	120	128	136	135	139	
Malta and Gozo	3.4				100	101	116	114	118	121	124	
Nigeria	0.4	105	109	99	100	106	108	105	105			
Federation of Rhodesia and Nyasaland	2.0				100	105	109	114	113	113	113	
South Africa	1.7			98	100	102	104	105	108	109	109	
United Kingdom	2.3	99	97	96	100	104	108	108	111	113	117	120
France	3.3	88	94	97	100	103	108	113	118	118	119	124
Fed. Repub. of Germany	6.1	80	85	91	100	104	113	122	127	131	137	146
United States	1.5	97	96	97	100	99	105	106	107	106	110	112

*Average of last three years shown compared with average of first three years shown, compounded annually.

indicating general trends rather than precise year-to-year changes. The methods used to measure the estimates in constant prices differ widely; intercountry comparisons should, therefore, be made only with the necessary reservations. (*Compendium of Social Statistics: 1963* [United Nations, 1963], pp. 562-70.)

Table 3

The estimates in this table of total and per capita gross domestic product (G.D.P.) expressed in current U.S. dollars are designed to facilitate international comparisons of levels of economic activity. For most of the countries represented, the estimates have been prepared by converting the official G.D.P. figures by the prevailing dollar exchange rates. Population figures used in calculating per capita product are generally mid-year estimates reported in the United Nations' *Monthly Bulletin of Statistics*.

The estimates in this table should be considered as indicators of the total and per capita production of goods and services of the countries represented and not as measures of the standard of living

Table 5. *Percentage of Expenditure of Gross National Product on Fixed Capital Formation*

Country	1948	1950	1951	1952	1953	1954	1955	1957	1958	1959	1960	1961	1962
Australia	20				25				26			26	25
Barbados	22				20				30	27			
British Guiana				15	15				29		35		
Canada	20				23				25			22	21
Ceylon		9			10				12		13		14
Cyprus		14			14				17			15	21
Ghana							16		14			21	18
Jamaica		9			12				23		21	19	
Malaya, Federation of								8	10		9	15	
Malta						15			23			18	18
Mauritius						15			16			19	
New Zealand	18				22				22			22	22
Nigeria			6		9		12						
Federation of Rhodesia and Nyasaland						30			33			20	18
South Africa	24				26				23			20	19
Tanganyika						18			16			15	15
Trinidad and Tobago				23	21				29	32			31
United Kingdom	12				13				15			17	16
France			16		16				18			18	20
Federal Republic of Germany			19		20				22			25	25
United States	17				16				16			16	16

of their inhabitants. No particular significance should be attached to small differences between the estimates of two countries because of the margin of error inherent in the method of estimation. (*Year-book of National Accounts Statistics 1962* [United Nations, 1963], pp. 314-19.)

Table 4

The figures in this table relate to index numbers and average annual rates of growth of per capita private consumption expenditure at constant market prices. *Private consumption expenditure* comprises the value at market prices of final expenditure by households and private non-profit institutions on current goods and services less sales of similar goods (mainly second-hand) and services, plus value of gifts in kind (net) received from the rest of the world. Purchases by residents abroad, apart from those chargeable to business expense, are included and those made by visiting non-residents are excluded. Direct taxes and other current transfers paid by house-

Table 6. *Index Numbers of Agricultural Production All Commodities*
(1952/53-1956/57 = 100)

Country	1956/7	1957/8	1958/9	1959/60	1960/1	1961/2
Australia	105	99	119	119	123	126
Canada	109	93	97	100	106	93
Ceylon	102	106	110	111	115	121
India	108	107	111	114	120	121
Malaya, Federation of	108	108	110	119	123	126
New Zealand	105	109	115	120	122	124
Pakistan	104	103	103	108	111	115
South Africa	110	105	110	113	121	125
United Kingdom	107	105	101	110	116	120
France	102	105	105	111	125	122
Federal Republic of Germany	102	105	111	107	121	112
United States	103	99	106	109	110	110

holds and private non-profit institutions are excluded. Income in kind, such as food, shelter, and clothing furnished to employees is included at cost. Imputations are also made for rent in respect of owner-occupied dwellings and for the value of home-grown food consumed by farm families and others. The source of this table is the same as for Table 2, and the same caveats apply.

Table 5

Gross domestic fixed capital formation covers the value of purchases and own-account construction of fixed assets by enterprises, private non-profit institutions, and general government. Expenditure by households on durable goods other than new dwellings is treated as private consumption expenditure. All expenses directly related to the acquisition of capital goods, such as transportation and installation charges, fees for engineering, legal and other services, are included. (*Statistical Yearbook 1962* [United Nations, 1963], pp. 498-504; and *ibid.*, *1963*, pp. 523-528.)

Table 6

The all commodities index of agricultural production includes food, fibers, tobacco, industrial oilseeds, and rubber. (*Statistical Yearbook 1962* [United Nations, 1963], p. 91; and *ibid.*, *1963*, p. 116.)

Table 7

The index numbers for "General" industrial production cover mining, manufacturing, and electricity and gas, and do not cover,

Table 7. *Index Numbers of Industrial Production (1958 = 100)*

Country	1948	1953	1955	1956	1957	1958	1959	1960	1961	1962
Canada	62	84	92	100	101	100	108	108	112	121
India	64	74	85	92	96	100	108	120	129	138
New Zealand (manufacturing only)	60	76	88	88	95	100	103	114	119	
Pakistan		48	78	88	93	100	112	119	126	144
Rhodesia and Nyasaland, Federation of			83	94	103	100	119	127	131	127
South Africa (manufacturing only)	49	80	88	92	94	100	102	108	116	122
United Kingdom (including construction)	74	89	99	99	101	100	105	112	114	115
France (including construction)	55	72	84	89	97	100	101	109	114	120
Federal Republic of Germany (including construction)	27	66	85	92	97	100	108	119	125	131
United States	73	97	103	107	107	100	113	116	117	126
U.S.S.R.	27	59	74	82	91	100	111	122	133	146

unless otherwise indicated, construction. (*Statistical Yearbook 1962*
[United Nations, 1963], pp. 78-88; and *ibid., 1963*, pp. 92-102.)

Table 8

The general consumer price index (all items index) usually covers
all the main classes of expenditure (food, fuel and light, clothing,
rent, and miscellaneous), but exceptions have been indicated in footnotes in the original source. The indices are designed to show changes
over time in the price level of goods and services on which consumers in general or a defined population group, e.g., urban wage
earners, spend their incomes. The table headings show the town or
number of localities in which prices are recorded. Owing to differences in scope and in methods used for the compilation of the indices,
the statistics for the different countries shown in the table are not
uniformly representative of changes in price levels and vary in reliability from one country to another. (*Compendium of Social Statistics: 1963* [United Nations, 1963], pp. 353 and 446-52.)

Table 9

A wholesale price index refers to a representative list of commodities priced at a wholesale stage of distribution. It represents such
prices as those charged by representative manufacturers or producers
to wholesalers, prices charged by wholesalers to retailers, prices paid
by importers to producers, etc. (*Statistical Yearbook 1962* [United
Nations, 1963], pp. 474-79; and *ibid., 1963*, pp. 502-7.)

Table 8. *Consumer Price Indices for All Items: Yearly, 1950-61*
(1953 = 100)

Country	1950	1951	1952	1953	1954	1955	1956	1957	1958	1959	1960	1961
Aden (colony)		81		100	96	96	113	122	101	100	103	103
Australia (6 towns)	68	82	96	100	101	103	109	112	113	116	120	123
Barbados (Bridgetown)	77	86	100	100	99	101	101	104	107	108	110	112
British Guiana (2 urban areas)	84	90	100	100	103	106	108	101	102	105	106	107
Canada (11-33 towns)	89	98	101	100	101	101	102	106	108	110	111	112
Ceylon (Colombo)	95	99	98	100	100	99	99	101	103	104	102	103
Cyprus (4 towns)	82	92	96	100	104	110	119	127	133	135	136	135
Fiji Islands (5 towns)	83	90	101	100	105	105	109	110	108	109	100	101
Ghana (Accra)	88	103	105	100	102	104	108	109	109	112	113	121
Hong Kong	90	98	99	100	98	95	97	98	96	104	100	101
India (27 centers)	95	98	97	100	95	90	99	104	109	114	116	118
Jamaica (Kingston)	79	90	100	100	98	100	100	103	108	112	116	123
Kenya (Nairobi)	81	87	95	100	103	109	113	116	117	118	118	120
Malaya, Federation of (49 localities)												
Malay laborers	81	101	103	100	94	91	92	96	95	92	99	99
Chinese laborers	76	100	103	100	94	91	92	97	96	93	100	100
Malta (13 localities)	84	94	101	100	102	100	102	105	107	109	114	119
Mauritius	83	90	98	100	99	97	96	95	96	95	97	96
New Zealand	80	89	96	100	105	107	111	113	118	123	124	126
Nigeria (Lagos)			100	105	108	117	119	119	124	132	140	
Pakistan (Karachi)	85	88	90	100	98	94	97	106	110	106	113	115
Federation of Rhodesia and Nyasaland:												
Northern Rhodesia: (8 towns)												
European population	87	91	97	100	103	107	111	115	118	120	123	124
African population			97	100	101	103	106	107	107			
South Rhodesia (6 towns)	84	89	97	100	100	101	105	108	113	115	118	121
Sierra Leone (Freetown)	66	88	101	100	106	100	107	116	112	112	115	119
Singapore	79	97	101	100	93	91	92	94	92	92		
South Africa (9 towns)	83	89	97	100	102	105	107	110	114	115	117	119
Trinidad			98	100	101	106	107	109	114	117	119	121
Tanganyika (Dar es Salaam)		79	87	100	98	95	93	98	102	100	101	102
Uganda (Kampala)												
European & Asian population		89	94	100	104	110	117	119	121	122	123	125
African population								98	100	101	95	110
United Kingdom (23-200 areas)	81	89	97	100	102	106	112	116	119	120	121	125
France (Paris)	77	91	101	100	100	101	103	106	121	129	134	138
Federal Republic of Germany	92	100	102	100	100	102	104	107	109	110	111	114
United States (46 towns)	90	97	99	100	100	100	102	105	108	109	111	112
U.S.S.R.	127	116	110	100	95	95	95	95	97	96	95	95

Table 10

This table presents the percentage of population economically active, or crude labor-force participation rates, for both sexes. These data are considered to be basic background information for studying levels of living. *Crude participation* (or activity) *rates* are the num-

Table 9. *Wholesale Prices* (General Unless Otherwise Described)
(Index Numbers 1958 = 100)

Country	1948	1953	1954	1955	1956	1957	1958	1959	1960	1961	1962
Australia (basic materials)	51	96	95	98	101	102	100	101	107	103	100
Canada	85	97	95	96	99	100	100	101	101	102	105
India	88	95	90	82	92	98	100	104	111	113	115
New Zealand	67	92	92	93	96	97	100	102	102	102	102
Federation of Rhodesia and Nyasaland (building materials)	81	96	96	98	101	100	100	97	98	96	100
South Africa	63	93	94	97	98	100	100	100	101	101	101
United Kingdom (basic materials)			99	102	106	107	100	101	101	100	100
France	54	83	81	81	85	90	100	105	107	110	113
Federal Republic of Germany			96	97	99	100	100	99	100	102	103
United States	88	92	93	93	96	99	100	100	100	100	100

ber of economically active population of both sexes, all ages, per 100 total population. *Economically active population* is that part of the population which furnishes the supply of labor for the production of goods and services. This is the labor-force concept which comprises all persons of either sex engaged in, or actively seeking, productive work in some branch of the economy during a specified time near the census date.

Comparability of statistics on the economically active population, however, is subject to important limitations because of the differing definitions employed and the various methods of collecting and compiling the basic data. One of the most important variables is probably the treatment of persons who assist without pay in economic enterprises operated by other members of the household. In some countries these persons are classified as unpaid family workers and included in the economically active population while in others they are considered in the same category as housewives, retired persons, students, and so forth, and classified as inactive. The classification of persons with dual status also varies between countries, as does the treatment of members of the armed forces and inmates of institutions. Unemployed persons, especially those seeking work for the first time, are classified as economically active under the labor-force concept which is standard for this table, but they are considered to be inactive under the gainful-worker concept used in some countries. Differences between countries in the lower age limit for the enumeration and tabulation of economically active population also tends to impair the comparability of the crude participation rates and those for the youngest age

Table 10. *Economically Active Percentage of Population, All Ages*
(Latest Available Census)

Country	Census date	Per cent
Aden (colony)	1955	37.5
Australia	1954	41.2
Bahamas	1953	50.5
Barbados	1946	48.5
British Guiana	1946	39.8
Canada	1951	37.9
Ceylon	1953	36.8
Cyprus	1946	36.4
Ghana	1960	73.0
High Commission territories:		
Basutoland	1946	63.9
Swaziland	1956	22.8
Hong Kong	1956	38.7
India	1953-54	43.8
Jamaica	1953	41.4
Malaya, Federation of	1957	34.5
Malta and Gozo	1957	31.0
Mauritius	1952	32.9
New Zealand	1956	37.6
Nigeria (indigenous population)	1952-53	47.9
Brunei	1947	57.6
North Borneo	1951	68.8
Sarawak	1960	71.2
Pakistan	1951	30.7
Singapore	1957	33.2
South Africa:		
Indigenous population	1951	36.0
Non-indigenous population	1951	37.2
Trinidad and Tobago	1946	39.0
United Kingdom:		
England and Wales	1951	46.5
Zanzibar and Pemba	1948	59.2
France	1954	45.3
Federal Republic of Germany	1950	46.3
United States	1950	39.8
U.S.S.R.	1959	47.5

group. (*Compendium of Social Statistics: 1963* [United Nations, 1963],
pp. 349 and 365-71.)

Table 11

Illiteracy rates are presented in this table, as indicating the order
of magnitude of the illiteracy problem. Because of the rapid growth
of population in some countries during recent years, the number of
illiterates may, in a given case, be about the same over a period of
years, or even show some increase, although the corresponding per-

Table 11. *Percentage of Population 15 Years of Age and Over Unable to Read and Write* (Latest Available Census)

Country	Census date	Per cent
Aden (colony)	1946	79
Bahamas	1953	15
Barbados	1946	9
British Guiana	1946	24
Ceylon	1953	32
Cyprus	1946	39
High Commission territories:		
Basutoland	1946	65
Bechuanaland	1946	80
Swaziland	1956	77
(African population)		
Hong Kong	1961	29
India	1961	76
Jamaica	1953	23
Malaya, Federation of (excluding Europeans and nomadic aborigines)	1957	53
Malta and Gozo	1948	42
Mauritius:		
European language	1952	58
Non-European language	1952	48
Nigeria	1952-53	89
Brunei	1960	57
North Borneo	1960	76
Sarawak	1960	79
Pakistan	1951	81
Singapore	1957	50
South Africa (Bantu population)	1946	72
Trinidad and Tobago	1946	26
Uganda	1959	75
France	1946	4
United States	1959	2
U.S.S.R.	1959	2

centage may have decreased slightly. (*Compendium of Social Statistics: 1963* [United Nations, 1963], pp. 288 and 303-12.)

Table 12

The data presented in this table are based on national food balance sheets prepared by governments in collaboration with the Food and Agriculture Organization and, in the case of European countries, with the Organization for Economic Co-operation and Development. The food balance sheet starts from the data of production, trade, and movement in stocks for each foodstuff; makes appropriate deductions for the amounts used for animal feed, seed, and non-food purposes; and so arrives at the estimated quantity of food and nutrient supplies

Table 12. *Per Capita Calorie Levels as Percentages of Requirements*
Annual Averages 1951/52-1953/54 and 1957/58-1959/60

Country	1951/52-1953/54	1957/58-1959/60
Australia	121.9	123.5
Canada	115.5	117.4
Ceylon	86.9	88.6
India	73.9	83.9
Mauritius		100.9
New Zealand	126.9	130.3
Pakistan	88.9	88.0
South Africa	104.7	102.3
United Kingdom	118.3	125.1
France	112.3	115.4
Federal Republic of Germany	110.8	113.5
United States	121.6	120.1

available at the retail level for a given period, usually a year (July-June).

The food balance sheet is only a rough statistical method, subject to the following principal limitations. For a number of commodities, official statistics of production and trade are frequently inadequate, so that rough estimates have to be made. The range and accuracy of national statistics vary widely from country to country. Except in a few countries, practically no data are available on farm and commercial stocks whose yearly changes may appreciably affect the supplies of food. Quantities utilized for feed, seed, waste, and industrial purposes are frequently roughly determined in the absence of statistics on the utilization of individual commodities.

For these reasons, the results obtained for different countries are not fully comparable. (*Compendium of Social Statistics: 1963* [United Nations, 1963], pp. 161 and 163-64.)

Tables 13 and 14

The indices of employment shown in Table 13 refer to the general level of employment, covering all branches of economic activity, although in certain cases the component industries are not fully represented (in particular in the branches "agriculture, forestry, hunting, fishing" and "services.") The indices shown in Table 14 cover non-agricultural employment only, i.e., employment in all branches of economic activity except agriculture.

Table 13. *Employment Index General Level* (1958 = 100)

Country	1954	1955	1956	1957	1958	1959	1960	1961
Canada	92.1	94.2	98.1	100.5	100.0	102.8	104.6	106.3
Cyprus	97.7	98.5	99.3	100.3	100.0	99.4	99.7	101.3
Ghana	83.7	83.9	91.6	95.0	100	109.4	114.0	
Malta	92.7	89.4	93.3	95.8	100.0	98.7	99.8	100.6
New Zealand	92.0	93.9	95.5	97.6	100.0	101.2	103.4	106.0
Rhodesia and Nyasaland, Fed. of:								
Northern Rhodesia	89.8	94.2	98.3	103.1	100	95.6	94.6	91.5
Southern Rhodesia	86.3	89.6	94.6	98.1	100	99.9	101.5	98.1
Nyasaland	81.2	88.0	97.4	100.4	100	98.1	94.4	90.8
Singapore	105.1	102.7	117.2	107.7	100.0	96.0	86.5	88.0
Trinidad and Tobago				86.6	94.6	95.3*100.0	100.3	
Tanganyika	102.0	95.9	98.5	100.0	100.0	99.4	90.3	102.7
Uganda	97.0	97.7	97.6	99.0	100.0	98.5	100.6	97.2
United Kingdom	97.9	99.4	100.3	100.6	100.0	100.5	102.4	103.6
Federal Republic of Germany	86.4	91.2	95.8	98.8	100	103.0	105.5	107.7
United States	95.2	98.4	101.2	101.6	100.0	102.5	104.2	104.4
U.S.S.R.	86.6	88.6	92.6	97.3	100.0	103.5	113.6	120.9

*Average of February and November.

Statistics of employment usually relate to the total numbers at work at a specified date in each month or quarter, but sometimes to the average number over a given period. Usually no distinction is made between persons working full time and those working less than full time. Fluctuations in the numbers employed within a country reflect the influence, on the one hand, of factors connected with seasonal and other short-term variations in economic activity and, on the other, of long-term trends in the population, including changes in its industrial and social structure. For instance, where the trend in total numbers in the labor force is upwards, as is usually the case, index numbers of employment generally follow a similar trend. Where the index refers only to the wage earner and salaried employee group, which in most cases tends to become an increasingly large proportion of the total labor force, the series will also show a rising trend on this account. On the other hand, changes in institutional factors (for example, the raising of the statutory school-leaving age) may result in a decrease in the labor force. (International Labour Office, *Year Book of Labour Statistics*, 1962, pp. 73 and 100-115.)

Table 15

This table presents index numbers of real wages, taking into account the changes in the purchasing power of money wages as re-

Table 14. *Non-Agricultural Employment Index* (1958 = 100)

Country	1954	1955	1956	1957	1958	1959	1960	1961
Australia	93.6	96.8	98.5	99.0	100.0	101.9	105.3	104.9
Canada	93.2	95.8	102.4	104.0	100.0	101.5	100.7	100.2
Cyprus	89.0	93.1	97.4	98.6	100.0	98.5	99.2	100.0
Fiji	85.3	91.4	99.3	99.8	100.0	95.2	104.6	93.7
Ghana	84.7	82.2	90.6	95.2	100.0	106.5	110.8	
Kenya	93.5	106.9	105.2	105.1	100.0	100.5	102.0	98.2
Malta	86.0	85.0	91.5	94.1	100.0	95.7	97.6	99.5
New Zealand	89.8	92.6	94.9	97.1	100.0	101.7	104.4	107.7
Nigeria				94.8	100.0	100.0	98.7	
Rhodesia and Nyasaland, Fed. of:								
Northern Rhodesia	87.1	92.9	98.4	103.5	100.0	94.1	92.9	89.4
Southern Rhodesia	81.9	85.5	92.2	97.9	100.0	99.2	99.8	96.2
Nyasaland	82.7	88.5	97.1	100.0	100.0	97.1	93.3	90.4
Sierra Leone	86.7	86.7	100.0	103.3	100.0	100.0	96.7	111.4
Singapore	105.0	102.6	117.0	107.6	100.0	96.1	86.6	88.1
South Africa	88.8	92.9	96.4	99.6	100.0	100.6	101.1	101.9
Trinidad and Tobago			84.5	93.7	95.5*	100.0	101.3	
Tanganyika	101.6	97.4	104.4	100.8	100.0	96.0	87.6	90.5
Uganda	95.8	94.5	93.2	98.9	100.0	99.0	99.3	97.7
United Kingdom	97.4	99.1	100.2	100.6	100.0	100.6	102.8	104.3
France	94.4	95.4	96.6	99.2	100.0	98.6	99.2	99.8
Federal Republic of Germany	85.1	89.9	95.2	98.9	100.0	103.5	106.5	109.4
United States	95.3	98.5	101.9	102.9	100.0	103.8	105.7	105.2
U.S.S.R.		87.1	91.7	95.7	100.0	104.7	113.5	119.9

*Average of February and November.

vealed by consumer price indices. Owing to differences in coverage and reliability of the original data, the indices of real wages, obtained by dividing index numbers of money wages by index numbers of consumer prices, are subject to important reservations. They should not be interpreted as precise measures of fluctuations in the level of living of wage earners or wage earners' families: they are intended to show only the approximate trend in the purchasing power of average hourly wages over the items covered by the price index; they do not take into account fluctuations in income from other sources such as social security allowances; nor do the indices take into account the effect on aggregate weekly earnings of changes in total hours worked, variations in taxation payable by the workers, etc. Frequently the wages data refer to non-agricultural wage earners throughout the country, while the corresponding consumer price indices mostly cover only one city or a group of cities. (*Compendium of Social Statistics: 1963* [United Nations, 1963], pp. 353-54 and 482-88.)

Table 15. *Index Numbers of Real Wages in Non-Agricultural Industries: Yearly, 1950-1961*

Country	1950	1951	1952	1953	1954	1955	1956	1957	1958	1959	1960	1961
Australia	96	100	99	100	104	109	108	110	111	113	119	118
Canada	88	88	94	100	102	105	109	112	113	117	119	121
Ceylon	93	97	100	100	102	122	121	97	112	125	134	137
Cyprus	96	95	99	100	101	114	124	131	131	129	133	140
Ghana							100	99	109	111	112	119
Northern Rhodesia								100	102	104	111	
Singapore					100	110	128	131	132	135	137	139
South Africa	97	98	99	100	99	100	99	100	98	99	98	
Trinidad and Tobago				89	100	102	103	108	109	111	113	125
Tanganyika					100	112	143	161	157	160	181	198	208
United Kingdom		97	96	96	100	104	107	111	113	114	118	126	129
France		84	92	94	100	105	113	123	129	125	126	131	139
Federal Republic of Germany		84	89	94	100	102	107	113	121	127	132	143	154

Tables 16 and 17

The indices in Tables 16 and 17 provide analysis of the movement of the value of the aggregate exports or imports of each country shown into a component due to changes in price (unit value index) and a component due to changes in volume (quantum index). (*Statistical Yearbook, 1962* [United Nations, 1963], pp. 425 and 450-59; and *ibid., 1963,* pp. 478-87.)

Tables 18, 19, 20, 21 and 22

These tables make use of the latest annual data available in 1964 provided jointly by the United Nations, the International Monetary Fund, and the International Bank for Reconstruction and Development concerning the "direction of international trade." The data have been converted into United States dollars by the International Monetary Fund. Annual data are on a cumulative basis from January on, except for India and Pakistan for 1948 where data are for the year beginning April 1, 1948. There is some inconsistency among data of different countries as to inclusions and exclusions of certain items, in particular: military supplies, transit trade, and strategic materials. In general the territory to which the figures refer is the customs area of the country concerned as defined by the country itself for each period covered. Naturally, there was considerable redefinition of nations and customs areas between 1948 and 1959. Peculiarities of the data are described thoroughly in the original source.

Table 16. *Exports of Commonwealth Countries: Index Numbers by Countries* [*Volume/Price (unit value): 1958 = 100*]

Country		1948	1954	1955	1956	1957	1958	1959	1960	1961	1962
Australia	V	71	91	90	99	112	100	114	121	128	144
	P	107	124	112	104	116	100	88	98	92	94
British Guiana	V	70	98	106	105	106	100	105	129	—	—
	P	79	90	90	95	108	100	100	98	—	—
Canada	V	77	84	91	99	99	100	103	108	117	121
	P	80	95	96	99	101	100	103	102	98	96
Ceylon	V	78	97	102	98	93	100	99	103	107	115
	P	101	109	114	107	102	100	104	104	95	91
Cyprus	V	54	96	98	100	107	100	109	108	100	—
	P	82	102	110	127	105	100	96	95	97	—
East Africa (Kenya, Tanganyika, Uganda)	V	43	68	77	89	89	100	106	117	111	—
	P	105	123	116	110	107	100	98	96	95	—
Ghana	V	91	98	96	109	121	100	122	141	174	185
	P		111	94	76	72	100	89	78	63	58
India	V		97	106	102	110	100	107	101	105	112
	P		105	97	101	101	100	100	109	111	—
Jamaica	V	41	77	83	91	103	100	101	127	—	—
	P	92	88	92	92	107	100	97	96	—	—
Malaya, Federation of	V		94	100	103	105	100	109	123	133	136
	P		87	125	116	110	100	120	127	105	102
Mauritius	V	73	93	90	102	112	100	98	58	100	102
	P	97	97	96	101	102	100	102	110	102	103
New Zealand	V	81	85	89	94	94	100	109	107	110	—
	P	98	119	122	119	117	100	114	111	104	—
Nigeria	V	66	95	94	105	101	100	120	118	140	149
	P	107	118	104	98	99	100	105	106	99	94
Pakistan	V										
	P		111	108	102	109	100	94	114	158	—
Rhodesia and Nyasaland, Fed. of	V		93	85	96	103	100	125	135	140	145
	P		118	152	142	113	100	111	112	108	106
South Africa	V	48	81	91	97	103	100	112	116	124	—
	P	108	103	102	107	109	100	98	96	95	—
Trinidad and Tobago	V	—	66	72	87	92	100	114	130	—	—
	P	—	99	100	96	106	100	98	93	—	—
United Kingdom	V		90	96	102	104	100	104	110	112	115
	P		91	93	96	101	100	99	101	102	103
France	V	35	84	97	87	96	100	120	140	148	150
	P	113	97	98	103	104	100	92	97	96	96
Federal Republic of Germany	V		62	72	84	95	100	112	128	136	140
	P		95	95	100	102	100	99	101	106	107
United States	V	76	91	92	109	115	100	98	113	112	117
	P	92	93	94	97	101	100	101	101	104	104
U.S.S.R.	V			77	81	97	100	132	133	147	171
	P										

Table 17. *Imports of Commonwealth Countries: Index Numbers by Countries* [*Volume/Price (unit value): 1958 = 100*]

Country		1948	1954	1955	1956	1957	1958	1959	1960	1961	1962
Australia	V	65	94	114	108	92	100	101	118	140	114
	P	92	92	94	96	98	100	100	101	103	103
Canada	V	60	84	95	113	108	100	111	109	112	115
	P	83	94	93	96	101	100	99	99	98	97
Ceylon	V	61	88	86	94	99	100	111	104	97	—
	P		106	98	102	114	100	100	101	104	101
Cyprus	V	39	69	84	105	113	100	116	111	115	129
	P		91	96	100	105	100	98	96	96	—
East Africa (Kenya, Tanganyika, Uganda)	V		97	123	107	113	100	99	105	114	—
	P		99	99	102	102	100	100	104	98	—
Ghana	V	41	85	108	104	113	100	130	145	159	136
	P		99	97	100	101	100	103	106	106	102
India	V		79	83	98	111	100	110	—	—	—
	P		97	97	99	107	100	93	98	99	—
Jamaica	V	47	64	79	92	102	100	103	109	—	—
	P	95	79	88	96	101	100	103	104	—	—
Malaya, Federation of	V		74	95	104	104	100	106	128	134	152
	P		107	98	101	105	100	98	101	99	101
Malta	V	72	77	74	90	89	100	97	103	105	104
	P	123	95	99	102	105	100	100	99	98	96
Mauritius	V	52	73	84	77	89	100	102	118	115	118
	P	126	99	101	98	99	100	95	94	94	92
New Zealand	V	59	91	105	96	103	100	83	100	114	—
	P	95	93	95	97	100	100	98	99	100	—
Nigeria	V	26	66	82	91	89	100	109	123	129	121
	P	128	101	99	101	103	100	98	103	103	105
Pakistan	V										
	P		74	79	84	93	100	97	100	102	101
Rhodesia and Nyasaland, Fed. of	V		86	94	105	115	100	98	100	96	88
	P		92	94	96	98	100	97	99	103	103
South Africa	V	88	84	91	91	99	100	90	102	95	—
	P	104	95	95	98	100	100	97	98	96	—
Trinidad and Tobago	V		63	72	73	83	100	110	120	—	—
	P		93	98	100	104	100	98	103	—	—
United Kingdom	V		87	97	97	100	100	107	121	118	122
	P		101	104	106	108	100	99	100	98	97
France	V	56	72	82	95	101	100	98	117	127	144
	P	109	101	100	104	108	100	92	96	94	93
Federal Republic of Germany	V		60	74	83	92	100	118	139	149	170
	P		104	106	108	110	100	97	99	100	98
United States	V	64	76	85	92	95	100	119	114	112	128
	P	85	102	102	104	105	100	99	100	99	96
U.S.S.R.	V			68	78	83	100	120	130	134	149
	P										

23

The Changing Role of Sterling

J. S. G. Wilson*

I

The sterling area is a product of historical evolution. To some extent it owed its emergence to political factors, and over the years Commonwealth countries have formed the hard core. But economic factors largely provided the *raison d'être* for the banker-customer relationship which is of its essence. Originally, these arrangements derived from a particular pattern of trade. In simple terms, it consisted of the export of manufactured goods in exchange for imports of food and raw materials. Since the incomes of primary producing countries tend to fluctuate rather violently, they were inclined to build up balances in good years and to run them down in bad. Yet at no time was this trade confined to a particular political grouping and, in fact, Britain traded with the world.

In addition, London was during the nineteenth century a major source of capital and lent freely to the countries with which she traded. Although sometimes unwilling to spend the whole of her export proceeds on imports, she was prepared to lend, in this way making her export surplus available for investment in the development of countries overseas. In these ways, a regular supply of sterling was made available for worldwide use. There was confidence in its stability and it was freely accepted in payment of debts. Moreover, London already possessed an

* Professor of economics, University of Hull, England.

established banking and financial mechanism capable of servicing trade and investment on a worldwide scale. It was therefore convenient to hold sterling funds on deposit in London and to employ a market in which they could be invested profitably at short-term.

London became the world's banker, accepting deposits and lending both short- and long-term either for the purpose of financing trade or to assist development and economic expansion. As with domestic banking, it was necessary to maintain a reserve of cash so that these deposit liabilities (or sterling balances) could if necessary be converted into gold on demand. This was the basis of confidence in sterling.

Gradually, the pattern of trade changed and the rather simple dichotomy between manufacturing and primary producing countries gave way to the much more complex interrelationships of diversified economies, though many countries (including Britain) were rather slow to adjust their industrial structures in sympathy. Two world wars and the Great Depression of the 1930's undoubtedly hastened the changes that were taking place, though they did not initiate them. Disequilibrium in production and consumption led to trading difficulties and currency instability. With the devaluation of sterling in September, 1931, there was a marked loss of confidence. This accentuated the effects of the shrinking quantum of world trade, which of itself reduced the extent to which sterling could be used as an international currency. For the remainder of the interwar years, sterling became a managed currency, after 1932 through the agency of the Exchange Equalisation Account, supported by a degree of international co-operation based on the Tripartite Monetary Agreement signed in 1936 with the United States and France and later adhered to by a number of other countries as well. These changes, together with the importance of the United Kingdom market for many producers of foods and raw materials, brought into being a sterling bloc in the sense that some currencies attached themselves to sterling, virtually pegging their exchange rates to the pound and thereafter operating on the basis of a sterling exchange standard, any surplus balances being held on deposit in London.

What had once been an international monetary standard rapidly disintegrated into a number of managed national currencies with attached currency blocs, some protected by exchange control. Indeed, with the outbreak of World War II sterling also sought the protection of exchange control. This move was followed almost immediately by the several associated currencies, and, for the first time, the existence of a "sterling area" received formal recognition. Later, under the Exchange Control Act of 1947, the countries of the sterling area were to be defined as "the scheduled territories." The membership varied from time to time, depending on the exigencies of war, but the fundamental *raison d'être* for the link with sterling remained the underlying pattern of trade, artificial though the direction of this trade may sometimes have been, especially during the war years.

Moreover, the rate at which sterling was being supplied had been accelerated by a level of wartime imports that could not immediately be paid for by exports. In consequence, there was an embarrassingly large accumulation of sterling liabilities, the postwar repayment of which was by agreement with the creditors staggered over a period of some years, their liquidation being greatly assisted by a price inflation that in real terms did much to reduce the burden of debt.

Meanwhile, both during the war and earlier postwar years, the gold and dollar reserves of the sterling area were centralized in London. Some of the scheduled territories were net dollar earners; others maintained a more or less balanced position; while the remainder customarily ran a dollar deficit, which was financed by drawing dollars from the central pool against sterling balances held in London. But, apart from the colonial territories, there was no compulsion about this. Each country was free to make its own dollar arrangements if it so wished. Indeed, South Africa, without breaking completely with sterling, did elect to become a "fringe" country and assumed responsibility for settling her own hard currency debts, mainly by the export of gold; but she also continued to contribute to the sterling area's central reserves by selling gold in London against sterling. Again, when Ceylon (and later other countries) achieved independence, they elected to retain a portion of their dollar earnings as part of their own currency reserves.

There was also consultation and a co-operative attempt to co-ordinate the operations of the several exchange controls in the autonomous member countries. Nevertheless, such countries remained within the sterling area only because on a balance of considerations such membership was still from their point of view convenient and advantageous. The only actual regulation that the United Kingdom authorities could be said to have exercised over these years (and they still do) concerned access to the London capital market, where the applicants were required to queue.

II

The essence of sterling area arrangements was a banker-customer relationship, whereby the outer sterling area countries held a major part of their overseas reserves on deposit or invested largely at short-term in London. These sums would originally have been earned by exporters and would have accrued to commercial banks in the countries concerned. Usually the bulk of these funds would then pass to the central bank in exchange for deposits with itself, though the commercial banks often retain working balances which they hold (and invest) in London for their own account. Whether London funds are held by the central bank or by the commercial banks, their existence will contribute to the over-all liquidity of the relevant banking system; and in the absence of off-setting action by the monetary authorities concerned there will be an increased internal flow of money, some proportion of which will inevitably be spent on imports and thus draw down funds held in London.

The extent to which these operations are dependent on a

closely knit system of banking arrangements will be obvious. In effect London is acting as banker for the sterling area and, indeed, to some extent for much of the rest of the world as well. Funds are left on short-term deposits and, when necessary, are withdrawn by their owners. They may wish to spend in sterling, in which case the funds will accrue to another holder of sterling, and the transaction is effected virtually by means of a book-keeping entry in London; or they may wish to make payments in non-sterling countries and therefore require foreign currencies in exchange for their sterling holdings. Against its liability to repay short-term funds on deposit with it, London as the sterling area's banker must hold a gold and foreign exchange reserve, and it is against this reserve that sterling area customers draw when they need non-sterling exchange. Likewise, following the dismantling of exchange control over current account transactions, so may other customers also.

The position is further complicated by the United Kingdom's own trading commitments and her need of reserves to meet them. She must also be capable of accommodating any speculative movements that might develop against sterling (e.g., should there be fears of a devaluation), which given time would usually tend to be reversed. Thus importers can build up stocks and anticipate payments only within certain limits. Likewise, purchasers of United Kingdom goods in other countries cannot indefinitely postpone payment in anticipation of a possible settlement of their debt in depreciated pounds. If the basic level of reserves is adequate, "leads" and "lags" can always be accommodated. So, too, can the inflow and subsequent outflow of "hot money," occasioned, for example, by changes in the United Kingdom level of interest rates. It is only when reserves are at unduly low levels that speculation could force a devaluation. In the absence of any deep-seated maladjustments in the domestic economy, there is little to fear. It is only when a country is quite unable to export sufficient goods to pay for its imports that the case for devaluation is strong. It may then become necessary to choke off imports by raising their prices to the consumer, meanwhile encouraging exports by making them cheaper to foreign buyers. Even then devaluation might be deferred by imposing drastic import restrictions, though the extent to which the United Kingdom could do this—in view of the size of its raw material imports—is distinctly limited. These questions that relate to the United Kingdom's domestic economy also have an international significance. Obviously if the trading world is to continue to use sterling as a reserve currency, confidence in it must be maintained. A devaluation might well destroy that confidence, and it is important therefore to maintain the value of sterling in relation to other currencies. That can only be assured if the United Kingdom economy is itself kept in a healthy condition.

London's position in the sterling area has been likened to that of a banker. Deposit banking would not be possible whether on a domestic or international basis if all the customers required repayment at one and the same time. It is only because customers prefer to keep their surplus funds on deposit rather than themselves to hold the whole of those funds (e.g., in gold) that a banker can operate at all. Nevertheless, he must maintain a reserve so that he can meet on demand any request for repayment. At various times there has been much discussion about the adequacy of the reserves held by London, but only in the immediate postwar years was it really necessary for the United Kingdom to seek an accommodation with her creditors in order to space out the repayment of moneys due. The big wartime accumulations of sterling balances have now been eliminated, and current holdings represent what has been built up over the postwar years largely out of trading surpluses.

Since any running down of the sterling balances of one holder tends to be offset at least in part by a building up of the balances of another, it is possible successfully to operate a banking business on the basis of reserves of gold and foreign exchange that appear to be quite modest. Indeed, this is one of the main purposes of the arrangement—to use international reserves of liquidity as economically as possible. Moreover, it might well be argued that in the more stable postwar world there is less need for very high ratios of liquid assets to liabilities. If the world at large can be persuaded that sterling's banking operations can be run efficiently and safely on the basis of a reserve ratio of between 20 and 25 per cent, there is no reason why this should not become established as the appropriate convention.

The case is even stronger when account is taken (a) of the fact that by no means all sterling balances constitute "quick" liabilities and (b) of the existence of "secondary" reserves and standby credit facilities.

To a not inconsiderable extent, the London balances of overseas sterling countries represent reserve funds of various kinds, some of them being earmarked for special purposes, such as currency reserves or sinking or pension funds. Of such balances, the central monetary institutions of overseas sterling countries hold a sizable proportion, something approximating £1,000 million of which is invested in British government and government-guaranteed stocks (this excludes Treasury bills). There is no necessary reason why these assets should continue to be held in sterling securities, though it is important to hold a high proportion of such reserves in external form, in order to accommodate any drain due to a balance-of-payments deficit. As several of the former colonial territories have gained their independence, they have in fact considered the possibility of investing their overseas balances in more than one center. At the same time, there are distinct advantages when the time comes for sale, if the relevant securities can be realized on a market capable of absorbing them without too drastic an impact on prices. Alternatively, reserves might be repatriated and held in gold, but if this dispersal of reserves became at all general it would mean that the total reserves available were being used less economically than they are when concentrated in a major world financial center. Nor will an investment income accrue on the gold so held.

The reserves maintained by marketing boards, for example, are intended for use in the event of a fall in the incomes of the producers concerned. In times of prosperity, when receipts are heavy, reserves are built up against the day when there might be a fall in export incomes. Moneys can then be paid out of the accumulated surplus. Whenever such payments have to be made disbursements are in local currencies, but, when an incomes-stabilization scheme is in operation, a fall in export incomes not offset by a decline in domestic incomes will necessarily impose a strain on the balance of payments as a result of the continued propensity to import. Overseas reserves will then have to be drawn upon to make good the deficit.

Although all member countries have borrowing rights at the International Monetary Fund, the relevance of "secondary" reserves additional to a nation's holdings of gold and foreign exchange was not generally appreciated prior to the Suez crisis of 1956, when sterling came under heavy pressure. In a sense, sterling thrives on crises. At other times it is merely taken for granted. The Suez crisis was provoked by political and military action and was primarily a crisis of confidence. In order to restore confidence, steps were taken to demonstrate the extent of sterling area liquidity by putting into the shop window some of the area's "secondary" reserves, the existence of which had sometimes tended to be overlooked. Liquidity is determined not merely by the amount of cash in hand, but also by borrowing rights and by the possibility of selling investments. On the basis of its borrowing rights, the United Kingdom arranged in December, 1956, to draw up to $1,300 million from the International Monetary Fund. Of this sum $561 million was drawn immediately and added to reserves. About the same time, it was disclosed that the United Kingdom held short-term U.S. Treasury securities of some $30 million and other longer-dated "hard currency" assets of a value estimated at between $750 and $1,000 millions. These were "secondary" reserves on any reckoning and it was decided to advertise not only their existence but also the extent to which they might be mobilized. It was therefore agreed with the U.S. Export-Import Bank that these securities should be pledged as collateral against a line of credit of $500 million. By this means it was clearly demonstrated that any serious drain of gold and dollars in order to pay for Western Hemisphere oil (or for any other reason) could easily be met without endangering the position of sterling.

Subsequently, more elaborate arrangements were introduced, whereby the central banks of a number of countries entered into agreements to co-operate in the mutual support of each other's currencies. Not only has further resort been made to the standby credit at the International Monetary Fund, but in December, 1961, a "gold pool" was set up by a number of central banks and currency swap arrangements were also made between the United States and several other countries.

Under the "gold pool" agreements, each participating country was given a quota for the amount of gold it was willing to provide against dollars. The total commitment was $270 million, divided between the U.S. ($135 million); Western Germany ($30 million); the U.K., France, and Italy ($25 million each); and Switzerland, Belgium, and the Netherlands ($10 million each). The pool is managed by the Bank of England, which may also make purchases on its behalf in any of the countries listed. Normally supplies come mainly from Russia (e.g., in order to obtain sterling) or private sellers, newly mined gold from South Africa being taken up by the Bank of England itself. At the end of each month the net balance between the month's sales and purchases is communicated to members and the deficit or surplus (as the case may be) is divided among them in accordance with their quotas. For example, speculation against the U.S. dollar in July, 1962, involved a gold drain of some $100 million. At this stage, the U.S. made a special contribution of $35 million in gold within the terms of the general arrangement that the pool should not bear the whole strain. This left a deficit of $65 million, for half of which the United States was also committed, leaving about $32 million to be financed by the European members. In the event of a surplus, as a result of net pool purchases, this is distributed amongst the eight member countries; i.e., the gold is sold to them by the Bank of England against dollars in proportion to their quotas. By accommodating sharp changes in the supply or demand for gold, to which the value of all International Monetary Fund currencies is related, the gold pool mechanism helps to stabilize the exchange values of the relevant currencies, by cushioning them, for example, against the whole impact of "hot" money movements.

An important additional step towards greater international monetary co-operation took the form of the currency swap arrangements between the central banks of the major countries of western Europe plus Canada and the U.S. By this means, additional support has been provided in particular for the two currencies most likely to be subjected to major strains, viz., sterling and the dollar in consequence of their widespread use for reserve purposes. Most of these swap arrangements were in fact developed to assist the United States in dealing with a persistent balance of payments deficit and, by October, 1963, the Federal Reserve Bank of New York had extended its network of reciprocal currency arrangements or "swaps" to include all the EEC countries, the U.K., Austria, Sweden, and Canada. It also had a swap agreement with the Bank for International Settlements. Of a total value of $1,800 million the largest was for $500 million with the Bank of England. The U.S. was also able to arrange for European holdings of dollars on a three-month basis to be converted into longer-term U.S. Treasury foreign currency bonds. At the end of August, 1963, these amounted to $705 million and were mainly in the hands of Western Germany, Italy, and Switzerland. Although much of this structure has been built up to assist the U.S. dollar, the arrangements are reciprocal and are available to support other currencies as well.

Meanwhile, the dollar guarantee for all sterling held by European central banks was formally ended as from March 1, 1963, when a revised European Monetary Agreement came into effect. This provided an automatic guarantee amounting to no more than the purely nominal figure of £11,250,000. This change was made at the request of the outer sterling area countries, which themselves had no guarantee in respect of their sterling holdings. Nevertheless, it is open to the Bank of England, if in the future it should be thought necessary, to offer guarantees against any particular European holdings that might be taken up specifically to assist sterling. As a result of these several arrangements, which followed and may in part have been occasioned by the general return to convertibility on current account at the end of 1958, it is clear that sterling is now tied in much more closely with the fortunes of other currencies, and the sterling area has in the process become more fully integrated with the world economy.

III

The U.K. has an "open" economy, as, indeed, have all other sterling area countries. In other words, the U.K. depends for her prosperity to a significant extent on overseas trade. The volume of that trade will in turn be a function of the prosperity of her customers. Despite the multilateral character of world trade, the ability of the U.K. to sell her goods abroad will in some measure be related to her capacity to absorb the exports of other countries. This in turn depends on the level of economic activity and incomes in the U.K. The nexus of sterling area (and world) trading arrangements is emphasized by the prominence given in day-to-day economic discussion to indices of commodity prices and the terms of trade.

As long as there remained a chronic dearth of dollars world trade was inevitably forced by controls into a somewhat artificial mold. But as dollars became more available as a result of (*a*) U.S. grants and loans for reconstruction and development, and (*b*) the consequential building up (especially in Europe) of the world's capacity to produce and to trade, controls and restrictions could be relaxed, and a more normal pattern of trade began to emerge. This had a two-way effect. Not only were dollars earned by exporting to and selling in the U.S., but the spending of dollars on U.S. goods exposed the domestic markets of many countries (including sterling countries) to greater competition from U.S. goods. Previously domestic markets had often been almost completely protected by exchange control and import licensing.

As import and exchange restrictions were relaxed, local industries that had mushroomed behind a wall of protection were subjected to much greater price competition and were thereby obliged to become more efficient, even though they sometimes successfully sought partial tariff protection.

As sterling became increasingly convertible—and, in the nature of things, it was a gradual process—the effects of world competition on the domestic economies of sterling area countries could be expected to become more marked. It was partly for this reason, for example, that 1957 proved to be such a difficult and troubled year. With freer world trading conditions, it became apparent that the underlying trading relationships within the sterling area were changing. Although Britain was anxious to maintain if not expand her Commonwealth markets for manufactured goods, her imports from Commonwealth countries were tending to decline. Meanwhile the outer sterling area countries were concerned to sell advantageously the primary products that still featured prominently amongst their exports, but Britain was now near saturation point as a food consumer and by no means the only important importer of raw materials.

Expanded sales of foods and raw materials from Commonwealth countries almost certainly lay elsewhere than in Britain. Moreover, if these markets were to be exploited to the full, it was likely that the outer sterling area countries would feel impelled to buy more from such countries as France, West Germany, Italy, Japan, and the U.S., and there was in fact a marked increase in Commonwealth trade (including that of the colonies) with, for example, western Europe. Sterling area exports to the U.S. and Canada also increased. In addition Australia (like Canada before her) had become a competitor with British industry (especially in Southeast Asia and the Pacific) in the export, for example, of electrical generators and motor cars.

All of these developments reflected structural changes, but the new trends were reinforced by the fact that the Ottawa preferential agreements dating from 1932 had been progressively undermined by inflation in consequence of the arrangement (e.g., in Australia and New Zealand) whereby British exports had enjoyed ad valorem preferences, while the preferences Britain had agreed to give were specific and therefore increasingly less valuable in real terms. At the same time, whatever hopes Britain had of increasing her trade with Commonwealth countries (and, in the capital goods field, these were not negligible), she was also interested in the possibilities of an expanding European market and, despite the difficulties of the European Free Trade Area negotiations and Britain's subsequent failure (in 1963) to join the EEC, the U.K. has in fact expanded steadily the volume of her trade with European countries.

Whatever the direction of their trade, the prosperity of countries producing foods and raw materials for export ultimately depends on that of the highly industrialized countries. Thus, the tendency for commodity prices to trend downwards for a whole decade until September, 1962 (though admittedly interrupted by occasional and temporary recoveries), was directly attributable to the state of demand in the world's leading industrial economies. On occasion, movements in commodity prices may be influenced both by political factors and, indeed, even by quite local developments, but the underlying and long-run determinants are economic and relate to the demands of the ultimate consumers. For example, the general strengthening of demand from the heavily industrialized countries was the basic reason for the steady improvement in commodity prices from September, 1962, onwards. By May, 1964, they were at their highest level for seven years. To a certain extent this rise could be explained by the incidence of a number of local factors, but these were exaggerative rather than causal. The fundamental reason for the rise was the fact that over this latter period practically all the major industrial countries had been putting their economies into top gear about the same time. Because of its long period of recession and its balance of payments difficulties, we had tended to forget, for example, the important role that is played by U.S. demand in world markets, but it is significant that commodity prices started to rise about the same time as

American economic activity began to recover. This reacted cumulatively upon the high rates of economic growth being achieved in Europe. To the associated increase in demand from that source, the U.K. latterly also began to add. It is clear that the sterling area is a much less self-contained unit than it was even a few years ago, and its constituent members depend even more directly for their prosperity on that of the world as a whole.

For most sterling area countries the combined effect of good commodity sales at rising prices was certainly favorable. Imports also increased but at a lower rate. Again, these developments reflect a fundamental economic relationship, and, indeed, the ebb and flow of the demand for primary products is an observed fact. Moreover, the demand from industrial countries, though it is related to fluctuations in their own levels of economic activity, is itself subject to leads and lags. Hence, primary producing countries often find themselves in balance-of-payments difficulties at a time when their customers can boast of a very sound reserve position.

Ordinarily, with the beginnings of industrial recovery, there will be an increased demand for raw materials, and the export incomes (and reserves, including sterling balances) of the primary producing countries will tend to rise. If export prices also rise, the terms of trade (i.e., the relation between the prices paid for imports and those received for exports) will tend to move against the industrial countries. Meanwhile, because of the rise in their export incomes, the primary producers will increase their orders of manufactured goods. While these orders are still in the pipeline, the reserves of the primary producers will continue to rise, encouraging them to increase their orders still further. Then, when the manufactured goods begin to arrive and have to be paid for, the reserves (and sterling balances) of the primary producers begin to tumble, and they are likely to experience balance-of-payments difficulties. Yet, because of these orders, the prosperity of the industrial countries (and their reserves) may continue for a time to go on increasing. Only when the now reduced spending power of the primary producing countries begins to be transmitted through reduced orders to the industrialized countries will the latter's balances of payments begin to come under pressure.

It is also necessary to emphasize in this context that important though intra-sterling area trade still is, a significant amount of trade has always taken place between sterling area countries and the outside world. Hence, the earnings of outer sterling area countries will derive in part from exports to non-sterling countries. Very frequently, the financial transactions will be cleared through London, where the foreign currencies that have been earned will be exchanged for sterling, which at least temporarily may then be allowed to accumulate and be held as a sterling balance, the foreign currencies being added to the U.K.'s reserves. For this reason, the balance-of-payments surpluses of outer sterling area countries (e.g., as a result of the recent rise in commodity prices) may at the appropriate phase of the upward swing in economic activity serve to offset or neutralize any tendency for a drain to develop on the U.K.'s gold and foreign currency reserves, though the additional reserves so gained by the U.K. will be balanced by—and be reflected in—an increase in the U.K.'s liabilities to the outer sterling area, i.e., in its holdings of sterling balances.

Broadly speaking, this then is the framework within which much of the sterling area's trade takes place. It helps to explain why, for example, in 1958—and despite the emergence of some recession—the U.K.'s balance of payments remained strong and her reserve position healthy. This situation continued into 1959, permitting the freeing from import restriction of a wide range of dollar and other goods, some repayment of outstanding debts, and the decision not to renew the standby credit with the IMF. Then, when the tide began to run the other way, with an emergent boom in the U.K., gradually the other members of the sterling area found their economies increasingly in better shape, even though the degree of recovery was rather uneven. The extent to which the effects of an increased demand in raw materials will percolate through to specific outer sterling area countries depends on the products most in demand and whether particular countries produce these materials or not. For similar reasons, when there is a price fall some countries will be more vulnerable than others, though some of the more important national economies are now becoming sufficiently diversified to absorb the impact of localized shocks to a much greater extent than was formerly the case. The most vulnerable are those with a national income dependent on no more than one or two major export commodities. It is they that commodity price equalization schemes would most obviously assist.

Over the long decade when commodity prices were trending downwards, the terms of trade enjoyed by the industrialized countries were favorable and all of them tended to gain at the expense of the less developed and primary producing countries of the world. The reasons are not far to seek and they are all too reminiscent of the experience of the 1930's. In brief, and despite the recent upward surge in commodity prices, the general downward trend which over the longer term is likely to continue is due to the impact of technological change. Nowadays, it is possible to produce foods and raw materials ever more efficiently, while technological developments in the industrialized countries have encouraged them to economize in the use of the traditional raw materials and sometimes to replace these with synthetics. As a result, natural products tend to be in surplus, and, during times of recession, the attempts of producers to compensate for lower prices by higher sales have tended to push surpluses to even higher levels. The situation has also been greatly aggravated by high-cost production of foods and raw materials in many of the industrialized countries on the basis of either protection or subsidy. Meanwhile, the industrialized countries are tending to export more and more to each other (and therefore to import more and more from each other), something (it may be remembered) that was also a feature of world trade patterns in pre-World War II days.

There seem to be two main reasons for these developments.

sufficiently reorientated to provide the basis for more trade—largely in terms of more manufactured goods.

The trends noticeable over the past few years might reasonably be expected to continue. Because developing countries will continue to develop, one must expect that their trade will tend to expand rather more rapidly than that of older industrial countries like Britain—the former start from a lower base level and the opportunities for rapid expansion (once the critical breakthrough is effected) are much greater in consequence. Hence, Britain's share of total sterling area trade will tend to fall. Moreover, to the extent that overseas sterling area countries develop trading patterns similar to those of the U.K., swings in their balances of payments will tend to synchronize with those of Britain much more than in the past, and, for the sterling area as a whole, this could periodically accentuate pressure on the reserves, whether these be centrally held in London or (as is increasingly the case) by the outer sterling area countries themselves (in gold and non-sterling currencies).[1]

Relatively, too, there has been some decline in the use made of sterling as an international reserve currency. The total of overseas sterling holdings (as Table 1 shows) has remained remarkably steady, but in real terms their value has certainly been reduced. Nevertheless, the use of sterling as a reserve currency continues, and, judging by the switches in ownership (the drawings of one country being offset by increases in the sterling holdings of another), sterling is still very actively employed both for trading and reserve purposes. In addition, it is much to be desired that other reserve currencies (like the U.S. dollar) should emerge to share the burdens of financing world trade and of effecting capital movements. This is the obvious consequence of increasing interdependence.

The mere accumulation of sterling balances is by no means the only indication of the amount of world trade currently being

1. "There is no particular pattern underlying these gold holdings which, as a proportion of reserves, vary from country to country. The reasons for holding gold have to be balanced against the need for sterling for international payments; and, unlike sterling, gold does not earn its keep." See "Overseas Sterling Holdings," Bank of England, *Quarterly Bulletin*, III (Dec., 1963), 266-67.

financed by sterling. But if (in very general terms) one can relate the amount of trade undertaken by means of sterling with the size of the balances maintained in sterling, then a good deal of financing still depends on London. Although the big wartime accumulations have now been eliminated, overseas sterling area countries still hold about two-thirds of the total (their funds also tend to be less volatile than those of other groups, having fluctuated over the past ten years between £2,478 million in 1960 and the high of £2,822 million in 1954). These holdings, it should be noted, represent what has been retained

Table 2. *Gross Holdings of Sterling, End-June, 1963*

A. Overseas sterling countries	£ Million
Australia, New Zealand, and South Africa	559
India, Pakistan, and Ceylon	225
Caribbean area	195
East, Central, and West Africa	390
Middle Eastern countries*	423
Far Eastern countries†	675
Other overseas sterling countries‡	296
Total overseas sterling countries	2,763

*Persian Gulf territories, Libya, and Jordan.
†Malaysia, Brunei, Hong Kong, and Burma.
‡Malta, Gibraltar, Mauritius, Fiji, and other dependent territories not elsewhere included; Cyprus, the Republic of Ireland, and Iceland.

B. Non-sterling countries	£ Million
EFTA countries	221
EEC countries	205
Other West European countries*	105
East European countries	41
Middle Eastern countries†	135
Far Eastern countries‡	154
North America§	113
Latin America‖	41
Other non-sterling countries	22
Total non-sterling countries	1,037

*Finland, Greece, Spain, Turkey, and Yugoslavia.
†Egypt, Iran, Iraq, Israel, Lebanon, Saudi Arabia, Sudan, Syria, and Yemen.
‡China, Indonesia, Japan, Thailand, Formosa, Cambodia, Laos, Vietnam, Korea, and the Philippines.
§United States and dependencies, and Canada.
‖Other independent countries of the American continent.

Source: Bank of England, *Quarterly Bulletin*, III (Dec., 1963).

over the postwar years out of trading surpluses. Moreover, now that funds can be moved fairly freely, the decision whether or not to hold reserves in sterling increasingly depends on considerations of commercial and financial advantage. In other words, if countries continue to hold sterling balances, they do so from choice.

IV

The other main contribution that London has been able to offer to the outer sterling area over a long period of years is access to its capital market. Although the funds available to meet their investment requirements are much less than is needed, many Commonwealth countries continue to look primarily to London for the external capital necessary to develop their economies. Very largely, this reflects the advantage of an established connection. It is true that by no means all needs of these countries can be met by borrowing in London, and, in the earlier postwar years, new borrowings had to compete also with releases from the wartime accumulations of sterling balances. But by insisting that borrowers take their turn in the queue, the authorities have been able to enforce a degree of rationing and to ensure that quite substantial sums are raised without forcing rates up to exorbitant levels. In addition, Commonwealth countries can and do borrow elsewhere. Several of them have borrowed, for example, from the World Bank, and issues have also been made in certain other capital markets— e.g., New York, Switzerland, and Amsterdam.

To some extent, London's capacity to lend depends on the amount of savings being undertaken within the U.K. itself and not currently being absorbed by investment at home. But, in addition, the U.K. does a considerable entrepôt business. Indeed, the amounts made available from domestic sources over the postwar years have been substantially supplemented by an inflow of funds from other countries, which has permitted a net outflow to the sterling area. In effect, the U.K. has been acting as a banker-middleman—borrowing to relend. But these funds derive as much from permanent overseas investment in the U.K. as from the movement to London of temporary surplus balances. In recent years, the inflow of direct investment into the U.K. has been growing, and, in some years (e.g., in 1961, when it was £225 million) it has been quite substantial. This excludes oil and insurance, but includes for the year quoted the £131 million Ford take-over of its British subsidiary, as well as large foreign purchases of British securities. Likewise, much U.K. investment is direct (i.e., not funneled through the market) and the technique of setting up subsidiaries or branch plants has been practiced in

Table 3. *Capital Transactions* (£ millions)

	Total			Overseas sterling countries			Non-sterling countries		
	1959	1960	1961	1959	1960	1961	1959	1960	1961
Gross new investment abroad	55	48	38	42	35	32	13	13	6
Gross repayment from abroad	34	25	17	16	15	12	18	10	5
Net new investment (−) or repayment (+)	−21	−23	−21	−26	−20	−20	+ 5	− 3	− 1
Other capital transactions	+55	+59	+69	+23	+34	+32	+32	+25	+37
Total net cash inflow to UK (+) or outflow from UK (−)	+34	+36	+48	− 3	+14	+12	+37	+22	+36

Note: The signs conform to those normally used in balance of payments accounts, an increase in U.K. assets being shown—and a decrease +.

Source: Bank of England, *Quarterly Bulletin*, II (June, 1962), 104.

western Europe as well as in the Commonwealth. For a summary of the extent of capital transactions in recent years, see Table 3.

Nevertheless, lenders everywhere have been selective, and, in some countries, capital is particularly shy. This is partly due to the sheer ignorance of the investing public, when considering propositions that relate to loans outside one's own national borders. One way of overcoming this kind of difficulty is for London to develop further the entrepôt business it is already undertaking. By this means, it will be possible effectively to marry

London's expertise and experience with the flows of financial capital that could be made available for international investment from such countries as Western Germany and France. Even though a particular national economy may be too small to support an international capital market, it may nevertheless be able to participate in capital export by using the services of a larger center, which can provide the necessary degree of breadth both to make capital available in appropriately large amounts and to facilitate, if necessary, the withdrawal of funds by being able to sell securities in a ready market. The size of a market is also important when considering its vulnerability to movements of "hot money."

Another example of London's initiative is the developing entrepôt business based on Euro-dollar operations.[2] These were stimulated by the coming of non-resident convertibility, which enabled non-residents to exchange European currencies without restriction into dollars. The business in Euro-dollars derives from the acceptance of dollar claim deposits by banks (chiefly in Europe) and the lending of these claims to other customers typically for short periods. The large increase in supplies of funds to this market consists mainly of foreign-owned dollar claims as a result of the U.S. balance-of-payments deficit. The demand comes from a wide range of customers, including both those who require dollars to finance international trade and American corporations that (because of the size of transactions and the rapid turnover) find the funds in this market cheaper than loans available from traditional lenders at home. In addition, such dollars may be used to buy other currencies which can then be lent in foreign markets, subject to a hedge against the exchange risk.

The loan arranged in October, 1963, for the City of Copenhagen by a London house heading an international syndicate was a further instance of entrepôt business par excellence. The loan was not intended for the British investor at all, the bonds being resold by the syndicate at par in the various capital mar-

2. See J. S. G. Wilson, "The Internationalisation of Capital Markets," *Three Banks Review*, No. 62, June, 1964, pp. 3-24.

kets of Europe, primarily with a view to attracting non-resident Swiss francs. It is probable that this technique of arranging long-term loans in the currencies of other countries (which is an extension of the Euro-dollar technique) will be increasingly developed as the internationalization of the world's capital markets proceeds.

Indeed, this development indicates the probable direction of change. With the emergence of a U.S. balance of payments deficit (though this will eventually be reduced to manageable proportions), the dollar has become more available, and an interesting new relationship has developed with the pound, such that the two together are better able to bear the burdens of providing international reserve currency facilities. Likewise, the pattern of the Euro-dollar market has suggested a means of linking together a number of the world's capital markets and provides a broader base for supplying the needs of the developing countries. It is possibly through this door, too, that sterling (and the dollar) will glide into a wider currency grouping, and, ultimately, no doubt the sterling area as such will disappear. If the world's financial and capital markets became integrated in this way, an even wider range of transactions would be channeled through the centers of London and New York and the world's main trading and reserve currencies could expect to be even more heavily in demand. The development of a new international financial mechanism is certainly one way of assisting the growth in world trade on which the raising of living standards in part depends. The role to be played by sterling over the course of the next decade may thus be even more significant than in its nineteenth-century heyday.

24

External Economic Aid to Underdeveloped Countries of the Commonwealth

Calvin B. Hoover*

An analysis of external economic aid to the underdeveloped countries of the Commonwealth might be restricted to aid from countries *outside* the Commonwealth. This would be almost entirely United States aid. However, since a part of foreign economic aid to underdeveloped countries of the Commonwealth has come from the developed countries of the Commonwealth, I shall also analyze this form of economic aid. The consideration of economic aid from Commonwealth countries is all the more essential since the proportion from Commonwealth sources seems likely to increase.

Economic aid to the underdeveloped countries of the Commonwealth can be understood only as part of worldwide international economic aid. There has been a close connection between economic aid from outside and inside the Commonwealth from the beginning. In the first place, aid from the United States under the Marshall Plan facilitated the economic revival of the United Kingdom following World War II. The government of the U.K. could otherwise hardly have permitted utilization of the large sterling balances which largely reflected expenditures it incurred in the common war effort. The privilege of utilizing these balances was of great importance to Commonwealth countries, such as India, in meeting their balance of payments deficits. In the early days of the Marshall Plan, we included the exports

* James B. Duke Professor of Economics, Duke University.

so financed in what we called "unrequited exports," meaning that no compensating imports of goods or services were being currently received by what might be called the donor country.

There can be little doubt that present international economic aid does not exist simply on account of current justification and rationalization, but because this aid got "spliced on" to foreign economic aid which began for other reasons. The current system of international economic aid thus owes its origin largely to the Marshall Plan. Lend-lease aid had been furnished as a means of winning the war. UNRRA was provided as a means of immediate postwar relief to our allies. Marshall Plan aid was furnished originally primarily to prevent the spread of Communism in Europe.[1] Gradually Marshall Plan aid became aid justified for reasons other than the original one, and eventually aid for underdeveloped countries could be separated out from Marshall Plan aid. It could be justified both on grounds of preventing a Communist take-over and on the grounds of furnishing the means for economic and political stability. At the present time, aid has come to be justified primarily on the humanitarian grounds of enabling these countries to build the economic foundations for a higher standard of living. Original justifications faded into later ones almost imperceptibly.

In the beginning, there was no differentiated program for Commonwealth countries. Indeed, there is even now no category of United States aid for Commonwealth countries as a class. With the development of the Colombo Plan and with the planning of a special program for India, however, the United States aid program came to have certain characteristics tailored for particular Commonwealth countries.

Just as the motivation for the U.S. foreign aid program changed through time, and just as different motivations overlapped each other, so have the forms of the aid changed and overlapped. The Draper Report[2] listed the major post-World War

1. Calvin B. Hoover, "Foreign Economic Aid and Communism," *Journal of Political Economy*, LIX (Feb., 1951), 1-13. The writer was a member of the President's Committee on Foreign Aid which formulated the Marshall Plan in 1947.
2. "Conclusions Concerning the Mutual Security Program," *Letter to the President of the United States from the President's Committee to Study the United*

II foreign assistance programs as of that date: UNRRA (UN Relief Rehabilitation); GARIOA (Government Aid and Relief in Occupied Areas); Assistance to Philippines; Assistance to China; Assistance to Greece and Turkey; "Point Four" (Inst. of Inter-American Affairs and Tech. Co-op.); Marshall Plan; MDAP (Mutual Defense Assistance Program); British Loan; MSP (Mutual Security Program); Agricultural Surpluses (Public Law 480); Contributions to UN Assistance Programs; Export-Import Bank. Although a number of these programs have been "phased out," others have been added, including the Alliance for Progress, applicable only to Latin America, and "Food for Peace," which has taken over the disposal of agricultural surpluses under Public Law 480. From fiscal 1946 through fiscal 1963, U.S. aid to Foreign Assistance Act countries amounted in obligations and loan authorizations to $104 billion. Of this total, over $71 billion was economic aid.[3]

Almost without exception, each of these programs came to include elements which had not originally been intended. For example, under the Mutual Defense Assistance Program, there came to be an item called "Defense Support." Quite large expenditures under this item came to be for items which were not of a military nature at all; they simply supported the economy of the particular country in order to assist it in providing for defense expenditures.

United States economic aid to the underdeveloped countries of the Commonwealth has now become part of a more comprehensive program of aid to the less developed countries both within and without the Commonwealth by the countries of the OEEC. The total flow of long-term financial resources from governmental sources to less developed countries and to international agencies providing aid and assistance to these countries from the twelve OEEC countries which participated in the Development Aid Committee amounted in 1962 to $5,957 million.

States Military Assistance Program and the Committee's Final Report (Aug. 17, 1959) (Washington: G.P.O., 1959), p. 17.

3. Statistics and Reports Division, Agency for International Development, *U.S. Aid to Foreign Assistance Act Countries (Preliminary)* (Aug. 22, 1963), p. 1.

The twelve participating countries were Belgium, Canada, Denmark, France, Germany, Italy, Japan, the Netherlands, Norway, Portugal, the United Kingdom, and the United States. Of the total, the United States provided 3,606 millions; the United Kingdom, 417 millions; Canada, 50 millions. During the seven-year period from 1957 through 1962 for which comparable figures are readily available, total annual governmental aid increased from $3,206 million to $5,957 million. During the same period, the figure for the United States increased from $1,996 to $3,606 millions, while that for the U.K. increased from $205 million to $417 million.

During the same seven-year period, net private investment by these twelve countries in the less developed countries remained without trend at slightly less than $2,500 millions. There are certain statistical and conceptual difficulties about adding governmental and private investment together, but if one did combine the amounts, the total in 1962 would have been about $8,400 million. Thus, almost three-fourths of the financial resources provided the less developed countries were from governmental sources. To arrive at any of these totals, quite disparate amounts have to be lumped together. Thus it makes a great difference both to the recipient and to the donor country whether the aid furnished is in the form of a non-repayable grant, whether the interest is 2 per cent or 4 per cent, if a loan, whether the length of the interest-free grace period before repayment is required is long or short, if such is provided, whether the loans are "tied" or not, and the like.[4] We can be sure that statistics on such complex matters as those with which we are here concerned, coming from different sources and covering time periods with different terminal dates, will not quite coincide.

Intra-Commonwealth financial aid to less developed countries was largely from the United Kingdom.[5] For 1962-63 aid

4. These data are from a report by Willard L. Thorp, Chairman Development Assistance Committee, *Development Assistance Efforts and Policies, 1963 Review* (O.E.C.D., Sept., 1963), Table 1, p. 79. In *ibid.*, Table 3, p. 81, there is a breakdown which indicates the differences in the form of the financial aid by countries for 1962. (See Appendixes A and B.)

5. For fiscal 1961-62 Canadian economic aid to Commonwealth countries

from the U.K. amounted to a total of roughly £123 million, divided almost equally between the colonial territories and independent Commonwealth countries. The table in the appendix shows the breakdown between grants and loans. In addition, the figure of £15 million for loans to other countries is shown, and an amount of roughly £10 million for aid through international organizations is also shown.[6] During fiscal 1962, U.S. aid to Foreign Assistance Act political divisions which were either members of the Commonwealth or British colonial territories amounted to $1,403.3 million. This was a little less than 40 per cent of all United States economic aid advanced to underdeveloped countries.[7] It was roughly four times the amount of aid extended by the U.K. to Commonwealth countries and colonial territories. U.K. loans have been extended for maximum periods of twenty-five years with a grace period of seven years before repayment begins. The intention to extend the maximum period to thirty years and the grace period to ten years in some cases has been announced by the British government.

In any analysis of external aid to underdeveloped countries of the Commonwealth, the Colombo Plan merits particular attention. As has been apparent in the presentation thus far, almost all forms of foreign aid are commingled in complex relationships. This is particularly true of the Colombo Plan. The Colombo Plan was exclusively a Commonwealth affair in its origin in the Consultative Committee set up at a meeting of the Commonwealth governments in Sydney, Australia, in May, 1950. This committee, meeting in London in September of that year, drew up a blueprint of the Colombo Plan, setting forth six-year development plans for seven Commonwealth coun-

amounted to about 52 million dollars. Data furnished by the Canadian Institute of International Affairs, derived from External Aid Office, *Report on Canadian External Aid Program, and Public Accounts of Canada* (Ottawa: Queen's Printer, 1961 and 1962). Annual economic aid to the less well-developed countries from New Zealand amounted to about £NZ3 million ($8.4 million) of which about half went to Commonwealth countries. Australian economic aid amounted to £A9,889,500. (See Appendices E, F, and G.)

6. H. M. Treasury, *Aid to Developing Countries* (London: H.M.S.O., Sept., 1963), p. 15. (See Appendix C.)

7. See Appendix D.

tries of South and Southeast Asia, Ceylon, India, Pakistan, Malaya, Singapore, North Borneo, and Sarawak. The governments of the United Kingdom, Australia, Canada, and New Zealand also participated. The meeting identified some of the problems of the area, and suggested the ways in which external aid could help in its development.[8] Other countries not members of the Commonwealth were invited to join the Colombo Plan organization; Burma, Cambodia, Indonesia, Laos, Nepal, the Philippines, Thailand, Vietnam, Japan, and the United States later did so.

From the beginning of the Colombo Plan to about the middle of 1959, total external aid to the countries of South and Southeast Asia amounted to some $6,500 million or roughly £2,300 million, including both capital aid and technical assistance. Of this amount, the United States furnished about $5,660 million, or about £2,021 million. The United Kingdom furnished about £150 million, Canada $352 million, Australia £31 million and New Zealand over £9 million pounds. India had committed 133 million rupees to Nepal for her first five-year plan. Japan had committed about 600 million yen for Colombo Plan aid. Thus over 85 per cent of the aid from outside the area was furnished by the United States.[9] Assistance under the plan covers substantially all forms of socioeconomic development, including scientific development of agriculture, irrigation, basic industries, sanitation and disease control, nutrition, village development programs, national highways and roads, community development programs, training of students abroad, and many others.

In addition to economic aid from the developed countries of the free world, a substantial amount of economic aid has been furnished by what used to be called the "Sino-Soviet bloc." Such estimates of Sino-Soviet aid as are available are not readily comparable with statistics of those of and from the free world. For what it may be worth, one estimate shows the amount of Sino-

8. *The Colombo Plan, Facts and Figures* (2nd ed.; Colombo Plan Bureau, 1960), p. 1.

9. *The Colombo Plan, Questions and Answers* (3rd ed.; Colombo Plan Bureau, 1960), pp. 1-18.

Soviet economic aid to all underdeveloped countries from 1955 through 1960 to have been $7.1 billion. This may be compared with economic aid of $9.3 billion furnished by the free world, excluding the United States.[10] During the same period, total economic aid by the United States, primarily to underdeveloped countries, amounted to $28 billion.[11]

Economic aid from the Sino-Soviet bloc has been largely in the form of repayable short-term credits at rates of interest which are low in comparison with commercial rates, but which are much more onerous than the terms for loans and grants by the United States. Underdeveloped countries would strenuously oppose the use of interest and amortization on their aid loans from the United States for the purchase of current exports. Sino-Soviet aid to underdeveloped countries, however, has largely amounted to the barter of munitions and capital equipment for the exports of these countries rather than "aid" in the usual sense.

Soviet Russia claims to have advanced credits amounting to 15 per cent of India's foreign currency expenditures during that country's second five-year plan.[12] In repayment, the Soviet Union took 25 per cent of India's small raw hides, 50 per cent of her black pepper, 20 per cent of her raw wool, 25 per cent of her castor oil, and 10 per cent of her cashew nuts. In addition, the Soviet Union imported increasing quantities of jute material and bags, leather footwear, woolen fabrics, coconut fibre goods, and handicraft wares;[13] Soviet aid to Commonwealth countries between January, 1954, and June, 1962, was limited to four countries: India $810 million, Pakistan $35 million, Ghana $95 million, and Ceylon $30 million.[14]

10. "Foreign Aid of Other Free World Countries" in Bureau of Public Affairs, Department of State, *Proposed Mutual Defense and Assistance Programs FY 1964 —Summary Presentation to the Congress* (Washington: G.P.O., 1963).

11. Agency for International Development, Statistics and Reports Division, U.S. *Foreign Assistance and Assistance from International Organizations, July 1, 1945—June 30, 1962* (Washington, 1963), p. 1.

12. V. Rimalov, *Economic Cooperation Between the U.S.S.R. and Underdeveloped Countries* (translated from the Russian; Moscow: Foreign Languages Publishing House), p. 46.

13. *Ibid.*, p. 96.

14. Joint Economic Committee, United States Congress, "The External Impact," *Dimensions of Soviet Economic Power* (Washington, 1962), Part VI.

The Chinese Communist portion of economic assistance to underdeveloped countries dropped sharply to $115 million in 1962 from $446 million in 1961. This reduction reflected the critical economic situation in China. Communist Chinese economic aid to Commonwealth countries during the period 1954-62 was limited to $37 million to Ceylon and $20 million to Ghana.

Since such a large proportion of economic aid to the underdeveloped countries of the Commonwealth has come from the United States, it is perhaps admissible to analyze both the accomplishments and difficulties of such aid primarily in terms of United States aid. This amounts to analyzing United States foreign aid in general since there has been no category of aid to the Commonwealth as such.

The economic, as distinguished from the political, rationale of United States economic aid has been that the more underdeveloped a country, the smaller the proportion of the national income which can be saved and devoted to capital investment. As a consequence, the more underdeveloped a country is, the higher the proportion of capital investment which must come from foreign aid. It is further assumed that the increase in national income will be largely dependent upon the amount of capital invested so that a capital coefficient can be calculated. This capital coefficient in turn depends upon the assumption that the labor force employed by the additional capital investment is in essence surplus labor. However, the more underdeveloped a country is, the less its initial capacity to carry out efficient programs of national development. This is due to the initial absence of planning, administrative, technical, and entrepreneurial skills. Consequently, during the early years, foreign economic aid, while a large proportion of investment, need be only modest in total amount.

This line of argument assumes that a foreign aid cycle can be expected, by which the amounts of aid to a given country would increase as it developed until national income reached a point where a growing proportion of the increasing national income could be saved and devoted to capital investment. Eventually, it would be expected that the country would become able to furnish its own capital out of domestic savings except for such foreign capital as would be invested at commercial rates and terms.[15] Such a concept of a cycle in foreign economic aid is based largely upon the Keynesian "consumption function," which holds that the wealthier a society, the larger the proportion of its income it is willing to devote to saving. The validity of the Keynesian consumption function has been vigorously questioned by a number of economists.

The results of our economic aid to underdeveloped countries do not yet either confirm or disprove the reality of such an assumed cycle of aid, first increasing and then decreasing. So far, we have been only in the increasing phase of the alleged cycle, at least in terms of the demands for economic aid by underdeveloped countries.

It is not feasible to attempt a survey for each of the countries of the Commonwealth of the economic effects of foreign aid, but the experience of one country, India, may be examined. India could hardly be considered typical since the amount of aid has been larger than that given any other underdeveloped country, since the Indian economy is much the largest, and since both the planning apparatus and statistical data are much more sophisticated than for other underdeveloped countries. It has been estimated that something like 25 per cent of capital investment funds are currently being provided out of foreign economic aid.[16] While there have been fluctuations in the annual rate of economic growth, it has averaged about 3.5 per cent to 4 per cent during the period 1950-51 to 1962-63.[17] On account of the high rate of population increase (some 2.4 per cent annually), this economic

15. For a more comprehensive policy statement along this line, see Max Millikan and W. W. Rostow, "The Magnitude of Capital Requirements," *A Proposal: Key to an Effective Foreign Policy* (New York, 1957), chap. x.

16. For an analysis of the relation between foreign aid and domestic investment see "Finance and Foreign Exchange" in Government of India Planning Commission, *Second Five Year Plan* (New Delhi, 1956), pp. 77-102.

17. Testimony of William S. Gaud, Assistant Administrator, Bureau of Near East and South Asia, A.I.D., *Hearings before The Committee on Foreign Affairs, House of Representatives, 85th Congress, 1st Sess., April 5-May 10, 1963* (Washington, 1963), p. 429.

growth has meant only a very moderate increase in per capita income of perhaps 1.5 per cent annually. In the absence of foreign aid there probably would have been no per capita increase in national income. To this extent foreign economic aid to India has been productive.

There was some evidence of a slight acceleration in the rate of growth of industrial production. The first three years of the second five-year plan produced a growth rate in real per capita income of about 2 per cent per annum.[18] During the last several years, however, there has been very little increase in agricultural production, and this tends to slow down the rate of increase in national income. The effect of greatly increased expenditures for defense following the Chinese invasion cannot yet be estimated but will certainly slow down the rate of capital investment in civilian industry.

While the effects of foreign economic aid to the other countries of the Commonwealth are not closely comparable to those in India, it may be assumed that the effects have been positive, i.e., that national income has been greater than would otherwise have been the case.

Since the United States has furnished much the greater part of economic aid to underdeveloped countries, including those of the Commonwealth, the United States government has increasingly urged that a greater share of the aid be furnished by the other developed countries. As a result of this urging, at least in part, the share of other countries in aid furnished has been increasing somewhat.[19]

At the same time, profound dissatisfaction with the whole foreign aid program has been rapidly growing. Deeper congressional cuts in the foreign aid proposals of President Ken-

18. Government of India Planning Commission, *Second Five Year Plan Progress Report, 1958-59*, p. 2.

19. From 1956 to 1961 the United States' annual aid level rose by 71 per cent. The combined aid level of other D.A.C. of OEEC countries rose by 112 per cent. These countries together with the U.S. furnished about 98 per cent of total bilateral public assistance from free world sources. Bureau of Public Affairs, Department of State, "Foreign Aid of Other Free-World Countries," *Proposed Mutual Defense and Assistance Programs FY 1964—Summary Presentation to the Congress.*

nedy were made during the 1963-64 Congressional session than ever before. The immediate cause for concern is, of course, our balance-of-payments difficulties for which our economic aid is so substantially responsible. Beyond this immediate concern, however, there are others more basic.

First, there is the fear that the burden of foreign aid will be never-ending and, indeed, may even increase. All foreign aid programs have been "sold" to the American people with the argument that they would be only temporary. Now, eighteen years after the close of World War II, Congress and the public are becoming skeptical. Pointing out that economic aid to western Europe under the Marshall Plan was productive and did terminate does not end the skepticism. The answer is given that the countries of western Europe already possessed the technology, scientific and entrepreneurial personnel, saving habits, and political stability necessary to attain the impressive rates of economic growth which they have reached. United States economic aid consisted in essence only of filling up the depleted industrial pipelines and supplying the complementary circulating capital essential for goods to pour off the conveyor belts of the European economy. Hence, it is felt that the Marshall Plan does not furnish an analogy for the situation of the underdeveloped countries. Parenthetically, it is pointed out that substantial amounts of financial aid for military purposes are still being furnished to Europe, long after European economic revival had taken place.

Second, it is felt that economic aid by the United States to underdeveloped countries serves largely to facilitate the building up of armaments by these countries for use against each other. There is little doubt that our economic aid to Egypt and Israel, to Algeria and Morocco, to India and Pakistan has enabled these countries to maintain larger military forces and armaments than they otherwise would have done. However, it should be pointed out that United States economic aid has been not at all responsible for the hostility between these pairs of countries. The most extreme case is probably that of Indonesia, where I feel that our economic aid has probably encouraged Sukarno in his aggressive foreign policy, for it has assuredly facilitated that aggressive policy.

Third, the United States Congress and the public are greatly disturbed over the dilemma of whether aid is or is not to have "strings attached." If the United States government furnishes economic aid to Yugoslavia or Poland, for example, what amounts to the transfer of some part of that aid to Cuba raises serious problems. The furnishing of either military or economic aid to Pakistan or India while the Kashmir dispute is unresolved also presents great difficulties. Quite a different sort of problem also involves the question of whether aid should have strings attached. By a curious coincidence, within twenty-four hours after our press announced that additional emergency economic aid had been advanced to the Indonesian government in the amount of $17 million for the purchase of spare parts, it also announced that President Sukarno had ordered $20 million worth of luxury passenger airliners. Similarly, when a country receives large grants in aid while simultaneously using its domestic financial resources to construct palaces for its rulers, provide luxurious limousines for its delegates to the United Nations, build sports stadiums or the like, the American public is outraged. Yet even to express disapproval is to risk the charge that strings are being attached to economic aid.

Finally, the high rate of population growth in most of the underdeveloped countries receiving aid is profoundly disturbing. What good is economic aid if it enables a 3 per cent rate of economic growth when the population increases at the same, or at a higher rate? It has been proposed that some aid be earmarked for disseminating information on birth control and even that United States technical personnel participate in the dissemination and popularization of such information. Here is intervention in the social customs of other countries with a vengeance! Here is certainly aid with strings attached! While such participation by the United States in the restriction of population in particular countries is inadvisable, it is not unreasonable for the

United States to say, in effect, "How you control the increase in population is no other country's responsibility, but we cannot ask our taxpayers to underwrite a population increase which nullifies the productive results of economic aid."

The revolt in the United States against foreign economic aid resulted in the recommendation by the Senate Foreign Relations Committee that aid on the present basis be terminated within the next two or three years. The Committee suggested that the United States should shift most of its aid away from the bilateral approach to a multilateral basis through such agencies as the International Bank. The Committee had come to recognize that the dissatisfaction of recipient countries with the amounts of aid and its administration was a greater liability than the wasting asset of gratitude for aid rendered. The Committee recognized also that since aid had to have strings attached if it was not to be wasted, these strings could be pulled by an international agency as they never could be under bilateral aid.

It may be that aid through Public Law 480, the "Food for Peace" program, will remain on a bilateral basis since this program is primarily designed to dispose of United States agricultural surpluses. Even this program is running into serious difficulties. It is naturally not popular with the competitors of the United States in world markets, such as Canada. It is not popular with the farmers of the countries receiving grain since the imported grain limits their own markets. (Recently, Uganda refused to accept any more Public Law 480 supplies for this reason.)

It appears then that the less developed countries of the Commonwealth as well as other countries in this category will have to look to international agencies for a greatly increased proportion of economic aid. Instead of the 10 per cent of aid from such sources at the present time,[20] it seems possible that within a few years the proportion would be more than 50 per cent.

20. "At present the multilateral institutions generate a flow of resources about one-tenth the size of the aggregate of free world bilateral assistance." Bureau of Public Affairs, Department of State, "Foreign Aid of Other Free-World Countries," *Proposed Mutual Defense and Assistance Programs F.Y. 1964—Summary Presentation to the Congress,* p. 9.

It would be a happy solution if an increasing amount of economic aid to underdeveloped countries could come from private investment from the more developed countries. Private corporate investment is usually accompanied by the technical and managerial skills required for its effective utilization. Such investment has to meet the tests of the market with respect to its relative profitability. The governments of the underdeveloped countries would, nevertheless, need to set up priorities on the provision of foreign exchange for the payment of the profits on such investments. Such priorities would need to forbid the utilization of scarce foreign exchange to enable the repatriation of profits invested in, say, the cosmetics industry.

The prospect for an increase in private corporate investments in underdeveloped countries is not at all favorable. It has been pointed out that the annual totals have not been increasing. This is not surprising when we review the recent nationalization of foreign investments in Egypt, Algeria, Indonesia, and Cuba. Other inhibitions on foreign private investment can be just as effective as outright nationalization. The cancellation of the contracts of foreign oil companies in Argentina, the dispossession of foreign owners of public utilities and the wiping out of profits through a multitude of special financial burdens in Brazil, the threatened elimination of all profits of foreign oil companies in Peru through taxation, the combination of high taxes and of wages far above the national average of the American copper companies in Chile are drying up foreign private investment in South America. No such confiscation of foreign investments has yet occurred in Commonwealth countries, but private investors are not likely to differentiate closely among the less developed countries.

Whatever the amounts and kinds of external aid, and whatever the organizational forms under which it is furnished, by far the greater part of the economic resources necessary for economic growth in underdeveloped countries must come from the internal resources of these countries. It is totally unlikely that the more developed countries would be willing and able to furnish the major portions of the funds required.

Furthermore, any substantial increase in the amount of external aid might well produce unfortunate results for the less well developed countries receiving it. If external aid is allowed to facilitate too great a rise in domestic incomes, it would be almost impossible either to bring about adequate internal saving to support capital investment or to develop the exports necessary to pay for the imports essential to economic development. For the less well developed countries to become permanently pensioners of particular previously developed countries would be an intolerable relationship. There have been some indications that the proportion of capital investment attainable from domestic sources of the underdeveloped countries is greater than had at one time been believed. It is true that underdeveloped countries show no willingness to go through the centuries-long process of saving which provided the present capital stock of the more developed countries. Further to encourage "the revolution of rising expectations" of underdeveloped countries with respect to foreign aid would constitute a maximum disservice, and I have not done so. This observation may, I hope, excuse the bluntness of my conclusions.

Table 1. *The Total Flow of Long-Term Financial Resources, by Country, 1956-62* (U.S. $ million)

Official flow, net*	1956	1957	1958	1959	1960	1961	1962
Belgium	20	20	23	79	101	92	97
Canada	29	48	92	60	75	62	50
Denmark	3	2	5	14	6	7	9
France	648	819	884	832	837	943	996
Germany	149	300	278	337	324	589	427
Italy	36	155	45	43	55	66	66
Japan	61	58	254	112	125	214	165
Netherlands	48	23	39	49	47	69	86
Norway	8	8	—	4	10	9	1
Portugal	3	3	1	17	37	30	37
United Kingdom	205	234	276	375	402	441	417
United States	1,996	2,083	2,388	2,310	2,817	3,493	3,606
Total D.A.C. countries	3,206	3,753	4,285	4,232	4,836	6,015	5,957
Total private investment, net	2,440	3,369	2,669	2,222	2,582	2,636†	(2,443)†
Total official and private net	5,646	7,122	6,954	6,454	7,418	8,651†	(8,400)†

*This flow includes all non-military grants in cash and in kind as well as lending from official sources for maturities exceeding 5 years.

†See footnotes † and ‡, Table 2.

Source: Report by Willard L. Thorp, *Development Assistance Efforts and Policies, 1963 Review* (OECD, Sept., 1963).

Table 4. *U.S. Aid to Foreign Assistance Act Countries of the Common-wealth by Region and Country Fiscal Year 1962* (millions of dollars)

Region and country	Total economic
Ceylon	5.7
Cyprus	8.7
India	775.1
Pakistan	403.9
Jamaica	2.0
Trinidad and Tobago	11.7
British Guiana	1.5
British Honduras	0.9
Hong Kong	3.4
Malaya	0.9
Ghana	130.1
Kenya	11.4
Nigeria	25.2
Rhodesia & Nyasaland	2.8
Sierra Leone	2.5
Tanganyika	13.2
Uganda	4.2
Zanzibar	0.1
Total	1,403.3

Source: Agency for International Development Statistics and Reports Division, *U. S. Foreign Assistance and Assistance from International Organizations, July 1, 1945, June 30, 1962* (Revised), pp. 5-7.

Table 5. *Canada's External Aid 1950-1962**
(million dollars Canadian)

Economic aid programs	Fiscal year 1961-62	Total from 1950 to March 31/62
(a) Bilateral		
Colombo Plan	50.00	381.68
Canada-West Indies Aid Program	1.34	6.45
Commonwealth Technical Assistance	.08	.42
Commonwealth Scholarship and Fellowship Plan	.67	1.05
Special Commonwealth Africa Aid Program	1.22	1.22
French-Speaking Africa Assistance Program	.07	.07
Total	53.38	390.89
(b) Multilateral		
UN Technical Assistance (EPTA)	2.22	17.07
UN Children's Fund (UNICEF)	.65	7.00
UN Special Fund	2.42	6.28
Miscellaneous grants†	.06	.38
Total	5.35	30.73
Contributions to special aid programs		
(a) refugees		
Hungarian refugees	—	16.22
IRO, UNREF, and UNHCR	.29	3.74
Palestine refugees (UNRWA)	2.00	13.35
Far Eastern Refugees (ICEM)	.06	.33
Tubercular Refugee Programme (WRY)	.11	.71
Total	2.46	34.35
(b) Other		
UN Korean Reconstruction Agency	—	7.75
Wheat/flour to India, Pakistan, Ceylon	—	34.96
Miscellaneous relief (in kind)‡	.02	15.75
UN Fund for the Congo	—	.99
Total	.02	59.45
Loans and advances		
Colombo Plan countries for purchase of Canadian wheat and flour	—	34.97
UN for Suez Canal clearance	—	1.00
International Finance Corporation	—	3.52
International Bank	—	9.99
International Development Ass'n.	7.19	15.70
Total	7.19	65.18
Total aid	68.40	580.60

*This table excludes NATO Mutual Aid, advances to the International Monetary Fund, and Canada's assessed share of costs of international programs and budgets. The table lists expenditures which are sometimes less than appropriations.

†Of which (in rounded figures): Operative program of the International Atomic Energy Agency (IAEA)$117,000 (1959-62); gift of uranium to IAEA $62,000 (1959); Malaria Eradication Program of WHO $100,000 (1960); UN Technical Assistance Training Centre in B.C. $30,000 (1959-61); and Freedom from HungerCampaign of FAO $23,000 (1960).

‡Mostly dry skimmed milk, canned pork, wheat, and flour.

Source: External Aid Office, *A Report on Canadian External Aid Programmes* and *Public Accounts of Canada, 1961 and 1962* (Ottawa: Queen's Printer, 1961 and 1962).

Table 6. *New Zealand Charges for and Incidental to International Organizations: Proportion of Expenses* (£)

	1962-63
Codex Alimentaries Commission	350
General Agreement on Tariffs and Trade	3,000
Intergovernmental Maritime Consultative Committee	950
International Labor Organization	19,000
Permanent Court of Arbitration	375
Southeast Asia Treaty Organization	26,650
South Pacific Commission	35,950
United Nations Food and Agriculture Organization	28,650
United Nations Organization	25
World Health Organization	32,800
Membership costs	**147,750**
International and other organizations: grants and contributions—	
Colombo Plan	1,000,000
Commonwealth Education Scheme	38,550
International Red Cross	4,000
Special Commonwealth Aid to Africa Plan	100,000
Southeast Asia Treaty Organization—	
Assistance toward cost of training security personnel in Malaya	1,500
Assistance toward Thai community development project	10,000
Graduate School of Engineering, expenses of lectures and scholarship grants	7,250
United Nations agencies—	
European refugees in China	20,000
International Children's Emergency Fund Appeal	75,000
Relief and Works Agency for Palestine refugees	50,000
United Nations Association of New Zealand	1,200
United Nations military observers in Kashmir and Palestine: pay of seconded New Zealand personnel	14,750
United Nations Special Fund	50,000
United Nations Technical Assistance Scheme	100,000
Grants and contributions	**1,472,250**

Source: "Estimates of the Expenditures of the Government of New Zealand for the Year Ending 31 March 1963," *New Zealand, General Assembly, House of Representatives, Appendix to the Journals,* pp. 90-91.

APPENDIX: Australia's External Aid

Australian contributions to international organizations for the budgetary year 1962-63 were estimated at £1,061,600, international development and relief at £8,827,900, of which £2,810,000 was for economic development, and £1,990,000 for technical assistance under the Colombo Plan. £1,000,000 was to be provided by special appropriation for the Indus Basin Development Plan. The total is £9,889,500.

It has been argued that the grant of £20,879,000 for Papua and New Guinea should be included in Australian foreign aid, but they are not so included in the Australian budget.

Source: The Parliament of Australia, *Estimates of Receipts and Expenditure for the Year Ending 30th June 1963* (Canberra, 1962), p. 19.

Index

Wilson, J. S. G., xv, 525 n. *See chapter by*, 503-26
Wilson, Robert R., xv, 90 n., 180 n., 182 n., 190 n. *See chapter by*, 172-93
Winch, D. N., 213 n.
Wolfson Foundation, 130, 132
Woodruff, Philip (*pseud.*). *See* Mason
Wright, H. R. C., 212 n.

Yalem, R. J., 325 n.
Yaounde Agreement, 338

Young, G. M., 215 n.
Yugoslavia, 6, 182, 376, 538. *Statistics for*: sterling holdings, 522

Zambia, 26, 249, 273, 345, 428
Zanzibar, 10, 94, 102 n., 111 n., 117, 240, 241, 242, 404, 428. *Statistics for*: aid, 545; gross domestic product, 482; labor force, 489. *See also* Tanzania
Zinner, Paul E., 368 n.

Date

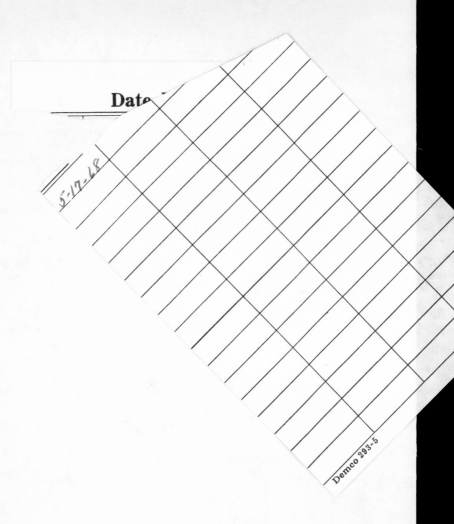

5-17-68

Demco 293-5